THE BASEBALL MANIAC'S ALMANAC

3RD EDITION

THE BASEBALL MANIAC'S ALMANAC

3RD EDITION

The ABSOLUTELY, POSITIVELY, and WITHOUT QUESTION GREATEST Book of FACTS, FIGURES, and ASTONISHING LISTS EVER COMPLIED

Edited by Bert Randolph Sugar
with Stuart Shea

SPORTS
PUBLISHING

Sports Publishing books may be purchased in bulk at special discounts for sales promo-
tion, corporate gifts, fund-raising, or educational purposes. Special editions can also be
created to specifications. For details, contact the Special Sales Department, Sports
Publishing, 307 West 36th Street, 11th Floor, New York, NY 10018 or sportspubbooks@sky-
horsepublishing.com.

Sports Publishing® is a registered trademark of Skyhorse Publishing, Inc.®, a Delaware
corporation.

Visit our website at www.sportspubbooks.com

10 9 8 7 6 5 4 3 2 1

Library of Congress Cataloging-in-Publication Data available on file.

ISBN: 978-1-61321-061-1

Printed in the United States of America

CONTENTS

Foreword   xxxi

Part 1   **Individual Statistics**   1

1   **Batting**   3

Base Hits   3

Most Hits by Decade   3
Evolution of Singles Record   4
Most Hits, Season   4
Base Hit Leaders by State of Birth   4
Players with 200 Hits and 40 Home Runs, Season   5
Players with 200 Base Hits and Fewer Than 40 Extra-Base Hits,
    Season (Post-1900)   6
Players with 3000 Hits, Career   6
Most Hits by Position, Season   7
Players Hitting for the Cycle Two or More Times (Post 1900)   7
Most Times at Bat Without a Hit, Season   7
Players with 200 Hits in Each of First Three Major League Seasons   7
Players with 600 Total Hits in First Three Major League Seasons   7
Players with 200-Hit Seasons in Each League   8
Players with 200 Hits in Five Consecutive Seasons   8

v

Rookies with 200 or More Hits   8

Teammates Finishing One-Two in Base Hits   8

Players Getting 1000 Hits Before Their 25th Birthday   9

Players with 10000 At Bats and Fewer Than 3000 Hits, Career   9

Players with 200 Hits, Batting Under .300, Season   9

Players with 2500 Hits and Career .300 Batting Average Never Winning
    Batting Title (Post-1900),   9

Former Negro Leaguers with 1500 Major League Hits   10

Players with 2500 Career Hits, Never Having a 200-Hit Season   10

Latino Players with 2500 Hits   11

3000 Hits, 500 Home Runs, and a .300 Batting Average, Career   11

Most Hits by Switch-Hitter, Career   11

Most Hits by Catcher, Career   11

Most Singles, Career   11

Fewest Singles, Season (Min. 150 Games)   12

Most Singles, Season   13

20 Triple Seasons (Since 1930)   13

Largest Differential Between League Leader in Hits and Runner-Up   14

Batting Average   14

Evolution of Batting Average Record   14

Highest Batting Average by Position, Season   14

Highest Batting Average by Decade (2000 At Bats)   15

Highest Batting Average for a Rookie   16

Top 10 Rookie Batting Averages, Each League (Min. 100 Games)   16

Lifetime Batting Averages of 20-Year Players (Not Including Pitchers)   16

Players Never Hitting Below .270 in Career (Min. 10 Years)   17

Players Batting .300 for 10 or More Consecutive Seasons From Start of
    Career   17

.400 Hitters and How Their Team Finished   17

.400 Hitters Versus League Batting Average (Post-1900)   18

Players Hitting .370 Since Ted Williams's .406 Season (1941)   18

Players Hitting .300 in Rookie *and* Final Seasons
(Post-1900; Min. Five Years)   18

Players Hitting .300 in Each of First 10 Seasons   19

Players Hitting .300 in Their Only Major League Season (Post-1900;
Min. 100 Games, 300 At Bats)   19

Players Batting .350 with 50 Home Runs   19

Players 40 or Older* Hitting .300 (Min. 50 Games)   19

Players Hitting .325 for Two or More Different Clubs (Post-1945)   20

Batting Title   21

Closest Batting Races   21

Teammates Finishing One-Two in Batting Race   22

Switch-Hitting Batting Champions   22

Catchers Winning Batting Titles   23

Batting Champions on Last-Place Teams   23

Batting Title Winners Without a Home Run   23

Batting Champions Driving in Fewer Than 40 Runs   23

Batting Champions with 100 Strikeouts in Year They Led League   23

Lowest Batting Averages to Lead League   23

Highest Batting Average *Not* to Win Batting Title   24

Runners-Up for Batting Titles in Both Leagues   25

Players Winning Batting Title in Season *After* Joining New Club   25

Players Changing Team in Season *After* Winning Batting Title   25

Largest Margin Between Batting Champion and Runner-Up   26

Champions Whose Next Season's Batting Average Declined the Most   26

Lowest Lifetime Batting Averages for Players Who Led League   27

Two-Time Batting Champions with Lifetime Batting Averages
Below .300   27

Years in Which Right-Handed Batters Won Batting Titles in
Both Leagues   28

Fewest Strikeouts For Batting Champions 28

Home Runs 28

Evolution of Home Run Record 28

Most Home Runs by Decade 29

Career Home Run Leaders by Zodiac Sign 30

All-Time Home Run Leaders by First Letter of Last Name 30

Home Run Leaders by State of Birth 30

500th Home Run of 500 Home Run Hitters 31

Most Home Runs in First Three Seasons in Majors 32

Most Home Runs for One Club 32

Most Home Runs by Position, Career 33

Most Home Runs Not Leading League, Season 33

Most Home Runs, Never Leading League, Career 34

Most Inside-the-Park Home Runs, Career (Post-1898) 34

Players with 10 or More Letters in Last Name, Hitting 40 or More Home
   Runs in Season 34

Most Home Runs, Month by Month 34

Most Home Runs by Position, Season* 35

Players Leading League in Home Runs for Different Teams 35

Players with 40 Home Run Seasons in Each League 36

Players Hitting a Total of 100 Home Runs in Two Consecutive Seasons 36

Players with First 20-Home Run Season After 35th Birthday 37

Shortstops with at Least Seven Consecutive 20-Home Run Seasons 37

Players Hitting Four Home Runs in One Game 38

Career Home Runs by Players Hitting Four Home Runs in One Game 38

Players with Three Home Runs in One Game, Fewer Than 10 in Season 39

Rookies Hitting 30 or More Home Runs 39

Former Negro Leaguers Who Led Major Leagues in Home Runs 39

Players with 50 Home Runs, Batting Under .300, Season 40

Players Hitting 49 Home Runs in Season, Never Hitting 50 40

Most Multi-Home Run Games 40

Players Hitting Two Grand Slams, Same Game   41

Most Home Runs by Age   41

Teenagers Hitting Grand Slams   41

Oldest Players to Hit Grand Slams   41

Oldest Home Run Champions*   42

Most Career Home Runs by Players Hitting Home Run on First Pitch
   in Majors   42

Players Hitting Home Run in First Time At Bat, Never Hitting Another   43

Most At Bats, No Home Runs, Career   43

Most Consecutive At Bats Without a Home Run   43

Lowest Batting Average for Home Run Leaders, Season (Post-1900)   44

Players Hitting 30 or More Home Runs in First Three Seasons   44

Reverse 30–30 Club: Players with 30 Home Runs and 30 Errors,
   Season   44

Players Increasing Their Home Run Production in Seven Consecutive
   Seasons   45

Most Home Runs by Switch-Hitters, Career   45

Most Home Runs by Catcher, Season*   45

Most Home Runs by Catcher, Career*   46

300 Career Home Runs and 100 Home Runs, Both Leagues   46

Most Home Runs Hit in One Ballpark, Career   46

Players Whose Home Run in "Cycle" Was Grand Slam   47

Players with the Highest Percentage of Team's Total Home Runs, Season   47

Shortstops Leading League in Home Runs   47

Most Home Runs by Left-Handed Hitting Shortstops   48

Players Hitting Home Runs in 20 Consecutive Seasons Played   48

Players with 100 Home Runs, Three Different Teams   48

Players with 40-Home Run Seasons Before 25th Birthday   48

Players with More Home Runs Than Strikeouts, Season
   (Min. 10 Home Runs)   49

Largest Differential Between Leader in Home Runs and Runner-Up   51

Most Home Runs, Last Season in Majors   51

Fewest Career Home Runs for League Leader (Post-1920)   52

Runs Batted In   52

Evolution of RBI Record   52
Most RBIs by Decade   53
Career RBI Leaders by First Letter of Last Name   54
Teammates Finishing One-Two in RBIs   54
Largest Differential Between League Leader in RBIs and Runner-Up   55
Career RBI Totals, Players Hitting 500 Home Runs   56
Players Driving in 100 Runs in First Two Seasons in Majors   56
Players Driving in 500 Runs in First Four Years of Career   56
Catchers with 100 RBIs and 100 Runs Scored, Season   56
Catchers Hitting .300 with 30 Home Runs and 100 RBIs, Season   57
Players with 40 or More Home Runs and Fewer Than 100 RBIs, Season   57
Players with More Than 100 RBIs and Fewest Home Runs, Season   57
Players with Most Career RBIs, Never Leading League   58
Players with 1000 Career RBIs, Never Driving in 100 in One Season   58
Batters Driving in 100 Runs with Three Different Teams   58
Players Driving in 130 Teammates During Season   59
Players Driving in 100 Runs, Season, in Each League   60
Players with More RBIs Than Games Played, Season (Min. 100 Games)   62
Players Driving in 20 Percent of Their Team's Runs, Season   63
Players with Lowest Batting Average for 100-RBI Season   63
Players on Last-Place Teams Leading League in RBIs, Season   64
Players Driving in 95 or More Runs in Season Three Times, Never 100   64

Runs Scored   64

Evolution of Runs Scored Record   64
Most Runs Scored by Decade   64
Players with More Runs Scored Than Games Played, Season (Min. 100
    Games)   65
Players Scoring 1000 Runs in Career, Never 100 in One Season   66

Most Runs Scored by Position, Season 66

Walks 67

Evolution of Batters' Walks Record 67
Players with 1000 Walks, 2000 Hits, and 300 Home Runs, Career 67
Players Leading League in Base Hits and Walks, Season 68
Players with 200 Base Hits and 100 Walks, Season 68
Players with More Walks Than Hits, Season (Min. 100 Walks) 69
Players Hitting 40 or More Home Runs, with More Home Runs
    Than Walks, Season 70
Players with 90 Walks in Each of First Two Seasons 70

Strikeouts 70

Players with 100 More Career Strikeouts Than Hits
    (Min. 375 strikeouts) 70
Players with 500 At Bats and Fewer Than 10 Strikeouts, Season 71
Players with 200 Hits and 100 Strikeouts, Season 72
Players with 40 Home Runs and Fewer Than 50 Strikeouts, Season 73
Players with 100 More Strikeouts Than RBIs, Season 73
Toughest Batters to Strike Out, Career* 74

Pinch Hits 74

Highest Batting Average for Pinch Hitter, Season (Min. 25 At Bats) 74

Extra-Base Hits 74

Evolution of Total Bases Record 74
Players with 100 Extra-Base Hits, Season 75
Players with 400 Total Bases, Season 75
Evolution of Doubles Record 76
Players Hitting 40 Home Runs and 40 Doubles, Season 76
Evolution of Triples Record 77

Leaders in Doubles and Triples, Season   77

Leaders in Doubles and Home Runs, Season   78

Leaders in Triples and Home Runs, Season   78

Players Hitting 20 Home Runs, 20 Triples, and 20 Doubles, Season   78

Players Leading League in Doubles, Triples, and Home Runs During
   Career (Post-1900)   79

Players Since World War II with 100 Doubles, Triples, Home Runs,
   and Stolen Bases, Career   79

Players with 200 Hits and Fewer than 40 Extra-Base Hits, Season   80

Most Doubles by Position, Season   80

Most Triples by Position, Season   80

Most Total Bases by Position, Season   81

Stolen Bases   81

Evolution of Stolen Base Record   81

Most Stolen Bases by Position, Season   81

Most Stolen Bases by Decade   82

Teammates Combining for 125 Stolen Bases, Season   83

Players Stealing 30 Bases for 10 Consecutive Seasons   83

Players Leading League in Stolen Bases and Total Bases, Season   83

Players with 200 Home Runs and 200 Stolen Bases, Career   84

Players with 400 Home Runs and 10 Steals of Home, Career   84

Players with 200 Hits, 20 Home Runs, and 20 Stolen Bases, Season   85

Players with 10 Doubles, Triples, Home Runs, and Steals in Each of First
   Three Seasons in Majors   85

Players Who Have Stolen Second, Third, and Home in Same Inning   85

Most Stolen Bases by Catcher, Season   86

Most Stolen Bases by Catcher, Career   86

Players with 50 Stolen Bases and 100 RBIs, Season   86

Most Stolen Bases by Home Run Champion, Season   87

Players Stealing Bases in Four Decades   87

Batting Miscellany   87

    Most Times Leading League in Offensive Category   87

    Most Consecutive Seasons Leading League in Offensive Category   88

    Players Leading in All Triple Crown Categories, but Not
      in Same Year*   89

    Highest Offensive Career Totals by Players Who Never Led League   90

    Career Offensive Leaders by Players Under Six Feet Tall   90

    Largest Margin Between League Leaders and Runners-Up   90

    Evolution of Slugging Average Record   91

    Players Hitting Safely in at Least 135 Games in Season   91

    Players Hitting for the Cycle in Natural Order (Single, Double, Triple,
      Home Run)   91

    Highest Slugging Average by Position, Season   92

    Most Times Awarded First Base on Catcher's Interference or
      Obstruction   92

    Winners of Two "Legs" of Triple Crown Since Last Winner*   92

2   **Pitching**   93

Wins   93

    Most Victories by Decade   93

    Pitchers with the Most Career Wins by First Letter of Last Name   94

    Pitchers with the Most Career Victories by Zodiac Sign   94

    Pitchers with the Most Victories by State of Birth   94

    Pitchers with Five or More Consecutive 20-Win Seasons (Post-1900)   95

    100-Game Winners, Both Leagues   95

    Pitchers with 500 Major League Decisions   96

    Most Wins, Major and Minor Leagues Combined   96

    Most Wins For One Team   97

    Pitchers with 100 More Wins Than Losses, Career   97

    Pitchers with Most Career Wins, Never Leading League in One Season   98

200-Game Winners, Never Winning 20 Games in Season 98

Pitchers with 100 Wins and 500 Hits, Career 98

Victories in Most Consecutive Seasons 99

Most Wins in a Season Without a Complete Game 99

Most Career Wins by Pitchers Six and a Half Feet Tall or Taller 99

Most Career Wins by Pitchers Under Six Feet Tall 99

Pitchers Winning 20 Games in Season Split Between
    Two Teams (Post-1900) 100

Pitchers Winning 20 Games with 3 Different Teams 100

Oldest Pitchers to Win 20 Games for First Time 100

Youngest Pitchers to Win 20 Games 101

Rookies Winning 20 Games 101

Most Seasons Logged Before First 20-Win Season 102

Rookie Pitchers with 20 Wins and 200 Strikeouts 102

Pitchers Winning 20 Games in Rookie Year, Fewer Than
    20 Balance of Career 102

20-Game Winners Who Didn't Win 20 More Games in
    Career (Post-1900) 102

Pitchers Winning 20 Games in Last Season in Majors 102

Earliest 20-Game Winner During Season 102

Most Wins After Turning 40 103

Pitchers on Losing Teams, Leading League in Wins 103

20-Game Winners on Last-Place Teams 103

20-Game Winners with Worst Lifetime Winning Percentage
    (Post-1900) 104

"Pure" 20-Game Winners (Pitchers with 20 or More
    Wins Than Losses) 104

Lefties Winning 20 Games Twice Since World War II 105

Pitchers with 20-Win Seasons After Age 40 106

Pitchers Leading Both Leagues in Wins, Season 106

20-Game Winners One Season, 20-Game Losers the Next 107

20-Game Winners and Losers, Same Season 107

Pitchers Who Led League in Wins in Successive Seasons   107

Most Pitching Wins for One Season   108

Most Total Wins, Two Pitchers on Same Staff, Career Together
   as Teammates   109

Most Wins, Right-Hander and Left-Hander on Same Staff, Season   109

Largest Differential Between League Leader in Wins and Runner-Up   110

Highest Percentage of Team's Total Wins for Season   111

300-Game Winners with Fewer Than 200 Losses   111

Pitchers Winning 300 Games, Never Striking Out 200
   Batters, Season   111

Won-Loss Percentage of 300-Game Winners   111

Shutouts   112

Evolution of Shutout Record   112

20-Game Winners with No Complete Game Shutouts   112

Most Shutouts by a Rookie   113

Pitchers Leading League in Wins, No Complete Game Shutouts   113

Most Career Starts, No Shutouts   113

Most Career Shutouts, Never Led League   114

Pitchers with Shutouts in First Two Major League Starts   114

Most Hits Allowed by Pitcher Pitching Shutout   114

Players with Highest Percentage of Shutouts to Games Started, Career   114

Losses   115

Most Losses by Decade   115

Evolution of Pitchers' Losses Record   116

Pitchers with Seven or More Consecutive Losing Seasons   116

Pitchers with 150 Wins with More Losses Than Wins, Career   117

Pitchers on Winning Teams, Leading League in Losses, Season   117

Pitchers Winning 20 Games in Rookie Year, Losing 20 in Second Year   118

300-Game Winners with Fewer Than 200 Losses   118

Earned Run Average   118

    Best ERA by Decade (Min. 1000 Innings)   118

    Teammates Finishing One-Two in ERA, Season   119

    Pitchers with 3000 Innings Pitched and an ERA Lower Than 3.00
       (Post–1900)   120

    Pitchers Leading League in ERA After Their 40th Birthday   121

    ERA Under 2.00, Season (Since 1920)   121

    Pitchers with Losing Record, Leading League in ERA   121

    20-Game Winners with 4.00 ERA, Season   121

    20-Game Losers with ERA Below 2.00   122

    ERA Leaders with Fewer Than 10 Wins   122

    Pitchers with Lowest ERA in Both Leagues   122

    ERA Leaders with 25 or More Wins, Season   123

    ERAs of 300-Game Winners   124

Strikeouts   124

    Evolution of Strikeout Record   124

    Most Strikeouts by Decade   125

    Members of Same Pitching Staff Finishing One-Two in
       Strikeouts, Season   126

    Pitchers Leading League with 100 More Strikeouts Than Runner-Up   126

    Pitchers with 3000 Strikeouts, Never Leading League   127

    Pitchers Striking Out 1000 Batters Before Their 24th Birthday   127

    Most Times Striking Out 10 or More Batters in a Game, Career   127

    Pitchers Averaging 10 Strikeouts per Nine Innings, Season   127

    Pitchers with Combined Total of 500 Strikeouts and Walks, Season   128

    Pitchers Striking Out the Side on Nine Pitches   129

    Pitchers with 200 Strikeouts and Fewer Than 50 Walks, Season   129

    Rookie Pitchers Striking Out 200 Batters   130

    Rookies Leading League in Strikeouts   131

    Pitchers Leading League in Strikeouts, 10 or More Years Apart   131

Oldest Pitchers to Lead League in Strikeouts   131
Strikeout Leaders on Last-Place Teams   132

Walks   132

Pitchers Walking 20 or Fewer Batters, Season (Min. 200 Innings)   132
Fewest Walks, Season (Min. One Inning Pitched Each Team Game)   132
Pitchers Walking Fewer Than One Batter Every Nine Innings, Season
    (min. 160 1P)   132
Highest Percentage of Walks to Innings Pitched, Season   133

Low-Hit Games   133

Pitchers Losing No-Hit Games   133
Pitchers with a No-Hitter in First Major League Start   134
Pitchers with a One-Hitter in First Major League Game   134
Last Outs in Perfect Games*   134
Perfect Game Pitchers, Career Wins   135
26-Batter Perfect Games (Spoiled by 27th Batter)   135
Most Walks Given Up by No-Hit Pitchers, Game   135
Pitchers Pitching No-Hitters in 20-Loss Season   136
Pitchers Hitting Home Runs in No-Hit Games   136
Pitchers Throwing No-Hitters in Consecutive Seasons   136
No-Hitters Pitched Against Pennant-Winning Teams   136
No-Hit Pitchers Going Winless the Next Season after
    Pitching a No-Hitter   136
Back-to-Back One-Hit Games (Post-1900)   137
Rookies Throwing No-Hitters   137

Saves/Reliefs   138

Evolution of Saves Record   138
Pitchers with 100 Wins and 100 Saves, Career   138
Relief Pitchers with the Most Wins, Season   139

Most Games Won by Relief Pitcher, Career   139

Teams with Two Pitchers with 20 Saves, Season   139

Pitchers Having 20-Win Seasons and 20-Save Seasons, Career   139

Pitchers with 15 Saves and 15 Wins in Relief, Same Season   140

Pitching Miscellany   140

Best Winning Percentage by Decade (100 Decisions)   140

Most Seasons Leading League in Pitching Category   141

Most Consecutive Seasons Leading League in Pitching Category   142

Most Consecutive Scoreless Innings Pitched   142

Highest Career Pitching Totals by Pitchers Who Never Led League   143

Career Pitching Leaders Under Six Feet Tall   143

Pitching's Triple Crown Winners (Led League in Wins, ERA,
    and Strikeouts, Same Season)   144

Most Home Runs Given Up, Season   144

Most Home Runs Given Up, Career   145

Pitchers Giving Up Most Grand Slams, Season   145

Pitchers with 2000 Innings Pitched, Allowing No Grand Slams 145

20-Game Winners Batting .300, Same Season 146

Pitchers with Two Seasons of 1.000 Batting Averages (Post-1900)   146

Evolution of Complete Games Record   146

Most Games Started By a Pitcher, Career   147

Highest Percentage of Complete Games to Games Started   147

Pitchers Starting 20 Games in 20 Consecutive Seasons   147

Evolution of Record for Most Games Pitched in a Season   148

Evolution of Innings Pitched Record   148

Most Wild Pitches, Season (Since 1900)   148

Last Legal Spitball Pitchers   148

Left-Handed Pitchers Appearing in More Than 700 Games, Career   149

Pitchers Who Pitched for Both Yankees and Mets and
    Threw No-Hitters   149

Pitchers Who Have Stolen Home   149

3 **Hall of Fame**   151

First Players Elected to Hall of Fame from Each Position   151

Highest Lifetime Batting Average for Hall of Fame Pitchers   151

Hall of Famers with Lifetime Batting Averages Below .265 (Excluding
    Pitchers)   151

Hall of Famers with Lowest Marks in Offensive Categories*   152

Teams Fielding Most Future Hall of Fame Players   152

Infields Fielding Four Future Hall of Famers   152

Hall of Fame Pitchers Who Batted Right and Threw Left   152

Switch-Hitting Pitchers in Hall of Fame   152

Hall of Fame Pitchers Who Played Most Games at Other Positions   153

Hall of Fame Position Players Who Also Pitched   153

Hall of Fame Pitchers with Losing Records   153

Leading Career Pitching Marks by Those Eligible for Hall of Fame
    but Not In   153

Leading Career Batting Marks by Those Eligible for Hall of Fame
    but Not In   154

Most Career Hits by Players Eligible for Hall of Fame but Not In   154

Most Career Wins by Pitchers Eligible for Hall of Fame but Not In   154

Most Career Home Runs by Players Eligible for Hall of Fame but
    Not In   154

Hall of Fame Inductees Receiving 90 Percent of Vote   154

Won-Lost Percentage of Hall of Famers Elected as Players Who Managed in
    Majors   155

Hall of Famers Making Last Out in World Series   157

Hall of Famers Who Played for the Harlem Globetrotters   157

Hall of Famers Who Died on Their Birthday   157

4 Awards 159

Most Valuable Player 159

Unanimous Choice for MVP 159
Closest Winning Margins in MVP Voting 159
Widest Winning Margins in MVP Voting 160
Won MVP Award in Consecutive Years, by Position 160
Teammates Finishing One-Two in MVP Balloting 160
Triple Crown Winners *Not* Winning MVP 161
MVPs on Nonwinning Teams 161
MVPs *Not* Batting .300, Hitting 30 Home Runs, or
    Driving in 100 Runs (Not Including Pitchers) 161
Pitchers Winning MVP Award 162
Players Winning MVP Award First Season in League 162
MVPs Receiving Fewer First-Place Votes Than Runner-Up 162
Teams with Most Consecutive MVP Awards 162
Players Winning MVP Award with Two Different Teams 163
MVPs with Fewest Hits 163
Switch-Hitting MVPs 163

Cy Young Award 163

Pitchers Winning 25 Games, *Not* Winning Cy Young Award 163
Pitchers Winning 20 Games Only Once and Cy Young Award
    Same Season 164
Cy Young Winners *Not* in Top 10 in League in ERA, Season 164
Relief Pitchers Winning Cy Young Award 164
Cy Young Winners Increasing Their Number of Victories the Following
    Season 164
Won Both Cy Young and MVP Same Season 165
Cy Young Winners with Higher Batting Averages Than That Year's Home Run
    Leader 165

Rookie of the Year   165

   Rookie of the Year Winners on Team Other Than the
      One First Played On   165
   Relief Pitchers Winning Rookie of the Year   165
   Rookie of the Year on Pennant-Winning Teams   165
   Rookies of the Year Elected to Hall of Fame   166

Gold Gloves   166

   Most Gold Gloves, by Position   166

5   **Managers**   167
   Winningest Managers by First Letter of Last Name   167
   Winningest Managers by Zodiac Sign   167
   Managers During Most Presidential Administrations   168
   Managers Winning 1000 Games with One Franchise   168
   Managers with Over 1000 Career Wins and sub-.500
      Winning Percentage   168
   Managers with Most Career Victories for Each Franchise   170
   Best Winning Percentage as Manager with One Team (Post-1900;
      Min. 150 Games)   171
   Managers with 500 Wins in Each League   171
   Played in 2000 Games, Managed in 2000 Games   171
   Managers Managing 100-Loss Teams After 1000th Career Victory   171
   Managers with Both 100 Wins and 100-Loss Seasons   171
   Former Pitchers Winning Pennants as Managers (Post-1900)   172
   Managers Taking Over World Series Teams in Midseason   172
   Managers Replaced While Team Was in First Place   172
   Managers Winning Pennant in First Year as Manager of Team   172
   Managers Undefeated in World Series Play   173
   Managers with Fewest Career Wins to Win World Series   173
   Managers with Most Career Wins *Never* to Manage a World Series Team
      (Post-1903)   173

Pennant-Winning Managers with Fewest Career Wins (Since 1900) 173

Most Times Managing the Same Club 174

Managers with Best Winning Percentage for First Five Full Years of
   Managing 174

Managers Never Experiencing a Losing Season (Post-1900;
   Min. Two Full Seasons) 174

Career One-Game Managers 174

Managers Managing in Civilian Clothes 175

Managers Who Were Lawyers 175

Pennant-Winning Managers Who Won Batting Titles 175

Managers with Same Initials as Team They Managed 175

Playing Managers After 1950 175

1000 Wins as Manager and 2000 Hits as Player 176

6 **Fielding** 177

Most Games Played by Position, Career 177

Most Consecutive Games Played at Each Position 177

Players Who Played 1000 Games at Two Positions, Career 177

Unassisted Triple Plays 178

Most No-Hitters Caught 178

Games Caught by Left-Handed Catchers 179

Players Pitching and Catching, Same Game 180

Most Times Catchers Charged with Errors Due to Interference 180

7 **Relatives** 181

Father-Son Combinations with 250 Home Runs, Career 181

Brother Batteries* 181

Twins Who Played Major League Baseball 182

Hall of Famers Whose Sons Played in Majors 182

Players with Two Sons Who Played in Majors 182

Brother Double-Play Combinations 183

Most Home Runs, Brothers 183

Pitching Brothers Each Winning 20 Games in Same Season 184
Hall of Famers' Brothers Who Played 10 or More Seasons in Majors
(Post-1900) 184
Father-Son Tandems Who Both Played for Same Manager 184
Sons Who Played for Their Fathers 184
Best Won-Lost Percentage for Pitching Brothers 184
Most Total Combined Career Wins for Pitching Brothers 186
Pitching Brothers Facing Each Other, Regular Season 187
Most Career Victories by Father-Son Combination (Post-1900) 187
Brothers Who Played Together on Three Major League Teams 188

8 **World Series** 189
Teams Never to Trail in a World Series 189
Highest Batting Average for a World Series Team 189
Lowest Batting Average for a World Series Team 189
Most Regular Season Losses, Reaching World Series 190
Players Hitting .500 in World Series (Min. 10 At Bats) 190
0-for-the Series (10 or More At Bats) 191
Players on World Series–Winning Teams in Both Leagues 191
Pitchers in World Series with Highest Slugging Average 192
World Series–Ending Hits 193
Pitchers in World Series with 300 Career Wins 193
Players on World Series Teams in Three Decades 193
Players with World Series Home Runs in Three Decades 194
Player-Managers on World Series–Winning Teams 194
World Series-Winning Managers Who Never Played in Majors 195
Leaders in Offensive Categories, Never Appearing in World Series
(Post-1903) 195
Most Seasons, Never Appearing in World Series (Post-1903) 195
Playing Most Games, Never Appearing in World Series (Post-1903) 196
Players with the Most Home Runs, Never Appearing in World Series 196
Players with Highest Lifetime Batting Average, Never Appearing in
World Series (Post-1903; Min. 10 Seasons) 196

Players with Most Hits, Never Appearing in World Series (Post-1903)   196

Leaders in Pitching Categories, Never Pitching in World Series
    (Post-1903)   197

Pitchers with Most Wins, Never Appearing in World Series
    (Post-1903)   197

Pitchers with World Series Wins in Both Leagues   197

Pitchers with World Series Losses in Both Leagues   197

Players Whose Home Run Won World Series Game 1–0   197

Brothers Who Were World Series Teammates   198

Brothers Facing Each Other in World Series   198

Fathers and Sons in World Series Competition   198

Batting Average of .400 Hitters in World Series Play   198

Batting Averages of .400 in World Series Play   198

Players Hitting World Series Home Runs in Each League   199

World Series Inside-The-Park Home Runs   199

World Series Teams Using Six Different Starting Pitchers   199

Rookies Starting Seventh Game of World Series   199

Players Playing Four Different Positions in World Series Competition,
    Career   200

Players Stealing Home in World Series Game   200

Pitchers Hitting Home Runs in World Series Play   200

Cy Young Winners Facing Each Other in World Series Games   200

World Series in Which Neither Team Had a 20-Game Winner   200

Pitchers with Lowest ERA in Total World Series Play (Min. 25 Innings)   201

World Series Grand Slams   201

Players on Three Different World Series Clubs   202

Players Playing for 2 Different World Series Champions
    in Successive Years   202

Players with Same Lifetime Batting Average as Their World Series Overall
    Average   203

Batting Champions Facing Each Other in World Series   203

Home Run Champions Facing Each Other in World Series   203

Players Hitting Home Run in First World Series At Bat   203

World Series Pitchers with Most Losses, Season   203

Teams Winning a World Series in First Year in New Ballpark   204

Pitchers on World Series Winning Teams, Both Winning 20 Games and *All*
    of Their Team's Series Victories   204

Teams' Overall Won-Lost Percentage in World Series Games Played   204

Oldest Players to Appear in World Series   205

Players with 3000 Hits Playing in World Series   205

9 **All-Star Game**   207

Players Who Made All-Star Roster After Starting Season in Minors   207

Pitchers Winning All-Star Game and World Series Game,
    Same Season   207

Pitchers Who Pitched More Than Three Innings in One All-Star Game   207

All-Star Game Managers Who Never Managed in World Series   207

Brothers Selected to Play in All-Star Game, Same Season   207

Players Hitting Home Runs in All-Star Game and World Series,
    Same Season   208

Fathers and Sons, Both of Whom Played in All-Star Games   208

Pitchers with No Victories, Named to All-Star Team   208

Oldest Players Named to All-Star Team   208

10 **Teams**   209

Teams' Won-Lost Percentage by Decade   209

Clubs Winning 100 Games, Not Winning Pennant   213

Pennant Winners One Year, Losing Record Next (Post-1900)   214

Pennant-Winning Season After Losing Record Year Before   214

Teams Winning 100 Games in a Season, 3 Years in a Row   215

Largest Increase in Games Won by Team Next Season   215
Largest Decrease in Games Won Next Season   216
Teams with Worst Won-Lost Percentage   216
Teams Hitting .300   217
Teams with Three 20-Game Winners   217
Teams with 30-Game Winners, Not Winning Pennant   218
Teams Leading or Tied for First Place Entire Season   218
Teams Scoring in Every Inning   218
Most Lopsided Shutouts   219

11   **Miscellany**   221
Players with Both Little League and Major League World Series Teams   221
Olympians (in Sports Other Than Baseball) Who Played
   Major League Baseball   221
Babe Ruth's Yearly Salary   221
Players Leading N.Y. Yankees in Home Runs One Season,
   Playing Elsewhere Next Season   222
Billy Martin's Fights   222
Four-Decade Players   222
First Players Chosen in Draft by Expansion Teams   223
Last Active Player Once Playing for . . .   223
Last Players Born in Nineteenth Century to Play in Majors   224
First Players Born in Twentieth Century to Play in Majors   224
Second African American to Play for Each of 16 Original
   Major League Teams   224
Players Having Same Number Retired on Two Different Clubs   224
Major Leaguers Who Played Pro Football in Same Year(s)   225
Performances by Oldest Players   225
Oldest Players, by Position   226
Youngest Players to Play in Majors   226
Youngest Players, by Position   226

Players Who Played During Most Presidential Administrations   227

Players Playing Most Seasons with One Address (One Club, One City in
     Majors)   227

Players Who Played 2500 Games in One Uniform (Post-1900)   228

Players Playing Most Seasons in City of Birth   228

Players with Same Surname as Town of Birth   228

Players with Longest Given Names   228

Players with Palindromic Surnames*   228

Most Common Last Names in Baseball History   229

Number of Major League Players by First Letter of Last Name*   229

Third Basemen on Tinker-to-Evers-to-Chance Chicago Cubs Teams*   229

First Designated Hitter for Each Major League Team   229

Players Killed as Direct Result of Injuries Sustained in
     Major League Games   230

Players Who Played for Three New York Teams   230

Players Who Played for Both Original and Expansion
     Washington Senators   231

Players Who Played for Both K.C. A's and K.C. Royals   231

Players Who Played for Both Milwaukee Braves and
     Milwaukee Brewers   231

Pitchers Who Gave Up Most Hits to Pete Rose   231

Pitchers Who Gave Up Home Runs to Both Mark McGwire and
     Barry Bonds in Their Record-Breaking Seasons (1998 and 2001)   232

Major League Shortstops from San Pedro de Macoris,
     Dominican Republic   232

Players Born on Leap Year Day (February 29)   232

Players Who Played on Four of California's Five Major League Teams   232

Tallest Players in Major League History   233

Shortest Players in Major League History   233

Teammates the Longest   233

Teammates with 300 Wins and 500 Home Runs   234

New Baseball Stadiums Built Since 2005   234

Players Traded for Themselves   234

Players Wearing Numbers "0" and "00"   234

Part 2   **Team-by-Team Histories**   235

American League   237

Baltimore Orioles   237

Boston Red Sox   241

Chicago White Sox   247

Cleveland Indians   252

Detroit Tigers   258

Kansas City Royals   264

Los Angeles Angels of Anaheim   267

Minnesota Twins   270

New York Yankees   273

Oakland A's   280

Seattle Mariners   284

Tampa Bay Rays   286

Texas Rangers   288

Toronto Blue Jays   290

National League   293

Arizona Diamondbacks   293

Atlanta Braves   295

Chicago Cubs   299

Cincinnati Reds   305

Colorado Rockies   311

Florida Marlins   313

Houston Astros   315

Los Angeles Dodgers   318

Milwaukee Brewers   322

New York Mets   325

Philadelphia Phillies   328

Pittsburgh Pirates   334

St. Louis Cardinals   340

San Diego Padres   347

San Francisco Giants   350

Washington Nationals   353

Franchises No Longer in Existence   357

Boston Braves   357

Brooklyn Dodgers   361

New York Giants   365

Philadelphia Athletics   370

St. Louis Browns   374

Washington Senators   377

FOREWORD

Statistics (or as they are known in their circumcised, smaller version of the word, "stats") have been a part of baseball—indeed, the very mortar of the sport—since the dawn of the game, even if in the beginning their number was so few they could be entered on a postcard with more than enough room left for an oversized one-cent stamp and a generous message. And those few reduced to paper could be called statistics only in the same way raisins could be called fruit—technically and only in a manner of speaking.

Take, for example, one of the very first recorded: that of the number of miles traveled by the first professional baseball team, the Cincinnati Red Stockings, as they criss-crossed the country in 1869, their first year in existence. One of the early recordkeepers estimated that the Red Stockings had covered some 11,877 miles, playing in 57 games—of which they won 56 and tied one. However, one historian, ever Thomas the Doubter, doubling back on the historic breadcrumbs laid down by the Red Stockings, discovered that Harry Wright's team had played at least 80 games in their inaugural season and figured they had many a mile more to go than that originally estimated.

Many of those early records set down by recordkeepers were something of a hit-or-miss proposition—mostly miss. One of those came on the afternoon of Thursday, September 6, 1883, when Cap Anson's Chicago White Stockings set a record by scoring 18 runs in the seventh inning against the Detroit Wolverines. However, when the report of the game was wired to the *Detroit Free Press,* as well as other papers around the country, most of the details of the game were MIA. The sporting editor of the Free Press, taking note of the omissions, apologized to his readers, writing that the paper "would be pleased to submit the full score of this remarkable game to its readers, but the Western Union Telegraph Company, which has no excuse for its poor service, has furnished it bobtailed and in ludicrous deformity . . . the Company was requested to supply the missing links, but the head operator declined to do so."

There were several other instances of reporters or Western Union operatives exhibiting a polite fiction of the non-existence of such relevant statistics, several times omitting the names of batterymates. However, here it must be noted that many's the time in those early days of organized-and-disorganized-baseball, even the pitcher and the catcher didn't know the names of their batterymates. Such was the case in 1897 when the pitcher and the catcher of the Louisville team were as unfamiliar to one another as two shipwrecked survivors coming ashore on a wave-swept beach, neither knowing the name of the other. None of their teammates knew their names either, both having just joined the team—the pitcher the day before; the catcher being signed on a trial basis just before the game. When the pitcher was asked by writers who his catcher was, he answered, "Couldn't tell you, first time I ever saw him." The catcher's answer to the identity of the pitcher was ditto. Still at a loss as to the names of the two, the writers now approached manager Fred Clarke and asked the same question. As lost as Robinson Crusoe without a boat, all Clarke could do was point to the name "Weddel" on the scorecard and say, "This man will pitch." Then, pointing to the tall man putting on his catcher's gear, said, "And that tall fellow over there will catch." Calling over to his catcher, Clarke had him spell out his name for the writers, which he did: "S-c-h-r-e-c-k-e-n-g-o-s-t." Then, asked by the writers if the "Weddel" on the scorecard was the correct spelling, Clarke shrugged his shoulders and responded, "Don't know, you'll have to ask him." They did, discovering it was spelled "Waddell." (Ironically, after their dual Major League debut, Ossee Schreckengost and Rube Waddell's faces would become as recognizable to one another as those seen in the mirror every morning as they became batterymates for six seasons with the Philadelphia Athletics.)

The shoddy record keeping of the time also resulted in several other records being overlooked, there being no mention of the-then-record 11 RBIs in one game by Baltimore Oriole Wilbert Robinson nor the 27 home runs by Chicago White Stocking Ned Williamson in 1884, both records forgotten by the time they were broken—Robinson's by Jim Bottomley and Williamson's by Babe Ruth.

Ernest Lanigan, baseball's first great historian, noted that the omission of Williamson's season record of 27 home runs was occasioned by the fact that whenever Henry Chadwick—known as "The Father of Baseball," but whom Lanigan called "that human eliminator"—wrote on the subject of home runs, "which variety of hits he detested . . . (he) eliminated them from the guides."

Early records were thus cut and restitched to fit any pattern the recordkeeper wanted, many of their entries unable to stand up to the slightest investigation. In one classic case Wee Willie Keeler was credited by the Baltimore scorekeeper with four hits in a 1897 game versus St. Louis. However, St. Louis sportswriter Frank Houseman, pulling up the game to study its roots, wrote the following rundown of Keeler's run-up of hits: "Down in Baltimore, Keeler sent two flies to (Bud) Larry, who muffed both of them. Then he hit to (Fred) Hartman, who fumbled the ball and threw wild. Then Keeler made a good single. The next morning, four hits appeared to Keeler's credit in the Baltimore papers." Houseman couldn't resist adding, "Talk about stuffing records."

And, as if it wasn't enough that telegraphers or writers "stuffed" a player's performance, sometimes they even "stuffed" the line-up itself. In one of those moments that inspires a reference to A. Lincoln's sonnet about "fooling all the people . . . ," a St. Louis Western Union operative up in the press box named Lou Proctor, in a "Forgive us our Press Passes" moment, inserted his own name in a 1912 St. Louis Browns boxscore, fooling even the MacMillan Baseball Encyclopedia editors who included it in their first edition, giving him equal standing with "Moonlight" Graham before discovering the error and dropping Proctor from its later editions.

As sportswriters and fans voyaged, Columbus-like, into the new world of baseball statistics, commissions and omissions weren't the only problems they faced. One of those problems was the determinate criteria for stolen bases, there being no baseline (good word, that!) of agreed-upon standards. At given times over the years, runners were given credit for a stolen base when they scored from third on a fly out, when they took two bases on an infield out, when they were the successful half of a double-steal when the other half was thrown out, or even when they overslid a base and were tagged out.

Other statistics, like strikeouts, runs scored and batted in, and sacrifices, hitherto unaccountable in whole or in part, came late to the table and were incorporated into baseball's growing world of stats—soon to be joined by others.

Still, with annuals like the early day *Reach* and *Spalding Guides* and Balldom as well as *The Sporting Life Base Ball Guide and Handbook* and the while-you-get-your-haircut weeklies serving up heaping platefuls of statistics to satisfy the appetite of ever-increasingly hungry fans for such fare, statistics took on a life of their own, framing the game and providing a basis of comparison of the past and the present.

As baseball archaeologists like the aforementioned Lanigan began spackling the cracks by correcting some of the early statistics that had been recorded with all the innocence of Adam naming the animals on his first day in the Garden by early recordkeepers even they created problems of their own. One such error occurred when the *Reach Guide* of 1903, in a typographical error, credited Nap Lajoie with 43 triples in 1897 when the actual number of triples should have read 23. And so, when Pirate outfielder Owen Wilson, better known as "Chief," began belting the ball all over the lot, hitting seven triples against Chicago and Cincinnati pitching, five against St. Louis and New York, and three each versus Philadelphia and Brooklyn, sportswriters took little note of his feat, figuring his total of 36 still seven shy of Lajoie's "43." It would take some of baseball's best archaeologists to dig back through Lajoie's game-by-game record to exhume his real total and properly acknowledge Wilson's record.

By the 1920s, recordkeeping had approached the foothills of accuracy as statistical cryptographers resurrected and decoded the facts and figures of earlier historians, thus providing a correction to baseball's past. No longer random and haphazard, baseball statistics now had a relativism to earlier-day records and accomplishments, ensuring that no feat would vanish down the hole of history—for baseball records, like everything else, except maybe Eve telling Adam about all the men she could have married, are relative.

It was that thesis of baseball relativity that enabled Lanigan to compare Tip O'Neill's otherworldly .492 batting average in 1887 (later amended to .485) to Babe Ruth's .378 in his great offensive year of 1921 when he hit 59 home runs and drove in 171 runs. Pointing out that in 1887 batters received credit for base hits when they walked, producing helium-like averages, he calculated that Ruth would have an equally lofty .509 in '21 had his then-record of 145 bases on balls counted as hits.

In fact, it was the explosion of the long ball (as personified by The Babe, who held the original copyright) that changed the game. And along with it, its statistics. Suddenly, the trickle of records became a Niagara as statisticians wore a carload of pencils down to their stubs recording them as records lasting about as long as Hollywood bridegrooms.

As the game continued to evolve, so too did the statistics, growing with the game. And nothing proved that the body of statistics was growing at an exponential rate more than a quiz show back in the '50s called "The $64,000 Question," where one contestant, a Georgian housewife named Myrtle Powers, was asked to name the seven players who "had a lifetime total of 3,000 or more hits." Ms. Powers correctly answered: "Ty Cobb, Honus Wagner, Nap Lajoie, Eddie Collins, Tris Speaker, Cap Anson, and Paul Waner," the number who had climbed that statistical mountain over the past 80-plus years. Now, a half-century later, a total of 27 players, almost a fourfold number, have reached that magic mark.

But, even as baseball's "official" recordkeepers continue to col-lect each and every statistic from the obvious to the most minute, amateur historians who OD on baseball stats continue to find omissions and commissions—such as an extra run batted in by Hack Wilson in his record-setting 190 RBI season of 1930, an extra triple in the lifetime total of Lou Gehrig, and a double-counting of a two-for-three day by Ty Cobb in 1910, which would have cost him the batting title to Nap Lajoie by one point. (Such a finding of an error even occurred in that Holiest of Holy places, the Base-ball Hall of Fame, when an eagle-eyed fan standing in front of the Babe Ruth plaque noted that the inscription for his playing days read "1915–1935" and pointed out to the powers-that-be that Ruth had first played for the Red Sox in 1914, not 1915.)

Now I had always considered myself as part of that amateur array of baseballogists, one of a large group of enthusiasts who accumulate lists of stats, especially those with more variations on the theme than even Mussorgsky had imagined.

But it wasn't until I met a fellow traveler in stats named Jack McClain that I realized that my variations were as nothing compared to those Jack had conceived—his lists defying normal categorization, like "Most Pitching Wins by Zodiac Sign," "Most Home Runs by State of Birth," et cetera, etc., etc., etc.—the et ceteras going on for about five pages or more. We decided on the spot to collaborate on a book of what we called "fun stats," a novel approach of combining our efforts into one volume that would be different from anything before.

Unfortunately, Jack passed away before we had finished our book, leaving me to carry on alone. But over the years, I have continued to develop list after list—so many, in fact, they are available at a discount. And now, with the able assistance of many others, including Bill Francis of the Baseball Hall of Fame, Cornell Richardson, the Office of the Baseball Commissioner, Mark Weinstein, Parker Bena, Frances J. Buonarota, Jason Katzman, and a cast of hundreds, if not thousands, it is my pleasure to give you a different perspective (call it a "different view from the same pew," if you will) on America's second most popular pastime: baseball statistics.

—Bert Randolph Sugar

THE BASEBALL
MANIAC'S
ALMANAC
3RD EDITION

PART 1
Individual Statistics

BATTING

Base Hits

Most Hits by Decade

Pre-1900		1900-1909		1910-1919	
3012	Cap Anson	1847	Honus Wagner	1948	Ty Cobb
2467	Roger Connor	1677	Sam Crawford	1821	Tris Speaker
2303	Jim O'Rourke	1660	Nap Lajoie	1682	Eddie Collins
2296	Dan Brouthers	1566	Willie Keeler	1556	Clyde Milan
2258	Bid McPhee	1559	Ginger Beaumont	1548	Joe Jackson
2134	Jimmy Ryan	1460	Cy Seymour	1535	Jake Daubert
2127	Hugh Duffy	1431	Elmer Flick	1516	Zack Wheat
2107	Monte Ward	1396	Fred Clarke	1502	Home Run Baker
2086	George Van Haltren	1387	Fred Tenney	1481	Heinie Zimmerman
2084	Ed McKean	1373	Bobby Wallace	1475	Ed Konetchy

1920-1929		1930-1939		1940-1949	
2085	Rogers Hornsby	1959	Paul Waner	1578	Lou Boudreau
2010	Sam Rice	1865	Charlie Gehringer	1563	Bob Elliott
1924	Harry Heilmann	1845	Jimmie Foxx	1512	Dixie Walker
1900	George Sisler	1802	Lou Gehrig	1432	Stan Musial
1808	Frankie Frisch	1786	Earl Averill	1407	Bobby Doerr
1734	Babe Ruth	1700	Al Simmons	1402	Tommy Holmes
1698	Joe Sewell	1697	Ben Chapman	1376	Luke Appling
1623	Charlie Jamieson	1676	Chuck Klein	1328	Bill Nicholson
1570	Charlie Grimm	1673	Mel Ott	1310	Marty Marion
1569	George Kelly	1650	Joe Cronin	1304	Phil Cavarretta

1950-59		1960-69		1970-79	
1875	Richie Ashburn	1877	Roberto Clemente	2045	Pete Rose
1837	Nellie Fox	1819	Hank Aaron	1787	Rod Carew
1771	Stan Musial	1776	Vada Pinson	1686	Al Oliver
1675	Alvin Dark	1744	Maury Wills	1617	Lou Brock
1605	Duke Snider	1692	Brooks Robinson	1565	Bobby Bonds
1551	Gus Bell	1690	Curt Flood	1560	Tony Perez
1526	Minnie Minoso	1651	Billy Williams	1552	Larry Bowa
1517	Red Schoendienst	1635	Willie Mays	1550	Ted Simmons
1499	Yogi Berra	1603	Frank Robinson	1549	Amos Otis
1491	Gil Hodges	1592	Ron Santo	1548	Bobby Murcer

continued on next page

1980-89		1990-99		2000-11	
1731	Robin Yount	1754	Mark Grace	2428	Ichiro Suzuki
1642	Eddie Murray	1747	Rafael Palmeiro	2281	Derek Jeter
1639	Willie Wilson	1728	Craig Biggio	2108	Miguel Tejada
1597	Wade Boggs	1713	Tony Gwynn	2092	Vladimir Guerrero
1553	Dale Murphy	1678	Roberto Alomar	2073	Albert Pujols
1547	Harold Baines	1622	Ken Griffey Jr.	2061	Michael Young
1539	Andre Dawson	1589	Cal Ripken Jr.	2043	Johnny Damon
1507	Rickey Henderson	1584	Dante Bichette	2020	Juan Pierre
1504	Alan Trammell	1573	Fred McGriff	1994	Bobby Abreu
1497	Dwight Evans	1568	Paul Molitor	1756	Todd Helton

Evolution of Singles Record

American League

1901	Nap Lajoie, Phila. A's	154
1903	Patsy Dougherty, Bost. Red Sox	161
1904	Willie Keeler, N.Y. Yankees	164
1906	Willie Keeler, N.Y. Yankees	166
1911	Ty Cobb, Det. Tigers	169
1920	George Sisler, St. L. Browns	171
1921	Jack Tobin, St. L. Browns	179
1925	Sam Rice, Wash. Senators	182
1980	Willie Wilson, K.C. Royals	184
1985	Wade Boggs, Bost. Red Sox	187
2001	Ichiro Suzuki, Sea. Mariners	192
2004	Ichiro Suzuki, Sea. Mariners	225

National League (Post-1900)

1900	Willie Keeler, Bklyn. Dodgers	179
1901	Jesse Burkett, St. L. Cardinals	180
1927	Lloyd Waner, Pitt. Pirates	198

Most Hits, Season

American League

Ichiro Suzuki, Sea. Mariners, 2004	262
George Sisler, St. L. Browns, 1920	257
Al Simmons, Phila. A's, 1925	253
Ty Cobb, Det. Tigers, 1911	248
George Sisler, St. L. Browns, 1922	246
Ichiro Suzuki, Sea. Mariners, 2001	242
Heine Manush, St. L. Browns, 1928	241
Wade Boggs, Bost. Red Sox, 1985	240
Darin Erstad, Anaheim, 2000	240

National League (Post-1900)

Lefty O'Doul, Phila. Phillies, 1929	254
Bill Terry, N.Y. Giants, 1930	254
Rogers Hornsby, St. L. Cardinals, 1922	250
Chuck Klein, Phila. Phillies, 1930	250
Babe Herman, Bklyn. Dodgers, 1930	241

Base Hit Leaders by State of Birth

Alabama	Hank Aaron (Mobile)	3771
Alaska	Josh Phelps (Anchorage)	380
Arizona	Billy Hatcher (Williams)	1146
Arkansas	Lou Brock (El Dorado)	3023
California	Eddie Murray (Los Angeles)	3255
Colorado	Roy Hartzell (Golden)	1146
Connecticut	Roger Connor (Waterbury)	2467

Delaware	Delino DeShields (Seaford)	1548
Florida	Andre Dawson (Miami)	2774
Georgia	Ty Cobb (Narrows)	4189
Hawaii	Shane Victorino (Wailuku)	908
Idaho	Harmon Killebrew (Payette)	2086
Illinois	Robin Yount (Danville)	3142
Indiana	Sam Rice (Morocco)	2987

Iowa	Cap Anson (Marshalltown)	3012	Oregon	Dale Murphy (Portland)	2111
Kansas	Johnny Damon (Fort Riley)	2723	Pennsylvania	Stan Musial (Donora)	3630
Kentucky	Pee Wee Reese (Ekron)	2170	Rhode Island	Nap Lajoie (Woonsocket)	3242
Louisiana	Mel Ott (Gretna)	2876	South Carolina	Jim Rice (Anderson)	2452
Maine	George Gore (Saccarappa)	1612	South Dakota	Dave Collins (Rapid City)	1335
Maryland	Cal Ripken Jr. (Havre de Grace)	3184	Tennessee	Vada Pinson (Memphis)	2757
Massachusetts	Rabbit Maranville (Springfield)	2605	Texas	Tris Speaker (Lake Whitney)	3514
Michigan	Charlie Gehringer (Fowlerville)	2839	Utah	Duke Sims (Salt Lake City)	580
Minnesota	Paul Molitor (St. Paul)	3319	Vermont	Carlton Fisk (Bellows Falls)	2356
Mississippi	Dave Parker (Grenada)	2712	Virginia	Willie Horton (Arno)	1993
Missouri	Jake Beckley (Hannibal)	2934	Washington	Ryne Sandberg (Spokane)	2386
Montana	John Lowenstein (Wolf Point)	881	West Virginia	George Brett (Glen Dale)	3154
Nebraska	Wade Boggs (Omaha)	3010	Wisconsin	Al Simmons (Milwaukee)	2927
Nevada	Marty Cordova (Las Vegas)	938	Wyoming	Mike Lansing (Rawlings)	1124
New Hampshire	Arlie Latham (West Lebanon)	1836	American Samoa	Tony Solaita	336
New Jersey	Derek Jeter (Pequannock)	3088	District of Columbia	Maury Wills	2134
New Mexico	Vern Stephens (McAllister)	1859	Puerto Rico	Roberto Clemente	3000
New York	Carl Yastrzemski (Southampton)	3419	Virgin Islands	Horace Clarke	1230
North Carolina	Luke Appling (High Point)	2749			
North Dakota	Darin Erstad (Jamestown)	1697			
Ohio	Pete Rose (Cincinnati)	4256			
Oklahoma	Paul Waner (Harrah)	3152			

Players with 200 Hits and 40 Home Runs, Season

American League	Hits	Home Runs	National League (Post-1900)	Hits	Home Runs
Babe Ruth, N.Y. Yankees, 1921	204	59	Rogers Hornsby, St. L. Cardinals, 1922	250	42
Babe Ruth, N.Y. Yankees, 1923	205	41	Rogers Hornsby, Chi. Cubs, 1929	229	40
Babe Ruth, N.Y. Yankees, 1924	220	46	Chuck Klein, Phila. Phillies, 1929	219	43
Lou Gehrig, N.Y. Yankees, 1927	218	47	Chuck Klein, Phila. Phillies, 1930	250	40
Lou Gehrig, N.Y. Yankees, 1930	220	41	Hank Aaron, Milw. Braves, 1963	201	44
Lou Gehrig, N.Y. Yankees, 1931	211	46	Billy Williams, Chi. Cubs, 1970	205	42
Jimmie Foxx, Phila. A's, 1932	213	58	Ellis Burks, Colo. Rockies, 1996	211	40
Jimmie Foxx, Phila. A's, 1933	204	48	Mike Piazza, L.A. Dodgers, 1997	201	40
Lou Gehrig, N.Y. Yankees, 1934	210	49	Larry Walker, Colo. Rockies, 1997	208	49
Lou Gehrig, N.Y. Yankees, 1936	205	49	Vinny Castilla, Colo. Rockies, 1998	206	46
Hal Trosky, Cleve. Indians, 1936	216	42	Todd Helton, Colo. Rockies, 2000	216	42
Joe DiMaggio, N.Y. Yankees, 1937	215	46	Albert Pujols, St. L. Cardinals, 2003	212	43
Hank Greenberg, Det. Tigers, 1937	200	40			
Al Rosen, Cleve. Indians, 1953	201	43			
Jim Rice, Bost. Red Sox, 1970	213	46			
Mo Vaughn, Bost. Red Sox, 1996	207	44			
Albert Belle, Chi. White Sox, 1998	200	49			
Alex Rodriguez, Sea. Mariners, 1998	213	42			
Mo Vaughn, Bost. Red Sox, 1998	205	40			
Alex Rodriguez, Tex. Rangers, 2001	201	52			

Players with 200 Base Hits and Fewer Than 40 Extra-Base Hits, Season (Post-1900)

American League	Hits	Extra-Base Hits	National League (Post-1900)	Hits	Extra-Base Hits
Johnny Pesky, Bost. Red Sox, 1947	207	35	Willie Keeler, Bklyn. Dodgers, 1900	204	29
Nellie Fox, Chi. White Sox, 1954	201	34	Willie Keeler, Bklyn. Dodgers, 1901	202	32
Harvey Kuenn, Det. Tigers, 1954	201	39	Milt Stock, St. L. Cardinals, 1920	204	34
Cesar Tovar, Minn. Twins, 1971	204	33	Milt Stock, Bklyn. Dodgers, 1925	202	38
Rod Carew, Minn. Twins, 1974	218	38	Lloyd Waner, Pitt. Pirates, 1927	223	25
Ichiro Suzuki, Sea. Mariners, 2004	262	37	Chick Fullis, Phila. Phillies, 1933	200	38
Ichiro Suzuki, Sea. Mariners, 2006	224	38	Richie Ashburn, Phila. Phillies, 1953	205	36
Ichiro Suzuki, Sea. Mariners, 2007	238	35	Richie Ashburn, Phila. Phillies, 1958	215	39
Ichiro Suzuki, Sea. Mariners, 2008	213	33	Maury Wills, L.A. Dodgers, 1962	208	28
Ichiro Suzuki, Sea. Mariners, 2010	214	39	Curt Flood, St. L. Cardinals, 1964	211	33
			Matty Alou, Pitt. Pirates, 1970	201	30
			Ralph Garr, Atl. Braves, 1971	219	39
			Dave Cash, Phila. Phillies, 1974	206	39
			Tony Gwynn, S.D. Padres, 1984	213	36

Players with 3000 Hits, Career

	Hits	Date of 3000th Hit	Opposing Pitcher
Pete Rose	4256	May 5, 1978	Steve Rogers, Mont. Expos (NL)
Ty Cobb	4189	Aug. 19, 1921	Elmer Myers, Bost. Red Sox (AL)
Hank Aaron	3771	May 17, 1970	Wayne Simpson, Cin. Reds (NL)
Stan Musial	3630	May 13, 1958	Moe Drabowsky, Chi. Cubs (NL)
Tris Speaker	3514	May 17, 1925	Tom Zachary, Wash. Senators (AL)
Honus Wagner	3420	June 9, 1914	Erskine Mayer, Phila. Phillies (NL)
Carl Yastrzemski	3419	Sept. 12, 1979	Jim Beattie, N.Y. Yankees (AL)
Paul Molitor	3319	Sept. 16, 1996	Jose Rosado, K.C. Royals (AL)
Eddie Collins	3315	June 3, 1925	Rip Collins, Det. Tigers (AL)
Willie Mays	3283	July 18, 1970	Mike Wegener, Mont. Expos (NL)
Eddie Murray	3255	June 30, 1995	Mike Trombley, Minn. Twins (AL)
Nap Lajoie	3242	Sept. 27, 1914	Marty McHale, N.Y. Yankees (AL)
Cal Ripken Jr.	3184	Apr. 15, 2000	Hector Carrasco, Minn. Twins (AL)
George Brett	3154	Sept. 30, 1992	Tim Fortugno, Cal. Angels (AL)
Paul Waner	3152	June 19, 1942	Rip Sewell, Pitt. Pirates (NL)
Robin Yount	3142	Sept. 9, 1992	Jose Mesa, Cleve. Indians (AL)
Tony Gwynn	3141	Aug. 6, 1999	Dan Smith, Mont. Expos (NL)
Dave Winfield	3110	Sept. 16, 1993	Dennis Eckersley, Oak. A's (AL)
Craig Biggio	3060	June 28, 2007	Aaron Cook, Colo. Rockies (NL)
Derek Jeter	3088	July 9, 2011	David Price, Tampa Bay Rays (AL)
Rickey Henderson	3055	Oct. 7, 2001	John Thomson, Colo. Rockies (NL)
Rod Carew	3053	Aug. 4, 1985	Frank Viola, Minn. Twins (AL)
Lou Brock	3023	Aug. 13, 1979	Dennis Lamp, Chi. Cubs (NL)
Rafael Palmeiro	3020	July 15, 2005	Joel Piniero, Sea. Mariners (AL)
Cap Anson	3012	July 18, 1897	George Blackburn, Balt. Orioles (NL)
Wade Boggs	3010	Aug. 7, 1999	Chris Haney, Cleve. Indians (AL)
Al Kaline	3007	Sept. 24, 1974	Dave McNally, Balt. Orioles (AL)
Roberto Clemente	3000	Sept. 30, 1972	Jon Matlack, N.Y. Mets (NL)

Most Hits by Position, Season

American League

First Base ....257............George Sisler, St. L. Browns, 1920

Second Base ....232 ....Nap Lajoie, Phila. A's, 1901

Third Base ....240 ....Wade Boggs, Bost. Red Sox, 1985

Shortstop ....219 ....Derek Jeter, N.Y. Yankees, 1999

Outfield ....262 ....Ichiro Suzuki, Sea. Mariners, 2004

Catcher ....199 ....Ivan Rodriguez, Tex. Rangers, 1999

Pitcher ....52 ....George Uhle, Cleve. Indians, 1923

Designated Hitter ...216 ....Paul Molitor, Milw. Brewers, 1991

National League (Post-1900)

First Base ....254 ....Bill Terry, N.Y. Giants, 1930

Second Base ....250 ......Rogers Hornsby, St. L. Cardinals, 1922

Third Base ....231 ....Fred Lindstrom, N.Y. Giants, 1928 and 1930

Shortstop ....211 .....Garry Templeton, St. L. Cardinals, 1978

Outfield ....254 ....Lefty O'Doul, Phila. Phillies, 1929

Catcher ....201 ....Mike Piazza, L.A. Dodgers, 1997

Pitcher ....47 ....Red Lucas, Cin. Reds, 1927

Players Hitting for the Cycle Two or More Times (Post-1900)

Three Times

Babe Herman, Bklyn. Dodgers (NL), 1931 (2); Chi. Cubs (NL), 1933   Bob Meusel, N.Y. Yankees (AL), 1921, 1922, 1928

Two Times

Ken Boyer, St. L. Cardinals (NL), 1961, 1964

Cesar Cedeno, Cin. Reds (NL), 1972, 1976

Fred Clarke, Pitt. Pirates (NL), 1901, 1903

Mickey Cochrane, Phila. A's (AL), 1932, 1933

Joe Cronin, Wash. Senators (AL), 1929; Bost. Red Sox (AL), 1940

Joe DiMaggio, N.Y. Yankees (AL), 1937, 1948

Bobby Doerr, Bost. Red Sox (AL), 1944, 1947

Jim Fregosi, L.A. Angels (AL), 1964, 1968

Lou Gehrig, N.Y. Yankees (AL), 1934, 1937

Chuck Klein, Phila. Phillies (NL), 1931, 1933

John Olerud, Sea. Mariners (AL) 2001, N.Y. Mets (NL) 1997

George Sisler, St. L. Browns (AL), 1920, 1921

Chris Speier Mont. Expos (NL) 1978, S.F. Giants (NL) 1988

Arky Vaughan, Pitt. Pirates (NL), 1933, 1939

Bob Watson, Hous. Astros (NL), 1977; Bost. Red Sox (AL), 1979

Wally Westlanke, Pitt. Pirates (NL), 1948, 1949

Brad Wilkerson, Mont. Expos (NL) 2003, Was. Nationals (NL) 2005

Most Times at Bat Without a Hit, Season

American League

61 ....Bill Wight, Chi. White Sox, 1950

46 ....Karl Drews, St. L. Browns, 1949

41 ....Ernie Koob, St. L. Browns, 1916

39 ....Ed Rakow, Det. Tigers, 1964

31 ....Bob Miller, Minn. Twins, 1969

National League (Post-1900)

70.........................Bob Buhl, Milw. Braves–Chi. Cubs, 1962

47...Ron Herbel, S.F. Giants, 1964

41 ....Randy Tate, N.Y. Mets, 1975

40 ....Jason Burgemin, Was. Nationals, 2008

40 ....Joey Hamilton, S.D.Podras, 1994

38 ....Darryl Kile, Hous. Astros, 1991

37....................................Evgenio Velez, S.F. Giants, 2011

36.......................................Harry Parker, N.Y. Mets, 1974

Players with 200 Hits in Each of First Three Major League Seasons

Willie Keeler, Balt. Orioles (NL) ....1894 (219), 1895 (221), and 1896 (214)

Johnny Pesky, Bost. Red Sox (AL) ....1942 (205), 1946 (208), and 1947 (207)

Ichiro Suzuki, Sea. Mariners (AL) ....2001 (242), 2002 (208), and 2003 (212)

Lloyd Waner, Pitt. Pirates (NL) ....1927 (223), 1928 (221), and 1929 (234)

Players with 600 Total Hits in First Three Major League Seasons

	Seasons–Hits	Total Hits
Earle Combs	1925–203; 1926–181; 1927–231	615
Joe DiMaggio	1936–206; 1937–215; 1938–194	615
Willie Keeler	1894–219; 1895–221; 1896–214	654
Johnny Pesky	1942–205; 1946–208; 1947–207	620
Al Simmons	1924–183; 1925–253; 1926–199	635

Ichiro Suzuki 2001–242; 2002–202; 2003–212 662
Lloyd Waner 1927–223; 1928–221; 1929–234 678
Paul Waner 1926–180; 1927–237; 1928–223 640

Players with 200-Hit Seasons in Each League

Bill Buckner .... Chi. Cubs (NL), 1982
Bost. Red Sox (AL), 1985
Nap Lajoie .... Phila. A's (AL), 1901
Cleve. Naps (AL), 1904, 1906, and 1910
Phila. Phillies (NL), 1898

Al Oliver .... Tex. Rangers (AL), 1980
Mont. Expos (NL), 1982
Steve Sax .... L.A. Dodgers (NL), 1986
N.Y. Yankees (AL), 1989
George Sisler .... St. L. Browns (AL), 1920–22, 1925, and 1927
Bost. Braves (NL), 1929

Players with 200 Hits in Five Consecutive Seasons

	Seasons
Ichiro Suzuki, Sea. Mariners (AL), 2001–10	10
Willie Keeler, Balt. Orioles (NL), 1894–98, and Bklyn. Dodgers (NL), 1899–1901	8
Wade Boggs, Bost. Red Sox (AL), 1983–89	7
Chuck Klein, Phila. Phillies (NL), 1929–33	5
Al Simmons, Phila. A's (AL), 1929–32, and Chi. White Sox (AL), 1933	5
Charlie Gehringer, Det. Tigers (AL), 1933–37	5

Rookies with 200 or More Hits

American League

Ichiro Suzuki, Sea. Mariners, 2001	242
Joe Jackson, Cleve. Indians, 1911	233
Tony Oliva, Minn. Twins, 1964	217
Dale Alexander, Det. Tigers, 1929	215
Harvey Kuenn, Det. Tigers, 1953	209
Kevin Seitzer, K.C. Royals, 1987	207
Hal Trosky, Cleve. Indians, 1934	206
Joe DiMaggio, N.Y. Yankees, 1936	206
Johnny Pesky, Bost. Red Sox, 1942	205
Earle Combs, N.Y. Yankees, 1925	203
Roy Johnson, Det. Tigers, 1929	201
Dick Wakefield, Det. Tigers, 1943	200

National League (Post-1900)

Lloyd Waner, Pitt. Pirates, 1927	223
Johnny Frederick, Bklyn. Dodgers, 1929	209
Billy Herman, Chi. Cubs, 1932	206
Vada Pinson, Cin. Reds, 1959*	205
Juan Pierre, Colo. Rockies, 2001	202
Dick Allen, Phila. Phillies, 1964	201

*Not a rookie by present standards.

Teammates Finishing One-Two in Base Hits

American League

Season	Team	Leader	Hits	Runner-Up	Hits
1908	Det. Tigers	Ty Cobb	188	Sam Crawford	184
1915	Det. Tigers	Ty Cobb	208	Sam Crawford	183
1919	Det. Tigers (Tie)	Bobby Veach	191	Ty Cobb	191
1923	Cleve. Indians	Charlie Jamieson	222	Tris Speaker	218
1927	N.Y. Yankees	Earl Combs	231	Lou Gehrig	218
1929	Det. Tigers (Tie)	Dale Alexander	215	Charlie Gehringer	215
1938	Bost. Red Sox	Joe Vosmik	201	Doc Cramer	198
1956	Det. Tigers	Harvey Kuenn	196	Al Kaline	194
1960	Chi. White Sox	Minnie Minoso	184	Nellie Fox	175
1965	Minn. Twins	Tony Oliva	185	Zoilo Versalles	182
1982	Milw. Brewers	Robin Yount	210	Cecil Cooper	205
1993	Tor. Blue Jays	Paul Molitor	211	John Olerud	200
2001	Sea. Manners	Ichiro Suzuki	242	Bret Bane	206

National League (Post-1900)

Season	Team	Leader	Hits	Runner-Up	Hits
1910	Pitt. Pirates (Tie)	Bobby Byrne	178	Honus Wagner	178
1920	St. L. Cardinals	Rogers Hornsby	218	Milt Stock	204
1927	Pitt. Pirates	Paul Waner	237	Lloyd Waner	223
1933	Phila. Phillies	Chuck Klein	223	Chick Fullis	200
1952	St. L. Cardinals	Stan Musial	194	Red Schoendienst	188
1957	Milw. Braves	Red Schoendienst	200*	Hank Aaron	198
1965	Cin. Reds	Pete Rose	209	Vada Pinson	204
1979	St. L. Cardinals	Garry Templeton	211	Keith Hernandez	210
2008	N.Y. Mets	Jose Reyer	204	David Wright	189

*Schoendienst had 78 with N.Y. Giants and 122 hits with Braves in 1957.

Players Getting 1000 Hits Before Their 25th Birthday

Ty Cobb, Det. Tigers (AL), 1911	24 years, 4 months
Mel Ott, N.Y. Giants (NL), 1933	24 years, 5 months
Al Kaline, Det. Tigers (AL), 1959	24 years, 7 months
Freddie Lindstrom, N.Y. Giants (NL), 1930	24 years, 8 months
Buddy Lewis, Wash. Senators (AL), 1941	24 years, 9 months
Robin Yount, Milw. Brewers (AL), 1980	24 years, 11 months

Players with 10000 At Bats and Fewer Than 3000 Hits, Career

	At Bats	Hits		At Bats	Hits
Brooks Robinson (1955–77)	10654	2848	Rabbit Maranville (1912–33, 1935)	10078	2605
Omar Vizquel (1989–2011)	10433	2841	Frank Robinson (1956–76)	10006	2943
Luis Aparicio (1956–73)	10230	2677			

Players with 200 Hits, Batting Under .300, Season

	Hits	Batting Average
Juan Pierre, Chic. Cubs (NL), 2006	204	.292
Jo-Jo Moore, N.Y. Giants (NL), 1935	201	.295
Maury Wills, L.A. Dodgers (NL), 1962	208	.299
Lou Brock, St. L. Cardinals (NL), 1967	206	.299
Matty Alou, Pitt. Pirates (NL), 1970	201	.297
Ralph Garr, Atl. Braves (NL), 1973	200	.299
Buddy Bell, Tex. Rangers (AL), 1979	200	.299
Bill Buckner, Bost. Red Sox (AL), 1985	201	.299

Players with 2500 Hits and Career .300 Batting Average, Never Winning Batting Title (Post-1900)

	Career Hits	Career Batting Average
Paul Molitor	3319	.306
Eddie Collins	3314	.333
Derek Jeter	3088	.313
Sam Rice	2987	.322
Sam Crawford	2925*	.309
Frankie Frisch	2880	.316
Mel Ott	2876	.304
Roberto Alomar	2724	.300
Vladimir Guerrero	2590	.318

*1899 totals not included.

Former Negro Leaguers with 1500 Major League Hits

3771—Hank Aaron, Milw. Braves (NL), 1954–65; Atl. Braves (NL), 1966–74; Milw. Brewers (AL), 1975–76. (Played in the Negro Leagues with Indianapolis Clowns.)

3283—Willie Mays, N.Y. Giants (NL), 1951–52, 1954–57; S.F. Giants (NL), 1958–71; N.Y. Mets (NL), 1972–73. (Played in the Negro Leagues with Chattanooga Choo-Choos, 1947; Birmingham Black Barons, 1948–50.)

2583—Ernie Banks, Chi. Cubs (NL), 1953–71. (Played in the Negro Leagues with Kansas City Monarchs, 1950–53.)

1963—Minnie Minoso, Cleve. Indians (AL), 1949, 1951, 1958–59; Chi. White Sox (AL), 1951–57, 1960–61, 1964, 1976, 1980; St. L. Cardinals (NL), 1962; Wash. Senators (AL), 1963. (Played in the Negro Leagues with New York Cubans.)

1889—Jim "Junior" Gilliam, Bklyn. Dodgers (NL), 1953–57; L.A. Dodgers (NL), 1958–66. (Played in the Negro Leagues with Nashville Black Vols, 1946; Baltimore Elite Giants, 1946–51)

1518—Jackie Robinson, Bklyn. Dodgers (NL), 1947–56. (Played in the Negro Leagues with Kansas City Monarchs, 1944–45.)

1515—Larry Doby, Cleve. Indians (AL), 1947–55; Chi. White Sox (AL), 1956–57, 1959. (Played in the Negro Leagues with Newark Eagles, 1942–43, 1946–47.)

Players with 2500 Career Hits, Never Having a 200-Hit Season

	Career Hits	Most in One Season
Carl Yastrzemski (1961–83)	3419	191 (1962)
Eddie Murray (1977–97)	3255	186 (1980)
Dave Winfield (1973–95)	3110	193 (1984)
Cap Anson (1871–97)	3081	187 (1886)
Rickey Henderson (1979–2003)	3055	179 (1980)
Jake Beckley (1888–1907)	2930	190 (1900)
Mel Ott (1926–47)	2876	191 (1935)
Harold Baines (1980–98)	2866	198 (1985)
Brooks Robinson (1955–77)	2848	194 (1964)
Ivan Rodriguez (1991–2011)	2844	199 (1999)
Omar Vizquel (1989–2011)	2841	191 (1999)
Ken Griffey (1989–2010)	2781	185 (1997)
Andre Dawson (1976–96)	2774	189 (1983)
Tony Perez (1964–86)	2732	186 (1970)
Barry Bonds (1987–2007)	2730	181 (1993)
Roberto Alomar (1988–2004)	2724	193 (1996)
Rusty Staub (1963–85)	2716	186 (1971)
Luis Aparicio (1956–73)	2677	182 (1966)
George Davis (1890–1909)	2683	195 (1893)
Ted Williams (1939–42, 1946–60)	2654	194 (1949)
Chipper Jones (1993, 1995–2011)	2615	189 (2001)
Rabbit Maranville (1912–33, 1935)	2605	198 (1922)
Tim Raines (1979–2002)	2605	194 (1986)
Reggie Jackson (1967–87)	2584	158 (1973)
Manny Ramirez (1993–2011)	2574	185 (2003)
Ernie Banks (1953–71)	2583	193 (1958)
Willie Davis (1960–76, 1979)	2561	198 (1971)
Joe Morgan (1963–84)	2517	167 (1973)
Jimmy Ryan (1885–1900, 1902–03)	2502	185 (1898)

Latino Players with 2500 Hits

3053	Rod Carew	2732	Tony Perez
3020	Rafael Palmeiro	2724	Roberto Alomar
3000	Roberto Clemente	2677	Luis Aparicio
2844	Ivan Rodriguez*	2591	Luis Gonzalez
2841	Omar Vizquel*	2586	Julio Franco
2775	Alex Rodriguez*	2574	Manny Ramirez
2757	Vada Pinson		

*Active through 2011.

3000 Hits, 500 Home Runs, and a .300 Batting Average, Career

	Hits	Runs	Batting Average		Hits	Runs	Batting Average
Hank Aaron	3771	755	.305	Willie Mays	3283	660	.302

Most Hits by Switch-Hitter, Career

4256	Pete Rose (1963–86)	2724	Roberto Alomar (1988–2004)
3255	Eddie Murray (1977–97)	2665	Max Carey (1910–29)
2880	Frankie Frisch (1919–37)	2665	George Davis (1890–1909)
2841	Omar Vizquel (1989–2011)		

Most Hits by Catcher, Career

2844	Ivan Rodriguez (1999–2011)	2195	Jason Kendall (1996–2010)
2472	Ted Simmons (1968–88)	2150	Yogi Berra (1946–65)
2356	Carlton Fisk (1977–97)	2127	Mike Piazza (1992–2007)
2342	Joe Torre (1960–77)	2092	Gary Carter (1974–92)

Most Singles, Career

3215	Pete Rose (1963–86)	2163	Doc Cramer (1929–48)
3053	Ty Cobb (1905–28)	2162	Luke Appling (1930–50)
2643	Eddie Collins (1906–30)	2161	Nellie Fox (1947–65)
2614	Cap Anson (1871–1897)	2156	Eddie Murray (1977–97)
2513	Willie Keeler (1892–1910)	2154	Roberto Clemente (1955–72)
2424	Honus Wagner (1897–1917)	2130	Jake Beckley (1888–1907)
2404	Rod Carew (1967–85)	2121	George Sisler (1915–22, 1924–30)
2383	Tris Speaker (1907–28)	2119	Richie Ashburn (1948–62)
2378	Tony Gwynn (1982–98)	2108	Luis Aparicio (1956–73)
2366	Paul Molitor (1978–98)	2106	Cal Ripken Jr. (1981–98)
2340	Nap Lajoie (1896–1916)	2104	Zack Wheat (1909–27)
2294	Hank Aaron (1954–1976)	2097	Sam Crawford (1899–1917)
2291	Derek Jeter (1995–2011)	2056	Lave Cross (1887–1907)
2273	Jesse Burkett (1890–1905)	2046	Craig Biggio (1988–2007)
2271	Sam Rice (1915–34)	2035	Al Kaline (1953–74)
2262	Carl Yastrzemski (1961–83)	2033	George Brett (1973–93)
2253	Stan Musial (1941–44, 1946–63)	2033	Lloyd Waner (1927–45)
2253	Wade Boggs (1982–98)	2030	Brooks Robinson (1955–77)
2247	Lou Brock (1961–79)	2030	Fred Clarke (1894–1911, 1913–15)
2243	Paul Waner (1926–45)	2028	George Van Haltren (1887–1903)
2234	Omar Vizquel (1989–2011)	2020	Rabbit Maranville (1912–33, 1935)
2182	Rickey Henderson (1979–2003)	2017	Max Carey (1910–29)
2182	Robin Yount (1974–93)	2017	Dave Winfield (1973–95)
2171	Frankie Frisch (1919–37)		

Fewest Singles, Season (Min. 150 Games)

American League

Singles		Games	Total Hits
53	Mark McGwire, Oak. A's, 1991	154	97
53	Mark Reynolds, Balt. Oridles, 2011	155	118
56	Jose Bautista, Tor. Blue Jays, 2011	161	148
58	Gene Tenace, Oak. A's, 1974	158	102
59	Nick Swisher, N.Y. Yankees, 2009	150	124
61	Mike Pagliarulo, N.Y. Yankees, 1987	150	122
61	Carlos Delgado, Tor. Blue Jays, 1997	153	136
62	Ed Brinkman, Wash. Senators II, 1965	154	82
62	Gorman Thomas, Milw. Brewers, 1979	156	136
64	Harmon Killebrew, Minn. Twins, 1962	155	134
64	Tom McCraw, Chi. White Sox, 1966	151	89
65	Reggie Jackson, Oak. A's, 1969	152	151
66	Glenn Hoffman, Bost. Red Sox, 1982	150	98
66	Tom Brunansky, Minn. Twins, 1983	151	123
66	Jose Canseco, Tor. Blue Jays, 1998	151	138
66	Troy Glaus, Ana. Angels, 2001	161	147
67	Monte Cross, Phila. A's, 1904	153	95
67	Tom Tresh, N.Y. Yankees, 1968	152	99
67	Mickey Tettleton, Det. Tigers, 1993	152	128
67	Jeromy Burnitz, Milw. Brewers, 1997	153	139
67	B.J. Upton, Tampa Bay Rays, 2010	154	127
68	Harmon Killebrew, Wash. Senators, 1959	153	132
68	Tom Brookens, Det. Tigers, 1985	156	115
68	Darrell Evans, Det. Tigers, 1985	151	125
68	Carlton Fisk, Chi. White Sox, 1985	153	129
68	Mark McGwire, Oak. A's, 1990	156	123
68	Mickey Tettleton, Det. Tigers, 1992	157	125
68	Carlos Santana, Clev. Indians, 2011	155	132
69	Jesse Barfield, N.Y. Yankees, 1990	153	117

National League (Post-1900)

Singles		Games	Total Hits
49	Barry Bonds, S.F. Giants, 2001	153	156
53	Carlos Pena, Chi. Cubs, 2011	153	111
55	Andruw Jones, Atl. Braves, 1997	153	92
56	Jose Valentin, Milw. Brewers, 1998	151	96
57	Adam Dunn, Cin. Reds, 2005	160	134
58	Mark McGwire, St. L. Cardinals, 1999	153	145
59	Adam Dunn, Cin. Reds/Ariz. D'backs, 2008	158	122
61	Shane Andrews, Mont. Expos, 1998	150	117
61	Mark McGwire, St. L. Cardinals, 1998	155	152
63	Willie McCovey, S.F. Giants, 1970	152	143
63	Mike Schmidt, Phila. Phillies, 1979	160	137
65	Mike Schmidt, Phila. Phillies, 1975	158	140
65	Adam Dunn, Cin. Reds, 2006	160	131
66	Todd Hundley, N.Y. Mets, 1996	153	140
66	Mike Stanton, Flor. Marlins, 2011	150	135
67	Jeff Conine, Flor. Marlins, 1997	151	98
68	Greg Vaughn, Cin. Reds, 1999	153	135

68	Brian Giles, Pitt. Pirates, 2002	153	148
69	Gil Hodges, Bklyn. Dodgers, 1952	153	129
69	Kevin Elster, N.Y. Mets, 1989	151	106
69	Jeromy Burnitz, Milw. Brewers, 2000	161	131
69	Jeromy Burnitz, N.Y. Mets, 2002	154	103
69	Adam Dunn, Cin. Reds, 2007	152	138
69	Adam Dunn, Was. Nationals, 2010	158	145

Most Singles, Season

American League

Singles		Total Hits
225	Ichiro Suzuki, Sea. Mariners, 2004	262
203	Ichiro Suzuki, Sea. Mariners, 2007	238
192	Ichiro Suzuki, Sea. Mariners, 2001	242
187	Wade Boggs, Bost. Red Sox, 1985	240
186	Ichiro Suzuki, Sea. Mariners, 2006	224
184	Willie Wilson, K.C. Royals, 1980	230
182	Sam Rice, Wash. Senators, 1925	227
180	Rod Carew, Minn. Twins, 1974	218
180	Ichiro Suzuki, Sea. Mariners, 2008	213
179	Jack Tobin, St. L. Browns, 1921	236
179	Ichiro Suzuki, Sea. Mariners, 2009	225
178	George Sisler, St. L. Browns, 1922	246
176	George Sisler, St. L. Browns, 1925	224

National League (Post-1900)

Singles		Total Hits
198	Lloyd Waner, Pitt. Pirates, 1927	223
184	Juan Pierre, Flor. Marlins, 2004	221
183	Matty Alou, Pitt. Pirates, 1969	231
181	Jesse Burkett, St. L. Cardinals, 1901	226
181	Lefty O'Doul, Phila. Phillies, 1929	254
181	Lloyd Waner, Pitt. Pirates, 1929	234
181	Richie Ashburn, Phila. Phillies, 1951	221
181	Pete Rose, Cin. Reds, 1973	230
180	Lloyd Waner, Pitt. Pirates, 1928	221
180	Ralph Garr, Atl. Braves, 1971	219
179	Maury Wills, L.A. Dodgers, 1962	208
178	Paul Waner, Pitt. Pirates, 1937	219
178	Curt Flood, St. L. Cardinals, 1964	211
177	Bill Terry, N.Y. Giants, 1930	254
177	Tony Gwynn, S.D. Padres, 1984	213
176	Richie Ashburn, Phila. Phillies, 1958	215
176	Willie Keeler, Bklyn. Dodgers, 1900	204

20 Triple Seasons (Since 1930)

American League			National League (Post-1900)		
1930	Earle Combs, N.Y. Yankees	22	1930	Adam Comorosky, Pitt. Pirates	23
1935	Joe Vosmik, Cleve. Indians	20	1931	Bill Terry, N.Y. Giants	20
1941	Jeff Heath, Cleve. Indians	20	1943	Stan Musial, St. L. Cardinals	20
1945	Snuffy Stirnweiss, N.Y. Yankees	22	1946	Stan Musial, St. L. Cardinals	20
1949	Dale Mitchell, Cleve. Indians	23	1957	Willie Mays, S.F. Giants	20

1979 George Brett, K.C. Royals 20

1985 Willie Wilson, K.C. Royals 21

2000 Cristian Guzman, Minn. Twins............................20

2007 Curtis Granderson, Det. Tigers 23

1996 Lance Johnson, N.Y. Mets 21

2007 Jimmy Rollins, Phila. Phillies................................20

Largest Differential Between League Leader in Hits and Runner-Up

American League

Differential	Season	Leader	Hits	Runner-Up	Hits
+46	2004	Ichiro Suzuki, Sea. Mariners	262	Michael Young, Tex. Rangers	216
+42	1901	Nap Lajoie, Phila. A's	232	John Anderson, Milw. Brewers	190
+37	1974	Rod Carew, Minn. Twins	218	Tommy Davis, Balt. Orioles	181
+36	2001	Ichiro Suzuki, Sea. Mariners	242	Bret Boone, Sea. Mariners	206
+35	1917	Ty Cobb, Det. Tigers	225	George Sisler, St. L. Browns	190
+35	1922	George Sisler, St. L. Browns	246	Ty Cobb, Det. Tigers	211
+33	1910	Nap Lajoie, Cleve. Indians	227	Ty Cobb, Det. Tigers	194
+33	1920	George Sisler, St. L. Browns	257	Eddie Collins, Chi. White Sox	224
+31	1928	Heinie Manush, St. L. Browns	241	Lou Gehrig, N.Y. Yankees	210
+29	1985	Wade Boggs, Bost. Red Sox	240	Don Mattingly, N.Y. Yankees	211
+27	1945	Snuffy Stirnweiss, N.Y. Yankees	195	Wally Moses, Chi. White Sox	168
+27	1977	Rod Carew, Minn. Twins	239	Ron LeFlore, Det. Tigers	212
+26	1925	Al Simmons, Phila. A's	253	Sam Rice, Wash. Senators	227
+26	2000	Darin Erstad, Ana. Angels	240	Johnny Damon, K.C. Royals	214

National League (Post-1900)

Differential	Season	Leader	Hits	Runner-Up	Hits
+44	1946	Stan Musial, St. L. Cardinals	228	Dixie Walker, Bklyn. Dodgers	184
+40	1948	Stan Musial, St. L. Cardinals	230	Tommy Holmes, Bost. Braves	190
+35	1922	Rogers Hornsby, St. L. Cardinals	250	Carson Bigbee, Pitt. Pirates	215
+34	1987	Tony Gwynn, S.D. Padres	218	Pedro Guerrero, L.A. Dodgers	184
+30	1973	Pete Rose, Cin. Reds	230	Ralph Garr, Atl. Braves	200
+27	1945	Tommy Holmes, Bost. Braves	224	Goody Rosen, Bklyn. Dodgers	197

Batting Average

Evolution of Batting Average Record

American League	National League (Pre-1900)	National League (Post-1900)
1901 Nap Lajoie, Phila. A's .... .426	1876 Ross Barnes, Chi. Cubs .... .404	1900 Honus Wagner, Pitt. Pirates .... .381
	1879 Cap Anson, Chi. Cubs .... .407	1901 Jesse Burkett, St. L. Cardinals .... .382
	1887 Cap Anson, Chi. Cubs .... .421	1921 Rogers Hornsby, St. L. Cardinals .... .397
	1894 Hugh Duffy, Bost. Braves ..... .438	1922 Rogers Hornsby, St. L. Cardinals .... .401
		1924 Rogers Hornsby, St. L. Cardinals .... .424

Highest Batting Average by Position, Season

American League	National League (Post-1900)
First Base .... .420 .....George Sisler, St. L. Browns, 1922	First Base .... .401 ....Bill Terry, N.Y. Giants, 1930

Second Base...... .426.............Nap Lajoie, Phila. A's, 1901

Third Base......... .390........George Brett, K.C. Royals, 1980

Shortstop .... .388............................Luke Appling, Chi. White Sox, 1936

Outfield............. .420................Ty Cobb, Det. Tigers, 1911

Catcher .... .365...........Joe Mauer, Minn. Twins, 2009

Pitcher .... .433 ....Walter Johnson, Wash. Senators, 1925

Designated Hitter .... .356..............................Edgar Martinez, Sea. Mariners, 1995

Second Base...... .424 ....Rogers Hornsby, St. L. Cardinals, 1924

Third Base .... .379.......Fred Lindstrom, N.Y. Giants, 1930

Shortstop .... .385........Arky Vaughan, Pitt. Pirates, 1935

Outfield............. .398........Lefty O'Doul, Phila. Phillies, 1929

Catcher .... .367 .....Babe Phelps, Bklyn. Dodgers, 1936

Pitcher .... .427 ....Jack Bentley, N.Y. Giants, 1923

Highest Batting Average by Decade (2000 At Bats)

Pre-1900
.384.........................Willie Keeler
.356..........................Jesse Burkett
.349.........................Billy Hamilton
.345...........................Ed Delahanty
.342......................Dan Brouthers
.342...................................Dave Orr
.341.......................Pete Browning
.340................................Joe Kelley
.338.............................Jake Stenzel
.336.........................John McGraw

1900–09
.352............................Honus Wagner
.346 ....Nap Lajoie
.338 ....Mike Donlin
.337 ....Ty Cobb
.312 ....Jesse Burkett
.312 ....Elmer Flick
.311 ....Willie Keeler
.311 ....Cy Seymour
.310 ....George Stone
.309 ....Ginger Beaumont

1910–19
.387 ....Ty Cobb
.354 ....Joe Jackson
.344................................Tris Speaker
.331..................................George Sisler
.326 ....Eddie Collins
.321 ....Nap Lajoie
.314....................................Edd Roush
.313 ....Sam Crawford
.313 ....Benny Kauff
.310 ....Home Run Baker
.310................................Vin Campbell
.310 ....Rogers Hornsby

1920–29
.382 ....Rogers Hornsby
.364 ....Harry Heilmann
.357 ....Ty Cobb
.356 ....Al Simmons
.356 ....Paul Waner
.355 ....Babe Ruth
.354 ....Tris Speaker
.347...............................George Sisler
.346 ....Eddie Collins
.342 ....Fats Fothergill

1930–39
.352 ....Bill Terry
.346 ....Johnny Mize
.345 ....Lefty O'Doul
.343 ....Lou Gehrig
.341 ....Joe DiMaggio
.338 ....Joe Medwick
.336 ....Jimmie Foxx
.336 ....Paul Waner
.331 ....Charlie Gehringer
.331 ....Babe Ruth

1940–49
.356 ....Ted Williams
.346................................Stan Musial
.325 ....Joe DiMaggio
.321 ....Barney McCosky
.316 ....Johnny Pesky
.312 ....Enos Slaughter
.311 ....Luke Appling
.311 ....Dixie Walker
.308 ....Taffy Wright
.305 ....George Kell
.305 ....Joe Medwick

1950–59
.336 ....Ted Williams
.330 ....Stan Musial
.333.............................Hank Aaron
.317 ....Willie Mays
.314 ....Harvey Kuenn
.313 ....Richie Ashburn
.311 ....Al Kaline
.311 ....Mickey Mantle
.311 ....Jackie Robinson
.308 ....George Kell
.308................................Duke Snider

1960–69
.328 ....Roberto Clemente
.312.................................Matty Alou
.309 ....Pete Rose
.308 ....Hank Aaron
.308 ....Tony Oliva
.304 ....Frank Robinson
.300 ....Dick Allen
.300 ....Willie Mays
.297 ....Curt Flood
.297 ....Manny Mota

1970–79
.343 ....Rod Carew
.320..............................Bill Madlock
.317 ....Dave Parker
.314 ....Pete Rose
.311 ....Lyman Bostock
.310 ....George Brett
.310 ....Ken Griffey Sr.
.310...................................Jim Rice
.307 ....Ralph Garr
.300 ....Fred Lynn

continued on next page

1980–89	1990–99	2000–11
.352....................................Wade Boggs	.344...............................Tony Gwynn	.328..............................Albert Pujols
.332......................................Tony Gwynn	.328..................................Mike Piazza	.326.................................Ichiro Suzuki
.323.................................Don Mattingly	.322..............................Edgar Martinez	.324......................................Todd Helton
.323...................................Kirby Puckett	.320................................Frank Thomas	.323.......................................Joe Mauer
.314..Rod Carew	.318......................................Derek Jeter	.322....................................Barry Bonds
.311...................................George Brett	.313.....................................Paul Molitor	.318........................Vladimir Guerrero
.308................................Pedro Guerrero	.313......................................Larry Walker	.317..............................Miguel Cabrera
.307..Al Oliver	.312..................................Kirby Puckett	.315....................................Matt Holliday
.305.....................................Robin Yount	.310.....................................Mark Grace	.315................................Manny Ramirez
.304...Will Clark	.310...................................Kenny Lofton	.312.......................................Ryan Braun

Highest Batting Average for a Rookie

American League	National League (Post-1900)
.408..................................Joe Jackson, Cleve. Indians, 1911	.373..........................George Watkins, St. L. Cardinal, 1930
.350..............................Ichiro Suzuki, Sea. Mariners, 2001	.355....................................Lloyd Waner, Pitt. Pirates, 1927
.343.................................Dale Alexander, Det. Tigers, 1929	.354.......................................Kiki Cuyler, Pitt. Pirates, 1924
.343.......................................Jeff Heath, Cleve. Indians, 1938	.352...Hack Miller, Chi. Cubs, 1922
.342.............................Patsy Dougherty, Bost. Red Sox, 1902	.350............................Cuckoo Christiansen, Cin. Reds, 1926
.342.......................................Earle Combs, N.Y. Yankees, 1925	.336...................................Paul Waner, Pitt. Pirates, 1926
.337..Ike Boone, Bost. Red Sox, 1924	

Top 10 Rookie Batting Averages, Each League (Min. 100 Games)

American League	National League (Post-1900)
.408..................................Joe Jackson, Cleve. Indians, 1911	.373........................George Watkins, St. L. Cardinals, 1930
.350..............................Ichiro Suzuki, Sea. Mariners, 2001	.355....................................Lloyd Waner, Pitt. Pirates, 1927
.349..................................Wade Boggs, Bost. Red Sox, 1982	.354.......................................Kiki Cuyler, Pitt. Pirates, 1924
.343.................................Dale Alexander, Det. Tigers, 1929	.352...Hack Miller, Chi. Cubs, 1922
.343.......................................Jeff Heath, Cleve. Indians, 1938	.350............................Cuckoo Christiansen, Cin. Reds, 1926
.342.............................Patsy Dougherty, Bost. Red Sox, 1902	.339..................................Lonnie Smith, Phila. Phillies, 1980
.342.......................................Earle Combs, N.Y. Yankees, 1925	.336...........................Paul Waner, Pitt. Pirates, 1926
.337..Ike Boone, Bost. Red Sox, 1924	.333...........................Richie Ashburn, Phila. Phillies, 1948
.334..................................Heinie Manush, Det. Tigers, 1923	.330...................................Rico Carty, Milw. Braves, 1964
.334...................................Charlie Keller, N.Y. Yankees, 1939	.329...............................Johnny Mize, St. L. Cardinals, 1936
.331................................Mickey Cochrane, Phila. A's, 1925	.329..............................Albert Pujols, St. L. Cardinals, 2001
.331......................................Earl Averill, Cleve. Indians, 1929	.328....................Johnny Frederick, Bklyn. Dodgers, 1929
.331.................................Johnny Pesky, Bost. Red Sox, 1942	.322....................................Alvin Dark, Bost. Braves, 1948
.331.......................................Fred Lynn, Bost. Red Sox, 1975	

Lifetime Batting Averages of 20-Year Players (Not Including Pitchers)

.366........................Ty Cobb (24 years)	.331.................Stan Musial (22 years)	.304...............Manny Mota (20 years)
.359............Rogers Hornsby (23 years)	.328.............Honus Wagner (21 years)	.304.........................Mel Ott (22 years)
.345.................Tris Speaker (22 years)	.325.................Jimmie Foxx (20 years)	.303.................Pete Rose (24 years)
.342.................Babe Ruth (22 years)	.322....................Sam Rice (20 years)	.302.............Willie Mays (22 years)
.338.................Tony Gwynn (20 years)	.312...................Fred Clarke (21 years)	.301...................Joe Cronin (20 years)
.338...................Nap Lajoie (21 years)	.310..............Luke Appling (20 years)	.298.............Julio Franco (23 years)
.334..................Al Simmons (20 years)	.308................Jake Beckley (20 years)	.298............Joe Judge (20 years)
.334....................Cap Anson (22 years)	.306..............Paul Molitor (21 years)	.295.............George Davis (20 years)
.333................Eddie Collins (25 years)	.305..............Hank Aaron (23 years)	.297..............Gabby Hartnett (20 years)
.333..................Paul Waner (20 years)	.305..............George Brett (21 years)	.297....................Al Kaline (22 years)

.296 ....Doc Cramer (20 years)	.284 ...,,,,,,,,....Ken Griffey Jr. (22 years)	.271 ....Joe Morgan (22 years)
.294 ....Tim Raines (23 years)	.283 ....Dave Winfield (22 years)	.270 ....Willie McCovey (22 years)
.294 ....Frank Robinson (21 years)	.282 ....Willie Stargell (21 years)	.269.................Carlton Fisk (24 years)
.293 ....Phil Cavarretta (22 years)	.282 ....Elmer Valo (20 years)	.268............Bobby Wallace (25 years)
.292 ....Lave Cross (21 years)	.280 ....Jimmy Dykes (22 years)	.267 ....Brian Downing (20 years)
.290 ....Charlie Grimm (20 years)	.279 ....Andre Dawson (21 years)	.267...............Jay Johnstone (20 years)
.289 ....Harold Baines (22 years)	.279 ....Rickey Henderson (25 years)	.267........Brooks Robinson (23 years)
.289 ....Bill Buckner (22 years)	.279 ....Tony Perez (23 years)	.266 ....Ron Fairly (21 years)
.287 ....Eddie Murray (21 years)	.279 ....Rusty Staub (23 years)	.263 ....Jack O'Connor (21 years)
.286............Johnny Cooney (20 years)	.278 ....Deacon McGuire (26 years)	.261 ....Kid Gleason (22 years)
.286 ....Mickey Vernon (20 years)	.277 ....Harry Davis (22 years)	.259 ....Luke Sewell (20 years)
.285.................Max Carey (20 years)	.277 ....Jim Thome (21 years)	.258 ....Rabbit Maranville (23 years)
.285 ....Ted Simmons (21 years)	.276.............Cal Ripken Jr. (21 years)	.256........Harmon Killebrew (22 years)
.285 ....Alan Trammell (20 years)	.273 ....Bob O'Farrell (21 years)	.255 ....Gary Gaetti (20 years)
.285..........Carl Yastrzemski (23 years)	.272 ....Bill Dahlen (22 years)	.248 ....Darrell Evans (21 years)
.285 ....Robin Yount (20 years)	.272 ....Omar Vizquel (23 years)	.248 ....Graig Nettles (22 years)
	.271 ....Tim McCarver (21 years)	.233.............Rick Dempsey (24 years)

Players Never Hitting Below .270 in Career (Min. 10 Years)

	Lifetime Batting Average	Lowest Batting Average	Seasons
Cap Anson (1876–97)	.334	.272 (1892)	22
Sam Rice (1915–34)	.322	.293 (1934)	20
Rod Carew (1967–85)	.328	.273 (1968)	19
Tony Gwynn (1982–2000)	.338	.289 (1982)	19
Derek Jeter (1995–2011)	.313	.270 (2010)	17
Vladimir Guerrero (1996–2011)	.318	.290 (2011)	16
George Sisler (1915–22, 1924–30)	.340	.285 (1915)	15
Joe Sewell (1920–33)	.312	.272 (1932)	14
Mickey Cochrane (1925–37)	.320	.270 (1936)	13
Bruce Campbell (1930–42)	.290	.275 (1941)	13
Bibb Falk (1920–31)	.314	.285 (1921)	12
Fats Fothergill (1922–33)	.325	.281 (1930)	12
Earle Combs (1924–35)	.325	.282 (1935)	12
Juan Pierre (2000–11)	.296	.275 (2010)	12
Dom DiMaggio (1940–42, 1946–53)	.298	.283 (1941, 1947)	11
Ichiro Suzuki (2001–11)	.326	.272 (2011)	11
Albert Pujols (2001–11)	.328	.299 (2011)	11
Homer Summa (1920, 1922–30)	.302	.272 (1929)	10

Players Batting .300 for 10 or More Consecutive Seasons From Start of Career

15 ....Ted Williams (1939–42, 1946–51, 1954–58)	11 ...,,,,,,,,,,,...........................Al Simmons (1924–34)
12 ....Paul Waner (1926–37)	10 ....Wade Boggs (1982–91)
	10 ....Albert Pujols (2001–10)

.400 Hitters and How Their Team Finished

American League

	Batting Average	Team's Wins–Losses	Place	Games Behind
Nap Lajoie, Phila. A's, 1901	.427	74–62	4	9½
Ty Cobb, Det. Tigers, 1911	.420	89–65	2	13½
Joe Jackson, Cleve. Indians, 1911	.408	80–73	3	22

continued on next page

Ty Cobb, Det. Tigers, 1912......................... .409 .... 69–84 .... 6 ....36½
George Sisler, St. L. Browns, 1920 .... .407 .... 76–77 .... 4 ....21½
George Sisler, St. L. Browns, 1922 .... .420 .... 93–6l 2 1
Ty Cobb, Det. Tigers, 1922....................... .401 .... 79–75 .... 3 15
Harry Heilmann, Det. Tigers, 1923............. .403 .... 83–71 .... 2 16
Ted Williams, Bost. Red Sox, 1941 .... .406 .... 84–70 .... 2 17

National League (Post-1900)

	Batting Average	Team's Wins–Losses	Place	Games Behind
Rogers Hornsby, St. L. Cardinals, 1922	.401	85–69	3	8
Rogers Hornsby, St. L. Cardinals, 1924	.424	65–89	6	28½
Rogers Hornsby, St. L. Cardinals, 1925	.403	77–76	4	18
Bill Terry, N.Y. Giants, 1930	.401	87–67	3	5

.400 Hitters Versus League Batting Average (Post-1900)

	Batting Average	League Batting Average	Differential
Nap Lajoie, Phila. A's (AL), 1901	.426	.277	+.149
Ty Cobb, Det. Tigers (AL), 1911	.420	.273	+.147
Ty Cobb, Det. Tigers (AL), 1912	.409	.265	+.144
Rogers Hornsby, St. L. Cardinals (NL), 1924	.424	.283	+.141
Ted Williams, Bost. Red Sox (AL), 1941	.406	.266	+.140
George Sisler, St. L. Browns (AL), 1922	.420	.284	+.136
Joe Jackson, Cleve. Indians (AL), 1911	.408	.273	+.135
George Sisler, St. L. Browns (AL), 1920	.407	.283	+.124
Harry Heilmann, Det. Tigers (AL), 1923	.403	.282	+.121
Ty Cobb, Det. Tigers (AL), 1922	.401	.284	+.117
Rogers Hornsby, St. L. Cardinals (NL), 1925	.403	.292	+.111
Rogers Hornsby, St. L. Cardinals (NL), 1922	.401	.292	+.109
Bill Terry, N.Y. Giants (NL), 1930	.401	.303	+.098

Players Hitting .370 Since Ted Williams's .406 Season (1941)

American League

Ted Williams, Bost. Red Sox, 1957	.388
Rod Carew, Minn. Twins, 1977	.388
George Brett, K.C. Royals, 1980	.390
Nomar Garciaparra, Bost. Red Sox, 2000	.372
Ichiro Suzuki, Sea. Mariners, 2004	.372

National League

Stan Musial, St. L. Cardinals, 1948	.376
Tony Gwynn, S.D. Padres, 1987	.370
Andres Galarraga, Colo. Rockies, 1993	.370
Tony Gwynn, S.D. Padres, 1994	.394
Tony Gwynn, S.D. Padres, 1997	.372
Larry Walker, Colo. Rockies, 1999	.379
Todd Helton, Colo. Rockies, 2000	.372

Players Hitting .300 in Rookie and Final Seasons (Post-1900; Min. Five Years)

First Year

Richie Ashburn	Phila. Phillies (NL), 1948	.333
Wade Boggs	Bost. Red Sox (AL), 1982	.349
Tony Cuccinello	Cin. Reds (NL), 1930	.312
Fats Fothergill	Det. Tigers (AL), 1923	.315
Joe Jackson	Cleve. Indians (AL), 1911	.408
Del Pratt	St. L. Browns (AL), 1912	.302
Ted Williams	Bost. Red Sox (AL), 1939	.327

Final Year

N.Y. Mets (NL), 1962	.306
T.B. Devil Rays (AL), 1999	.301
Chi. White Sox (AL), 1945	.308
Bost. Red Sox (AL), 1933	.344
Chi. White Sox (AL), 1920	.382
Det. Tigers (AL), 1924	.303
Bost. Red Sox (AL), 1960	.316

Players Hitting .300 in Each of First 10 Seasons

17 ....Willie Keeler (1892–1906)
15 ....Ted Williams (1939–42, 1946–51, 1954–58)
11 ....Al Simmons (1924–34)
10 ....Wade Boggs (1982–91)
10 ....Albert Pujols (2001–10)

Players Hitting .300 in Their Only Major League Season (Post-1900; Min. 100 Games, 300 At Bats)

Buzz Arlett, Phila. Phillies (NL), 1931 .... .313
Tex Vache, Bost. Red Sox (AL), 1925 .... .313
Irv Waldron, Milw. Brewers–Wash. Senators (AL), 1901 .... .311

Players Batting .350 with 50 Home Runs

American League

	Batting Average	Home Runs
Babe Ruth, N.Y. Yankees, 1920	.356	54
Babe Ruth, N.Y. Yankees, 1921	.378	59
Babe Ruth, N.Y. Yankees, 1927	.356	60
Jimmie Foxx, Phila. A's, 1932	.364	58
Mickey Mantle, N.Y. Yankees, 1956	.353	52

National League

	Batting Average	Home Runs
Hack Wilson, Chi. Cubs, 1930	.356	56

Players 40 or Older* Hitting .300 (Min. 50 Games)

American League

	Age	Batting Average
Ty Cobb, Phila. A's, 1927	40	.357
Sam Rice, Wash. Senators, 1930	40	.349
Paul Molitor, Minn. Twins, 1996	40	.341
Eddie Collins, Phila. A's, 1927	40	.338
Ted Williams, Bost. Red Sox, 1958	40	.328
Ty Cobb, Phila. A's, 1928	41	.323
Sam Rice, Wash. Senators, 1932	42	.323
Bert Campaneris, N.Y. Yankees, 1983	41	.322
Ted Williams, Bost. Red Sox, 1960	41	.316
Rickey Henderson, N.Y. Yankees, 1999	42	.315
Luke Appling, Chi. White Sox, 1948	41	.314
Harold Baines, Balt. Orioles–Cleve. Indians	40	.312
Sam Rice, Wash. Senators, 1931	41	.310
Birdie Tebbetts, Bost. Red Sox, 1950	40	.310
Luke Appling, Chi. White Sox, 1947	40	.306
Paul Molitor, Minn. Twins, 1997	41	.305
Bing Miller, Bost. Red Sox, 1935	41	.304
Enos Slaughter, N.Y. Yankees, 1958	42	.304
Wade Boggs, T.B. Devil Rays, 1999	40	.301
Luke Appling, Chi. White Sox, 1949	42	.301

National League

	Age	Batting Average
Cap Anson, Chi. Colts, 1894	43	.388
Barry Bonds, S.F. Giants, 2004	40	.362
Moises Alou, N.Y. Mets 2007	40	.341
Cap Anson, Chi. Colts, 1895	44	.335
Cap Anson, Chi. Colts, 1896	45	.331
Stan Musial, St. L. Cardinals, 1962	41	.330
Tony Perez, Cin. Reds, 1985	43	.328
Jack Saltzgaver, Pitt. Pirates, 1945	40	.325
Pete Rose, Phila. Phillies, 1984	40	.325
Tony Gwynn, S.D. Padres, 2001	41	.324
Johnny Cooney, Bost. Braves, 1941	40	.319
Rickey Henderson, N.Y. Mets, 1999	40	.315
Cap Anson, Chi. Colts, 1893	42	.314
Al Nixon, Phila. Phillies, 1927	41	.312
Paul Waner, Bklyn. Dodgers, 1943	40	.311
Julio Franco, Atl. Braves, 2004	46	.309
Orator Jim O'Rourke, N.Y. Giants, 1893	40	.304
Andres Galarraga, S.F. Giants, 2003	42	.301
Gabby Hartnett, N.Y. Giants, 1941	40	.300

*As of September of that year.

Players Hitting .325 for Two or More Different Clubs (Post-1945)

Roberto Alomar	Tor. Blue Jays (AL)	1993	.326
	Balt. Orioles (AL)	1996	.328
		1997	.333
	Cleve. Indians (AL)	2001	.336
Moises Alou	Mont. Expos (NL)	1994	.339
	Hous. Astros (NL)	2000	.355
		2001	.331
Albert Belle	Cleve. Indians (AL)	1994	.357
	Chi. White Sox (AL)	1998	.328
Wade Boggs	Bost. Red Sox (AL)	1982	.349
		1983	.361
		1984	.325
		1985	.368
		1986	.357
		1987	.363
		1988	.366
		1989	.330
		1991	.332
	N.Y. Yankees (AL)	1994	.342
Ellis Burks	Colo. Rockies (NL)	1996	.344
	S.F. Giants (NL)	2000	.344
Miguel Cabrera	Flo. Marlins (NL)	2006	.339
	Det. Tigers (AL)	2010	.328
		2011	.344
Rod Carew	Minn. Twins (AL)	1969	.332
		1970	.366
		1973	.350
		1974	.364
		1975	.359
		1976	.331
		1977	.388
		1978	.333
	Cal. Angels (AL)	1980	.331
		1983	.339
Vladimir Guerrero	Mont. Expos (NL)	2000	.345
		2002	.336
	L.A. Angels (AL)	2004	.337
		2006	.329
Carney Lansford	Bost. Red Sox (AL)	1981	.336
	Oak. A's (AL)	1989	.336
Kenny Lofton	Cleve. Indians (AL)	1993	.325
		1994	.349
	Atl. Braves (NL)	1997	.333
	Phila. Phillies (NL)	2005	.335
Bill Madlock	Chi. Cubs (NL)	1975	.354
		1976	.339
	Pitt. Pirates (NL)	1981	.341
Paul Molitor	Milw. Brewers (AL)	1987	.353
	Tor. Blue Jays (AL)	1993	.332
		1994	.341
	Minn. Twins (AL)	1996	.341
John Olerud	Tor. Blue Jays (AL)	1993	.363
	N.Y. Mets (NL)	1998	.354
Mike Piazza	L.A. Dodgers (NL)	1995	.346

	1996	.336
	1997	.362
N.Y. Mets (NL)	1998	.348
Manny Ramirez .... Cleve. Indians (AL)	1997	.328
	1999	.333
	2000	.351
Bost. Red Sox (AL)	2002	.349
	2003	.325
L.A. Dodgers (AL)	2008	.332
Mickey Rivers .... N.Y. Yankees (AL)	1977	.326
Tex. Rangers (AL)	1980	.333
Ivan Rodriguez .... Tex. Rangers (AL)	1999	.332
	2000	.347
Det. Tigers (AL)	2004	.334
Pete Rose .... Cin. Reds (NL)	1968	.335
	1969	.348
	1973	.338
Phila. Phillies (NL)	1979	.331
	1981	.325
Gary Sheffield .... S.D. Padres (NL)	1992	.330
L.A. Dodgers (NL)	2000	.325
Atl. Braves (NL)	2003	.330
Al Zarilla .... St. L. Browns (AL)	1948	.329
Bost. Red Sox (AL)	1950	.325

Batting Title

Closest Batting Races

American League

Spread	Season		Batting Average
.0001	1945	Snuffy Stirnweiss, N.Y. Yankees	.3085
		Tony Cuccinello, Chi. White Sox	.3084
.0001	1949	George Kell, Det. Tigers	.3429
		Ted Williams, Bost. Red Sox	.3428
.0004	1970	Alex Johnson, Cal. Angels	.3290
		Carl Yastrzemski, Bost. Red Sox	.3286
.0006	1935	Buddy Myer, Wash. Senators	.3490
		Joe Vosmik, Cleve. Indians	.3484
.0009	1982	Willie Wilson, K.C. Royals	.3316
		Robin Yount, Milw. Brewers	.3307
.0010	1910	Ty Cobb, Det. Tigers	.3851
		Nap Lajoie, Cleve. Indians	.3841
.0012	1976	George Brett, K.C. Royals	.3333
		Hal McRae, K.C. Royals	.3321
.0012	2003	Bill Mueller, Bost. Red Sox	.3263
		Manny Ramirez, Bost. Red Sox	.3251
.0016	1953	Mickey Vernon, Wash. Senators	.3372
		Al Rosen, Cleve. Indians	.3356
.0017	1928	Goose Goslin, Wash. Senators	.3794
		Heinie Manush, St. L. Browns	.3777
.0022	1930	Al Simmons, Phila. A's	.3809
		Lou Gehrig, N.Y. Yankees	.3787
.0022	2008	Joe Mauer, Minn. Twins	.3284
		Dustin Pedroia, Bost. Red Sox	.3262

National League (Post-1900)

Spread	Season		Batting Average
.0002	2003	Albert Pujols, St. L. Cardinals	.3587
		Todd Helton, Colo. Rockies	.3585
.0003	1931	Chick Hafey, St. L. Cardinals	.3489
		Bill Terry, N.Y. Giants	.3486
.0011	1991	Terry Pendleton, Atl. Braves	.3191
		Hal Morris, Cin. Reds	.3180
.0013	1911	Honus Wagner, Pitt. Pirates	.3340
		Doc Miller, Bost. Braves	.3327
.0016	1918	Zack Wheat, Bklyn. Dodgers	.3349
		Edd Roush, Cin. Reds	.3333
.0022	1976	Bill Madlock, Chi. Cubs	.3385
		Ken Griffey Sr., Cin. Reds	.3363

Teammates Finishing One-Two in Batting Race

American League

Season	Team	Leader	Batting Average	Runner-Up	Batting Average
1907	Det. Tigers	Ty Cobb	.350	Sam Crawford	.323
1908	Det. Tigers	Ty Cobb	.324	Sam Crawford	.311
1919	Det. Tigers	Ty Cobb	.384	Bobby Veach	.355
1921	Det. Tigers	Harry Heilmann	.394	Ty Cobb	.389
1942	Bost. Red Sox	Ted Williams	.356	Johnny Pesky	.331
1958	Bost. Red Sox	Ted Williams	.388	Pete Runnels	.322
1959	Det. Tigers	Harvey Kuenn	.353	Al Kaline	.327
1961	Det. Tigers	Norm Cash	.361	Al Kaline	.324
1976	K.C. Royals	George Brett	.333	Hal McRae	.332
1977	Minn. Twins	Rod Carew	.388	Lyman Bostock	.336
1984	N.Y. Yankees	Don Mattingly	.343	Dave Winfield	.340
1993	Tor. Blue Jays	John Olerud	.363	Paul Molitor	.332
2003	Bost. Red Sox	Bill Mueller	.326	Manny Ramirez	.325

National League (Post-1900)

Season	Team	Leader	Batting Average	Runner-Up	Batting Average
1903	Pitt. Pirates	Honus Wagner	.355	Fred Clarke	.351
1923	St. L. Cardinals	Rogers Hornsby	.384	Jim Bottomley	.371
1925	St. L. Cardinals	Rogers Hornsby	.403	Jim Bottomley	.367
1926	Cin. Reds	Bubbles Hargrave	.353	Cuckoo Christenson	.350
1933	Phila. Phillies	Chuck Klein	.368	Spud Davis	.349
1937	St. L. Cardinals	Joe Medwick	.374	Johnny Mize	.364
1954	N.Y. Giants	Willie Mays	.354	Don Mueller	.342

Switch-Hitting Batting Champions

American League

Mickey Mantle, N.Y. Yankees, 1956	.353	Bernie Williams, N.Y. Yankees, 1998 ... .339
Willie Wilson, K.C. Royals, 1982	.332	Bill Mueller, Bost. Red Sox, 2003 ... .326

National League (Post-1900)

Pete Rose, Cin. Reds, 1968	.335	Willie McGee, St. L. Cardinals, 1990 ... .335*
Pete Rose, Cin. Reds, 1969	.348	Terry Pendleton, Atl. Braves, 1991 ... .319
Pete Rose, Cin. Reds, 1973	.338	Chipper Jones, Atl. Braves, 2008 ... .364
Willie McGee, St. L. Cardinals, 1985	.353	Jose Reyes, N.Y. Mets, 2011 ... .337
Tim Raines, Mont. Expos, 1986	.334	*Also with Oak. A's (AL).

Catchers Winning Batting Titles

Bubbles Hargrave, Cin. Reds (NL), 1926 .... .353 (326 at bats, 115 hits)
Ernie Lombardi, Cin. Reds (NL), 1938 .... .342 (489 at bats, 167 hits)
Ernie Lombardi, Bost. Braves (NL), 1942 .... .330 (309 at bats, 102 hits)
Joe Mauer, Minn. Twins (AL), 2006 .... .347 (521 at bats, 181 hits)
Joe Mauer, Minn. Twins (AL), 2008 .... .328 (536 at bats, 176 hits)
Joe Mauer, Minn. Twins (AL), 2009 .... .365 (523 at bats, 191 hits)

Batting Champions on Last-Place Teams

American League		National League (Post-1900)	
Dale Alexander, Bost. Red Sox, 1932*	.367	Larry Doyle, N.Y. Giants, 1915	.320
Edgar Martinez, Sea. Mariners, 1992	.343	Richie Ashburn, Phila. Phillies, 1958	.350
Ichiro Suzuki, Sea. Mariners, 2004	.373	Tony Gwynn, S.D. Padres, 1987	.370
		Willie McGee, St. L. Cardinals, 1990**	.335
		Tony Gwynn, S.D. Padres, 1994	.394
		Tony Gwynn, S.D. Padres, 1997	.372
*Also with Det. Tigers (AL)		Larry Walker, Colo. Rockies, 1999	.379
**Also with Oak. A's (AL)		Larry Walker, Colo. Rockies, 2001	.350

Batting Title Winners Without a Home Run

Ginger Beaumont, Pitt. Pirates (NL), 1902 .... .357
Zack Wheat, Bklyn. Dodgers (NL), 1918 .... .335
Rod Carew, Minn. Twins (AL), 1972 .... .318

Batting Champions Driving in Fewer Than 40 Runs

	Batting Average	RBIs
Richie Ashburn, Phila. Phillies (NL), 1958	.350	33
Pete Runnels, Bost. Red Sox (AL), 1960	.320	35
Matty Alou, Pitt. Pirates (NL), 1966	.342	27

Batting Champions with 100 Strikeouts in Year They Led League

Roberto Clemente, Pitt. Pirates (NL), 1967	.357	103 strikeouts
Dave Parker, Pitt. Pirates (NL), 1977	.338	107 strikeouts
Alex Rodriguez, Sea. Mariners (AL), 1996	.358	104 strikeouts
Larry Walker, Col. Rockies (NL), 2001	.350	103 strikeouts
Derek Lee, Chi. Cubs (NL), 2005	.335	109 strikeouts
Matt Holliday, Col. Rockies (NL), 2007	.340	126 strikeouts
Hanley Ramirez, Flo. Marlins (NL), 2009	.342	101 strikeouts
Carlos Gonzalez, Col. Rockies (NL), 2010	.336	135 strikeouts

Lowest Batting Averages to Lead League

American League		National League (since 1900)	
.301	Carl Yastrzemski, Bost. Red Sox, 1968	.313	Tony Gwynn, S.D. Padres, 1988
.306	Elmer Flick, Cleve. Indians, 1905	.319	Terry Pendleton, Atl. Braves, 1991
.309	Snuffy Stirnweiss, N.Y. Yankees, 1945	.320	Larry Doyle, N.Y. Giants, 1915
.316	Frank Robinson, Balt. Orioles, 1966	.321	Edd Roush, Cin. Reds, 1919
.318	Rod Carew, Minn. Twins, 1972	.323	Bill Madlock, Pitt. Pirates, 1983
.320	Pete Runnels, Bost. Red Sox, 1960	.324	Bill Buckner, Chi. Cubs, 1980
.321	Carl Yastrzemski, Bost. Red Sox, 1963	.325	Dick Groat, Pitt. Pirates, 1960
.321	Tony Oliva, Minn. Twins, 1965	.326	Tommy Davis, L.A. Dodgers, 1962
.323	Tony Oliva, Minn. Twins, 1964	.328	Hank Aaron, Milw. Braves, 1956
.324	Ty Cobb, Det. Tigers, 1908	.329	Jake Daubert, Bklyn. Dodgers 1914

.326................................Bill Mueller, Bost. Red. Sox, 2003   .329...........................Roberto Clemente, Pitt. Pirates, 1965

.330.............................Ernie Lombardi, Bost. Braves, 1942

.330.............................Gary Sheffield, S.D. Padres, 1992

Highest Batting Average *Not* to Win Batting Title

American League

Batting Average	Season		Winner
.408	1911	Joe Jackson	Ty Cobb (.420)
.401	1922	Ty Cobb	George Sisler (.420)
.395	1912	Joe Jackson	Ty Cobb (.409)
.393	1923	Babe Ruth	Harry Heilmann (.403)
.392	1927	Al Simmons	Harry Heilmann (.398)
.389	1921	Ty Cobb	Harry Heilmann (.394)
.389	1925	Tris Speaker	Harry Heilmann (.393)
.388	1920	Tris Speaker	George Sisler (.407)
.387	1925	Al Simmons	Harry Heilmann (.393)
.383	1910	Ty Cobb	Nap Lajoie (.384)
.383	1912	Tris Speaker	Nap Lajoie (.384)
.382	1920	Joe Jackson	George Sisler (.407)
.379	1930	Lou Gehrig	Al Simmons (.381)
.378	1921	Babe Ruth	Harry Heilmann (.394)
.378	1928	Heinie Manush	Goose Goslin (.379)
.378	1922	Tris Speaker	George Sisler (.425)
.378	1936	Earl Averill	Luke Appling (.388)
.378	1911	Sam Crawford	Ty Cobb (.420)
.378	1925	Ty Cobb	Harry Heilmann (.393)
.376	1902	Ed Delahanty	Nap Lajoie (.378)
.376	1920	Babe Ruth	George Sisler (.407)

National League (Post-1900)

Batting Average	Season		Winner
.393	1930	Babe Herman	Billy Terry (.401)
.386	1930	Chuck Klein	Billy Terry (.401)
.383	1930	Lefty O'Doul	Billy Terry (.401)
.381	1929	Babe Herman	Lefty O'Doul (.398)
.380	1929	Rogers Hornsby	Lefty O'Doul (.398)
.379	1930	Fred Lindstrom	Bill Terry (.401)
.375	1924	Zack Wheat	Rogers Hornsby (.424)
.373	1930	George Watkins	Bill Terry (.401)
.372	1929	Bill Terry	Lefty O'Doul (.398)
.371	1923	Jim Bottomley	Rogers Hornsby (.384)
.370	1928	Paul Waner	Rogers Hornsby (.387)
.368	1994	Jeff Bagwell	Tony Gwynn (.394)
.368	1930	Paul Waner	Bill Terry (.401)
.367	1900	Elmer Flick	Honus Wagner (.381)
.367	1925	Jim Bottomley	Rogers Hornsby (.403)
.367	1936	Babe Phelps	Paul Waner (.373)
.366	1930	Pie Traynor	Bill Terry (.401)

Runners-Up for Batting Titles in Both Leagues

American League				National League	
Mike Donlin	Balt. Orioles, 1901	.341	Cin. Reds, 1903		.351
			Cin. Reds–N.Y. Giants, 1904		.329
			N.Y. Giants, 1908		.334
Willie Keeler	N.Y. Yankees, 1904	.343	Bklyn. Dodgers, 1901		.355
	N.Y. Yankees, 1905	.302	Bklyn. Dodgers, 1902		.338
Al Oliver	Tex. Rangers, 1978	.324	Pitt. Pirates, 1974		.321
Frank Robinson	Balt. Orioles, 1967	.311	Cin. Reds, 1962		.342

Players Winning Batting Title in Season *After* Joining New Club

American League

Nap Lajoie (.426), Phila. A's, 1901	Jumped from Phila. Phillies (NL)
Ed Delahanty (.376), Wash. Senators, 1902	Jumped from Phila. Phillies (NL)
Tris Speaker (.386), Cleve. Indians, 1916	Traded from Bost. Red Sox
Frank Robinson (.316), Balt. Orioles, 1966	Traded from Cin. Reds
Alex Johnson (.329), Cal. Angels, 1970	Traded from Cin. Reds
Carney Lansford (.336), Bost. Red Sox, 1981	Traded from Cal. Angels
Bill Mueller (.326), Bost. Red Sox, 2003	Free agent

National League (Post-1900)

Hal Chase (.339), Cin. Reds, 1916	Jumped from Federal League
Rogers Hornsby (.387), Bost. Braves, 1928	Traded from N.Y. Giants
Lefty O'Doul (.398), Phila. Phillies, 1929	Traded from N.Y. Giants
Debs Garms (.355), Pitt. Pirates, 1940	Traded from Bost. Braves
Ernie Lombardi (.330), Bost. Braves, 1942	Traded from Cin. Reds
Matty Alou (.342), Pitt. Pirates, 1966	Traded from S.F. Giants
Al Oliver (.331), Mont. Expos, 1982	Traded from Tex. Rangers (AL)
Terry Pendleton (.319), Atl. Braves, 1991	Traded from St. L. Cardinals
Gary Sheffield (.330), S.D. Padres, 1992	Traded from Milw. Brewers (AL)
Andres Galarraga (.370), Colo. Rockies, 1993	Free agent

Players Changing Team in Season *After* Winning Batting Title

American League

Nap Lajoie (.426), Phila. A's, 1901	Sold to Cleve. Indians, June 1902
Ferris Fain (.327), Phila. A's, 1952	Traded to Chi. White Sox, Jan. 1953
Harvey Kuenn (.353), Det. Tigers, 1959	Traded to Cleve. Indians in off-season for Rocky Colavito
Pete Runnels (.326), Bost. Red Sox, 1962	Traded to Hous. Astros in off-season for Roman Mejias
Rod Carew (.333), Minn. Twins, 1978	Traded to Cal. Angels in off-season for Ken Landreaux and 3 other players

National League (Post-1900)

Chick Hafey (.349), St. L. Cardinals, 1931	Traded to Cin. Reds, Apr. 1932
Chuck Klein (.368), Phila. Phillies, 1933	Traded to Chi. Cubs in off-season for 2 players and $65,000
Bill Madlock (.339), Chi. Cubs, 1976	Traded to S.F. Giants in off-season for Bobby Murcer and 2 other players
Willie McGee (.335), St. L. Cardinals, 1990	Traded to Oak. A's, end-of-season, 1990
Gary Sheffield (.330), S.D. Padres, 1992	Traded to Flor. Marlins, midseason, 1993

Largest Margin Between Batting Champion and Runner-Up

American League

Margin	Season	Winner	Batting Average	Runner-Up	Batting Average
+.086	1901	Nap Lajoie, Phila. A's	.426	Mike Donlin, Balt. Orioles	.340
+.052	1977	Rod Carew, Minn. Twins	.388	Lyman Bostock, Minn. Twins	.336
+.048	1974	Rod Carew, Minn. Twins	.364	Jorge Orta, Chi. White Sox	.316
+.047	1941	Ted Williams, Bost. Red Sox	.406	Cecil Travis, Wash. Senators	.359
+.044	1973	Rod Carew, Minn. Twins	.350	George Scott, Milw. Brewers	.306
+.038	1904	Nap Lajoie, Cleve. Indians	.381	Willie Keeler, N.Y. Yankees	.343
+.038	1980	George Brett, K.C. Royals	.390	Cecil Cooper, Milw. Brewers	.352
+.037	1915	Ty Cobb, Det. Tigers	.369	Eddie Collins, Chi. White Sox	.332
+.037	1961	Norm Cash, Det. Tigers	.361	Al Kaline, Det. Tigers	.324
+.033	1904	Nap Lajoie, Cleve. Indians	.376	Willie Keeler, N.Y. Yankees	.343
+.033	1985	Wade Boggs, Bost. Red Sox	.368	George Brett, K.C. Royals	.335
+.032	2004	Ichiro Suzuki, Sea. Mariners	.372	Melvin Mora, Balt. Orioles	.340
+.031	2010	Josh Hamilton, Tex. Rangers	.359	Miguel Cabrera, Det. Tigers	.328
+.031	1993	John Olerud, Tor. Blue Jays	.363	Paul Molitor, Tor. Blue Jays	.332
+.030	1909	Ty Cobb, Det. Tigers	.377	Eddie Collins, Phila. A's	.347
+.030	1917	Ty Cobb, Det. Tigers	.383	George Sisler, St. L. Browns	.353
+.030	1918	Ty Cobb, Det. Tigers	.382	George Burns, Phila. A's	.352

National League (Post-1900)

Margin	Season	Winner	Batting Average	Runner-Up	Batting Average
+.049	1924	Rogers Hornsby, St. L. Cardinals	.424	Zack Wheat, Bklyn. Dodgers	.375
+.047	1922	Rogers Hornsby, St. L. Cardinals	.401	Ray Grimes, Chi. Cubs	.354
+.046	1947	Harry Walker, St. L. Cardinals–Phila. Phillies	.363	Bob Elliott, Bost. Braves	.317
+.045	1921	Rogers Hornsby, St. L. Cardinals	.397	Edd Roush, Cin. Reds	.352
+.043	1948	Stan Musial, St. L. Cardinals	.376	Richie Ashburn, Phila. Phillies	.333
+.043	1999	Larry Walker, Colo. Rockies	.379	Luis Gonzalez, Ariz. D'backs	.336
+.041	1970	Rico Carty, Atl. Braves	.366	Joe Torre, St. L. Cardinals	.325
+.036	1925	Rogers Hornsby, St. L. Cardinals	.403	Jim Bottomley, St. L. Cardinals	.367
+.036	1940	Debs Garms, Pitt. Pirates	.355	Ernie Lombardi, Cin. Reds	.319
+.033	1985	Willie McGee, St. L. Cardinals	.353	Pedro Guerrero, L.A. Dodgers	.320
+.032	1935	Arky Vaughan, Pitt. Pirates	.385	Joe Medwick, St. L. Cardinals	.353
+.032	1946	Stan Musial, St. L. Cardinals	.365	Tommy Holmes, Bost. Braves	.333
+.032	1974	Ralph Garr, Atl. Braves	.353	Al Oliver, Pitt. Pirates	.321
+.032	1987	Tony Gwynn, S.D. Padres	.370	Pedro Guerrero, L.A. Dodgers	.338
+.032	2002	Barry Bonds, S.F. Giants	.370	Larry Walker, Col. Rockies	.338

Champions Whose Next Season's Batting Average Declined the Most

American League

	Seasons/Batting Averages	Change
Norm Cash, Det. Tigers	1961 (.361), 1962 (.243)	–.118
George Sisler, St. L. Browns*	1922 (.420), 1924 (.305)	–.115
Julio Franco, Tex. Rangers	1991 (.341), 1992 (.234)	–.107
Goose Goslin, Wash. Senators	1928 (.379), 1929 (.288)	–.091
Lew Fonseca, Cleve. Indians	1929 (.369), 1930 (.279)	–.090
Babe Ruth, N.Y. Yankees	1924 (.378), 1925 (.290)	–.088
Mickey Vernon, Wash. Senators	1946 (.353), 1947 (.265)	–.088
Dale Alexander, Det. Tigers–Bost. Red Sox	1932 (.367), 1933 (.281)	–.086

National League (Post-1900)

	Seasons/Batting Averages	Change
Willie McGee, St. L. Cardinals	1985 (.353), 1986 (.256)	–.097
Cy Seymour, Cin. Reds (N.Y. Giants)	1905 (.377), 1906 (.286)	–.091
Debs Garms, Pitt. Pirates	1940 (.355), 1941 (.264)	–.091
Rico Carty, Atl. Braves*	1970 (.366), 1972 (.277)	–.089
Rogers Hornsby, St. L. Cardinals	1925 (.403), 1926 (.317)	–.086
Richie Ashburn, Phila. Phillies	1958 (.350), 1959 (.266)	–.084
Lefty O'Doul, Bklyn. Dodgers (N.Y. Giants)	1932 (.368), 1933 (.284)	–.084

*Missed season after winning batting championship.

Lowest Lifetime Batting Averages for Players Who Led League

.268	Snuffy Stirnweiss (1943–52)	Led AL with .309 in 1945
.270	Terry Pendleton (1984–98)	Led NL with .319 in 1991
.271	Norm Cash (1958–74)	Led AL with .361 in 1961
.281	Derrek Lee (1997–2011)	Led NL with .335 in 2005
.281	Bobby Avila (1949–59)	Led AL with .341 in 1954
.284	Fred Lynn (1974–89)	Led AL with .333 in 1979
.285	Carl Yastrzemski (1961–83)	Led AL with .321 in 1963
		Led AL with .326 in 1967
		Led AL with .301 in 1968
.286	Mickey Vernon (1939–43, 1946–60)	Led AL with .353 in 1946
		Led AL with .337 in 1953
.286	Dick Groat (1952, 1955–67)	Led NL with .325 in 1960
.288	Alex Johnson (1964–76)	Led AL with .329 in 1970
.288	Paul O'Neill (1985–2001)	Led AL with .359 in 1994
.289	Bill Buckner (1969–90)	Led NL with .324 in 1980
.290	Larry Doyle (1907–20)	Led NL with .320 in 1915
.290	Ferris Fain (1947–55)	Led AL with .344 in 1951
		Led AL with .327 in 1952
.290	Billy Williams (1959–76)	Led NL with .333 in 1972
.290	Carney Lansford (1978–88)	Led AL with .336 in 1981
.291	Sherry Magee (1904–19)	Led NL with .331 in 1910
.291	Hal Chase (1905–19)	Led NL with .339 in 1916
.291	Pete Runnels (1951–64)	Led AL with .320 in 1960
		Led AL with .326 in 1962
.291	Bill Mueller (1996–2006)	Led AL with .326 in 2003

Two-Time Batting Champions with Lifetime Batting Averages Below .300

Willie McGee (1982–99)	.295	Won NL batting titles in 1985 and 1990
Tommy Davis (1959–76)	.294	Won NL batting titles in 1962 and 1963
Ferris Fain (1947–55)	.290	Won AL batting titles in 1951 and 1952
Dave Parker (1973–91)	.290	Won NL batting titles in 1977 and 1978
Pete Runnels (1951–64)	.291	Won AL batting titles in 1960 and 1962
Mickey Vernon (1939–43, 1946–60)	.286	Won AL batting titles in 1946 and 1953
Carl Yastrzemski (1961–83)	.285	Won AL batting titles in 1963, 1967, and 1968

Years in Which Right-Handed Batters Won Batting Titles in Both Leagues

Season	American League	National League
1903	Nap Lajoie, Cleve. Indians	Honus Wagner, Pitt. Pirates
1904	Nap Lajoie, Cleve. Indians	Honus Wagner, Pitt. Pirates
1921	Harry Heilmann, Det. Tigers	Rogers Hornsby, St. L. Cardinals
1923	Harry Heilmann, Det. Tigers	Rogers Hornsby, St. L. Cardinals
1925	Harry Heilmann, Det. Tigers	Rogers Hornsby, St. L. Cardinals
1931	Al Simmons, Phila. A's	Chick Hafey, St. L. Cardinals
1938	Jimmie Foxx, Bost. Red Sox	Ernie Lombardi, Cin. Reds
1949	George Kell, Det. Tigers	Jackie Robinson, Bklyn. Dodgers
1954	Bobby Avila, Cleve. Indians	Willie Mays, N.Y. Yankees
1959	Harvey Kuenn, Det. Tigers	Hank Aaron, Milw. Braves
1970	Alex Johnson, Cal. Angels	Rico Carty, Atl. Braves
1981	Carney Lansford, Bost. Red Sox	Bill Madlock, Pitt. Pirates
1992	Edgar Martinez, Sea. Mariners	Gary Sheffield, S.D. Padres
2005	Michael Young, Tex. Rangers	Derrek Lee, Chi. Cubs
2007	Magglio Ordonez, Chi. White Sox	Matt Holliday, Col. Rockies

Fewest Strikeouts For Batting Champions

American League			National League		
Strikeouts		Batting Average	Strikeouts		Batting Average
9	Nap Lajoie, Phila. Athletics, 1901	.426	6	Debs Garms, Pitt. Pirates, 1940	.355
13	George Kell, Det. Tigers, 1949	.343	12	Ernie Lombardi, Bost. Braves, 1942	.330
14	George Sisler, St. L. Browns, 1922	.420	14	Paul Waner, Pitt. Pirates, 1927	.380
16	Harry Heilmann, Det. Tigers, 1927	.398	14	Ernie Lombardi, Cin. Reds, 1938	.342
19	Nap Lajoie, Cleve. Indians, 1904	.376	15	Tony Gwynn, S.D.Padres, 1995	.368
19	George Sisler, St. L. Browns, 1920	.407	17	Zack Wheat, Bklyn. Dodgers, 1918	.335
19	Goose Goslin, Wash. Senators, 1928	.379	17	Honus Wagner, Pitt. Pirates, 1903	.355
20	Tris Speaker, Cleve. Indians, 1916	.386	17	Bubbles Hargrove, Cin. Reds, 1926	.353
20	Joe DiMaggio, N.Y. Yankees, 1939	.381	17	Henry Wagner, Pitts. Pirates, 1903	.355
20	Ferris Fain, Phila. Athletics, 1951	.344	18	Arky Vaughan, Pitt. Pirates, 1935	.385
			18	Stan Musial, St. L. Cardinals, 1943	.357
			18	Bill Buckner, Chic. Cubs, 1980	.324
			19	Edd Roush, Cin. Reds, 1919	.321
			19	Lefty O'Doul, Phila. Athletics, 1926	.398
			19	Tony Gwynn, S.D.Padres, 1994	.394
			20	Lefty O'Doul, Brooklyn Dodgers, 1932	.368

Home Runs

Evolution of Home Run Record

American League

1901	Nap Lajoie, Phila. Athletics	14	1921	Babe Ruth, N.Y. Yankees	59
1902	Socks Seybold, Phila. Athletics	16	1927	Babe Ruth, N.Y. Yankees	60
1919	Babe Ruth, Bost. Red Sox	29	1961	Roger Maris, N.Y. Yankees	61
1920	Babe Ruth, N.Y. Yankees	54			

National League (Pre-1900)

1876	George Hall, Phila. Athletics	5	1883	Buck Ewing, N.Y. Gothams	10
1879	Charley Jones, Bost. Beaneaters	9	1884	Ned Williamson, Chi. Colts	27

National League (Post-1900)

1900	Herman Long, Bost. Braves 12	1929	Chuck Klein, Phila. Phillies....................43
1901	Sam Crawford, Cin. Reds 16	1930	Hack Wilson, Chi. Cubs 56
1911	Wildfire Schulte, Chi. Cubs...................21	1998	Mark McGwire, St. L. Cardinals 70
1915	Gavvy Cravath, Phila. Phillies 24	2001	Barry Bonds, S.F. Giants 73
1922	Rogers Hornsby, St. L. Cardinals 42		

Most Home Runs by Decade

Pre-1900
138	Roger Connor
126	Sam Thompson
122	Harry Stovey
106	Mike Tiernan
106	Dan Brouthers
102	Hugh Duffy
100	Jimmy Ryan
97	Cap Anson
94	Fred Pfeffer
80	Ed Delahanty

1900–09
67	Harry Davis
58	Piano Legs Hickman
57	Sam Crawford
54	Buck Freeman
51	Socks Seybold
51	Honus Wagner
47	Nap Lajoie
43	Cy Seymour
40	Jimmy Williams
40	Hobe Ferris

1910–19
116	Gavvy Cravath
83	Fred Luderus
76	Home Run Baker
75	Frank Schulte
64	Larry Doyle
61	Sherry Magee
58	Heinie Zimmerman
57	Fred Merkle
55	Vic Saier
52	Owen Wilson

1920–29
467	Babe Ruth
250	Rogers Hornsby
202	Cy Williams
190	Ken Williams
146	Jim Bottomley
146	Lou Gehrig
146	Bob Meusel
142	Harry Heilmann
137	Hack Wilson
134	George Kelly

1930–39
415	Jimmie Foxx
347	Lou Gehrig
308	Mel Ott
241	Wally Berger
238	Chuck Klein
218	Earl Averill
206	Hank Greenberg
198	Babe Ruth
190	Al Simmons
186	Bob Johnson

1940–49
234	Ted Williams
217	Johnny Mize
211	Bill Nicholson
189	Rudy York
181	Joe Gordon
180	Joe DiMaggio
177	Vern Stephens
173	Charlie Keller
168	Ralph Kiner
164	Bobby Doerr

1950–59
326	Duke Snider
310	Gil Hodges
299	Eddie Mathews
280	Mickey Mantle
266	Stan Musial
256	Yogi Berra
250	Willie Mays
239	Ted Kluszewski
232	Gus Zernial
228	Ernie Banks

1960–69
393	Harmon Killebrew
375	Hank Aaron
350	Willie Mays
316	Frank Robinson
300	Willie McCovey
288	Frank Howard
278	Norm Cash
269	Ernie Banks
256	Mickey Mantle
254	Orlando Cepeda

1970–79
296	Willie Stargell
292	Reggie Jackson
290	Johnny Bench
280	Bobby Bonds
270	Lee May
252	Dave Kingman
252	Graig Nettles
235	Mike Schmidt
226	Tony Perez
225	Reggie Smith

1980–89
313	Mike Schmidt
308	Dale Murphy
274	Eddie Murray
256	Dwight Evans
250	Andre Dawson
230	Darrell Evans
225	Tony Armas
225	Lance Parrish
223	Dave Winfield
216	Jack Clark

1990–99
405	Mark McGwire
382	Ken Griffey Jr.
361	Barry Bonds
351	Albert Belle
339	Juan Gonzalez
332	Sammy Sosa
328	Rafael Palmeiro
303	Jose Canseco
301	Frank Thomas
300	Fred McGriff
300	Matt Williams

2000–11
481	Alex Rodriguez
408	Jim Thome
445	Albert Pujols
348	Manny Ramirez
324	Carlos Delgado
317	Barry Bonds
365	Adam Dunn
357	Vladimir Guerrero
354	Lance Berkman
369	David Ortiz

Career Home Run Leaders by Zodiac Sign

Aquarius (Jan. 20–Feb. 18) ....Hank Aaron 755
Pisces (Feb. 19–Mar. 20)...Mel Ott 511
Aries (Mar. 21–Apr. 19) ....Gil Hodges 370
Taurus (Apr. 20–May 20).............................Willie Mays 660
Gemini (May 21–June 21) ....Manny Ramirez 555
Cancer (June 22–July 22) ....Harmon Killebrew 573
Leo (July 23–Aug. 22)   ....Barry Bonds 762
Virgo (Aug. 23–Sept. 22)...........................Jim Thome* 604
Libra (Sept. 23–Oct. 23)..........................Mark McGwire 583
Scorpio (Oct. 24–Nov. 21) ....Ken Griffey Jr. 630
Sagittarius (Nov. 22–Dec. 21) ....Dave Kingman 442
Capricorn (Dec. 22–Jan. 19) ....Willie McCovey 521
*Still active.

All-Time Home Run Leaders by First Letter of Last Name

A	Hank Aaron (1954–76) 755		O	Mel Ott (1926–47)..........................511
B	Barry Bonds (1986–2007) 762		P	Rafael Palmeiro (1986–2005) 569
C	Jose Canseco (1985–2001) 462		Q	Carlos Quentin* (2006–) 121
D	Carlos Delgado (1993–2009) 473		R	Babe Ruth (1914–35).......................714
E	Darrell Evans (1969–89) 414		S	Sammy Sosa (1989–2007) 609
F	Jimmie Foxx (1925–42, 1944–45).......534		T	Jim Thome* (1991–)........................604
G	Ken Griffey Jr. (1989–2010) 630		U	Willie Upshaw (1978, 1980–88)........123
H	Frank Howard (1958–73) 382		V	Greg Vaughn (1989–2003) 355
I	Raul Ibañez* (1996–)......................252		W	Ted Williams (1939–42, 1946–60).....521
J	Reggie Jackson (1967–87) 563		X	[No player]
K	Harmon Killebrew (1954–75)............573		Y	Carl Yastrzemski (1961–83) 452
L	Carlos Lee* (1999–).......................349		Z	Todd Zeile (1989–2004) 253
M	Willie Mays (1951–52, 1954–73) 660			*Still active.
N	Graig Nettles (1967–88) 390			

Home Run Leaders by State of Birth

Alabama ....Hank Aaron (Mobile).................................755
Alaska...Josh Phelps (Anchorage)............................64
Arizona ....Ian Kinsler (Tucson)...............................124
Arkansas ....Brooks Robinson (Little Rock), Pat Burrell (Eureka Springs)...........292
California..Barry Bonds (Riverside)............................762
Colorado..Johnny Frederick (Denver)..........................85
Connecticut.......................................Mo Vaughn (Norwalk)...............................328
Delaware ....Dave May (New Castle), Randy Bush (Dover), and John Mabry (Wilmington) 96
Florida...Gary Sheffield (Tampa)............................509
Georgia...Frank Thomas (Columbus)...........................521
Hawaii..Mike Lum (Honolulu).................................90
Idaho ....Harmon Killebrew (Payette)........................573
Illinois..Jim Thome (Peoria)................................604
Indiana ....Gil Hodges (Princeton)............................370
Iowa ....Hal Trosky (Norway)................................228
Kansas ....Tony Clark (Newton)................................251
Kentucky ....Jay Buhner (Louisville)...........................310
Louisiana ....Mel Ott (Gretna)..................................511

Maine ....Del Bissonette (Winthrop) 68

Maryland..Babe Ruth (Baltimore)...................................714

Massachusetts...Jeff Bagwell (Boston)..................................449

Michigan ....John Mayberry (Detroit) and Kirk Gibson (Pontiac)...................................255

Minnesota ....Dave Winfield (St. Paul)...................................465

Mississippi...Ellis Burks (Vicksburg)...................................352

Missouri..Yogi Berra (St. Louis)...................................358

Montana ....John Lowenstein (Wolf Point)...................................116

Nebraska ....Wade Boggs (Omaha)...................................118

Nevada ....Marty Cordova (Las Vegas)...................................122

New Hampshire ....Phil Plantier (Manchester).....................................91

New Jersey ....Eric Karros (Hackensack)...................................282

New Mexico ....Ralph Kiner (Santa Rita)...................................369

New York...Alex Rodriguez* (Manhattan)...................................629

North Carolina ....Mark Grace (Winston-Salem), Ray Durham (Charlotte)...................................192

North Dakota...Travis Hafner (Jamestown)...................................189

Ohio...Mike Schmidt (Dayton)...................................548

Oklahoma...Mickey Mantle (Spavinaw)...................................536

Oregon...Dave Kingman (Pendleton)...................................442

Pennsylvania...Ken Griffey Jr. (Donora)...................................630

Rhode Island...Paul Konerko (Providence)...................................396

South Carolina...Jim Rice (Anderson)...................................382

South Dakota ....Jason Kubel (Belle Fourche)...................................104

Tennessee...Todd Helton (Knoxville)...................................347

Texas...Frank Robinson (Beaumont)...................................586

Utah ....Duke Sims (Salt Lake City)...................................100

Vermont...Carlton Fisk (Bellows Falls)...................................376

Virginia ....Willie Horton (Arno)...................................325

Washington...Ron Santo (Seattle)...................................342

West Virginia ....George Brett (Glen Dale)...................................317

Wisconsin...Al Simmons (Milwaukee)...................................307

Wyoming...John Buck (Kemmerer)...................................106

American Samoa ....Tony Solaita.....................................50

District of Columbia...Don Money...................................176

Puerto Rico ....Carlos Delgado...................................473

Virgin Islands...Ellie Hendricks.....................................62

*Still active.

500th Home Run of 500 Home Run Hitters

Hitter	Career Home Runs	Date of 500th Home Run	Pitcher
Barry Bonds	762	Apr. 17, 2004	Terry Adams, L.A. Dodgers
Hank Aaron	755	July 14, 1968	Mike McCormick, S.F. Giants
Babe Ruth	714	Aug. 11, 1929	Willis Hudlin, Cleve. Indians
Ken Griffey	630	June 6, 2004	Matt Morris, St. L. Cardinals
Alex Rodriguez*	629	Aug. 4, 2007	Kyle Davies, K.C. Royals
Willie Mays	616	Sept. 13, 1965	Don Nottebart, Atl. Braves
Sammy Sosa	609	Apr. 4, 2004	Scott Sullivan, Cin. Reds
Jim Thome*	604	Sept. 16, 2007	Dustin Mosley, L.A. Dodgers
Frank Robinson	586	Sept. 13, 1971	Fred Schuman, Det. Tigers

continued on next page

Hitter	Career Home Runs	Date of 500th Home Run	Pitcher
Mark McGwire	583	Aug. 5, 1999	Andy Ashley, S.D. Padres
Harmon Killebrew	573	Aug. 10, 1971	Mike Cuellar, Balt. Orioles
Rafael Palmeiro	569	May 11, 2003	Dave Elder, Cleve. Indians
Reggie Jackson	563	Sept. 17, 1984	Bud Black, K.C. Royals
Manny Ramirez	555	May 31, 2008	Chad Bradford, Balt. Orioles
Mike Schmidt	548	Apr. 18, 1987	Don Robinson, Pitt. Pirates
Mickey Mantle	536	May 14, 1967	Stu Miller, Balt. Orioles
Jimmy Foxx	534	Sept. 24, 1940	George Caster, Phila. A's
Willie McCovey	521	June 30, 1978	Jamie Easterly, Atl. Braves
Frank Thomas	521	June 28, 2007	Carlos Silva, Minn. Twins
Ted Williams	521	June 17, 1960	Wynn Hankins, Cleve. Indians
Ernie Banks	512	May 12, 1970	Pat Jarvis, Atl. Braves
Eddie Mathews	512	July 14, 1967	Juan Marichal, S.F. Giants
Mel Ott	511	Aug. 1, 1945	John Hutchings, Bost. Braves
Gary Sheffield	509	Apr. 17, 2009	Mitch Stetter, Milw. Brewers
Eddie Murray	504	Sept. 6, 1996	Felipe Lira, Det. Tigers

*Still active.

Most Home Runs in First Three Seasons in Majors

114	Ralph Kiner, Pitt. Pirates (NL)	1946 (23), 1947 (51), and 1948 (40)
114	Albert Pujols, St. L. Cardinals (NL)	2001 (37), 2002 (34), and 2003 (43)
112	Eddie Mathews, Bost./Milw. Braves (NL)	1952 (25), 1953 (47), and 1954 (40)
107	Joe DiMaggio, N.Y. Yankees (AL)	1936 (29), 1937 (46), and 1938 (32)
107	Mark Teixeira, Tex. Rangers (AL)	2003 (26), 2004 (38), and 2005 (43)

Most Home Runs for One Club

733	Hank Aaron	Milw./Atl. Braves* (NL) (1954–74)
659	Babe Ruth	N.Y. Yankees (AL) (1920–34)
646	Willie Mays	N.Y./S.F. Giants* (NL) (1951–52, 1954–72)
586	Barry Bonds	S.F. Giants (NL) (1993–2007)
573	Sammy Sosa	Chi. Cubs (NL) (1989–2004)
565	Harmon Killebrew	Wash. Senators/Minn. Twins* (AL) (1954–74)
548	Mike Schmidt	Phila. Phillies (NL) (1972–89)
536	Mickey Mantle	N.Y. Yankees (AL) (1951–68)
521	Ted Williams	Bost. Red Sox (AL) (1939–42, 1946–60)
512	Ernie Banks	Chi. Cubs (NL) (1953–71)
511	Mel Ott	N.Y. Giants (NL) (1926–47)
493	Lou Gehrig	N.Y. Yankees (AL) (1923–39)
493	Eddie Mathews	Bost./Milw./Atl. Braves* (NL) (1952–66)
475	Stan Musial	St. L. Cardinals (NL) (1941–44, 1946–63)
475	Willie Stargell	Pitt. Pirates (NL) (1962–82)
469	Willie McCovey	S.F. Giants (NL) (1959–80)
454	Chipper Jones	Atl. Braves (1993–2001)
452	Carl Yastrzemski	Bost. Red Sox (AL) (1961–83)
449	Jeff Bagwell	Hous. Astros (NL) (1991–2005)

*Franchises that moved.

Most Home Runs by Position, Career

First Base ....583 ....Mark McGwire
Second Base ....278 ....Jeff Kent
Third Base ....509 ....Mike Schmidt
Shortstop ....381 ....Cal Ripken Jr.
                                                                                  344 ....Alex Rodriguez
Outfield...762 ....Barry Bonds
Catcher..358 ....Mike Piazza*
Pitcher..36 ....Wes Ferrell
Designated Hitter...244 ....Edgar Martinez

*While in lineup at position indicated.

Most Home Runs *Not* Leading League, Season

American League

Home Runs	Season		Winner
54	1961	Mickey Mantle, N.Y. Yankees	Roger Maris (61), N.Y. Yankees
52	2002	Jim Thome, Cleve. Indians	Alex Rodriguez (57), Tex. Rangers
50	1996	Brady Anderson, Balt. Orioles	Mark McGwire (52), Oak. A's
50	1938	Jimmie Foxx, Bost. Red Sox	Hank Greenberg (58), Det. Tigers
49	1998	Albert Belle, Chi. White Sox	Ken Griffey Jr. (56), Sea. Mariners
49	1996	Ken Griffey Jr., Sea. Mariners	Mark McGwire (52), Oak. A's
49	2001	Jim Thome, Cleve. Indians	Alex Rodriguez (52), Tex. Rangers
48	1969	Frank Howard, Wash. Senators II	Harmon Killebrew (49), Minn. Twins
48	1996	Albert Belle, Cleve. Indians	Mark McGwire (52), Oak. A's
47	1999	Rafael Palmeiro, Tex. Rangers	Ken Griffey Jr. (48), Sea. Mariners
47	1969	Reggie Jackson, Oak. A's	Harmon Killebrew (49), Minn. Twins
47	1996	Juan Gonzalez, Tex. Rangers	Mark McGwire (52), Oak. A's
47	1927	Lou Gehrig, N.Y. Yankees	Babe Ruth (60), N.Y. Yankees
47	2001	Rafael Palmeiro, Tex. Rangers	Alex Rodriguez (52), Tex. Rangers
47	1987	George Bell, Tor. Blue Jays	Mark McGwire (49), Oak. A's
47	2005	David Oritz, Bost. Red Sox	Alex Rodriguez (98), N.Y. Yankees
46	1961	Jim Gentile, Balt. Orioles	Roger Maris (61), N.Y. Yankees
46	1961	Harmon Killebrew, Minn. Twins	Roger Maris (61), N.Y. Yankees

National League

Home Runs	Season		Winner
66	1998	Sammy Sosa, Chi. Cubs	Mark McGwire (70), St. L. Cardinals
64	2001	Sammy Sosa, Chi. Cubs	Barry Bonds (73), S.F. Giants
63	1999	Sammy Sosa, Chi. Cubs	Mark McGwire (65), St. L. Cardinals
57	2001	Luis Gonzalez, Ariz. D'backs	Barry Bonds (73), S.F. Giants
50	1998	Greg Vaughn, S.D. Padres	Mark McGwire (70), St. L. Cardinals
49	2000	Barry Bonds, S.F. Giants	Sammy Sosa (50), Chi. Cubs
49	2001	Todd Helton, Colo. Rockies	Barry Bonds (73), S.F. Giants
49	2001	Shawn Green, L.A. Dodgers	Barry Bonds (73), S.F. Giants
49	2006	Albert Pujols, St. L. Cardinals	Ryan Howard (58), Phila. Phillies
49	1971	Hank Aaron, Atl. Braves	Willie Stargell (48), Pitt. Pirates
47	2000	Jeff Bagwell, Hous. Astros	Sammy Sosa (50), Chi. Cubs
47	1955	Ted Kluszewski, Cin. Reds	Willie Mays (51), N.Y. Giants
47	2007	Ryan Howard, Phila. Phillies	Prince Fielder (50), Milw. Brewers

Most Home Runs, Never Leading League, Career

569	....	Rafael Palmeiro (1986–2005)
521	....	Frank Thomas (1990–2008)
509	....	Gray Sheffield (1988–2009)
475	....	Stan Musial (1941–44, 1946–63)
473	....	Carlos Delgado (1993–2009)
465	....	Dave Winfield (1973–95)
454	....	Chipper Jones (1993–2011)
449	....	Jeff Bagwell (1991–2005)
449	....	Vladimir Guerrero (1996–2011)
431	....	Cal Ripken Jr. (1981–2001)
428	....	Jason Giambi (1995–2011)
427	....	Mike Piazza (1992–2007)
426	....	Billy Williams (1959–76)
399	....	Al Kaline (1953–74)
396	....	Joe Carter (1983–98)
396	....	Paul Konerko (1997–2011)

Most Inside-the-Park Home Runs, Career (Post-1898)

51	....	Sam Crawford (1899–1917)
48	....	Tommy Leach (1898–1918)
47	....	Ty Cobb (1905–28)
29	....	Edd Roush (1913–29, 1931)
22	....	Rabbit Maranville (1912–35)
21	....	Sam Rice (1915–34)
16	....	Kiki Cuyler (1920–37)
15	....	Ben Chapman (1930–48)
14	....	Tris Speaker (1907–28)
14	....	Honus Wagner (1897–1917)

Players with 10 or More Letters in Last Name, Hitting 40 or More Home Runs in Season

	Season	Home Runs
Roy Campanella, Bklyn. Dodgers (NL)	1953	41
Ted Kluszewski, Cin. Reds (NL)	1953	40
	1954	49
	1955	47
Rico Petrocelli, Bost. Red Sox (AL)	1969	40
Carl Yastrzemski, Bost. Red Sox (AL)	1967	44
	1969	40
	1970	40

Most Home Runs, Month by Month

American League

March	1	....	Many players
Apr.	14	....	Alex Rodriguez, N.Y. Yankees, 2007
May	16	....	Mickey Mantle, N.Y. Yankees, 1956
June	15	....	Babe Ruth, N.Y. Yankees, 1930
			Bob Johnson, Phila. A's, 1934
			Roger Maris, N.Y. Yankees, 1961
July	16	....	Albert Belle, Chi. White Sox, 1998
Aug.	18	....	Rudy York, Det. Tigers, 1937
Sept.	17	....	Babe Ruth, N.Y. Yankees, 1927
			Albert Belle, Cleve. Indians, 1995
Oct.	4	....	Gus Zernial, Chi. White Sox, 1950
			George Brett, K.C. Royals, 1985
			Ron Kittle, Chi. White Sox, 1985
			Wally Joyner, Cal. Angels, 1987
			Jose Cruz Jr., Tor. Blue Jays, 2001

National League

	2	....	Vinny Castilla, Colo. Rockies, 1998
	14	....	Albert Pujols, St. L. Cardinals, 2007
	17	....	Barry Bonds, S.F. Giants, 2001
	20	....	Sammy Sosa, Chi. Cubs, 1998
	16	....	Mark McGwire, St. L. Cardinals, 1999
	17	....	Willie Mays, S.F. Giants, 1965
			Sammy Sosa, Chi. Cubs, 2001
	16	....	Ralph Kiner, Pitt. Pirates, 1949
	5	....	Richie Sexson, Milw. Brewers, 2001
			Sammy Sosa, Chi. Cubs, 2001

Most Home Runs by Position, Season*

American League		
First Base	58 ....Hank Greenberg, Det. Tigers, 1938
Second Base	39.........Alfonso Soriano, N.Y. Yankees, 2002
Third Base	47 ....Troy Glaus, Ana. Angels, 2000
Shortstop	57 ....Alex Rodriguez, Tex. Rangers, 2002
Outfield	61 ....Roger Maris, N.Y. Yankees, 1961
Catcher	35................Terry Steinbach, Oak. A's, 1996
	35 ....Ivan Rodriguez, Tex. Rangers, 1999
Pitcher	9................Wes Ferrell, Cleve. Indians, 1931
Designated Hitter	47 ....David Ortiz, Bost. Red Sox, 2006

National League		
First Base	69 ......Mark McGwire, St. L. Cardinals, 1998
Second Base	42 .....Rogers Hornsby, St. L. Cardinals, 1922
	42.............Davey Johnson, Atl. Braves, 1973
Third Base	48 ....Mike Schmidt, Phila. Phillies, 1980
	48............Adrian Beltre, L.A. Dodgers, 2004
Shortstop	47...................Ernie Banks, Chi. Cubs, 1958
Outfield	71.................Barry Bonds, S.F. Giants, 2001
Catcher	43 ....Javy Lopez, Atl. Braves, 2003
Pitcher	7 ....Don Newcombe, Bklyn. Dodgers, 1955
	7 ....Don Drysdale, L.A. Dodgers, 1965

*While in lineup at position indicated.

Players Leading League in Home Runs for Different Teams

Tony Armas	Oak. A's (AL)	1981	22
	Bost. Red Sox (AL)	1984	43
Sam Crawford	Cin. Reds (NL)	1901	16
	Det. Tigers (AL)	1908	7
		1914	8
Jimmie Foxx	Phila. A's (AL)	1932	58
		1933	48
		1935	36
	Bost. Red Sox (AL)	1939	35
Reggie Jackson	Oak. A's (AL)	1973	32
		1975	36
	N.Y. Yankees (AL)	1980	41
	Cal. Angels (AL)	1982	39
Dave Kingman	Chi. Cubs (NL)	1979	48
	N.Y. Mets (NL)	1982	37
Fred McGriff	Tor. Blue Jays (AL)	1989	36
	S.D. Padres (NL)	1992	35
Mark McGwire	Oak. A's (AL)	1987	49
		1996	52
	St. L. Cardinals (NL)	1998	70
		1999	65
Johnny Mize	St. L. Cardinals (NL)	1939	28
		1940	43
	N.Y. Giants (NL)	1947	51 (Tie)
		1948	40 (Tie)
Babe Ruth	Bost. Red Sox (AL)	1918	11
		1919	29
	N.Y. Yankees (AL)	1920	54
		1921	59
		1923	41
		1924	46

continued on next page

		1926	47
		1927	60
		1928	54
		1929	46
		1930	49
		1931	46 (Tie)
Cy Williams	Chi. Cubs (NL)	1916	12
	Phila. Phillies (NL)	1920	15
		1923	41

Players with 40 Home Run Seasons in Each League

Mark McGwire	Oak. A's (AL)	1987	49
		1992	42
		1996	52
		1997	58*
	St. L. Cardinals (NL)	1998	70
		1999	65
Jim Thome	Cleve. Indians (AL)	1997	40
		2001	49
		2002	52
	Chi. White Sox (AL)	2006	42
	Phila. Philles (NL)	2003	47
		2004	42
Ken Griffey Jr.	Sea. Mariners (AL)	1993	45
		1994	40
		1996	49
		1997	56
		1998	56
		1999	48
	Cin. Reds (NL)	2000	40
Darrell Evans	Atl. Braves (NL)	1973	41
	Det. Tigers (AL)	1958	40

*34 with Oak. A's (AL) and 24 with St. L. Cardinals (NL).

Players Hitting a Total of 100 Home Runs in Two Consecutive Seasons

Total Home Runs

Mark McGwire, St. L. Cardinals (NL), 1998 (70) and 1999 (65)	135
Sammy Sosa, Chi. Cubs (NL), 1998 (66) and 1999 (63)	129
Barry Bonds, S.F. Giants (NL), 2000 (49) and 2001 (73)	122
Barry Bonds, S.F. Giants (NL), 2001 (73) and 2002 (46)	119
Babe Ruth, N.Y. Yankees (AL), 1927 (60) and 1928 (54)	114
Sammy Sosa, Chi. Cubs (NL), 2000 (50) and 2001 (64)	114
Babe Ruth, N.Y. Yankees (AL), 1920 (54) and 1921 (59)	113
Sammy Sosa, Chi. Cubs (NL), 1999 (63) and 2000 (50)	113
Sammy Sosa, Chi. Cubs (NL), 2001 (64) and 2002 (49)	113
Ken Griffey Jr., Sea. Mariners (AL), 1997 (56) and 1998 (56)	112
Alex Rodriguez, Tex. Rangers (AL), 2001 (52) and 2002 (57)	109
Babe Ruth, N.Y. Yankees (AL), 1926 (47) and 1927 (60)	107
Jimmie Foxx, Phila. A's (AL), 1932 (58) and 1933 (48)	106
Ken Griffey Jr., Sea. Mariners (AL), 1996 (49) and 1997 (56)	105
Ryan Howard, Phila. Philles (NL) 2006 (58) and 2007 (47)	105
Ken Griffey Jr., Sea. Mariners (AL), 1998 (56) and 1999 (48)	104

Alex Rodriguez, Tex. Rangers (AL), 2002 (57) and 2003 (47) 104
Ralph Kiner, Pitt. Pirates (NL), 1949 (54) and 1950 (47)..101
David Ortiz, Bost. Red Sox (AL) 2005 (47) and 2006 (54)..101
Roger Maris, N.Y. Yankees (AL), 1960 (39) and 1961 (61) 100

Players with First 20-Home Run Season After 35th Birthday

	Season	Home Runs	35th Birthday
Cy Williams, Phila. Phillies (NL)	1922	26	Dec. 21, 1921
Charlie Gehringer, Det. Tigers (AL)	1938	20	May 11, 1938
Luke Easter, Cleve. Indians (AL)	1950	28	Aug. 4, 1949
Mickey Vernon, Wash. Senators (AL)	1954	20	Apr. 22, 1953
John Lowenstein, Balt. Orioles (AL)	1982	24	Jan. 27, 1982
Frank White, K.C. Royals (AL)	1985	20	Sept. 4, 1985
Buddy Bell, Cin. Reds (NL)	1986	20	Aug. 27, 1986

Shortstops with at Least Seven Consecutive 20-Home Run Seasons

	Season	Home Runs
Cal Ripken Jr., Balt. Orioles (AL) (10 seasons)	1982	28
	1983	27
	1984	27
	1985	26
	1986	25
	1987	27
	1988	23
	1989	21
	1990	21
	1991	34
Alex Rodriguez, Tex. Rangers (AL) (8 seasons)	1996	36
	1997	23
	1998	44
	1999	42
	2000	41
	2001	52
	2002	57
	2003	47
Miguel Tejada (8 seasons) ... Oak. A's (AL) (5 seasons)	1999	21
	2000	30
	2001	31
	2002	34
	2003	27
Balt. Orioles (AL) (3 seasons)	2004	34
	2005	26
	2006	24
Ernie Banks, Chi. Cubs (NL) (7 seasons)	1955	44
	1956	28
	1957	43*
	1958	47
	1959	45
	1960	41
	1961	29**

*Played 58 games at third base.
**Played 28 games in outfield, 76 at first.

Players Hitting Four Home Runs in One Game

American League

Batter	Date	Opposing Pitcher(s)
Lou Gehrig, N.Y. Yankees	June 3, 1932	George Earnshaw (3 home runs) and Roy Mahaffey (1 home run), Phila. A's
Pat Seerey, Chi. White Sox	July 18, 1948	Carl Scheib (2 home runs), Bob Savage (1 home run), and Lou Brissie (1 home run), Phila. A's
Rocky Colavito, Cleve. Indians	June 10, 1959	Jerry Walker (2 home runs), Arnold Portocarrero (1 home run), and Ernie Johnson (1 home run), Balt. Orioles
Mike Cameron, Sea. Mariners	May 2, 2002	Jon Rauch (1 home run) and Jim Parque (3 home runs), Chi. White Sox
Carlos Delgado, Tor. Blue Jays	Sept. 26, 2003	Jorge Sosa (2 home runs), Joe Kennedy (1 home run), and Lance Carter (1 home run), T.B. Devil Rays

National League

Batter	Date	Opposing Pitcher(s)
Bobby Lowe, Bost. Braves	May 30, 1894	Icebox Chamberlain (4 home runs), Cin. Reds
Ed Delahanty, Phila. Phillies	July 13, 1896	Adonis Bill Terry (4 home runs), Chi. Cubs
Chuck Klein, Phila. Phillies	July 10, 1936	Jim Weaver (1 home run), Mace Brown (2 home runs), and Bill Swift (1 home run), Pitt. Pirates
Gil Hodges, Bklyn. Dodgers	Aug. 31, 1950	Warren Spahn (1 home run), Normie Roy (1 home run), Bob Hall (1 home run), and Johnny Antonelli (1 home run), Bost. Braves
Joe Adcock, Milw. Braves	July 31, 1954	Don Newcombe (1 home run), Erv Palica (1 home run), Pete Wojey (1 home run), and Johnny Podres (1 home run), Bklyn. Dodgers
Willie Mays, S.F. Giants	Apr. 30, 1961	Lew Burdette (2 home runs), Seth Morehead (1 home run), and Don McMahon (1 home run), Milw. Braves
Mike Schmidt, Phila. Phillies	Apr. 17, 1976	Rick Reuschel (2 home runs), Mike Garman (1 home run), and Paul Reuschel (1 home run), Chi. Cubs
Bob Horner, Atl. Braves	July 6, 1986	Andy McGaffigan (3 home runs) and Jeff Reardon (1 home run), Mont. Expos
Mark Whiten, St. L. Cardinals	Sept. 7, 1993	Larry Luebbers (1 home run), Mike Anderson (2 home runs), and Rob Dibble (1 home run), Cin. Reds
Shawn Green, L.A. Dodgers	May 23, 2002	Glendon Rusch (1 home runs), Brian Mallette (2 home runs), and Jose Cabrera (1 home run), Milw. Brewers

Career Home Runs by Players Hitting Four Home Runs in One Game

American League

Batter	Date	Result	Career Home Run
Lou Gehrig, N.Y. Yankees	June 3, 1932	N.Y. Yankees 20, Phila. Athletics 13	493
Carlos Delgado, Tor. Blue Jays	Sept. 25, 2003	Tor. Blue Jays 10, T.B. Devil Rays 8	473
Rocky Colavito, Cleve. Indians	June 10, 1959	Cleve. Indians 11, Balt. Orioles 8	374
Mike Cameron, Sea. Mariners	May 2, 2002	Sea. Mariners 15, Chi. White Sox 4	278*
Pat Seerey, Chi. White Sox	July 18, 1948	Chi. White Sox 12, Phila. Athletics 11	86

National League

Batter	Date	Result	Career Home Run
Willie Mays, S.F. Giants	June 30, 1961	S.F. Giants 14, Milw. Brewers 4	660
Mike Schmidt, Phila. Phillies	Apr. 17, 1976	Phila. Phillies 18, Chi. Cubs 16	548
Gil Hodges, Bklyn. Dodgers	Aug. 31, 1950	Blyn. Dodgers 19, Bost. Braves 3	370
Joe Adcock, Milw. Brewers	July 31, 1954	Milw. Brewers 15, Bklyn. Dodgers 7	336
Shawn Green, L.A. Dodgers	May 23, 2002	L.A. Dodgers 16, Milw. Brewers 3	328

Chuck Klein, Phila. Phillies ....July 10, 1936........Phila. Phillies 9, Pitt. Pirates 6 300
Bob Horner, Atl. Braves ....July 6, 1986 ....Mont. Expos 11, Atl. Braves 8...218
Mark Whiten, St. L. Cardinals ....Sept. 7, 1993....St. L. Cardinals 15, Cin. Reds 2 105
' Ed Delahanty, Phila. Phillies ....July 13, 1896.......Chi. Cubs 9, Phila. Phillies 8..101
Bobby Lowe, Bost. Braves ....March 30, 1894....Bost. Braves 20, Cin. Reds 11 71

*Active player.

Players with Three Home Runs in One Game, Fewer Than 10 in Season

American League

	Home Runs
Mickey Cochrane, Phila. A's, 1925	6
Merv Connors, Chi. White Sox, 1938	6
Billy Glynn, Cleve. Indians, 1954	5
Preston Ward, K.C. A's, 1958	6
Don Leppert, Wash. Senators II, 1963	6
Joe Lahoud, Bost. Red Sox, 1969	9
Fred Patek, Cal. Angels, 1980	5
Juan Beniquez, Balt. Orioles, 1986	6

National League (Post-1900)

	Home Runs
Hal Lee, Bost. Braves, 1934	8
Babe Ruth, Bost. Braves, 1935	6
Clyde McCullough, Chi. Cubs, 1942	5
Jim Tobin, Bost. Braves, 1942	6
Tommy Brown, Bklyn. Dodgers, 1950	8
Del Wilber, Phila. Phillies, 1951	8
Jim Pendleton, Milw. Braves, 1953	7
Bob Thurman, Cin. Reds, 1956	8
Roman Mejias, Pitt. Pirates, 1958	5
Gene Oliver, Atl. Braves, 1966	8
Mike Lum, Atl. Braves, 1970	7
George Mitterwald, Chi. Cubs, 1974	7
Pete Rose, Cin. Reds, 1978	7
Karl Rhodes, Chi. Cubs, 1994	8
Cory Snyder, L.A. Dodgers, 1994	6
Bobby Estalella, Phila. Phillies, 1999	4
Todd Hollandsworth, Colo. Rockies, 2001	6
Damion Easley, Ariz. Diamondbacks, 2006	9

Rookies Hitting 30 or More Home Runs

Mark McGwire, Oak. A's (AL), 1987	49	Earl Williams, Atl. Braves (NL), 1971	33
Wally Berger, Bost. Braves (NL), 1930	38	Jose Canseco, Oak. A's (AL), 1986	33
Frank Robinson, Cin. Reds (NL), 1956	38	Tony Oliva, Minn. Twins (AL), 1964	32
Al Rosen, Cleve. Indians (AL), 1950	37	Chris Young, Ariz. Diamondbacks (NL), 2007	32
Albert Pujols, St. L. Cardinals (NL), 2001	37	Ted Williams, Bost. Red Sox (AL), 1939	31
Hal Trosky, Cleve. Indians (AL), 1934	35	Jim Hart, S.F. Giants (NL), 1964	31
Rudy York, Det. Tigers (AL), 1937	35	Bob Allison, Wash. Senators (AL), 1959	30
Walt Dropo, Bost. Red Sox (AL), 1950	34	Willie Montanez, Phila. Phillies (NL), 1971	30
Ryan Braun, Milw. Brewers (NL), 2007	34	Pete Incaviglia, Tex. Rangers (AL), 1986	30
Jimmie Hall, Minn. Twins (AL), 1963	33	Matt Nokes, Det. Tigers (AL), 1987	30

Former Negro Leaguers Who Led Major Leagues in Home Runs

Hank Aaron	Atl. Braves (NL)	1967	39
	Atl. Braves (NL)	1966	44
	Milw. Brewers (NL)	1963	44
	Milw. Brewers (NL)	1957	44
	(Played in Negro Leagues with Indianapolis Clowns, 1952.)		
Willie Mays	S.F. Giants (NL)	1965	52
	S.F. Giants (NL)	1964	47
	S.F. Giants (NL)	1962	49
	N.Y. Giants (NL)	1955	51
	(Played in Negro Leagues with Chattanooga Choo-Choos, 1947; Birmingham Black Barons, 1948–50.)		

continued on next page

Ernie Banks ....Chi. Cubs (NL)..1960.....................................41
Chi. Cubs (NL)..1958.....................................47
(Played in Negro Leagues with Kansas City Monarchs, 1950–53.)
Larry Doby ....Cleve. Indians (AL)...........................1954.....................................32
Cleve. Indians (AL)...........................1952.....................................32
(Played in Negro Leagues with Newark Eagles, 1942–43, 1946–47.)

Players with 50 Home Runs, Batting Under .300, Season

	Home Runs	Batting Average
Mark McGwire, St. L. Cardinals (NL), 1998	70	.299
Brady Anderson, Balt. Orioles (AL), 1996	50	.297
Prince Fielder, Milw. Brewers (NL), 2007	50	.297
Sammy Sosa, Chi. Cubs (NL), 1999	63	.288
David Ortiz, Bost. Red Sox (AL), 2006	54	.287
Ken Griffey Jr., Sea. Mariners (AL), 1998	56	.284
Mark McGwire, St. L. Cardinals (NL), 1999	65	.278
Cecil Fielder, Det. Tigers (AL), 1990	51	.277
Mark McGwire, Oak. A's (AL)–St. L. Cardinals (NL), 1997	58	.274
Greg Vaughn, S.D. Padres (NL), 1998	50	.272
Roger Maris, N.Y. Yankees (AL), 1961	61	.269
Andruw Jones, Atl. Braves (NL), 2005	51	.263
Jose Bautista, Tor. Blue Jays (AL) 2010	54	.260

Players Hitting 49 Home Runs in Season, Never Hitting 50

American League

Lou Gehrig, N.Y. Yankees, 1934 and 1936
Harmon Killebrew, Minn. Twins, 1964 and 1969
Frank Robinson, Balt. Orioles, 1966

National League

Ted Kluszewski, Cin. Reds, 1954
Andre Dawson, Chi. Cubs, 1987
Larry Walker, Colo. Rockies, 1997
Shawn Green, L.A. Dodgers, 2001
Todd Helton, Colo. Rockies, 2001*
Albert Pujols, St. L. Cardinals, 2006*
*Still active.

Most Multi-Home Run Games

Seasons

72	Babe Ruth (1914–35)
71	Barry Bonds (1986–2007)
69	Sammy Sosa (1989–2007)
67	Mark McGwire (1986–2001)
63	Willie Mays (1951–52; 1954–73)
62	Hank Aaron (1954–76)
59	Alex Rodriguez (1994–2011)
55	Jimmie Foxx (1925–42; 1944–45)
55	Ken Griffey Jr. (1989–2010)
54	Frank Robinson (1956–76)
54	Marry Ramirez (1993–2011)

Players Hitting Two Grand Slams, Same Game

American League

Tony Lazzeri, N.Y. Yankees, May 24, 1936
Jim Tabor, Bost. Red Sox, July 4, 1939
Rudy York, Bost. Red Sox, July 27, 1946
Jim Gentile, Balt. Orioles, May 9, 1961
Jim Northrup, Det. Tigers, June 24, 1968
Frank Robinson, Balt. Orioles, June 26, 1970
Robin Ventura, Chi. White Sox, Sept. 4, 1995
Chris Hoiles, Balt. Orioles, Aug. 14, 1998
Nomar Garciaparra, Bost. Red Sox, May 10, 1999
Bill Mueller, Bost. Red Sox, July 29, 2003

National League

Tony Cloninger, Atl. Braves, July 3, 1966
Fernando Tatis, St. L. Cardinals, Apr. 23, 1999*
Josh Willingham, Was. Nationals, July 17, 2009
*Same inning.

Most Home Runs by Age

Teens

24	Tony Conigliaro
19	Mel Ott
18	Phil Cavarretta
16	Ken Griffey Jr
13	Mickey Mantle

Twenties

424	Alex Rodriguez
382	Ken Griffey, Jr.
376	Jimmie Foxx
370	Eddie Mathews
366	Albert Pujols
361	Mickey Mantle
342	Hank Aaron

Thirties

444	Barry Bonds
424	Babe Ruth
396	Rafael Palmeiro
371	Hank Aaron
356	Jim Thome
354	Mark McGwire
349	Willie Mays

Forties

72	Carlton Fisk
67	Darryl Evans
59	Dave Winfield
59	Barry Bonds
48	Carl Yastrzemski

Teenagers Hitting Grand Slams

Scott Stratton, Louisville Colonels (AA), May 27, 1889 ... 19 years, 7 months
George S. Davis, Cleve. Spiders (NL), May 30, 1890 ... 19 years, 9 months
Eddie Onslow, Det. Tigers (AL), Aug. 22, 1912 ... 19 years, 6 months
Phil Cavarretta, Chi. Cubs (NL), May 16, 1936 ... 19 years, 10 months
Al Kaline, Det. Tigers (AL), June 11, 1954 ... 19 years, 6 months
Harmon Killebrew, Wash. Senators (AL), June 11, 1954 ... 19 years, 11 months
Vada Pinson, Cin. Reds (NL), Apr. 18, 1958 ... 19 years, 8 months
Tony Conigliaro, Bost. Red Sox (AL), June 3, 1964 ... 19 years, 5 months

Oldest Players to Hit Grand Slams

American League

Julio Franco, Atl. Braves, June 25, 2005 ... 46 years, 10 months
Minnie Minoso, Wash. Senators II, July 24, 1963 ... 41 years, 5 months
Rafael Palmeiro, Balt. Orioles, June 4, 2005 ... 40 years, 9 months
Darrell Evans, Det. Tigers, Sept. 5, 1987 ... 40 years, 3 months
Matt Stairs, Tor. Blue Jays, May 14, 2008 ... 40 years, 3 months
Mickey Vernon, Cleve. Indians, Apr. 25, 1958 ... 40 years, 0 months

National League

Julio Franco, Atl. Braves, June 3, 2004	45 years, 10 months
Cap Anson, Chi. Cubs, Aug. 1, 1894	42 years, 3 months
Craig Biggio, Houst. Astros, July 29, 2007	41 years, 8 months
Matt Stairs, Phila. Phillies, September 10, 2009	41 years, 7 months
Honus Wagner, Pitt. Pirates, July 29, 1915	41 years, 5 months
Craig Biggio, Houst. Astros, April 20, 2007	41 years, 5 months
Stan Musial, St. L. Cardinals, June 23, 1961	40 years, 7 months
Hank Aaron, Atl. Braves, June 4, 1974	40 years, 3 months
Hank Aaron, Atl. Braves, Apr. 26, 1974	40 years, 2 months

Oldest Home Run Champions*

American League

	Age	Home Runs
Darrell Evans, Det. Tigers, 1985	38 years, 5 months	40
Babe Ruth, N.Y. Yankees, 1931	36 years, 8 months	46
Reggie Jackson, Cal. Angels, 1982	36 years, 5 months	39
Hank Greenberg, Det. Tigers, 1946	35 years, 9 months	44
Babe Ruth, N.Y. Yankees, 1930	35 years, 8 months	49

National League (Post-1900)

	Age	Home Runs
Cy Williams, Phila. Phillies, 1927	39 years, 10 months	30
Gavvy Cravath, Phila. Phillies, 1919	38 years, 7 months	12
Gavvy Cravath, Phila. Phillies, 1918	37 years, 7 months	8
Barry Bonds, S.F. Giants, 2001	37 years, 3 months	73
Mike Schmidt, Phila. Phillies, 1986	37 years, 1 month	37
Gavvy Cravath, Phila. Phillies, 1917	36 years, 7 months	12
Mark McGwire, St. L. Cardinals, 1999	36 years, 0 months	65
Cy Williams, Phila. Phillies, 1923	35 years, 10 months	41
Johnny Mize, N.Y. Giants, 1948	35 years, 9 months	40
Sam Thompson, Phila. Phillies, 1895	35 years, 7 months	18
Hank Sauer, Chi. Cubs, 1952	35 years, 7 months	37
Andres Galarraga, Colo. Rockies, 1996	35 years, 4 months	47
Jack Fournier, Bklyn. Dodgers, 1924	35 years, 1 month	27
Mike Schmidt, Phila. Phillies, 1984	35 years, 1 month	35
Mark McGwire, St. L. Cardinals, 1998	35 years, 0 months	70

*As of October that year.

Most Career Home Runs by Players Hitting Home Run on First Pitch in Majors

360 Gary Gaetti, Minn. Twins (AL), Sept. 20, 1981	55 Junior Felix, Tor. Blue Jays (AL), May 14, 1989
284 Will Clark, S.F. Giants (NL), Apr. 8, 1986	38 Brant Alyea, Wash. Senators II (AL), Sept. 12, 1965
260 Tim Wallach, Mont. Expos (NL), Sept. 6, 1980	35 Al Woods, Tor. Blue Jays (AL), Apr. 7, 1977
238 Earl Averill, Cleve. Indians (AL), Apr. 16, 1929	34 Chris Richard, St. L. Cardinals, July 17, 2000
202 Bill White, N.Y. Giants (NL), May 7, 1956	32 Ikaz Matsui, N.Y. Mets, April 6, 2004
195 Jay Bell, Cleve. Indians (AL), Sept. 29, 1986	25 J.P. Arencibia, Tor. Blue Jays (AL), August 7, 2010
182 Terry Steinbach, Oak. A's (AL), Sept. 12, 1986	21 Chuck Tanner, Milw. Braves (NL), Apr. 12, 1955
142 Wally Moon, St. L. Cardinals (NL), Apr. 13, 1954	14 Andy Phillips, N.Y. Yankees, Sept. 26, 2004
125 Bob Nieman, St. L. Browns (AL), Sept. 13, 1951	12 George Vico, Det. Tigers (AL), Apr. 20, 1948
115 Marcus Thames, N.Y. Yankees, June 10, 2002	8 Jim Bullinger, Chi. Cubs (NL), June 8, 1992
114 Whitey Lockman, N.Y. Giants (NL), July 5, 1945	5 Adam Wainwright, St. L. Cardinals, May 24, 2006

82........Kevin Kouzmanoff, Clev. Indians, September 2, 2006

79 ,,,,,,,,,,,,,,,Bert Campaneris, K.C. A's (AL), July 23, 1964

69.................Clyde Vollmer, Cin. Reds (NL), May 31, 1942

3..............Clise Dudley, Bklyn. Dodgers (NL), Apr. 27, 1929

3.................Jay Gainer, Colo. Rockies (NL), May 14, 1993

2..................Frank Ernaga, Chi. Cubs (NL), May 24, 1957

1............Eddie Morgan, St. L. Cardinals (NL), Apr. 14, 1936

1 ....Bill Lefebvre, Bost. Red Sox (AL), June 10, 1938

1 ....Don Rose, Cal. Angels (AL), May 24, 1972

1 ....Mark Saccomanno, Houst. Astros, Sept. 8, 2008

1 ....Tom Milone, Was. Nationals, Sept. 3, 2011

1 ....Daniel Nava, Bos. Red Sox, June 12, 2010

1 ....Gene Stechschulte, St.L. Cardinals, April 27, 2001

1 ....Estéban Yan, T.B. Rays, June 4, 2000

Players Hitting Home Run in First Time At Bat, Never Hitting Another

American League

Luke Stuart, St. L. Browns, Aug. 8, 1921 (Career: 1921)

Bill Lefebvre, Bost. Red Sox, June 10, 1938 (Career: 1938–39, 1943–44)

Hack Miller, Det. Tigers, Apr. 23, 1944 (Career: 1944–45)

Bill Roman, Det. Tigers, Sept. 30, 1964 (Career: 1964–65)

Don Rose, Cal. Angels, May 24, 1972 (Career: 1971–72, 1974)

Dave Machemer, Cal. Angels, June 21, 1978 (Career: 1978–79)

Andre David, Minn. Twins, June 29, 1984 (Career: 1984, 1986)

Esteban Yan, T.B. Rays, June 4, 2000 (Career: 1996–2006)

National League (Post-1900)

Eddie Morgan, St. L. Cardinals, Apr. 14, 1936 (Career: 1936–37)

Dan Bankhead, Bklyn. Dodgers, Aug. 26, 1947 (Career: 1947, 1950–51)

Hoyt Wilhelm, N.Y. Giants, Apr. 23, 1952 (Career: 1952–72)

Cuno Barragan, Chi. Cubs, Sept. 1, 1961 (Career: 1961–63)

Jose Sosa, Hous. Astros, July 30, 1975 (Career: 1975–76)

Dave Eiland, S.D. Padres, Apr. 10, 1992 (Career: 1988–93, 1995, 1998–2000)

Mitch Lyden, Flor. Marlins, June 6, 1993 (Career: 1993)

Gene Stechschulte, St. L Cardinals, Apr. 17, 2001 (Career: 2000–2002)

David Matranga, Hous. Astros, June 27, 2003 (Career: 2003)

Most At Bats, No Home Runs, Career

2335	Bill Holbert (1876–88)	
1931	Tom Oliver (1930–33)	
1904	Irv Hall (1943–46)	
1466	Pat Deasley (1881–88)	
1441	Tommy Bond (1876–84)	
1426	Roxy Walters (1915–25)	
1364	Paul Cook (1884–91)	
1354	Don Sutton (1966–89)	
1297	Joe McGinnity (1899–1908)	
1287	Waite Hoyt (1918–38)	

Most Consecutive At Bats Without a Home Run

3347	Tommy Thevenow	Sept. 22, 1926–end of career, 1938
3278	Eddie Foster	Apr. 20, 1916–end of career, 1923
3246	Al Bridwell	Start of career, 1905 Apr. 30, 1913
3186	Terry Turner	July 16, 1906–June 30, 1914
3104	Sparky Adams	July 26, 1923–June 30, 1931
1021	Jack McCarthy	June 28, 1899–end of career, 1907
2701	Lee Tannehill	Sept. 2, 1903–July 31, 1910
2663	Doc Cramer	Sept. 8, 1935–May 21, 1940
2617	Donie Bush	Aug. 29, 1915–Aug. 21, 1920
2568	Mike Tresh	May 19, 1940–Apr. 20, 1948

2480	Bill Bergen	June 3, 1901–Sept. 6, 1909
2426	Joe Sugden	May 31, 1895–end of career, 1912
2423	Emil Verban	Start of career, 1944–Sept. 6, 1948
2401	Everett Scott	Aug. 1, 1914–Apr. 26, 1920

Lowest Batting Average for Home Run Leaders, Season (Post-1900)

Batting Average		Home Runs
.204	Dave Kingman, N.Y. Mets (NL), 1982	37
.227	Carlos Pena, T.B. Rays (AL), 2009	39
.232	Gavvy Cravath, Phila. Phillies (NL), 1918	8
.241	Fred Odwell, Cin. Reds (NL), 1905	9
.242	Harmon Killebrew, Minn. Twins (AL), 1959	42
.243	Harmon Killebrew, Minn. Twins (AL), 1962	48
.244	Wally Pipp, N.Y. Yankees (AL), 1917	9
.244	Ralph Kiner, Pitt. Pirates (NL), 1952	37
.244	Gorman Thomas, Milw. Brewers (AL), 1979	45
.245	Gorman Thomas, Milw. Brewers (AL), 1982	39
.247	Tim Jordan, Bklyn. Dodgers (NL), 1908	12
.247	Ralph Kiner, Pitt. Pirates (NL), 1946	23
.248	Darrell Evans, Det. Tigers (AL), 1985	40
.249	Mike Schmidt, Phila. Phillies (NL), 1975	38

Players Hitting 30 or More Home Runs in First Three Seasons

Jose Canseco, Oak. A's (AL)	1986 (33), 1987 (31), and 1988 (42*)
Mark McGwire, Oak. A's (AL)	1987 (49*), 1988 (32), and 1989 (33)
Albert Pujols, St. L. Cardinals (NL)	2001 (37), 2002 (34), and 2003 (43)
Ryan Braun, Milw. Brewers (NL)	2007 (34), 2008 (37), 2009 (32)

*Led the league.

Reverse 30–30 Club: Players with 30 Home Runs and 30 Errors, Season

American League	Home Runs	Errors	National League (Post-1900)	Home Runs	Errors
Harmon Killebrew, Wash. Senators, 1959	42	30	Rogers Hornsby, St. L. Cardinals, 1922	42	30
Mark Reynolds, Balt. Orioles, 2011	37	31	Rogers Hornsby, St. L. Cardinals, 1924	39	34
			Ernie Banks, Chi. Cubs, 1958	47	32
			Tony Perez, Cin. Reds, 1969	37	32
			Tony Perez, Cin. Reds, 1970	40	35
			Davey Johnson, Atl. Braves, 1973	43	30
			Pedro Guerrero, L.A. Dodgers, 1983	32	30
			Howard Johnson, N.Y. Mets, 1991	38	31

Players Increasing Their Home Run Production in Seven Consecutive Seasons

Tim McCarver	St. L. Cardinals (NL), 1960	0
	St. L. Cardinals (NL), 1961	1
	St. L. Cardinals (NL), 1963	4
	St. L. Cardinals (NL), 1964	9
	St. L. Cardinals (NL), 1965	11
	St. L. Cardinals (NL), 1966	12
	St. L. Cardinals (NL), 1967	14
Jimmy Piersall	Bost. Red Sox (AL), 1950	0
	Bost. Red Sox (AL), 1952	1
	Bost. Red Sox (AL), 1953	3
	Bost. Red Sox (AL), 1954	8
	Bost. Red Sox (AL), 1955	13
	Bost. Red Sox (AL), 1956	14
	Bost. Red Sox (AL), 1957	19
Eddie Robinson	Cleve. Indians (AL), 1942	0
	Cleve. Indians (AL), 1946	3
	Cleve. Indians (AL), 1947	14
	Cleve. Indians (AL), 1948	16
	Wash. Senators (AL), 1949	18
	Wash. Senators–Chi. White Sox (AL), 1950	21
	Chi. White Sox (AL), 1951	29
John Shelby	Balt. Orioles (AL), 1981	0
	Balt. Orioles (AL), 1982	1
	Balt. Orioles (AL), 1983	5
	Balt. Orioles (AL), 1984	6
	Balt. Orioles (AL), 1985	7
	Balt. Orioles (AL), 1986	11
	L.A. Dodgers (NL), 1987	22
Cy Williams	Chi. Cubs (NL), 1917	5
	Phila. Phillies (NL), 1918	6
	Phila. Phillies (NL), 1919	9
	Phila. Phillies (NL), 1920	15
	Phila. Phillies (NL), 1921	18
	Phila. Phillies (NL), 1922	26
	Phila. Phillies (NL), 1923	41

Most Home Runs by Switch-Hitters, Career

536	Mickey Mantle (1951–68)
504	Eddie Murray (1977–97)
454	Chipper Jones (1993–)
358	Lance Berkman (1999–)
350	Chili Davis (1981–99)

Most Home Runs by Catcher, Season*

43	Javy Lopez, Atl. Braves (NL), 2003
41	Todd Hundley, N.Y. Mets (NL), 1996
40	Roy Campanella, Bklyn. Dodgers (NL), 1953
40	Mike Piazza, L.A. Dodgers (NL), 1997
40	Mike Piazza, N.Y. Mets (NL), 1999

38 ....Johnny Bench, Cin. Reds (NL), 1970
37 ....Gabby Hartnett, Chi. Cubs (NL), 1930
*While in lineup as catcher.

Most Home Runs by Catcher, Career*

376 ....Carlton Fisk (1977–97)
358..Mike Piazza (1992–2007)
327..Johnny Bench (1967–83)
306..Yogi Berra (1946–65)
298..Gary Carter (1974–92)
295..Lance Parrish (1977–95)
*While in lineup as catcher.

300 Career Home Runs and 100 Home Runs, Both Leagues

	American League	National League	Total
Adrina Beltre	163	197	310
Carlos Beltran	123	179	302
Bobby Bonds	135	197	332
Ellis Burks	177	175	352
Chili Davis	249	101	350
Carlos Delgado	336	137	473
Jim Edmonds	121	272	393
Darrell Evans	141	273	414
Shawn Green	119	209	328
Ken Griffey Jr.	420	210	501
Vladimir Guerrero	215	234	449
Frank Howard	259	123	382
David Justice	145	160	305
Carlos Lee	161	188	349
Lee May	126	228	354
Fred McGriff	224	269	493
Mark McGwire	363	220	583
Eddie Murray	396	108	504
Frank Robinson	262	324	586
Richie Sexson	164	142	306
Gary Sheffield	141	368	509
Reggie Smith	149	165	314
Alfonso Soriano	162	178	340
Greg Vaughn	229	126	355

*Still active.

Most Home Runs Hit in One Ballpark, Career

323..............................Mel Ott..Polo Grounds
293..............................Sammy Sosa..Wrigley Field
290..............................Ernie Banks..Wrigley Field
266..............................Mickey Mantle..Yankee Stadium
265..............................Mike Schmidt..Veterans Stadium
263..............................Frank Thomas..U.S. Cellular Field
259..............................Babe Ruth..Yankee Stadium
252..............................Stan Musial..Sportsman's Park
251..............................Lou Gehrig..Yankee Stadium
248..............................Ted Williams..Fenway Park
246..............................Harmon Killebrew..Metropolitan Stadium
237..............................Carl Yastrzemski..Fenway Park
236..............................Willie McCovey..Candlestick Park

231	Billy Williams	Wrigley Field
216	Chipper Jones	Turner Field
212	Ron Santo	Wrigley Field
212	Todd Helton	Coors Field
212	Norm Cash	Tiger Stadium

Players Whose Home Run in "Cycle" Was Grand Slam

American League

Nap Lajoie, Phila. A's, July 30, 1901
Tony Lazzeri, N.Y. Yankees, June 3, 1932
Jimmie Foxx, Phila. A's, Aug. 14, 1933
Jay Buhner, Sea. Mariners, July 23, 1993
Miguel Tejada, Oak. A's, Sept. 29, 2001
Jason Kubel, Minn. Twins, Apr. 17, 2009
Bengie Molina, Tex. Rangers, July 16, 2010

National League

Bill Terry, N.Y. Giants, May 29, 1928

Players with the Highest Percentage of Team's Total Home Runs, Season

American League

88%	Babe Ruth, Bost. Red Sox, 1919	29 of team's 33
73%	Babe Ruth, Bost. Red Sox, 1918	11 of team's 15
56%	Smokey Joe Wood, Cleve. Indians, 1918	5 of team's 9
55%	Goose Goslin, Wash. Senators, 1924	12 of team's 22
55%	Stan Spence, Wash. Senators, 1944	18 of team's 33
51%	Jimmie Foxx, Bost. Red Sox, 1938	50 of team's 98
50%	Erve Beck, Cleve. Indians, 1901	6 of team's 12
50%	Tilly Walker, Phila. A's, 1918	11 of team's 22
50%	Joe Judge, Wash. Senators, 1924	2 of team's 4
50%	Sam Chapman, Phila. A's, 1946	20 of team's 40

National League (Post-1900)

60%	Shad Barry, Phila. Phillies, 1902	3 of team's 5
60%	Jimmy Seckard, Bklyn. Dodgers, 1903	9 of team's 15
60%	Harry Lumley, Bklyn. Dodgers, 1904	9 of team's 15
58%	Wally Berger, Bost. Braves, 1930	38 of team's 66
56%	Wally Berger, Bost. Braves, 1931	19 of team's 34
56%	Bill Nicholson, Chi. Cubs, 1943	29 of team's 52
53%	Ed Konetchy, St. L. Cardinals, 1913	8 of team's 15
53%	Cy Williams, Phila. Phillies, 1927	30 of team's 57
52%	Dick Hoblitzel, Cin. Reds, 1911	11 of team's 21
50%	Homer Smoot, St. L. Cardinals, 1903	4 of team's 8
50%	Sherry Magee, Phila. Phillies, 1906	6 of team's 12
50%	Harry Lumley, Bklyn. Dodgers, 1907	9 of team's 18
50%	Wally Berger, Bost. Braves, 1933	27 of team's 54

Federal League

| 50% | Ed Konetchy, Pitt. Pirates, 1915 | 10 of team's 20 |

Shortstops Leading League in Home Runs

American League

| Vern Stephens, St. L. Browns, 1945 | 24 |
| Alex Rodriguez, Tex. Rangers, 2001 | 52 |

National League

| Ernie Banks, Chi. Cubs, 1958 | 47 |
| Ernie Banks, Chi. Cubs, 1959 | 45 |

Alex Rodriguez, Tex. Rangers, 2002...............................57
Alex Rodriguez, Tex. Rangers, 2003...............................47

Most Home Runs by Left-Handed Hitting Shortstops

Home Runs		Games at Short
96	Arky Vaughan (1932–43, 1947–48)	1485
70	Stephen Drew (2006–)	717
57	Tony Kubek (1957–65)	882
49	Joe Sewell (1920–33)	1216
42	Craig Reynolds (1975–89)	1240
40	Billy Klaus (1952–53, 1955–63)	426
28	Ozzie Guillen (1985–2000)	1896

Players Hitting Home Runs in 20 Consecutive Seasons Played

Rickey Henderson (1979–2003)	25	Ken Griffey Jr. (1959–2009)	21
Ty Cobb (1905–28)	24	Ron Fairly (1958–78)	21
Hank Aaron (1954–76)	23	Reggie Jackson (1967–87)	21
Carl Yastrzemski (1961–83)	23	Graig Nettles (1968–88)	21
Rusty Staub (1963–85)	23	Eddie Murray (1977–97)	21
Carlton Fisk (1971–93)	23	Harold Baines (1980–2000)	21
Stan Musial (1941–44, 1946–63)	22	Tim Raines (1981–99; 2001–02)	21
Willie Mays (1951–52, 1954–73)	22	Cal Ripken Jr. (1981–2001)	21
Al Kaline (1953–74)	22	Ivan Rodriguez (1991–)	21
Brooks Robinson (1956–77)	22	Mel Ott (1927–46)	20
Willie McCovey (1959–80)	22	Dwight Evans (1972–91)	20
Tony Perez (1965–86)	22	Brian Downing (1973–92)	20
Dave Winfield (1973–88, 1990–95)	22	George Brett (1974–93)	20
Gary Sheffield (1988–2009)	22	Robin Yount (1974–93)	20
Barry Bonds (1986–2007)	22	Andre Dawson (1977–96)	20
Babe Ruth (1915–35)	21	Tony Gwynn (1982–2001)	20
Frank Robinson (1956–76)	21	Rafael Palmiero (1986–2005)	20
Jim Thome (1991–)	21		

Players with 100 Home Runs, Three Different Teams

Darrell Evans	Atl. Braves (NL), 1969–76, 1989	131
	S.F. Giants (NL), 1976–83	142
	Det. Tigers (AL), 1984–88	141
Reggie Jackson	K.C./Oak. A's (AL), 1967–75, 1987	269
	N.Y. Yankees (AL), 1977–81	144
	Cal. Angels (AL), 1982–86	123
Alex Rodriguez*	Sea. Mariners (AL), 1994–2000	189
	Tex. Rangers (AL), 2001–03	156
	N.Y. Yankees (AL), 2004–	284

*Active player.

Players with 40-Home Run Seasons Before 25th Birthday

		Home Runs	Age
Hank Aaron	Milw. Braves (NL), 1957	44	23
Richie Allen	Phila. Phillies (NL), 1966	40	24
Ernie Banks	Chi. Cubs (NL), 1955	44	24
Johnny Bench	Cin. Reds (NL), 1970	45	22
	Cin. Reds (NL), 1972	40	24

Joe DiMaggio .... N.Y. Yankees (AL), 1937 .... 46 22
Adam Dunn .... Cin. Reds (NL), 2004 .... 46 24
Prince Fielder .... Milw. Brewers (NL), 2007 .... 50 23
Jimmie Foxx .... Phila. A's (AL), 1932 .... 58 .... 24*
Lou Gehrig .... N.Y. Yankees (AL), 1927 .... 47 24
Troy Glaus .... L.A. Angels (AL), 2000 .... 47 23
Ken Griffey Jr. .... Sea. Mariners (AL), 1993 .... 45 23
                                            Sea. Mariners (AL), 1994 .... 40 24
Reggie Jackson .... Oak. A's (AL), 1969 .... 47 23
Harmon Killebrew .... Wash. Senators (AL), 1959 .... 42 23
Ralph Kiner .... Pitt. Pirates (NL), 1947 .... 51 .... 24*
Chuck Klein .... Phila. Phillies (NL), 1929 .... 43 .... 24*
Mickey Mantle .... N.Y. Yankees (AL), 1956 .... 52 .... 24*
Eddie Mathews .... Milw. Braves (NL), 1953 .... 47 21
Willie Mays .... N.Y. Giants (NL), 1954 .... 41 23
                                            N.Y. Giants (NL), 1955 .... 51 24
Mark McGwire .... Oak. A's (AL), 1987 .... 49 23
Mel Ott .... N.Y. Giants (NL), 1929 .... 42 20
Albert Pujols .... St. L. Cardinals (NL), 2003 .... 43 23
                                            St. L. Cardinals (NL), 2004 .... 46 24
Alex Rodriguez .... Sea. Mariners (AL), 1998 .... 42 23
                                            Sea. Mariners (AL), 1999 .... 42 24
                                            Sea. Mariners (AL), 2000 .... 41 25
Hal Trosky .... Cleve. Indians (AL), 1936 .... 42 23
*Turned 25 during season.

Players with More Home Runs Than Strikeouts, Season (Min. 10 Home Runs)

American League

	Home Runs	Strikeouts	Differential
Lou Gehrig, N.Y. Yankees, 1934	49	31	+18
Joe DiMaggio, N.Y. Yankees, 1941	30	13	+17
Yogi Berra, N.Y. Yankees, 1950	28	12	+16
Ken Williams, St. L. Browns, 1925	25	14	+11
Joe DiMaggio, N.Y. Yankees, 1938	32	21	+11
Joe DiMaggio, N.Y. Yankees, 1939	30	20	+10
Ted Williams, Bost. Red Sox, 1941	37	27	+10
Joe DiMaggio, N.Y. Yankees, 1937	46	37	+9
Joe DiMaggio, N.Y. Yankees, 1948	39	30	+9
Lou Boudreau, Cleve. Indians, 1948	18	9	+9
Ken Williams, St. L. Browns, 1922	39	31	+8
Joe Sewell, N.Y. Yankees, 1932	11	3	+8
Bill Dickey, N.Y. Yankees, 1937	29	22	+7
Ted Williams, Bost. Red Sox, 1950	28	21	+7
Yogi Berra, N.Y. Yankees, 1951	27	20	+7
Yogi Berra, N.Y. Yankees, 1955	27	20	+7
Bill Dickey, N.Y. Yankees, 1936	22	16	+6
Yogi Berra, N.Y. Yankees, 1952	30	24	+6
Mickey Cochrane, Phila. A's, 1927	12	7	+5
Bill Dickey, N.Y. Yankees, 1938	27	22	+5
Ted Williams, Bost. Red Sox, 1955	28	24	+4
Charlie Gehringer, Det. Tigers, 1935	19	16	+3

continued on next page

American League

	Home Runs	Strikeouts	Differential
Bill Dickey, N.Y. Yankees, 1935	14	11	+3
Lou Gehrig, N.Y. Yankees, 1936	49	46	+3
Ted Williams, Bost. Red Sox, 1953	13	10	+3
Lou Skizas, K.C. A's, 1957	18	15	+3
Tris Speaker, Cleve. Indians, 1923	17	15	+2
Al Simmons, Phila. A's, 1930	36	34	+2
Bill Dickey, N.Y. Yankees, 1932	15	13	+2
Charlie Gehringer, Det. Tigers, 1936	15	13	+2
Vic Power, K.C. A's–Cleve. Indians, 1958	16	14	+2
George Brett, K.C. Royals, 1980	24	22	+2
Ken Williams, St. L. Browns, 1924	18	17	+1
Mickey Cochrane, Phila. A's, 1932	23	22	+1
Joe DiMaggio, N.Y. Yankees, 1940	31	30	+1
Joe DiMaggio, N.Y. Yankees, 1946	25	24	+1
Johnny Mize, N.Y., Yankees, 1950	25	24	+1
Yogi Berra, N.Y. Yankees, 1956	30	29	+1

National League

	Home Runs	Strikeouts	Differential
Tommy Holmes, Bost. Braves, 1945	28	9	+19
Ted Kluszewski, Cin. Reds, 1954	49	35	+14
Lefty O'Doul, Phila. Phillies, 1929	32	19	+13
Johnny Mize, N.Y. Giants, 1947	51	42	+9
Cap Anson, Chi. Colts, 1884	21	13	+8
Ernie Lombardi, N.Y. Giants, 1945	19	11	+8
Sam Thompson, Phila. Phillies, 1895	18	11	+7
Ted Kluszewski, Cin. Reds, 1955	47	40	+7
Jack Clements, Phila. Phillies, 1895	13	7	+6
Billy Southworth, St. L. Cardinals, 1926	16	10	+6
Ernie Lombardi, Cin. Reds, 1935	12	6	+6
Willard Marshall, N.Y. Giants, 1947	36	30	+6
Ted Kluszewski, Cin. Reds, 1953	40	34	+6
Bill Terry, N.Y. Giants, 1932	28	23	+5
Ernie Lombardi, Cin. Reds, 1938	19	14	+5
Stan Musial, St. L. Cardinals, 1948	39	34	+5
Mel Ott, N.Y. Giants, 1929	42	38	+4
Frank McCormick, Cin. Reds, 1941	17	13	+4
Andy Pafko, Chi. Cubs, 1950	36	32	+4
Ted Kluszewski, Cin. Reds, 1956	35	31	+4
Barry Bonds, S.F. Giants, 2004	45	41	+4
Dan Brouthers, Det. Wolverines, 1887	12	9	+3
Hugh Duffy, Bost. Braves, 1894	18	15	+3
Irish Meusel, N.Y. Giants, 1923	19	16	+3
Frank McCormick, Cin. Reds, 1944	20	17	+3
Johnny Mize, N.Y. Giants, 1948	40	37	+3
Don Mueller, N.Y. Giants, 1951	16	13	+3
Billy O'Brien, Wash. Statesmen, 1887	19	17	+2
Irish Meusel, N.Y. Giants, 1925	21	19	+2
Frank McCormick, Cin. Reds, 1939	18	16	+2
Tommy Holmes, Bost. Braves, 1944	13	11	+2
Lefty O'Doul, Phila. Phillies, 1930	22	21	+1

Lefty O'Doul, Bklyn. Dodgers, 1932 ....21 .... 20 ....+1
Arky Vaughan, Pitt. Pirates, 1935 ....19 ....18 ....+1
Ernie Lombardi, Cin. Reds, 1939 ....20 ....19 ....+1

Largest Differential Between Leader in Home Runs and Runner-Up

American League

Differential	Season	Leader	Home Runs	Runner-Up	Home Runs
+35	1920	Babe Ruth, N.Y. Yankees	54	George Sisler, St. L. Browns	19
+35	1921	Babe Ruth, N.Y. Yankees	59	Ken Williams, St. L. Browns, and Bob Meusel, N.Y. Yankees	24
+28	1926	Babe Ruth, N.Y. Yankees	47	Al Simmons, Phila. A's	19
+27	1928	Babe Ruth, N.Y. Yankees	54	Lou Gehrig, N.Y. Yankees	27
+20	1956	Mickey Mantle, N.Y. Yankees	52	Vic Wertz, Cleve. Indians	32
+19	1919	Babe Ruth, Bost. Red Sox	29	Home Run Baker, N.Y. Yankees, George Sisler, St. L. Browns, and Tilly Walker, Phila. A's	10
+19	1924	Babe Ruth, N.Y. Yankees	46	Joe Hauser, Phila. A's	27
+17	1932	Jimmie Foxx, Phila. A's	58	Babe Ruth, N.Y. Yankees	41
+15	2010	Jose Bautista, Tor. Blue Jays	54	Paul Konerko, Chi. White Sox	39
+14	1933	Jimmie Foxx, Phila. A's	48	Babe Ruth, N.Y. Yankees	34
+13	1927	Babe Ruth, N.Y. Yankees	60	Lou Gehrig, N.Y. Yankees	47
+12	1923	Babe Ruth, N.Y. Yankees	41	Ken Williams, St. L. Browns	29
+12	1978	Jim Rice, Bost. Red Sox	46	Don Baylor, Cal. Angels, and Larry Hisle, Milw. Brewers	34
+12	1990	Cecil Fielder, Det. Tigers	51	Mark McGwire, Oak. A's	39
+12	1997	Ken Griffey Jr., Sea. Mariners	56	Tino Martinez, N.Y. Yankees	44
+11	1929	Babe Ruth, N.Y. Yankees	46	Lou Gehrig, N.Y. Yankees	35

National League

Differential	Season	Leader	Home Runs	Runner-Up	Home Runs
+19	1923	Cy Williams, Phila. Phillies	41	Jake Fournier, Bklyn. Dodgers	22
+18	1940	Johnny Mize, St. L. Cardinals	43	Bill Nicholson, Chi. Cubs	25
+18	1949	Ralph Kiner, Pitt. Pirates	54	Stan Musial, St. L. Cardinals	36
+16	1922	Rogers Hornsby, St. L. Cardinals	42	Cy Williams, Phila. Phillies	26
+16	1930	Hack Wilson, Chi. Cubs	56	Chuck Klein, Phila. Phillies	40
+15	1925	Rogers Hornsby, St. L. Cardinals	39	Gabby Hartnett, Chi. Cubs	24
+14	1964	Willie Mays, S.F. Giants	47	Billy Williams, Chi. Cubs	33
+13	1899	Buck Freeman, Wash. Senators	25	Bobby Wallace, St. L. Cardinals	12
+13	1965	Willie Mays, S.F. Giants	52	Willie McCovey, S.F. Giants	39
+13	1980	Mike Schmidt, Phila. Phillies	48	Bob Horner, Atl. Braves	35
+12	1958	Ernie Banks, Chi. Cubs	47	Frank Thomas, Pitt. Pirates	35
+11	1915	Gavvy Cravath, Phila. Phillies	24	Cy Williams, Chi. Cubs	13
+11	1943	Bill Nicholson, Chi. Cubs	29	Mel Ott, N.Y. Giants	18
+11	1950	Ralph Kiner, Pitt. Pirates	47	Andy Pafko, Chi. Cubs	36
+11	1977	George Foster, Cin. Reds	52	Jeff Burroughs, Atl. Braves	41
+11	1989	Kevin Mitchell, S.F. Giants	47	Howard Johnson, N.Y. Mets	36

Most Home Runs, Last Season in Majors

35	Dave Kingman, Oak. A's (AL), 1986	21	Paul O'Neill, N.Y. Yankees (AL), 2001
29	Ted Williams, Bost. Red Sox (AL), 1960	21	Sammy Sosa, Tex. Rangers, 2007
29	Mark McGwire, St. L. Cardinals (NL), 2001	19	Joe Gordon, Cleve. Indians (AL), 1950
28	Barry Bonds, S.F. Giants (NL), 2007	19	Chili Davis, N.Y. Yankees (AL), 1999

27 ....Jermaine Dye, Chi. White Sox, 2009
25.........................Hank Greenberg, Pitt. Pirates (NL), 1947
24...........................Roy Cullenbine, Det. Tigers (AL), 1947
24........................Jack Graham, St. L. Browns (AL), 1949
23 ....Kirby Puckett, Minn. Twins (AL), 1995
23 ....Albert Belle, Balt. Orioles (AL), 2000
22 ....Phil Nevin, Tex. Ranges (AL), Chic. Cubs (NL), Minn. Twins (AL)
21 ....Dave Nilsson, Milw. Brewers (NL), 1999

19.............................George Brett, K.C. Royals (AL), 1993
19 .....Jose Guillen, K.C. Royals (AL), S.F. Giants (NL), 2010
18..............................Buzz Arlett, Phila. Phillies (NL), 1931
18...........................Ralph Kiner, Cleve. Indians (AL), 1955
18 ....Joe Adcock, Cal. Angels (AL), 1966
18......................Mickey Mantle, N.Y. Yankees (AL), 1968
18 ....Reggie Smith, S.F. Giants (NL), 1982
18 ....Rafael Palmeiro, Balt. Orioles (AL), 2005

Fewest Career Home Runs for League Leader (Post-1920)

American League

89..Nick Etten (N.Y. Yankees), led league in 1944 with 22
156...Bob Meusel (N.Y. Yankees), led league in 1925 with 33
160..Bill Melton (Chi. White Sox), led league in 1971 with 33
166..Tony Conigliaro (Bost. Red Sox), led league in 1965 with 32
192...Al Rosen (Cleve. Indians), led league in 1950 with 37 and in 1953 with 43
196...Ken Williams (St. L. Browns), led league in 1922 with 39
224...Bobby Grich (Cal. Angels), led league in 1981 with 22
235..Ben Oglivie (Milw. Brewers), led league in 1980 with 41
237...Gus Zernial (Phila. A's), led league in 1951 with 33
241..Jesse Barfield (Tor. Blue Jays), led league in 1986 with 40
247...Vern Stephens (St. L. Browns), led league in 1945 with 24

National League

88...Tommy Holmes (Bost. Braves), led league in 1945 with 28
135 ....Ripper Collins (St. L. Cardinals), led league in 1934 with 35
136...Jack Fournier (Bklyn. Dodgers), led league in 1924 with 27
148..George Kelly (N.Y. Giants), led league in 1921 with 23
205...Joe Medwick (St. L. Cardinals), led league in 1937 with 31
219...Jim Bottomley (St. L. Cardinals), led league in 1928 with 31
228...Howard Johnson (N.Y. Mets), led league in 1991 with 38
234 ....Kevin Mitchell (S.F. Giants), led league in 1989 with 47
235..Bill Nicholson (Chi. Cubs), led league in 1943 with 29 and in 1944 with 33
239...Dolph Camilli (Bklyn. Dodgers), led league in 1941 with 34
242 ....Wally Berger (Bost. Braves), led league in 1935 with 34
244 ....Hack Wilson (Chi. Cubs), led league in 1926 with 21, in 1927 with 30, in 1928 with 31, and in 1930 with 56
*Still active.

Runs Batted In

Evolution of RBI Record

American League

1901	Nap Lajoie, Phila. A's	125
1911	Ty Cobb, Det. Tigers	127
1912	Frank Baker, Phil. Athletics	130
1920	Babe Ruth, N.Y. Yankees	137
1921	Babe Ruth, N.Y. Yankees	170
1927	Lou Gehrig, N.Y. Yankees	175
1931	Lou Gehrig, N.Y. Yankees	184

National League (Pre-1900)

1876	Deacon White, Chi. White Stockings	60

1879	Charley Jones, Bost. Beaneaters	62
	John O'Rourke, Bost. Beaneaters	62
1880	Cap Anson, Chi. White Stockings	74
1881	Cap Anson, Chi. White Stockings	82
1882	Cap Anson, Chi. White Stockings	83
1883	Dan Brouthers, Buf. Bisons	97
1884	Cap Anson, Chi. White Stockings	102
1885	Cap Anson, Chi. White Stockings	108
1886	Cap Anson, Chi. White Stockings	147
1887	Sam Thompson, Det. Wolverines	166

National League (Post-1899)

1900	Elmer Flick, Phila. Phillies	110
1901	Honus Wagner, Pitt. Pirates	126
1910	Sherry Magee, Phila. Phillies	123
1913	Gavvy Cravath, Phila. Phillies	128
1922	Rogers Hornsby, St. L. Cardinals	152
1929	Hack Wilson, Chi. Cubs	159
1930	Hack Wilson, Chi. Cubs	191

Most RBIs by Decade

Pre-1900		1900–09		1910–19	
1880	Cap Anson	956	Honus Wagner	828	Ty Cobb
1323	Roger Connor	808	Sam Crawford	793	Home Run Baker
1302	Sam Thompson	793	Nap Lajoie	765	Heinie Zimmerman
1296	Dan Brouthers	688	Harry Davis	746	Sherry Magee
1218	Hugh Duffy	685	Cy Seymour	718	Tris Speaker
1135	Ed Delahanty	680	Jimmy Williams	718	Duffy Lewis
1124	Ed McKean	638	Bobby Wallace	697	Sam Crawford
1080	Jake Beckley	610	Harry Steinfeldt	687	Ed Konetchy
1072	Bid McPhee	597	Bill Dahlen	682	Eddie Collins
1021	Fred Pfeffer	590	"Piano Legs" Hickman	665	Gavvy Cravath

1920–29		1930–39		1940–49	
1331	Babe Ruth	1403	Jimmie Foxx	903	Bob Elliot
1153	Rogers Hornsby	1358	Lou Gehrig	893	Ted Williams
1133	Harry Heilmann	1135	Mel Ott	887	Bobby Doerr
1005	Bob Meusel	1081	Al Simmons	854	Rudy York
923	George Kelly	1046	Earl Averill	835	Bill Nicholson
885	Jim Bottomley	1036	Joe Cronin	824	Vern Stephens
860	Ken Williams	1003	Charlie Gehringer	786	Joe DiMaggio
827	George Sisler	979	Chuck Klein	759	Dixie Walker
821	Goose Goslin	937	Bill Dickey	744	Johnny Mize
821	Joe Sewell	893	Wally Berger	710	Joe Gordon

1950–59		1960–69		1970–79	
1031	Duke Snider	1107	Hank Aaron	1013	Johnny Bench
1001	Gil Hodges	1013	Harmon Killebrew	954	Tony Perez
997	Yogi Berra	1011	Frank Robinson	936	Lee May
972	Stan Musial	1003	Willie Mays	922	Reggie Jackson
925	Del Ennis	937	Ron Santo	906	Willie Stargell

continued on next page

863 ....Jackie Jensen	925 ....Ernie Banks	860 ....Rusty Staub
841 ....Mickey Mantle	896 ....Orlando Cepeda	856 ....Bobby Bonds
823 ....Ted Kluszewski	862 ....,Roberto Clemente	846 ....Carl Yastrzemski
817 ....Gus Bell	853 ....Billy Williams	840 ....Bobby Murcer
816 ....Larry Doby	836 ....Brooks Robinson	832 ....Bob Watson

1980–89	**1990–99**	**2000–11**
996 ....Eddie Murray	1099 ....Albert Belle	1430 ....Alex Rodriguez
929 ....Dale Murphy	1091 ....Ken Griffey Jr.	1329 ....Albert Pujols
929 ....Mike Schmidt	1076 ....Barry Bonds	1215 ....Vladimir Guerrero
900 ....Dwight Evans	1068 ....Juan Gonzalez	1214 ....David Ortiz
899 ....Dave Winfield	1068 ....Rafael Palmeiro	1202 ....Carlos Lee
895 ....Andre Dawson	1040 ....Frank Thomas	1178 ....Lance Berkman
868 ....Jim Rice	979 ....Dante Bichette	1149 ....Manny Ramirez
851 ....George Brett	975 ....Fred McGriff	1143 ....Miguel Tejada
835 ....Harold Baines	961 ....Jeff Bagwell	1131 ....Bobby Abreu
821 ....Robin Yount	960 ....Matt Williams	

Career RBI Leaders by First Letter of Last Name

A	Hank Aaron (1954–76) 2297	N	Graig Nettles (1967–88) 1314
B	Barry Bonds (1986–2007) 1996	O	Mel Ott (1926–47)....................................1860
C	Ty Cobb (1905–28)..1938	P	Rafael Palmeiro (1986–2005) 1835
D	Andre Dawson (1976–96) 1591	Q	Joe Quinn (1884–86, 1888–1901).....................795
E	Dwight Evans (1972–91) 1384	R	Babe Ruth (1914–35)..................................2213
F	Jimmie Foxx (1925–42, 1944–45)....................1922	S	Al Simmons (1924–41, 1943–44) 1827
G	Lou Gehrig (1923–39)....................................1995	T	Frank Thomas (1990–2008) 1704
H	Rogers Hornsby (1915–37)..............................1584	U	Chase Utley* (2003–)....................................694
I	Raul Ibañez* (1996–)....................................1054	V	Mickey Vernon (1939–43, 1946–60) 1311
J	Reggie Jackson (1967–87)...............................1702	W	Ted Williams (1939–42, 1946–60) 1839
K	Harmon Killebrew (1954–75)..........................1584	X	[No player]
L	Nap Lajoie (1896–1916).................................1599	Y	Carl Yastrzemski (1961–83).............................1844
M	Stan Musial (1941–44, 1946–63)...................1951	Z	Todd Zeile (1989–2004) 1110

*Still active.

Teammates Finishing One-Two in RBIs

American League

Season	Team	Leader	RBIs	Runner-Up	RBIs
1902 ....Bost. Americans...............Buck Freeman ....121 ....Piano Legs Hickman*...........110
1905 ....Phila. A's ....Harry Davis.......................83 ....Lave Cross..............................77
1908 ....Det. Tigers ....Ty Cobb ....108 ....Sam Crawford 80
1909 ....Det. Tigers ....Ty Cobb ....107 ....Sam Crawford 97
1910 ....Det. Tigers ....Sam Crawford ....120 ....Ty Cobb 91
1913 ....Phila. A's ....Home Run Baker ....126 ....Stuffy McInnis 90
1915 ....Det. Tigers ....Bobby Veach ....112 (Tie)..............Sam Crawford 112
1917 ....Det. Tigers ....Bobby Veach ....103 ....Ty Cobb 102
1926 ...............N.Y. Yankees ....Babe Ruth........................146 ....Tony Lazzeri ....114 (Tie)
1927 ...............N.Y. Yankees ....Lou Gehrig ....175 ....Babe Ruth...............................164
1928 ...............N.Y. Yankees ....Lou Gehrig ....142 (Tie)..............Babe Ruth...............................142
1931 ...............N.Y. Yankees ....Lou Gehrig ....184 ....Babe Ruth...............................163

American League

Season	Team	Leader	RBIs	Runner-Up	RBIs
1932	Phila. A's	Jimmie Foxx	169	Al Simmons	151
1940	Det. Tigers	Hank Greenberg	150	Rudy York	134
1949	Bost. Red Sox	Vern Stephens	159 (Tie)	Ted Williams	159
1950	Bost. Red Sox	Vern Stephens	144 (Tie)	Walt Dropo	144
1952	Cleve. Indians	Al Rosen	105	Larry Doby	104 (Tie)
1980	Milw. Brewers	Cecil Cooper	122	Ben Oglivie	118
1984	Bost. Red Sox	Tony Armas	123	Jim Rice	122
2011	N.Y. Yankees	Curtis Granderson	119	Robinson Canó	118

*Also with Cleveland part of the season.

National League (Post-1900)

Season	Team	Leader	RBIs	Runner-Up	RBIs
1900	Phila. Phillies	Elmer Flick	110	Ed Delahanty	109
1902	Pitt. Pirates	Honus Wagner	91	Tommy Leach	85
1904	N.Y. Giants	Bill Dahlen	80	Sam Mertes	78
1914	Phila. Phillies	Sherry Magee	103	Gavvy Cravath	100
1932	Phila. Phillies	Don Hurst	143	Chuck Klein	137
1960	Milw. Braves	Hank Aaron	126	Eddie Mathews	124
1965	Cin. Reds	Deron Johnson	130	Frank Robinson	113
1970	Cin. Reds	Johnny Bench	148	Tony Perez	129
1976	Cin. Reds	George Foster	121	Joe Morgan	111
1996	Colo. Rockies	Andres Galarraga	150	Dante Bichette	141

Largest Differential Between League Leader in RBIs and Runner-Up

American League

Differential	Season	Leader	RBIs	Runner-Up	RBIs
+51	1935	Hank Greenberg, Det. Tigers	170	Lou Gehrig, N.Y. Yankees	119
+36	1913	Home Run Baker, Phila. A's	126	Stuffy McInnis, Phila. A's, and Duffy Lewis, Bost. Red Sox	90
+32	1921	Babe Ruth, N.Y. Yankees	171	Harry Heilmann, Det. Tigers	139
+31	1926	Babe Ruth, N.Y. Yankees	145	George H. Bums, Cleve. Indians, and Tony Lazzeri, N.Y. Yankees	114
+30	1953	Al Rosen, Cleve. Indians	145	Mickey Vernon, Wash. Senators	115
+29	1910	Sam Crawford, Det. Tigers	120	Ty Cobb, Det. Tigers	91
+29	1911	Ty Cobb, Det. Tigers	144	Sam Crawford, Det. Tigers, and Home Run Baker, Phila A's	115
+29	1922	Ken Williams,. St. L. Browns	155	Bobby Veach, Det. Tigers	126
+29	1938	Jimmie Foxx, Bost. Red Sox	175	Hank Greenberg, Det. Tigers	146
+28	1908	Ty Cobb, Det. Tigers	108	Sam Crawford, Det. Tigers	80

National League (Post-1900)

Differential	Season	Leader	RBIs	Runner-Up	RBIs
+39	1937	Joe Medwick, St. L. Cardinals	154	Frank Demaree, Chi. Cubs	115
+35	1910	Sherry Magee, Phila. Phillies	123	Mike Mitchell, Cin. Reds	88
+33	1913	Gavvy Cravath, Phila. Phillies	128	Heinie Zimmerman, Chi. Cubs	95
+28	1915	Gavvy Cravath, Phila. Phillies	115	Sherry Magee, Phila. Phillies	87
+27	1943	Bill Nicholson, Chi. Cubs	128	Bob Elliott, Pitt. Pirates	101
+27	1957	Hank Aaron, Milw. Braves	132	Del Ennis, St. L. Cardinals	105

Career RBI Totals, Players Hitting 500 Home Runs

	HRs	RBIs		HRs	RBIs		HRs	RBIs
Barry Bonds	762	1996	Harmon Killebrew	573	1584	Frank Thomas	521	1704
Hank Aaron	755	2297	Rafael Palmeiro	569	1835	Ted Williams	521	1839
Babe Ruth	714	2213	Jim Thome*	604	1674	Ernie Banks	512	1636
Willie Mays	660	1903	Reggie Jackson	563	1702	Eddie Mathews	512	1453
Ken Griffey Jr.	630	1836	Mike Schmidt	548	1595	Mel Ott	511	1860
Sammy Sosa	609	1667	Manny Ramirez	555	1831	Gary Sheffield	509	1676
Frank Robinson	586	1812	Mickey Mantle	536	1509	Eddie Murray	504	1917
Mark McGwire	583	1414	Jimmie Foxx	534	1922			
Alex Rodriguez*	629	1893	Willie McCovey	521	1555	*Active player.		

Players Driving in 100 Runs in First Two Seasons in Majors

American League

Al Simmons, Phila. A's	1924 (102) and 1925 (129)
Tony Lazzeri, N.Y. Yankees	1926 (114) and 1927 (102)
Dale Alexander, Det. Tigers	1929 (137) and 1930 (135)
Hal Trosky, Cleve. Indians	1934 (142) and 1935 (113)
Joe DiMaggio, N.Y. Yankees	1936 (125) and 1937 (167)
Rudy York, Det. Tigers	1937 (103) and 1938 (127)
Ted Williams, Bost. Red Sox	1939 (145) and 1940 (113)
Jose Canseco, Oak. Athletics	1986 (117) and 1987 (113)
Wally Joyner, Cal. Angels	1986 (100) and 1987 (117)
Frank Thomas, Chi. White Sox	1991 (109) and 1992 (115)
Hideki Motsui, N.Y. Yankees	2003 (106) and 2004 (108)

National League (Post-1900)

Glenn Wright, Pitt. Pirates	1924 (111) and 1925 (121)
Pinky Whitney, Phila. Phillies	1928 (103) and 1929 (115)
Ray Jablonski, St. L. Cardinals	1953 (112) and 1954 (104)
Albert Pujols, St. L. Cardinals	2001 (130) and 2002 (127)

Players Driving in 500 Runs in First Four Years of Career

558	Joe DiMaggio, 1936–39, N.Y. Yankees (AL)
535	Hal Troksy, 1934–37, Clev. Indians (AL)
515	Ted Williams, 1939–42, Bost. Red Sox (AL)
504	Albert Pujols, 2001–04, St. L. Cardinals (NL)

Catchers with 100 RBIs and 100 Runs Scored, Season

American League

	RBIs	Runs
Mickey Cochrane, Phila. A's, 1932	112	118
Yogi Berra, N.Y. Yankees, 1950	124	116
Carlton Fisk, Bost. Red Sox, 1977	102	106
Darrell Porter, K.C. Royals, 1979	112	101
Ivan Rodriguez, Tex. Rangers, 1999	113	116

National League (Post-1900)

	RBIs	Runs
Roy Campanella, Bklyn. Dodgers, 1953	142	103
Johnny Bench, Cin. Reds, 1974	129	108

Mike Piazza, L.A. Dodgers, 1997 ....124 104
Mike Piazza, N.Y. Mets, 1999..124 100

Catchers Hitting .300 with 30 Home Runs and 100 RBIs, Season

American League

	Home Runs	RBIs	Batting Average
Rudy York,* Det. Tigers, 1937	35	103	.307
Ivan Rodriguez, Tex. Rangers, 1999	35	113	.332

National League (Post-1900)

	Home Runs	RBIs	Batting Average
Gabby Hartnett, Chi.Cubs, 1930	37	122	.339
Walker Cooper, N.Y. Giants, 1947	35	122	.305
Roy Campanella, Bklyn. Dodgers, 1951	33	108	.325
Roy Campanella, Bklyn. Dodgers, 1953	41	142	.312
Roy Campanella, Bklyn. Dodgers, 1955	32	107	.318
Joe Torre,** Atl. Braves, 1966	36	101	.315
Mike Piazza, L.A. Dodgers, 1993	35	112	.318
Mike Piazza, L.A. Dodgers, 1996	36	105	.336
Mike Piazza, L.A. Dodgers, 1997	40	124	.362
Mike Piazza, L.A. Dodgers–Flor. Marlins, 1990	32	111	.328
Mike Piazza, N.Y. Mets, 1999	40	124	.303
Mike Piazza, N.Y. Mets, 2000	38	113	.324
Javy Lopez, Atl. Braves, 2003	43	109	.328

*54 at catcher, 43 at other positions
**114 at catcher, 36 at other positions

Players with 40 or More Home Runs and Fewer Than 100 RBIs, Season

American League

	Home Runs	RBIs
Mickey Mantle, N.Y. Yankees, 1958	42	97
Mickey Mantle, N.Y. Yankees, 1960	40	94
Harmon Killebrew, Minn. Twins, 1963	45	96
Rico Petrocelli, Bost. Red Sox, 1969	40	97
Darrell Evans, Det. Tigers, 1985	40	94
Ken Griffey Jr., Sea. Mariners, 1994	40	90

National League (Post-1900)

	Home Runs	RBIs
Duke Snider, Bklyn. Dodgers, 1957	40	92
Hank Aaron, Atl. Braves, 1969	44	97
Hank Aaron, Atl. Braves, 1973	40	96
Davey Johnson, Atl. Braves, 1973	43	99
Matt Williams, S.F. Giants, 1994	43	96
Barry Bonds, S.F. Giants, 2003	45	90
Adam Dunn, Cin. Reds, 2006	40	92
Alfonso Soriano, Wash. Nationals, 2006	46	95
Adrian Gonzalez, S.D. Padres, 2009	40	99

Players with More Than 100 RBIs and Fewest Home Runs, Season

American League

	RBIs	Home Runs
Lave Cross, Phila. A's, 1902	108	0

Larry Gardner, Cleve. Indians, 1920 ....118 3
Larry Gardner, Cleve. Indians, 1921 ....115 3
Joe Sewell, Cleve. Indians, 1923............................109 3
Joe Sheely, Chi. White Sox, 1924 ....103 3
Billy Rogell, Det. Tigers, 1934.............................100 3

National League (Post-1900)

	RBIs	Home Runs
Ross Youngs, N.Y. Giants, 1921	102	3
Pie Traynor, Pitt. Pirates, 1928	124	3
Pie Traynor, Pitt. Pirates, 1931	103	2

Players with Most Career RBIs, Never Leading League

Willie Mays (1951–52, 1954–73)	1903	Tony Perez (1964–86)	1652
Rafael Palmeiro (1986–2005)	1775	Harold Baines (1980–2000)	1628
Frank Thomas (1990–2008)	1704	George Brett (1973–93)	1595
Cal Ripken Jr. (1981–2001)	1695	Al Kaline (1953–74)	1583
Gary Sheffield (1988–2004)	1676	Jake Beckley (1888–1907)	1575
Jim Thome (1991–)	1674	Chipper Jones (1993, 1995–)	1161

Players with 1000 Career RBIs, Never Driving in 100 in One Season

Pete Rose (1963–86)	1314	Jose Cruz (1970–88)	1077
Craig Biggio (1988–2007)	1175	Jimmy Dykes (1918–39)	1071
Mark Grace (1988–2003)	1146	Willie Davis (1960–79)	1053
Tommy Corcoran (1890–1907)	1135	Ron Fairly (1958–78)	1044
Johnny Damon (1995–)	1120	Bobby Murcer (1965–83)	1043
Rickey Henderson (1979–2003)	1115	Joe Judge (1915–34)	1037
Julio Franco (1982–94, 1996–97, 1999, 2001–07)	1110	Dusty Baker (1968–86)	1013
Charlie Grimm (1916, 1918–36)	1078	Amos Otis (1967–84)	1007

Batters Driving in 100 Runs with Three Different Teams

Richie Allen	Phila. Phillies (NL)	1966	110
	St. L. Cardinals (NL)	1970	101
	Chi. White Sox (AL)	1972	113
Adrian Beltre	L.A. Dodgers (NL)	2004	121
	Bost. Red. Sox (AL)	2010	102
	Tex. Rangers (AL)	2011	105
Orlando Cepeda	S.F. Giants (NL)	1959	105
		1961	142
		1962	114
	St. L. Cardinals (NL)	1967	111
	Atl. Braves (NL)	1970	111
Rocky Colavito	Cleve. Indians (AL)	1958	113
		1959	111
		1965	108
	Det. Tigers (AL)	1961	140
		1962	112
	K.C. Royals (AL)	1964	102
Vladimir Guerrero	Mont. Expos (NL)	1998	109
		1999	131
		2000	123
		2001	108
	L.A. Angels (AL)	2009	126

continued on next page

		2005	108
		2006	116
		2007	125
	Tex. Rangers (AL)	2010	115
Lee May	Cin. Reds (NL)	1969	110
	Houston Astros (NL)	1973	105
	Balt. Orioles (AL)	1976	109
Alex Rodriguez	Sea. Mariners (AL)	1996	123
		1998	124
		1999	111
		2000	132
	Tex. Rangers (AL)	2001	135
		2002	142
		2003	118
	N.Y. Yankees (AL)	2004	106
		2004	106
		2005	130
		2006	121
		2007	156
		2008	103
		2009	100
Gary Sheffield	S.D. Padres (NL)	1992	100
	Flor. Marlins (NL)	1996	120
	L.A. Dodgers (NL)	1999	116
		2000	100
		2001	101
	Atl. Braves (NL)	2003	132
	N.Y. Yankees (AL)	2004	121
		2005	123
Dave Winfield	S.D. Padres (NL)	1979	118
	N.Y. Yankees (AL)	1982	106
		1983	116
		1984	100
		1985	114
		1985	104
		1988	107
	Tor. Blue Jays (AL)	1992	108

Players Driving in 130 Teammates During Season

American League

	Teammates	Home Runs	RBIs
Hank Greenberg, Det. Tigers, 1937	143	40	183
Lou Gehrig, N.Y. Yankees, 1935	138	46	184
Ty Cobb, Det. Tigers, 1911	136	8	144
Lou Gehrig, N.Y. Yankees, 1930	133	41	174
Hank Greenberg, Det. Tigers, 1935	134	36	170

National League (Post-1900)

	Teammates	Home Runs	RBIs
Hack Wilson, Chi. Cubs, 1930	135	56	191
Chuck Klein, Phila. Phillies, 1930	130	40	170

Players Driving in 100 Runs, Season, in Each League

Bob Abreu	American League	N.Y. Yankees, 2007	101
		2008	100
		L.A. Angels, 2009	103
	National League	Phila. Phillies, 2001	110
		2003	101
		2004	105
		2005	102
Dick Allen	National League	Phila. Phillies, 1966	110
		St. L. Cardinals, 1970	101
	American League	Chi. White Sox, 1972	113
Carlos Beltran	American League	K.C. Royals, 1999	108
		2001	101
		2002	105
		2003	100
	National League	N.Y. Mets, 2006	116
		2007	112
		2008	112
Jason Bay	American League	Bost. Red Sox, 2009	119
	National League	Pitts. Pirates, 2005	101
		2006	104
Bobby Bonds	National League	S.F. Giants, 1971	102
	American League	Cal. Angels, 1977	115
Bill Buckner	National League	Chi. Cubs, 1982	105
	American League	Bost. Red Sox, 1985	110
		Bost. Red Sox, 1986	102
Jeff Burroughs	American League	Tex. Rangers, 1974	118
	National League	Atl. Braves, 1977	114
Miguel Cabrera	American League	Det. Tigers, 2008	127
		Det. Tigers, 2009	103
		Det. Tigers, 2010	126
		Det. Tigers, 2011	105
	National League	Fla. Marlins, 2004	112
		Fla. Marlins, 2005	116
		Fla. Marlins, 2006	114
		Fla. Marlins, 2007	119
Sam Crawford	National League	Cin. Reds, 1901	104
	American League	Det. Tigers, 1910	120
		Det. Tigers, 1911	115
		Det. Tigers, 1912	109
		Det. Tigers, 1914	104
		Det. Tigers, 1915	112
Adrian Gonzalez	American League	Bost. Red Sox, 2011	117
	National League	S.D. Padres, 2007	100
		S.D. Padres, 2008	119
		S.D. Padres, 2010	101
Ken Griffey Jr.	American League	Sea. Mariners, 1991	100
		Sea. Mariners, 1992	103
		Sea. Mariners, 1993	109
		Sea. Mariners, 1996	140
		Sea. Mariners, 1997	147
		Sea. Mariners, 1998	146
		Sea. Mariners, 1999	134
	National League	Cin. Reds, 2000	118

Vladimir Guerrero	American League	L.A. Angels, 2004	126
		L.A. Angels, 2005	108
		L.A. Angels, 2006	116
		L.A. Angels, 2007	125
		Texas Rangers, 2010	115
	National League	Mont. Expos, 1998	104
		Mont. Expos, 1999	131
		Mont. Expos, 2000	123
		Mont. Expos, 2001	108
		Mont. Expos, 2002	111
Frank Howard	National League	L.A. Dodgers, 1962	119
	American League	Wash. Senators II, 1968	106
		Wash. Senators II, 1969	111
		Wash. Senators II, 1970	126
Nap Lajoie	National League	Phila. Phillies, 1897	127
		Phila. Phillies, 1898	127
	American League	Phila. A's, 1901	125
		Cleve. Blues, 1904	102
Carlos Lee	American League	Chi. White Sox, 2003	113
	National League	Milw. Brewers, 2005	114
		Hous. Astros, 2007	119
		2008	100
		2009	102
Mike Lowell	American League	Bost. Red Sox, 2007	120
	National League	Fld. Marlins, 2001	100
		2003	105
Lee May	National League	Cin. Reds, 1969	110
		Hous. Astros, 1973	105
	American League	Balt. Orioles, 1976	109
Fred McGriff	National League	S.D. Padres, 1991	106
		S.D. Padres–Atl. Braves, 1993	101
		Chi. Cubs, 2002	103
	American League	T.B. Devil Rays, 1999	104
		T.B. Devil Rays, 2000	106
Mark McGwire	American League	Oak. A's, 1987	118
		Oak. A's, 1990	108
		Oak. A's, 1992	104
		Oak. A's, 1995	113
	National League	St. L. Cardinals, 1998	147
		St. L. Cardinals, 1999	147
Tony Perez	National League	Cin. Reds, 1967	102
		Cin. Reds, 1969	122
		Cin. Reds, 1970	129
		Cin. Reds, 1973	101
		Cin. Reds, 1974	101
		Cin. Reds, 1975	109
	American League	Bost. Red Sox, 1980	105
Frank Robinson	National League	Cin. Reds, 1959	125
		Cin. Reds, 1961	124
		Cin. Reds, 1962	136
		Cin. Reds, 1965	113
	American League	Balt. Orioles, 1966	122
		Balt. Orioles, 1969	100

continued on next page

Gary Sheffield	National League	S.D. Padres, 1992	100
		Flor. Marlins, 1996	120
		L.A. Dodgers, 1999	101
		L.A. Dodgers, 2000	109
		L.A. Dodgers, 2001	100
		Atl. Braves, 2003	132
	American League	N.Y. Yankees, 2004	121
		N.Y. Yankees, 2005	123
Richie Sexson	American League	Cle. Indians, 1999	116
		Sea. Mariners, 2005	121
		Sea. Mariners, 2006	107
	National League	N.Y. Yankees, 2001	125
		N.Y. Yankees, 2002	102
		Milw. Brewer, 2003	124
Ken Singleton	National League	Mont. Expos, 1973	103
	American League	Balt. Orioles, 1979	111
		Balt. Orioles, 1980	104
Rusty Staub	National League	N.Y. Mets, 1975	105
	American League	Det. Tigers, 1977	101
		Det. Tigers, 1978	121
Dick Stuart	National League	Pitt. Pirates, 1961	117
	American League	Bost. Red Sox, 1963	118
		Bost. Red Sox, 1964	114
Jim Thome	American League	Cleve. Indians, 1996	116
		Cleve. Indians, 1997	102
		Cleve. Indians, 1999	108
		Cleve. Indians, 2000	106
		Cleve. Indians, 2001	124
		Cleve. Indians, 2002	118
		Chi. White Sox, 2006	109
	National League	Phila. Phillies, 2003	131
		Phila. Phillies, 2004	105
Richie Zisk	National League	Pitt. Pirates, 1974	100
	American League	Chi. White Sox, 1977	101

Players with More RBIs Than Games Played, Season (Min. 100 Games)

American League

	RBIs	Games	Differential
Lou Gehrig, N.Y. Yankees, 1931	184	155	+29
Hank Greenberg, Det. Tigers, 1937	183	154	+29
Al Simmons, Phila. A's, 1930	165	138	+27
Jimmie Foxx, Bost. Red Sox, 1938	175	149	+26
Lou Gehrig, N.Y. Yankees, 1927	175	155	+20
Lou Gehrig, N.Y. Yankees, 1930	174	154	+20
Babe Ruth, N.Y. Yankees, 1921	171	152	+19
Babe Ruth, N.Y. Yankees, 1929	154	135	+19
Babe Ruth, N.Y. Yankees, 1931	163	145	+18
Hank Greenberg, Det. Tigers, 1935	170	152	+18
Manny Ramirez, Cleve. Indians, 1999	165	147	+18
Joe DiMaggio, N.Y. Yankees, 1937	167	151	+16
Jimmie Foxx, Phila. A's, 1932	169	154	+15

Al Simmons, Phila. A's, 1929	157	143	+14
Jimmie Foxx, Phila. A's, 1933	163	149	+14
Babe Ruth, N.Y. Yankees, 1927	164	151	+13
Lou Gehrig, N.Y. Yankees, 1934	165	154	+11
Hal Trosky, Cleve. Indians, 1936	162	151	+11
Juan Gonzalez, Tex. Rangers, 1996	144	134	+10
Babe Ruth, N.Y. Yankees, 1930	153	145	+8
Walt Dropo, Bost. Red Sox, 1950	144	136	+8
Joe DiMaggio, N.Y. Yankees, 1939	126	120	+6
Babe Ruth, N.Y. Yankees, 1932	137	133	+4
Vern Stephens, Bost. Red Sox, 1949	159	155	+4
Ted Williams, Bost. Red Sox, 1949	159	155	+4
Kirby Puckett, Minn. Twins, 1994	112	108	+4
Manny Ramirez, Cleve. Indians, 2000	122	118	+4
Ken Williams, St. L. Browns, 1925	105	102	+3
Jimmie Foxx, Phila. A's, 1930	156	153	+3
Juan Gonzalez, Tex. Rangers, 1998	157	154	+3
Ken Williams, St. L. Browns, 1922	155	153	+2
Al Simmons, Phila. A's, 1927	108	106	+2
Lou Gehrig, N.Y. Yankees, 1937	159	157	+2
Hank Greenberg, Det. Tigers, 1940	160	148	+2
Joe DiMaggio, N.Y. Yankees, 1948	155	153	+2
Joe DiMaggio, N.Y. Yankees, 1940	133	132	+1
George Brett, K.C. Royals, 1980	118	117	+1

National League (Post-1900)

	RBIs	Games	Differential
Hack Wilson, Chi. Cubs, 1930	190	155	+35
Chuck Klein, Phila. Phillies, 1930	170	156	+14
Hack Wilson, Chi. Cubs, 1929	159	150	+9
Jeff Bagwell, Hous. Astros, 1994	116	110	+6
Rogers Hornsby, St. L. Cardinals, 1925	143	138	+5
Met Ott, N.Y. Giants, 1929	151	150	+1

Players Driving in 20 Percent of Their Team's Runs, Season

Nate Colbert, S.D. Padres (NL), 1972	111 of 488	22.75%
Wally Berger, Bost. Braves (NL), 1935	130 of 575	22.61%
Ernie Banks, Chi. Cubs (NL), 1959	143 of 673	21.25%
Sammy Sosa, Chi. Cubs (NL), 2001	160 of 777	20.59%
Jim Gentile, Balt. Orioles (AL), 1961	141 of 691	20.40%
Bill Buckner, Chi. Cubs (NL), 1981	75 of 370	20.27%
Bill Nicholson, Chi. Cubs (NL), 1943	128 of 632	20.25%
Frank Howard, Wash. Senators II (AL), 1968	106 of 524	20.23%
Babe Ruth, Bost. Red Sox (AL), 1919	114 of 565	20.18%
Frank Howard, Wash. Senators II (AL), 1970	126 of 626	20.13%

Players with Lowest Batting Average for 100-RBI Season

	RBIs	Batting Average
Tony Armas, Bost. Red Sox (AL), 1983	107	.218
Carlos Peña, T.B. Rays (AL), 2009	100	.227
Roy Sievers, Wash. Senators (AL), 1954	102	.232
Joe Carter, S.D. Padres (NL), 1990	115	.232
Ruben Sierra, Oak. Athletics (AL), 1993	101	.233
Joe Carter, Tor. Blue Jays (AL), 1997	102	.234

continued on next page

	RBIs	Batting Average
Mark McGuire, Oak. Athletics (AL), 1990	108	.235
Adam Dunn, Cin. Reds (NL), Ariz. Diamondbacks (NL), 2008	100	.236
Jose Canseco, Tor. Blue Jays (AL), 1998	107	.237
Jeff King, K.C. Royals (AL), 1997	112	.238
Carlton Fisk, Chi. White Sox (AL), 1985	107	.238
Gorman Thomas, Milw. Brewers (AL), 1980	105	.239
Phil. Plantier, S.D. Padres (NL), 1993	100	.240
Jose Canseco, Oak. A's (AL), 1986	117	.240
Tony Batista. Mont. Expos (NL), 2004	110	.241
Ron Cey, L.A. Dodgers (NL), 1977	110	.241
Harmon Killebrew, Minn. Twins (AL), 1959	105	.242

Players on Last-Place Teams Leading League in RBIs, Season

	RBIs		RBIs
Wally Berger, Bost. Braves (NL), 1935	130	Andre Dawson, Chi. Cubs (NL), 1987	137
Roy Sievers, Wash. Senators (AL), 1957	114	Alex Rodriguez, Tex. Rangers (AL), 2002	142
Frank Howard, Wash. Senators II (AL), 1970	126		

Players Driving in 95 or More Runs in Season Three Times, Never 100

Donn Clendenon (1961–72)	1965	96
	1966	98
	1970	97
Kevin McReynolds (1983–94)	1986	96
	1987	95
	1988	99
Arky Vaughan (1932–43, 1947–48)	1933	97
	1935	99
	1940	95

Runs Scored

Evolution of Runs Scored Record

American League

1901	Nap Lajoie, Phila. A's	145	1920	Babe Ruth, N.Y. Yankees	158
1911	Ty Cobb, Det. Tigers	147	1921	Babe Ruth, N.Y. Yankees	177

National League (Pre-1900)

1876	Ross Barnes, Chi. White Stockings	126	1894	Billy Hamilton, Phila. Phillies	198
1886	King Kelly, Chi. White Stockings	155			

National League (Post-1899)

1900	Roy Thomas, Phila. Phillies	132	1929	Rogers Hornsby, Chi. Cubs	156
1901	Jesse Burkett, St. L. Cardinals	142	1930	Chuck Klein, Phila. Phillies	158
1925	Kiki Cuyler, Pitt. Pirates	144			

Most Runs Scored by Decade

Pre-1900		1900–09		1910–19	
1722	Cap Anson	1014	Honus Wagner	1051	Ty Cobb
1684	Bid McPhee	885	Fred Clarke	991	Eddie Collins
1620	Roger Connor	862	Roy Thomas	967	Tris Speaker
1523	Dan Brouthers	835	Ginger Beaumont	958	Donie Bush

1523	Tom Brown	828	Tommy Leach	868	Harry Hooper
1523	Billy Hamilton	813	Sam Crawford	765	Joe Jackson
1492	Harry Stovey	807	Jimmy Sheckard	758	Clyde Milan
1480	Arlie Latham	806	Nap Lajoie	745	Larry Doyle
1470	Hugh Duffy	799	Fielder Jones	733	Home Run Baker
1445	Orator Jim O'Rourke	797	Willie Keeler	727	Max Carey
				727	Jake Daubert

1920–29		**1930–39**		**1940–49**	
1365	Babe Ruth	1257	Lou Gehrig	951	Ted Williams
1195	Rogers Hornsby	1244	Jimmie Foxx	815	Stan Musial
1001	Sam Rice	1179	Charlie Gehringer	803	Bob Elliott
992	Frankie Frisch	1102	Earl Averill	764	Bobby Doerr
962	Harry Heilmann	1095	Mel Ott	758	Lou Boudreau
896	Lu Blue	1009	Ben Chapman	743	Bill Nicholson
894	George Sisler	973	Paul Waner	721	Dom DiMaggio
868	Charlie Jamieson	955	Chuck Klein	708	Vern Stephens
830	Ty Cobb	930	Al Simmons	704	Dixie Walker
830	Tris Speaker	885	Joe Cronin	684	Joe DiMaggio

1950–59		**1960–69**		**1970–79**	
994	Mickey Mantle	1091	Hank Aaron	1068	Pete Rose
970	Duke Snider	1050	Willie Mays	1020	Bobby Bonds
952	Richie Ashburn	1013	Frank Robinson	1005	Joe Morgan
948	Stan Musial	916	Roberto Clemente	861	Amos Otis
902	Nellie Fox	885	Vada Pinson	845	Carl Yastrzemski
898	Minnie Minoso	874	Maury Wills	843	Lou Brock
898	Eddie Yost	864	Harmon Killebrew	837	Rod Carew
890	Gil Hodges	861	Billy Williams	833	Reggie Jackson
860	Alvin Dark	816	Ron Santo	816	Bobby Murcer
848	Yogi Berra	811	Al Kaline	792	Johnny Bench

1980–89		**1990–99**		**2000–09**	
1122	Keith Hernandez	1091	Barry Bonds	1331	Alex Rodriguez
957	Robin Yount	1042	Craig Biggio	1291	Albert Pujols
956	Dwight Evans	1002	Ken Griffey Jr.	1283	Derek Jeter
938	Dale Murphy	968	Frank Thomas	1275	Johnny Damon
866	Tim Raines	965	Rafael Palmeiro	1203	Bobby Abreu
858	Eddie Murray	951	Roberto Alomar	1127	Ichiro Suzuki
845	Willie Wilson	950	Chuck Knoblauch	1124	Todd Helton
832	Mike Schmidt	946	Tony Phillips	1097	Lance Berkman
828	Paul Molitor	932	Rickey Henderson	1080	Jimmy Rollins
823	Wade Boggs	921	Jeff Bagwell	1072	Vladimir Guerrero

Players with More Runs Scored Than Games Played, Season (Min. 100 Games)

American League

	Runs	Games	Differential
Babe Ruth, N.Y. Yankees, 1921	177	152	+25
Babe Ruth, N.Y. Yankees, 1920	158	142	+16
Nap Lajoie, Phila. A's, 1901	145	131	+14
Al Simmons, Phila. A's, 1930	152	138	+14
Lou Gehrig, N.Y. Yankees, 1936	167	155	+12
Babe Ruth, N.Y. Yankees, 1928	163	154	+9

Lou Gehrig, N.Y. Yankees, 1932 ....163 ....155...+8
Babe Ruth, N.Y. Yankees, 1927 ....158 ....151...+7
Jimmie Foxx, Bos. Red Sox, 1939 ....130 ....124...+6
Babe Ruth, N.Y. Yankees, 1930 ....150 ....145...+5
Babe Ruth, N.Y. Yankees, 1931 ....149 ....145...+4
Rickey Henderson, N.Y. Yankees, 1985.............146 ....143...+3
Ty Cobb, Det. Tigers, 1911 ....147 ....146...+1

National League (Post-1900)

	Runs	Games	Differential
Chuck Klein, Phila. Phillies, 1930	158	156	+2

Players Scoring 1000 Runs in Career, Never 100 in One Season

	Career Runs	Most in One Season
Luis Aparicio (1956–73)	1335	98 (1959)
Harold Baines (1980–2001)	1299	89 (1982)
Chili Davis (1981–99)	1240	87 (1984)
Willie Randolph (1975–92)	1239	99 (1980)
Brooks Robinson (1955–77)	1232	91 (1966)
Graig Nettles (1967–88)	1193	99 (1977)
Rusty Staub (1963–85)	1189	98 (1970)
Al Oliver (1968–85)	1189	96 (1974)
Bert Campaneris (1964–81, 1983)	1181	97 (1970)
Buddy Bell (1972–89)	1151	89 (1979, 1988)
Steve Garvey (1969–87)	1143	95 (1974)
Deacon White (1871–90)	1140	82 (1884)
Gary Gaetti (1981–2000)	1130	95 (1987)
Jack Clark (1975–92)	1118	93 (1987)
Jimmy Dykes (1918–39)	1108	93 (1925)
Edd Roush (1913–29, 1931)	1099	95 (1926)
Paul Hines (1872–91)	1083	94 (1884)
Bill Buckner (1969–90)	1077	93 (1982)
Ted Simmons (1968–88)	1074	84 (1980)
Bob Elliott (1939–53)	1064	99 (1948)
Bobby Wallace (1894–1918)	1057	99 (1897)
Tony Fernandez (1983–2000)	1057	91 (1986)
Paul O'Neill (1985–2001)	1041	95 (1998)
Jose Cruz (1970–88)	1036	96 (1984)
Bobby Grich (1970–86)	1033	93 (1976)
Gary Carter (1974–92)	1025	91 (1982)
Kid Gleason (1888–1908, 1912)	1020	95 (1905)
Harry Davis (1895–1917)	1001	94 (1906)

Most Runs Scored by Position, Season

American League

First Base ....167 ....Lou Gehrig, N.Y. Yankees, 1936
Second Base ..145 ....Nap Lajoie, Phila. A's, 1901
Third Base .....141 ....Harlond Clift, St. L. Browns, 1936
Shortstop ....141 ......Alex Rodriguez, Sea. Mariners, 1996
Outfield ....177 ....Babe Ruth, N.Y. Yankees, 1921
Catcher ....118 ....Mickey Cochrane, Phila. A's, 1932

National League

First Base ....152 ....Jeff Bagwell, Hous. Astros, 2000
Second Base ...156 ....Rogers Hornsby, Chi. Cubs, 1929
Third Base ......130 ....Pete Rose, Cin. Reds, 1976
Shortstop ....139 ....Jimmy Rollins, Phila. Phillies, 2008
Outfield ....158 ....Chuck Klein, Phila. Phillies, 1930
Catcher ....112 ....Jason Kendall, Pitt. Pirates, 2000

Pitcher ....31 ....Jack Coombs, Phila. A's, 1911   **Pitcher** ....25 ....Claude Hendrix, Pitt Pirates, 1912
Designated
Hitter ....133 ....Paul Molitor, Milw. Brewers, 1991

Walks

Evolution of Batters' Walks Record

American League

1901	Dummy Hoy, Chi. White Sox	86
1902	Topsy Hartsel, Phila. A's	87
1905	Topsy Hartsel, Phila. A's	121
1920	Babe Ruth, N.Y. Yankees	150
1923	Babe Ruth, N.Y. Yankees	170

National League (Pre-1900)

1876	Ross Barnes, Chi. Cubs	20
1879	Charley Jones, Bost. Beaneaters	29
1881	John Clapp, Cleve. Spiders	35
1883	Tom York, Cleve. Spiders	37
1884	George Gore, Chi. Cubs	61
1885	Ned Williamson, Chi. Cubs	75
1886	George Gore, Chi. Cubs	102
1890	Cap Anson, Chi. Cubs	113
1892	John Crooks, St. L. Cardinals	136

National League (Post-1900)

1900	Roy Thomas, Phila. Phillies	115
1910	Miller Huggins, St. L. Cardinals	116
1911	Jimmy Sheckard, Chi. Cubs	147
1945	Eddie Stanky, Bklyn. Dodgers	148
1996	Barry Bonds, S.F. Giants	151
1998	Mark McGwire, St. L. Cardinals	162
2001	Barry Bonds, S.F. Giants	177
2002	Barry Bonds, S.F. Giants	198
2004	Barry Bonds, S.F. Giants	232

Players with 1000 Walks, 2000 Hits, and 300 Home Runs, Career

	Walks	Hits	Home Runs
Barry Bonds (1986–2007)	2558	2935	762
Babe Ruth (1914–35)	2062	2873	714
Ted Williams (1939–42, 1946–60)	2021	2654	521
Carl Yastrzemski (1961–83)	1845	3419	452
Mickey Mantle (1951–68)	1733	2415	536
Jim Thome* (1991–)	1725	2181	604
Mel Ott (1926–47)	1708	2876	511
Frank Thomas (1990–2008)	1667	2468	521
Darrell Evans (1969–89)	1605	2223	414
Stan Musial (1941–44, 1946–63)	1599	3630	475
Harmon Killebrew (1954–75)	1559	2086	573
Lou Gehrig (1923–39)	1508	2721	493
Mike Schmidt (1972–89)	1507	2234	548
Gary Sheffield (1988–2009)	1475	2689	509

Willie Mays (1951–52, 1954–73) ....1464 ....3283 660
Jimmie Foxx (1925–42, 1944–45)............................1452 ....2646 534
Eddie Mathews (1952–68)..1444 ....2315 512
Ken Griffey (1989–2010) ....1312 ....2781 630
Frank Robinson (1956–76) ....1420 ....2943 586
Hank Aaron (1954–76)..1402 ....3771 755
Jeff Bagwell (1991–2005) ....1401 ....2314 449
Dwight Evans (1972–91) ....1391 ....2446 385
Reggie Jackson (1967–87)...1375 ....2584 563
Rafael Palmeiro (1986–2005) ....1353 ....3020 569
Willie McCovey (1959–80) ....1345 ....2211 521
Eddie Murray (1977–97)...1333 ....3255 504
Manny Ramirez (1993–2011) ....1329 ....2574 555
Ken Griffey Jr. (1989–2010).....................................1312 ....2781 630
Fred McGriff (1986–2004) ....1305 ....2484 493
Edgar Martinez (1987–2004) ....1283 ....2247 309
Al Kaline (1953–74) ....1277 ....3007 399
Todd Helton* (1997–2010) ....1256 ....2363 347
Dave Winfield (1973–95)...1216 ....3110 465
Chili Davis (1981–99)..1194 ....2380 350
Alex Rodriguez* (1994–)...1166 ....2775 629
Cal Ripken Jr. (1981–2001).......................................1129 ....3164 431
Luis Gonzales (1990–2008).......................................1155 ....2591 354
Carlos Delgado (1993–2009) ....1109 ....2038 473
Ron Santo (1960–74)..1108 ....2254 342
George Brett (1973–93)...1096 ....3154 317
Graig Nettles (1967–88)..1088 ....2225 390
Harold Baines (1980–2000) ....1054 ....2855 384
Billy Williams (1959–76)...1045 ....2711 426
Rogers Hornsby (1915–37)..1038 ....2930 301
*Active player.

Players Leading League in Base Hits and Walks, Season

American League

	Hits	Walks
Carl Yastrzemski, Bost. Red Sox, 1963	183	95

National League (Post-1900)

	Hits	Walks
Rogers Hornsby, St. L. Cardinals, 1924	227	89
Richie Ashburn, Phila. Phillies, 1958	215	97

Players with 200 Base Hits and 100 Walks, Season

American League			National League (Post-1900)		
	Hits	Walks		Hits	Walks
Ty Cobb, Det. Tigers, 1915	208	118	Woody English, Chi. Cubs, 1930	214	100
Babe Ruth, N.Y. Yankees, 1921	204	145	Hack Wilson, Chi. Cubs, 1930	208	105
Babe Ruth, N.Y. Yankees, 1923	205	170	Stan Musial, St. L. Cardinals, 1949	207	107
Babe Ruth, N.Y. Yankees, 1924	200	142	Stan Musial, St. L. Cardinals, 1953	200	105
Lou Gehrig, N.Y. Yankees, 1927	218	109	Todd Helton, Colo. Rockies, 2000	216	103
Lou Gehrig, N.Y. Yankees, 1930	220	101	Todd Helton, Colo. Rockies, 2003	209	111
Lou Gehrig, N.Y. Yankees, 1931	211	117			

American League

Jimmie Foxx, Phila. A's, 1932 ....213 116
Lou Gehrig, N.Y. Yankees, 1932 ....208 138
Lou Gehrig, N.Y. Yankees, 1934 ....210 109
Lou Gehrig, N.Y. Yankees, 1936 ....205 130
Lou Gehrig, N.Y. Yankees, 1937 ....200 127
Hank Greenberg, Det. Tigers, 1937 ....200 102
Wade Boggs, Bost. Red Sox, 1986 ....207 105
Wade Boggs, Bost. Red Sox, 1987 ....200 105
Wade Boggs, Bost. Red Sox, 1988 ....214 125
Wade Boggs, Bost. Red Sox, 1989 ....205 107
John Olerud, Tor. Blue Jays, 1993 ....200 114
Bernie Williams, N.Y. Yankees, 1999 ....202 100

Players with More Walks Than Hits, Season (Min. 100 Walks)

American League

	Walks	Hits	Differential
Roy Cullenbine, Dat. Tigers, 1947	137	104	+33
Eddie Yost, Wash. Senators, 1956	151	119	+32
Max Bishop, Phila. A's, 1929	128	110	+18
Max Bishop, Phila. A's, 1930	128	111	+17
Eddie Joost, Phila. A's, 1949	149	138	+11
Max Bishop, Phila. A's, 1926	116	106	+10
Gene Tenace, Oak. A's, 1974	110	102	+8
Mickey Tettleton, Balt. Orioles, 1990	106	99	+7
Max Bishop, Phila. A's, 1932	110	104	+6
Toby Harrah, Tex. Rangers, 1985	113	107	+6
Mickey Tettleton, Tex. Ranges, 1995	107	102	+5
Jack Cust, Oak. Athletics, 2007	105	101	+4
Eddie Joost, Phila. A's, 1947	114	111	+3
Ted Williams, Bost. Red Sox, 1954	136	133	+3
Mickey Mantle, N.Y. Yankees, 1968	106	103	+3
Max Bishop, Phila. A's, 1927	105	103	+2
Mickey Mantle, N.Y. Yankees, 1962	122	121	+1

National League (Post-1900)

	Walks	Hits	Differential
Barry Bonds, S.F. Giants, 2004	232	135	+97
Barry Bonds, S.F. Giants, 2002	198	149	+49
Barry Bonds, S.F. Giants, 2005	132	94	+38
Jim Wynn, Atl. Braves, 1976	127	93	+34
Wes Westrum, N.Y. Giants, 1951	104	79	+25
Gene Tenace, S.D. Padres, 1977	125	102	+23
Jack Clark, S.D. Padres, 1984	132	110	+22
Barry Bonds, S.F. Giants, 2001	177	156	+21
Jack Clark, St. L. Cardinals, 1987	136	120	+16
Barry Bonds, S.F. Giants, 2006	115	99	+16
Jim Wynn, Hous. Astros, 1969	148	133	+15
Barry Bonds, S.F. Giants, 2003	148	133	+15
Jack Clark, S.D. Padres, 1990	104	89	+15
Rickey Henderson, S.D. Padres, 1996	125	112	+13
Gene Tenace, S.D. Padres, 1978	101	90	+11

Mark McGwire, St. L. Cardinals, 1998.............................162.............................152.............................+10
Gary Sheffield, Flo. Marlins, 1997 ....121.............................111.............................+10
Morgan Ensberg, Hou. Astros, 2006 ....101.............................91.............................+10
Jim Wynn, L.A. Dodgers, 1975.............................110.............................102.............................+8
Eddie Stanky, Bklyn. Dodgers, 1945.............................148.............................143.............................+5
Eddie Stanky, Bklyn. Dodgers, 1946.............................137.............................132.............................+5
Hank Greenberg, Pitt. Pirates, 1947.............................104.............................100.............................+4

Players Hitting 40 or More Home Runs, with More Home Runs Than Walks, Season

American League

	Home Runs	Walks	Differential
Tony Armas, Bost. Red Sox, 1984	43	32	+11
Juan Gonzalez, Tex. Rangers, 1993	46	37	+9
Juan Gonzalez, Tex. Rangers, 1997	42	33	+9
George Bell, Tor. Blue Jays, 1987	47	39	+8
Juan Gonzalez, Tex. Rangers, 1992	43	35	+8
Hal Trosky, Cleve. Indians, 1936	42	36	+6
Tony Batista, Tor. Blue Jays, 2000	41	35	+6
Juan Gonzalez, Tex. Rangers, 1996	47	45	+2

National League (Post-1900)

	Home Runs	Walks	Differential
Dante Bichette, Colo. Rockies, 1995	40	22	+18
Andre Dawson, Chi. Cubs, 1987	49	32	+17
Matt Williams, S.F. Giants, 1994	43	33	+10
Javy Lopez, Atl. Braves, 2003	43	33	+10
Orlando Cepeda, S.F. Giants, 1961	46	39	+7
Andres Galarraga, Colo. Rockies, 1996	47	40	+7
Sammy Sosa, Chi. Cubs, 1996	40	34	+6
Vinny Castilla, Colo. Rockies, 1998	46	40	+6
Vinny Castilla, Colo. Rockies, 1996	40	35	+5
Dave Kingman, Chi. Cubs, 1979	48	45	+3

Players with 90 Walks in Each of First Two Seasons

Jack Crooks, Columbus Solons (AA) ....1890 (96) and 1891 (103)
Alvin Davis, Sea. Mariners (AL) ....1984 (97) and 1985 (90)
Ferris Fain, Phila. A's (AL) ....1947 (95) and 1948 (113)
Roy Thomas, Phila. Phillies (NL).............................1899 (115) and 1900 (115)
Ted Williams, Bost. Red Sox (AL) ....1939 (107) and 1940 (96)

Strikeouts

Players with 100 More Career Strikeouts Than Hits (Min. 375 strikeouts)

	Strikeouts	Hits	Differential
Rob Deer (1984–1996)	1409	853	+556
Adam Dunn* (2001–)	1809	1312	+497
Russell Branyan* (1998–)	1118	682	+436
Mark Reynolds* (2007–)	963	598	+365
Carlos Pena* (2001–)	1292	982	+310
Jack Cust* (2001–)	819	510	+309
Gorman Thomas (1973–86)	1339	1051	+288
Dave Nicholson (1960–1967)	573	301	+272

Bo Jackson (1986–1994) ....841 ....598 ....+243
Dave Kingman (1971–86)..........................1816...........................1575........................+241
Mark Bellhorn (1997–2007)........................723 ....484..........................+239
Pete Incaviglia (1986–98) ....1277...........................1043........................+234
Jose Hernandez (1991–2006) ....1391...........................1166........................+225
Mike Cameron* (1995–) ....1901...........................1700........................+201
Jim Thome* (1991–) ....2487...........................2287........................+200
Kelly Shoppach* (2005–) ....489 ....289..........................+200
Melvin Nieves (1992–98)...........................483 ....284..........................+199
Ron Karkovice (1986–1997)........................749 ....574..........................+175
Mickey Tettleton (1984–97) ....1307...........................1132........................+175
Mark Reynolds* (2007–) ....556 ....381..........................+175
Pat Burrell* (2000–)..................................1564...........................1393........................+171
Ruben Rivera (1995–2003) ....510 ....343..........................+167
Ryan Howard* (2004–)..............................1207...........................1043........................+164
Brad Wilkerson (2001–08) ....947 ....788..........................+159
Jonny Gomes* (2003–) ....726 ....573..........................+153
Greg Maddux (1986–2008) ....419 ....272..........................+147
Steve Balboni (1981–93)............................856 ....714..........................+142
Bob Gibson (1959–75) ....415 ....274..........................+141
Tom Egan (1965–1975) ....336 ....196..........................+140
Shane Andrews (1995–2002).......................515 ....375..........................+140
Bill Hall* (2002–)......................................964 ....825..........................+139
Ray Oyler (1965–1970)..............................359 ....221..........................+138
Don Lock (1962–69)..................................776 ....642..........................+134
Wily Mo Pena (2002–)* ....559 ....425..........................+134
Jay Buhner (1987–2001) ....1406...........................1273........................+133
Juson LaRue* (1999–)................................760 ....628..........................+132
Miguel Olivo* (2002–)................................940 ....815..........................+125
Warren Spahn (1947–65) ....487 ....363..........................+124
Craig Wilson (2001–07)..............................643 ....527..........................+116
Ryan Langerhans* (2002–)..........................385 ....280..........................+105
Todd Hundley (1990–2003).........................988 ....883..........................+105
Gary Pettis (1982–92)................................958 ....855..........................+103
Dean Palmer (1989–2003)..........................1332...........................1229........................+103
Brandon Inge* (2001–)..............................1183...........................1081........................+102
Ian Stewart* (2007–) ....396 ....293..........................+103
*Still active.

Players with 500 At Bats and Fewer Than 10 Strikeouts, Season

American League (Post-1913)*

	At Bats	Strikeouts
Stuffy McInnis, Bost. Red Sox, 1921	584	9
Stuffy McInnis, Cleve. Indians, 1922	537	5
Eddie Collins, Chi. White Sox, 1923	505	8
Joe Sewell, Cleve. Indians, 1925	608	4
Joe Sewell, Cleve. Indians, 1926	578	7
Homer Summa, Cleve. Indians, 1926	581	9
Joe Sewell, Cleve. Indians, 1927	569	7
Tris Speaker, Wash. Senators, 1927	523	8
Joe Sewell, Cleve. Indians, 1928	588	9
Mickey Cochrane, Phila. A's, 1929	514	8

Sam Rice, Wash. Senators, 1929	616	9
Joe Sewell, Cleve. Indians, 1929	578	4
Joe Sewell, N.Y. Yankees, 1932	503	3
Joe Sewell, N.Y. Yankees, 1933	524	4
Lou Boudreau, Cleve. Indians, 1948	560	9
Dale Mitchell, Cleve. Indians, 1952	511	9

National League (Post-1910)*

	At Bats	Strikeouts
Charlie Hollocher, Chi. Cubs, 1922	592	5
Stuffy McInnis, Bost. Braves, 1924	581	6
Pie Traynor, Pitt. Pirates, 1929	540	7
Freddy Leach, N.Y. Giants, 1931	515	9
Lloyd Waner, Pitt. Pirates, 1933	500	8
Tommy Holmes, Bost. Braves, 1945	636	9
Emil Verban, Phila. Phillies, 1947	540	8

*Official strikeouts first recorded by American League in 1913 and National League in 1910.

Players with 200 Hits and 100 Strikeouts, Season

American League

	Hits	Strikeouts
Hank Greenberg, Det. Tigers, 1937	200	101
Ron LeFlore, Det. Tigers, 1977	212	121
Jim Rice, Bost. Red Sox, 1977	206	120
Jim Rice, Bost. Red Sox, 1978	213	126
Alex Rodriguez, Sea. Mariners, 1996	215	104
Mo Vaughn, Bost. Red Sox, 1996	207	154
Derek Jeter, N.Y. Yankees, 1998	203	119
Alex Rodriguez, Sea. Mariners, 1998	213	121
Mo Vaughn, Bost. Red Sox, 1998	205	144
Derek Jeter, N.Y. Yankees, 1999	219	116
Alex Rodriguez, Tex. Rangers, 2001	201	131
Bret Boone, Sea. Mariners, 2001	206	110
Alfonso Soriano, N.Y. Yankees, 2002	209	157
Michael Young, Tex. Rangers, 2003	204	103
Derek Jeter, N.Y. Yankees, 2005	202	117
Derek Jeter, N.Y. Yankees, 2006	214	102
Derek Jeter, N.Y. Yankees, 2007	206	100
Michael Young, Tex. Rangers, 2007	201	107
Adrian Gonzalez, Bost. Red Sox, 2011	213	119

National League (Post-1900)

	Hits	Strikeouts
Bill White, St. L. Cardinals, 1963	200	100
Dick Allen, Phila. Phillies, 1964	201	138
Lou Brock, Chi. Cubs–St. L. Cardinals, 1964	200	127
Roberto Clemente, Pitt. Pirates, 1966	202	109
Lou Brock, St. L. Cardinals, 1967	206	109
Roberto Clemente, Pitt. Pirates, 1967	209	103
Bobby Bonds, S.F. Giants, 1970	200	189
Lou Brock, St. L. Cardinals, 1971	200	107

continued on next page

National League (Post-1900)

	Hits	Strikeouts
Dave Parker, Pitt. Pirates, 1977	215	107
Ryne Sandberg, Chi. Cubs, 1984	200	101
Ellis Burks, Colo. Rockies, 1996	211	114
Craig Biggio, Hous. Astros, 1998	210	113
Chase Utley, Phila. Phillies, 2006	203	132
Matt Holliday, Colo. Rockies, 2007	216	126
Ryan Braun, Milw. Brewers, 2009	203	121

Players with 40 Home Runs and Fewer Than 50 Strikeouts, Season

American League

	Home Runs	Strikeouts
Lou Gehrig, N.Y. Yankees, 1934	49	31
Lou Gehrig, N.Y. Yankees, 1936	49	46
Joe DiMaggio, N.Y. Yankees, 1937	46	37
Ted Williams, Bost. Red Sox, 1949	43	48
Al Rosen, Cleve. Indians, 1953	43	48

National League

	Home Runs	Strikeouts
Mel Ott, N.Y. Giants, 1929	42	38
Johnny Mize, St. L. Cardinals, 1940	43	49
Johnny Mize, N.Y. Giants, 1947	51	42
Johnny Mize, N.Y. Giants, 1948	40	37
Ted Kluszewski, Cin. Reds, 1953	40	34
Ted Kluszewski, Cin. Reds, 1954	49	35
Ted Kluszewski, Cin. Reds, 1955	47	40
Hank Aaron, Atl. Braves, 1969	44	47
Barry Bonds, S.F. Giants, 2002	46	47
Barry Bonds, S.F. Giants, 2004	45	41

Players with 100 More Strikeouts Than RBIs, Season

American League

	Strikeouts	RBIs	Differential
Austin Jackson, Det. Tigers, 2011	181	45	+136
Adam Dunn, Chi. White Sox, 2011	177	42	+135
Austin Jackson, Det. Tigers, 2010	170	41	+129
Jack Cust, Oak. Athletics, 2008	197	77	+120
Jack Cust, Oak. Athletics, 2009	185	70	+115
Mark Reynolds, Balt. Orioles, 2011	196	86	+110
Rob Deer, Milw. Brewers, 1987	186	80	+106
Curtis Granderson, Det. Tigers, 2006	174	68	+106
Dave Nicholson, Chi. White Sox, 1963	175	70	+105
Ron LeFlore, Det. Tigers, 1975	139	37	+102

National League (Post-1900)

	Strikeouts	RBIs	Differential
Drew Stubbs, Cin. Reds, 2011	205	44	+161
Mark Reynolds, Ariz. Diamondbacks, 2010	211	85	+126
Mark Reynolds, Ariz. Diamondbacks, 2009	223	102	+121
Mark Reynolds, Ariz. Diamondbacks, 2008	204	97	+107
Jose Hernandez, Milw. Brewers, 2002	188	73	+115
Bobby Bonds, S.F. Giants, 1970	189	78	+111
Jose Hernandez, Milw. Brewers, 2001	185	78	+107
Adam Dunn, Cin. Reds, 2006	194	92	+102

Toughest Batters to Strike Out, Career*

	At Bats	Strikeouts
Joe Sewell (1920–33)	7132	113 (1 every 63 at bats)
Lloyd Waner (1927–45)	7772	173 (1 every 45 at bats)
Nellie Fox (1947–65)	9232	216 (1 every 43 at bats)
Tommy Holmes (1942–52)	4992	122 (1 every 41 at bats)
Tris Speaker (1913–28)	7899	220 (1 every 36 at bats)
Stuffy McInnis (1913–27)	6667	189 (1 every 35 at bats)
Frankie Frisch (1919–37)	9112	272 (1 every 34 at bats)
Andy High (1922–34)	4440	130 (1 every 34 at bats)
Sam Rice (1915–34)	9269	276 (1 every 33 at bats)
Johnny Cooney (1921–44)	3372	107 (1 every 32 at bats)

*Batter strikeouts not recorded until 1913 in American League and 1910 in National League.

Pinch Hits

Highest Batting Average for Pinch Hitter, Season (Min. 25 At Bats)

American League

.467	Smead Jolley, Chi. White Sox, 1931	14-for-30
.457	Rick Miller, Bost. Red Sox, 1983	16-for-35
.452	Elmer Valo, K.C. A's, 1955	14-for-31
.450	Gates Brown, Det. Tigers, 1968	18-for-40
.433	Ted Easterly, Cleve. Indians–Chi. White Sox, 1912	13-for-30
.433	Randy Bush, Minn. Twins, 1986	13-for-30
.429	Joe Cronin, Bost. Red Sox, 1943	18-for-42
.429	Don Dillard, Cleve. Indians, 1961	15-for-35
.419	Dick Williams, Balt. Orioles, 1962	13-for-31
.414	Jose Offerman, Minn. Twins, 2004	12-for-29
.412	Bob Hansen, Milw. Brewers, 1974	14-for-34

National League (Post-1900)

.486	Ed Kranepool, N.Y. Mets, 1974	17-for-35
.472	Seth Smith, Col. Rockies, 2009	17-for-36
.465	Frenchy Bordagaray, St. L. Cardinals, 1938	20-for-43
.455	Bill Spiers, Hous. Astros, 1997	15-for-33
.455	Jorge Piedra, Col. Rockies, 2005	15-for-33
.452	Jose Pagan, Pitt. Pirates, 1969	19-for-42
.452	Mark Johnson, Pitts. Pirates, 1996	19-for-31
.433	Milt Thompson, Atl. Braves, 1985	13-for-30
.425	Candy Maldonado, S.F. Giants, 1986	17-for-40
.419	Bob Bowman, Phila. Phillies, 1958	13-for-31
.419	Richie Ashburn, N.Y. Mets, 1962	13-for-31
.415	Merritt Ranew, Chi. Cubs, 1963	17-for-41

Extra-Base Hits

Evolution of Total Bases Record

American League

1901	Nap Lajoie, Phila. A's	350
1911	Ty Cobb, Det. Tigers	367
1920	George Sisler, St. L. Browns	399
1921	Babe Ruth, N.Y. Yankees	457

National League (Pre-1900)

1876.................................Ross Barnes, Chi. White Stockings.................................190
1879.................................Paul Hines, Providence Grays.................................197
1883.................................Dan Brouthers, Buff. Bisons.................................243
1884.................................Abner Dalrymple, Chi. Cubs.................................263
1886.................................Dan Brouthers, Det. Wolverines.................................284
1887 ....Sam Thompson, Det. Wolverines.................................308
1893.................................Ed Delahanty, Phil. Phillies.................................347
1894.................................Hugh Duffy, Bost. Beaneaters.................................374

National League (Post-1900)

1921 ....Rogers Hornsby, St. L. Cardinals.................................378
1922 ....Rogers Hornsby, St. L. Cardinals.................................450

Players with 100 Extra-Base Hits, Season

	Doubles	Triples	Home Runs	Total
Babe Ruth, N.Y. Yankees (AL), 1921	44	16	59	119
Lou Gehrig, N.Y. Yankees (AL), 1927	52	18	47	117
Chuck Klein, Phila. Phillies (NL), 1930	59	8	40	107
Barry Bonds, S.F. Giants (NL), 2001	32	2	73	107
Todd Helton, Colo. Rockies (NL), 2001	54	2	49	105
Chuck Klein, Phila. Phillies (NL), 1932	50	15	38	103
Hank Greenberg, Det. Tigers (AL), 1937	49	14	40	103
Stan Musial, St. L. Cardinals (NL), 1948	46	18	39	103
Albert Belle, Cleve. Indians (AL), 1995	52	1	50	103
Todd Helton, Colo. Rockies (NL), 2000	59	2	42	103
Sammy Sosa, Chi. Cubs (NL), 2001	34	5	64	103
Rogers Hornsby, St. L. Cardinals (NL), 1922	46	14	42	102
Lou Gehrig, N.Y. Yankees (AL), 1930	42	17	41	100
Jimmie Foxx, Phila. A's (AL), 1932	33	9	58	100
Luis Gonzalez, Ariz. D'backs (NL), 2001	36	7	57	100

Players with 400 Total Bases, Season

American League

Babe Ruth, N.Y. Yankees, 1921.................................457
Lou Gehrig, N.Y. Yankees, 1927 447
Jimmie Foxx, Phila. A's, 1932.................................438
Lou Gehrig, N.Y. Yankees, 1930 419
Joe DiMaggio, N.Y. Yankees, 1937.................................418
Babe Ruth, N.Y. Yankees, 1927.................................417
Lou Gehrig, N.Y. Yankees, 1931.................................410
Lou Gehrig, N.Y. Yankees, 1934 409
Jim Rice, Bost. Red Sox, 1978.................................406
Hal Trosky, Cleve. Indians, 1936 405
Jimmie Foxx, Phila. A's, 1933.................................403
Lou Gehrig, N.Y. Yankees, 1936 403

National League (Post-1900)

Rogers Hornsby, St. L. Cardinals, 1922.................................450
Chuck Klein, Phila. Phillies, 1930 445
Stan Musial, St. L. Cardinals, 1948 429
Sammy Sosa, Chi. Cubs, 2001.................................425
Hack Wilson, Chi. Cubs, 1930.................................423
Chuck Klein, Phila. Phillies, 1932 420
Luis Gonzalez, Ariz. Diamondbacks, 2001.................................419
Babe Herman, Bklyn. Dodgers, 1930.................................416
Sammy Sosa, Chi. Cubs, 1998.................................416
Barry Bonds, S.F. Giants, 2001.................................411
Rogers Hornsby, Chi. Cubs, 1929.................................409
Larry Walker, Colo. Rockies, 1997.................................409
Joe Medwick, St. L. Cardinals, 1937.................................406
Chuck Klein, Phila. Phillies, 1929.................................405
Todd Helton, Colo. Rockies, 2000.................................405
Todd Helton, Colo. Rockies, 2001.................................402
Hank Aaron, Milw. Braves, 1959 400

Evolution of Doubles Record

American League

1901	Nap Lajoie, Phila. A's	48
1904	Nap Lajoie, Cleve. Blues	49
1910	Nap Lajoie, Cleve. Naps	51
1912	Tris Speaker, Bost. Red Sox	53
1923	Tris Speaker, Cleve. Indians	59
1926	George H. Burns, Cleve. Indians	64
1931	Earl Webb, Bost. Red Sox	67

National League (Pre-1900)

1876	Ross Barnes, Chi. White Stockings	21
	Dick Higham, Hartford Dark Blues	21
	Paul Hines, Chi. White Stockings	21
1878	Dick Higham, Providence Grays	22
1879	Charlie Eden, Cleve. Spiders	31
1882	King Kelly, Chi. White Stockings	37
1883	Ned Williamson, Chi. White Stockings	49
1894	Hugh Duffy, Bost. Beaneaters	51
1899	Ed Delahanty, Phila. Phillies	55

National League (Post-1899)

1900	Honus Wagner, Pitt. Pirates	45
1922	Rogers Hornsby, St. L. Cardinals	46
1928	Paul Waner, Pitt. Pirates	50
1929	Johnny Frederick, Bklyn. Dodgers	52
1930	Chuck Klein, Pitt. Pirates	59
1932	Paul Waner, Pitt. Pirates	62
1936	Joe Medwick, St. L. Cardinals	64

Players Hitting 40 Home Runs and 40 Doubles, Season

American League

	Home Runs	Doubles
Babe Ruth, N.Y. Yankees, 1921	59	44
Babe Ruth, N.Y. Yankees, 1923	41	45
Lou Gehrig, N.Y. Yankees, 1927	47	52
Lou Gehrig, N.Y. Yankees, 1930	41	42
Lou Gehrig, N.Y. Yankees 1934	49	40
Hal Trosky, Cleve. Indians, 1936	42	45
Hank Greenberg, Det. Tigers, 1937	40	49
Hank Greenberg, Det. Tigers, 1940	41	50
Albert Belle, Cleve. Indians, 1995	50	52
Albert Belle, Chi. White Sox, 1998	49	48
Juan Gonzalez, Tex. Rangers, 1998	45	50
Shawn Green, Tor. Blue Jays, 1999	42	45
Frank Thomas, Chi. White Sox, 2000	43	44
Carlos Delgado, Tor. Blue Jays, 2000	41	57
Manny Ramirez, Bost. Red Sox, 2004	43	44
David Ortiz, Bost. Red Sox, 2004	41	47
David Ortiz, Bost. Red Sox, 2005	47	40
Mark Teixeira, Tex. Rangers, 2005	43	41

continued on next page

National League (Post-1900)

	Home Runs	Doubles
Rogers Hornsby, St. L. Cardinals, 1922	42	46
Chuck Klein, Phila. Phillies, 1929	43	45
Chuck Klein, Phila. Phillies, 1930	40	59
Willie Stargell, Pitt. Pirates, 1973	44	43
Ellis Burks, Colo. Rockies, 1996	40	45
Larry Walker, Colo. Rockies, 1997	49	46
Jeff Bagwell, Hous. Astros, 1997	43	40
Chipper Jones, Atl. Braves, 1999	45	41
Todd Helton, Colo. Rockies, 2000	42	59
Richard Hidalgo, Hous. Astros, 2000	44	42
Todd Helton, Colo. Rockies, 2001	49	54
Albert Pujols, St. L. Cardinals, 2003	43	51
Albert Pujols, St. L. Cardinals, 2004	46	51
Derrek Lee, Chi. Cubs, 2005	46	50
Alfonso Soriano, Was. Nationals, 2006	46	41
Albert Pujols, St. L. Cardinals, 2009	47	45

Evolution of Triples Record

American League

1901	Jimmy Williams, Balt. Orioles	21
1903	Sam Crawford, Det. Tigers	25
1912	Joe Jackson, Cleve. Indians	26

National League (Pre-1900)

1876	Ross Barnes, Chi. White Stockings	14
1882	Roger Connor, Troy Haymakers	18
1884	Buck Ewing, N.Y. Gothams	20
1887	Sam Thompson, Det. Wolverines	23
1890	Long John Reilly, Cin. Reds	26
1893	Perry Werden, St. L. Cardinals	29
1894	Heinie Reitz, Balt. Orioles	31

National League (Post-1899)

1900	Honus Wagner, Pitt. Pirates	22
1911	Larry Doyle, N.Y. Giants	25
1912	Owen Wilson, Pitt. Pirates	36

Leaders in Doubles and Triples, Season

American League

	Doubles	Triples
Ty Cobb, Det. Tigers, 1908	36	20
Ty Cobb, Det. Tigers, 1911	47	24
Ty Cobb, Det. Tigers, 1917	44	23
Bobby Veach, Det. Tigers, 1919	45	17
Charlie Gehringer, Det. Tigers, 1929	45	19
Joe Vosmik, Cleve. Indians, 1935	47	20
Zoilo Versalles, Minn. Twins, 1964	45	12
Cesar Tovar, Minn. Twins, 1970	36	13

National League (Post-1900)

	Doubles	Triples
Honus Wagner, Pitt. Pirates, 1900	45	22
Honus Wagner, Pitt. Pirates, 1908	39	19
Rogers Hornsby, St. L. Cardinals, 1921	44	18
Stan Musial, St. L. Cardinals, 1943	48	20
Stan Musial, St. L. Cardinals, 1946	50	20
Stan Musial, St. L. Cardinals, 1948	46	18
Stan Musial, St. L. Cardinals, 1949	41	13
Lou Brock, St. L. Cardinals, 1968	46	14

Leaders in Doubles and Home Runs, Season

American League

	Doubles	Home Runs
Nap Lajoie, Phila. A's, 1901	48	14
Tris Speaker, Bost. Red Sox, 1912	53	10 (Tie)
Hank Greenberg, Det. Tigers, 1940	50	41
Ted Williams, Bost. Red Sox, 1949	39	43
Albert Belle, Cleve. Indians, 1995	52	50

National League (Post-1900)

	Doubles	Home Runs
Heinie Zimmerman, Chi. Cubs, 1912	41	14
Rogers Hornsby, St. L. Cardinals, 1922	46	42
Chuck Klein, Phila. Phillies, 1933	44	28
Joe Medwick, St. L. Cardinals, 1937	56	31 (Tie)
Willie Stargell, Pitt. Pirates, 1973	43	44

Leaders in Triples and Home Runs, Season

American League

	Triples	Home Runs
Mickey Mantle, N.Y. Yankees, 1955	11 (Tie)	37
Jim Rice, Bost. Red Sox, 1978	15	46

National League (Post-1900)

	Triples	Home Runs
Tommy Leach, Pitt. Pirates, 1902	22	6
Harry Lumley, Bklyn. Dodgers, 1904	18	9
Jim Bottomley, St. L. Cardinals, 1928	20	31 (Tie)
Willie Mays, N.Y. Giants, 1955	15 (Tie)	51

Players Hitting 20 Home Runs, 20 Triples, and 20 Doubles, Season

American League

	Doubles	Triples	Home Runs
Jeff Heath, Cleve. Indians, 1941	32	20	24
George Brett, K.C. Royals, 1979	42	20	23

continued on next page

National League (Post-1900)

	Doubles	Triples	Home Runs
Curtis Granderson, Det. Tigers, 2007	38	23	23
Wildfire Schulte, Chi. Cubs, 1911	30	21	21
Jim Bottomley, St. L. Cardinals, 1928	42	20	31
Willie Mays, N.Y. Giants, 1957	26	20	35
Jimmy Rollins, Phila. Phillies, 2007	38	20	30

Players Leading League in Doubles, Triples, and Home Runs During Career (Post-1900)

Jim Bottomley	Doubles: 1925 (44) and 1926 (40)
	Triples: 1928 (20)
	Home Runs: 1928 (31)
Ty Cobb	Doubles: 1908 (36), 1911 (47), and 1917 (44)
	Triples: 1908 (20), 1911 (24), 1917 (24), and 1918 (14)
	Home Runs: 1909 (9)
Sam Crawford	Doubles: 1909 (35)
	Triples: 1902 (23), 1903 (25), 1910 (19), 1913 (23), 1914 (26), and 1915 (19)
	Home Runs: 1908 (7)
Lou Gehrig	Doubles: 1927 (52)
	Triples: 1926 (20)
	Home Runs: 1931 (46), 1934 (49), and 1936 (49)
Rogers Hornsby	Doubles: 1920 (44), 1921 (44), and 1922 (46)
	Triples: 1917 (17) and 1921 (18)
	Home Runs: 1922 (42) and 1925 (39)
Johnny Mize	Doubles: 1941 (39)
	Triples: 1938 (16)
	Home Runs: 1939 (28), 1940 (43), 1947 (51-Tie), and 1948 (40-Tie)

Players Since World War II with 100 Doubles, Triples, Home Runs, and Stolen Bases, Career

	Doubles	Triples	Home Runs	Stolen Bases
George Brett (1973–93)	665	137	317	201
Lou Brock (1961–79)	486	141	149	938
Carl Crawford (2002–)	244	112	115	427
Johnny Damon (1995–)	516	107	231	404
Willie Davis (1960–79)	395	138	182	398
Steve Finley (1989–2007)	449	124	304	320
Kenny Lofton (1991–2007)	383	116	130	622
Willie Mays (1951–73)	523	140	660	338
Paul Molitor (1978–98)	605	114	234	504
Vada Pinson (1958–75)	485	127	256	305
Tim Raines (1979–2002)	430	113	170	808
Jimmy Rollins (2000–)	399	100	170	373
Pete Rose (1963–86)	746	135	160	198
Juan Samuel (1983–98)	287	102	161	396
Mickey Vernon (1939–60)	490	120	172	137
Robin Yount (1974–93)	583	126	251	271

Players with 200 Hits and Fewer than 40 Extra-Base Hits, Season

American League

	Hits	Extra-Base Hits
Cesar Tovar, Minn. Twins, 1971	204	33
Ichiro Suzuki, Sea. Mariners, 2008	213	33
Nellie Fox, Chi. White Sox, 1954	201	34
Steve Sax, N.Y. Yankees, 1989	205	34
Johnny Pesky, Bost. Red Sox, 1947	207	35
Ichiro Suzuki, Sea. Mariners, 2007	238	35
Ichiro Suzuki, Sea. Mariners, 2004	262	37
Rod Carew, Minn. Twins, 1974	218	38
Ichiro Suzuki, Sea. Mariners, 2006	224	38
Harvey Kuenn, Det. Tigers, 1954	201	39
Ichiro Suzuki, Sea. Mariners, 2010	214	39

National League (Post-1900)

	Hits	Extra-Base Hits
Lloyd Waner, Pitt. Pirates, 1927	223	25
Maury Wills, L.A. Dodgers, 1962	208	29
Matty Alou, Pitt. Pirates, 1970	201	30
Willie Keeler, Bklyn. Dodgers, 1901	202	33
Curt Flood, St. L. Cardinals, 1964	211	33
Milt Stock, St. L. Cardinals, 1920	204	34
Richie Ashburn, Phila. Phillies, 1953	205	36
Tony Gwynn, S.D. Padres, 1984	213	36
Juan Pierre, Fla. Mariners, 2003	204	36
Juan Pierre, Fla. Mariners, 2004	221	37
Milt Stock, Bklyn. Dodgers, 1925	202	38
Chick Fullis, Phila. Phillies, 1933	200	38
Tony Gwynn, S.D. Padres, 1989	203	38
Richie Ashburn, Phila. Phillies, 1958	215	39
Ralph Garr, Atl. Braves, 1971	219	39
Dave Cash, Phila. Phillies, 1974	213	39
Juan Pierre, Col. Rockies, 2001	202	39

Most Doubles by Position, Season

American League

First Base......64......George H. Burns, Cleve. Indians, 1926
Second Base..60.........Charlie Gehringer, Det. Tigers, 1936
Third Base.....56.................George Kell, Det. Tigers, 1950
Shortstop.......56 .Nomar Garciaparra, Bost. Red Sox, 2002
Outfield.........67 ....Earl Webb, Bost. Red Sox, 1931
Catcher..........47 ....Ivan Rodriguez, Tex. Rangers, 1996
Pitcher...........13....Smokey Joe Wood, Bost. Red Sox, 1912
                    13..............Red Ruffing, Bost. Red Sox, 1928

Designated Hitter.........52 ....Edgar Martinez, Sea. Mariners, 1995
                    52 ....Edgar Martinez, Sea. Mariners, 1996
                    52 ....David Ortiz, Bost. Red Sox, 2007

National League (Post-1900)

First Base.........59 ....Todd Helton, Colo. Rockies, 2000
Second Base...57.Billy Herman, Chi. Cubs, 1935 and 1936
Third Base......53...............Jeff Cirillo, Colo. Rockies, 2000
                    53 ......Freddick Sanchez, Pitts. Pirates, 2006
Shortstop........54 ...Mark Grudzielanek, Mont. Expos, 1997
Outfield..........64 ....Joe Medwick, St. L. Cardinals, 1936
Catcher...........42............Terry Kennedy, S.D. Padres, 1982
                    42 ....Brian McCann, Atl. Braves, 2008
Pitcher.............11.....................Red Lucas, Cin. Reds, 1932

Most Triples by Position, Season

American League

First Base......20 ....Lou Gehrig, N.Y. Yankees, 1926
Second Base..22.......Snuffy Stirnweiss, N.Y. Yankees, 1945
Third Base.....22.......Bill Bradley, Cleve. Indians, 1903
Shortstop.......21 ....Bill Keister, Balt. Orioles, 1901
Outfield.........26 ....Joe Jackson, Cleve. Indians, 1912
                    26 ....Sam Crawford, Det. Tigers, 1914
Catcher..........12 ....Mickey Cochrane, Phila. A's, 1928
                    12 ....Eddie Ainsmith, Det. Tigers, 1919
Pitcher...........6 ....Jesse Tannehill, N.Y. Yankees, 1904
                    6 ....Walter Johnson, Wash. Senators, 1913

Designated Hitter.........13 ....Paul Molitor, Milw. Brewers, 1991

National League (Post-1900)

First Base........22 ....Jake Daubert, Cin. Reds, 1922
Second Base...25 ....Larry Doyle, N.Y. Giants, 1911
Third Base......22 ....Tommy Leach, Pitt. Pirates, 1902
Shortstop........20 ....Honus Wagner, Pitt. Pirates, 1912
                    20 ....Jimmy Rollins, Phila. Phillies, 2007
Outfield   36 ....Owen Wilson, Pitt. Pirates, 1912
Catcher...........13 ....Johnny Kling, Chi. Cubs, 1903
                    13.......Tim McCarver, St. L. Cardinals, 1966
Pitcher............6 ....Claude Hendrix, Pitt. Pirates, 1912

Most Total Bases by Position, Season

American League

First Base.......447 ....Lou Gehrig, N.Y. Yankees, 1927

Second Base ..381 ......Alfonso Soriano, N.Y. Yankees, 2002

Third Base .....376 ....Alex Rodriguez, N.Y. Yankees, 2007

Shortstop ....393 ....Alex Rodriguez, Tex. Rangers, 2001

Outfield ....457 ....Babe Ruth, N.Y. Yankees, 1921

Catcher ....335 ....Ivan Rodriguez, Tex. Rangers, 1999

Pitcher ....80 ....Wes Ferrell, Cleve. Indians, 1931

Designated

  Hitter ....363............David Ortiz, Bost. Red Sox, 2005

National League (Post-1900)

First Base........405 ....Todd Helton, Colo. Rockies, 2000

Second Base ...450 ..Rogers Hornsby, St. L. Cardinals, 1922

Third Base ......380 ....Vinny Castilla, Colo. Rockies, 1998

Shortstop........380.........Jimmy Rollins, Phila. Phillies, 2007

Outfield ....445...........Chuck Klein, Phila. Phillies, 1930

Catcher...........355 ....Mike Piazza, L.A. Dodgers, 1997

                       355 ....Johnny Bench, Cin. Reds, 1970

Pitcher............74 ....Don Newcombe, Bklyn. Dodgers, 1955

Stolen Bases

Evolution of Stolen Base Record

American League

1901	Frank Isbell, Chi. White Sox	52
1907	Ty Cobb, Det. Tigers	53
1909	Ty Cobb, Det. Tigers	76
1910	Eddie Collins, Phila. A's	81
1911	Ty Cobb, Det. Tigers	83
1912	Clyde Milan, Wash. Senators	88
1915	Ty Cobb, Det. Tigers	96
1980	Rickey Henderson, Oak. A's	100
1982	Rickey Henderson, Oak. A's	130

National League (Pre-1900)

1886	Ed Andrews, Phila. Phillies	56
1887	Monte Ward, N.Y. Gothams	111

National League (Post-1899)

1900	George Van Haltren, N.Y. Giants	45
	Patsy Donovan, St.L. Cardinals	
1901	Honus Wagner, Pitt. Pirates	49
1903	Jimmy Sheckard, Bklyn. Dodgers	67
	Frank Chance, Chi. Cubs	67
1910	Bob Bescher, Cin. Reds	70
1911	Bob Bescher, Cin. Reds	81
1962	Maury Wills, L.A. Dodgers	104
1974	Lou Brock, St. L. Cardinals	118

Most Stolen Bases by Position, Season

American League

First Base.......52............Frank Isbell, Chi. White Sox, 1901

Second Base ..81 ....Eddie Collins, Phila. A's, 1910

Third Base .....74..............Fritz Maisel, N.Y. Yankees, 1914

Shortstop ....62..............Bert Campaneris, Oak. A's, 1968

Outfield ....130 ....Rickey Henderson, Oak. A's, 1982

Catcher ....36 ....John Wathan, K.C. Royals, 1982

National League (Post-1900)

First Base........67...............Frank Chance, Chi. Cubs, 1903

Second Base ...77...........Davey Lopes, L.A. Dodgers, 1975

Third Base ......59 ....Art Devlin, N.Y. Giants, 1905

Shortstop........104 ....Maury Wills, L.A. Dodgers, 1962

Outfield..........118...........Lou Brock, St. L. Cardinals, 1974

Catcher...........26..............Jason Kendall, Pitt. Pirates, 1998

Pitcher ....10......Nixey Callahan, Chi. White Sox, 1901   **Pitcher** ....8.................Bill Dineen, Bost. Braves, 1901
Designated
Hitter ....22...................Gary Sheffield, Det. Tigers, 2007
....Paul Molitor, Tor. Blue Jays, 1993
....Hal; McRae, K.C. Royals, 1976

Most Stolen Bases by Decade

Pre-1900	1900–09	1910–19
862 ....Billy Hamilton	487 ....Honus Wagner	576.......................................Ty Cobb
741 ....Arlie Latham	359 ....Frank Chance	489 ....Eddie Collins
657 ....Tom Brown	305 ....Sam Mertes	434 ....Clyde Milan
568 ....Bid McPhee	295 ....Jimmy Sheckard	392 ....Max Carey
558.........................Dummy Hoy	275 ....Elmer Flick	364 ....Bob Bescher
548..........................Hugh Duffy	252 ....Jimmy Slagle	340 ....Tris Speaker
540..........................Monte Ward	250 ....Frank Isbell	324 ....Donie Bush
509 ....Harry Stovey	239 ....Fred Clarke	293 ....George J. Burns
494 ....George Van Haltren	239 ....Wid Conroy	286 ....Buck Herzog
473................................Mike Griffin	239 ....Fielder Jones	285 ....Burt Shotton

1920–29	1930–39	1940–49
346 ....Max Carey	269 ....Ben Chapman	285 ....George Case
310 ....Frankie Frisch	176 ....Bill Werber	130 ....Snuffy Stirnweiss
254 ....Sam Rice	158 ....Lyn Lary	126 ....Wally Moses
214..........................George Sisler	158 ....Gee Walker	117 ....Johnny Hopp
210 ....Kiki Cuyler	136 ....Pepper Martin	108 ....Pee Wee Reese
180 ....Eddie Collins	118 ....Kiki Cuyler	108 ....Mickey Vernon
175 ....Johnny Mostil	115 ....Roy Johnson	93.................................Joe Kuhel
167 ....Bucky Harris	101.............................Charlie Gehringer	91 ....Luke Appling
145 ....Cliff Heathcote	100..................................Pete Fox	90 ....Bob Dillinger
144................................Jack Smith	100..................................Stan Hack	88 ....Jackie Robinson

1950–59	1960–69	1970–79
179 ....Willie Mays	535 ....Maury Wills	551 ....Lou Brock
167 ....Minnie Minoso	387.................................Lou Brock	488 ....Joe Morgan
158 ....Richie Ashburn	342 ....Luis Aparicio	427 ....Cesar Cedeno
150 ....Jim Rivera	292 ....Bert Campaneris	380 ....Bobby Bonds
134 ....Luis Aparicio	240 ....Willie Davis	375 ....Davey Lopes
134...........................Jackie Jensen	208 ....Tommy Harper	344 ....Fred Patek
132..............................Jim Gilliam	204 ....Hank Aaron	336................................Bert Campaneris
124 ....Pee Wee Reese	202 ....Vada Pinson	324 ....Billy North
121 ....Billy Bruton	161 ....Don Buford	294 ....Ron LeFlore
109 ....Jackie Robinson	157 ....Tony Taylor	294 ....Amos Otis

1980–89	1990–99	2000–11
838.........................Rickey Henderson	478 ....Otis Nixon	554 ....Juan Pierre
583..................................Tim Raines	463 ....Rickey Henderson	427 ....Carl Crawford
472 ....Vince Coleman	433 ....Kenny Lofton	423 ....Ichiro Suzuki
451 ....Willie Wilson	393 ....Delino DeShields	373 ....Jimmy Rollins
364 ....Ozzie Smith	381 ....Marquis Grissom	370 ....Jose Reyes
333 ....Steve Sax	343 ....Barry Bonds	340 ....Bobby Abreu
331 ....Lonnie Smith	335 ....Chuck Knoblauch	333 ....Chone Figgins
307 ....Brett Butler	319 ....Craig Biggio	302 ....Rafael Furcal

| 293 | Mookie Wilson | 311 | Roberto Alomar | 301 | Scott Podsednik |
| 284 | Dave Collins | 297 | Lance Johnson | 294 | Johnny Damon |

Teammates Combining for 125 Stolen Bases, Season

American League

Rickey Henderson (130) and Davey Lopes (28), Oak. A's, 1982	158
Rickey Henderson (108) and Mike Davis (33), Oak. A's, 1983	141
Clyde Milan (75) and Danny Moeller (62), Wash. Senators, 1913	137
Ty Cobb (96) and Donie Bush (35), Det. Tigers, 1915	131
Ty Cobb (76) and Donie Bush (53), Det. Tigers, 1909	129
Bill North (75) and Bert Campaneris (54), Oak. A's, 1976	129
Rickey Henderson (100) and Dwayne Murphy (26), Oak. A's, 1980	126

National League (Post-1900)

Vince Coleman (110) and Willie McGee (56), St. L. Cardinals, 1985	166
Ron LeFlore (96) and Rodney Scott (63), Mont. Expos, 1980	159
Vince Coleman (109) and Ozzie Smith (43), St. L. Cardinals, 1987	152
Lou Brock (118) and Bake McBride (30), St. L. Cardinals, 1974	148
Vince Coleman (107) and Ozzie Smith (31), St. L. Cardinals, 1986	138
Vince Coleman (81) and Ozzie Smith (57), St. L. Cardinals, 1988	138
Maury Wills (104) and Willie Davis (32), L.A. Dodgers, 1962	136

Players Stealing 30 Bases for 10 Consecutive Seasons

	Seasons
Rickey Henderson, 1979–93	15
Lou Brock, 1964–77	14
Ty Cobb, 1907–18	12
Tim Raines, 1981–92	12
Honus Wagner, 1899–1909	11
Willie Wilson, 1978–88	11
Brett Butler, 1983–93	11
Bert Campaneris, 1965–74	10
Otis Nixon, 1988–97	10
Juan Pierre, 2001–10	10

Players Leading League in Stolen Bases and Total Bases, Season

American League

	Stolen Bases	Total Bases
Ty Cobb, Det. Tigers, 1907	49	286
Ty Cobb, Det. Tigers, 1909	76	296
Ty Cobb, Det. Tigers, 1911	83	367
Ty Cobb, Det. Tigers, 1915	96	274
Ty Cobb, Det. Tigers, 1917	55	336
Snuffy Stirnweiss, N.Y. Yankees, 1945	33	301

National League (Post-1900)

	Stolen Bases	Total Bases
Honus Wagner, Pitt. Pirates, 1904	53	255
Honus Wagner, Pitt. Pirates, 1907	61	264
Honus Wagner, Pitt. Pirates, 1908	53	308
Chuck Klein, Phila. Phillies, 1932	20	420

Players with 200 Home Runs and 200 Stolen Bases, Career

	Home Runs	Stolen Bases
Hank Aaron (1954–76)	755	240
Bobby Abreu* (1996–)	284	393
Roberto Alomar (1988–2004)	210	474
Brady Anderson (1988–2002)	210	315
Jeff Bagwell (1991–2005)	449	202
Don Baylor (1970–88)	338	285
Carles Beltran* (1998–)	302	293
Craig Biggio (1988–2007)	291	414
Barry Bonds (1986–2007)	762	514
Bobby Bonds (1968–81)	332	461
George Brett (1973–93)	317	201
Mike Cameron* (1995–)	278	297
Jose Canseco (1985–2001)	462	200
Joe Carter (1983–98)	396	231
Johnny Damon* (1995–)	231	404
Eric Davis (1984–94, 1996–2001)	282	349
Andre Dawson (1976–96)	438	314
Steve Finley (1989–2007)	304	320
Ron Gant (1987–2003)	321	243
Kirk Gibson (1979–95)	255	284
Marquis Grissom (1989–2005)	227	429
Rickey Henderson (1979–2003)	297	1406
Reggie Jackson (1967–87)	563	228
Derek Jeter* (1996–)	240	339
Howard Johnson (1982–95)	228	231
Ray Lankford (1990–2002, 2004)	238	258
Willie Mays (1951–52, 1954–73)	660	338
Paul Molitor (1978–98)	234	504
Raul Mondesi (1993–2005)	271	229
Joe Morgan (1963–84)	268	689
Vada Pinson (1958–75)	256	305
Frank Robinson (1956–76)	586	204
Alex Rodriguez* (1994–)	629	305
Ryne Sandberg (1981–97)	282	344
Reggie Sanders (1991–2007)	305	304
Gary Sheffield (1988–2009)	509	253
Alfonso Soriano* (1999–)	370	264
Sammy Sosa (1989–2005, 2007)	609	234
Darryl Strawberry (1983–99)	335	221
Larry Walker (1989–2005)	383	230
Devon White (1985–2001)	208	346
Dave Winfield (1973–88, 1990–95)	465	223
Jimmy Wynn (1963–77)	291	225
Robin Yount (1974–93)	251	271

*Active player.

Players with 400 Home Runs and 10 Steals of Home, Career

	Home Runs	Steals of Home
Lou Gehrig	493	15
Babe Ruth	714	10

Players with 200 Hits, 20 Home Runs, and 20 Stolen Bases, Season

American League

	Hits	Home Runs	Stolen Bases
Joe Carter, Clev. Indians, 1986	200	29	29
Kirby Puckett, Minn. Twins, 1986	223	31	20
Alan Trammell, Det. Tigers, 1987	205	28	21
Paul Molitor. Tor. Blue Jays, 1993	211	22	22
Nomar Garciaparra, Bost. Red Sox, 1997	209	30	22
Alex Rodriguez, Sea. Mariners, 1998	213	42	46
Darin Erstad, Ana. Angels, 2000	240	25	28
Alfonso Soriano, N.Y. Yankees, 2002	209	39	41
Jacoby Ellsbury, Bost. Red Sox, 2011	212	32	39

National League

	Hits	Home Runs	Stolen Bases
Babe Herman, Bklyn. Dodgers, 1929	217	21	21
Chuck Klein, Phila. Phillies, 1932	226	38	20
Willie Mays, S.F. Giants, 1958	208	29	31
Vada Pinson, Cin. Reds, 1959	205	20	21
Hank Aaron, Milw. Braves, 1963	201	44	31
Vada Pinson, Cin. Reds, 1963	204	22	27
Vada Pinson, Cin. Reds, 1965	205	22	21
Lou Brock, St. L. Cardinals, 1967	206	21	52
Bobby Bonds, S.F. Giants, 1970	200	26	48
Marquis Grissom, Atl. Braves, 1996	207	23	28
Ellis Burks, Colo. Rockies, 1996	211	40	32
Larry Walker, Colo. Rockies, 1997	208	49	33
Craig Biggio, Hous. Astros, 1998	210	20	50
Vladimir Guerrero, Mont. Expos, 2002	206	39	40
Hanley Ramirez, Flor. Marlins, 2007	212	29	51
Ryan Braun, Milw. Brewers, 2009	203	32	20

Players with 10 Doubles, Triples, Home Runs, and Steals in Each of First Three Seasons in Majors

		Doubles	Triples	Home Runs	Steals
Ben Chapman	N.Y. Yankees (AL), 1930	31	10	10	14
	N.Y. Yankees (AL), 1931	28	11	17	61
	N.Y. Yankees (AL), 1932	41	15	10	38
Juan Samuel	Phila. Phillies (NL), 1984	36	19	15	72
	Phila. Phillies (NL), 1985	31	13	19	53
	Phila. Phillies (NL), 1986	36	12	16	42
	Phila. Phillies (NL), 1987	37	15	28	35

Players Who Have Stolen Second, Third, and Home in Same Inning

American League	National League (Post-1900)
Dave Fultz, Phila. A's, Sept. 4, 1902	Honus Wagner, Pitt. Pirates, Sept. 25, 1907
Wild Bill Donovan, Det. Tigers, May 7, 1906	Hans Lobert, Cin. Reds, Sept. 27, 1908
Bill Coughlin, Det. Tigers, June 4, 1906	Honus Wagner, Pitt. Pirates, May 2, 1909

Ty Cobb, Det. Tigers, July 22, 1909
Ty Cobb, Det. Tigers, July 12, 1911
Ty Cobb, Det. Tigers, July 4, 1912
Joe Jackson, Cleve. Indians, Aug. 11, 1912
Eddie Collins, Phila. A's, Sept. 22, 1912
Eddie Ainsmith, Wash. Senators, June 26, 1913
Red Faber, Chi. White Sox, July 14, 1915
Don Moeller, Wash. Senators, July 19, 1915
Fritz Maisel, N.Y. Yankees, Aug. 17, 1915
Buck Weaver, Chi. White Sox, Sept. 6, 1919
Bobby Roth, Wash. Senators, May 31, 1920
Bob Meusel, N.Y. Yankees, May 16, 1927
Jack Tavener, Det. Tigers, July 10, 1927
Jack Tavener, Det. Tigers, July 25, 1928
Don Kolloway, Chi. White Sox, June 28, 1941
Rod Carew, Minn. Twins, May 18, 1969
Dave Nelson, Tex. Rangers, Aug. 30, 1974
Paul Molitor, Milw. Brewers, July 26, 1987
Devon White, L.A. Angels, Sept. 9, 1989
Chris Stynes, K.C. Royals, May 12, 1996

Dode Paskert, Cin. Reds, May 23, 1910
Wilbur Good, Chi. Cubs, Aug. 18, 1915
Jim Johnstone, Bklyn. Dodgers, Sept. 22, 1916
Greasy Neale, Cin. Reds, Aug. 15, 1919
Max Carey, Pitt. Pirates, Aug. 13, 1923
Max Carey, Pitt. Pirates, May 26, 1925
Harvey Hendrick, Bklyn. Dodgers, June 12, 1928
Pete Rose, Phila. Phillies, May 11, 1980
Dusty Baker, S.F. Giants, June 27, 1984
Eric Young, Colo. Rockies, June 30, 1996
Jayson Werth, Phila. Phillies, May 12, 2009
Dee Gordon, L.A. Dodgers, July 1, 2011

Most Stolen Bases by Catcher, Season

36 ....John Wathan, K.C. Royals (AL), 1982	24..............Ray Schalk, Chi. White Sox (AL), 1914
30..............Ray Schalk, Chi. White Sox (AL), 1916	23 ....Johnny Kling, Chi. Cubs (NL), 1903
28 ....John Wathan, K.C. Royals (AL), 1983*	22..............Jason Kendall, Pitts. Pirates (NL), 1999
26 ....Jason Kendall, Pitts. Pirates (NL), 1998	22..............Jason Kendall, Pitts. Pirates (NL), 2000
25..............Johnny Kling Chi. Cubs (NL), 1902	21..............Benito Santiago, S.D. Padres (NL), 1987
25..............Roger Bresnahan, N.Y. Giants (NL), 1906*	21..............B.J. Surhoff, Milw. Brewers (AL), 1988
25..............John Stearns, N.Y. Mets (NL), 1978	21..............Craig Biggio, Hous. Astros (NL), 1989
25 ....Ivan Rodriguez, Tex. Rangers (AL), 1999	21..............Russell Martin, L.A. Dodgers (NL), 2007
25 ....Craig Biggio, Hous. Astros (NL), 1990	20..............Red Dooin, Phila. Phillies (NL), 1908

*Caught in majority of games played during season.

Most Stolen Bases by Catcher, Career

212..............Roger Bresnahan (1900–15)*	102..............Brad Ausmus (1993–2010)
189..............Jason Kendall (1996–2010)	92..............Billy Sullivan (1899–14)
177..............Ray Schalk (1912–29)	91..............Benito Santiago (1986–2005)
133..............Red Dooin (1902–16)	91..............John Stearns (1975–84)
128..............Carlton Fisk (1969–93)	87..............Ivy Wingo (1911–29)
127..............Ivan Rodriguez (1991–)	86..............Eddie Ainsmith (1910–24)
124..............Johnny Kling (1900–13)	86..............Jimmie Wilson (1923–40)
121..............Wally Schang (1913–31)	80..............Tony Pena (1980–1997)
105..............John Wathan (1976–85)*	

*Caught in majority of games played during career.

Players with 50 Stolen Bases and 100 RBIs, Season

	Stolen Bases	RBIs
Sam Mertes, N.Y. Giants (NL), 1905	52	108
Honus Wagner, Pitt. Pirates (NL), 1905	57	101
Ty Cobb, Det. Tigers (AL), 1908	53	119
Honus Wagner, Pitt. Pirates (NL), 1908	53	109
Ty Cobb, Det. Tigers (AL), 1909	76	107

Ty Cobb, Det. Tigers (AL), 1911 ....83 127
Ty Cobb, Det. Tigers (AL), 1917 ....55 102
George Sisler, St. L. Browns (AL), 1922...................................51 105
Ben Chapman, N.Y. Yankees (AL), 1931................................61 122
Cesar Cedeno, Hous. Astros (NL), 1974................................57 102
Joe Morgan, Cin. Reds (NL), 1976..60 111
Eric Davis, Cin. Reds (NL), 1987 ....50 100
Barry Bonds, S.F. Giants (NL), 1990 ....52 114

Most Stolen Bases by Home Run Champion, Season

American League

76...Ty Cobb, Det. Tigers, 1909 (9 home runs)
52 ....Tris Speaker, Bost. Red Sox, 1912 (10 home runs-Tie)
40 ....Home Run Baker, Phila. A's, 1912 (10 home runs-Tie)
40 ....Jose Canseco, Oak. A's, 1988 (42 home runs)
38 ....Home Run Baker, Phila. A's, 1911 (11 home runs)
37 ....Ken Williams, St. L. Browns, 1922 (39 home runs)
36 ....Harry Davis, Phila. A's, 1905 (8 home runs)
34 ....Home Run Baker, Phila. A's, 1913 (12 home runs)
??   ....Nap Lajoie, Phila. A's, 1901 (14 home runs)
26 ....Jose Canseco, Oak. A's, 1991 (44 home runs)

National League (Post-1900)

67 ....Jimmy Sheckard, Bklyn. Dodgers, 1903 (9 home runs)
48..Red Murray, N.Y. Giants, 1909 (7 home runs)
40...Matt Kemp L.A. Dodgers, 2011 (39 home runs)
33 ....Larry Walker, Colo. Rockies, 1997 (49 home runs)
31 ....Hank Aaron, Atl. Braves, 1963 (44 home runs)
30...Harry Lumley, Bklyn. Dodgers, 1904 (9 home runs)
30..Howard Johnson, N.Y. Mets, 1991 (38 home runs)
29 ....Mike Schmidt, Phila. Phillies, 1975 (38 home runs)
29 ....Darryl Strawberry, N.Y. Mets, 1988 (39 home runs)
29 ....Barry Bonds, S.F. Giants, 1993 (26 home runs)
25 ....Tommy Leach, Pitt. Pirates, 1902 (6 home runs)
25 ....Ryne Sandberg, Chi. Cubs, 1990 (40 home runs)

Players Stealing Bases in Four Decades

	Decades	Total
Rickey Henderson (1979–2003)	1970s (33), 1980s (838), 1990s (463), 2000s (72)	1406
Tim Raines (1979–99, 2001–02)	1970s (2), 1980s (583), 1990s (222), 2000s (1)	808
Omar Vizquel (1989–)	1980s (1) 1990s (237), 2000s (151), 2010s (12)	401
Ted Williams (1939–42, 1946–60)	1930s (2), 1940s (14), 1950s (7), 1960s (1)	24

Batting Miscellany
Most Times Leading League in Offensive Category

American League

	Seasons	
Base Hits	8	Ty Cobb, 1907–09, 1911–12, 1915, 1917, and 1919
Singles	10	Ichiro Suzuki, 2001–10
Doubles	8	Tris Speaker, 1912, 1914, 1916, 1918, and 1920–23

Triples ....5.................Sam Crawford, 1903, 1910, and 1913–15
Home Runs.......................................12................Babe Ruth, 1918–21, 1923–24, and 1926–31
Total Bases ....6.................Ty Cobb, 1907–09, 1911, 1915, and 1917
                                               6.................Babe Ruth, 1919, 1921, 1923–24, 1926, and 1928
                                               6.................Ted Williams, 1939, 1942, 1946–47, 1949, and 1951
Slugging Percentage....................13................Babe Ruth, 1918–24 and 1926–31
Batting Average ....12................Ty Cobb, 1907–15 and 1917–19
Runs...8.................Babe Ruth, 1919–21, 1923–24, and 1926–28
RBIs..6.................Babe Ruth, 1919–21, 1923, 1926, and 1928
Walks..11................Babe Ruth, 1920–21, 1923–24, 1926–28, and 1930–33
Strikeouts...7.................Jimmie Foxx, 1929–31, 1933, 1935–36, and 1941
Stolen Bases....................................12................Rickey Henderson, 1980–86, 1988–91, 1998

National League (Post-1900)

Base Hits..7.................Pete Rose, 1965, 1968, 1970, 1972–73, 1976, and 1981
Singles ....4.................Ginger Beaumont, 1902–04 and 1907
                                               4.................Lloyd Waner, 1927–29 and 1931
                                               4.................Richie Ashburn, 1951, 1953, and 1957–58
                                               4.................Maury Wills, 1961–62, 1965, and 1967
Doubles..8.................Stan Musial, 1943–44, 1946, 1948–49, and 1952–54
Triples ....5.................Stan Musial, 1943, 1946, 1948–49, and 1951
Home Runs.......................................8.................Mike Schmidt, 1974–76, 1980–81, 1983–84, and 1986
Total Bases ....8.................Hank Aaron, 1956–57, 1959–61, 1963, 1967, and 1969
Slugging Percentage....................11................Rogers Hornsby, 1917–25 and 1928–29
Batting Average ....8.................Honus Wagner, 1900, 1903–04, 1906–09, and 1911
Runs ....5.................Rogers Hornsby, 1921–22, 1924, 1927, and 1929
                                               5.................Stan Musial, 1946, 1948, 1951–52, and 1954
RBIs ....4.................Honus Wagner, 1901–02 and 1908–09
                                               4.................Rogers Hornsby, 1920–22 and 1925
                                               4.................Hank Aaron, 1957, 1960, 1963, and 1966
                                               4.................Mike Schmidt, 1980–81, 1984, and 1986
Walks ....10................Barry Bonds, 1992, 1994–97, 2000–2004
Strikeouts...6.................Vince DiMaggio, 1937–38 and 1942–45
Stolen Bases....................................10................Max Carey, 1913, 1915–18, 1920, and 1922–25

Most Consecutive Seasons Leading League in Offensive Category

	American League		National League (Post-1900)	
	Seasons		Seasons	
Batting Average	9	Ty Cobb, 1907–15	6	Rogers Hornsby, 1920–25
Slugging Percentage	7	Babe Ruth, 1918–24	6	Rogers Hornsby, 1920–25
Runs	3	Ty Cobb, 1909–11	3	Chuck Klein, 1930–32
	3	Eddie Collins, 1912–14	3	Duke Snider, 1953–55
	3	Babe Ruth, 1919–21 and 1926–28	3	Pete Rose, 1974–76
	3	Ted Williams, 1940–42	3	Albert Pujols, 2003–05
	3	Mickey Mantle, 1956–58		
Base Hits	5	Ichiro Suzuki, 2001–10	3	Ginger Beaumont, 1902–04
			3	Rogers Hornsby, 1920–22
			3	Frank McCormick, 1938–40
Singles	10	Ichiro Suzuki, 2001–10	3	Ginger Beaumont, 1902–04
			3	Lloyd Waner, 1927–29
				Ryan Theriot, 2008–10

Doubles	4	Tris Speaker, 1920–23	4	Honus Wagner, 1906–09
Triples	3	Elmer Flick, 1905–07	3	Garry Templeton, 1977–79
	3	Sam Crawford, 1913–15		
	3	Zoilo Versalles, 1963–65		
	3	Carl Crawford, 2004–06		
Home Runs	6	Babe Ruth, 1926–31	7	Ralph Kiner, 1946–52
Total Bases	3	Ty Cobb, 1907–09	4	Honus Wagner, 1906–09
	3	Jim Rice, 1977–79	4	Chuck Klein, 1930–33
RBIs	3	Ty Cobb, 1907–09	3	Rogers Hornsby, 1920–22
	3	Babe Ruth, 1919–21	3	Joe Medwick, 1936–38
			3	George Foster, 1976–78
Walks	4	Babe Ruth, 1930–33	5	Barry Bonds, 2000–2004
	4	Ted Williams, 1946–49		
Strikeouts	4	Vince DiMaggio, 1942–45	4	Hack Wilson, 1927–30
	4	Reggie Jackson, 1968–71		
Stolen Bases	9	Luis Aparicio, 1956–64	6	Maury Wills, 1960–65

Players Leading in All Triple Crown Categories, but Not in Same Year*

Hank Aaron..................Batting: 1956 (.328) and 1959 (.355)
Home Runs: 1957 (44), 1963 (44 Tie), 1966 (44), and 1967 (39)
RBIs: 1957 (132), 1960 (126), 1963 (130), and 1966 (127)

Barry Bonds..................Batting: 2002 (.370) and 2004 (.363)
Home Runs: 1993 (46) and 2001 (73)
RBIs: 1993 (123)

Dan Brouthers.................Batting: 1882 (.368), 1883 (.374), 1889 (.373), 1891 (.350), and 1892 (.335)
Home Runs: 1881 (8) and 1886 (11)
RBIs: 1892 (97)

Miguel Cabrera...............Batting: 2011 (.344)
Home Runs: 2008 (37)
RBIs: 2010 (126)

Ed Delahanty ....Batting: 1899 (.410) and 1902 (.376)
Home Runs: 1893 (19) and 1896 (13)
RBIs: 1893 (146), 1896 (126), and 1899 (137)

Joe DiMaggio ....Batting: 1939 (.381) and 1940 (.352)
Home Runs: 1937 (46) and 1948 (39)
RBIs: 1941 (125) and 1948 (155)

Johnny Mize ....Batting: 1939 (.349)
Home Runs: 1939 (28), 1940 (43), 1947 (51 Tie), and 1948 (40 Tie)
RBIs: 1940 (137), 1942 (110), and 1947 (138)

Marry Ramirez................Batting: 2002 (.349)
Home Runs: 2004 (43)
RBIs: 1999 (155)

Albert Pujols ....Batting: 2003 (.348)
Home Runs: 2009 (41)
2010 (42)
RBIs: 2010 (118)

Babe Ruth.....................Batting: 1924 (.378)
Home Runs: 1918 (11), 1919 (29), 1920 (54), 1921 (59), 1923 (41), 1924 (46), 1926 (47), 1927 (60), 1928 (54), 1929 (46), 1930 (49), and 1931 (46 Tie)
RBIs: 1919 (114), 1920 (137), 1921 (171), 1923 (131), 1926 (146), and 1928 (142 Tie)

*Includes only players who *never* won triple crown.

Highest Offensive Career Totals by Players Who Never Led League

American League		
Base Hits	3315	Eddie Collins
Singles	2262	Carl Yastrzemski
Doubles	539	Al Simmons
Triples	223	Tris Speaker
Home Runs	544	Rafael Palmeiro
Total Bases	4854	Paul Molitor
Batting Average	.356	Joe Jackson
Slugging Average	.556	Carlos Delgado
Runs	1882	Tris Speaker
RBIs	1740	Rafael Palmeiro
Walks	1381	Tris Speaker
Strikeouts	1916	Alex Rodriguez
Stolen Bases	504	Paul Molitor

National League (Post-1900)		
Base Hits	3060	Craig Biggio
Singles	2424	Honus Wagner
Doubles	601	Barry Bonds
Triples	177	Rabbit Maranville
Home Runs	475	Stan Musial
Total Bases	5752	Pete Rose
Batting Average	.336	Riggs Stephenson
Slugging Average	.588	Vladimir Guerrero
Runs	1561	Chipper Jones
RBIs	1903	Willie Mays
Walks	1566	Pete Rose
Strikeouts	1753	Craig Biggio
Stolen Bases	550	Cesar Cedeno

Career Offensive Leaders by Players Under Six Feet Tall

Games Played	3562	Pete Rose (5'11")
At Bats	14053	Pete Rose (5'11")
Base Hits	4256	Pete Rose (5'11")
Singles	3115	Pete Rose (5'11")
Doubles	793	Tris Speaker (5'11½")
Triples	222	Tris Speaker (5'11")
Home Runs	660	Willie Mays (5'10½")
Extra-Base Hits	1323	Willie Mays (5'10½")
Total Bases	6066	Willie Mays (5'10½")
Runs	2295	Rickey Henderson (5'10")
RBIs	1903	Willie Mays (5'10½")
Walks	2190	Rickey Henderson (5'10")
Strikeouts	1753	Craig Biggio (5'11")
Batting Average	.358	Rogers Hornsby (5'11")
Slugging Average	.577	Rogers Hornsby (5'11")
Stolen Bases	1406	Rickey Henderson (5'10")

Largest Margin Between League Leaders and Runners-Up

American League

	Margin	Season	Leader		Runner-Up	
Batting Average	.086	1901	Nap Lajoie, Phila. A's	.426	Mike Donlin, Balt. Orioles	.340
Hits	46	2004	Ichiro Suzuki, Sea. Mariners	262	Michael Young, Tex. Rangers	216
Doubles	15	1910	Nap Lajoie, Cleve. Indians	51	Ty Cobb, Det. Tigers	36
Triples	10	1949	Dale Mitchell, Cleve. Indians	23	Bob Dillinger, St. L. Browns	13
Home Runs	35	1920	Babe Ruth, N.Y. Yankees	54	George Sisler, St. L. Browns	19
Runs Scored	45	1921	Babe Ruth, N.Y. Yankees	177	Jack Tobin, St. L. Browns	132
RBIs	51	1935	Hank Greenberg, Det. Tigers	170	Lou Gehrig, N.Y. Yankees	119
Total Bases	92	1921	Babe Ruth, N.Y. Yankees	457	Harry Heilmann, Det. Tigers	365
Slugging Average	.240	1921	Babe Ruth, N.Y. Yankees	.846	Harry Heilmann, Det. Tigers	.606
Stolen Bases	76	1982	Rickey Henderson, Oak. A's	130	Damaso Garcia, Tor. Blue Jays	54
Walks	72	1923	Babe Ruth, N.Y. Yankees	170	Joe Sewell, Cleve. Indians	98

National League

	Margin	Season	Leader		Runner-Up	
Batting Average	.049	1924	Rogers Hornsby, St. L. Cardinals	.424	Zack Wheat, Bklyn. Dodgers	.375
Hits	44	1946	Stan Musial, St. L. Cardinals	228	Dixie Walker, Bklyn. Dodgers	184
Doubles	16	1904	Honus Wagner, Pitt. Pirates	44	Sam Mertes, N.Y. Giants	28
Triples	16	1912	Owen Wilson, Pitt. Pirates	36	Honus Wagner, Pitt. Pirates	20
Home Runs	19	1923	Cy Williams, Phila. Phillies	41	Jack Fournier, Bklyn. Dodgers	22
Runs Scored	29	1909	Tommy Leach, Pitt. Pirates	126	Fred Charles, Pitt. Pirates	97
RBIs	39	1937	Joe Medwick, St. L. Cardinals	154	Frank Demaree, Chi. Cubs	115
Total Bases	136	1922	Rogers Hornsby, St. L. Cardinals	450	Irish Meusel, N.Y. Giants	314
Slugging Average	.177	2002	Barry Bonds, S.F. Giants	.799	Brian Giles, Pitt. Pirates	.622
Stolen Bases	72	1962	Maury Wills, L.A. Dodgers	104	Willie Davis, L.A. Dodgers	32
Walks	105	2004	Barry Bonds, S.F. Giants	232	Bobby Abreu, Phila. Phillies	127
					Lance Berkman, Hous. Astros	127
					Todd Helton, Colo. Rockies	127

Evolution of Slugging Average Record

American League

1901	Nap Lajoie, Phila. A's	.643
1919	Babe Ruth, Bost. Red Sox	.657
1920	Babe Ruth, N.Y. Yankees	.847

National League (Pre-1900)

1876	Ross Barnes, Chi. White Stockings	.590
1894	Sam Thompson, Phila. Phillies	.696

National League (Post-1899)

1922	Rogers Hornsby, St. L. Cardinals	.722
1925	Rogers Hornsby, St. L. Cardinals	.756
2001	Barry Bonds, S.F. Giants	.863

Players Hitting Safely in at Least 135 Games in Season

American League

Wade Boggs, Bost. Red Sox, 1985 (240 hits in 161 games, .368 batting average)

Derek Jeter, N.Y. Yankees, 1999 (219 hits in 158 games, .349 batting average)

Ichiro Suzuki, Sea. Mariners, 2001 (242 hits in 157 games, .350 batting average)

National League (Post-1900)

Rogers Hornsby, St. L. Cardinals, 1922 (250 hits in 154 games, .401 batting average)

Chuck Klein, Phila. Phillies, 1930 (250 hits in 156 games, .386 batting average)

Players Hitting for the Cycle in Natural Order (Single, Double, Triple, Home Run)

American League

Fats Fothergill, Det. Tigers, Sept. 26, 1926
Tony Lazzeri, N.Y. Yankees, June 3, 1932
Charlie Gehringer, Det. Tigers, May 27, 1939
Leon Culberson, Bost. Red Sox, July 3, 1943
Bob Watson, Bost. Red Sox, Sept. 15, 1979
Jose Valentin, Chi. White Sox, Apr. 27, 2000
Gary Matthews Jr., Tex. Rangers, Sept. 13, 2006

National League (Post-1900)

Bill Collins, Bost. Braves, Oct. 6, 1910
Jim Hickman, N.Y. Mets, Aug. 7, 1963
Ken Boyer, St. L. Cardinals, June 16, 1964
Billy Williams, Chi. Cubs, July 17, 1966
Tim Foli, Mont. Expos, Apr. 22, 1976
John Mabry, St. L. Cardinals, May 18, 1996
Brad Wilkerson, Mont. Expos, June 24, 2003

Highest Slugging Average by Position, Season

American League

First Base ..... .765 ....Lou Gehrig, N.Y. Yankees, 1927
Second Base .... .643 ....Nap Lajoie, Phila. A's, 1901
Third Base .... .664 ....George Brett, K.C. Royals, 1980
Shortstop ...... .631 ......Alex Rodriguez, Sea. Mariners, 1996
Outfield .... .847 ....Babe Ruth, N.Y. Yankees, 1920
Catcher .... .617 ....Bill Dickey, N.Y. Yankees, 1936
Pitcher .... .621 ....Wes Ferrell, Cleve. Indians, 1931
Designated Hitter .... .628 .....Edgar Martinez, Sea. Mariners, 1995

National League (Post-1900)

First Base .... .752 ....Mark McGwire, St. L. Cardinals, 1998
Second Base .... .756 ...Rogers Hornsby, St. L. Cardinals, 1925
Third Base ... .644 ....Mike Schmidt, Phila. Phillies, 1981
Shortstop ..... .614 ....Ernie Banks, Chi. Cubs, 1958
Outfield .... .863 ....Barry Bonds, S.F. Giants, 2001
Catcher .... .638 ....Mike Piazza, L.A. Dodgers, 1997
Pitcher .... .632 ...Don Newcombe, Bklyn. Dodgers, 1955

Most Times Awarded First Base on Catcher's Interference or Obstruction

29 ....Pete Rose (1963–86)
18 ....Julian Javier (1960–72)
18...Dale Berra (1977–87)
17 ....Roberto Kelly (1988–2000)
17 ....Andy Van Slyke (1983–95)
16 ....Bob Stinson (1969–80)
13 ....Phil Nakso (1954–87)
13 ....Carl Crawford (2002–)
13 ....Darin Erstad (1996–2009)
12 ....Hector Torres (1968–77)
12...Craig Counsell (1995–)

Winners of Two "Legs" of Triple Crown Since Last Winner*

American League

Dick Allen, Chi. White Sox, 1972 ....37 home runs, 113 RBIs (batting avg. .308, third behind Rod Carew's .318)
Jim Rice, Bost. Red Sox, 1978.....................46 home runs, 139 RBIs (batting avg. .315, third behind Rod Carew's .333)
Alex Rodriguez, Tex. Rangers, 2002............57 home runs, 142 RBIs (batting avg. .300, twenty-third behind Manny Ramirez's .349)
David Ortiz, Bost. Red Sox, 2006 ....54 home runs, 137 RBIs (batting avg. .287, thirty-ninth behind Joe Mauer's .347
Alex Rodriguez, N.Y. Yankees, 2007 ....54 home runs, 156 RBIs (batting avg. .314, thirteenth behind Magglio Ordonez's .363
Mark Teixeira, N.Y. Yankees, 2009 ....39 home runs, 122 RBIs (batting avg. .292, thirty-first behind Joe Mauer's .365)

National League

George Foster, Cin. Reds, 1977 ....52 home runs, 149 RBIs (batting avg. .320, third behind Dave Parker's .338)
Mike Schmidt, Phila. Phillies, 1981 ....31 home runs, 91 RBIs (batting avg. .316, fourth behind Bill Madlock's .341)
Dante Bichette, Colo. Rockies, 1995 ....40 home runs, 128 RBIs (batting avg. .340, third behind Tony Gwynn's .368)
Todd Helton, Colo. Rockies, 2000..............147 RBIs, .372 batting avg. (42 home runs, sixth behind Sammy Sosa's 50)
Ryan Howard, Phila. Phillies, 2006............58 home runs, 199 RBIs, .313 batting avg. (ninth behind Freddy Sanchez's .344)
Matt Holliday, Colo. Rockies, 2007............137 RBIs, .340 batting avg. (36 home runs, behind Prince Fielder's .50)
Ryan Howard, Phila. Phillies, 2008............48 home runs, 146 RBIs, .251 batting avg. (sixty-second behind Chipper Jones .364)
Albert Pujols, St.L. Cardinals, 2010 ....42 home runs, 118 RBIs, .312 batting avg. (sixth behind Carlos Gonzalez, .336)
Matt Kemp. L.A. Dodgers, 2011................39 home runs, 126 RBIs, .324 batting avg. (third behind Jose Reyés, .337)
*Carl Yastrzemski, 1967.

2

Wins

Most Victories by Decade

Pre-1900		1900–09		1910–19	
361	Pud Galvin	236	Christy Mathewson	265	Walter Johnson
342	Tim Keefe	230	Cy Young	208	Grover C. Alexander
328	John Clarkson	218	Joe McGinnity	162	Eddie Cicotte
309	Hoss Radbourn	192	Jack Chesbro	156	Hippo Vaughn
307	Mickey Welch	188	Vic Willis	149	Slim Sallee
297	Kid Nichols	186	Eddie Plank	144	Rube Marquard284
Tony Mullane	183	Rube Waddell	140	Eddie Plank	
267	Cy Young	166	Sam Leever	137	Christy Mathewson
265	Jim McCormick	160	Jack Powell	135	Claude Hendrix
258	Gus Weyhing	157	George Mullin	126	Hooks Dauss

1920–29		1930–39		1940–49	
190	Burleigh Grimes	199	Lefty Grove	170	Hal Newhouser
166	Eppa Rixley	188	Carl Hubbell	137	Bob Feller
165	Grover C. Alexander	175	Red Ruffing	133	Rip Sewell
163	Herb Pennock	170	Wes Ferrell	129	Dizzy Trout
161	Waite Hoyt	165	Lefty Gomez	122	Dutch Leonard
156	Urban Shocker	158	Mel Harder	122	Bucky Walters
154	Eddie Rommel	156	Larry French	114	Mort Cooper
153	Jesse Haines	150	Tommy Bridges	111	Claude Passeau
152	George Uhle	148	Paul Derringer	105	Kirby Higbe
149	Red Faber	147	Dizzy Dean	105	Bobo Newsom
				105	Harry Brecheen

1950–59		1960–69		1970–79	
202	Warren Spahn	191	Juan Marichal	186	Jim Palmer
199	Robin Roberts	164	Bob Gibson	184	Gaylord Perry
188	Early Wynn	158	Don Drysdale	178	Steve Carlton
155	Billy Pierce	150	Jim Bunning	178	Ferguson Jenkins
150	Bob Lemon	142	Jim Kaat	178	Tom Seaver
128	Mike Garcia	141	Larry Jackson	169	Catfish Hunter
126	Lew Burdette	137	Sandy Koufax	166	Don Sutton
126	Don Newcombe	134	Jim Maloney	164	Phil Niekro
121	Whitey Ford	131	Milt Pappas	155	Vida Blue
116	Johnny Antonelli	127	Camilo Pascual	155	Nolan Ryan

continued on next page

	1980-89		1990-99		2000-11
162	Jack Morris	176	Greg Maddux	179	Roy Halladay
140	Dave Steib	164	Tom Glavine	176	C. C. Sabathia
137	Bob Welch	152	Roger Clemens	170	Tim Hudson
128	Charlie Hough	150	Randy Johnson	161	Mark Buehrle
128	Fernando Valenzuela	143	Kevin Brown	159	Roy Oswalt
123	Bert Blyleven	143	John Smoltz	159	Andy Pettitte
122	Nolan Ryan	141	David Cone	155	Derek Lowe
119	Jim Clancy	136	Mike Mussina	151	Javier Vasquez
117	Frank Viola	135	Chuck Finley	149	Jamie Moyer
116	Rick Sutcliffe	130	Scott Erickson	147	Livan Hernandez

Pitchers with the Most Career Wins by First Letter of Last Name

A	Grover C. Alexander	373	N	Kid Nichols	361
B	Bert Blyleven	287	O	Al Orth	204
C	Roger Clemens	354	P	Eddie Plank	326
D	Hooks Dauss, Paul Derringer	223	Q	John P. Quinn	247
E	Dennis Eckersley	197	R	Nolan Ryan	324
F	Bob Feller	266	S	Warren Spahn	363
G	Pud Galvin	361	T	Frank Tanana	240
H	Carl Hubbell	253	U	George Uhle	200
I	Jason Isringhausen	48	V	Dazzy Vance	197
J	Walter Johnson	417	W	Mickey Welch	307
K	Tim Keefe	341	X	[No pitcher]	
L	Ted Lyons	260	Y	Cy Young	511
M	Christy Mathewson	373	Z	Tom Zachary	186

Pitchers with the Most Career Victories by Zodiac Sign

Aquarius (Jan. 20–Feb. 18)	Nolan Ryan	324
Pisces (Feb. 19–Mar. 20)	Grover C. Alexander	373
Aries (Mar. 21–Apr. 19)	Cy Young	511
Taurus (Apr. 20–May 20)	Warren Spahn	363
Gemini (May 21–June 21)	Tommy John	288
Cancer (June 22–July 22)	John Clarkson	327
Leo (July 23–Aug. 22)	Christy Mathewson	373
Virgo (Aug. 23–Sept. 22)	Kid Nichols	360
Libra (Sept. 23–Oct. 23)	Robin Roberts	286
Scorpio (Oct. 24–Nov. 21)	Walter Johnson	417
Sagittarius (Nov. 22–Dec. 21)	Old Hoss Radbourn	310
Capricorn (Dec. 22–Jan. 19)	Pud Galvin	361

Pitchers with the Most Victories by State of Birth

Alabama	Don Sutton (Clio)	324	Delaware	Sadie McMahon (Wilmington)	177
Alaska	Curt Schilling (Anchorage)	216	Florida	Steve Carlton (Miami)	329
Arizona	John Denny (Prescott)	123	Georgia	Kenny Rogers (Savannah)	219
Arkansas	Lon Warneke (Mount Ida)	193	Hawaii	Charlie Hough (Honolulu)	216
California	Tom Seaver (Fresno)	311	Idaho	Larry Jackson (Nampa)	194
Colorado	Roy Halladay (Denver)	188	Illinois	Robin Roberts (Springfield)	286
Connecticut	Bill Hutchinson (New Haven)	182	Indiana	Tommy John (Terre Haute)	288

Iowa	Bob Feller (Van Meter)	266		

Iowa ....Bob Feller (Van Meter).......................266
Kansas....................Walter Johnson (Humboldt).............417
Kentucky ....Gus Weyhing (Louisville) 264
Louisiana................Ted Lyons (Sulphur) 260
Maine ....Bob Stanley (Portland).....................115
Maryland ....Lefty Grove (Lonaconing) 300
Massachusetts ....Tim Keefe (Cambridge)....................341
Michigan.................Jim Kaat (Zeeland)..........................283
Minnesota ....Jack Morris (St.Paul) 254
Mississippi..............Guy Bush (Aberdeen) 176
Missouri ....Pud Galvin (St. Louis) 361
Montana ....Dave McNally (Billings) 184
Nebraska ....Grover C. Alexander (Elba) 373
Nevada..................Barry Zito (Las Vegas) 145
New Hampshire ....Mike Flanagan (Manchester)...........167
New Jersey..............Al Leiter (Toms River).......................162
New Mexico ....Wade Blasingame (Deming)..............46
New York ....Warren Spahn (Buffalo)...................363
North Carolina ....Gaylord Perry (Williamston) 314
North Dakota ....Rick Helling (Devils Lake)................93

Ohio.......................Cy Young (Gilmore) 511
Oklahoma ....Allie Reynolds (Bethany) 182
Oregon ....Mickey Lolich (Portland)..................217
Pennsylvania...........Christy Mathewson (Factoryville) 373
Rhode Island...........Tom Lovett (Providence) 88
South Carolina........Bobo Newsom (Hartsville)...............211
South Dakota...........Floyd Bannister (Pierre) 134
Tennessee ....Bob Caruthers (Memphis) 218
Texas ....Greg Maddux (San Angelo)............355
Utah ....Bruce Hurst (St. George).................145
Vermont ....Ray Fisher (Middlebury) 100
Virginia..................Eppa Rixey (Culpepper)...................266
Washington ....Todd Stottlemyre (Sunnyside)...........138
West Virginia..........Wilbur Cooper (Bearsville)...............216
Wisconsin ....Kid Nichols (Madison).....................361
Wyoming ....Tom Browning (Casper) 123

District of Columbia..Doc White 189
Puerto Rico ....Javier Vazquez (Ponce) 165
Virgin Islands...........Al McBean (Charlotte Amalie)...........67

Pitchers with Five or More Consecutive 20-Win Seasons (Post-1900)

	Seasons
Christy Mathewson, N.Y. Giants (NL), 1903–14	12
Walter Johnson, Wash. Senators (AL), 1910–19	10
Lefty Grove, Phila. A's (AL), 1927–33	7
Three Finger Brown, Chi. Cubs (NL), 1906–11	6
Robin Roberts, Phila. Phillies (NL), 1950–55	6
Warren Spahn, Milw. Braves (NL), 1956–61	6
Ferguson Jenkins, Chi. Cubs (NL), 1967–72	6
Grover C. Alexander, Phila. Phillies (NL), 1913–17	5
Carl Hubbell, N.Y. Giants (NL), 1933–37	5
Catfish Hunter, Oak. A's (AL), 1971–74, and N.Y. Yankees (AL), 1975	5

100-Game Winners, Both Leagues

	American League	National League	Total Wins
Al Orth	104 (1902–09)	100 (1895–1901)	204
Kevin Brown	102 (1986–95, 2004–05)	109 (1996–2003)	211
Pedro Martinez	117 (1998–2004)	102 (1992–97, 2005–09)	219
Jim Bunning	118 (1955–63)	106 (1964–71)	224
Dennis Martinez	141 (1976–86, 1994–98)	104 (1986–93)	245
Ferguson Jenkins	115 (1974–81)	169 (1965–73, 1982–83)	284
Randy Johnson	164 (1989–98, 2005–06)	139 (1988–89, 1998–2004, 2007–09)	303
Gaylord Perry	139 (1972–77, 1980, 1982–83)	175 (1962–71, 1978–79, 1981)	314
Nolan Ryan	189 (1972–79, 1989–93)	135 (1966–71, 1980–88)	324
Cy Young	221 (1901–11)	290 (1890–1900, 1911)	511

Pitchers with 500 Major League Decisions

	Wins–Losses	Total
Cy Young (1890–1911)	511–316	827
Walter Johnson (1907–27)	417–279	696
Pud Galvin (1875, 1879–92)	361–308	669
Nolan Ryan (1966–93)	324–292	616
Warren Spahn (1942, 1946–65)	363–245	608
Phil Niekro (1964–87)	318–274	592
Greg Maddux (1986–2008)	355–277	582
Grover C. Alexander (1911–30)	373–208	581
Don Sutton (1966–88)	324–256	580
Gaylord Perry (1962–83)	314–265	579
Steve Carlton (1965–88)	329–244	573
Kid Nichols (1890–1901, 1904–06)	361–208	569
Tim Keefe (1880–93)	342–225	567
Christy Mathewson (1900–16)	373–188	561
Early Wynn (1939, 1941–44, 1946–63)	300–244	544
Roger Clemens (1984–2007)	354–184	538
Bert Blyleven (1970–92)	287–250	537
Robin Roberts (1948–66)	286–245	531
Jim Kaat (1959–83)	283–237	520
Eddie Plank (1901–17)	326–194	520
Tommy John (1963–74, 1976–89)	288–231	519
Mickey Welch (1880–92)	307–210	517
Eppa Rixey (1912–17, 1919–33)	266–251	517
Tom Seaver (1967–86)	311–205	516
Ferguson Jenkins (1965–83)	284–226	510
Tom Glavine (1987–2008)	305–203	508
John Clarkson (1882, 1884–94)	328–178	506
Tony Mullane (1881–94)	284–220	504
Old Hoss Radbourn (1880–91)	309–194	503

Most Wins, Major and Minor Leagues Combined

Total		Majors	Minors
526	Cy Young	511	15
481	Joe McGinnity	246	235
444	Kid Nichols	360	84
418	Grover C. Alexander	373	45
417	Walter Johnson	417	0
415	Warren Spahn	363	52
412	Lefty Grove	300	112
398	Christy Mathewson	373	25
391	Greg Maddux	355	36
369	Gaylord Perry	314	55
366	Early Wynn	300	66
364	Roger Clemens	354	10
361	Pud Galvin	361	0
361	Phil Niekro	318	43
360	Tony Freitas	25	335
355	Joe Martina	6	349
353	Steve Carlton	329	24
350	Bobo Newsom	211	139

348	Stan Coveleski	215	133
348	Don Sutton	324	24
348	Bill Thomas	0	348
347	John P. Quinn	247	100
345	Nolan Ryan	324	21
342	Burleigh Grimes	270	72
341	Tim Keefe	341	0
338	Gus Weyhing	264	74
334	Tom Glavine	305	29
332	Red Faber	254	78
332	Dazzy Vance	197	135
331	Randy Johnson	303	28
331	Alex McColl	4	327

Most Wins For One Team

American League

417 ....Walter Johnson, Wash. Senators (1907–27)
284 ....Eddie Plank, Phila. A's (1900–14)
268 ....Jim Palmer, Balt. Orioles (1965–84)
266 ....Bob Feller, Cleve. Indians (1936–41, 1945–56)
260 ....Ted Lyons, Chi. White Sox (1923–42, 1946)
254 ....Red Faber, Chi. White Sox (1914–33)
236 ....Whitey Ford, N.Y. Yankees (1950, 1953–67)
231 ....Red Ruffing, N.Y. Yankees (1930–42, 1945–46)
223 ....Mel Harder, Cleve. Indians (1928–47)
222 ....Hooks Dauss, Det. Tigers (1912–26)
209 ....George Mullin, Det. Tigers (1902–13)
207 ....Bob Lemon, Cleve. Indians (1946–58)
207 ....Mickey Lolich, Det. Tigers (1963–75)
200 ....Hal Newhouser, Det. Tigers (1939–53)

National League

372 ....Christy Mathewson, N.Y. Giants (1900–16)
356 ...Warren Spahn, Bost.–Milw. Braves (1942, 1946–64)
329 ....Kid Nichols, Bost. Braves (1890–1901)
266 ....Phil Niekro, Atl. Braves (1966–83)
253 ....Carl Hubbell, N.Y. Giants (1928–43)
251 ....Bob Gibson, St. L. Cardinals (1959–75)
244 ....Tom Glavine, Atl. Braves (1987–2002, 2008)
241 ....Steve Carlton, Phila. Phillies (1972–86)
241 ....Cy Young, Cleve. Spiders (1890–98)
238 ....Juan Marichal, S.F. Giants (1960–73)
238 ....Mickey Welch, N.Y. Giants (1885–92)
234 ....Robin Roberts, Phila. Phillies (1948–61)
233...........Amos Rusie, N.Y. Giants (1890–95, 1827–98)
233..............Don Sutton, L.A. Dodgers (1966–80, 1988)
218..........................Pud Galvin, Buff. Bisons (1879–85)
210 ....Jesse Haines, St. L. Cardinals (1920–37)
205 ....Al Spalding, Bost. Red Stockings (1871–75)
202 ....Wilbur Cooper, Pitt. Pirates (1912–24)
201 ....Charlie Root, Chi. Cubs (1926–41)

Pitchers with 100 More Wins Than Losses, Career

	Wins	Losses	Differential
Cy Young (1890–1911)	511	315	+196
Christy Mathewson (1900–16)	373	188	+185
Roger Clemens (1984–2007)	354	184	+170
Grover C. Alexander (1911–30)	373	208	+165
Lefty Grove (1925–41)	300	141	+159
Kid Nichols (1890–1901, 1904–06)	360	205	+155
John Clarkson (1882, 1884–94)	327	177	+150
Walter Johnson (1907–27)	417	279	+138
Randy Johnson (1988–2009)	303	166	+137
Eddie Plank (1901–17)	326	194	+132
Whitey Ford (1950, 1953–67)	236	106	+130
Greg Maddux (1986–2008)	355	227	+128
Bob Caruthers (1884–92)	218	97	+121
Pedro Martinez (1992–2009)	219	100	+119

continued on next page

Tim Keefe (1880–93)............................341.........................223........................+118
Warren Spahn (1942, 1946–65) ....363.........................245........................+118
Jim Palmer (1965–84) ....268.........................152........................+116
Old Hoss Radbourn (1880–91)................310.........................196........................+114
Tom Seaver (1967–86) ....311.........................205........................+106
Joe McGinnity (1899–1908) ....246.........................141........................+105
Bob Feller (1936–41, 1945–56) ....266.........................162........................+104
Tom Glavine (1987–2008) ....305.........................203........................+102
Andy Pettitte 1995–2010).......................240.........................138........................+102
Juan Marichal (1960–75) ....243.........................142........................+101

Pitchers with Most Career Wins, Never Leading League in One Season

Pud Galvin (1875, 1879–92).......................361
Eddie Plank (1901–17) 327
Nolan Ryan (1966–88) 324
Don Sutton (1966–88)..................................324
Mickey Welch (1880–92)...............................309
Tommy John (1963–74, 1976–89)................288
Bert Blyleven (1970–92) 287

Tony Mullane (1881–84, 1886–94) 285
Gus Weyhing (1887–1901)............................264
Red Faber (1914–33).....................................254
Vic Willis (1898–1910)...................................249
John P. Quinn (1909–15, 1918–33) 247
Jack Powell (1897–1912) 246

200-Game Winners, Never Winning 20 Games in Season

	Career Wins	Most in One Season
Dennis Martinez (1976–98)	245	16 (1978, 1982, 1989, and 1992)
Frank Tanana (1973–93)	240	19 (1976)
Jerry Reuss (1969–90)	220	18 (1975, 1980)
Kenny Rogers (1989–2008)	219	18 (2004)
Charlie Hough (1970–94)	216	18 (1987)
Milt Pappas (1957–73)	209	17 (1971, 1972)
Chuck Finley (1986–2002)	200	18 (1990, 1991)
Tim Wakefield (1991–93, 1995-2011)	200	16(1995, 2005)

Pitchers with 100 Wins and 500 Hits, Career

	Wins	Hits
George Bradley (1875–84, 1886, 1888)	174	523
Charlie Buffinton (1882–93)	231	543
Bob Caruthers (1884–96)	218	694
Dave Foutz (1884–96)	147	1254
Pud Galvin (1875, 1879–92)	361	554
Kid Gleason (1888–1908, 1912)	134	1944
Guy Hecker (1882–90)	177	822
Walter Johnson (1907–27)	417	549
Bobby Mathews (1871–87)	298	505
Win Mercer (1894–1902)	131	502
Tony Mullane (1881–84, 1886–94)	285	661
Old Hoss Radbourn (1880–91)	310	585
Red Ruffing (1924–42, 1945–47)	273	521
Al Spalding (1871–78)	255	620
Jack Stivetts (1889–99)	207	592
Adonis Terry (1884–97)	197	595
Monte Ward (1878–84)	161	2123
Jim Whitney (1881–90)	192	559
Smokey Joe Wood (1908–15, 1917–22)	116	553
Cy Young (1890–1911)	511	623

Victories in Most Consecutive Seasons

Seasons		Seasons	
26	Nolan Ryan, 1968–93	21	Bert Blyleven, 1970–90
24	Roger Clemens, 1984–2007	21	Walter Johnson, 1907–27
24	Don Sutton, 1966–1988	21	Joe Niekro, 1967–87
23	Greg Maddux, 1986–2008	21	Jerry Reuss, 1969–89
23	Jim Kaat, 1960–82	21	Eppa Rixey, 1912–17, 1919–33
23	Dennis Martinez, 1976–98	21	Red Ruffing, 1925–42, 1945–47*
23	Phil Niekro, 1965–87	21	Frank Tanana, 1973–93
22	Steve Carlton, 1966–87	21	David Wells, 1987–2007
22	Charlie Hough, 1973–94	20	Red Faber, 1914–33
22	Randy Johnson, 1989–2009	20	Lindy McDaniel, 1956–75
22	Tom Glavine, 1987–2008	20	Tom Seaver, 1967–86
22	Gaylord Perry, 1962–83	20	Warren Spahn, 1946–65
22	Early Wynn, 1941–44, 1946–63*	20	Kenny Rogers, 1989–2008
22	Cy Young, 1890–1911		

*Missing years were spent in military service.

Most Wins in a Season Without a Complete Game

American League		National League	
20	Roger Clemens, N.Y. Yankees, 2001	19	Roy Oswalt, Hous. Astros, 2002
20	Mike Mussina, N.Y. Yankees, 2008	19	Jake Peavy, S.D. Padres, 2007
18	Roger Clemens, N.Y. Yankees, 2004	18	Roy Face, Pitt. Pirates, 1959
18	Bartolo Colon, Cleve. Indians, 2004	18	Kent Bottenfield, St. L. Cardinals, 1999
18	Daisuke Matsuzaka, Bost. Red Sox, 2008	18	Woody Williams, St. L. Cardinals, 2003
18	Phil Hughes, N.Y. Yankees, 2010	18	Chris Capuano, Milw. Brewers, 2005
17	Bill Campbell, Minn. Twins, 1976	17	Andy Pettitte, Hous. Astros, 2005
17	John Hiller, Det. Tigers, 1974	17	Ted Lilly, Chi. Cubs, 2008
17	Milt Wilcox, Det. Tigers, 1984	17	Edison Volquez, Cin. Reds, 2008
17	C. C. Sabathia, Cleve. Indians, 2001		
17	Kenny Rogers, Det. Tigers, 2006		
17	Tim Wakefield, Bost. Red Sox, 2007		
17	Scott Feldman, Tex. Rangers, 2009		

Most Career Wins by Pitchers Six and a Half Feet Tall or Taller

303	Randy Johnson (1988–2009)	6'10"	171	Rick Sutcliffe (1976, 1978–94)	6'7"
200	Chuck Finley (1986–2002)	6'6"	166	Derek Lowe* (1997–)	6'6"
188	Roy Halladay* (1998–)	6'6"	155	Andy Benes (1989–2002)	6'6"
177	John Candelaria (1975–93)	6'7"	146	Ron Reed (1966–84)	6'6"
176	C. C. Sabathia* (2001–09)	6'7"	144	Chris Carpenter* (1997–)	6'6"

* Still active.

Most Career Wins by Pitchers Under Six Feet Tall

361	Pud Galvin (1875, 1879–92)	5'8"	237	Clark Griffith (1891–1914)	5'6"
361	Kid Nichols (1890–1901, 1904–06)	5'10½"	236	Whitey Ford (1950, 1953–67)	5'10"
341	Tim Keefe (1880–93)	5'10½"	229	Will White (1877–86)	5'9½"
328	John Clarkson (1882, 1884–94)	5'10"	228	George Mullin (1902–15)	5'11"
326	Eddie Plank (1901–17)	5'11½"	223	Hooks Dauss (1912–26)	5'10½"
309	Old Hoss Radbourn (1881–91)	5'9"	219	Pedro Martinez (1992–2009)	5'11"
307	Mickey Welch (1880–92)	5'8"	218	Bob Caruthers (1884–92)	5'7"
284	Tony Mullane (1881–84, 1886–94)	5'10½"	218	Earl Whitehill (1923–39)	5'9½"
270	Burleigh Grimes (1916–34)	5'10"	217	Freddie Fitzsimmons (1925–43)	5'11"

continued on next page

265	Jim McCormick (1878–87)	5'10½"
264	Gus Weyhing (1887–96, 1899–1901)	5'10"
260	Ted Lyons (1923–42, 1946)	5'11"
246	Joe McGinnity (1899–1908)	5'11"
245	Jack Powell (1897–1912)	5'11"
239	Three Finger Brown (1903–16)	5'10"

216	Wilbur Cooper (1912–26)	5'11½"
215	Stan Coveleski (1912, 1916–28)	5'11"
211	Billy Pierce (1945, 1948–64)	5'10"
209	Eddie Cicotte (1905, 1908–20)	5'9"
208	Carl Mays (1915–29)	5'11½"
201	Charlie Root (1923, 1926–41)	5'10½"

Pitchers Winning 20 Games in Season Split Between Two Teams (Post-1900)

Joe McGinnity, 21–18	1902	Balt. Orioles (AL), 13–10	N.Y. Giants (NL), 8–8	
Bob Wicker, 20–9	1903	St. L. Cardinals (NL), 0–0	Chi. Cubs (NL), 20–9	
Patsy Flaherty, 20–11	1904	Chi. White Sox (AL), 1–2	Pitt. Pirates (NL), 19–9	
John Taylor, 20–12	1906	St. L. Cardinals (NL), 8–9	Chi. Cubs (NL), 12–3	
Bobo Newsom, 20–11	1939	St. L. Browns (AL), 3–1	Det. Tigers (AL), 17–10	
Red Barrett, 23–12	1945	Bost. Braves (NL), 2–3	St. L. Cardinals (NL), 21–9	
Hank Borowy, 21–7	1945	N.Y. Yankees (AL), 10–5	Chi. Cubs (NL), 11–2	
Virgil Trucks, 20–10	1953	St. L. Browns (AL), 5–4	Chi. White Sox (AL), 15–6	
Tom Seaver, 21–6	1977	N.Y. Mets (NL), 7–3	Cin. Reds (NL), 14–3	
Rick Sutcliffe, 20–6	1984	Cleve. Indians (AL), 4–5	Chi. Cubs (NL), 16–1	
Bartolo Colon, 20–8	2002	Cleve. Indians (AL), 10–4	Mont. Expos (NL), 10–4	

Pitchers Winning 20 Games with 3 Different Teams

Grover Cleveland Alexander	Phila. Phillies	1911, 1913, 1914, 1915, 1916, 1917
	Chi. Cubs	1920, 1923
	St. L. Cardinals	1927
Roger Clemens	Bost. Red Sox	1986, 1987, 1990
	Tor. Blue Jays	1997, 1998
	N.Y. Yankees	2001
Claude Hendrix	Pitts. Pirates	1912
	Chi. Whales (FL)	1914
	Chi. Cubs	1918
Carl Mays	Bost. Red Sox	1917, 1918
	N.Y. Yankees	1920, 1921
	Cin. Reds	1924
Joe McGinnity	Balt. Orioles	1899, 1901
	Bklyn. Dodgers	1900
	N.Y. Giants	1903, 1904, 1905, 1906
Gaylord Perry	S.F. Giants	1966, 1970
	Cleve. Indians	1972, 1974
	S.D. Padres	1978
Cy Young	Cleve. Spiders	1891–98
	St. L. Cardinals	1899
	Bost. Red Sox	1901–04, 1907

Oldest Pitchers to Win 20 Games for First Time

American League	Age	Wins–Losses	National League (Post-1899)	Age	Wins–Losses
Mike Mussina, N.Y. Yankees, 2008	39	20–9	Curt Davis, St. L. Cardinals, 1939	36	22–16
Jamie Moyer, Sea. Mariners, 2001	38	20–6	Rip Sewell, Pitt. Pirates, 1943	36	21–9

Allie Reynolds, N.Y. Yankees, 1952.........37 20–8
David Wells, Tor. Blue Jays, 2000 ....37 20–8
Spud Chandler, N.Y. Yankees, 1943........36 20–4
Thorton Lee, Chi. White Sox, 1941 ....35........22–11
Dick Donovan, Cleve. Indians, 1962........35......20–10☐
Earl Whitehill, Wash. Senators, 1933......34 22–8
Roger Wolff, Wash. Senators, 1945 ....34........20–10
Rube Walberg, Phil. Athletics, 1931 ....34........20–12

Preacher Roe, Bklyn. Dodgers, 1951 ......36............22–3
Murray Dickson, Pitt. Pirates, 1951 ....35.........20–16
Slim Sallee, Cin. Reds, 1919 ....34............21–7
Jim Turner, Bost. Braves, 1937 ....34.........20–11
Whit Wyatt, Bklyn. Dodgers, 1941........34.........22–10
Sal Maglie, N.Y. Giants, 1951..............34............23–6
Sal Maglie, N.Y. Giants, 1951..............34............23–6
Sam Jones, S.F. Giants, 1959 ....34.........21–15
Tommy John, L.A. Dodgers, 1977..........34............20–7
Joe Niekro, Hous. Astros, 1979 ....34.........21–11
Mike Krukow, S.F. Giants, 1986.............34............20–9

Youngest Pitchers to Win 20 Games

American League

	Age	Wins–Losses
Bob Feller, Cleve. Indians, 1939	20 years, 10 months	24–9
Bret Saberhagen, K. C. Royals, 1985	21 years, 5 months	20–6
Babe Ruth, Bost. Red Sox, 1916	21 years, 7 months	23–12
Wes Ferrell, Cleve. Indians, 1929	21 years, 8 months	21–10
Bob Feller, Cleve. Indians, 1980	21 years, 10 months	27–11

National League (Post-1900)

	Age	Wins–Losses
Dwight Gooden, N.Y. Mets, 1985	20 years, 10 months	24–4
Christy Mathewson, N. Y. Giants, 1901	20 years, 1 month	20–17
Al Mamaux, Pitt. Pirates, 1915	21 years, 4 months	21–8
Ralph Branca, Bklyn. Dodgers, 1947	21 years, 9 months	21–12
Nick Maddox, Pitts. Pirates, 1908	21 years, 10 months	23–8

Rookies Winning 20 Games

American League

Roscoe Miller, Det. Tigers, 1901 23–13
Roy Patterson, Chi. White Sox, 1901 20–16
Ed Summers, Det. Tigers, 1908.................24–12
Russ Ford, N.Y. Yankees, 1910.................26–6
Vean Gregg, Cleve. Indians, 1911 23–7
Reb Russell, Chi. White Sox, 1913.............21–17
Scott Perry, Phila. A's, 1918 21–19
Wes Ferrell, Cleve. Indians, 1929 21–10
Monte Weaver, Wash. Senators, 1932 22–10
Dave "Boo" Ferriss, Bost. Red Sox, 1945.....21–10
Gene Bearden, Cleve. Indians, 1948...........20–7
Alex Kellner, Phila. A's, 1949 20–12
Bob Grim, N.Y. Yankees, 1954............ 20–6

National League (Post-1900)

Christy Mathewson, N.Y. Giants, 1901......................20–17
Henry Schmidt, Bklyn. Bridegrooms, 1903.................21–13
Jake Weimer, Chi. Cubs, 1903 21–9
Irv Young, Bost. Braves, 1905.................................20–21
George McQuillan, Phila. Phillies, 1908....................23–17
King Cole, Chi. Cubs, 1910 20–4
Grover C. Alexander, Phila. Phillies, 1911.................28–13
Larry Cheney, Chi. Cubs, 1912 26–10
Jeff Pfeffer, Bklyn. Dodgers, 1914 23–12
Lou Fette, Bost. Braves, 1937..................................20–10
Cliff Melton, N.Y. Giants, 1937 20–9
Jim Turner, Bost. Braves, 1937................................20–11
Johnny Beazley, St. L. Cardinals, 1942......................21–6
Bill Voiselle, N.Y. Giants, 1944................................21–16
Larry Jansen, N.Y. Giants, 1947...............................21–5
Harvey Haddix, St. L. Cardinals, 1953......................20–9
Tom Browning, Cin. Reds, 1985...............................20–9

Most Seasons Logged Before First 20-Win Season

Seasons		20-Win Season
18	Mike Mussina (1991–2008)*	20–9 in 2008
14	Tommy John (1963–74, 1976–89)	20–7 in 1977
14	Jamie Moyer (1986–91, 1993–)	20–6 in 2001
13	Red Ruffing (1924–42, 1945–47)	20–12 in 1936
13	David Wells (1987–2007)	20–8 in 2000
12	Slim Sallee (1908–21)	21–7 in 1919
12	Lee Meadows (1915–29)	20–9 in 1926
12	Whit Wyatt (1929–45)	22–10 in 1941
11	Wee Willie Sherdel (1918–32)	21–10 in 1928
11	Earl Whitehill (1923–39)	22–8 in 1933
11	Early Wynn (1939, 1941–44, 1946–63)	20–13 in 1951
11	Allie Reynolds (1942–54)	20–8 in 1952
10	Mike Krukow (1976–89)	20–9 in 1986
9	Rube Walberg (1923–37)	20–12 in 1931
9	Preacher Roe (1938, 1944–54)	??–?? in 1951

Rookie Pitchers with 20 Wins and 200 Strikeouts

	Wins–Losses	Strikeouts
Christy Mathewson, N.Y. Giants (NL), 1901	20–17	221
Russ Ford, N.Y. Yankees (AL), 1910	26–6	209
Grover C. Alexander, Phila. Phillies (NL), 1911	28–13	227

Pitchers Winning 20 Games in Rookie Year, Fewer Than 20 Balance of Career

	Rookie Year	Career
Roscoe Miller, Det. Tigers (AL) (1901–04)	23–13 (1901)	39–46
Henry Schmidt, Bklyn. Bridegrooms (NL) (1903)	21–13 (1903)	21–13
Johnny Beazley, St. L. Cardinals (NL) (1941–42, 1946–49)	21–6 (1942)	31–12

20-Game Winners Who Didn't Win 20 More Games in Career (Post-1900)

Roscoe Miller, Det. Tigers (AL) (1901–04)	23 wins (1901)	16 rest of career
Henry Schmidt, Bklyn. Bridegrooms (NL) (1903)	21 wins (1903)	0 rest of career
Buck O'Brien, Bost. Red Sox (AL) (1911–13)	20 wins (1912)	9 rest of career
Bill James, Bost. Braves (NL) (1913–15, 1919)	26 wins (1914)	11 rest of career
George McConnell, Chi. Whales (FL) (1909, 1912–16)	25 wins (1915)	16 rest of career
Johnny Beazley, St. L. Cardinals (NL) (1941–42, 1946–49)	21 wins (1942)	10 rest of career
Mike Mussina, N.Y. Yankees (AL) (2001–08)*	20 wins (2008)	0 rest of career

Bolit Oroler (AL), (1991–2000),R
* Retired after 2008 season

Pitchers Winning 20 Games in Last Season in Majors

Mike Mussina, N.Y. Yankees (AL), 2008	20–9	Henry Schmidt, Bklyn. Dodgers (NL), 1903	21–13
Eddie Cicotte, Chi. White Sox (AL), 1920	21–10	Lefty Williams, Chi. White Sox (AL), 1920	22–14
Sandy Koufax, L.A. Dodgers (NL), 1966	27–9		

Earliest 20-Game Winner During Season
American League

		Final Record
July 25, 1931	Lefty Grove, Phila. Athletics	31–4

July 27, 1968 ....Denny McLain, Det. Tigers 31–6

National League

	Final Record
July 19, 1912.............................Rube Marquard, N.Y. Giants..26–11

Most Wins After Turning 40

		Total Career Wins				Total Career Wins
121	Phil Niekro	318		71	Nolan Ryan	324
103	Jamie Moyer*	267		67	Charlie Hough	216
96	John Picus Quinn	247		61	Roger Clemens	354
75	Cy Young	511		54	David Wells	239
75	Warren Spahn	363		54	Hoyt Wilhelm	143
73	Randy Johnson	303				

*Still active.

Pitchers on Losing Teams, Leading League in Wins

American League

Pitcher	Wins–Losses	Team Record
Walter Johnson, Wash. Senators, 1916	25–20	76–77
Eddie Rommel, Phila. A's, 1922	27–13	65–89
Ted Lyons, Chi. White Sox, 1927	22–14	70–83
Bob Feller, Cleve. Indians, 1941	25–13	75–79
Bob Feller, Cleve. Indians, 1946	26–15	68–86
Jim Perry, Cleve. Indians, 1960	18–10	76–78
Gaylord Perry, Cleve. Indians, 1972	24–16	72–84
Wilbur Wood, Chi. White Sox, 1973	24–20	77–85
Roger Clemens, Bost. Red Sox, 1987	20–9	78–84
Kevin Brown, Tex. Rangers, 1992	21–11	77–85
Roger Clemens, Tor. Blue Jays, 1997	21–7	76–86

National League (Post-1900)

Pitcher	Wins–Losses	Team Record
Grover C. Alexander, Phila. Phillies, 1914	27–15	74–80
Grover C. Alexander, Chi. Cubs, 1920	27–14	75–79
Dazzy Vance, Bklyn. Dodgers, 1925	22–9	68–85
Jumbo Elliott, Phila. Phillies, 1931	19–14 (Tie)	66–88
Heine Meine, Pitt. Pirates, 1931	19–13 (Tie)	75–79
Ewell Blackwell, Cin. Reds, 1947	22–8	73–81
Warren Spahn, Bost. Braves, 1949	21–14	75–79
Robin Roberts, Phila. Phillies, 1954	23–15	75–79
Larry Jackson, Chi. Cubs, 1964	24–11	76–86
Bob Gibson, St. L. Cardinals, 1970	23–7	76–86
Steve Carlton, Phila. Phillies, 1972	27–10	59–97
Randy Jones, S.D. Padres, 1976	22–14	73–89
Phil Niekro, Atl. Braves, 1979	21–20	66–94
Fernando Valenzuela, L.A. Dodgers, 1986	21–11	73–89
Rick Sutcliffe, Chi. Cubs, 1987	18–10	76–85
Greg Maddux, Chi. Cubs, 1992	20–11	78–84
Brandon Webb, Ariz. D'backs, 2006	16–8	76–86

20-Game Winners on Last-Place Teams

American League

Pitcher	Wins–Losses	Team Record
Scott Perry, Phila. A's, 1918	20–19	52–76

Howard Ehmke, Bost. Red Sox, 1923............................20–17 61–91
Sloppy Thurston, Chi. White Sox, 1924 ....20–14 66–87
Ned Garver, St. L. Browns, 1951 ....20–12 52–102
Nolan Ryan, Cal. Angels, 1974 ....22–16 68–94
Roger Clemens, Tor. Blue Jays, 1997 ....21–7 76–86

National League (Post-1900)

Pitcher	Wins–Losses	Team Record
Noodles Hahn, Cin. Reds, 1901	22–19	52–87
Steve Carlton, Phila. Phillies, 1972	27–10	59–97
Phil Niekro, Atl. Braves, 1979	21–20	66–94

20-Game Winners with Worst Lifetime Winning Percentage (Post-1900)

	Percentage	Lifetime	20-Win Season(s)
Scott Perry	.376	41–68	1918
Irv Young	.397	62–94	1905
Pete Schneider	.399	57–86	1917
Ben Cantwell	.413	76–108	1933
Joe Oeschger	.417	83–116	1921
Tom Hughes	.427	128–172	1903
Willie Sudhoff	.430	102–135	1903
Roger Wolff	.430	52–69	1945
Frank Allen	.431	50–66	1915
Otto Hess	.434	69–90	1906
Bob Harmon	.436	103–133	1911
Al Schulz	.440	48–61	1915
Vem Kennedy	.441	104–132	1936
Patsy Flaherty	.443	66–83	1904
Bob Groom	.446	121–150	1912
Oscar Jones	.446	45–56	1903
Randy Jones	.448	100–123	1975, 1976
Ned Garver	.451	129–157	1951
George McConnell	.452	42–51	1915
Chick Fraser	.454	176–212	1901

"Pure" 20-Game Winners (Pitchers with 20 or More Wins Than Losses)

American League

Cy Young, Bost. Americans, 1901............................33–10
Cy Young, Bost. Americans, 1902............................32–11
Jack Chesbro, N.Y. Highlanders, 1904....................41–12
Ed Walsh, Chi. White Sox, 1908..............................40–15
George Mullin, Det. Tigers, 1909 29–8
Jack Coombs, Phila. A's, 1910 31–9
Russ Ford, N.Y. Highlanders, 1910.........................26–6
Smokey Joe Wood, Bost. Red Sox, 1912 34–5
Walter Johnson, Wash. Senators, 1912.....................32–12
Eddie Plank, Phila. A's, 1912 26–6
Walter Johnson, Wash. Senators, 1913.....................36–7
Eddie Cicotte, Chi. White Sox, 1919.........................29–7
Lefty Grove, Phila. A's, 1930 28–5
Lefty Grove, Phila. A's, 1931 31–4
Lefty Gomez, N.Y. Yankees, 1934...........................26–5
Hal Newhouser, Det. Tigers, 1944 29–9

National League (Post-1900)

Joe McGinnity, Bklyn. Bridegrooms, 1900..................29–9
Jack Chesbro, Pitt. Pirates, 1902.............................28–6
Joe McGinnity, N.Y. Giants, 1904............................35–8
Christy Mathewson, N.Y. Giants, 1904......................33–12
Christy Mathewson, N.Y. Giants, 1905 31–8
Three Finger Brown, Chi. Cubs, 1906 26–6
Three Finger Brown, Chi. Cubs, 1908 29–9
Christy Mathewson, N.Y. Giants, 1908......................37–11
Grover C. Alexander, Phila. Phillies, 1914.................31–10
Grover C. Alexander, Phila. Phillies, 1916.................33–12
Dazzy Vance, Bklyn. Dodgers, 1923.........................28–6
Dizzy Dean, St. L. Cardinals, 1934...........................30–7
Carl Hubbell, N.Y. Giants, 1935 26–6
Robin Roberts, Phila. Phillies, 1951..........................28–7
Don Newcombe, Bklyn. Dodgers, 1955.....................27–7
Sandy Koufax, L.A. Dodgers, 1962...........................25–5

Whitey Ford, N.Y. Yankees, 1961 25–4

Denny McLain, Det. Tigers, 1968..............................31–6

Ron Guidry, N.Y. Yankees, 1978 25–3

Roger Clemens, Bost. Red Sox, 1986 24–4

Dwight Gooden, N.Y. Mets, 1985..............................24–4

Lefties Winning 20 Games Twice Since World War II

American League

Vida Blue	Oakland A's	1971	24
	Oakland A's	1973	20
	Oakland A's	1975	22
Mike Cuellar	Balt. Orioles	1969	23
	Balt. Orioles	1970	24
	Balt. Orioles	1974	22
Whitey Ford	N.Y. Yankees	1961	25
	N.Y. Yankees	1963	24
Ron Guidry	N.Y. Yankees	1978	25
	N.Y. Yankees	1983	21
	N.Y. Yankees	1985	22
Tommy John*	N.Y. Yankees	1979	21
	N.Y. Yankees	1980	22
Jim Kaat	Minn. Twins	1966	25
	Chi. White Sox	1974	21
	Chi. White Sox	1975	20
Mickey Lolich	Det. Tigers	1971	25
	Det. Tigers	1972	22
Dave McNally	Balt. Orioles	1968	22
	Balt. Orioles	1969	20
	Balt. Orioles	1970	24
	Balt. Orioles	1971	21
Jamie Moyer	Sea. Mariners	2001	21
	Sea. Mariners	2003	21
Hal Newhouser	Det. Tigers	1946	26
	Det. Tigers	1948	21
Mel Parnell	Bost. Red Sox	1949	25
	Bost. Red Sox	1953	21
Andy Pettitte	N.Y. Yankees	1996	21
	N.Y. Yankees	2003	21
Billy Pierce	Chi. White Sox	1956	20
	Chi. White Sox	1957	20
Wilbur Wood	Chi. White Sox	1971	22
	Chi. White Sox	1972	24
	Chi. White Sox	1973	24
	Chi. White Sox	1974	20

National League

Johnny Antonelli	N.Y. Giants	1954	21
	N.Y. Giants	1956	20
Steve Carlton	St. L. Cardinals	1971	20
	Phila. Phillies	1972	27
	Phila. Phillies	1976	20
	Phila. Phillies	1977	23
	Phila. Phillies	1980	24
	Phila. Phillies	1982	23

continued on next page

Tom Glavine	Atl. Braves	1991	20
	Atl. Braves	1992	20
	Atl. Braves	1993	22
	Atl. Braves	1998	20
	Atl. Braves	2000	21

National League

Randy Johnson**	Ariz. D'backs	2001	21
	Ariz. D'backs	2002	24
Randy Jones	S.D. Padres	1975	20
	S.D. Padres	1976	22
Sandy Koufax	L.A. Dodgers	1963	25
	L.A. Dodgers	1965	26
	L.A. Dodgers	1966	27
Claude Osteen	L.A. Dodgers	1969	20
	L.A. Dodgers	1972	20
Howie Pollet	St. L. Cardinals	1946	21
	St. L. Cardinals	1949	20
Warren Spahn	Bost. Braves	1947	21
	Bost. Braves	1949	21
	Bost. Braves	1950	21
	Bost. Braves	1951	22
	Milw. Braves	1953	23
	Milw. Braves	1954	21
	Milw. Braves	1956	20
	Milw. Braves	1957	21
	Milw. Braves	1958	22
	Milw. Braves	1959	21
	Milw. Braves	1960	21
	Milw. Braves	1961	21
	Milw. Braves	1963	23

*Also won 20 games in 1977 with the L.A. Dodgers.
**Also won 20 games in 1997 with the Sea. Mariners

Pitchers with 20-Win Seasons After Age 40

		Age	Season	Wins–Losses
Grover C. Alexander	St. L. Cardinals (NL)	40	1927	21–10
Jamie Moyer*	Sea. Mariners (AL)	40	2003	21–7
Phil Niekro	Atl. Braves (NL)	40	1979	21–20
Gaylord Perry	S.D. Padres (NL)	40	1978	21–6
Eddie Plank	St. L. Terriers (FL)	40	1915	21–11
Warren Spahn	Milw. Braves (NL)	40	1961	21–13
	Milw. Braves (NL)	42	1963	23–7
Cy Young	Bost. Americans (AL)	40	1907	21–15
	Bost. Americans (AL)	41	1908	21–11

*Still active.

Pitchers Leading Both Leagues in Wins, Season

American League			National League		
Jack Chesbro	N.Y. Highlanders, 1904	41–13	Pitt. Pirates, 1902		28–6
Roy Halladay	Tor. Blue Jays, 2003	22–7	Phila. Phillies, 2010		21–10
Ferguson Jenkins	Tex. Rangers, 1974	25–12 (Tie)	Chi. Cubs, 1971		24–13
Gaylord Perry	Cleve. Indians, 1972	24–16 (Tie)	S.F. Giants, 1970		23–13 (Tie)
			S.D. Padres, 1978		21–6

Curt Schilling.........Bost. Red Sox, 2004 ....21–6.............Ariz. D'backs, 2001 22–6
Cy Young ....Bost. Americans, 1901 ....33–10.............Cleve. Spiders, 1892 ....36–12 (Tie)
                      Bost. Americans, 1902 ....32–11.............Cleve. Spiders, 1895 35–10
                      Bost. Americans, 1903 28–9

20-Game Winners One Season, 20-Game Losers the Next

American League

George Mullin, Det. Tigers ....21–18 (1906)...20–20 (1907)
Al Orth, N.Y. Highlanders ....27–17 (1906)..27–21 (1907)
Russ Ford, N.Y. Highlanders....................................22–11 (1911)..13–21 (1912)
Walter Johnson, Wash. Senators ....27–13 (1915)..25–20 (1916)
Hooks Dauss, Det. Tigers ....21–9 (1919)...13–21 (1920)
Bobo Newsom, Det. Tigers ....21–5 (1940)...12–20 (1941)
Alex Kellner, Phila. A's...20–12 (1949)...8–20 (1950)
Mel Stottlemyre, N.Y. Yankees ....20–9 (1965)...12–20 (1966)
Luis Tiant, Cleve. Indians ....21–9 (1968)...9–20 (1969)
Stan Bahnsen, Chi. White Sox.................................21–16 (1972)..18–21 (1973)
Wilbur Wood, Chi. White Sox.................................24–17 (1972)..24–20 (1973)
Wilbur Wood, Chi. White Sox.................................20–19 (1974)..16–20 (1975)

National League (Post-1900)

Joe McGinnity, Bklyn. Bridegrooms (NL), Balt. Orioles (AL)............28–8 (1900).............................26–20 (1901)
Vic Willis, Bost. Braves....................................20–17 (1901)..27–20 (1902)
Togie Pittinger, Bost. Braves................................27–16 (1902)..18–22 (1903)
Jack Taylor, St. L. Cardinals................................20–19 (1904)..15–21 (1905)
Irv Young, Bost. Braves.....................................20–21 (1905)..16–25 (1906)
Nap Rucker, Bklyn. Dodgers................................22–18 (1911)..18–21 (1912)
Rube Marquard, N.Y. Giants................................23–10 (1913)..12–22 (1914)
Eppa Rixey, Phila. Phillies ....22–10 (1916)..16–21 (1917)
Joe Oeschger, Bost. Braves.................................20–14 (1921)...6–21 (1922)
Murray Dickson, Pitt. Pirates...............................20–16 (1951)..14–21 (1952)
Larry Jackson, Chi. Cubs ....24–11 (1964)..14–21 (1965)
Steve Carlton, Phila. Phillies ....27–10 (1972)..13–20 (1973)
Jerry Koosman, N.Y. Mets..................................21–10 (1976)...8–20 (1977)

20-Game Winners and Losers, Same Season

American League

Joe McGinnity, Balt. Orioles, 1901 26–20
Bill Dineen, Bost. Americans, 1902 21–21
George Mullin, Det. Tigers, 1905 21–21
George Mullin, Det. Tigers, 1907 20–20
Jim Scott, Chi. White Sox, 1913................................20–20
Walter Johnson, Wash. Senators, 1916.........................25–20
Wilbur Wood, Chi. White Sox, 1973 24–20

National League (Post-1900)

Vic Willis, Bost. Braves, 1902 27–20
Joe McGinnity, N.Y. Giants, 1903............................31–20
Irv Young, Bost. Braves, 1905...................................20–21
Phil Niekro, Atl. Braves, 1979 21–20

Pitchers Who Led League in Wins in Successive Seasons

American League

Seasons
 4 ....Walter Johnson, Wash, Senators, 1913–16

National League

Seasons
 5 ....Warren Spahn, Milw. Braves, 1957–61

continued on next page

3...........................Cy Young, Bost. Americans, 1901–03

4..............Grover C. Alexander, Phila. Phillies, 1914–17

American League

National League

Seasons

3..............................Bob Feller, Cleve. Indians, 1939–41
3.........................Hal Newhouser, Det. Tigers, 1944–46
3.............................Jim Palmer, Balt. Orioles, 1975–77
2..............................Jack Coombs, Phila A's, 1910–11
2.....................................Lefty Grove, Phila A's, 1930–31
2.................General Crowder, Wash. Senators, 1932–33
2..............................Bob Feller, Cleve. Indians, 1946–47
2...........................Bob Lemon, Cleve. Indians, 1954–55
2...........................Denny McLain, Det. Tigers, 1968–69
2.....................Wilbur Wood, Chi. White Sox, 1972–73
2........................Catfish Hunter, Oak. A's, 1974–75
2.......................La Marr Hoyt, Chi. White Sox, 1982–83
2.......................Roger Clemens, Bost. Red Sox, 1986–87
2.......................Roger Clemens, Tor. Blue Jays, 1997–98
2.........................C. C. Sabathia, N.Y. Yankees, 2009–10

Seasons

4........................Robin Roberts, Phila. Phillies, 1952–55
3............................Bill Hutchison, Chi. Colts, 1890–92
3...........................Kid Nichols, Bost. Braves, 1896–98
3...........................Tom Glavine, Atl. Braves, 1991–93
2..................Tommy Bond, Bos. Red Caps, 1877–78
2.............Old Hoss Radbourn, Prov. Grays, 1883–84
2..................Joe McGinnity, Balt. Orioles, 1899–1900
2........................Joe McGinnity, N.Y. Giants, 1903–04
2..................Christy Mathewson, N.Y. Giants, 1907–08
2....................Dazzy Vance, Bklyn. Dodgers, 1924–25
2.........................Pat Malone, Chi. Cubs, 1929–30
2.........................Dizzy Dean, St. L. Cardinals, 1934–35
2.....................Carl Hubbell, N.Y. Giants, 1936–37
2.......................Bucky Walters, Cin. Reds, 1939–40
2..................Mort Cooper, St. L. Cardinals, 1942–43
2.......................Warren Spahn, Bost. Braves, 1949–50
2.....................Sandy Koufax, L.A. Dodgers, 1965–66
2............................Greg Maddux, Atl. Braves, 1994–95

Most Pitching Wins for One Season

Pitcher	Wins	Year	Team
Old Hoss Radbourn	59	1884	Prov. Grays (NL)
John Clarkson	53	1885	Chi. White Stockings (NL)
Guy Hecker	52	1884	Loui. Colonels (AA)
John Clarkson	49	1889	Bost. Beaneaters (NL)
Charlie Buffinton	48	1884	Bost. Beaneaters (NL)
Old Hoss Radbourn	48	1883	Prov. Grays (NL)
Al Spalding	47	1876	Chi. White Stockings (NL)
John Ward	47	1879	Prov. Grays (NL)
Pud Galvin	46	1884	Buff. Bisons (NL)
Pud Galvin	46	188	Buff. Bisons (NL)
Matt Kilroy	46	1887	Balt. Orioles (AA)
George Bradley	45	1876	St. L. Brown Stockings (NL)
Silver King	45	1888	St. L. Browns (AA)
Jim McCormick	45	1880	Cleve. Blues (NL)
Bill Hutchinson	44	1891	Chi. Colts (NL)
Mickey Welch	44	1885	N.Y. Giants (NL)
Tommy Bond	43	1897	Bost. Red Caps (NL)
Larry Corcoran	43	1880	Chi. White Stockings (NL)
Billy Taylor	43	1884	Phila. Athletics (AA) St. L. Maroons (UA)
Will White	43	1879	Cin. Reds (NL)
Will White	43	1883	Cin. Red Stockings (AA)
Lady Baldwin	42	1886	Det. Wolverines (NL)
Bill Hutchinson	42	1890	Chi. Colts (NL)
Tim Keefe	42	1886	N.Y. Giants (NL)
Jack Chesbro	41	1904	N.Y. Highlanders (AL)

Dave Foutz	41	1886	St. L. Browns (AA)
Tim Keefe	41	1883	N.Y. Metropolitans (AA)
Ed Morris	41	1886	Pitt. Alleghenys (AA)
Charlie Sweeney	41	1884	Prov. Grays (NL)
			St. L. Maroons (UA)
Tommy Bond	40	1877	Bost. Red Caps (NL)
Tommy Bond	40	1878	Bost. Red Caps (NL)
Bob Caruthers	40	1885	St. L. Browns (AA)
Bob Caruthers	40	1889	Bklyn. Bridegrooms (AA)
Jim McCormick	40	1884	Cleve. Blues (NL)
			Cin. Outlaw Reds (UA)
Bill Sweeney	40	1884	Balt. Monumentals (UA)
Ed Walsh	40	1908	Chi. White Sox (AL)
Will White	40	1882	Cin. Red Stockings (AA)

Most Total Wins, Two Pitchers on Same Staff, Career Together as Teammates

American League

440	Eddie Plank (247) and Chief Bender (193), Phila. A's (1903–14)
408	Lefty Grove (257) and Rube Walberg (151), Phila. A's (1925–33) and Bost. Red Sox (1934–37)
408	Red Ruffing (219) and Lefty Gomez (189), N.Y. Yankees (1930–42)
361	Hal Newhouser (200) and Dizzy Trout (161), Det. Tigers (1939–52)
355	Bob Lemon (201) and Bob Feller (154), Cleve. Indians (1946–56)
349	Early Wynn (177) and Bob Lemon (172), Cleve. Indians (1949–58)
332	Ed Walsh (190) and Doc White (142), Chi. White Sox (1904–13)
331	Bob Lemon (192) and Mike Garcia (139), Cleve. Indians (1948–58)

National League

443	Warren Spahn (264) and Lew Burdette (179), Bost./Milw. Braves (1951–63)
433	Christy Mathewson (297) and Hooks Wiltse (136), N.Y. Giants (1904–14)
358	Carl Hubbell (204) and Hal Schumacher (154), N.Y. Giants (1931–42)
347	Greg Maddux (178) and Tom Glavine (169), Atl. Braves (1993–2002)
342	Christy Mathewson (191) and Joe McGinnity (151), N.Y. Giants (1902–08)
340	Sam Leever (172) and Deacon Phillippe (168), Pitt. Pirates (1900–10)
340	Don Drysdale (177) and Sandy Koufax (163), Bklyn./L.A. Dodgers (1956–66)
336	Juan Marichal (202) and Gaylord Perry (134), S.F. Giants (1962–71)
326	Robin Roberts (212) and Curt Simmons (114), Phila. Phillies (1948–50, 1952–60)
318	Three Finger Brown (182) and Ed Reulbach (136), Chi. Cubs (1905–13)
317	Bob Friend (176) and Vern Law (141), Pitt. Pirates (1951, 1954–65)

Most Wins, Right-Hander and Left-Hander on Same Staff, Season

American League

58	Ed Walsh (RH, 40) and Doc White (LH, 18), Chi. White Sox, 1908
56	Hal Newhouser (RH, 29) and Dizzy Trout (LH, 27), Det. Tigers, 1944
53	Walter Johnson (RH, 36) and Joe Boehling (LH, 17), Wash. Senators, 1913
52	Eddie Cicotte (RH, 29) and Lefty Williams (LH, 23), Chi. White Sox, 1919
52	Lefty Grove (LH, 31) and George Earnshaw (RH, 21), Phila. A's, 1931
51	Doc White (LH, 27) and Ed Walsh (RH, 24), Chi. White Sox, 1907
51	Jack Coombs (RH, 28) and Eddie Plank (LH, 23), Phila. A's, 1911
50	Ed Killian (LH, 25) and Bill Donovan (RH, 25), Det. Tigers, 1907

continued on next page

50 ....Lefty Grove (LH, 28) and George Earnshaw (RH, 22), Phila. A's, 1930

American League

48 ....Mel Parnell (LH, 25) and Ellis Kinder (RH, 23), Bost. Red Sox, 1949
48 ....Denny McLain (RH, 31) and Mickey Lolich (LH, 17), Det. Tigers, 1968
47 ....Cy Young (RH, 26) and Jesse Tannehill (LH, 21), Bost. Red Sox, 1904
47 ....Jack Coombs (RH, 31) and Eddie Plank (LH, 16), Phila. A's, 1910
47 ....Smokey Joe Wood (RH, 34) and Ray Collins, (LH, 13), Bost. Red Sox, 1912
47 ....Eddie Plank (LH, 26) and Jack Coombs (RH, 21), Phila. A's, 1912
46 ....Babe Ruth (LH, 24) and Carl Mays (RH, 22), Bost. Red Sox, 1917
46 ....General Crowder (RH, 24) and Earl Whitehill (LH, 22), Wash. Senators, 1933
46 ....Hooks Dauss (RH, 24) and Harry Coveleski (LH, 22), Det. Tigers, 1915

National League (Post-1900)

60 ....Christy Mathewson (RH, 37) and Hooks Wiltse (LH, 23), N.Y. Giants, 1908
55 ....Grover C. Alexander (RH, 33) and Eppa Rixey (LH, 22), Phila. Phillies, 1916
50 ....Christy Mathewson (RH, 26) and Rube Marquard (LH, 24), N.Y. Giants, 1911
49 ....Rube Marquard (LH, 26) and Christy Mathewson (RH, 23), N.Y. Giants, 1912
49 ....Sandy Koufax (LH, 26) and Don Drysdale (RH, 23), L.A. Dodgers, 1965
48 ....Jack Chesbro (RH, 28) and Jesse Tannehill (LH, 20), Pitt. Pirates, 1902
48 ....Joe McGinnity (RH, 35) and Hooks Wiltse (LH, 13), N.Y. Giants, 1904
48 ....Christy Mathewson (RH, 25) and Rube Marquard (LH, 23), N.Y. Giants, 1913
47 ....Randy Johnson (LH, 24) and Curt Schilling (RH, 23), Ariz. D'backs, 2002
47 ....Dolf Luque (RH, 27) and Eppa Rixey (LH, 20), Cin. Reds, 1923
46 ....Christy Mathewson (RH, 31) and Hooks Wiltse (LH, 15), N.Y. Giants, 1905
46 ....Three Finger Brown (RH, 26) and Jack Pfiester (LH, 20), Chi. Cubs, 1906
46 ....Grover C. Alexander (RH, 30) and Eppa Rixey (LH, 16), Phila. Phillies, 1917
46 ....Grover C. Alexander (RH, 27) and Hippo Vaughn (LH, 19), Chi. Cubs, 1920

Largest Differential Between League Leader in Wins and Runner-Up

American League

Differential		Leader	Runner(s)-Up
+16	1908	Ed Walsh, Chi. White Sox (40)	Addie Joss, Cleve. Indians (24)
			Ed Summers, Det. Tigers (24)
+15	1904	Jack Chesbro, N.Y. Yankees (41)	Eddie Plank, Phila. A's (26)
			Cy Young, Bost. Americans (26)
+13	1913	Walter Johnson, Wash. Senators (36)	Cy Falkenberg, Cleve. Indians (23)
+9	1931	Lefty Grove, Phila. A's (31)	Wes Ferrell, Cleve. Indians (22)
+9	1968	Denny McLain, Det. Tigers (31)	Dave McNally, Balt. Orioles (22)
+8	1902	Cy Young, Bost. Americans (32)	Rube Waddell, Phila. A's (24)

National League (Post-1900)

+10	1952	Robin Roberts, Phila. Phillies (28)	Sal Maglie, N.Y. Giants (18)
+9	1915	Grover C. Alexander, Phila. Phillies (31)	Dick Rudolph, Bost. Braves (22)
+8	1900	Joe McGinnity, Bklyn. Bridegrooms (28)	Bill Dineen, Bost. Braves (20)
			Brickyard Kennedy, Bklyn. Dodgers (20)
			Deacon Phillippe, Pitt. Pirates (20)
			Jesse Tannehill, Pitt. Pirates (20)
+8	1905	Christy Mathewson, N.Y. Giants (31)	Togie Pittinger, Phila. Phillies (23)
+8	1908	Christy Mathewson, N.Y. Giants (37)	Three Finger Brown, Chi. Cubs (29)
+8	1916	Grover C. Alexander, Phila. Phillies (33)	Jeff Pfeffer, Bklyn. Dodgers (25)

Highest Percentage of Team's Total Wins for Season

American League

45.6%	Jack Chesbro (N.Y. Highlanders, 1904)	41 of team's 92 wins
45.5%	Ed Walsh (Chi. White Sox, 1908)	40 of team's 88 wins
41.8%	Cy Young (Bost. Americans, 1901)	33 of team's 79 wins
41.7%	Joe Bush (Phila. A's, 1916)	15 of team's 36 wins
41.6%	Cy Young (Bost. Red Sox, 1902)	32 of team's 77 wins
41.5%	Eddie Rommel (Phila. A's, 1922)	27 of team's 65 wins
40.3%	Red Faber (Chi. White Sox, 1921)	25 of team's 62 wins
40.0%	Walter Johnson (Wash. Senators, 1913)	36 of team's 90 wins
39.1%	Walter Johnson (Wash. Senators, 1911)	25 of team's 64 wins
38.9%	Elmer Myers (Phila. A's, 1916)	14 of team's 36 wins
38.5%	Ned Garver (St. L. Browns, 1951)	20 of team's 52 wins
38.5%	Scott Perry (Phila. A's, 1918)	20 of team's 52 wins
38.2%	Joe McGinnity, (Balt. Orioles, 1901)	26 of team's 68 wins
38.2%	Bob Feller (Cleve. Indians, 1946)	26 of team's 68 wins
37.9%	Walter Johnson (Wash. Senators, 1910)	25 of team's 66 wins

National League (Post-1900)

45.8%	Steve Carlton (Phila. Phillies, 1972)	27 of team's 39 wins
42.3%	Noodles Hahn (Cin. Reds, 1901)	22 of team's 52 wins
39.2%	Irv Young (Bost. Braves, 1905)	20 of team's 51 wins
38.5%	Christy Mathewson (N.Y. Giants, 1901)	20 of team's 52 wins
37.8%	Christy Mathewson (N.Y. Giants, 1908)	37 of team's 98 wins
37.3%	Slim Sallee (St. L. Cardinals, 1913)	19 of team's 51 wins
37.0%	Togie Pittinger (Bost. Braves, 1902)	27 of team's 73 wins
37.0%	Vic Willis (Bost. Braves, 1902)	27 of team's 73 wins
36.9%	Joe McGinnity (N.Y. Giants, 1903)	31 of team's 84 wins

300-Game Winners with Fewer Than 200 Losses

Differential		Wins	Losses
+185	Christy Mathewson (1900–16)	373	188
+170	Roger Clemens (1984–2007)	354	184
+154	Lefty Grove (1925–41)	300	141
+151	John Clarkson (1882, 1884–94)	327	176
+137	Randy Johnson (1988–2009)	303	166
+124	Eddie Plank (1901–17)	305	181
+117	Old Hoss Radbourn (1880–91)	308	191

Pitchers Winning 300 Games, Never Striking Out 200 Batters, Season

Pitcher	Wins	Most Strikeouts (Season)
Tom Glavine	305	192 (1991)
Warren Spahn	363	191 (1960)
Early Wynn	300	184 (1957)

Won-Loss Percentage of 300-Game Winners

Won-Loss Percentage	Player	Years	Record
.680	Lefty Grove	(1925–41)	300–141
.665	Christy Mathewson	(1900–16)	373–188
.658	Roger Clemens	(1984–2007)	354–184

continued on next page

Won-Loss Percentage	Player	Years	Record.
.648	John Clarkson	(1882–94)	328–178
.646	Randy Johnson	(1988–2009)	303–166
.642	Grover C. Alexander	(1911–30)	373–208
.634	Kid Nichols	(1890–1906)	361–208
.627	Eddie Plank	(1901–17)	326–194
.619	Cy Young	(1900–11)	511–316
.614	Old Hoss Radbourn	(1880–91)	310–194
.610	Greg Maddux	(1986–2008)	355–227
.603	Tim Keefe	(1880–93)	341–225
.603	Tom Seaver	(1967–86)	311–205
.600	Tom Glavine	(1987–2008)	305–203
.599	Walter Johnson	(1907–27)	417–279
.597	Warren Spahn	(1946–65)	363–245
.594	Mickey Welch	(1880–92)	307–210
.574	Steve Carlton	(1965–88)	329–244
.559	Don Sutton	(1966–88)	324–256
.551	Early Wynn	(1939, 1941–44, 1946–63)	300–244
.542	Gaylord Perry	(1962–83)	314–265
.540	Pud Galvin	(1879–92)	361–308
.537	Phil Niekro	(1964–87)	318–274
.526	Nolan Ryan	(1966, 1968–93)	324–292

Shutouts

Evolution of Shutout Record

American League

1901	Clark Griffith, Chi. White Sox	5
	Cy Young, Bost. Americans	5
1903	Cy Young, Bost. Americans	7
1904	Cy Young, Bost. Americans	10
1908	Ed Walsh, Chi. White Sox	11
1910	Jack Coombs, Phila. A's	13

National League (Pre-1900)

1876	George Bradley, St. L. Brown Stockings	16

National League (Post-1899)

1900	Clark Griffith, Chi. Cubs	4
	Noodles Hahn, Cin. Reds	4
	Kid Nichols, Bost. Braves	4
	Cy Young, St. L. Cardinals	4
1901	Jack Chesbro, Pitt. Pirates	6
	Al Orth, Phila. Phillies	6
	Vic Willis, Bost. Braves	6
1902	Jack Chesbro, Pitt. Pirates	8
	Christy Mathewson, N.Y. Giants	8
	Jack Taylor, Chi. Cubs	8
1904	Joe McGinnity, N.Y. Giants	9
1908	Christy Mathewson, N.Y. Giants	11
1915	Grover C. Alexander, Phila. Phillies	12
1916	Grover C. Alexander, Phila. Phillies	16

20-Game Winners with No Complete Game Shutouts

American League

Wins	Losses		
26	7	Joe Bush, N.Y. Yankees, 1922
24	15	General Crowder, Wash. Senators, 1933
23	5	Barry Zito, Oak. A's, 2002
22	14	Lefty Williams, Chi. White Sox, 1920
22	11	Earl Wilson, Det. Tigers, 1967
21	10	C. C. Sabathia, N.Y. Yankees, 2010
21	9	Esteban Loaiza, Chi. White Sox, 2003
21	9	Dave Stewart, Oak. A's, 1989

National League (Post-1900)

Wins	Losses		
24	12	Ron Bryant, S.F. Giants, 1973
23	12	Christy Mathewson, N.Y. Giants, 1912
21	12	Three Finger Brown, Chi. Cubs, 1911
21	10	Willie Sherdel, St. L. Cardinals, 1928
21	10	Jose Lima, Hous. Astros, 1999
20	19	Pete Schneider, Cin. Reds, 1917

21........8 ....Andy Pettitte, N.Y. Yankees, 1996
21........8 ....Andy Pettitte, N.Y. Yankees, 2001/2003
21........8 ....Bartolo Colon, L.A. Angels, 2005
21........7 ....Jamie Moyer, Sea. Mariners, 2003
21........6 ....Curt Schilling, Bost. Red Sox, 2004
20........9 ....Hugh Bedient, Bost. Red Sox, 1912
20.......16....................Bobo Newsom, St. L. Browns, 1938
20.......12....................Alex Kellner, Phila. A's, 1949
20.......12....................Dave Boswell, Minn. Twins, 1969
20.......13....................Luis Tiant, Bost. Red Sox, 1973
20........9 ....Bill Gullickson, Det. Tigers, 1991
20........7 ....David Cone, N.Y. Yankees, 1998
20........3..................Roger Clemens, N.Y. Yankees, 2001
20........6 ....Jamie Moyer, Sea. Mariners, 2001
20........4 ....Pedro Martinez, Bost. Red Sox, 2002
20........7 ....Josh Beckett, Bost. Red Sox, 2007
20........9 ....Mike Mussina, N.Y. Yankees, 2008

Most Shutouts by a Rookie

American League		National League	
0	Russ Ford, 1910 N.Y. Yankees	8	Fernando Valenzuela, 1981 L.A. Dodgers
	Reb Russell, 1913 Chi. White Sox	7	Irv Young, 1905 Bost. Braves
7	Harry Krause, 1909 Phila. Athletics		George McQuillan, 1908 Phila. Phillies
6	Red Glad, 1904 St. L. Browns		Grover Cleveland Alexander, 1911 Phila. Phillies
	Gene Bearden, 1948 Cleve. Indians		Jerry Koosman, 1968 N.Y. Mets
		6	Harvey Haddix, 1953 St. L. Cardinals
			Ewell Blackwell, 1946 Cin. Reds

Pitchers Leading League in Wins, No Complete Game Shutouts

American League		National League (Post-1900)	
Wins Losses		**Wins Losses**	
24.......15............General Crowder, Wash. Senators, 1933		24........12 ....Ron Bryant, S.F. Giants, 1973	
23........5................................Barry Zito, Oak. A's, 2002		19.........8 ....Adam Wainwright, St. L. Cardinals, 2009	
22........6....................Tex Hughson, Bost. Red Sox, 1942		19.........6 ....Jake Peavy, S.D. Padres, 2007	
22.......11...........................Earl Wilson, Det. Tigers, 1967		16.........9 ....Brad Penny, L.A. Dodgers, 2006	
21........8 ....Andy Pettitte, N.Y. Yankees, 1996		16.........8 ....Derek Lowe, L.A. Dodgers, 2006	
21........8 ....Bartolo Colon, L.A. Angels, 2005		16.........7 ....Carlos Zambrano, Chi. Cubs, 2006	
21........7 ....C. C. Sabathia, N.Y. Yankees, 2010			
21........6 ....Curt Schilling, Bost. Red Sox, 2004			
20........9 ....Bill Gullickson, Det. Tigers, 1991			
20........7 ....David Cone, N.Y. Yankees, 1998			
20........7 ....Josh Beckett, Bost. Red Sox, 2007			
18.......10....................Bob Lemon, Cleve. Indians, 1955			
14..........6 ....Johan Santana, Minn. Twins, 2006			

Most Career Starts, No Shutouts

		Wins–Losses
203	Jason Bere (1993–2003)	71–65
201	Adam Eaton (2000–09)	71–68
187	Nate Robertson (2002–10)	57–77
167	Tony Armas (1999–2008)	53–65
154	Jeremy Guthrie (2004–)	97–65
153	Paul Wilson (1996–2005)	40–58

Most Career Shutouts, Never Led League

Shutouts		Overall Record
50	Rube Waddell (1897, 1899–1910)	191–145
49	Ferguson Jenkins (1965–83)	284–226
46	Doc White (1901–13)	190–157
45	Phil Niekro (1964–87)	318–274
42	Catfish Hunter (1965–79)	224–166
41	Chief Bender (1903–17, 1925)	210–127
40	Mickey Welch (1880–92)	311–207
40	Ed Reulbach (1905–17)	181–105
40	Claude Osteen (1957, 1959–75)	196–195
40	Mel Stottlemyre (1964–74)	164–139

Pitchers with Shutouts in First Two Major League Starts

American League

	Season Record	Shutouts
Joe Doyle, N.Y. Highlanders, 1906	2–2	2
Johnny Marcum, Phila. A's, 1933	3–2	2
Hal White, Det. Tigers, 1941	12–12	4
Boo Ferriss, Bost. Red Sox, 1945	21–10	5
Tom Phoebus, Balt. Orioles, 1966	2–1	2

National League (Post-1900)

	Season Record	Shutouts
Al Worthington, N.Y. Giants, 1953	4–8	2
Karl Spooner, Bklyn. Dodgers, 1954	2–0	2

Most Hits Allowed by Pitcher Pitching Shutout

American League

14	Milt Gaston, Wash. Senators, July 10, 1928
13	Mudcat Grant, Minn. Twins, July 15, 1964
12	Bob Shawkey, N. Y. Yankees, June 13, 1920
12	Duster Mails, Cleve. Indians, July 10, 1926
12	Stan Bahnsen, Chi. White Sox, June 21, 1973

National League (Post-1900)

14	Larry Cheney, Chi. Cubs, Sept. 14, 1913
13	Dizzy Dean, St. L. Cardinals, April 20, 1937
13	Bill Lee, Chi. Cubs, Sept. 17, 1938
12	Pol Perritt, N.Y. Giants, Sept. 14, 1917
	Rube Benton, N.Y. Giants, Aug. 28, 1920
	Leon Cadore, Bklyn. Dodgers, Sept. 4, 1920
	George Smith, Phila. Phillies, Aug. 12, 1921
	Hal Schumacher, N.Y. Giants, July 19, 1934
	Fritz Ostermueller, Pitt. Pirates, May 17, 1947
	Lew Burdette, Milw. Braves, May 26, 1959
	Bob Friend, Pitt. Pirates, Sept. 24, 1959
	Rick Reuschel , Chi. Cubs, June 20, 1974
	Dennis Martinez, Mont. Expos, June 2, 1998

Players with Highest Percentage of Shutouts to Games Started, Career

	Games Started	Shutouts	Percentage
Ed Walsh (1904–17)	315	57	18.10
Smokey Joe Wood (1908–15, 1917–20)	158	28	17.72
Addie Joss (1902–10)	260	46	17.69
Three Finger Brown (1903–16)	332	57	17.17
Walter Johnson (1907–27)	666	110	16.52

Grover C. Alexander (1911–30)................598................90 ....15.05
Lefty Leifield (1905–13, 1918–20)................217................32 ....14.75
Rube Waddell (1897, 1899–1910)................340................50 ....14.71
Christy Mathewson (1900–16)................552................80 ....14.49
Spud Chandler (1937–47)................184................26 ....14.13
Nap Rucker (1907–16)................273................38 ....13.92
Mort Cooper (1938–47, 1949)................239................33 ....13.81
Ed Reulbach (1905–17)................299................40 ....13.38
Babe Adams (1906–07, 1909–26)................355................47 ....13.24
Eddie Plank (1901–17)................527................69 ....13.09
Sam Leever (1898–1910)................299................39 ....13.04

Losses

Most Losses by Decade

Pre-1900

308 ....Pud Galvin
225................Gus Weyhing
225................Tim Keefe
220................Tony Mullane
214................Jim McCormick
210................Mickey Welch
204................Jim Whitney
194................Adonis Terry
194................Old Hoss Radbourn
178................John Clarkson

1900–09

172................Vic Willis
163 ....Jack Powell
146................Cy Young
143................Al Orth
141................Bill Dineen
139................Rube Waddell
138................Harry Howell
135................Long Tom Hughes
134................Chick Fraser
134................George Mullin

1910–19

143 ....Walter Johnson
124................Bob Groom
122................Bob Harmon
120................Eddie Cicotte
117................Red Ames
114................Slim Sallee
110................Hippo Vaughn
104................Claude Hendrix
104................Ray Caldwell
103................Rube Marquard
103................Pet Ragan

1920–29

146................Dolf Luque
142................Eppa Rixey
137 ....Howard Ehmke
135................Slim Harriss
130................Burleigh Grimes
128................Jimmy Ring
124................George Uhle
122................Tom Zachary
119 ....Jesse Haines
118................Sad Sam Jones

1930–39

137................Paul Derringer
134................Larry French
123................Mel Harder
119 ....Bump Hadley
115................Wes Ferrell
115................Ted Lyons
112................Ed Brandt
111................Danny MacFayden
107................Earl Whitehill
106................Willis Hudlin

1940–49

123................Dutch Leonard
120................Bobo Newsom
119 ....Dizzy Trout
118................Hal Newhouser
100................Sid Hudson
92................Johnny Vander Meer
92 ....Early Wynn
90 ....Bucky Walters
89................Ken Raffensberger
88................Jim Tobin

1950–59

149 ....Robin Roberts
131................Warren Spahn
127................Bob Friend
124................Murry Dickson
123................Bob Rush
121................Billy Pierce
119 ....Early Wynn
117................Ned Garver
113................Chuck Stobbs
100................Alex Kellner

1960–69

133................Jack Fisher
132................Dick Ellsworth
132................Larry Jackson
126................Don Drysdale
121 ....Claude Osteen
119 ....Jim Kaat
118................Jim Bunning
111................Don Cardwell
105................Bob Gibson
105................Ken Johnson

1970–79

151 ....Phil Niekro
146 ....Nolan Ryan
133................Gaylord Perry
130................Ferguson Jenkins
128................Bert Blyleven
127................Jerry Koosman
126 ....Steve Carlton
123................Wilbur Wood
117................Mickey Lolich
117 ....Rick Wise

continued on next page

	1980–89		**1990–99**		**2000–11**
126	Jim Clancy	116	Andy Benes	149	Livan Hernandez
122	Frank Tanana	115	Tim Belcher	137	Javier Vasquez
119	Jack Morris	113	Bobby Witt	128	Derek Lowe
118	Bob Knepper	112	Jaime Navarro	124	Barry Zito
114	Charlie Hough	110	Tom Candiotti	122	Kevin Millwood
109	Floyd Bannister	108	Scott Erickson	119	Mark Buehrle
109	Rich Dotson	108	Chuck Finley	119	Jon Garland
109	Dave Steib	101	John Burkett	118	Jeff Suppan
107	Mike Moore	101	Mike Morgan	113	Tim Wakefield
104	Nolan Ryan	100	Terry Mulholland	109	A. J. Burnett

Evolution of Pitchers' Losses Record

American League

1901	Pete Dowling, Milw. Brewers–Cleve. Indians	25
1904	Happy Townsend, Wash. Senators	25

National League (Pre-1900)

1876	Jim Devlin, Louis. Colonels	35
1879	George Bradley, Troy Trojans	40
	Jim McCormick, Cleve. Spiders	40
1880	Will White, Cin. Reds	42
1883	John Coleman, Phila. Quakers	48

National League (Post-1899)

1900	Bill Carrick, N.Y. Giants	22
1901	Dummy Taylor, N.Y. Giants	27
1905	Vic Willis, Bost. Braves	29

Pitchers with Seven or More Consecutive Losing Seasons

Seasons

10........Bill Bailey, St. L. Browns (AL), 1908–12; Balt. (FL), 1913; Balt.–Chi. (FL), 1914; Det. Tigers (AL), 1918; and St. L. Cardinals (NL), 1921–22

10........Ron Kline, Pitt. Pirates (NL), 1952, 1955–59; St. L. Cardinals (NL), 1960; L.A. Angels–Det. Tigers (AL), 1961; Det. Tigers (AL), 1962; and Wash. Senators II (AL), 1963

9........Milt Gaston, St. L. Browns (AL), 1926–27; Wash. Senators (AL), 1928; Bost. Red Sox (AL), 1929–31; and Chi. White Sox (AL), 1932–34

8........Pete Broberg, Wash. Senators II (AL), 1971; Tex. Rangers (AL), 1972–74; Milw. Brewers (AL), 1975–76; Chi. Cubs (NL), 1977; and Oak. A's (AL), 1978

8........Jack Fisher, Balt. Orioles (AL), 1961–62; S.F. Giants (NL), 1963; N.Y. Mets (NL), 1964–67; and Chi. White Sox (AL), 1968

8........Bill Hart, Phila. A's (AA), 1886–87; Bklyn. Trolley Dodgers (NL), 1892; Pitt. Pirates (NL), 1895; St. L. Cardinals (NL), 1896–97; Pitt. Pirates (NL), 1898; and Cleve. Indians (AL), 1901

8........Ken Raffensberger, Cin. Reds (NL), 1940–41; Phila. Phillies (NL), 1943–46; Phila. Phillies–Cin. Reds (NL), 1947; and Cin. Reds (NL), 1948

8........Charlie Robertson, Chi. White Sox (AL), 1919 and 1922–25; St. L. Browns (AL), 1926; and Bost. Braves (NL), 1927–28

8........Socks Seibold, Phila. A's (AL), 1916–17 and 1919; and Bost. Braves (NL), 1929–33

7........Boom Boom Beck, St. L. Browns (AL), 1928; Bklyn. Dodgers (NL), 1933–34; and Phila. Phillies (NL), 1939–42

7........Bert Cunningham, Bklyn. Bridegrooms (AA), 1887; Balt. Orioles (AA), 1888–89; Phila. Quakers–Buffalo Bisons (Players), 1890; Balt. Orioles (AA), 1891; and Louis. Colonels (NL), 1895–96

7........Bill Dietrich, Phila. A's (AL), 1933–35; Phila. A's–Wash. Senators I–Chi. White Sox (AL), 1936; and Chi. White Sox (AL), 1937–39

7........Jesse Jefferson, Balt. Orioles–Chi. White Sox (AL), 1975; Chi. White Sox (AL), 1976; Tor. Blue Jays (AL), 1977–79;

Tor. Blue Jays (AL)–Pitt. Pirates (NL), 1980; and Cal. Angels (AL), 1981

7........Howie Judson, Chi. White Sox (AL), 1948–52; and Cin. Reds (NL), 1953–54

7........Dick Littlefield, Det. Tigers–St. L. Browns (AL), 1952; St. L. Browns (AL), 1953; Balt. Orioles (AL)–Pitt. Pirates (NL), 1954; Pitt. Pirates (NL), 1955; Pitt. Pirates–St. L. Cardinals–N.Y. Giants (NL), 1956; Chi. Cubs (NL), 1957; and Milw. Braves (NL), 1958

7........Skip Lockwood, Sea. Pilots (AL), 1969; Milw. Brewers (AL), 1970–73; Cal. Angels (AL), 1974; and N.Y. Mets (NL), 1975

7........Duane Pillette, N.Y. Yankees (AL), 1949; N.Y. Yankees–St. L. Browns (AL), 1950; St. L. Browns (AL), 1951–53; and Balt. Orioles (AL), 1954–55

7........Eric Rasmussen, St. L. Cardinals (NL), 1976–77; St. L. Cardinals–S.D. Padres (NL), 1978; S.D. Padres (NL), 1979–80; St. L. Cardinals (NL), 1982; and St. L. Cardinals (NL)–K.C. Royals (AL), 1983

7........Buck Ross, Phila. A's (AL), 1936–40; Phila. A's–Chi. White Sox (AL), 1941; and Chi. White Sox (AL), 1942

7........Jack Russell, Bost. Red Sox (AL), 1926–31; and Bost. Red Sox–Cleve. Indians (AL), 1932

7........Herm Wehmeier, Cin. Reds (NL), 1949–53; Cin. Reds–Phila. Phillies (NL), 1954; and Phila. Phillies (NL), 1955

7........Bob Weiland, Chi. White Sox (AL), 1929–31; Bost. Red Sox (AL), 1932–33; Bost. Red Sox–Cleve. Indians (AL), 1934; and St. L. Browns (AL), 1935

7........Carlton Willey, Milw. Braves (NL), 1959–62; and N.Y. Mets (NL), 1963–65

Pitchers with 150 Wins with More Losses Than Wins, Career

Jack Powell (1897–1912)	245–254
Bobo Newsom (1929–30, 1932, 1934–40, 1942–53)	211–222
Bob Friend (1951–66)	197–230
Jim Whitney (1881–90)	191–204
Tom Zachary (1918–36)	186–191
Chick Fraser (1896–1909)	175–212
Livan Hernandez (1996–)	174–176
Murry Dickson (1939–40, 1942–43, 1946–59)	172–181
Danny Darwin (1978–98)	171–182
Bill Dineen (1898–1909)	170–177
Pink Hawley (1892–1901)	167–179
Red Donahue (1893, 1895–1906)	164–175
Mike Moore (1982–95)	161–176
Bump Hadley (1926–41)	161–165
Ted Breitenstein (1891–1901)	160–170
Mark Baldwin (1887–93)	154–165
Rudy May (1965–83)	152–156
Tom Candiotti (1983–99)	151–164
Jim Slaton (1971–86)	151–158

Pitchers on Winning Teams, Leading League in Losses, Season

American League

Pitcher	Wins–Losses	Team Wins–Losses
Bill Dineen, Bost. Americans, 1902	21–21	77–60
Herman Pillette, Det. Tigers, 1923	14–19 (Tie)	83–71
Hal Newhouser, Det. Tigers, 1947	17–17	85–69
Brian Kingman, Oak. A's, 1980	8–20	83–79
Bert Blyleven, Minn. Twins, 1988	10–17	91–71

National League (Post-1900)

Pitcher	Wins–Losses	Team Wins–Losses
Dick Rudolph, Bost. Braves, 1915	22–19 (Tie)	83–69
Dolf Luque, Cin. Reds, 1922	13–23	86–68

Wilbur Cooper, Pitt. Pirates, 1923 ....17–19 87–67
Charlie Root, Chi. Cubs, 1926 ....18–17 (Tie) 82–72
Rip Sewell, Pitt. Pirates, 1941 ....14–17 81–73
Ron Kline, Pitt. Pirates, 1958...................13–16 84–70
Bob Friend, Pitt. Pirates, 1959...................8–19 78–76
Phil Niekro, Atl. Braves, 1980...................15–18 81–80
Ken Hill, St. L. Cardinals, 1989...................7–15 86–76
Doug Drabek, Hous. Astros, 1993...................9–18 85–7
Livan Hernandez, S.F. Giants, 2002...................12–16 95–66
Jason Marquis, St. L. Cardinals, 2006...................14–16 83–78
Derek Lowe, Atl. Braves, 2011 ....9–17 89–73

Pitchers Winning 20 Games in Rookie Year, Losing 20 in Second Year

Roscoe Miller, Det. Tigers (AL), 1901 (23–13), 1902 (7–20)   Alex Kellner, Phila. A's (AL), 1949 (20–12), 1950 (8–20)

300-Game Winners with Fewer Than 200 Losses

	Wins	Losses
Christy Mathewson (1900–16)	373	188
Roger Clemens (1984–2007)	354	184
John Clarkson (1882, 1884–94)	328	178
Eddie Plank (1901–17)	326	194
Old Hoss Radbourn (1880–91)	309	194
Randy Johnson (1988–2009)	303	166
Lefty Grove (1925–41)	300	141

Earned Run Average

Best ERA by Decade (Min. 1000 Innings)

Pre-1900		1900–09		1910–19	
1.89	Jim Devlin	1.63	Three Finger Brown	1.59	Walter Johnson
2.10	Monte Ward	1.68	Ed Walsh	1.97	Smoky Joe Wood
2.25	Tommy Bond	1.72	Ed Reulbach	1.98	Ed Walsh
2.28	Will White	1.87	Addie Joss	2.09	Grover C. Alexander
2.36	Larry Corcoran	1.98	Christy Mathewson	2.15	Carl Mays
2.43	Terry Larkin	2.11	Rube Waddell	2.19	Babe Ruth
2.43	Jim McCormick	2.12	Cy Young	2.20	Jeff Pfeffer
2.50	George Bradley	2.13	Orval Overall	2.22	Dutch Leonard
2.62	Tim Keefe	2.19	Frank Smith	2.25	Eddie Plank
2.67	Charlie Ferguson	2.20	Lefty Leifield	2.28	Fred Toney
		2.20	Doc White		

1920–29		1930–39		1940–49	
3.04	Grover C. Alexander	2.71	Carl Hubbell	2.67	Spud Chandler
3.09	Lefty Grove	2.91	Lefty Grove	2.68	Max Lanier
3.09	Dolf Luque	2.96	Dizzy Dean	2.74	Harry Brecheen
3.10	Dazzy Vance	3.21	Bill Lee	2.84	Hal Newhouser
3.20	Stan Coveleski	3.23	Lon Warneke	2.90	Bob Feller
3.24	Eppa Rixey	3.24	Lefty Gomez	2.93	Mort Cooper
3.24	Tommy Thomas	3.38	Hal Schumacher	2.94	Tex Hughson

1920–29		1930–39		1940–49	
3.33	Urban Shocker	3.42	Larry French	2.94	Claude Passeau
3.33	Walter Johnson	3.42	Van Lingle Mungo	2.97	Bucky Walters
3.34	Red Faber	3.50	Curt Davis	2.99	Howie Pollet
3.36	Wilbur Cooper	3.50	Paul Derringer		
		3.50	Charlie Root		

1950–59		1960–69		1970–79	
2.66	Whitey Ford	2.16	Hoyt Wilhelm	2.58	Jim Palmer
2.79	Hoyt Wilhelm	2.36	Sandy Koufax	2.61	Tom Seaver
2.92	Warren Spahn	2.57	Juan Marichal	2.88	Bert Blyleven
3.06	Billy Pierce	2.74	Bob Gibson	2.89	Rollie Fingers
3.07	Allie Reynolds	2.76	Mike Cuellar	2.92	Gaylord Perry
3.12	Eddie Lopat	2.77	Dean Chance	2.93	Andy Messersmith
3.14	Bob Buhl	2.81	Tommy John	2.93	Frank Tanana
3.18	Johnny Antonelli	2.83	Don Drysdale	2.97	Jon Matlack
3.19	Sal Maglie	2.83	Whitey Ford	2.98	Mike Marshall
3.28	Early Wynn	2.83	Joe Horlen	3.01	Don Wilson
		2.83	Bob Veale		

1980–89		1990–99		2000–09	
2.64	Dwight Gooden	2.54	Greg Maddux	2.98	Tim Lincecum
2.69	Orel Hershiser	2.74	Jose Rijo	3.01	Pedro Martinez
3.06	Roger Clemens	2.83	Pedro Martinez	3.10	Johan Santana
3.08	Dave Righetti	3.02	Roger Clemens	3.20	Roy Halladay
3.13	Dave Dravecky	3.14	Randy Johnson	3.21	Roy Oswalt
3.13	John Tudor	3.21	David Cone	3.24	Felix Hernandez
3.14	Nolan Ryan	3.21	Tom Glavine	3.27	Brandon Webb
3.19	Fernando Valenzuela	3.25	Kevin Brown	3.28	John Smoltz
3.21	Bob Welch	3.31	Curt Schilling	3.31	Jared Weaver
3.22	Sid Fernandez	3.32	John Smoltz	3.34	Randy Johnson
				3.34	Roger Clemens
				3.50	Tim Hudson

Teammates Finishing One-Two in ERA, Season

American League

Season	Team	Leader	ERA	Runner-Up	ERA
1914	Bost. Red Sox	Dutch Leonard	1.01	Rube Foster	1.65
1924	Wash. Senators	Walter Johnson	2.72	Tom Zachary	2.75
1927	N.Y. Yankees	Wilcy Moore	2.28	Waite Hoyt	2.63
1933	Cleve. Indians	Monte Pearson	2.33	Mel Harder	2.95
1943	N.Y. Yankees	Spud Chandler	1.64	Tiny Bonham	2.27
1944	Det. Tigers	Dizzy Trout	2.12	Hal Newhouser	2.22
1945	Det. Tigers	Hal Newhouser	1.81	Al Benton	2.02
1949	Cleve. Indians	Gene Bearden	2.43	Bob Lemon	2.82 (Tie)
1957	N.Y. Yankees	Bobby Shantz	2.45	Tom Sturdivant	2.54
1963	Chi. White Sox	Gary Peters	2.33	Juan Pizarro	2.39
1966	Chi. White Sox	Gary Peters	1.98	Joel Horlen	2.43
1967	Chi. White Sox	Joel Horlen	2.06	Gary Peters	2.28
1968	Cleve. Indians	Luis Tiant	1.60	Sam McDowell	1.81
1979	N.Y. Yankees	Ron Guidry	2.78	Tommy John	2.97
1996	Tor. Blue Jays	Juan Guzman	2.93	Pat Hentgen	3.22
2002	Bost. Red Sox	Pedro Martinez	2.26	Derek Lowe	2.58
1901	Pitt. Pirates	Jesse Tannehill	2.18	Deacon Phillippe	2.22

continued on next page

1906	Chi. Cubs	Three Finger Brown	1.04	Jack Pfiester	1.56
1907	Chi. Cubs	Jack Pfiester	1.15	Carl Lundgren	1.17
1912	N.Y. Giants	Jeff Tesreau	1.96	Christy Mathewson	2.12

National League (Post-1900)

Season	Team	Leader	ERA	Runner-Up	ERA
1918	Chi. Cubs	Hippo Vaughn	1.74	Lefty Tyler	2.00
1919	Chi. Cubs	Grover C. Alexander	1.72	Hippo Vaughn	1.79
1923	Cin. Reds	Dolf Luque	1.93	Eppa Rixey	2.80
1925	Cin. Reds	Dolf Luque	2.63	Eppa Rixey	2.88
1931	N.Y. Giants	Bill Walker	2.26	Carl Hubbell	2.66
1935	Pitt. Pirates	Cy Blanton	2.58	Bill Swift	2.70
1942	St. L. Cardinals	Mort Cooper	1.78	Johnny Beazley	2.13
1943	St. L. Cardinals	Howie Pollet	1.75	Max Lanier	1.90
1944	Cin. Reds	Ed Heusser	2.38	Bucky Walters	2.40
1945	Chi. Cubs	Hank Borowy*	2.13	Ray Prim	2.40
1956	Milw. Braves	Lew Burdette	2.70	Warren Spahn	2.78
1957	Bklyn. Dodgers	Johnny Podres	2.66	Don Drysdale	2.69
1959	S.F. Giants	Sam Jones	2.83	Stu Miller	2.84
1964	L.A. Dodgers	Sandy Koufax	1.74	Don Drysdale	2.18
1974	Atl. Braves	Buzz Capra	2.28	Phil Niekro	2.38
1981	Hous. Astros	Nolan Ryan	1.69	Bob Knepper	2.18
2001	Ariz. D'backs	Randy Johnson	2.49	Curt Schilling	2.98
2005	Hous. Astros	Roger Clemens	1.87	Andy Pettitte	2.39

*Also with N.Y. Yankees (3.13 ERA)

Pitchers with 3000 Innings Pitched and an ERA Lower Than 3.00 (Post-1900)

	Innings	ERA
Three Finger Brown (1903–16)	3172	2.06
Christy Mathewson (1901–16)	4755	2.11
Cy Young (1901–11)	3312	2.12
Walter Johnson (1907–27)	5914	2.17
Eddie Plank (1905–17)	4496	2.35
Eddie Cicotte (1905–20)	3226	2.38
Doc White (1901–13)	3041	2.39
Chief Bender (1903–25)	3017	2.46
Vic Willis (1901–10)	3106	2.50
Grover C. Alexander (1911–30)	5189	2.56
Pete Alexander (1911–30)	5190	2.56
Red Ames (1905–19)	3069	2.65
Whitey Ford (1950, 1953–67)	3170	2.75
Jack Powell (1901–12)	3161	2.75
George Mullin (1902–13)	3687	2.82
Jim Palmer (1965–84)	3948	2.86
Tom Seaver (1967–86)	4782	2.86
Juan Marichal (1960–75)	3507	2.89
Stanley Coveleski (1912, 1916–28)	3082	2.89
Wilbur Cooper (1912–26)	3480	2.89
Bob Gibson (1959–75)	3884	2.91
Carl Mays (1915–29)	3020	2.92
Don Drysdale (1956–69)	3432	2.95
Carl Hubbell (1928–43)	3589	2.97

Pitchers Leading League in ERA After Their 40th Birthday

	Age	ERA
Ted Lyons, Chi. White Sox (AL), 1942	42	2.10
Spud Chandler, N.Y. Yankees (AL), 1947	40	2.46
Nolan Ryan, Hous. Astros (NL), 1987	40	2.76

ERA Under 2.00, Season (Since 1920)

American League

1.60	Luis Tiant, 1968 Cleve. Indians
1.64	Spud Chandler, 1943 N.Y. Yankees
1.65	Dean Chance, 1964 L.A. Angels
1.74	Ron Guidry, 1978 N. Y. Yankees
1.74	Pedro Martinez, 2000 Bost. Red Sox

National League

1.12	Bob Gibson, 1968 St. L. Cardinals
1.53	Dwight Gooden, 1986 N.Y. Mets
1.56	Greg Maddux, 1994 Atl. Braves
1.63	Greg Maddux, 1995 Atl. Braves
1.66	Carl Hubbell, 1933 N.Y. Giants
1.69	Nolan Ryan, 1981 Hous. Astros
1.73	Sandy Koufax, 1966 L.A. Dodgers
1.74	Sandy Koufax, 1964 L.A. Dodgers
1.87	Roger Clemens, 2005 Hous. Astros

Pitchers with Losing Record, Leading League in ERA

American League

	ERA	Wins–Losses
Ed Siever, Det. Tigers, 1902	1.91	8–11
Ed Walsh, Chi. White Sox, 1910	1.27	18–20
Stan Coveleski, Cleve. Indians, 1923	2.76	13–14
Kevin Millwood, Cleve. Indians, 2005	2.86	9–11

National League (Post-1900)

	ERA	Wins–Losses
Rube Waddell, Pitt. Pirates, 1900	2.37	8–13
Dolf Luque, Cin. Reds, 1925	2.63	16–18
Dave Koslo, N.Y. Giants, 1949	2.50	11–14
Stu Miller, S.F. Giants, 1958	2.47	6–9
Nolan Ryan, Hous. Astros, 1987	2.76	8–16
Joe Magrane, St. L. Cardinals, 1988	2.18	5–9

20-Game Winners with 4.00 ERA, Season

American League

	ERA	Wins–Losses
Bobo Newsom, St. L. Browns, 1938	5.08	20–16
Vern Kennedy, Chi. White Sox, 1936	4.63	21–9
George Earnshaw, Phila. A's, 1930	4.44	22–13
Rick Helling, Tex. Rangers, 1998	4.41	20–7
Lefty Gomez, N.Y. Yankees, 1932	4.21	24–7
Wes Ferrell, Bost. Red Sox, 1936	4.19	20–15
Tim Hudson, Oak. A's, 2000	4.14	20–6
David Wells, Tor. Blue Jays, 2000	4.11	20–8
Monte Weaver, Wash. Senators, 1932	4.08	22–10
George Uhle, Cleve. Indians, 1922	4.07	22–16

Billy Hoeft, Det. Tigers, 1956...4.06...20–14
Jack Morris, Tor. Blue Jays, 1992...4.04...21–6
Andy Pettitte, N.Y. Yankees, 2003..4.02...21–8
Vic Raschi, N.Y. Yankees, 1950...4.00...21–8

National League (Post-1899)

	ERA	Wins–Losses
Ray Kremer, Pitt. Pirates, 1930	5.02	20–12
Jim Merritt, Cin. Reds, 1970	4.08	20–12
Lew Burdette, Milw. Braves, 1959	4.07	21–15
Murry Dickson, Pitt. Pirates, 1951	4.02	20–16

20-Game Losers with ERA Below 2.00

American League

	ERA	Wins–Losses
Ed Walsh, Chi. White Sox, 1910	1.27	18–20
Walter Johnson, Wash. Senators, 1916	1.89	25–20
Jim Scott, Chi. White Sox, 1913	1.90	20–20
Harry Howell, St. L. Browns, 1905	1.98	15–22

National League

	ERA	Wins–Losses
Kaiser Wilhelm, Bklyn. Dodgers, 1908	1.87	16–22

ERA Leaders with Fewer Than 10 Wins

American League

Wins		ERA
6	Steve Ontiveros, Oak. Athletics, 1994*	2.65
8	Ed Siever, Det. Tigers, 1902	1.91
9	Kevin Millwood, Cleve. Indians, 2005	2.86

National League

Wins		ERA
5	Joe Magrane, St. L. Cardinals, 1988	2.18
6	Stu Miller, S.F. Giants, 1958	2.47
8	Rube Waddell, Pitt. Pirates, 1900	2.37
	Fred Anderson, N.Y. Giants, 1917	1.44
	Nolan Ryan, Hous. Astros, 1987	2.76
9	Craig Swan, N.Y. Mets, 1978	2.43

*Strike-shortened season.

Pitchers with Lowest ERA in Both Leagues

Roger Clemens	1986 Bost. Red Sox (AL)	2.48
	1990 Bost. Red Sox (AL)	1.93
	1991 Bost. Red Sox (AL)	2.62
	1992 Bost. Red Sox (AL)	2.41
	1997 Tor. Blue Jays (AL)	2.05
	1998 Tor. Blue Jays (AL)	2.65
	2005 Hous. Astros (NL)	1.87
Randy Johnson	1995 Sea. Mariners (AL)	2.48
	1999 Ariz. D'backs (NL)	2.49
	2001 Ariz. D'backs (NL)	2.49
	2002 Ariz. D'backs (NL)	2.32
Pedro Martinez	1997 Mont. Expos (NL)	1.90
	1999 Bost. Red Sox (AL)	2.07
	2000 Bost. Red Sox (AL)	1.74
	2002 Bost. Red Sox (AL)	2.26
	2003 Bost. Red Sox (AL)	2.22

Johan Santana	2004 Minn. Twins (AL)	2.61
	2006 Minn. Twins (AL)	2.77
	2008 N.Y. Mets (NL)	2.54
Rube Waddell	1900 Pittsburg* Pirates (NL)	2.37
	1905 Phila. Athletics (AL)	1.48
Hoyt Wilhelm	1952 N.Y. Giants (NL)	2.43
	1959 Balt. Orioles (AL)	2.19
Cy Young	1892 Cleve. ?? (NL)	1.93
	1901 Bost. Red Sox (AL)	1.62

*Spelled Pittsburg without the "h" in 1900.

ERA Leaders with 25 or More Wins, Season

American League

	ERA	Wins
Cy Young, Bost. Americans, 1901	1.62	33
Rube Waddell, Phila. A's, 1905	1.48	26
Walter Johnson, Wash. Senators, 1912	1.39	32
Walter Johnson, Wash. Senators, 1913	1.14	36
Eddie Cicotte, Chi. White Sox, 1917	1.53	28
Red Faber, Chi. White Sox, 1921	2.48	25
Lefty Grove, Phila. A's, 1930	2.54	28
Lefty Grove, Phila. A's, 1931	2.06	31
Lefty Grove, Phila. A's, 1932	2.84	25
Lefty Gomez, N.Y. Yankees, 1934	2.33	26
Bob Feller, Cleve. Indians, 1940	2.61	27
Dizzy Trout, Det. Tigers, 1944	2.12	27
Hal Newhouser, Det. Tigers, 1945	1.81	25
Hal Newhouser, Det. Tigers, 1946	1.94	26
Mel Parnell, Bost. Red Sox, 1949	2.77	25
Catfish Hunter, Oak. A's, 1974	2.49	25
Ron Guidry, N.Y. Yankees, 1978	1.74	25

National League (Post-1900)

	ERA	Wins
Sam Leever, Pitt. Pirates, 1903	2.06	25
Joe McGinnity, N.Y. Giants, 1904	1.61	35
Christy Mathewson, N.Y. Giants, 1905	1.28	31
Three Finger Brown, Chi. Cubs, 1906	1.04	26
Christy Mathewson, N.Y. Giants, 1908	1.43	37
Christy Mathewson, N.Y. Giants, 1909	1.14	25
Christy Mathewson, N.Y. Giants, 1911	1.99	26
Christy Mathewson, N.Y. Giants, 1913	2.06	25
Grover C. Alexander, Phila. Phillies, 1915	1.22	31
Grover C. Alexander, Phila. Phillies, 1916	1.55	33
Grover C. Alexander, Chi. Cubs, 1920	1.91	27
Dolf Luque, Cin. Reds, 1923	1.93	27
Dazzy Vance, Bklyn. Dodgers, 1924	2.16	28
Carl Hubbell, N.Y. Giants, 1936	2.31	26
Bucky Walters, Cin. Reds, 1939	2.29	27
Sandy Koufax, L.A. Dodgers, 1963	1.88	25
Sandy Koufax, L.A. Dodgers, 1965	2.04	26
Sandy Koufax, L.A. Dodgers, 1966	1.73	27
Steve Carlton, Phila. Phillies, 1972	1.97	27

continued on next page

ERAs of 300-Game Winners

	ERA	Wins
Christy Mathewson (1900–16)	2.13	373
Walter Johnson (1907–27)	2.17	417
Eddie Plank (1901–17)	2.35	326
Grover C. Alexander (1911–30)	2.56	373
Cy Young (1890–1911)	2.63	511
Tim Keefe (1880–93)	2.63	342
Old Hoss Radbourn (1880–91)	2.68	309
Mickey Welch (1880–92)	2.71	307
John Clarkson (1882, 1884–94)	2.81	328
Tom Seaver (1967–86)	2.86	311
Pud Galvin (1879–92)	2.87	361
Kid Nichols (1890–1901, 1904–06)	2.96	361
Lefty Grove (1925–41)	3.06	300
Warren Spahn (1942, 1946–65)	3.09	363
Gaylord Perry (1962–83)	3.11	314
Roger Clemens (1984–2007)	3.12	354
Greg Maddux (1986–2008)	3.16	355
Nolan Ryan (1966, 1968–93)	3.19	324
Steve Carlton (1965–88)	3.22	329
Don Sutton (1966–88)	3.26	324
Randy Johnson (1988–2009)	3.29	303
Phil Niekro (1967–87)	3.35	318
Tom Glavine (1987–2008)	3.54	305
Early Wynn (1939, 1941–44, 1946–63)	3.54	300

Strikeouts

Evolution of Strikeout Record

American League

1901	Cy Young, Bost. Americans	158
1902	Rube Waddell, Phila. A's	210
1903	Rube Waddell, Phila. A's	302
1904	Rube Waddell, Phila. A's	349
1973	Nolan Ryan, Cal. Angels	383

National League (Pre-1900)

1876	Jim Devlin, Louis. Grays	122
1877	Tommy Bond, Bost. Red Caps	170
1878	Tommy Bond, Bost. Red Caps	182
1879	Monte Ward, Prov. Grays	239
1880	Larry Corcoran, Chi. White Stockings	268
1883	Jim Whitney, Bost. Red Caps	345
1884	Old Hoss Radbourn, Prov. Grays	441

National League (Post-1899)

1900	Noodles Hahn, Cin. Reds	132
1901	Noodles Hahn, Cin. Reds	239
1903	Christy Mathewson, N.Y. Giants	267
1961	Sandy Koufax, L.A. Dodgers	269
1963	Sandy Koufax, L.A. Dodgers	306
1965	Sandy Koufax, L.A. Dodgers	382

Most Strikeouts by Decade

Pre-1900		1900–09		1910–19	
2564	Tim Keefe	2251	Rube Waddell	2219	Walter Johnson
1978	John Clarkson	1799	Christy Mathewson	1539	Grover C. Alexander
1944	Amos Rusie	1565	Cy Young	1253	Hippo Vaughn
1850	Mickey Welch	1342	Eddie Plank	1141	Rube Marquard
1830	Old Hoss Radbourn	1304	Vic Willis	1104	Eddie Cicotte
1803	Tony Mullane	1293	Wild Bill Donovan	1028	Bob Groom
1799	Pud Galvin	1237	Jack Chesbro	1020	Claude Hendrix
1704	Jim McCormick	1209	Jack Powell	938	Lefty Tyler
1700	Charlie Buffinton	1115	Long Tom Hughes	926	Larry Cheney
1650	Gus Weyhing	1105	Doc White	913	Willie Mitchell

1920–29		1930–39		1940–49	
1464	Dazzy Vance	1337	Lefty Gomez	1579	Hal Newhouser
1018	Burleigh Grimes	1313	Lefty Grove	1396	Bob Feller
904	Dolf Luque	1281	Carl Hubbell	1070	Bobo Newsom
895	Walter Johnson	1260	Red Ruffing	972	Johnny Vander Meer
837	Lefty Grove	1207	Tommy Bridges	930	Dizzy Trout
824	Howard Ehmke	1144	Dizzy Dean	863	Kirby Higbe
808	George Uhle	1022	Van Lingle Mungo	791	Allie Reynolds
804	Red Faber	1018	Paul Derringer	779	Dutch Leonard
788	Bob Shawkey	1006	Bump Hadley	772	Mort Cooper
753	Urban Shocker	963	Bobo Newsom	760	Virgil Trucks

1950–59		1960–69		1970–79	
1544	Early Wynn	2071	Bob Gibson	2678	Nolan Ryan
1516	Robin Roberts	2019	Jim Bunning	2304	Tom Seaver
1487	Billy Pierce	1910	Don Drysdale	2097	Steve Carlton
1464	Warren Spahn	1910	Sandy Koufax	2082	Bert Blyleven
1093	Harvey Haddix	1840	Juan Marichal	1907	Gaylord Perry
1072	Bob Rush	1663	Sam McDowell	1866	Phil Niekro
1026	Johnny Antonelli	1585	Jim Maloney	1841	Ferguson Jenkins
1000	Mike Garcia	1435	Jim Kaat	1767	Don Sutton
994	Sam Jones	1428	Bob Veale	1600	Vida Blue
983	Bob Turley	1391	Camilo Pascual	1587	Jerry Koosman

1980–89		1990–99		2000–11	
2167	Nolan Ryan	2538	Randy Johnson	2284	Javier Vasquez
1644	Fernando Valenzuela	2101	Roger Clemens	2182	Randy Johnson*
1629	Jack Morris	1928	David Cone	2017	C. C. Sabathia
1480	Bert Blyleven	1893	John Smoltz	1877	Johan Santana
1457	Bob Welch	1784	Chuck Finley	1839	Roy Halladay
1433	Steve Carlton	1764	Greg Maddux	1821	Josh Beckett
1380	Dave Stieb	1656	Andy Benes	1769	Roy Oswalt
1363	Charlie Hough	1581	Kevin Brown	1683	Barry Zito
1360	Mario Soto	1561	Curt Schilling	1620	Pedro Martinez
1356	Floyd Bannister	1534	Pedro Martinez	1488	Mike Mussina

Members of Same Pitching Staff Finishing One-Two in Strikeouts, Season

American League

Season	Team	Leader	Strikeouts	Runner-Up	Strikeouts
1905	Phila. A's	Rube Waddell	287	Eddie Plank	210
1918	Wash. Senators	Walter Johnson	162	Jim Shaw	129
1919	Wash. Senators	Walter Johnson	147	Jim Shaw	128
1927	Phila. A's	Lefty Grove	174	Rube Walberg	136
1929	Phila. A's	Lefty Grove	170	George Earnshaw	149
1930	Phila. A's	Lefty Grove	209	George Earnshaw	193
1931	Phila. A's	Lefty Grove	175	George Earnshaw	152
1935	Det. Tigers	Tommy Bridges	163	Schoolboy Rowe	140
1944	Det. Tigers	Hal Newhouser	187	Dizzy Trout	144
1948	Cleve. Indians	Bob Feller	164	Bob Lemon	147
1949	Det. Tigers	Virgil Trucks	153	Hal Newhouser	144
1953	Chi. White Sox	Billy Pierce	186	Virgil Trucks	149*
1976	Cal. Angels	Nolan Ryan	327	Frank Tanana	261
1990	Tex. Rangers	Nolan Ryan	232	Bobby Witt	221

National League (Post-1900)

Season	Team	Leader	Strikeouts	Runner-Up	Strikeouts
1903	N.Y. Giants	Christy Mathewson	267	Joe McGinnity	171
1905	N.Y. Giants	Christy Mathewson	206	Red Ames	198
1920	Chi. Cubs	Grover C. Alexander	173	Hippo Vaughn	131 (Tie)
1924	Bklyn. Dodgers	Dazzy Vance	262	Burleigh Grimes	135
1960	L.A. Dodgers	Don Drysdale	246	Sandy Koufax	197
1961	L.A. Dodgers	Sandy Koufax	269	Stan Williams	205
1962	L.A. Dodgers	Don Drysdale	232	Sandy Koufax	216
1987	Hous. Astros	Nolan Ryan	270	Mike Scott	233
1990	N.Y. Mets	David Cone	233	Dwight Gooden	223
2001	Ariz. D'backs	Randy Johnson	372	Curt Schilling	293
2002	Ariz. D'backs	Randy Johnson	334	Curt Schilling	316
2003	Chi. Cubs	Kerry Wood	266	Mark Prior	245

Federal League

Season	Team	Leader	Strikeouts	Runner-Up	Strikeouts
1914	Ind. Hoosiers	Cy Falkenberg	236	Earl Moseley	205

*Trucks also pitched 16 games with St. L. Browns, striking out 47; 102 strikeouts with Chi. White Sox.

Pitchers Leading League with 100 More Strikeouts Than Runner-Up

American League

Season	Leader	Strikeouts	Runner-Up	Strikeouts
1903	Rube Waddell, Phila. A's	302	Wild Bill Donovan, Det. Tigers	187
1904	Rube Waddell, Phila. A's	349	Jack Chesbro, N.Y. Highlanders	239
1973	Nolan Ryan, Cal. Angels	383	Bert Blyleven, Minn. Twins	258
1974	Nolan Ryan, Cal. Angels	367	Bert Blyleven, Minn. Twins	249
1993	Randy Johnson, Sea. Mariners	308	Mark Langston, Cal. Angels	196
1999	Pedro Martinez, Bost. Red Sox	313	Chuck Finley, Ana. Angels	200

National League (Post-1900)

Season	Leader	Strikeouts	Runner-Up	Strikeouts
1924	Dazzy Vance, Bklyn. Dodgers	262	Burleigh Grimes, Bklyn. Dodgers	135
1965	Sandy Koufax, L.A. Dodgers	382	Bob Veale, Pitt. Pirates	276
1979	J. R. Richard, Hous. Astros	313	Steve Carlton, Phila. Phillies	213
1999	Randy Johnson, Ariz. D'backs	364	Kevin Brown, L.A. Dodgers	221
2000	Randy Johnson, Ariz. D'backs	347	Chan Ho Park, L.A. Dodgers	217

Pitchers with 3000 Strikeouts, Never Leading League

Don Sutton (1966–88)	3574	Gaylord Perry (1962–83)	3534

Pitchers Striking Out 1000 Batters Before Their 24th Birthday

	Number of Strikeouts on 24th Birthday	Date of Birth
Bob Feller (1936–41)	1233	Nov. 3, 1918
Bert Blyleven (1970–74)	1094	Apr. 6, 1951
Dwight Gooden (1984–88)	1067	Nov. 16, 1964

Most Times Striking Out 10 or More Batters in a Game, Career

215	Nolan Ryan
212	Randy Johnson
110	Roger Clemens
108	Pedro Martinez
97	Sandy Koufax
93	Curt Schilling
84	Steve Carlton
74	Sam McDowell
74	Bob Gibson
70	Tom Seaver
70	Rube Waddell

Pitchers Averaging 10 Strikeouts per Nine Innings, Season

American League

	Average	Strikeouts	Innings
Pedro Martinez, Bost. Red Sox, 1999	13.20	313	213
Randy Johnson, Sea. Mariners, 1995	12.35	294	214
Randy Johnson, Sea. Mariners, 1997	12.30	291	213
Pedro Martinez, Bost. Red Sox, 2000	11.78	284	217
Nolan Ryan, Tex. Rangers, 1989	11.32	301	239
Erik Bedard, Balt. Orioles, 2007	10.93	221	182
Randy Johnson, Sea. Mariners, 1993	10.86	300	255
Pedro Martinez, Bost. Red Sox, 2002	10.79	239	199
Sam McDowell, Cleve. Indiana, 1965	10.71	325	273
Randy Johnson, Sea. Mariners, 1994	10.67	204	172
Nolan Ryan, Cal. Angels, 1973	10.57	383	326
Nolan Ryan, Tex. Rangers, 1991	10.56	203	173
Johan Santana, Minn. Twins, 2004	10.46	265	228
Nolan Ryan, Cal. Angels, 1972	10.43	329	284
Sam McDowell, Cleve. Indians, 1966	10.42	225	194
Scott Kazmir, T. B. Rays, 2007	10.41	239	207

continued on next page

American League

	Average	Strikeouts	Innings
Roger Clemens, Tor. Blue Jays, 1998	10.39	271	234
Nolan Ryan, Cal. Angels, 1976	10.35	327	284
Randy Johnson, Sea. Mariners, 1992	10.31	241	210
Nolan Ryan, Cal. Angels, 1977	10.26	341	299
David Cone, N.Y. Yankees, 1997	10.25	222	195
Nolan Ryan, Tex. Rangers, 1990	10.24	232	204

National League

	Average	Strikeouts	Innings
Randy Johnson, Ariz. D'backs, 2001	13.41	372	249
Kerry Wood, Chi. Cubs, 1998	12.58	233	166
Randy Johnson, Ariz. D'backs, 2000	12.56	347	248
Randy Johnson, Ariz. D'backs, 1999	12.06	364	271
Randy Johnson, Ariz. D'backs, 2002	11.56	334	260
Nolan Ryan, Hous. Astros, 1987	11.48	270	211
Dwight Gooden, N.Y. Mets, 1984	11.39	276	218
Pedro Martinez, Mont. Expos, 1997	11.37	305	241
Kerry Wood, Chi. Cubs, 2003	11.35	266	211
Curt Schilling, Phila. Phillies, 1997	11.29	319	254
Kerry Wood, Chi. Cubs, 2001	11.20	217	174
Hideo Nomo, L.A. Dodgers, 1995	11.10	236	191
Oliver Perez, Pitts. Pirates, 2004	10.97	239	196
Curt Schilling, Ariz. D'backs, 2002	10.97	316	259
Randy Johnson, Ariz. Diamondbacks, 2004	10.62	290	246
Sandy Koufax, L.A. Dodgers, 1962	10.55	216	184
Zack Greinke, Milw. Brewers, 2011	10.54	201	172
Tim Lincecum, S. F. Giants, 2008	10.51	265	227
Mark Prior, Chi. Cubs, 2003	10.43	245	211
Tim Lincecum, S. F. Giants, 2009	10.42	261	225

Pitchers with Combined Total of 500 Strikeouts and Walks, Season

American League

	Strikeouts	Walks	Total
Bob Feller, Cleve. Indians, 1946	348	153	501
Nolan Ryan, Cal. Angels, 1973	383	162	545
Nolan Ryan, Cal. Angels, 1974	367	202	569
Nolan Ryan, Cal. Angels, 1976	327	183	510
Nolan Ryan, Cal. Angels, 1977	341	204	545

National League

[None]

Pitchers Striking Out the Side on Nine Pitches

American League

Rube Waddell, Phila. A's, July 1, 1902 (3rd inning)

Sloppy Thurston, Chi. White Sox, Aug. 22, 1923 (12th inning)

Lefty Grove, Phila. A's, Aug. 23, 1928 (2nd inning)

Lefty Grove, Phila. A's, Sept. 27, 1928 (7th inning)

Billy Hoeft, Det. Tigers, Sept. 7, 1953 (7th inning, 2nd game)

Jim Bunning, Det. Tigers, Aug. 2, 1959 (9th inning)

Al Downing, N.Y. Yankees, Aug. 11, 1967 (2nd inning, 1st game)

Nolan Ryan, Cal. Angels, July 9, 1972 (2nd inning)

Ron Guidry, N.Y. Yankees, Aug. 7, 1984 (9th inning, 2nd game)

Jeff Montgomery, K.C. Royals, Apr. 29, 1990 (8th inning)

Pedro Martinez, Bost. Red Sox, May 18, 2002 (1st inning)

Rich Hardon, Oak. A's, June 8, 2008 (1st inning)

Felix Hernandez, Sea. Mariners, June 17, 2008 (4th inning)

A. J. Burnett, N. Y. Yankees, June 20, 2009 (3rd inning)

Rafael Soriano, T. B Rays, August 23, 2010 (9th inning)

National League (Post-1900)

Pat Ragan, Bklyn. Dodgers, Oct. 5, 1914 (8th inning, 2nd game)

Hod Eller, Cin. Reds, Aug. 21, 1917 (9th inning)

Joe Oeschger, Bost. Braves, Sept. 8, 1921 (4th inning, 1st game)

Dazzy Vance, Bklyn. Dodgers, Sept. 14, 1924 (3rd inning)

Warren Spahn, Bost. Braves, July 2, 1949 (2nd inning)

Sandy Koufax, L.A. Dodgers, June 30, 1962 (1st inning)

Sandy Koufax, L.A. Dodgers, Apr. 18, 1964 (3rd inning)

Bob Bruce, Hous. Astros, Apr. 19, 1964 (8th inning)

Nolan Ryan, N.Y. Mets, Apr. 19, 1968 (3rd inning)

Bob Gibson, St. L. Cardinals, May 12, 1969 (7th inning)

Milt Pappas, Chi. Cubs, Sept. 24, 1971 (4th inning)

Lynn McGlothen, St. L. Cardinals, Aug. 19, 1975 (2nd inning)

Bruce Sutter, Chi. Cubs, Sept. 8, 1977 (9th inning)

Jeff Robinson, Pitt. Pirates, Sept. 7, 1987 (8th inning)

Rob Dibble, Cin. Reds, June 4, 1989 (8th inning)

Andy Ashby, Phila. Phillies, June 15, 1991 (4th inning)

David Cone, N.Y. Mets, Aug. 30, 1991 (5th inning)

Pete Harnisch, Hous. Astros, Sept. 6, 1991 (7th inning)

Trevor Wilson, S.F. Giants, June 7, 1992 (9th inning)

Mel Rojas, Mont. Expos, May 11, 1994 (9th inning)

Mike Magnante, Hous. Astros, Aug. 22, 1997 (9th inning)

Randy Johnson, Ariz. D'backs, Aug. 23, 2001 (6th inning)

Jason Isringhausen, St. L. Cardinals, Apr. 13, 2002 (9th inning)

Byung-Hyun Kim, Ariz. D'backs, May 11, 2002 (8th inning)

Brian Lawrence, S.D. Padres, June 12, 2002 (3rd inning)

Brandon Backe, Hous. Astros, Apr. 15, 2004 (8th inning)

Ben Sheets, Milw. Brewers, June 13, 2004 (3rd inning)

Latroy Hawkins, Chi. Cubs, Sept. 11, 2004 (9th inning)

Rick Helling, Milw. Brewers, June 20, 2006 (1st inning)

Buddy Carlyle, Atl. Braves, July 6, 2007 (4th inning)

Ross Ohlendorf, Pitt. Pirates, Sept. 5, 2009 (7th inning)

Jordan Zimmermann, Wash. Senators, May 6, 2011 (2nd inning)

Juan Perez, Phila. Phillies, July 8, 2011 (10th inning)

Pitchers with 200 Strikeouts and Fewer Than 50 Walks, Season

American League

	Strikeouts	Walks
Cy Young, Bost. Americans, 1904	200	29
Cy Young, Bost. Americans, 1905	210	30
Walter Johnson, Wash. Senators, 1913	243	38
Jim Kaat, Minn. Twins, 1967	211	42
Ferguson Jenkins, Tex. Rangers, 1974	225	45
Pedro Martinez, Bost. Red Sox, 1999	313	37
Pedro Martinez, Bost. Red Sox, 2000	284	32
Mike Mussina, Balt. Orioles, 2000	210	46
Mike Mussina, N.Y. Yankees, 2001	214	42
Pedro Martinez, Bost. Red Sox, 2002	239	40
Pedro Martinez, Bost. Red Sox, 2003	206	47
Roy Halladay, Tor. Blue Jays, 2003	204	32

American League

	Strikeouts	Walks
Curt Schilling, Bost. Red Sox, 2004	203	35
Randy Johnson, N.Y. Yankees, 2005	211	47
Johan Santana, Minn. Twins, 2005	238	45
Johan Santana, Minn. Twins, 2006	245	47
C. C. Sabathia, Cleve. Indians, 2007	209	37
Ervin Santana, L.A. Angels, 2008	214	47
Roy Halladay, Tor. Blue Jays, 2008	206	39
Roy Halladay, Tor. Blue Jays, 2009	208	35

National League (Post-1900)

	Strikeouts	Walks
Christy Mathewson, N.Y. Giants, 1908	259	42
Jim Bunning, Phila. Phillies, 1964	219	46
Juan Marichal, S.F. Giants, 1965	240	46
Juan Marichal, S.F. Giants, 1966	222	36
Gaylord Perry, S.F. Giants, 1966	201	40
Juan Marichal, S.F. Giants, 1968	218	46
Tom Seaver, N.Y. Mets, 1968	205	48
Ferguson Jenkins, Chi. Cubs, 1971	263	37
Shane Reynolds, Hous. Astros, 1996	2004	44
Greg Maddux, Atl. Braves, 1998	204	45
Kevin Brown, S.D. Padres, 1998	257	49
Kevin Brown, L.A. Dodgers, 2000	216	47
Curt Schilling, Ariz. D'backs, 2001	293	39
Javier Vazquez, Mont. Expos, 2001	208	44
Curt Schilling, Ariz. D'backs, 2002	316	33
Jason Schmidt, S.F. Giants, 2003	208	46
Randy Johnson, Ariz. D'backs, 2004	290	44
Ben Sheets, Milw. Brewers, 2004	264	32
Pedro Martinez, N.Y. Mets, 2005	208	47
Dan Haren, Ariz. D'backs, 2008	206	40
Javier Vazquez, Atl. Braves, 2008	238	44
Dan Haren, Ariz. D'backs, 2009	223	38
Roy Halladay, Phila. Phillies, 2010	219	30
Zeck Greinke, Milw. Brewers, 2011	201	45
Roy Halladay, Phila. Phillies, 2011	220	35
Cliff Lee, Phila. Phillies, 2011	238	42

Rookie Pitchers Striking Out 200 Batters

American League

Herb Score, Cleve. Indians, 1955	245
Russ Ford, N.Y. Highlanders, 1910	209
Bob Johnson, K.C. Royals, 1970	206
Mark Langston, Sea. Mariners, 1984	204
Daisuke Matsuzaka, Bost. Red Sox, 2007	201

National League (Post-1900)

Dwight Gooden, N.Y. Mets, 1984	276
Hideo Nomo, L.A. Dodgers, 1995	236
Kerry Wood, Chi. Cubs, 1998	233
Grover C. Alexander, Phila. Phillies, 1911	227
Tom Hughes, Chi. Cubs, 1901	225

Christy Mathewson, N.Y. Giants, 1901 221
John Montefusco, S.F. Giants, 1975...215
Don Sutton, L.A. Dodgers, 1966 209
Gary Nolan, Cin. Reds, 1966...206
Tom Griffin, Hous. Astros, 1969...200

Rookies Leading League in Strikeouts

American League		National League (Post-1900)	
Lefty Grove, Phila. A's, 1925	116	Dazzy Vance, Bklyn. Dodgers, 1922	134
Allie Reynolds, Cleve. Indians, 1943	151	Dizzy Dean, St. L. Cardinals, 1932	191
Herb Score, Cleve. Indians, 1955	245	Bill Voiselle, N.Y. Giants, 1944	161
Mark Langston, Sea. Mariners, 1984	204	Sam Jones, Chi. Cubs, 1955	198
		Jack Sanford, S.F. Giants, 1957	188
		Fernando Valenzuela, L.A. Dodgers, 1981	180
		Dwight Gooden, N.Y. Mets, 1984	276
		Hideo Nomo, L.A. Dodgers, 1995	236

Pitchers Leading League in Strikeouts, 10 or More Years Apart

Steve Carlton	Phila. Phillies (NL), 1972	Phila. Phillies (NL), 1982 and 1983
Roger Clemens	Bost. Red Sox (AL), 1988	Tor. Blue Jays (AL), 1998
Bob Feller	Cleve. Indians (AL), 1938	Cleve. Indians (AL), 1948
Randy Johnson	Sea. Mariners (AL), 1992	Ariz. D'backs (NL), 2002 and 2004
Walter Johnson	Wash. Senators (AL), 1910	Wash. Senators (AL), 1924
Nolan Ryan	Cal. Angels (AL), 1972	Hous. Astros (NL), 1987 and 1988

Oldest Pitchers to Lead League in Strikeouts

American League			National League		
Age		Strikeouts	Age		Strikeouts
43	Nolan Ryan, Tex. Rangers, 1990	232	41	Nolan Ryan, Hous. Astros, 1988	228
42	Nolan Ryan, Tex. Rangers, 1989	301	41	Randy Johnson, Ariz. D'backs, 2004	290
38	Early Wynn, Chi. White Sox, 1958	184	40	Nolan Ryan, Hous. Astros, 1987	270
37	Early Wynn, Chi. White Sox, 1957	154	39	Randy Johnson, Ariz. D'backs, 2002	334
36	Walter Johnson, Wash. Senators, 1924	158	38	Phil Niekro, Atl. Braves, 1977	262
36	Roger Clemens, Tor. Blue Jays, 1998	271	38	Steve Carlton, Phila. Phillies, 1983	275
35	Walter Johnson, Wash. Senators, 1923	130	38	Randy Johnson, Ariz. D'backs, 2001	372
35	Allie Reynolds, N.Y. Yankees, 1952	160	37	Dazzy Vance, Bklyn. Dodgers, 1928	200
35	Roger Clemens, Tor. Blue Jays, 1997	257	37	Steve Carlton, Phila. Phillies, 1982	286
			37	Randy Johnson, Ariz. D'backs, 2000	347
			36	Dazzy Vance, Bklyn. Dodgers, 1927	184
			36	Randy Johnson, Ariz. D'backs, 1999	364
			35	Dazzy Vance, Bklyn. Dodgers, 1926	140
			35	Jim Bunning, Phila. Phillies, 1967	193
			35	Steve Carlton, Phila. Phillies, 1980	286
			35	Randy Johnson, Ariz. D'backs, 1999	364

Strikeout Leaders on Last-Place Teams

American League		National League	
Sam McDowell, 1969 Cleve. Indians	279	Kirby Higbe, 1940 Phila. Phillies	134
Nolan Ryan, 1974 Calif. Angels	367	Sam Jones, 1956 Chi. Cubs	176
Frank Tanana, 1975 Calif. Angels	269	Steve Carlton, 1972 Phila. Phillies	310
Scott Kazmir, 2007, T.B. Devil Rays	239	Phil Niekro, 1977 Atl. Braves	262
		Randy Johnson, 2004 Ariz. D'backs	290

Walks

Pitchers Walking 20 or Fewer Batters, Season (Min. 200 Innings)

	Walks	Pitcher's Record
Babe Adams, Pitt. Pirates (NL), 1920	18 (in 263 innings)	17–13
Red Lucas, Cin. Reds (NL), 1933	18 (in 219⅔ innings)	10–16
Cliff Lee, Sea. Mariners/Tex. Rangers, 2010	18 (in 212⅓ innings)	12–9
Bob Tewksbury, St. L. Cardinals (NL), 1992	20 (in 233 innings)	16–5
Greg Maddux, Atl. Braves (NL), 1997	20 (in 232⅔ innings)	19–4
Slim Sallee, Cin. Reds (NL), 1919	20 (in 227⅔ innings)	21–7
Bob Tewksbury, St. L. Cardinals (NL), 1993	20 (in 213⅔ innings)	17–10
David Wells, N.Y. Yankees (AL), 2003	20 (in 213 innings)	15–7
La Marr Hoyt, S.D. Padres (NL), 1985	20 (in 210⅓ innings)	16–8

Fewest Walks, Season (Min. One Inning Pitched Each Team Game)

American League			Innings	National League			Innings
9	Carlos Silva, 2005 Minn. Twins		188⅓	13	Bret Saberhagen, 1994 N.Y. Mets		177⅓
18	John Lieber, 2004 N.Y. Yankees		176⅔	15	Babe Adams, 1922 Pitt. Pirates		171½
18	Cliff Lee, 2010 Sea. Mariners/Tex. Rangers		212⅓	18	Babe Adams, 1920 Pitt. Pirates		263
				18	Red Lucas, 1993 Cin. Reds		219⅔
				18	Bill Burns, 1908 Pitt. Pirates		165
				18	Babe Adams, 1921 Pitt. Pirates		160
				19	Dennis Eckersley, 1985 Chi. Cubs		169⅓

Pitchers Walking Fewer Than One Batter Every Nine Innings, Season (min. 160 1P)

American League

	Walks	Innings
Cy Young, Bost. Americans, 1901	37	371
Cy Young, Bost. Americans, 1903	37	342
Cy Young, Bost. Americans, 1904	29	380
Cy Young, Bost. Americans, 1905	30	321
Cy Young, Bost. Americans, 1906	25	288
Addie Joss, Cleve. Indians, 1908	30	325
Bill Burns, Wash. Senators, 1908	18	164
Walter Johnson, Wash. Senators, 1913	38	346
Tiny Bonham, N. Y. Yankees, 1942	24	226
David Wells, N. Y. Yankees, 2003	20	213
Jon Lieber, N. Y. Yankees, 2004	18	177
Carlos Silva, Minn. Twins, 2005	9	188
Cliff Lee, Sea. Mariners/Tex. Rangers, 2010	18	212

National League (Post-1900)

	Walks	Innings
Deacon Phillippe, Pitts. Pirates, 1902	26	272
Jesse Tannehill, Pitts. Pirates, 1902	25	231

Deacon Phillippe, Pitts. Pirates, 1903	29	289
Christy Mathewson, N.Y. Giants, 1913	21	306
Christy Mathewson, N.Y. Giants, 1914	23	312
Babe Adams, Pitt. Pirates, 1919	23	263
Slim Sallee, Cin. Reds, 1919	20	228
Babe Adams, Pitt. Pirates, 1920	18	263
Grover C. Alexander, Chi. Cubs, 1923	30	305
Red Lucas, Cin. Reds, 1933	18	220
LaMarr Hoyt, S.D. Padres, 1985	20	210
Bob Tewksbury, St. L. Cardinals, 1992	20	233
Bob Tewksbury, St. L. Cardinals, 1993	20	213
Bret Saberhagen, N.Y. Mets, 1994	13	177
Greg Maddux, Atl. Braves, 1995	23	210
Greg Maddux, Atl. Braves, 1997	20	232
David Wells, S.D. Padres, 2004	20	196

Highest Percentage of Walks to Innings Pitched, Season

American League

	Walks	Innings	Percentage
Tommy Byrne, N.Y. Yankees/St. L. Browns, 1951	150	144	1.041
Bobby Witt, Tex. Rangers, 1987	140	143	.979
Tommy Byrne, N.Y. Yankees, 1949	179	196	.913
Bobby Witt, Tex. Rangers, 1986	143	157	.911
Randy Johnson, Sea. Mariners, 1991	152	201	.756
Bob Feller, Cleve. Indians, 1938	200	278	.748
Bob Turley, Balt. Orioles, 1954	181	247	.732
Bob Turley, N.Y. Yankees, 1955	177	247	.716
Bump Hadley, Chi. White Sox–St. L. Browns, 1932	171	248	.689
Randy Johnson, Sea. Mariners, 1992	144	210	.686
Bobo Newsom, Wash. Senators–Bost. Red Sox, 1937	167	275	.607
Nolan Ryan, Cal. Angels, 1974	202	333	.607
John Wycoff, Phila. A's, 1915	165	276	.598
Bobo Newsom, St. L. Browns, 1938	192	330	.582

National League (Post-1900)

	Walks	Innings	Percentage
Ray Golden, St. L. Cardinals, 1911	129	149	.866
Sam Jones, Chi. Cubs, 1955	185	242	.764

Low-Hit Games

Pitchers Losing No-Hit Games

American League

Earl Moore, Cleve. Indians (vs. White Sox), May 9, 1901 .... Allowed 2 hits and 4 runs in 10th, lost 2–4

Tom Hughes, N.Y. Highlanders (vs. Cleve. Naps), Aug. 30, 1910 .... Allowed hit in 10th by Harry Niles, lost 0–5 in 11 innings

Jim Scott, Chi. White Sox (vs. Wash. Senators), May 14, 1914 .... Allowed hit in 10th by Chick Gandil, lost 0–1

Bobo Newsom, St. L. Browns (vs. Bost. Red Sox), Sept. 18, 1934 .... Allowed hit in 10th by Roy Johnson, lost 1–2

Steve Barber (8⅔ innings) and Stu Miller (⅓ inning),
    Balt. Orioles (vs. Det. Tigers), Apr. 30, 1967 .... Lost on wild pitch and error. 1–2

National League

Red Ames, N.Y. Giants (vs. Bklyn. Dodgers), Apr. 15, 1909 .... Allowed hit in 10th by Whitey Alperman and lost 0–3 in 13 innings

Hippo Vaughn*, Chi. Cubs (vs. Cin. Reds), May 2, 1917 .... Allowed 2 hits in 10th, lost 0–1

Johnny Klippstein (7 innings), Hersh Freeman (1 inning), and
    Joe Black (2⅓ innings), Cin. Reds (vs. Milw. Braves),
    May 26, 1956 .... Black gave up 1 hit in 10th and 3 in 11th, lost 1–2

Harvey Haddix, Pitt. Pirates (vs. Milw. Braves), May 26, 1959 .... Pitched 12 perfect innings, gave up hit in 13th, lost 0–1

Ken Johnson, Hous. Astros (vs. Cin. Reds), Apr. 23, 1964 .... Johnson lost 0–1 after 2 Astro errors in 9th

Jim Maloney, Cin. Reds (vs. N.Y. Mets), June 14, 1965 .... Allowed home run to Johnny Lewis in 11th-inning, lost 0–1

Mark Gardner, Mont. Expos (vs. L.A. Dodgers), July 26, 1991 .... Allowed hit in 10th, lost 0–1

Pedro Martinez (9 innings) and Mel Rojas (1 inning),
    Mont. Expos (vs. S.D. Padres), June 3, 1995 .... Allowed hit in 10th after 9 perfect innings, won 1–0

*Vaughn lost to Cincinnati's Jim Toney, who also pitched a no-hitter.

Pitchers with a No-Hitter in First Major League Start

Ted Breitenstein, St. L. Browns (vs. Louis. Colonels) (AA), Oct. 4, 1891 (final score: 8–0)
Bumpus Jones, Cin. Reds (vs. Pitt. Pirates) (NL), Oct. 15, 1892 (final score: 7–1)
Bobo Holloman, St. L. Browns (vs. Phila. A's) (AL), May 6, 1953 (final score: 6–0)

Pitchers with a One-Hitter in First Major League Game

Addie Joss, Cleve. Indians (AL), Apr. 26, 1902
Ed Albrecht, St. L. Browns (AL), October 2, 1949
Mike Fornieles, Wash. Senators (AL), Sept. 2, 1952
Juan Marichal, S.F. Giants (NL), July 19, 1960

Bill Rohr, Bost. Red Sox (AL), Apr. 14, 1967
Jimmy Jones, S.D. Padres (NL), Sept. 21, 1986

Last Outs in Perfect Games*

Lee Richmond, Worc. Brown Stockings (NL) (vs. Cleve.
Spiders, NL), June 12, 1880 (final: 1–0).....................Last out: second baseman George Creamer
John M. Ward, Prov. Grays (NL) (vs. Buff. Bisons, NL),
June 17, 1880 (final: 5–0)..........................Last out: pitcher Pud Galvin
Cy Young, Bost. Red Sox (AL) (vs. Phila. A's, AL), May 5, 1904
(final: 3–0)...........................Last out: pitcher Rube Waddell (fly out to center)
Addie Joss, Cleve. Indians (AL) (vs. Chi. White Sox, AL),
Oct. 2, 1908 (final: 1–0)...................Last out: pinch hitter John Anderson (ground out to third)
Ernie Shore, Bost. Red Sox (AL) (vs. Wash. Senators, AL),
June 23, 1917 (final: 4–0)...................Last out: pinch hitter Mike Menosky (pop out to second)
Charley Robertson, Chi. White Sox (AL) (vs. Det. Tigers, AL),
Apr. 30, 1922 (final: 2–0)...................Last out: pinch hitter John Bassler (fly out to left)
Don Larsen, N.Y. Yankees (AL) (vs. Bklyn. Dodgers, NL)
(World Series), Oct. 8, 1956 (final: 2–0) ....Last out: pinch hitter Dale Mitchell (strikeout)
Harvey Haddix, Pitt. Pirates (NL) (vs. Milw. Braves, NL),
May 26, 1959 (final: 0–1)...................Last batter: first baseman Joe Adcock (double in 13th inning)
Jim Bunning, Phila. Phillies (NL) (vs. N.Y. Mets, NL),
June 21, 1964 (final: 6–0)...................Last out: pinch hitter John Stephenson (strikeout)
Sandy Koufax, L.A. Dodgers (NL) (vs. Chi. Cubs, NL),
Sept. 9, 1965 (final: 1–0)...................Last out: pinch hitter Harvey Kuenn (strikeout)
Catfish Hunter, Oak. A's (AL) (vs. Minn. Twins, AL),
May 8, 1968 (final: 4–0)...................Last out: pinch hitter Rich Reese (strikeout)
Len Barker, Cleve. Indians (AL) (vs. Tor. Blue Jays, AL),
May 15, 1981 (final: 3–0)...................Last out: pinch hitter Ernie Whitt (fly out to center)
Mike Witt, Cal. Angels (AL) (vs. Tex. Rangers, AL),
Sept. 30, 1984 (final: 1–0)...................Last out: Marv Foley (ground out to second)
Tom Browning, Cin. Reds (NL) (vs. L.A. Dodgers, NL),
Sept. 16, 1988 (final: 1–0)...................Last out: pinch hitter Tracy Woodson (strikeout)
Dennis Martinez, Mont. Expos (NL) (vs. L.A. Dodgers, NL),
July 28, 1991 (final: 2–0)...................Last out: pinch hitter Chris Gwynn (fly out to center)
Kenny Rogers, Tex. Rangers (AL) (vs. Cal. Angels, AL),
July 29, 1994 (final: 4–0)...................Last out: Gary DiSarcina (fly out to center)
Pedro Martinez, Mont. Expos (NL) (vs. S.D. Padres, NL),
June 3, 1995 (final: 1–0) ....Last out: Martinez gave up hit in 10th, relieved by Mel
Rojas who retired Ken Caminiti on pop-up to third
David Wells, N.Y. Yankees (AL) (vs. Minn. Twins, AL),
May 17, 1998 (final: 4–0)...................Last out: Pat Meares (fly out to center)
David Cone, N.Y. Yankees (AL) (vs. Mont. Expos, NL),
July 18, 1999 (final: 5–0)...................Last out: Orlando Cabrera (foul pop to third)
Randy Johnson, Ariz. D'backs (NL) (vs. Atl. Braves, NL),
May 18, 2004 (final: 2–0)...................Last out: pinch hitter Eddie Perez (strikeout)
Mark Buehrle, Chi. White Sox (AL) (vs. T.B. Rays, AL),
July 23, 2009 (final: 5–0)...................Last out: Jason Bartlett (ground out to shortstop)

Dallas Braden, Oak. A's (AL) (vs. T.B. Rays, AL),

May 9, 2010 (final: 4–0)...Last out: Gabe Kapler (ground out to shortstop)

Roy Halladay, Phila. Phillies (NL) (vs Fla. Marlins NL),

May 29, 2010 (final: 1–0)..Last out: pinch hitter Ronny Paulino (ground out to third)

*27 batters up, 27 out.

Perfect Game Pitchers, Career Wins

Cy Young (1890–1911)...511
Randy Johnson (1988–2009)..303
Dennis Martinez (1976–98)..245
David Wells (1988–2007) 239
Jim Bunning (1955–71)..224
Catfish Hunter (1965–79)...224
Pedro Martinez (1992–2009)...219
Kenny Rogers (1989–2008)..219
David Cone (1986–2001, 2003)...194
Roy Halladay*(1998–) 188
Sandy Koufax (1955–66) 165
Monte Ward (1878–84) 161
Mark Buehrle* (2000–) 161
Addie Joss (1902–10)..160
Harvey Haddix (1952–65) 136
Tom Browning (1984–95) 123
Mike Witt (1981–91, 1993) 117
Don Larsen (1953–65, 1967) 81
Lee Richmond (1879–83, 1886)...75
Len Barker (1976–85, 1987) 74
Ernie Shore (1912, 1914–17, 1919–20) 65
Charlie Robertson (1919, 1922–28)..49
Dallas Braden* (2007–) 26

*Still active.

26-Batter Perfect Games (Spoiled by 27th Batter)

	Spoiler
Hooks Wiltse, N.Y. Giants (vs. Phila. Phillies) (NL), July 4, 1908	George McQuillan, hit by pitch
Tommy Bridges, Det. Tigers (vs. Wash. Senators) (AL), Aug. 5, 1932	Dave Harris, singled
Billy Pierce, Chi. White Sox (vs. Wash. Senators) (AL), June 28, 1958	Ed FitzGerald, doubled
Milt Pappas, Chi. Cubs (vs. S.D. Padres) (NL), Sept. 2, 1972	Larry Stahl, walked
Milt Wilcox, Det. Tigers (vs. Chi. White Sox) (AL), Apr. 15, 1983	Jerry Hairston, singled
Ron Robinson, Cin. Reds (vs. Mont. Expos) (NL), May 2, 1988	Wallace Johnson, singled
Dave Stieb, Tor. Blue Jays (vs. N.Y. Yankees) (AL), Aug. 4, 1989	Roberto Kelly, doubled
Brian Holman, Sea. Mariners (vs. Oak. A's) (AL), Apr. 20, 1990	Ken Phelps, home run
Mike Mussina, N.Y. Yankees (vs. Bost. Red Sox) (AL), Sept. 2, 2001	Carl Everett, singled
Armando Galarraga, Det. Tigers (vs. Cleve. Indians) (AL), June 2010	Jason Donald, infield hit

Most Walks Given Up by No-Hit Pitchers, Game

11 ....Blue Moon Odom (9 in 5 innings) and Francisco Barrios (2 in 4 innings), Chi. White Sox (vs. Oakland A's) (AL),
July 28, 1976, won 6–0

10 ....Jim Maloney, Cin. Reds (vs. Chi. Cubs) (NL), Aug. 19, 1965, won 1–0

10 ....Steve Barber (10 in 8⅔ innings) and Stu Miller (0 in ⅓ inning), Balt. Orioles (vs. Det. Tigers) (AL),
Apr. 30, 1967, lost 1–2

9 ....John Klippstein (7 in 7 innings), Hersh Freeman (0 in 1 inning), and Joe Black (2 in 1 inning), Cin. Reds
(vs. Milw. Braves) (NL), May 26, 1956, lost 1–2

9 ................A.J. Burnett, Fla. Marlins (vs.S.D. Padres) (NL), May 12, 2001, won 3–0

continued on next page

8 ....Amos Rusie, N.Y. Giants (vs. Bklyn. Bridegrooms) (NL), July 31, 1891, won 6–0
8 ....Johnny Vander Meer, Cin. Reds (vs. Bklyn. Dodgers) (NL), June 15, 1938, won 6–0
8 ....Cliff Chambers, Pitt. Pirates (vs. Bost. Braves) (NL), May 6, 1951, won 3–0
8 ....Dock Ellis, Pitt. Pirates (vs. S.D. Padres) (NL), June 12, 1970, won 2–0
8 ....Nolan Ryan, Cal. Angels (vs. Minn. Twins) (AL), Sept. 28, 1974, won 4–0
8 ....Edwin Jackson, Ariz. Diamondbacks (vs.T.B. Rays) (AL), June 25, 2010, won 1–0
7 ....Bobo Newsom, St. L. Browns (vs. Bost. Red Sox) (AL), Sept. 18, 1934, lost 1–2
7 ....Sam Jones, Chi. Cubs (vs. Pitt. Pirates) (NL), May 12, 1955, won 4–0
7 ....Burt Hooton, Chi. Cubs (vs. Phila. Phillies) (NL), Apr. 16, 1972, won 4–0
7 ....Bill Stoneman, Mont. Expos (vs. N.Y. Mets) (NL), Oct. 2, 1972, won 7–0
7 ....Joe Cowley, Chi. White Sox (vs. Cal. Angels) (AL), Sept. 19, 1986, won 7–1
7 ....Tommy Greene, Phila. Phillies (vs. Mont. Expos (NL), May 23, 1991, won 2–0
7 ....Matt Young, Bost. Red Sox (vs. Cleve. Indians) (AL), April 12, 1992, lost 1–2

Pitchers Pitching No-Hitters in 20-Loss Season

	Wins	Losses
Joe Bush, Phila. A's (vs. Cleve. Indians), Aug. 26, 1916	15	22
Sam Jones, Chi. Cubs (vs. Pitt. Pirates), May 12, 1955	14	20
Harry McIntire, Bklyn. Dodgers* (vs. Pitt. Pirates), Aug. 1, 1906	12	21
Bobo Newsom, St. L. Browns* (vs. Bost. Red Sox), Sept. 18, 1934	16	20
Nap Rucker, Bklyn. Dodgers (vs. Bost. Braves), Sept. 5, 1908	18	20

*Lost in extra innings.

Pitchers Hitting Home Runs in No-Hit Games

	Opposing Pitcher(s)
Wes Ferrell, Cleve. Indians (vs. St. L. Cardinals) (NL), Apr. 29, 1931	Sam Gray
Jim Tobin, Bost. Braves (vs. Bklyn. Dodgers) (NL), Apr. 27, 1944	Fritz Ostermueller
Earl Wilson, Bost. Red Sox (vs. L.A. Angels) (AL), June 26, 1962	Bo Belinsky
Rick Wise, Phila. Phillies (vs. Cin. Reds) (NL), June 23, 1971	Ross Grimsley and Clay Carroll (2)

Pitchers Throwing No-Hitters in Consecutive Seasons

4 ....Sandy Koufax, L.A. Dodgers, 1962–65
3 ....Nolan Ryan, Cal. Angels, 1973–75
2 ....Warren Spahn, Milw. Braves, 1960–61
2 ....Steve Busby, K.C. Royals, 1973–74

No-Hitters Pitched Against Pennant-Winning Teams

American League

Ernie Koob, St. L. Browns (vs. Chi. White Sox), May 5, 1917
Bob Groom, St. L. Browns (vs. Chi. White Sox), May 6, 1917
Virgil Trucks, Det. Tigers (vs. N.Y. Yankees), Aug. 25, 1952
Hoyt Wilhelm, Balt. Orioles (vs. N.Y. Yankees), Sept. 20, 1958
Jim Bibby, Tex. Rangers (vs. Oak. A's), July 30, 1973
Dick Bosman, Cleve. Indians (vs. Oak. A's), July 19, 1974
Nolan Ryan, Tex. Rangers (vs. Oak. A's), June 11, 1990
Mark Buehrle, Chi. White Sox (vs. T.B. Rays), July 23, 2009

National League (Post-1900)

Tex Carleton, Bklyn. Dodgers (vs. Cin. Reds), Apr. 30, 1940
Bob Moose, Pitt. Pirates (vs. N.Y. Mets), Sept. 20, 1969
Bob Gibson, St. L. Cardinals (vs. Pitt. Pirates), Aug. 14, 1971
Nolan Ryan, Hous. Astros (vs. L.A. Dodgers), Sept. 26, 1981
Tom Browning, Cin. Reds (vs. L.A. Dodgers), Sept. 16, 1988 (perfect game)
Roy Oswalt, Pete Munro, Kirk Saarloos, Brad Lidge, Octavio Dotel, and Billy Wagner, Hous. Astros (vs. N.Y. Yankees, AL), June 11, 2003

No-Hit Pitchers Going Winless the Next Season After Pitching No-Hitter

American League

Weldon Henley, Phila. A's (vs. St. L. Browns), July 22, 1905
Tom Hughes, N.Y. Highlanders (vs. Cleve. Indians), Aug. 30 1910

National League (Post-1900)

Mal Eason, Bklyn. Dodgers (vs. St. L. Cardinals), July 20, 1906*
Jeff Pfeffer, Bost. Braves (vs. Cin. Reds), May 8, 1907

Addie Joss, Cleve. Indians (vs. Chi. White Sox), Apr. 20, 1910*

Ernie Koob, St. L. Browns (vs. Chi. White Sox), May 5, 1917

Ernie Shore, Bost. Red Sox (vs. Wash. Senators), June 23, 1917

Bobo Holloman, St. L. Browns (vs. Phila. A's), May 6, 1953**

Mel Parnell, Bost. Red Sox (vs. Chi. White Sox), July 14, 1956*

Bob Keegan, Chi. White Sox (vs. Wash. Senators), Aug. 20, 1957

Joe Cowley, Chi. White Sox (vs. Cal. Angels), Sept. 19, 1986

Mike Witt, Cal. Angels (vs. Sea. Mariners), Apr. 11, 1990***

Mike Flanagan, Balt. Orioles (vs. Oak. A's), July 13, 1991***

Mark Williamson, Balt. Orioles (vs. Oak. A's), July 13, 1991***

Tex Carleton, Bklyn. Dodgers (vs. Cin. Reds), Apr. 30, 1940*

Clyde Shoun, Cin. Reds (vs. Bost. Braves), May 15, 1944

Ed Head, Bklyn. Dodgers (vs. Bost. Braves), Apr. 23, 1946*

Jim Maloney, Cin. Reds (vs. Hous. Astros), Apr. 30, 1969

Fernando Valenzuela, L.A. Dodgers (vs. St. L. Cardinals), June 29, 1990

Ricardo Rincon, Pitt. Pirates (vs. Hous. Astros), July 12, 1997***

*Last Major League season.
**Only Major League season.
***Pitched no-hitter in tandem with other pitcher(s).

Back-to-Back One-Hit Games (Post-1900)

Rube Marquard, N.Y. Giants (NL) ....Aug. 28 and Sept. 1, 1911
Lon Warneke, Chi. Cubs (NL) ....Apr. 17 and Apr. 22, 1934
Mort Cooper, St. L. Cardinals (NL) ....May 31 and June 4, 1943
Whitey Ford, N.Y. Yankees (AL) ....Sept. 2 and Sept. 7, 1955
Sam McDowell, Cleve. Indians (AL) ....Apr. 25 and May 1, 1966
Dave Steib, Tor. Blue Jays (AL) ....Sept. 24 and Oct. 1, 1988

Rookies Throwing No-Hitters

American League

Pitcher	Date	Result
Clay Buchholz**	Sept. 1, 2007	Bost. Red Sox vs. Balt. Orioles, 10–0
Wilson Alvarez**	Aug. 11, 1991	Chi. Cubs at Balt. Orioles, 7–0
Mike Warren	Sept. 29, 1983	Oak. A's vs. Chi. Cubs, 3–0
Jim Bibby	July 30, 1973	Tex. Rangers at Oak. A's, 6–0
Steve Busby	Apr. 27, 1973	K.C. Royals at Det. Tigers, 3–0
Vida Ble	Sept. 21, 1970	Oak. A's vs. Minn. Twins, 6–0
Bo Belinsky	May 5, 1962	L.A. Dodgers vs. Balt. Orioles, 2–0
Bobo Holloman*	May 6, 1953	St. L. Browns vs. Phila. Athletics, 6–0
Bill McCahan	Sept. 3, 1947	Phila. Athletics vs. Wash. Senators, 3–0
Vern Kennedy	Aug. 31, 1935	Chi. White Sox vs. Cleve. Indians, 5–0
Charlie Robertson	April 30, 1922	Chi. White Sox vs. Cleve. Indians, 2–0 (PG)

*First Major League Start.
**Second Major League Start.

National League

Pitcher	Date	Result
Anibal Sanchez	Sept. 6, 2006	Flor. Mariners vs. Ariz. D'backs, 2–0
Bud Smith	Sept. 3, 2001	St. L. Cardinals at S.D. Padres, 4–0
Jose Jimenez	June 25, 1999	St. L. Cardinals vs. Ariz. D'backs, 1–0
Burt Hooton	April 16, 1972	Chi. Cubs vs. Phila. Phillies, 4–0
Don Wilson	June 18, 1967	Hous. Astros vs. Atl. Braves, 2–0
Sam Jones	May 12, 1955	Chi. Cubs vs. Pitt. Pirates, 4–0
Paul Dean	Sept. 21, 1934	St. L. Cardinals vs. Bklyn. Dodgers, 3–0
Jeff Tesreau	Sept. 6, 1912	N.Y. Giants at Phila. Phillies, 3–0
Nick Maddox	Sept. 20, 1907	Pitt. Pirates vs. Bklyn. Dodgers, 2–1
Christy Mathewson	July 15, 1901	N.Y. Dodgers vs. St. L. Cardinals, 5–0

Saves/Reliefs
Evolution of Saves Record

American League

1901	Bill Hoffer, Cleve. Indians	3
1908	Ed Walsh, Chi. White Sox	6
1909	Frank Arellanes, Bost. Americans	8
1912	Ed Walsh, Chi. White Sox	10
1913	Chief Bender, Phila. A's	13
1924	Firpo Marberry, Wash. Senators	15
1926	Firpo Marberry, Wash. Senators	22
1949	Joe Page, N.Y. Yankees	27
1961	Luis Arroyo, N.Y. Yankees	29
1966	Jack Aker, K.C. A's	32
1970	Ron Perranoski, Minn. Twins	34
1972	Sparky Lyle, N.Y. Yankees	35
1973	John Hiller, Det. Tigers	38
1983	Dan Quisenberry, K.C. Royals	45
1986	Dave Righetti, N.Y. Yankees	46
1990	Bobby Thigpen, Chi. White Sox	57
2008	Francisco Rodriguez, L.A. Angels	62

National League (Post-1899)

1900	Frank Kitson, Bklyn. Dodgers	4
1904	Joe McGinnity, N.Y. Giants	5
1905	Claude Elliott, Bost. Braves	6
1906	Cecil Ferguson, N.Y. Giants	7
1911	Three Finger Brown, Chi. Cubs	13
1931	John P. Quinn, Phila. Phillies	15
1947	Hugh Casey, Bklyn. Dodgers	18
1950	Jim Konstanty, Phila. Phillies	22
1954	Jim Hughes, Bklyn. Dodgers	24
1960	Lindy McDaniel, St. L. Cardinals	26
1962	Roy Face, Pitt. Pirates	28
1965	Ted Abernathy, Chi. Cubs	31
1970	Wayne Granger, Cin. Reds	35
1972	Clay Carroll, Cin. Reds	37
1984	Bruce Sutter, St. L. Cardinals	45
1991	Lee Smith, St. L. Cardinals	47
1993	Randy Myers, Chi. Cubs	53
2002	John Smoltz, Atl. Braves	55

Pitchers with 100 Wins and 100 Saves, Career

	Wins	Saves
Dennis Eckersley (1975–98)	197	390
Roy Face (1953, 1955–69)	104	193
Rollie Fingers (1968–85)	114	341
Dave Giusti (1962, 1964–77)	100	145
Tom Gordon (1988–2009)	138	158
Goose Gossage (1972–94)	124	310
Ellis Kinder (1946–57)	102	102

Ron Kline (1952, 1955–70)..............................114 108
Firpo Marberry (1923–36) 148 101
Lindy McDaniel (1955–75) 141 172
Stu Miller (1952–54, 1956–68) 105 154
Ron Reed (1966–84)..............................146 103
John Smoltz (1998–2009) 213 154
Bob Stanley (1977–89) 115 132
Hoyt Wilhelm (1952–72)..............................143 227

Relief Pitchers with the Most Wins, Season

American League

John Hiller, Det. Tigers, 1974 17–14
Bill Campbell, Minn. Twins, 1976 17–5
Tom Johnson, Minn. Twins, 1977 16–7
Dick Radatz, Bost. Red Sox, 1964 16–9
Luis Arroyo, N.Y. Yankees, 1961 15–5
Dick Radatz, Bost. Red Sox, 1963 15–6
Eddie Fisher, Chi. White Sox, 1965 15–7

*Started two games, no decisions

National League (Post-1900)

Roy Face, Pitt. Pirates, 1959 18–1
Jim Konstanty, Phila. Phillies, 1950 16–7
Ron Perranoski, L.A. Dodgers, 1963 16–3
Mace Brown, Pitt. Pirates, 1938 ....15–9*
Hoyt Wilhelm, N.Y. Giants, 1952 15–3
Mike Marshall, L.A. Dodgers, 1974 15–12
Dale Murray, Mont. Expos, 1975...............................15–8

Most Games Won by Relief Pitcher, Career

Hoyt Wilhelm (1952–72)..............................124
Lindy McDaniel (1955–75)..............................119
Goose Gossage (1972–94)..............................115
Rollie Fingers (1968–85)..............................107
Sparky Lyle (1967–82)..............................99
Roy Face (1953–69)..............................96
Gene Garber (1969–87)..............................94
Kent Tekulve (1974–89)..............................94
Mike Marshall (1967–81)..............................92

Teams with Two Pitchers with 20 Saves, Season

1965..........Chi. White Sox (AL) ....Eddie Fisher.................24 ....Hoyt Wilhelm 20
1983..........S.F. Giants (NL) ....Greg Minton ....22 ....Gary Lavelle...............20
1986..........N.Y. Mets (NL)...............................Roger McDowell ....22 ....Jesse Orosco 21

Pitchers Having 20-Win Seasons and 20-Save Seasons, Career

		Wins	Saves
Dennis Eckersley	Bost. Red Sox (AL), 1978	20	
	Oak. A's (AL), 1988		45
	Oak. A's (AL), 1989		33
	Oak. A's (AL), 1990		48
	Oak. A's (AL), 1991		43
	Oak. A's (AL), 1992		51
	Oak. A's (AL), 1993		36
	Oak. A's (AL), 1995		29
	St. L. Cardinals (NL), 1996		30
	St. L. Cardinals (NL), 1997		36
Mudcat Grant	Minn. Twins (AL), 1965	21	
	Oak. A's (AL)–Pitt. Pirates (NL), 1970		24

continued on next page

	Wins	Saves
Ellis Kinder .... Bost. Red Sox (AL), 1949 23		
.... Bost. Red Sox (AL), 1953		27
Johnny Sain .... Bost. Braves (NL), 1946 20		
.... Bost. Braves (NL), 1947 21		
.... Bost. Braves (NL), 1948 24		
.... Bost. Braves (NL), 1950 20		
.... N.Y. Yankees (AL), 1954		22
John Smoltz .... Atl. Braves (NL), 1996 24		
.... Atl. Braves (NL), 2002		55
.... Atl. Braves (NL), 2003		45
.... Atl. Braves (NL), 2004		45
Wilbur Wood .... Chi. White Sox (AL), 1970		21
.... Chi. White Sox (AL), 1971 22		
.... Chi. White Sox (AL), 1972 24		
.... Chi. White Sox (AL), 1973 24		
.... Chi. White Sox (AL), 1974 20		

Pitchers with 15 Saves and 15 Wins in Relief, Same Season

American League

	Wins	Saves
Luis Arroyo, N.Y. Yankees, 1961	15	29
Dick Radatz, Bost. Red Sox, 1963	15	25
Dick Radatz, Bost. Red Sox, 1964	16	29
Eddie Fisher, Chi. White Sox, 1965	15	24
Bill Campbell, Minn. Twins, 1976	17	20
Tom Johnson, Minn. Twins, 1977	16	15

National League (Post-1900)

	Wins	Saves
Jim Konstanty, Phila. Phillies, 1950	16	22
Joe Black, Bklyn. Dodgers, 1952	15	15
Ron Perranoski, L.A. Dodgers, 1963	16	21
Mike Marshall, L.A. Dodgers, 1974	15	21

Pitching Miscellany

Best Winning Percentage by Decade (100 Decisions)

Pre-1900		1900–09		1910–19	
.701	Bill Hoffer	.713	Ed Reulbach	.682	Smokey Joe Wood
.690	Dave Foutz	.697	Sam Leever	.675	Grover C. Alexander
.688	Bob Caruthers	.689	Three Finger Brown	.663	Chief Bender
.665	Larry Corcoran	.678	Christy Mathewson	.659	Babe Ruth
.663	Kid Nichols	.636	Ed Walsh	.657	Eddie Plank
.650	Ted Lewis	.634	Hooks Wiltse	.656	Doc Crandall
.648	John Clarkson	.634	Jack Pfiester	.650	Walter Johnson
.640	Lady Baldwin	.634	Joe McGinnity	.643	Christy Mathewson
.639	Cy Young	.633	Jesse Tannehill	.621	Jack Coombs
.630	Nig Cuppy	.631	Deacon Phillippe	.615	Jeff Tesreau

1920–29		1930–39		1940–49	
.660	Ray Kremer	.724	Lefty Grove	.714	Spud Chandler
.638	Carl Mays	.706	Johnny Allen	.640	Tex Hughson
.627	Urban Shocker	.686	Firpo Marberry	.640	Harry Brecheen
.626	Freddie Fitzsimmons	.650	Lefty Gomez	.629	Howie Pollet
.626	Lefty Grove	.648	Dizzy Dean	.626	Mort Cooper
.620	Dazzy Vance	.644	Carl Hubbell	.626	Bob Feller
.615	Art Nehf	.641	Red Ruffing	.621	Max Lanier
.612	Waite Hoyt	.634	Monte Pearson	.619	Schoolboy Rowe
.611	Grover C. Alexander	.629	Lon Warneke	.613	Warren Spahn
.599	Stan Coveleski	.602	Bill Lee	.605	Rip Sewell

1950–59		1960–69		1970–79	
.708	Whitey Ford	.695	Sandy Koufax	.686	Don Gullett
.669	Allie Reynolds	.685	Juan Marichal	.648	John Candelaria
.667	Eddie Lopat	.673	Whitey Ford	.647	Pedro Borbon
.663	Sal Maglie	.667	Denny McLain	.644	Jim Palmer
.643	Vic Raschi	.626	Jim Maloney	.638	Tom Seaver
.633	Don Newcombe	.621	Dave McNally	.624	Catfish Hunter
.618	Bob Buhl	.610	Bob Gibson	.613	Tommy John
.615	Bob Lemon	.596	Ray Culp	.612	Gary Nolan
.612	Early Wynn	.593	Bob Purkey	.610	Clay Carroll
.607	Warren Spahn	.582	Dick Hall	.607	Luis Tiant

1980–89		1990–99		2000–09	
.719	Dwight Gooden	.682	Pedro Martinez	.691	Jon Lester
.679	Roger Clemens	.673	Mike Mussina	.691	Pedro Martinez
.639	Ted Higuera	.667	Randy Johnson	.682	Roger Clemens
.613	Ron Darling	.667	Greg Maddux	.678	Roy Halladay
.612	John Tudor	.653	Tom Glavine	.658	Johan Santana
.607	Ron Guidry	.642	Kick Rueter	.653	Adam Wainwright
.605	Sid Fernandez	.638	Andy Pettitte	.652	Justin Verlander
.605	Orel Hershiser	.631	Roger Clemens	.650	Curt Schilling
.605	Dennis Rasmussen	.626	Jose Rijo	.647	Randy Johnson
.602	Jimmy Key	.624	David Cone	.647	C. C. Sabathia

Most Seasons Leading League in Pitching Category

American League

	Seasons	
Games Pitched	6	Firpo Marberry, 1924–26, 1928–29, and 1932
Complete Games	6	Walter Johnson, 1910–11 and 1913–16
Innings Pitched	5	Walter Johnson, 1910 and 1913–16
	5	Bob Feller, 1939–41 and 1946–47
Games Won	6	Walter Johnson, 1913–16, 1918, and 1924
Games Lost	4	Bobo Newsom, 1934–35, 1941, and 1945
	4	Pedro Ramos, 1958–61
Won-Lost Percentage	5	Lefty Grove, 1929–31, 1933, and 1939
ERA	9	Lefty Grove, 1926, 1929–32, 1935–36, and 1938–39
Strikeouts	12	Walter Johnson, 1910, 1912–19, 1921, and 1923–24
Shutouts	7	Walter Johnson, 1911, 1913–15, 1918–19, and 1924
Saves	5	Firpo Marberry, 1924–26, 1929, and 1932
	5	Dan Quisenberry, 1980 and 1982–85

continued on next page

National League (Post-1900)

Seasons

Games Pitched	6	Joe McGinnity, 1900 and 1903–07
Complete Games	9	Warren Spahn, 1949, 1951, and 1957–63
Innings Pitched	7	Grover C. Alexander, 1911–12, 1914–17, and 1920
Games Won	8	Warren Spahn, 1949–50, 1953, and 1957–61
Games Lost	4	Phil Niekro, 1977–80
Won-Lost Percentage	4	Tom Seaver, 1969, 1975, 1979, and 1981
ERA	5	Christy Mathewson, 1905, 1908–09, 1911, and 1913
	5	Grover C. Alexander, 1915–17 and 1919–20
	5	Sandy Koufax, 1962–66
Strikeouts	7	Dazzy Vance, 1922–28
Shutouts	7	Grover C. Alexander, 1911, 1913, 1915–17, 1919, and 1921
Saves	5	Bruce Sutter, 1979–82 and 1984

Most Consecutive Seasons Leading League in Pitching Category

American League

Seasons

Winning Percentage	3	Lefty Grove, 1929–31
ERA	4	Lefty Grove, 1929–32
Shutouts	3	Walter Johnson, 1913–15
Strikeouts	8	Walter Johnson, 1912–19
Saves	4	Dan Quisenberry, 1982–85

National League (Post-1900)

Seasons

Winning Percentage	3	Ed Reulbach, 1906–08
ERA	5	Sandy Koufax, 1962–66
Shutouts	3	Grover C. Alexander, 1915–17
Strikeouts	7	Dazzy Vance, 1922–28
Saves	4	Three Finger Brown, 1908–11
	4	Bruce Sutter, 1979–82

Most Consecutive Scoreless Innings Pitched

American League

Innings

55⅔	Walter Johnson, 1913 Wash. Senators
53	Jack Coombs, 1910 Phila. Athletics
45	Doc White, 1904 Chi. White Sox*
45	Cy Young, 1904 Bost. Red Sox*
43⅔	Rube Waddell, 1905 Phila. Athletics
42	Rube Foster, 1914 Bost. Red Sox

*Left-handed.

National League

Innings

59	Orel Hershiser, 1988 L.A. Dodgers
58⅔	Don Drysdale, 1968 L.A. Dodgers
47	Bob Gibson, 1968 St. L. Cardinals
45⅓	Carl Hubbell, 1933 N.Y. Giants*
45	Sal Maglie, 1950 N.Y. Giants
44	Ed Reulbach, 1908 Chi. Cubs

Highest Career Pitching Totals by Pitchers Who Never Led League

American League	National League

Games Pitched

1042 ....Mariano Rivera   1119 ....John Franco

Complete Games

395...............................Eddie Plank   290 ....Eppa Rixey

Innings Pitched

4269...............................Eddie Plank   5282...............................Don Sutton

Games Won

254...............................Red Faber   324...............................Don Sutton

Games Lost

279 ....Walter Johnson   245 ....Warren Spahn

Winning Percentage (Min. 100 Wins)

.691 ....Jon Lester   .647...............................Three Finger Brown

ERA

2.35...............................Eddie Plank   2.23...............................Orval Overall

Strikeouts

2416 ....Luis Tiant   3574...............................Don Sutton

Shutouts

47 ....Rube Waddell   43 ....Phil Niekro

Saves

358 ....Troy Percival   422...............................Billy Wagner

Career Pitching Leaders Under Six Feet Tall

Games Pitched	1119	John Franco (5'10")
Games Won	361	Pud Galvin (5'8")
Games Won	361	Kid Nichols (5'10")
Games Lost	308	Pud Galvin (5'8")
Winning Percentage (Min. 150 Wins)	.690	Whitey Ford (5'10")
ERA (Min. 100 Wins)	2.03	Smoky Joe Wood (5'11")
Complete Games	639	Pud Galvin (5'8")
Innings Pitched	5941	Pud Galvin (5'8")
Games Started	681	Pud Galvin (5'8")
Strikeouts	3154	Pedro Martinez (5'11")
Shutouts	69	Eddie Plank (5'11½")
Walks	1570	Gus Weyhing (5'10")
Saves	424	John Franco (5'10")

Pitching's Triple Crown Winners (Led League in Wins, ERA, and Strikeouts, Same Season)

American League

	Wins	ERA	Strikeouts
Cy Young, Bost. Americans, 1901	33	1.62	158
Rube Waddell, Phila. A's, 1905	26	1.48	287
Walter Johnson, Wash. Senators, 1913	36	1.09	243
Walter Johnson, Wash. Senators, 1918	23	1.27	162
Walter Johnson, Wash. Senators, 1924	23	2.72	158
Lefty Grove, Phila. A's, 1930	28	2.54	209
Lefty Grove, Phila. A's, 1931	31	2.06	175
Lefty Gomez, N.Y. Yankees, 1934	26	2.33	158
Lefty Gomez, N.Y. Yankees, 1937	21	2.33	194
Bob Feller, Cleve. Indians, 1940	27	2.61	261
Hal Newhouser, Det. Tigers, 1945	25	1.81	212
Roger Clemens, Tor. Blue Jays, 1997	21	2.05	292
Roger Clemens, Tor. Blue Jays, 1998	20	2.65	271
Pedro Martinez, Bost. Red Sox, 1999	23	2.07	313
Johan Santana, Minn. Twins, 2006	19	2.77	245
Justin Verlander, Det. Tigers, 2011	24	2.40	250

National League (Post-1900)

	Wins	ERA	Strikeouts
Christy Mathewson, N.Y. Giants, 1905	31	1.27	206
Christy Mathewson, N.Y. Giants, 1908	37	1.43	259
Grover C. Alexander, Phila. Phillies, 1915	31	1.22	241
Grover C. Alexander, Phila. Phillies, 1916	33	1.55	167
Grover C. Alexander, Phila. Phillies, 1917	30	1.86	201
Hippo Vaughn, Chi. Cubs, 1918	22	1.74	148
Grover C. Alexander, Chi. Cubs, 1920	27	1.91	173
Dazzy Vance, Bklyn. Dodgers, 1924	28	2.16	262
Bucky Walters, Cin. Reds, 1939	27	2.29	137
Sandy Koufax, L.A. Dodgers, 1963	25	1.88	306
Sandy Koufax, L.A. Dodgers, 1965	26	2.04	382
Sandy Koufax, L.A. Dodgers, 1966	27	1.73	317
Steve Carlton, Phila. Phillies, 1972	27	1.97	310
Dwight Gooden, N.Y. Giants, 1985	24	1.53	268
Randy Johnson, Ariz. D'backs, 2002	24	2.32	334
Jake Peavy, S.D. Padres, 2007	19	2.54	240
Clayton Kershaw, L. A. Dodgers, 2011	21	2.28	248

Most Home Runs Given Up, Season

American League

50	Bert Blyleven, Minn. Twins, 1986 (in 271 innings)
46	Bert Blyleven, Minn. Twins, 1987 (in 267 innings)
44	Jamie Moyer, Sea. Mariners, 2004 (in 202 innings)
43	Pedro Ramos, Wash. Senators, 1957 (in 231 innings)
42	Denny McLain, Det. Tigers, 1966 (in 264 innings)
41	Rick Helling, Tex. Rangers, 1999 (in 219 innings)

40 ....Ralph Terry, N.Y. Yankees, 1962 (in 298 innings)
40 ....Orlando Pena, K.C. A's, 1964 (in 219 innings)
40...Ferguson Jenkins, Tex. Rangers, 1979 (in 259 innings)
40...Jack Morris, Det. Tigers, 1986 (in 267 innings)
40...Shawn Boskie, Cal. Angels, 1996 (in 189 innings)
40..Brad Radke, Minn. Twins, 1996 (in 232 innings)
40...Ramon Ortiz, Ana. Angels, 2002 (in 217 innings)

National League (Post-1900)

48 ....Jose Lima, Hous. Astros, 2000 (in 196 innings)
46 ....Robin Roberts, Phila. Phillies, 1956 (in 297 innings)
46...Bronson Arroyo, 2011 (in 199 innings)
43...Eric Milton, Phila. Phillies, 2004 (in 201 innings)
41 ....Robin Roberts, Phila. Phillies, 1955 (in 305 innings)
41 ....Phil Niekro, Atl. Braves, 1979 (in 229 innings)
40...Robin Roberts, Phila. Phillies, 1957 (in 249 innings)
40...Phil Niekro, Atl. Braves, 1979 (in 342 innings)
40 ....Eric Milton, Cin. Reds, 2005 (in 186 innings)

Most Home Runs Given Up, Career

511 ,,,,,,,,,,, ...Jamie Moyer* (1986–91, 1993–)
505 ....Robin Roberts (1948–66)
484 ....Ferguson Jenkins (1965–83)
482 ....Phil Niekro (1964–87)
472 ....Don Sutton (1966–88)
448 ....Frank Tanana (1973–93)
434 ....Warren Spahn (1942, 1946–65)
430 ....Bert Blyleven (1970–92)
418 ....Tim Wakefield* (1992–)
414 ....Steve Carlton (1965–88)
411 ....Randy Johnson (1988–2009)
407 ....David Wells (1987–2007)
399 ....Gaylord Perry (1962–83)
*Still active.

Pitchers Giving Up Most Grand Slams, Season

American League	National League
4 Ray Narleski, Det. Tigers, 1959	4 Tug McGraw, Phila. Phillies, 1979
Mike Schooler, Sea. Mariners, 1992	Chan Ho Park, L.A. Dodgers, 1999
	Matt Clement, S.D. Padres, 2000

Pitchers with 2000 Innings Pitched, Allowing No Grand Slams

Old Hoss Radbourn (1880–91)	4535	Herb Pennock (1912–17, 1919–34)	3560
Eddie Plank (1901–17)	4505	Dazzy Vance (1915, 1918, 1922–35)	2967
Jim McCormick (1878–87)	4275	Joaquin Andujar (1976–88)	2153
Jim Palmer (1965–84)	3948	Gary Peters (1959–72)	2081

20-Game Winners Batting .300, Same Season

American League			National League (Post-1900)		
	Wins	**Batting Average**		**Wins**	**Batting Average**
Clark Griffith, Chi. White Sox, 1901	24	.303	Brickyard Kennedy, Bklyn. Bridegrooms, 1900	20	.301
Cy Young, Bost. Americans, 1903	28	.321	Jesse Tannehill, Pitt. Pirates, 1900	20	.336
Ed Killian, Det. Tigers, 1907	25	.320	Claude Hendrix, Pitt. Pirates, 1912	24	.322
Jack Coombs, Phila. A's, 1911	29	.319	Burleigh Grimes, Bklyn. Dodgers, 1920	23	.306
Babe Ruth, Bost. Red Sox, 1917	24	.325	Wilbur Cooper, Pitt. Pirates, 1924	20	.346
Carl Mays, N.Y. Yankees, 1921	27	.343	Pete Donahue, Cin. Reds, 1926	20	.311
Joe Bush, N.Y. Yankees, 1922	26	.326	Burleigh Grimes, Pitt. Pirates, 1928	25	.321
George Uhle, Cleve. Indians, 1923	26	.361	Curt Davis, St. L. Cardinals, 1939	22	.381
Joe Shaute, Cleve. Indians, 1924	20	.318	Bucky Walters, Cin. Reds, 1939	27	.325
Walter Johnson, Wash. Senators, 1925	20	.433	Johnny Sain, Bost. Braves, 1947	21	.346
Ted Lyons, Chi. White Sox, 1930	22	.311	Don Newcombe, Bklyn. Dodgers, 1955	20	.359
Wes Ferrell, Cleve. Indians, 1931	22	.319	Warren Spahn, Milw. Braves, 1958	22	.333
Schoolboy Rowe, Det. Tigers, 1934	24	.303	Don Drysdale, L.A. Dodgers, 1965	23	.300
Wes Ferrell, Bost. Red Sox, 1935	25	.347	Bob Gibson, St. L. Cardinals, 1970	23	.303
Red Ruffing, N.Y. Yankees, 1939	21	.307	Mike Hampton, Hous. Astros, 1999	22	.311
Ned Garver, St. L. Browns, 1951	20	.305			
Catfish Hunter, Oak. A's, 1971	21	.350			
Catfish Hunter, Oak. A's, 1973	21	1.000			

Pitchers with Two Seasons of 1.000 Batting Averages (Post-1900)

Nick Altrock	Wash. Senators, 1924	1-for-1 (1 game)
	Wash. Senators, 1929	1-for-1 (1 game)
Clark Griffith	Wash. Senators, 1913	1-for-1 (1 game)
	Wash. Senators, 1914	1-for-1 (1 game)
Scott Linebrink	S. F./Hous., 2000	1-for-1 (11 games)
	S.D. Padres, 2006	1-for-1 (73 games)
John Morris	Sea. Pilots, 1969	1-for-1 (6 games)
	S.F. Giants, 1974	1-for-1 (17 games)
Felix Rodriguez	S.F. Giants, 2002	1-for-1 (78 games)
	S.F. Giants, 2003	1-for-1 (81 games)
Al Schroll	Bost. Red Sox, 1958	1-for-1 (5 games)
	Chi. Cubs, 1960	1-for-1 (2 games)
Lefty Weinert	Phila. Phillies, 1919	2-for-2 (1 game)
	Phila. Phillies, 1921	1-for-1 (8 games)
Matt Wise	Milw. Brewers, 2005	1-for-1 (49 games)
	Milw. Brewers, 2007	1-for-1 (56 games)
Esteban Yan	T.B. Rays, 2000	1-for-1 (43 games)
	St. L. Cardinals, 2003	1-for-1 (39 games)

Evolution of Complete Games Record

American League

1901	Joe McGinnity, Balt. Orioles	39	1904	Jack Chesbro, N.Y. Yankees	48
1902	Cy Young, Bost. Red Sox	41			

National League (Pre-1900)

1876	Jim Devlin, Louis. Colonels	66	1879	Will White, Cin. Reds	75

National League (Post-1899)

1900	Pink Hawley, N.Y. Giants	34	1902	Vic Willis, Bost. Braves	45
1901	Noodles Hahn, Cin. Reds	41			

Most Games Started By a Pitcher, Career

Starts		Starts	
815	Cy Young (1890–1911)	682	Tom Glavine (1987–2008)
773	Nolan Ryan (1968–93)	666	Walter Johnson (1907–27)
756	Don Sutton (1966–88)	665	Warren Spahn (1942, 1946–65)
740	Greg Maddux (1986–2008)	647	Tom Seaver (1967–86)
716	Phil Niekro (1964–87)	628	Jamie Moyer (1986–91, 1993–)
709	Steve Carlton (1965–88)	625	Jim Kaat (1959–83)
707	Roger Clemens (1984–2007)	616	Frank Tanana (1973–93)
700	Tommy John (1963–74, 1976–89)	612	Early Wynn (1939, 1941–44, 1946–63)
690	Gaylord Perry (1962–83)	609	Robin Roberts (1948–66)
688	Pud Galvin (1875, 1879–92)	603	Randy Johnson (1988–2009)
685	Bert Blyleven (1970–92)	600	Grover C. Alexander (1911–30)

Highest Percentage of Complete Games to Games Started

		Games Started	Complete Games
.898	Cy Young (1900–11*)	404	363
.825	George Mullin (1902–15)	428	353
.820	Vic Willis (1900–10*)	395	324
.797	Walter Johnson (1907–27)	666	531
.793	Jack Powell (1900–12*)	406	322
.788	Christy Mathewson (1900–16)	529	435
.775	Eddie Plank (1900–17)	529	410
.736	Ted Lyons (1923–42, 1946)	484	356
.728	Grover C. Alexander (1911–30)	600	437
.652	Lefty Grove (1925–41)	457	298
.632	Burleigh Grimes (1916–34)	497	314
.623	Red Ruffing (1924–42, 1945–47)	538	335
.574	Warren Spahn (1942, 1946–65)	665	382

*Record only from 1900.

Pitchers Starting 20 Games in 20 Consecutive Seasons

	Seasons	Teams
Nolan Ryan	22	N.Y.Mets (NL), 1971; Cal. Angels (AL), 1972–79; Hous. Astros (NL), 1980–88; Tex. Rangers (AL), 1989–92;
Don Sutton, 1966–87	22	L.A. Dodgers (NL), 1966–80, 1988; Hous. Astros (NL), 1980–82; Milw. Brewers (AL), 1982–85; Oak. A's (AL), 1985; Cal. Angels (AL), 1986–88
Greg Maddux, 1987–2008	22	Chi. Cubs (NL), 1987–92; Atl. Braves (NL), 1993–2003; Chi. Cubs (NL), 2004–06; L.A. Dodgers (NL), 2006, S.D. Padres (NL), 2007–08; L.A. Dodgers (NL), 2008
Phil Niekro, 1965–87	21	Atl. Braves (NL), 1967–83, N.Y. Yankees (AL), 1984–85; Cleve. Indians (AL), 1986–87;
Cy Young, 1891–1910	20	Cleve. Spiders (NL), 1891–98; St. L. Cardinals (NL), 1899–1900; Bost. Americans (AL), 1901–08; Cleve. Naps (AL), 1909–11; Bost. Braves (NL), 1911
Tom Seaver, 1967–86	20	N.Y. Mets (NL), 1967–77, 1983; Cin. Reds (NL), 1977–82; Chi. White Sox (AL), 1984–86; Bost. Red Sox (AL), 1986
Roger Clemens, 1986–2005	20	Bost. Red Sox (AL), 1986–96; Tor. Blue Jays (AL), 1997–98; N.Y. Yankees (AL), 1999–2003; Hous. Astros (NL), 2004–05
Tom Glavine, 1988–2007	20	Atl. Braves (NL), 1988–2002; N.Y. Mets (NL), 2003–07

Evolution of Record for Most Games Pitched in a Season

American League		
1901	Joe McGinnity, Balt. Orioles	48
1904	Jack Chesbro, N.Y. Yankees	55
1907	Ed Walsh, Chi. White Sox	56
1908	Ed Walsh, Chi. White Sox	66
1953	Ellis Kinder, Bost. Red Sox	69
1960	Mike Fornieles, Bost. Red Sox	70
1963	Stu Miller, Balt. Orioles	71
1964	John Wyatt, K.C. A's	81
1965	Eddie Fisher, Chi. White Sox	82
1968	Wilbur Wood, Chi. White Sox	88
1979	Mike Marshall, Minn. Twins	90

National League (Pre-1900)

1876	Jim Devlin, Louis. Colonels	68
1879	Will White, Cin. Reds	76

National League (Post-1899)

1900	Bill Carrick, N.Y. Giants	45
1902	Vic Willis, Bost. Braves	51
1903	Joe McGinnity, N.Y. Giants	55
1908	Christy Mathewson, N.Y. Giants	56
1942	Ace Adams, N.Y. Giants	61
1943	Ace Adams, N.Y. Giants	70
1950	Jim Konstanty, Phila. Phillies	74
1965	Ted Abernathy, Chi. Cubs	84
1969	Wayne Granger, Cin. Reds	90
1973	Mike Marshall, Mont. Expos	92
1974	Mike Marshall, L.A. Dodgers	106

Evolution of Innings Pitched Record

American League

1901	Joe McGinnity, Balt. Orioles	382
1902	Cy Young, Bost. Americans	385
1904	Jack Chesbro, N.Y. Highlanders	455
1908	Ed Walsh, Chi. White Sox	464

National League (Pre-1900)

1876	Jim Devlin, Louis. Colonels	622
1879	Will White, Cin. Reds	680

National League (Post-1899)

1900	Joe McGinnity, Bklyn. Bridegrooms	343
1901	Noodles Hahn, Cin. Reds	375
1902	Vic Willis, Bost. Braves	410
1903	Joe McGinnity, N.Y. Giants	434

Most Wild Pitches, Season (Since 1900)

American League

26	Juan Guzman, 1993 Tor. Blue Jays
25	A.J.Burnett, 2011 N.Y. Yankees
24	Jack Morris, 1987 Det. Tigers
23	Tim Leary, 1990 N.Y. Yankees

National League

30	Red Ames, 1905 N.Y. Giants
27	Tony Cloninger, 1966 Atl. Braves
26	Larry Cheney, 1914 Chi. Cubs
23	Christy Mathewson, 1901 N.Y. Giants
23	Matt Clement, 2000 S.D. Padres

Last Legal Spitball Pitchers

American League

Doc Ayers	(1913–21)
Ray Caldwell	(1910–21)
Stan Coveleski	(1912–28)
Urban Faber	(1914–33)
Hub Leonard*	(1913–25)
Jack Quinn	(1909–33)
Allan Russell	(1915–25)
Urban Shocker	(1916–28)
Allan Sothoron	(1914–26)

*Left-hander.

National League

Bill Doak	(1912–29)
Phil Douglas	(1912–22)
Dana Fillingim	(1915–25)
Ray Fisher	(1910–20)
Marvin Goodwin	(1916–25)
Burleigh Grimes	(1916–34)
Claude Hendrix	(1911–20)
Clarence Mitchell*	(1911–32)
Dick Rudolph	(1910–27)

Left-Handed Pitchers Appearing in More Than 700 Games, Career

Jesse Orosco (1979, 1981–2003)	1252	Rick Honeycutt (1977–97)	797
Mike Stanton (1989–2007)	1178	Steve Kline (1997–2007)	796
John Franco (1984–2005)	1119	Buddy Groom (1992–2005)	786
Dan Plesac (1986–2003)	1064	Darold Knowles (1965–80)	765
Eddie Guardado (1993–2009)	908	Mark Guthrie (1989–2003)	765
Arthur Rhodes* (1991–)	900	Kenny Rogers (1989–2008)	762
Sparky Lyle (1967–82)	899	Tommy John (1963–74, 1976–89)	760
Jim Kaat (1959–83)	898	Warren Spahn (1942, 1946–65)	750
Paul Assenmacher (1986–99)	884	Tom Burgmeier (1968–84)	745
Mike Myers (1995–2007)	883	Gary Lavelle (1974–87)	745
Alan Embree (1992–2009)	882	Willie Hernandez (1977–89)	744
Billy Wagner (1995–2010)	853	Steve Carlton (1965–88)	741
Tug McGraw (1965–84)	824	Ron Perranoski (1961–73)	737

*Still active.

Pitchers Who Pitched for Both Yankees and Mets and Threw No-Hitters

No-Hitter

John Candelaria (Mets, 1987; Yankees, 1988–89) ....With Pitt. Pirates (vs. L.A. Dodgers), Aug. 9, 1976

David Cone (Mets, 1987–92; Yankees, 1995–99) ....With Yankees (vs. Mont. Expos), July 18, 1999 (perfect game)

Dock Ellis (Yankees, 1976–77; Mets, 1979) ....With Pitt. Pirates (vs. S.D. Padres), June 12, 1970

Dwight Gooden (Mets, 1984–94; Yankees, 1996–97)...........With Yankees (vs. Sea. Mariners), May 14, 1996

Al Leiter (Yankees, 1987–89; Mets, 1998–2004) ....With Flor. Marlins (vs. Colo. Rockies), May 11, 1996

Kenny Rogers (Yankees, 1996–97; Mets, 1999) ....With Tex. Rangers (vs. Cal. Angels), July 28, 1994 (perfect game)

Pitchers Who Have Stolen Home

American League

Frank Owen, Chi. White Sox (vs. Wash. Senators), Aug. 2, 1904

Bill Donovan, Det. Tigers (vs. Cleve. Indians), May 7, 1906

Frank Owen, Chi. White Sox (vs. St. L. Browns), Apr. 27, 1908

Ed Walsh, Chi. White Sox (vs. N.Y. Yankees), June 13, 1908

Ed Walsh, Chi. White Sox (vs. St. L. Browns), June 2, 1909

Eddie Plank, Phila. A's (vs. Chi. White Sox), Aug. 30, 1909

Jack Warhop, N.Y. Yankees (vs. Chi. White Sox), Aug. 27, 1910

Jack Warhop, N.Y. Yankees (vs. St. L. Browns), July 12, 1912

Red Faber, Chi. White Sox (vs. Phila. A's), July 14, 1915

Reb Russell, Chi. White Sox (vs. Bost. Red Sox), Aug. 7, 1916

Babe Ruth, Bost. Red Sox (vs. St. L. Browns), Aug. 24, 1918

Dickie Kerr, Chi. White Sox (vs. N.Y. Yankees), July 8, 1921

Red Faber, Chi. White Sox (vs. St. L. Browns), Apr. 23, 1923

George Mogridge, Wash. Senators (vs. Chi. White Sox), Aug. 15, 1923

Joe Haynes, Chi. White Sox (vs. St. L. Browns), Sept. 1, 1944

Fred Hutchinson, Det. Tigers (vs. St. L. Browns), Aug. 29, 1947

Harry Dorish, St. L. Browns (vs. Wash. Senators), June 2, 1950

National League (Post-1900)

John Menafee, Chi. Cubs (vs. Bklyn. Dodgers), July 15, 1902

Joe McGinnity, N.Y. Giants (vs. Bklyn. Dodgers), Aug. 8, 1903

Joe McGinnity, N.Y. Giants (vs. Bost. Braves), Apr. 29, 1904

Christy Mathewson, N.Y. Giants (vs. Bost. Braves), Sept. 12, 1911

Leon Ames, N.Y. Giants (vs. Bklyn. Dodgers), May 22, 1912

Christy Mathewson, N.Y. Giants (vs. Bost. Braves), June 28, 1912

Slim Sallee, N.Y. Giants (vs. St. L. Cardinals), July 22, 1913

Sherry Smith, Bklyn. Dodgers (vs. N.Y. Giants), Apr. 16, 1916

Tom Seaton, Chi. Cubs (vs. Cin. Reds), June 23, 1916

Bob Steele, N.Y. Giants (vs. St. L. Cardinals), July 26, 1918

Hippo Vaughn, Chi. Cubs (vs. N.Y. Giants), Aug. 9, 1919

Dutch Reuther, Cin. Reds (vs. Chi. Cubs), Sept. 3, 1919

Jesse Barnes, N.Y. Giants (vs. St. L. Cardinals), July 27, 1920

Dutch Reuther, Bklyn. Dodgers (vs. N.Y. Giants), May 4, 1921

Johnny Vander Meer, Cin. Reds (vs. N.Y. Giants), Sept. 23, 1943

Bucky Walters, Cin. Reds (vs. Pitt. Pirates), Apr. 20, 1946

Don Newcombe, Bklyn. Dodgers (vs. Pitt. Pirates), May 26, 1955

Curt Simmons, St. L. Cardinals (vs. Phila. Phillies), Sept. 1, 1963

Pascual Perez, Atl. Braves (vs. S.F. Giants), Sept. 7, 1984

Rick Sutcliffe, Chi. Cubs (vs. Phila. Phillies), July 29, 1988

Kevin Ritz, Colo. Rockies (vs. S.D. Padres), June 5, 1997

Darren Dreifort, L.A. Dodgers (vs. Tex. Rangers), June 12, 2001

3

HALL OF FAME

First Players Elected to Hall of Fame from Each Position

First Base ....Cap Anson, 1939
George Sisler, 1939
Second Base...Nap Lajoie, 1937
Third Base...Jimmy Collins, 1945
Shortstop...Honus Wagner, 1936
Left Field...Fred Clarke, 1945
Center Field...Ty Cobb, 1936
Right Field ....Babe Ruth, 1936
Catcher..Roger Bresnahan, 1945
King Kelly, 1945
Right-Handed Pitcher ....Walter Johnson, 1936
Christy Mathewson, 1936
Left-Handed Pitcher ....Eddie Plank, 1946
Rube Waddell, 1946
Relief Pitcher ....Hoyt Wilhelm, 1985
Designated Hitter...Paul Molitor, 2004

Highest Lifetime Batting Average for Hall of Fame Pitchers

	At Bats	Hits	Average
Red Ruffing (1924–42, 1945–47)	1937	521	.269
Burleigh Grimes (1916–34)	1535	380	.248
Amos Rusie (1889–98, 1901)	1730	428	.247
Walter Johnson (1907–27)	2324	547	.235
Old Hoss Radbourn (1880–91)	2487	585	.235
Ted Lyons (1923–42, 1946)	1563	364	.233
Bob Lemon (1941–42, 1946–58)	1183	274	.232
Catfish Hunter (1965–79)	658	149	.226
Kid Nichols (1890–1901, 1904–06)	2086	471	.226
Dizzy Dean (1930, 1932–41, 1947)	717	161	.225

Hall of Famers with Lifetime Batting Averages Below .265 (Excluding Pitchers)

Joe Tinker, shortstop (1902–16)...262...Elected 1946
Luis Aparicio, shortstop (1956–73)...262...Elected 1984
Reggie Jackson, outfield (1967–87)...262...Elected 1993
Ozzie Smith, shortstop (1978–96)...262...Elected 2002
Gary Carter, catcher (1974–92)..262...Elected 2003
Bill Mazeroski, second base (1956-72) ....260...Elected 2001
Rabbit Maranville, shortstop and second base (1912–35) ....258...Elected 1954

Harmon Killebrew, first base and third base (1954–75) .... .256 ....Elected 1984
Ray Schalk, catcher (1912–29)...Elected 1955

Hall of Famers with Lowest Marks in Offensive Categories*

Games...Ross Youngs (1917–26)..1211
At Bats..Roy Campanella (1948–57)...................................4205
Hits ....Roy Campanella (1948–57)...................................1161
Batting Average..Ray Schalk (1912–29) 253
Doubles ....Roy Campanella (1948–57)....................................178
Triples...Roy Campanella (1948–57) 18
Home Runs ....Ray Schalk (1912–29) and Johnny Evers (1902–17, 1922, 1929)....................12
Runs Scored ....Ray Schalk (1912–29) 579
Runs Batted In ....Johnny Evers (1902–17, 1922, 1929) 538
Stolen Bases..Ernie Lombardi (1931–47) 8

* Position players with at least 10 years.

Teams Fielding Most Future Hall of Fame Players

8 ..........N.Y. Giants (NL), 1923 ....Dave Bancroft (shortstop), Frankie Frisch (second base), Travis Jackson (infield),
George Kelly (first base), Casey Stengel (outfield), Bill Terry (first base), Hack Wilson
(outfield), and Ross Youngs (outfield)

8 ..........N.Y. Yankees (AL), 1930 ....Earle Combs (outfield), Bill Dickey (catcher), Lou Gehrig (first base), Lefty Gomez
(pitcher), Waite Hoyt (pitcher), Herb Pennock (pitcher), Red Ruffing (pitcher), and Babe
Ruth (outfield)

8 ..........N.Y. Yankees (AL), 1931 ....Earle Combs (outfield), Bill Dickey (catcher), Lou Gehrig (first base), Lefty Gomez
(pitcher), Herb Pennock (pitcher), Red Ruffing (pitcher), Babe Ruth (outfield), and Joe
Sewell (third base)

8 ..........N.Y. Yankees (AL), 1933 ....Earle Combs (outfield), Bill Dickey (catcher), Lou Gehrig (first base), Lefty Gomez
(pitcher), Herb Pennock (pitcher), Red Ruffing (pitcher), Babe Ruth (outfield), and Joe
Sewell (third base)

Infields Fielding Four Future Hall of Famers

N.Y. Giants (NL), 1925 ....First Base: Bill Terry   N.Y. Giants (NL), 1927 ....First Base: Bill Terry
Second Base: George Kelly   Second Base: Rogers Hornsby
Third Base: Fred Lindstrom   Third Base: Fred Lindstrom
Shortstop: Travis Jackson   Shortstop: Travis Jackson

N.Y. Giants (NL), 1926....................First Base: George Kelly
Second Base: Frankie Frisch
Third Base: Fred Lindstrom
Shortstop: Travis Jackson

Hall of Fame Pitchers Who Batted Right and Threw Left

Carl Hubbell (1928–43)   Eppa Rixey (1912–33)   Rube Waddell (1897, 1899–1910)
Sandy Koufax (1955–66)

Switch-Hitting Pitchers in Hall of Fame

Three Finger Brown (1903–16)   Ted Lyons (1923–42, 1946)   Kid Nichols (1890–1901, 1904–06)
Red Faber (1914–24, 1926–33)*   Rube Marquard (1908–24)**   Robin Roberts (1948–66)
Herb Pennock (1912–17, 1919–34)   Early Wynn (1946–63)***

* Batted right-handed in 1925.
** Batted left-handed in 1925.
*** Batted right-handed 1939–44.

Hall of Fame Pitchers Who Played Most Games at Other Positions

Games

John Clarkson (outfield: 27; third base: 4; first base: 2) 33

Bob Lemon (outfield: 14; third base: 2)..16

Walter Johnson (outfield)..15

Hall of Fame Position Players Who Also Pitched

Appearances

Cap Anson	3	1883 (2) and 1884 (1)
Jake Beckley	1	1902
Wade Boggs	2	1997 (1) and 1999 (1)
Roger Bresnahan	9	1897 (6), 1901 (2), and 1901 (1)
Dan Brouthers	4	1897 (3) and 1883 (1)
Jesse Burkett	23	1890 (21), 1894 (1), and 1902 (1)
Ty Cobb	3	1918 (2) and 1925 (1)
George Davis	3	1891
Buck Ewing	9	1882 (1), 1884 (1), 1885 (1), 1888 (2), 1889 (3), and 1890 (1)
Jimmie Foxx	10	1939 (1) and 1945 (9)
Harry Hooper	1	1913
George Kelly	1	1917
King Kelly	12	1880 (1), 1883 (1), 1884 (2), 1888 (3), 1890 (1), 1891 (3), and 1892 (1)
Tommy McCarthy	13	1884 (7), 1886 (1), 1888 (2), 1889 (1), 1891 (1), and 1894 (1)
Stan Musial	1	1952
Jim O'Rourke	6	1883 (2) and 1884 (4)
Sam Rice	9	1915 (4) and 1916 (5)
Babe Ruth	163	1914 (4), 1915 (32), 1916 (44), 1917 (41), and 1918 (20), 1919 (17), 1920 (1), 1921 (2), 1930 (1), and 1933 (1)
George Sisler	23	1915 (15), 1916 (3), and 1918 (2)
Tris Speaker	1	1914 (1)
Honus Wagner	2	1900 (1) and 1902 (1)
Bobby Wallace	57	1894 (4), 1895 (30), 1896 (22), and 1902 (1)
Ted Williams	1	1940

Hall of Fame Pitchers with Losing Records

Wins-Losses

Rollie Fingers (1968–82, 1984–85)...114–118

Satchel Paige (1948–49, 1951–53, 1965)..28–31

Leading Career Pitching Marks by Those Eligible for Hall of Fame but Not In

Most Games Pitched	Jesse Orosco (1979–2003)	1252
Most Games Started	Tommy John (1963–74, 1976–89)	700
Most Complete Games	Tony Mullane (1881–94)	468
Most Innings Pitched	Tommy John (1963–74, 1976–89)	4710
Most Walks Allowed	Bobo Newsom (1929–30, 1932, 1934–48, 1952–53)	1732
Most Strikeouts	Mickey Lolich (1963–79)	2832
Most Shutouts	Luis Tiant (1964–82)	49
Most Games Won	Tommy John (1963–74, 1976–89)	288
Most Games Lost	Jack Powell (1897–1912)	254
Lowest ERA	Orval Overall (1905–10, 1913)	2.23
Winning Percentage	Dave Foutz (1884–98)	.690

Leading Career Batting Marks by Those Eligible for Hall of Fame but Not In

Most Games Played	Rusty Staub (1963–85)	2951
Most At Bats	Rafael Palmeiro (1986–2005)	10472
Most Base Hits	Rafael Palmeiro (1986–2005)	3020
Most Doubles	Rafael Palmeiro (1986–2005)	585
Most Triples	Ed Konetchy (1907–21)	182
Most Home Runs	Rafael Palmeiro (1986–2005)	569
Most Runs Scored	Rafael Palmeiro (1986–2005)	1663
Most RBIs	Rafael Palmeiro (1986–2005)	1835
Most Walks	Eddie Yost (1944, 1946–62)	1614
Most Strikeouts	Andres Galarraga (1985–2004)	2003
Most Stolen Bases	Tim Raines (1979–2002)	808
Highest Lifetime Batting Average	Joe Jackson (1908–20)	.356
Highest Lifetime Slugging Average	Mark McGwire (1986–2001)	.588

Most Career Hits by Players Eligible for Hall of Fame but Not In

3020	Rafael Palmeiro (1986–2005)	2712	Dave Parker (1973–91)
2866	Harold Baines(1980–2001)	2705	Doc Cramer (1928–48)
2757	Vada Pinson (1958–75)	2666	Lave Cross (1887–1907)
2743	Al Oliver (1968–85)	2605	Tim Raines (1979–2002)
2716	Rusty Staub (1963–85)	2599	Steve Garvey (1969–87)
2715	Bill Buckner (1969–90)	2561	Willie Davis (1960–67)

Most Career Wins by Pitchers Eligible for Hall of Fame but Not In

288	Tommy John (1963–74, 1976–89)	254	Jack Morris (1977–94)
284	Tony Mullane (1881–94)	247	John P. Quinn (1909–33)
283	Jim Kaat (1959–83)	245	Dennis Martinez (1976–98)
265	Jim McCormick (1878–87)	245	Jack Powell (1897–1912)
264	Gus Weyhing (1887–1901)	240	Frank Tanana (1973–93)

Most Career Home Runs by Players Eligible for Hall of Fame but Not In

583	Mark McGwire (1986–2001)	384	Harold Baines (1980–2001)
569	Rafael Palmeiro (1986–2005)	383	Larry Walker (1989–2005)
493	Fred McGriff (1986–2004)	382	Frank Howard (1958–73)
462	Jose Canseco (1985–2001)	381	Albert Belle (1989–2000)
449	Jeff Bagwell (1991–2005)	378	Matt Williams (1987–2003)
442	Dave Kingman (1971–86)	377	Norm Cash (1958–74)
434	Juan Gonzalez (1989–2005)	374	Rocky Colavito (1955–68)
414	Darrell Evans (1969–89)	370	Gil Hodges (1943, 1947–63)
399	Andres Galarraga (1985–2004)	360	Greg Gaetti (1981–2000)
398	Dale Murphy (1976–93)	355	Gery Vaughn (1989–2003)
396	Joe Carter (1983–98)	354	Lee May (1965–82)
390	Graig Nettles (1967–88)	352	Ellis Burks (1987–2004)
385	Dwight Evans (1972–91)	351	Dick Allen (1963–77)

Hall of Fame Inductees Receiving 90 Percent of Vote

Tom Seaver, 1992 (425 ballots cast)	98.8	Bob Feller, 1962 (160 ballots cast)	93.8
Nolan Ryan, 1999 (491 ballots cast)	98.8	Reggie Jackson, 1993 (396 ballots cast)	93.6
Tony Gwynn, 2007 (545 ballots cast)	98.5	Ted Williams, 1966 (302 ballots cast)	93.4
Cal Ripken Jr., 2007 (545 ballots cast)	98.5	Stan Musial, 1969 (340 ballots cast)	93.2
Ty Cobb, 1936 (226 ballots cast)	98.2	Roberto Clemente, 1973 (424 ballots cast)	92.7

Hank Aaron, 1982 (415 ballots cast)............................97.8

Johnny Bench, 1989 (431 ballots cast)..........................96.4

Babe Ruth, 1936 (226 ballots cast)..............................95.1

Honus Wagner, 1936 (226 ballots cast) 95.1

Rickey Henderson, 2009 (539 ballots cast)...................94.8

Willie Mays, 1979 (432 ballots cast)...........................94.6

Carl Yastrzemski, 1989 (423 ballots cast) 94.6

Jim Palmer, 1990 (444 ballots cast) 92.5

Brooks Robinson, 1983 (374 ballots cast).....................92.0

Wade Boggs, 2005 (516 ballots cast).........................91.9

Christy Mathewson, 1936 (226 ballots cast) 90.7

Rod Carew, 1991 (401 ballots cast) 90.5

Roberto Alomar, 2011 (523 ballots cast)......................90.0

Won-Lost Percentage of Hall of Famers Elected as Players Who Managed in Majors

		Teams Managed	Career Wins–Losses
.593	Frank Chance	Chi. Cubs (NL), 1905–12	932–640
		N.Y. Yankees (AL), 1913–14	
		Bost. Red Sox (AL), 1923	
.582	Mickey Cochrane	Det. Tigers (AL), 1934–38	413–297
.576	Fred Clarke	Louis. Colonels (NL), 1897–99	1602–1179
		Pitt. Pirates (NL), 1900–15	
.575	Cap Anson	Chi. White Stockings/Colts (NL), 1879–97	1297–957
		N.Y. Giants (NL), 1898	
.562	Monte Ward	N.Y. Gothams (NL), 1884	394–307
		Bklyn. Wonders (PL), 1890	
		Bklyn. Bridegrooms (NL), 1891–92	
		N.Y. Giants (NL), 1893–94	
.555	Bill Terry	N.Y. Giants (NL), 1932–41	823–661
.553	Buck Ewing	N.Y. Giants (PL), 1890	489–395
		Cin. Reds (NL), 1895–99	
		N.Y. Giants (NL), 1900	
.551	Walter Johnson	Wash. Senators (AL), 1929–32	530–432
		Cleve. Indians (AL), 1933–35	
.546	Nap Lajoie	Cleve. Naps (AL), 1905–09	397–330
.544	Jimmy Collins	Bost. Americans (AL), 1901–06	464–389
.543	Bill Dickey	N.Y. Yankees (AL), 1946	57–48
.542	Tris Speaker	Cleve. Indians (AL), 1919–26	616–520
.541	King Kelly	Bost. Reds (PL), 1890	124–105
		Cin. Reds–Milw. Brewers (AA), 1891	
.540	Joe Cronin	Wash. Senators (AL), 1933–34	1236–1055
		Bost. Red Sox (AL), 1935–47	
.538	Hughie Jennings	Det. Tigers (AL), 1907–20	1131–972
.536	Gabby Hartnett	Chi. Cubs (NL), 1938–40	203–176
.530	Pie Traynor	Pitt. Pirates (NL), 1934–39	457–406
.522	Yogi Berra	N.Y. Yankees (AL), 1964	484–444
		N.Y. Mets (NL), 1972–75	
		N.Y. Yankees (AL), 1984–85	
.521	Eddie Collins	Chi. White Sox (AL), 1925–26	160–147
.521	Red Schoendienst	St. L. Cardinals (NL), 1965–76 and 1980	1028–944
.519	Ty Cobb	Det. Tigers (AL), 1921–26	479–444
.519	Bob Lemon	K.C. Royals (AL), 1970–72	432–401
		Chi. White Sox (AL), 1977–78	
		N.Y. Yankees (AL), 1978–79 and 1981–82	
.513	Frankie Frisch	St. L. Cardinals (NL), 1933–38	1137–1078
		Pitt. Pirates (NL), 1940–46	
		Chi. Cubs (NL), 1949–51	

continued on next page

		Teams Managed	Career Wins–Losses
.512	Joe Kelley	Cin. Reds (NL), 1902–05	337–321
		Bost. Rustlers (NL), 1908	
.498	Joe Gordon	Cleve. Indians (AL), 1958–60	305–308
		Det.Tigers (AL), 1960	
		K.C. Athletics (AL), 1961	
		K.C. Royals (AL), 1969	
.497	Joe Tinker	Cin. Reds (NL), 1913	304–308
		Chi. Whales (FL), 1914–15	
		Chi. Cubs (NL), 1916	
.488	Orator Jim O'Rourke	Buff. Bisons (NL), 1881–84	246–258
		Wash. Senators (NL), 1893	
.487	Lou Boudreau	Cleve. Indians (AL), 1942–50	1162–1224
		Bost. Red Sox (AL), 1952–54	
		K.C. A's (AL), 1955–57	
		Chi. Cubs (NL), 1960	
.485	Johnny Evers	Chi. Cubs (NL), 1913 and 1921	196–208
		Chi. White Sox (AL), 1924	
.482	Christy Mathewson	Cin. Reds (NL), 1916–18	164–176
.481	Eddie Mathews	Atl. Braves (NL), 1972–74	149–161
.476	Max Carey	Bklyn. Dodgers (NL), 1932–33	146–161
.476	Frank Robinson	Cleve. Indians (AL), 1975–77	913–1004
		S.F. Giants (NL), 1981–84	
		Balt. Orioles (AL), 1988–91	
		Mont. Expos (NL), 2002–04	
.475	George Sisler	St. L. Browns (AL), 1924–26	218–241
.467	Mel Ott	N.Y. Giants (NL), 1942–48	464–530
.460	Rogers Hornsby	St. L. Cardinals (NL), 1925–26	680–798
		Bost. Braves (NL), 1928	
		Chi. Cubs (NL), 1930–32	
		St. L. Browns (AL), 1933–37 and 1952	
		Cin. Reds (NL), 1952–53	
.444	Hugh Duffy	Milw. Brewers (AL), 1901	535–671
		Phila. Phillies (NL), 1904–06	
		Chi. White Sox (AL), 1910–11	
		Bost. Red Sox (AL), 1921–22	
.442	Three Finger Brown	St. L. Terriers (FL), 1914	50–63
.434	Rabbit Maranville	Chi. Cubs (NL), 1925	23–30
.432	Roger Bresnahan	St. L. Cardinals (NL), 1909–12	328–432
		Chi. Cubs (NL), 1915	
.432	Burleigh Grimes	Bklyn. Dodgers (NL), 1937–38	130–171
.430	Ted Lyons	Chi. White Sox (AL), 1946–48	185–245
.429	Cy Young	Bost. Puritans (AL), 1907	3–4
.429	Ted Williams	Wash. Senators II (AL), 1969–71	273–364
		Tex. Rangers (AL), 1972	
.425	Larry Doby	Chi. White Sox (AL), 1978	37–50
.408	Billy Herman	Pitt. Pirates (NL), 1947	189–274
		Bost. Red Sox (AL), 1964–66	

.407	Dave Bancroft	Bost. Braves (NL), 1924–27	249–363
.389	Bid McPhee	Cin. Reds (NL), 1901–02	79–124
.287	Bobby Wallace	St. L. Browns (AL), 1911–12	62–154
		Cin. Reds (NL), 1937	
.267	Pud Galvin	Buff. Bisons (NL), 1885	8–22
.266	Jim Bottomley	St. L. Browns (AL), 1937	21–58
.250	Luke Appling	K.C. A's (AL), 1967	10–30
.200	Honus Wagner	Pitt. Pirates (NL), 1917	1–4

Hall of Famers Making Last Out in World Series

1903	Honus Wagner (Pitt. Pirates, NL)	strikeout
1926	Babe Ruth (N.Y. Yankees, AL)	caught stealing
1938	Billy Herman (Chi. Cubs, NL)	ground out
1940	Earl Averill (Det. Tigers, AL)	ground out
1952	Pee Wee Reese (Bklyn. Dodgers, NL)	fly out
1958	Red Schoendienst (Milw. Brewers, NL)	fly out
1959	Luis Aparicio (Chi. White Sox, AL)	line out
1962	Willie McCovey (S.F. Giants, NL)	line out
1975	Carl Yazstremski (Bost. Red Sox, AL)	fly out
1984	Tony Gwynn (S.D. Padres, NL)	fly out

Hall of Famers Who Played for the Harlem Globetrotters

Ernie Banks

Lou Brock

Bob Gibson

Ferguson Jenkins

Satchel Paige

Hall of Famers Who Died on Their Birthday

Stanley "Bucky" Harris, born Nov. 8, 1896, and died Nov. 8, 1977

Charles "Gabby" Hartnett, born Dec. 20, 1900, and died Dec. 20, 1972

Joe Tinker, born July 27, 1880, and died July 27, 1948

4

AWARDS

Most Valuable Player
Unanimous Choice for MVP

American League

Ty Cobb, outfield, Det. Tigers, 1911
Babe Ruth, outfield, N.Y. Yankees, 1923
Hank Greenberg, first base, Det. Tigers, 1935
Al Rosen, third base, Cleve. Indians, 1953
Mickey Mantle, outfield, N.Y. Yankees, 1956
Frank Robinson, outfield, Balt. Orioles, 1966
Denny McLain, pitcher, Det. Tigers, 1968
Reggie Jackson, outfield, Oak. A's, 1973
Jose Canseco, outfield, Oak. A's, 1988
Frank Thomas, first base, Chi. White Sox, 1993
Ken Griffey Jr., outfield, Sea. Mariners, 1997

National League

Carl Hubbell, pitcher, N.Y. Giants, 1936
Orlando Cepeda, first base, St. L. Cardinals, 1967
Mike Schmidt, third base, Phila. Phillies, 1980
Jeff Bagwell, first base, Hous. Astros, 1994
Ken Caminiti, third base, S.D. Padres, 1996
Barry Bonds, outfield, S.F. Giants, 2002
Albert Pujols, first base, St. L. Cardinals, 2009

Closest Winning Margins in MVP Voting

American League

Margin	Season	MVP	Votes	Runner-Up	Votes
+1	1947	Joe DiMaggio, N.Y. Yankees	202	Ted Williams, Bost. Red Sox	201
+2	1928	Mickey Cochrane, Phila. A's	53	Heinie Manush, St. L. Browns	51
+2	1934	Mickey Cochrane, Det. Tigers	67	Charlie Gehringer, Det. Tigers	65
+3	1960	Roger Maris, N.Y. Yankees	225	Mickey Mantle, N.Y. Yankees	222
+3	1996	Juan Gonzalez, Tex. Rangers	290	Alex Rodriguez, Sea. Mariners	187
+4	1925	Roger Peckinpaugh, Wash. Senators	45	Al Simmons, Phila. A's	41
+4	1937	Charlie Gehringer, Det. Tigers	78	Joe DiMaggio, N.Y. Yankees	74
+4	1944	Hal Newhouser, Det. Tigers	236	Dizzy Trout, Det. Tigers	232
+4	1961	Roger Maris, N.Y. Yankees	202	Mickey Mantle, N.Y. Yankees	198

National League

Margin	Season	MVP	Votes	Runner-Up	Votes
0 (Tie)	1979	Keith Hernandez, St. L. Cardinals	216	Willie Stargell, Pitt. Pirates	216
+1	1944	Marty Marion, St. L. Cardinals	190	Bill Nicholson, Chi. Cubs	189
+2	1937	Joe Medwick, St. L. Cardinals	70	Gabby Hartnett, Chi. Cubs	68
+4	1911	Wildfire Schulte, Chi. Cubs	29	Christy Mathewson, N.Y. Giants	25
+5	1912	Larry Doyle, N.Y. Giants	48	Honus Wagner, Pitt. Pirates	43
+5	1955	Roy Campanella, Bklyn. Dodgers	226	Duke Snider, Bklyn. Dodgers	221

Widest Winning Margins in MVP Voting

American League

Margin	Season	MVP	Votes	Runner-Up	Votes
+183	1993	Frank Thomas, Chi. White Sox	392	Paul Molitor, Tor. Blue Jays	209
+169	1953	Al Rosen, Cleve. Indians	336	Yogi Berra, N.Y. Yankees	167
+169	1975	Fred Lynn, Bost. Red Sox	326	John Mayberry, K.C. Royals	157
+164	1973	Reggie Jackson, Oak. A's	336	Jim Palmer, Balt. Orioles	172
+157	1972	Dick Allen, Chi. White Sox	321	Joe Rudi, Oak. A's	164
+157	1982	Robin Yount, Milw. Brewers	385	Eddie Murray, Balt. Orioles	228
+150	1956	Mickey Mantle, N.Y. Yankees	336	Yogi Berra, N.Y. Yankees	186
+150	1988	Jose Canseco, Oak. A's	392	Mike Greenwell, Bost. Red Sox	242

National League

Margin	Season	MVP	Votes	Runner-Up	Votes
+215	2009	Albert Pujols, St. L. Cardinals	448	Hanley Ramirez, Flor. Marlins	233
+191	1994	Jeff Bagwell, Hous. Astros	392	Matt Williams, S.F. Giants	201
+172	2002	Barry Bonds, S.F. Giants	448	Albert Pujols, St. L. Cardinals	276
+166	1998	Sammy Sosa, Chi. Cubs	438	Mark McGwire, St. L. Cardinals	272
+164	2010	Joey Votto, Cin. Reds	443	Albert Pujols, St. L. Cardinals	279
+160	2001	Barry Bonds, S.F. Giants	438	Sammy Sosa, Chi. Cubs	278
+156	1999	Chipper Jones, Atl. Braves	432	Jeff Bagwell, Hous. Astros	276
+155	1996	Ken Caminiti, S.D. Padres	392	Mike Piazza, L.A. Dodgers	237

Won MVP Award in Consecutive Years, by Position

First Base	Jimmie Foxx, Phila. A's (AL), 1932–33
	Frank Thomas, Chi. White Sox (AL), 1993–94
	Albert Pujols, St. L. Cardinals (NL), 2008–09
Second Base	Joe Morgan, Cin. Reds (NL), 1975–76
Third Base	Mike Schmidt, Phila. Phillies (NL), 1980–81
Shortstop	Ernie Banks, Chi. Cubs (NL), 1959–60
Outfield	Mickey Mantle, N.Y. Yankees (AL), 1956–57
	Roger Maris, N.Y. Yankees (AL), 1960–61
	Dale Murphy, Atl. Braves (NL), 1982–83
	Barry Bonds, Pitt. Pirates (NL), 1992, and S.F. Giants (NL), 1993
	Barry Bonds, S.F. Giants (NL), 2001–04
Catcher	Yogi Berra, N.Y. Yankees (AL), 1954–55
Pitcher	Hal Newhouser, Det. Tigers (AL), 1944–45

Teammates Finishing One-Two in MVP Balloting

American League

Season	Team	Leader	Position	Runner-Up	Position
1934	Det. Tigers	Mickey Cochrane	Catcher	Charlie Gehringer	Second base
1944	Det. Tigers	Hal Newhouser	Pitcher	Dizzy Trout	Pitcher
1945	Det. Tigers	Hal Newhouser	Pitcher	Eddie Mayo	Second base
1956	N.Y. Yankees	Mickey Mantle	Outfield	Yogi Berra	Catcher
1959	Chi. White Sox*	Nellie Fox	Second base	Luis Aparicio	Shortstop
1960	N.Y. Yankees	Roger Maris	Outfield	Mickey Mantle	Outfield
1961	N.Y. Yankees	Roger Maris	Outfield	Mickey Mantle	Outfield
1962	N.Y. Yankees	Mickey Mantle	Outfield	Bobby Richardson	Second base
1965	Minn. Twins	Zoilo Versalles	Shortstop	Tony Oliva	Outfield

Season	Team	Leader	Position	Runner-Up	Position
1966	Balt. Orioles*	Frank Robinson	Outfield	Brooks Robinson	Third base
1968	Det. Tigers	Denny McLain	Pitcher	Bill Freehan	Catcher
1971	Oak. A's	Vida Blue	Pitcher	Sal Bando	Third base
1983	Balt. Orioles	Cal Ripken Jr.	Shortstop	Eddie Murray	First base

National League

Season	Team	Leader	Position	Runner-Up	Position
1914	Bost. Braves*	Johnny Evers	Second base	Rabbit Maranville	Shortstop
1941	Bklyn. Dodgers*	Dolph Camilli	First base	Pete Reiser	Outfield
1942	St. L. Cardinals	Mort Cooper	Pitcher	Enos Slaughter	Outfield
1943	St. L. Cardinals	Stan Musial	Outfield	Mort Cooper	Pitcher
1955	Bklyn. Dodgers	Roy Campanella	Catcher	Duke Snider	Outfield
1956	Bklyn. Dodgers	Don Newcombe	Pitcher	Sal Maglie	Pitcher
1960	Pitt. Pirates	Dick Great	Shortstop	Don Hoak	Third base
1967	St. L. Cardinals	Orlando Cepeda	First base	Tim McCarver	Catcher
1976	Cin. Reds	Joe Morgan	Second base	George Foster	Outfield
1989	S.F. Giants	Kevin Mitchell	Outfield	Will Clark	First base
1990	Pitt. Pirates	Barry Bonds	Outfield	Bobby Bonilla	Outfield
2000	S.F. Giants	Jeff Kent	Second base	Barry Bonds	Outfield

*Teammates finished one-two-three in voting (AL 1959: Early Wynn, pitcher; AL 1966: Boog Powell, first base; NL 1914: Bill James, pitcher; and NL 1941: Whit Wyatt, pitcher).

Triple Crown Winners *Not* Winning MVP

American League

Season	Triple Crown Winner	MVP Winner
1934	Lou Gehrig, N.Y. Yankees	Mickey Cochrane, Det. Tigers
1942	Ted Williams, Bost. Red Sox	Joe Gordon, N.Y. Yankees
1947	Ted Williams, Bost. Red Sox	Joe DiMaggio, N.Y. Yankees

National League

Season	Triple Crown Winner	MVP Winner
1912	Heinie Zimmerman, Chi. Cubs	Larry Doyle, N.Y. Giants
1933	Chuck Klein, Phila. Phillies	Carl Hubbell, N.Y. Giants

MVPs on Nonwinning Teams

American League

Team	Wins–Losses
Robin Yount, Milw. Brewers, 1989	81–81
Alex Rodriguez, Tex. Rangers, 2003	71–91

National League

Team	Wins–Losses
Hank Sauer, Chi. Cubs, 1952	77–77
Ernie Banks, Chi. Cubs, 1958	72–82
Ernie Banks, Chi. Cubs, 1959	74–80
Andre Dawson, Chi. Cubs, 1987	76–85
Barry Bonds, Pitt. Pirates, 1993	75–87

MVPs *Not* Batting .300, Hitting 30 Home Runs, or Driving in 100 Runs (Not Including Pitchers)

American League

Roger Peckinpaugh, Wash. Senators, 1925
Mickey Cochrane, Phila. A's, 1928
Yogi Berra, N.Y. Yankees, 1951
Elston Howard, N.Y. Yankees, 1963
Zoilo Versalles, Minn. Twins, 1965

National League

Johnny Evers, Bost. Braves, 1914
Bob O'Farrell, St. L. Cardinals, 1926
Marty Marion, St. L. Cardinals, 1944
Maury Wills, L.A. Dodgers, 1962
Kirk Gibson, L.A. Dodgers, 1988

Pitchers Winning MVP Award

American League	National League
Walter Johnson, Wash. Senators, 1912*	Dazzy Vance, Bklyn. Dodgers, 1924*
Walter Johnson, Wash. Senators, 1924**	Carl Hubbell, N.Y. Giants, 1933
Lefty Grove, Phila. A's, 1931	Dizzy Dean, St. L. Cardinals, 1934
Spud Chandler, N.Y. Yankees, 1943	Carl Hubbell, N.Y. Giants, 1936
Hal Newhouser, Det. Tigers, 1944	Bucky Walters, Cin. Reds, 1939
Hal Newhouser, Det. Tigers, 1945	Mort Cooper, St. L. Cardinals, 1942
Bobby Shantz, Phila. A's, 1952	Jim Konstanty, Phila. Phillies, 1950
Denny McLain, Det. Tigers, 1968	Don Newcombe, Bklyn. Dodgers, 1956
Vida Blue, Oak. A's, 1971	Sandy Koufax, L.A. Dodgers, 1963
Rollie Fingers, Milw. Brewers, 1981	Bob Gibson, St. L. Cardinals, 1968
Willie Hernandez, Det. Tigers, 1984	
Roger Clemens, Bost. Red Sox, 1986	
Dennis Eckersley, Oak. A's, 1992	

*Chalmers Award.
**League Award.

Players Winning MVP Award First Season in League

American League	National League
Frank Robinson, Balt. Orioles, 1966	Kirk Gibson, L.A. Dodgers, 1988
Dick Allen, Chi. White Sox, 1972	
Fred Lynn, Bost. Red Sox, 1975	
Willie Hernandez, Det. Tigers, 1984	
Ichiro Suzuki, Sea. Mariners, 2001	
Vladimir Guerrero, L.A. Angels, 2004	

MVPs Receiving Fewer First-Place Votes Than Runner-Up

American League

1944 Hal Newhouser (Det. Tigers pitcher) winner over Dizzy Trout (Det. Tigers pitcher), 236–232
1960 Roger Maris (N.Y. Yankees outfield) winner over Mickey Mantle (N.Y. Yankees outfield), 225–222
1991 Ivan Rodriguez (Tex. Rangers catcher) winner over Pedro Martinez (Bost. Red Sox pitcher), 252–239

National League

1966 Roberto Clemente (Pitt. Pirates outfield) winner over Sandy Koufax (L.A. Dodgers pitcher), 218–205

Teams with Most Consecutive MVP Awards

5	S.F. Giants (NL), 2000–04	Jeff Kent, second base, 2000
		Barry Bonds, outfield, 2001–04
4	N.Y. Yankees (AL), 1954–57	Yogi Berra, catcher, 1954 and 1955
		Mickey Mantle, outfield, 1956 and 1957
4	N.Y. Yankees (AL), 1960–63	Roger Maris, outfield, 1960 and 1961
		Mickey Mantle, outfield, 1962
		Elston Howard, catcher, 1963

Players Winning MVP Award with Two Different Teams

		MVP Seasons
Barry Bonds	Pitt. Pirates (NL)	1990 and 1992
	S.F. Giants (NL)	1993 and 2001–04
Mickey Cochrane	Phila. A's (AL)	1928
	Det. Tigers (AL)	1934
Jimmie Foxx	Phila. A's (AL)	1932–33
	Bost. Red Sox (AL)	1938
Rogers Hornsby	St. L. Cardinals (NL)	1925
	Chi. Cubs (NL)	1929
Frank Robinson	Cin. Reds (NL)	1961
	Balt. Orioles (AL)	1966
	Tex. Rangers (AL)	2003
Alex Rodriguez	N.Y. Yankees (AL)	2005 and 2007

MVPs with Fewest Hits

119 ... Willie Stargell, 1979, National League
124 ... Roger Peckinpaugh, 1925, American League
133 ... Barry Bonds, 2003, National League
135 ... Marty Marion, 1944, National League
135 ... Barry Bonds, 2004, National League

Switch-Hitting MVPs

American League

Mickey Mantle, N.Y. Yankees, 1956
Mickey Mantle, N.Y. Yankees, 1957
Mickey Mantle, N.Y. Yankees, 1962
Vida Blue, Oak. A's, 1971

National League

Frankie Frisch, St. L. Cardinals, 1931
Maury Wills, L.A. Dodgers, 1962
Pete Rose, Cin. Reds, 1973
Willie McGee, St. L. Cardinals, 1985
Terry Pendleton, Atl. Braves, 1991
Ken Caminiti, S.D. Padres, 1996
Chipper Jones, Atl. Braves, 1999
Jimmy Rollins, Phila. Phillies, 2007

Cy Young Award

Pitchers Winning 25 Games, *Not* Winning Cy Young Award

American League

		Wins–Losses	Cy Young Award Winner	Wins–Losses
1966	Jim Kaat, Minn. Twins	25–13	Sandy Koufax, L.A. Dodgers (NL)	27–9*
1971	Mickey Lolich, Det. Tigers	25–14	Vida Blue, Oak. A's	24–8
1974	Ferguson Jenkins, Tex. Rangers	25–12	Catfish Hunter, Oak. A's	25–12

National League

		Wins–Losses	Cy Young Award Winner	Wins–Losses
1963	Juan Marichal, S.F. Giants	25–8	Sandy Koufax, L.A. Dodgers	25–5*
1966	Juan Marichal, S.F. Giants	25–6	Sandy Koufax, L.A. Dodgers	27–9*
1968	Juan Marichal, S.F. Giants	26–9	Bob Gibson, St. L. Cardinals	22–9

*One winner, both leagues, 1956–67.

Pitchers Winning 20 Games Only Once and Cy Young Award Same Season

American League		National League	
	Wins		**Wins**
Jim Lonborg, Bost. Red Sox, 1967	22	Vern Law, Pitt. Pirates, 1960	20
Mike Flanagan, Balt. Orioles, 1979	23	Mike McCormick, S.F. Giants, 1967	22
Steve Stone, Balt. Orioles, 1980	25	Doug Drabek, Pitt. Pirates, 1990	22
Bob Welch, Oak. A's, 1990	27	John Smoltz, Atl. Braves, 1996	24
Pat Hentgen, Tor. Blue Jays, 1996	20	Chris Carpenter, St. L. Cardirals, 2005	21
Barry Zito, Oak. A's, 2002	23		
Roy Halladay, Tor. Blue Jays, 2003	22		
Johan Santana, Minn. Twins, 2004	20		
Cliff Lee, Cleve. Indians, 2008	22		

Cy Young Winners *Not* in Top 10 in League in ERA, Season

American League

	ERA	Place in League
Jim Lonborg, Bost. Red Sox, 1967	3.16	18th
LaMarr Hoyt, Chi. White Sox, 1983	3.66	17th

National League

	ERA	Place in League
Mike McCormick, S.F. Giants, 1967	2.85	16th

Relief Pitchers Winning Cy Young Award

American League	National League
Sparky Lyle, N.Y. Yankees, 1977	Mike Marshall, L.A. Dodgers, 1974
Rollie Fingers, Milw. Brewers, 1981	Bruce Sutter, Chi. Cubs, 1979
Willie Hernandez, Det. Tigers, 1984	Steve Bedrosian, Phila. Phillies, 1987
Dennis Eckersley, Oak. A's, 1992	Mark Davis, S.D. Padres, 1989
	Eric Gagne, L.A. Dodgers, 2003

Cy Young Winners Increasing Their Number of Victories the Following Season

American League

	Award-Winning Season	Next Season
Mike Cuellar, Balt. Orioles, 1969	23–11	24–8
David Cone, K.C. Royals, 1994	16–5	18–8
Felix Hernandez, Sea. Mariners, 2010	13–12	14–14

National League

	Award-Winning Season	Next Season
Warren Spahn, Milw. Braves, 1957	21–11	22–11
Sandy Koufax, L.A. Dodgers, 1965	26–8	27–9
Steve Bedrosian, Phila. Phillies, 1987	5–3	6–6
Greg Maddux, Atl. Braves, 1994	16–6	19–2
Pedro Martinez, Mont. Expos, 1997	17–8	19–7
Randy Johnson, Ariz. D'backs, 1999	17–9	19–7
Randy Johnson, Ariz. D'backs, 2000	19–7	21–6
Randy Johnson, Ariz. D'backs, 2001	21–6	24–5
Eric Gagne, L.A. Dodgers, 2003	2–3	7–3
Brandon Webb, Ariz. D'backs, 2007	16–8	18–10
Tim Lincecum, S.F. Giants, 2009	15–17	16–10

Won Both Cy Young and MVP Same Season

1968 ....Denny McLain, Det. Tigers	1956 ....Don Newcombe, Bklyn. Dodgers
1971 ....Vida Blue, Oak. A's	1963 ....Sandy Koufax, L.A. Dodgers
1981...Rollie Fingers, Milw. Brewers	1968 ....Bob Gibson, St. L. Cardinals
1984 ....Willie Hernandez, Det. Tigers	
1986..Roger Clemens, Bost. Red Sox	
1992...Dennis Eckersley, Oak. A's	

Cy Young Winners with Higher Batting Averages Than That Year's Home Run Leader

American League

	Cy Young Winner	Home Run Leader
1959	............................Early Wynn, Chi. White Sox, .244	...............................Harmon Killebrew, Minn. Twins, .242 (Tie)

National League (Post-1900)

	Cy Young Winner	Home Run Leader
1970	............................Bob Gibson, St. L. Cardinals, .303	...............................Johnny Bench, Cin. Reds, .293
1982	............................Steve Carlton, Phila. Phillies, .218	...............................Dave Kingman, N.Y. Mets, .204

Rookie of the Year

Rookie of the Year Winners on Team Other Than the One First Played On

Team First Played On

Tommie Agee, Chi. White Sox (AL), 1966	...................................First came up for 5 games with Cleve. Indians (AL), 1962
Jason Bay, Pitt. Pirates (NL), 2004	....First came up for 3 games with S.D. Padres (NL), 2003
Alfredo Griffin, Tor. Blue Jays (AL), 1979 (cowinner)	....................First came up for 12 games with Cleve. Indians (AL), 1976
Lou Piniella, K.C. Royals (AL), 1969	....First came up for 4 games with Balt. Orioles (AL), 1964
Hanley Ramirez, Fla. Marlins (NL), 2006	...................................First came up for 4 games with Bost. Red Sox (AL), 2005

Relief Pitchers Winning Rookie of the Year

American League	National League
Kazuhiro Sasaki, Sea. Mariners, 2000	Joe Black, Bklyn. Dodgers, 1952
Huston Street, Oak. A's, 2005	Butch Metzger, S.D. Padres, 1976 (Tie)
Andrew Bailey, Oak. A's, 2009	Steve Howe, L.A. Dodgers, 1980
Neftali Feliz, Tex. Rangers, 2010	Todd Worrell, St. L. Cardinals, 1986
	Scott Williamson, Cin. Reds, 1999

Rookie of the Year on Pennant-Winning Teams

American League	National League
Gil McDougald, second base and third base, N.Y. Yankees, 1951	Jackie Robinson, first base, Bklyn. Dodgers, 1947
Tony Kubek, outfield and shortstop, N.Y. Yankees, 1957	Alvin Dark, shortstop, Bost. Braves, 1948
Tom Tresh, shortstop, N.Y. Yankees, 1962	Don Newcombe, pitcher, Bklyn. Dodgers, 1949
Fred Lynn, outfield, Bost. Red Sox, 1975	Willie Mays, outfield, N.Y. Giants, 1951
Dave Righetti, pitcher, N.Y. Yankees, 1981	Joe Black, pitcher, Bklyn. Dodgers, 1952
Walt Weiss, shortstop, Oak. A's, 1988	Junior Gilliam, second base, Bklyn. Dodgers, 1953
Chuck Knoblauch, second base, Minn. Twins, 1991	Jim Lefebvre, second base, L.A. Dodgers, 1965
Derek Jeter, shortstop, N.Y. Yankees, 1996	Pat Zachry, pitcher, Cin. Reds, 1976
Dustin Pedroia, shortstop, Bost. Red Sox, 2007	Fernando Valenzuela, pitcher, L.A. Dodgers, 1981
Evan Longoria, third base, T.B. Rays, 2008	Vince Coleman, outfield, St. L. Cardinals, 1985
Neftali Feliz, pitcher, Tex. Rangers, 2010	Buster Posey, catcher, S.F. Giants, 2010

Rookies of the Year Elected to Hall of Fame

Rookie of the Year		HOF	Rookie of the Year		HOF
1947	Jackie Robinson	1962	1967	Tom Seaver	1992
1951	Willie Mays	1979	1967	Rod Carew	2003
1956	Frank Robinson	1982	1968	Johnny Bench	1989
1956	Luis Aparicio	1984	1972	Carlton Fisk	2000
1958	Orlando Cepeda	1999	1977	Eddie Murray	2003
1959	Willie McCovey	1986	1977	Andre Dawson	2010
1961	Billy Williams	1978	1982	Cal Ripken Jr.	2007

Gold Gloves

Most Gold Gloves, by Position

American League

First Base ....9 ....Don Mattingly (1985–89, 1991–94)
Second Base..10 ....Roberto Alomar (1991–96, 1998–2001)
Third Base .....16 ....Brooks Robinson (1960–75)
Shortstop ....9 ....Luis Aparicio (1958–62, 1964, 1966, 1968, 1970)
                     9 ....Omar Vizquel (1993–2001)
Outfield ....10 ....Al Kaline (1957–59, 1961–67)
                    10 ....Ken Griffey Jr. (1990–99)
                    10 ....Ichiro Suzuki* (2001–10)
Catcher ....13 ....Ivan Rodriguez* (1992–2001, 2004, 2006–07)
Pitcher...........14 ....Jim Kaat (1962–75)

*Still active.

National League

First Base ....11 ....Keith Hernandez (1978–88)
Second Base ......9 ....Ryne Sandberg (1983–91)
Third Base ....10 ....Mike Schmidt (1976–84, 1986)
Shortstop ....13 ....Ozzie Smith (1980–92)

Outfield ....12 ....Roberto Clemente (1961–72)
                      12..........................Willie Mays (1957–68)

Catcher ....10 ....Johnny Bench (1968–77)
Pitcher ....18 ....Greg Maddux (1990–2002, 2004–08)

5

MANAGERS

Winningest Managers by First Letter of Last Name

			Percentage
A	Sparky Anderson (1970–95)	2194–1834	.545
B	Dusty Baker* (1993–)	1484–1367	.521
C	Bobby Cox (1978–)	2504–2001	.521
D	Leo Durocher (1939–46, 1948–55, 1966–73)	2008–1709	.540
E	Buck Ewing (1890, 1895–1900)	489–395	.553
F	Frankie Frisch (1933–38, 1940–46, 1949–51)	1138–1078	.514
G	Clark Griffith (1901–20)	1491–1367	.522
H	Bucky Harris (1924–43, 1947–48, 1950–56)	2158–2219	.493
I	Arthur Irwin (1889, 1891–92, 1894–96, 1898–99)	416–427	.493
J	Davey Johnson* (1984–90, 1993–97, 1999–2000, 2011–)	1188–931	.561
K	Tom Kelly (1986–2000)	1140–1244	.478
L	Tony La Russa (1979–2011)	2728–2365	.536
M	Connie Mack (1894–96, 1901–50)	3731–3948	.486
N	Jerry Narron (2001–07)	291–341	.460
O	Steve O'Neill (1935–37, 1943–48, 1950–54)	1040–821	.559
P	Lou Piniella (1986–88, 1990–2010)	1885–1713	.517
Q	Frank Quilici (1972–75)	280–267	.494
R	Wilbert Robinson (1902, 1914–31)	1399–1398	.503
S	Casey Stengel (1934–36, 1938–43, 1949–60, 1962–65)	1905–1842	.508
T	Joe Torre (1977–84, 1990–2010)	2326–1997	.540
U	Bob Unglaub (1907)	9–20	.310
V	Bobby Valentine (1985–92, 1996–2002)	1117–1072	.510
W	Dick Williams (1967–69, 1971–88)	1571–1451	.520
X	[No manager]		
Y	Ned Yost* (2003–08, 2010–)	583–665	.467
Z	Don Zimmer (1972–73, 1976–82, 1988–91, 1999)	885–858	.508

*Still active.

Winningest Managers by Zodiac Sign

Aquarius (Jan. 20–Feb. 18)	Bill Rigney	1239
Pisces (Feb. 19–Mar. 20)	Sparky Anderson	2194
Aries (Mar. 21–Apr. 19)	John McGraw	2763
Taurus (Apr. 20–May 20)	Joe McCarthy	2125
Gemini (May 21–June 21)	Bobby Cox	2504
Cancer (June 22–July 22)	Joe Torre	2326
Leo (July 23–Aug. 22)	Leo Durocher	2008

continued on next page

Virgo (Aug. 23–Sept. 22) ....Lou Piniella...1835
Libra (Sept. 23–Oct. 23) ....Tony La Russa 2728
Scorpio (Oct. 24–Nov. 21) ....Bucky Harris..2158
Sagittarius (Nov. 22–Dec. 21)..Walter Alston 2040
Capricorn (Dec. 22–Jan. 19) ....Connie Mack 3637
*Still active.

Managers During Most Presidential Administrations

10............Connie Mack ....Cleveland, McKinley, T. Roosevelt, Taft, Wilson, Harding, Hoover, F. Roosevelt, Truman
7..............Gene Mauch..........................Eisenhower, Kennedy, L. Johnson, Nixon, Ford, Carter, Reagan
7..............John McGraw ....McKinley, T. Roosevelt, Taft, Wilson, Harding, Coolidge, Hoover
7..............Harry Wright..........................Grant, Hayes, Garfield, Arthur, Cleveland, B. Harrison, Cleveland
6..............Bobby Cox ....Carter, Reagan, G. Bush, Clinton, G. Bush, G. W. Bush, Obama
6..............Ralph Houk ....Kennedy, L. Johnson, Nixon, Ford, Carter, Reagan
6..............Tony La Russa ....Carter, Reagan, G. Bush, Clinton, G. W. Bush, Obama
6..............Bill McKechnie ....Wilson, Harding, Coolidge, Hoover, F. Roosevelt, Truman
6..............John McNamara ....Nixon, Ford, Carter, Reagan, G. Bush, Clinton
6..............Joe Torre ....Carter, Reagan, G. Bush, Clinton, G. W. Bush, Obama

Managers Winning 1000 Games with One Franchise

Connie Mack, Phila. A's (AL), 1901–50...3637
John McGraw, N.Y. Giants (NL), 1902–32 2658
Bobby Cox, Atl. Braves (NL), 1978–81 and 1990–2010...2149
Walter Alston, Bklyn./L.A. Dodgers (NL), 1954–76..2040
Tommy Lasorda, L.A. Dodgers (NL), 1976–96..1599
Earl Weaver, Balt. Orioles (AL), 1968–82 and 1985–86..1480
Joe McCarthy, N.Y. Yankees (AL), 1931–46..1460
Fred Clarke, Pitt. Pirates (NL), 1900–1915 1422
Tony La Russa, St. Louis Cardinals (NL) 1996–2011 1408
Wilbert Robinson, Bklyn. Robins (NL), 1914–31...1375
Bucky Harris, Wash. Senators (AL), 1924–28, 1935–42, and 1950–54 1336
Cap Anson, Chi. Colts/Cubs (NL), 1879–97..1288
Joe Torre, N.Y. Yankees (AL), 1996–2007..1173
Casey Stengel, N.Y. Yankees (AL), 1949–60...1149
Tom Kelly, Minn. Twins (AL), 1986–2001 1140
Hughie Jennings, Det. Tigers (AL), 1907–20 1131
Danny Murtaugh, Pitt. Pirates (NL), 1957–64, 1967, 1970–71, and 1973–76.....................1115
Miller Huggins, N.Y. Yankees (AL), 1918–29 1067
Mike Scioscia*, L.A. Angles (AL), 2000– 1066
Red Schoendienst, St. L. Cardinals (NL), 1965–76 and 1980 1028
Frank Selee, Bost. Beaneaters (NL), 1890–1901 1004
*Still active.

Managers with Over 1000 Career Wins and sub-.500 Winning Percentage

	Record	Percentage	
Bruce Bochy*	1360–1375	.497	S.D. Padres (NL), 1995–2005
....			S.F. Gaints (NL), 2007–

Lou Boudreau	1162–1224	.487	Cleve. Indians (AL), 1942–50
			Bost. Red Sox (AL), 1942–50
			K.C. Royals (AL), 1955–57
			Chi. Cubs (NL), 1960
Jimmy Dykes	1406–1541	.477	Chi. White Sox (AL), 1934–46
			Phila. Athletics (AL), 1951–53
			Balt. Orioles (AL), 1954
			Cin. Reds (NL), 1958
			Det. Tigers (AL), 1959–60
			Cleve. Indians (AL), 1960–61
Jim Fregosi	1028–1094	.484	Calif. Angels (AL), 1978–81
			Chi. White Sox (AL), 1986–88
			Phila. Phillies (NL), 1991–96
			Tor. Blue Jays (NL), 1999–2000
Bucky Harris	2158–2218	.493	Wash. Senators (AL), 1924–28, 1935–42, 1950–54
			Det. Tigers (AL), 1929–33, 1955–56
			Bost. Red Sox (AL), 1934
			Phila. Phillies (NL), 1943
			N.Y. Yankees (AL), 1947–48
Art Howe	1129–1137	.498	Hous. Astros (NL), 1989–93
			Oak. A's (AL), 1996–2002
			N.Y. Mets (NL), 2003–04
Tom Kelly	1140–1244	.478	Minn. Twins (AL), 1986–2001
Connie Mack	3731–3948	.486	Pitt. Pirates (NL), 1894–96
			Phila. Athletics (AL), 1901–50
Gene Mauch	1902–2037	.483	Phila. Phillies (NL), 1960–68
			Mont. Expos (NL), 1969–75
			Minn. Twins (AL), 1976–80
			Calif. Angels (AL), 1981–87
John McNamara	1168–1247	.484	Oak A's (AL), 1969–70
			S.D. Padres (NL), 1974–77
			Cin. Reds (NL), 1979–82
			Calif. Angels (AL), 1983–84, 1996
			Bost. Red Sox (AL), 1985–88
			Cleve. Indians (AL), 1900–91
Bill Rigney	1239–1321	.484	N.Y. Giants (NL), 1956–57
			S.F. Giants (NL), 1958–60
			L.A. Angels (AL), 1961–64
			Calif. Angels (AL), 1965–69
			Minn. Twins (AL), 1970–72
Frank Robinson	1065–1176	.475	Cleve. Indians (AL), 1975–77
			S.F. Giants (NL), 1981–84
			Balt. Orioles (AL), 1988–91
			Mont. Expos (NL), 2002–04
			Wash. Nationals (NL), 2005–06
Chuck Tanner	1352–1381	.495	Chi. White Sox (AL), 1970–75
			Oak. A's (AL), 1976
			Pitt. Pirates (NL), 1977–85
			Atl. Braves (NL), 1986–88

*Still active.

Managers with Most Career Victories for Each Franchise

American League

Balt. Orioles	Earl Weaver, 1968–82 and 1985–86	1480–1060	.583
Bost. Red Sox	Joe Cronin, 1935–47	1071–916	.539
Chi. White Sox	Jimmy Dykes, 1934–46	899–938	.489
Cleve. Indians	Lou Boudreau, 1942–50	728–649	.529
Det. Tigers	Hughie Jennings, 1907–20	1131–972	.538
K.C. A's	Harry Craft, 1957–59	162–196	.452
K.C. Royals	Whitey Herzog, 1975–79	410–304	.574
L.A./Cal./Ana. Angels	Mike Scioscia*, 2000–	1066–878	.548
Milw. Brewers	George Bamberger, 1978–80 and 1985–86	377–351	.518
Minn. Twins	Tom Kelly, 1986–2001	1140–1244	.478
N.Y. Yankees	Joe McCarthy, 1931–46	1460–867	.627
Oak. A's	Tony La Russa, 1986–95	798–673	.542
Phila. A's	Connie Mack, 1901–50	3627–3891	.482
Sea. Mariners	Lou Piniella, 1993–2002	840–711	.542
Sea. Pilots	Joe Schultz, 1969	64–98	.395
St. L. Browns	Jimmy McAleer, 1902–09	551–632	.466
T.B. Rays	Joe Maddon, 2006–	522–501	.510
Tex. Rangers	Ron Washington*, (2007–)	427–383	.527
Tor. Blue Jays	Cito Gaston, 1989–97, 2008–10)	894–837	.516
Wash. Senators	Bucky Harris, 1924–28, 1935–42, and 1950–54	1336–1416	.485
Wash. Senators II	Gil Hodges, 1963–67	321–445	.419

National League (Post-1900)

Ariz. D'backs	Bob Melvin, (2005–09)	337–340	.498
Atl. Braves	Bobby Cox, (1978–81 and 1990–2010)	2149–1709	.557
Bost. Braves	George Stallings, 1913–20	579–597	.492
Bklyn. Dodgers	Wilbert Robinson, 1914–31	1375–1341	.504
Chi. Cubs	Charlie Grimm, 1932–38, 1944–49, and 1960	946–784	.547
Cin. Reds	Sparky Anderson, 1970–78	863–586	.596
Colo. Rockies	Clint Hurdle, 2003–09	467–552	.452
Flor. Marlins	Fredi Gonzalez, (2007–10)	276–279	.497
Hous. Astros	Bill Virdon, 1975–82	544–522	.510
L.A. Dodgers	Walter Alston, 1958–76	1673–1355	.552
Milw. Braves	Fred Haney, 1956–59	341–231	.596
Mont. Expos	Gene Mauch, 1969–75	499–627	.443
N.Y. Giants	John McGraw, 1902–32	2658–1823	.593
N.Y. Mets	Davey Johnson, 1984–88	575–395	.593
Phila. Phillies	Charlie Manuel*, (2005–)	646–488	.570
Pitt. Pirates	Fred Clarke, 1900–15	1422–969	.595
St. L. Cardinals	Tony La Russa, 1996–2011	1408–1182	.544
S.D. Padres	Bruce Bochy*, 1995–2006	951–975	.494
S.F. Giants	Dusty Baker, 1993–2002	840–715	.540
Wash. Nationals	Manny Acta, 2007-09	158–252	.385

*Still active.

Best Winning Percentage as Manager with One Team (Post-1900; Min. 150 Games)

Percentage		Wins–Losses
.664	Frank Chance, Chi. Cubs (NL), 1905–12	768–389
.642	Chuck Dressen, Bklyn. Dodgers (NL), 1951–53	298–166
.642	Billy Southworth, St. L. Cardinals (NL), 1939–45	620–346
.632	Dick Howser, N.Y. Yankees (AL), 1978 and 1980	103–60
.627	Joe McCarthy, N.Y. Yankees (AL), 1931–46	1460–867
.623	Casey Stengel, N.Y. Yankees (AL), 1949–60	1149–696
.621	Jake Stahl, Bost. Red Sox (AL), 1912–13	144–88
.620	Bucky Harris, N.Y. Yankees (AL), 1947–48	191–117
.617	Al Lopez, Cleve. Indians (AL), 1951–56	570–354
.606	Joe McCarthy, Bost. Red Sox (AL), 1948–50	223–145
.605	Joe Torre, N.Y. Yankess (AL), 1996–2007	1173–767

Managers with 500 Wins in Each League

2728	Tony La Russa (1408 NL, 1320 AL)	1835	Lou Piniella (1264 AL, 571 NL)
2326	Joe Torre (1173 AL, 1153 NL)	1588	Jim Leyland (519 AL, 1069 NL)
2194	Sparky Anderson (1331 NL, 863 AL)	1571	Dick Williams (854 AL, 717 NL)
1905	Casey Stengel (1149 AL, 756 NL)	1168	John McNamara (665 AL, 503 NL)
1902	Gene Mauch (1145 NL, 757 AL)		

Played in 2000 Games, Managed in 2000 Games

	Games Played	Games Managed
Cap Anson	2276 (1876–97)	2296 (1879–98)
Fred Clarke	2245 (1894–1915)	2822 (1897–1915)
Joe Cronin	2124 (1926–45)	2315 (1933–47)
Jimmy Dykes	2282 (1918–39)	2960 (1934–46, 1951–54, 1958–61)
Frankie Frisch	2311 (1919–37)	2245 (1933–38, 1940–46, 1949–51)
Charlie Grimm	2164 (1916, 1918–36)	2370 (1932–38, 1944–49, 1952–56, 1960)
Joe Torre	2209 (1960–77)	4329 (1977–84, 1990–2010)
Dusty Baker*	2039 (1968–86)	2852 (1993–2006, 2008–)

*Still active.

Managers Managing 100-Loss Teams After 1000th Career Victory

Lou Boudreau, K.C. A's (AL), 1956
Leo Durocher, Chi. Cubs (NL), 1966
Jimmy Dykes, Balt. Orioles (AL), 1954
Ned Hanlon, Bklyn. Dodgers (NL), 1905
Ralph Houk, Det. Tigers (AL), 1975

Connie Mack, Phila. A's (AL), 1915–16, 1919–20, 1943, and 1946
Bill McKechnie, Bost. Braves (NL), 1935
Casey Stengel, N.Y. Mets (NL), 1962–64
Chuck Tanner, Pitt. Pirates (NL), 1985

Managers with Both 100 Wins and 100-Loss Seasons

	100 Wins	100 Losses
Sparky Anderson	Cin. Reds (NL) 1970, 1975, 1976	Det. Tigers (AL), 1989
Chuck Dressen	Bklyn. Dodgers (NL) 1953	Wash. Senators (AL) 1955
Leo Durocher	Bklyn. Dodgers (NL) 1941, 1942	Chi. Cubs (NL) 1966
Ralph Houk	N.Y. Yankees (AL), 1961, 1963	Det. Tigers (AL) 1957
Connie Mack	Phila. Athletics (AL), 1910, 1911, 1929, 1930, 1931	Phila. Athletics (AL), 1915, 1916, 1919, 1920, 1921, 1936, 1940, 1943, 1946, 1950

Bill McKechnie ....Cin. Reds (NL), 1940 ....Bost. Braves (NL), 1935
Casey Stengel ...........N.Y. Yankees (AL), 1954..N.Y. Mets (NL), 1962, 1963, 1964

Former Pitchers Winning Pennants as Managers (Post-1900)

Eddie Dyer, St. L. Cardinals (NL), 1946
Dallas Green, Phila. Phillies (NL), 1980
Clark Griffith, Chi. White Sox (AL), 1901
Roger Craig, S.F. Giants (NL), 1989

Fred Hutchinson, Cin. Reds (NL), 1961
Tommy Lasorda, L.A. Dodgers (NL), 1977–78, 1981, and 1988
Bob Lemon, N.Y. Yankees (AL), 1978 and 1981
Kid Gleason, Chi. White Sox (AL), 1919

Managers Taking Over World Series Teams in Midseason

American League

Season	Manager	Wins–Losses	Former Manager
1978	Bob Lemon, N.Y. Yankees*	48–20	Billy Martin (52–42), Dick Howser (0–1)
1981	Bob Lemon, N.Y. Yankees	13–15	Gene Michael (46–33)
1982	Harvey Kuenn, Milw. Brewers	72–49	Buck Rodgers (23–24)

National League

Season	Manager	Wins–Losses	Former Manager
1932	Charlie Grimm, Chi. Cubs	37–20	Rogers Hornsby (53–44)
1938	Gabby Hartnett, Chi. Cubs	44–27	Charlie Grimm (45–36)
1947	Burt Shotton, Bklyn. Dodgers	93–60	Clyde Sukeforth (1–0)
1983	Paul Owens, Phila. Phillies	47–30	Pat Corrales (43–42)
2003	Jack McKeon, Flor. Marlins*	75–49	Jeff Torborg (17–22)

*World Series winner.

Managers Replaced While Team Was in First Place

Season	Team	Former Manager	Wins–Losses	New Manager	Wins–Losses
1947	Bklyn. Dodgers (NL)	Clyde Sukeforth	1–0	Burt Shotton	93–60
1983	Phila. Phillies (NL)	Pat Corrales	43–42	Paul Owens	47–30

Managers Winning Pennant in First Year as Manager of Team

American League

Clark Griffith, Chi. White Sox, 1901
Hughie Jennings, Det. Tigers, 1907
Kid Gleason, Chi. White Sox, 1919
*Tris Speaker, Cleve. Indians, 1920
Bucky Harris, Wash. Senators, 1924
Joe Cronin, Wash. Senators, 1933
Mickey Cochrane, Det. Tigers, 1934
Ralph Houk, N.Y. Yankees, 1961
Yogi Berra, N.Y. Yankees, 1964
Dick Williams, Bost. Red Sox, 1967
**Bob Lemon, N.Y. Yankees, 1978
*Earl Weaver, Balt. Orioles, 1979
Jim Frey, K.C. Royals, 1980
Joe Torre, N.Y. Yankees, 1999
Terry Francona, Bost. Red Sox, 2004
Jim Leyland, Det. Tigers, 2006

National League

*Frank Chance, Chi. Cubs, 1906
Pat Moran, Phila. Phillies, 1915
Pat Moran, Cin. Reds, 1919
**Charlie Grimm, Chi. Cubs, 1932
**Gabby Hartnett, Chi. Cubs, 1938
Eddie Dyer, St. L. Cardinals, 1946
Burt Shotton, Bklyn. Dodgers, 1947
*Tommy Lasorda, L.A. Dodgers, 1977
Jim Leyland, Flor. Marlins, 1997
*Bob Brenly, Ariz. D'backs, 2001
**Jack McKeon, Flor. Marlins, 2003

*First full season as manager.

**Took over in mid-season.

Managers Undefeated in World Series Play

George Stallings, Bost. Braves (NL), 1914 ....4–0 over
   Phila. A's (AL)

Hank Bauer, Balt. Orioles (AL), 1966 ....4–0 over
   L.A. Dodgers (NL)

Lou Piniella, Cin. Reds (NL), 1990 ......4–0 over Oak. A's (AL)

Terry Francona, Bost. Red Sox (AL), 2004 ....4–0 over
   St. L. Cardinals (NL)

                                        2007 ....4–0 over
   Colo. Rockies (NL)

Ozzie Guillen, Chi. White Sox (AL), 2005..............4–0 over
   Hous. Astros

Managers with Fewest Career Wins to Win World Series

	Wins		Wins
Tom Kelly, Minn. Twins (AL), 1987	97	Mike Scioscia, Ana. Angels (AL), 2002	256
Eddie Dyer, St. L. Cardinals (NL), 1946	98	Joe Girardi, N.Y. Yankees (AL), 2009	269
Dallas Green, Phila. Phillies (NL), 1980	110	Pants Rowland, Chi. White Sox (AL), 1917	281
Ed Barrow, Bost. Red Sox (AL), 1918	172	Davey Johnson, N.Y. Mets (NL), 1986	296
Mickey Cochrane, Det. Tigers (AL), 1935	194	Johnny Keane, St. L. Cardinals (NL), 1964	317
Gabby Street, St. L. Cardinals (NL), 1931	195	Joe Altobelli, Balt. Orioles (AL), 1983	323
Jake Stahl, Bost. Red Sox (AL), 1912	224	Bill Carrigan, Bost. Red Sox (AL), 1916	323
Bill Carrigan, Bost. Red Sox (AL), 1915	232	Lemon, N.Y. Yankees (AL), 1978	379
Jimmy Collins, Bost. Red Sox (AL), 1903	247		

Managers with Most Career Wins *Never* to Manage a World Series Team (Post-1903)

	Wins	Seasons
Gene Mauch	1901	26 (1960–82, 1985–87)
Jimmy Dykes	1407	21 (1934–46, 1951–54, 1958–61)
Bill Rigney	1239	18 (1956–72, 1976)
Art Howe	1129	14 (1989–93, 1996–2004)
Frank Robinson	1065	14 (1975–77, 1981–84, 1988–91, 2002–06)
lipe Alou	1033	14 (1992–2001, 2003–06)
Bill Virdon	995	13 (1972–84)
Buck Showalter	985	13 (1992–95, 1998–2000, 2003–06, 2010–)
Paul Richards	923	12 (1951–61, 1976)
Jimy Williams	910	12 (1986–89, 1997–2004)
Don Zimmer	906	14 (1972–73, 1976–82, 1988–91, 1999)Ron
Ron Gardenhire	866	10 (2002–
Johnny Oates	797	11 (1991–2001)
Jim Tracy	792	10 (2001–07, 2009–)
Buck Rodgers	784	13 (1980–82, 1985–94)

Pennant-Winning Managers with Fewest Career Wins (Since 1900)

82	Gene Michael, 1981 N.Y. Yankees (AL)	162	Ralph Houk, 1961 N.Y. Yankees (AL)
140	Kid Gleason, 1919 Chi. White Sox (AL)	162	Jim Frey, 1980 K.C. Royals (AL)
133	Joe Cronin, 1933 Wash. Senators (AL)	164	Yogi Berra, 1964 N.Y. Yankees (AL)*
154	Mickey Cochrane, 1934 Det. Tigers (AL)	203	Gabby Hartnett, 1938 Chi. Cubs (NL)
155	Gabby Street, 1930 St. L. Cardinals (NL)	305	Mickey Cochrane, 1935 Det. Tigers (AL)*
156	Bucky Harris, 1924 Wash. Senators (AL)*	307	Bucky Harris, 1925 Wash. Senators (AL)
157	Paul Owens, 1983 Phila. Phillies (NL)	309	Gabby Street, 1931 St. L. Cardinals (NL)*
160	Harvey Kuenn, 1982 Milw. Brewers (AL)	324	Ralph Houk, 1962 N.Y. Yankees (AL)*

161 ....Paul Owens, 1983 Phila.Phillies (NL)   347 ....Ed Barrow, 1918 Bost. Red Sox (AL)*
*Won World Series.

Most Times Managing the Same Club

5 ....Billy Martin, N.Y. Yankees, 1975–78, 1979, 1983, 1985, and 1988
4 ....Danny Murtaugh, Pitt. Pirates, 1957–64, 1967, 1970–71, and 1973–76
3...Bucky Harris, Wash. Senators, 1924–28, 1935–42, and 1950–54
3 ....Charlie Grimm, Chi. Cubs, 1932–38, 1944–49, and 1960

Managers with Best Winning Percentage for First Five Full Years of Managing

	Wins–Losses	Percentage
Frank Chance, Chi. Cubs (NL), 1906–10	530–235	.693
Al Lopez, Cleve. Indians (AL), 1951–55	482–288	.626
Earl Weaver, Balt. Orioles (AL), 1969–73	495–303	.620
John McGraw, Balt. Orioles (NL), 1899; Balt. Orioles (AL), 1901; and N.Y. Giants (NL), 1903–05	449–277	.618
Davey Johnson, N.Y. Mets (NL), 1984–88	488–320	.604
Hughie Jennings, Det. Tigers (AL), 1907–11	455–308	.596
Leo Durocher, Bklyn. Dodgers (NL), 1939–43	457–310	.596
Sparky Anderson, Cin. Reds (NL), 1970–74	473–329	.590
Fielder Jones, Chi. White Sox (AL), 1904–07; and St. L. Terriers (FL), 1915	447–313	.588
Joe McCarthy, Chi. Cubs (NL), 1926–29; and N.Y. Yankees (AL), 1931	450–316	.587
Pat Moran, Phila. Phillies (NL), 1915–18; and Cin. Reds (NL), 1919	419–301	.582

Managers Never Experiencing a Losing Season (Post-1900; Min. Two Full Seasons)

	Winning Seasons	Wins–Losses	Percentage
Joe McCarthy (1926–46, 1948–50)	24	2136–1335	.614
Steve O'Neill (1935–37, 1943–48, 1950–54)	14	1039–819	.559
Eddie Dyer (1946–50)	5	446–325	.578
Eddie Kasko (1970–73)	4	345–295	.539
Joe Morgan (1989–91)	4	255–231	.525
Ossie Vitt (1938–40)	3	262–198	.570
Harvey Kuenn (1975, 1982–83)	3	160–118	.576
Ron Gardenhire (2002–06)	5	455–354	.562
Eddie Collins (1925–26)	2	160–147	.521
Dick Sisler (1964–65)	2	121–94	.563

Career One-Game Managers

American League		National League	
Bibb Falk, Cleve. Indians, 1933	1–0	Bill Holbert, Syr. Stars, 1879	0–1
Marty Martinez, Sea. Mariners, 1986	0–1	Vern Benson, Atl. Braves, 1977	1–0
Bob Schaefer, K.C. Royals, 1991	1–0	Bill Burwell, Pitt. Pirates, 1947	1–0
Jo-Jo White, Cleve. Indians, 1960	1–0	Andy Cohen, Phila. Phillies, 1960	1–0

Del Wilber, Tex. Rangers, 1973..................................1–0

Rudy York, Bost. Red Sox, 1959 0–1

Eddie Yost, Wash. Senators II, 1963 0–1

Roy Johnson, Chi. Cubs, 1944 1–0

Ted Turner, Atl. Braves, 1977 0–1

Brandon Hyde, Flor. Marlins, 2011 0–1

Managers Managing in Civilian Clothes

Bill Armour, Cleve. Indians (AL), 1902–04; and Det. Tigers (AL), 1905–06

Judge Emil Fuchs, Bost. Braves (NL), 1929

Connie Mack, Pitt. Pirates (NL), 1894–96; and Phila. A's (AL), 1901–50

John McGraw, N.Y. Giants (NL), 1930–32

Burt Shotton, Phila. Phillies (NL), 1928–33; Cin. Reds (NL), 1934; and Bklyn. Dodgers (NL), 1947–48 and 1949–50

George Stallings, Phila. Phillies (NL), 1897–99; Det. Tigers (AL), 1901; N.Y. Yankees (AL), 1909–10; and Bost. Braves (NL), 1913–20

Managers Who Were Lawyers

Bill Armour, Cleve. Indians (AL), 1902–04; Det. Tigers (AL), 1905–06

Judge Emil Fuchs, Bost. Braves (NL), 1929

Miller Huggins, St. L. Cardinals (NL), 1913–17; and N.Y. Yankees (AL), 1918–29

Hughie Jennings, Det. Tigers (AL), 1907–20

Tony La Russa, Chi. White Sox (AL), 1979–86; Oak. A's (AL), 1986–88; and St. L. Cardinals (NL), 1996–2011

Branch Rickey, St. L. Browns (AL), 1913–15; and St. L. Cardinals (NL), 1919–25

Muddy Ruel, St. Louis (AL), 1947

Monte Ward, N.Y. Gothams (NL), 1884; Bklyn. Wonders (PL), 1890; Bklyn. Bridegrooms (NL), 1891–92; and N.Y. Giants (NL), 1893–94

Pennant-Winning Managers Who Won Batting Titles

Manager of Pennant Winner	Batting Champion
Lou Boudreau............Cleve. Indians (AL), 1948 ....Cleve. Indians (AL), 1944 (.327)
Rogers Hornsby.........St. L. Cardinals (NL), 1926 ....St. L. Cardinals (NL), 1920 (.370), 1921 (.397), 1922 (.401), 1923 (.384), 1924 (.424), 1925 (.403) Bost. Braves (NL), 1928 (.387)
Harvey Kuenn ....Milw. Brewers (AL), 1982 ....Det. Tigers (AL), 1959 (.353)
Tris Speaker..............Cleve. Indians (AL), 1920 ....Cleve. Indians (AL), 1916 (.386)
Bill Terry...................N.Y. Giants (NL), 1933, 1936–37 .......................N.Y. Giants (NL), 1930 (.401)
Joe Torre ..................N.Y. Yankees (AL), 1996, 1998–2001, 2003............St. L. Cardinals (NL), 1971 (.363)

Managers with Same Initials as Team They Managed

Billy Barnie, Bklyn. Bridegrooms (1897–98)

Harry Craft, Hous. Colt .45s (1962)

Bill Dahlen, Bklyn. Dodgers (1910–13)

Dick Tracewski, Det. Tigers (1979)

Playing Managers After 1950

American League

Lou Boudreau (shortstop), Cleve., 1950 (81 games)

Lou Boudreau (shortstop), Bost., 1952 (4 games)

Fred Hutchinson (pitcher), Det., 1952–53 (12 games in 1952; 3 games in 1953)

Marty Marion (shortstop/third base), St. L. Browns, 1952–53 (67 games in 1952; 3 games in 1953)

Eddie Joost (infield), Phila. A's, 1954 (19 games)

Hank Bauer (outfield), K.C., 1961 (43 games)

Frank Robinson (designated hitter), Cleve., 1976 (36 games)

Don Kessinger (shortstop), Chi., 1979 (56 games)

National League

Tommy Holmes (outfield), Bost. Braves, 1951 (27 games)

Phil Cavaretta (first base), Chi., 1951–53 (89 games in 1951; 41 games in 1952; 27 games in 1953)

Eddie Stanky (second base), St. L., 1952–53 (53 games in 1952; 17 games in 1953)

Harry Walker (outfield), St. L., 1955 (11 games)

Solly Hemus (infield), St. L., 1959 (24 games)

El Tappe (catcher), Chi., 1962 (26 games)

Joe Torre (first base/pinch hitter), N.Y., 1977 (26 games)

Pete Rose (first base), Cin., 1984–86 (26 games in 1984; 119 games in 1985; 72 games in 1986)

1000 Wins as Manager and 2000 Hits as Player

Felipe Aloa ....Manager (1992–2003) 1033 wins
Player (1958–74) 2101 hits

Cap Anson ....Manager (1875, 1879–98) 2196 wins
Player (1871–97) 3012 hits

Fred Clarke..Manager (1897–15) 1602 wins
Player (1894–1915) 2678 hits

Joe Cronin ....Manager (1933–47) 1236 wins
Player (1926–45) 2285 hits

Jimmy Dykes ....Manager (1934–46, 1951–54, 1958–61) 1406 wins
Player (1918–38) 2256 hits

Frankie Frisch..Manager (1933–38, 1940–46, 1949–51) 1138 wins
Player (1919–37) 2880 hits

Charlie Grimm ....Manager (1932–38, 1944–49, 1952–56, 1960) 1287 wins
Player (1916, 1918–36) 2299 hits

Frank Robinson ....Manager (1975–77, 1981–84, 1988–91, 2002–03) 1065 wins
Player (1957–76) 2943 hits

Red Schoendienst ....Manager (1965–76, 1980, 1990) 1041 wins
Player (1945–63) 2449 hits

Joe Torre..Manager (1977–84, 1990–2010) 2326 wins
Player (1960–77) 2342 hits

6

FIELDING

Most Games Played by Position, Career

First Base	2413	Eddie Murray (1977–97)
Second Base	2650	Eddie Collins (1906, 1908–28)
Third Base	2870	Brooks Robinson (1955–77)
Shortstop	2699	Omar Vizquel (1989–)
Left Field	2715	Barry Bonds (1986–2007)
Centerfield	2832	Willie Mays (1951–52, 1954–73)
Right Field	2297	Roberto Clemente (1955–72)
Catcher	2427	Ivan Rodriguez (1991)
Pitcher	1252	Jesse Orosco (1979, 1981–2004)
Designated Hitter	1396	David Ortiz (1987–)

Most Consecutive Games Played at Each Position

American League

First Base	885	Lou Gehrig, N.Y. Yankees, 1925–30
Second Base	798	Nellie Fox, Chi. White Sox, 1955–60
Third Base	576	Eddie Yost, Wash. Senators, 1951–55
Shortstop	2216	Cal Ripken Jr., Balt. Orioles, 1983–95
Outfield	511	Clyde Milan, Wash. Senators, 1910–13
Catcher	312	Frankie Hayes, St. L. Browns–Phila. A's–Cleve. Indians, 1943–46
Pitcher	13	Dale Mohoric, Tex. Rangers, 1986

National League

First Base	652	Frank McCormick, Cin. Reds, 1938–42
Second Base	443	Dave Cash, Pitt. Pirates–Phila. Phillies, 1973–76
Third Base	364	Ron Santo, Chi. Cubs, 1964–66
Shortstop	584	Roy McMillan, Cin. Reds, 1951–55
Outfield	897	Billy Williams, Chi. Cubs, 1963–69
Catcher	217	Ray Mueller, Cin. Reds, 1943–44
Pitcher	13	Mike Marshall, L.A. Dodgers, 1974

Players Who Played 1000 Games at Two Positions, Career

Ernie Banks	1125 at shortstop	1259 at first base
Rod Carew	1130 at second base	1184 at first base
Ron Fairly	1218 at first base	1037 in the outfield
Stan Musial	1890 in the outfield	1016 at first base
Alex Rodriguez	1272 at shortstop	1071 at third base
Robin Yount	1479 at shortstop	1150 in center field
Babe Ruth	1054 in left field	1133 in right field

Unassisted Triple Plays

Neal Ball, shortstop, Cleve. Indians (vs. Bost. Red Sox) (AL), July 19, 1909, 2nd inning; Batter: Amby McConnell
  Ball spears McConnell's line drive, comes down on second to double up Heinie Wagner, and tags out Jake Stahl, coming from first.
Bill Wambsganss, second base, Cleve. Indians (vs. Bklyn. Dodgers) (AL), Oct. 10, 1920*, 5th inning; Batter: Clarence Mitchell
  "Wamby" catches Mitchell's liner, steps on second to retire Pete Kilduff, and wheels around to tag Otto Miller, coming down from first.
George H. Burns, first base, Bost. Red Sox (vs. Cleve. Indians) (AL), Sept. 14, 1923, 2nd inning; Batter: Frank Brower
  Burns takes Brower's line drive, reaches out and tags Walter Lutzke, who was on first base, and then rushes down to second to tag the base before base runner Joe Stephenson can return.
Ernie Padgett, shortstop, Bost. Braves (vs. Phila. Phillies) (NL), Oct. 6, 1923, 4th inning; Batter: Walter Holke
  Padgett takes Holke's line drive, tags second to retire Cotton Tierney, and then tags out Cliff Lee, coming into second.
Glenn Wright, shortstop, Pitt. Pirates (vs. St. L. Cardinals) (NL), May 7, 1925, 9th inning; Batter: Jim Bottomley
  Wright snares Bottomley's liner, touches second to retire Jimmy Cooney, and then tags out Rogers Hornsby, on his way into second.
Jimmy Cooney, shortstop, Chi. Cubs (vs. Pitt. Pirates) (NL), May 30, 1927, 4th inning; Batter: Paul Waner
  Cooney grabs Waner's line drive, doubles Lloyd Waner off second, and then tags out Clyde Barnhart, coming down from first.
Johnny Neun, first base, Det. Tigers (vs. Cleve. Indians) (AL), May 31, 1927, 9th inning; Batter: Homer Summa
  Neun snares Summa's liner, tags first to double up Charlie Jamieson, and then races down toward second to tag out base runner Glenn Myatt before he can return to second, ending the game.
Ron Hansen, shortstop, Wash. Senators II (vs. Cleve. Indians) (AL), July 29, 1968, 1st inning; Batter: Joe Azcue
  Hansen grabs Azcue's liner, steps on second to double up Dave Nelson, and then tags out Russ Snyder, barreling down from first.
Mickey Morandini, second base, Phila. Phillies (vs. Pitt. Pirates) (NL), Sept. 20, 1992, 6th inning; Batter: Jeff King
  Morandini makes a diving catch of King's line drive, runs to second to double off Andy Van Slyke, and then tags out Barry Bonds running down from first.
John Valentin, shortstop, Bost. Red Sox (vs. Sea. Mariners) (AL), July 8, 1994, 6th inning; Batter: Marc Newfield
  Valentin catches Newfield's line drive, steps on second to double up Mike Blowers, and then tags out Kevin Mitchell coming down from first.
Randy Velarde, second base, Oak. A's (vs. N.Y. Yankees) (AL), May 29, 2000, 6th inning; Batter: Shane Spencer
  Velarde catches Spencer's liner, tags Jorge Posada running from first to second, and then runs over to step on second to retire Tino Martinez.
Rafael Furcal, shortstop, Atl. Braves (vs. St. L. Cardinals) (NL), Aug. 10, 2003, 6th inning; Batter: Woody Williams
  Furcal grabs Williams's liner, steps on second to retire Mike Matheny, and then tags Orlando Palmeiro coming down the line from first.
Troy Tulowitzki, shortstop, Colo. Rockies (vs. Atl. Braves) (NL), Apr. 29, 2007, 7th inning; Batter: Chipper Jones
  Jones hits a line drive to Tulowitzki, who then steps on second to double up Kelly Johnson and tags Edgar Renteria between first and second base.
Asdrubal Cabrera, second base, Cleve. Indians (vs. Tor. Blue Jays) (AL), May 12, 2008, 5th inning; Batter: Lyle Overbay
  Overbay hits a line drive that is caught by a diving Cabrera, who steps on second to double up Kevin Mench and then tags out Marco Scutaro.
Eric Bruntlett, second base, Phila. Phillies (vs. N.Y. Mets) (NL), Aug. 23, 2009, 9th inning; Batter: Jeff Francoeur
  Francoeur hits a line drive to Bruntlett, who steps on second to double up Luis Castillo and then tags Daniel Murphy between first and second, ending the game.
*World Series game.

Most No-Hitters Caught

	Catcher	Pitcher
4	Ray Schalk, Chi. White Sox (AL)	Jim Scott, May 14, 1914, vs. Wash. Senators, 0–1*
		Joe Benz, May 31, 1914, vs. Cleve. Indians, 6–1
		Eddie Cicotte, Apr. 14, 1917, vs. St. L. Browns, 11–0
		Charlie Robertson, Apr. 30, 1922, vs. Det. Tigers, 2–0 (perfect game)

4.	Jason Varitek, Bost. Red Sox (AL)	Hideo Nomo, April 4, 2001, vs. Baltimore Orioles 3–0
		Derek Lowe, April 27, 2002, vs. Tampa Bay Rays, 10–0
		Clay Buchholz, September 1, 2007, vs. Balti. Orioles, 10–0
		Jon Lester, May 19, 2008, vs. K.C. Royals, 7–0
3	Alan Ashby, Hous. Astros (NL)	Ken Forsch, Apr. 7, 1979, vs. Atl. Braves, 6–0
		Nolan Ryan, Sept. 26, 1981, vs. L.A. Dodgers, 5–0
		Mike Scott, Sept. 25, 1986, vs. S.F. Giants, 2–0
3	Yogi Berra, N.Y. Yankees (AL)	Allie Reynolds, July 12, 1951, vs. Cleve. Indians, 1–0
		Allie Reynolds, Sept. 28, 1951, vs. Bost. Red Sox, 8–0
		Don Larsen, Oct. 8, 1956, vs. Bklyn. Dodgers, 2–0
		(World Series, perfect game)
3	Roy Campanella, Bklyn. Dodgers (NL)	Carl Erskine, June 19, 1952, vs. Chi. Cubs, 5–0
		Carl Erskine, May 12, 1956, vs. N.Y. Giants, 3–0
		Sal Maglie, Sept. 25, 1956, vs. Phila. Phillies, 5–0
3	Bill Carrigan, Bost. Red Sox (AL)	Smokey Joe Wood, July 29, 1911, vs. St. L. Browns, 5–0
		Rube Foster, June 16, 1916, vs. N.Y. Yankees, 2–0
		Dutch Leonard, Aug. 30, 1916, vs. St. L. Browns, 4–0
3	Del Crandall, Milw. Braves (NL)	Jim Wilson, June 12, 1954, vs. Phila. Phillies, 2–0
		Lew Burdette, Aug. 18, 1960, vs. Phila. Phillies, 1–0
		Warren Spahn, Sept. 16, 1960, vs. Phila. Phillies, 4–0
3	Lou Criger, Bost. Red Sox (AL)	Cy Young, May 5, 1904, vs. Phila. A's, 3–0 (perfect game)
		Bill Dineen, Sept. 27, 1905, vs. Chi. White Sox, 2–0
		Cy Young, June 30, 1908, vs. N.Y. Highlanders, 8–0
3	Johnny Edwards, Cin. Reds (NL)	Jim Maloney, Aug. 19, 1965, vs. Chi. Cubs, 1–0
		Jim Maloney, June 14, 1965, vs. N.Y. Mets, 0–1*
		George Culver, July 29, 1968, vs. Phila. Phillies, 6–1
3	Jim Hegan, Cleve. Indians (AL)	Don Black, July 10, 1947, vs. Phila. A's, 3–0
		Bob Lemon, June 30, 1948, vs. Det. Tigers, 2–0
		Bob Feller, July 1, 1951, vs. Det. Tigers, 2–1
3	Charles Johnson, Flor. Marlins (NL)	Al Leiter, May 11, 1996, vs. Colo. Rockies, 11–0
		Kevin Brown, June 10, 1997, vs. S.F. Giants, 9–0
		A. J. Burnett, May 12, 2001, vs. S.D. Padres, 3–0
3	Val Picinich, Phila. A's (AL)	Joe Bush, Aug. 26, 1916, vs. Cleve. Indians, 5–0
	Wash. Senators (AL)	Walter Johnson, July 1, 1920, vs.
		Bost. Red Sox, 1–0
	Bost. Red Sox (AL)	Howard Ehmke, Sept. 7, 1923, vs.
		Phila. A's, 4–0
3	Luke Sewell, Cleve. Indians (AL)	Wes Ferrell, Apr. 29, 1931, vs. St. L. Browns, 9–0
	Chi. White Sox (AL)	Vern Kennedy, Aug. 31, 1935, vs.
		Cleve. Indians, 5–0
		Bill Dietrich, June 1, 1937, vs. St. L. Browns, 8–0
3	Jeff Torborg, L.A. Dodgers (NL)	Sandy Koufax, Sept. 9, 1965, vs. Chi. Cubs, 1–0
		(perfect game)
		Bill Singer, July 20, 1970, vs. Phila. Phillies, 5–0
	Cal. Angels (AL)	Nolan Ryan, May 15, 1973, vs. K.C. Royals, 3–0

*No-hitter broken up in extra innings.

Games Caught by Left-Handed Catchers

1073	Jack Clements, 1884–1900	12	Charlie Krehmeyer, 1884–85
272	Sam Trott, 1880–85 and 1887–88	7	Joe Wall, 1901–02

202	Pop Tate, 1885–90
186	Sy Sutcliffe, 1885, 1888 –91
125	Bill Harbridge, 1876–**78**, 1880–83
99	Mike Hines, 1883–85, 1888
75	John Humphries, 1883–84
71	Fred Tenney, 1894–96, 1898, 1901
62	Phil Baker, 1883–84, 1886
52	Art Twineham, 1893–94
45	Jiggs Donahue, 1900–02
35	Dave Oldfield, 1883, 1885–86
34	Charlie Householder, 1882, 1884
21	Fergy Malone, 1876, 1884
16	Jack McMahon, 1892–93

5	Elmer Foster, 1884
3	Homer Hillebrand, 1905
3	Benny Distefano, 1989
2	Jim Egan, 1882
2	Dale Long, 1958
2	Mike Squires, 1980
1	John Mullen, 1876
1	Billy Redmond, 1878
1	Charlie Eden, 1879
1	Martin Powell, 1881
1	John Cassidy, 1887
1	Lefty Marr, 1889
1	Chris Short, 1961

Players Pitching and Catching, Same Game

American League

Bert Campaneris, K.C. A's	Sept. 8, 1965
Cesar Tovar, Minn. Twins	Sept. 22, 1968
Jeff Newman, Oak. A's	Sept. 14, 1977
Rick Cerone, N.Y. Yankees,	July 19 and Aug. 9, 1987
Scott Sheldon, Tex. Rangers,	Sept. 6, 2000
Shane Halter, Det. Tiger,	Oct. 1, 2000

National League (Post-1900)

Roger Bresnahan, St. L. Cardinals	Aug. 3, 1910

Most Times Catchers Charged with Errors Due to Interference

15	Milt May (1970–84)
12	John Bateman (1963–72)
10	Ted Simmons (1968–88)
10	Carlton Fisk (1969, 1971–93)
9	Clay Dalrymple (1960–71)
9	Tom Haller (1961–72)
9	Jerry Grote (1963–64, 1966–78, 1981)

9	Terry Kennedy (1978–91)
7	Manny Sanguillen (1967, 1969–80)
7	Barry Foote (1973–82)
6	John Stephenson (1964–73)
6	Gene Tenace (1969–83)
6	Gary Carter (1974–92)

7

RELATIVES

Father-Son Combinations with 250 Home Runs, Career

Total	Father	Home Runs	Son	Home Runs
1094	Bobby Bonds (1968–81)	332	Barry Bonds (1986–2007)	762
782	Ken Griffey Sr. (1973–91)	152	Ken Griffey Jr. (1989–2010)	630
549	Cecil Fielder (1985–88, 1990–98)	319	Prince Fielder (2005–)	230
538	Felipe Alou (1958–74)	206	Moises Alou (1990,1992–98, 2000–08)	332
458	Tony Perez (1964–86)	374	Eduardo Perez (1993–2000, 2002–06)	74
407	Gus Bell (1950–64)	206	Buddy Bell (1972–88)	201
407	Yogi Berra (1946–65)	358	Dale Berra (1977–87)	49
369	Jose Cruz (1970–88)	165	Jose Cruz, Jr. (1997–2008)	204
357	Bob Boone (1972–89)	105	Bret Boone (1992–2005)	252
342	Gary Matthews Sr. (1972–1987)	234	Gary Matthews Jr. (1999–2010)	108
324	Buddy Bell (1972–88)	201	David Bell (1995–2006)	123
294	Hal McRae (1968, 1970–87)	191	Brian McRae (1990–99)	103
284	Randy Hundley (1964–77)	82	Todd Hundley (1990–2003)	202
282	Earl Averill Sr. (1929–41)	238	Earl Averill Jr. (1956–63)	44
276	John Mayberry (1968–82)	255	John Mayberry, Jr. (2009–)	21
264	Jose Tartabull (1962–70)	2	Danny Tartabull (1984–97)	262
257	Jesse Barfield (1981–92)	241	Josh Barfield (2006–09)	16
257	Dolph Camilli (1933–45)	239	Doug Camilli (1960–69)	18
256	Ray Boone (1948–60)	151	Bob Boone (1972–89)	105
252	Jeff Burroughs (1970–85)	240	Sean Burroughs (2002–06, 2011)	12

Brother Batteries*

Jim and Ed Bailey	Cin. Reds (NL), 1959
Dick and Bill Conway	Balt. Orioles (AA), 1886
Mort and Walker Cooper	St. L. Cardinals (NL), 1940–45; and N.Y. Giants (NL), 1947
Ed and Bill Dugan	Rich. Virginias (AA), 1884
John and Buck Ewing	N.Y. Giants (NL), 1890–91
Wes and Rick Ferrell	Bost. Red Sox (AL), 1934–37; and Wash. Senators (AL), 1937–38
Milt and Alex Gaston	Bost. Red Sox (AL), 1929
Mike and John O'Neill	St. L. Cardinals (NL), 1902–03
Elmer and Johnny Riddle	Cin. Reds (NL), 1941 and 1944–45; and Pitt. Pirates (NL), 1948
Bobby and Billy Shantz	Phila. A's (AL), 1954; K.C. A's (AL), 1955; and N.Y. Yankees (AL), 1960
Larry and Norm Sherry	L.A. Dodgers (NL), 1960–62
Tom and Homer Thompson	N.Y. Yankees (AL), 1912
Lefty and Fred Tyler	Bost. Braves (NL), 1914
Will and Deacon White	Bost. Red Caps (NL), 1877; and Cin. Reds (NL) 1878–79
Pete and Fred Wood	Buff. Bisons (NL), 1885

*Pitcher listed first; catcher, second.

Twins Who Played Major League Baseball

Canseco.........Jose, outfield (1985–2001)
Ozzie, outfield (1990, 1992–93)
Cliburn ....Stan, catcher (1980)
Stu, pitcher (1984–85)
Edwards.........Marshall, outfield (1981–83)
Mike, second base (1977–80)
Grimes...........Ray, first base (1920–26)
Roy, second base (1920)
Hunter ....Bill, outfield (1912)
George, outfield and pitcher (1909–10)
Minor ....Ryan, first base (1998–2001)
Damon, first base (2000–04)

Jonnard ....Bubber, catcher (1920, 1922, 1926–27, 1929, 1935)
Claude, pitcher (1921–24, 1926, 1929)
O'Brien..........Eddie, shortstop, outfield, and pitcher (1953, 1955–58)
Johnny, infield and pitcher (1953, 1955–59)
Reccius ....John, outfield and pitcher (1882–88, 1890)
Phil, infield, outfield, and pitcher (1882–83)
Shannon ....Joe, outfield and second base (1915)
Red, shortstop (1915, 1917–21, 1926)

Hall of Famers Whose Sons Played in Majors

Father	Sons
Earl Averill Sr. (1929–41)	Earl Averill Jr. (1956, 1958–63)
Yogi Berra (1946–63, 1965)	Dale Berra (1977–87)
Eddie Collins Sr. (1906–30)	Eddie Collins Jr. (1939, 1941–42)
Freddie Lindstrom (1924–36)	Charlie Lindstrom (1958)
Connie Mack (1886–96)	Earle Mack (1910–11, 1914)
Orator Jim O'Rourke (1876–93, 1904)	Queenie O'Rourke (1908)
Tony Perez (1964–86)	Eduardo Perez (1993–2000, 2002–06)
George Sisler (1915–22, 1924–30)	Dick Sisler (1946–53)
	Dave Sisler (1956–62)
Ed Walsh Sr. (1904–17)	Ed Walsh Jr. (1928–30)
Tony Gwynn Sr. (1982–2001)	Tony Gwynn Jr.* (2006–)

*Still active.

Players with Two Sons Who Played in Majors

Father	Sons
Buddy Bell (1972–89)	David Bell (1995–2006)
	Mike Bell (2000)
Bob Boone (1972–90)	Aaron Boone (1997–2009)
	Bret Boone (1992–2005)
Jimmy Cooney (1890–92)	Jimmy Cooney (1917, 1919, 1924–28)
	Johnny Cooney (1921–44)
Dave Duncan (1964–76)	Chris Duncan (2005–09)
	Shelley Duncan* (2007–)
Larry Gilbert (1914–15)	Charlie Gilbert (1940–43, 1946–47)
	Tookie Gilbert (1950, 1953)
Jerry Hairston (1973–88)	Jerry Hairston Jr.* (1998–)
	Scott Hairston* (2004–)
Sam Hairston (1951)	Jerry Hairston (1973–88)
	John Hairston (1969)

continued on next page

Dave LaRoche (1970–83)..Adam LaRoche (2004–)

Andy LaRoche (2007–)

Manny Mota (1962–82)..Andy Mota (1991)

Jose Mota (1991–5)

Kevin Romine (1985–91)...Andrew Rumine*(2010–)

Austin Rumine*(2011–)

George Sisler (1915–22, 1924–30) ....Dave Sisler (1956–62)

Dick Sisler (1946–53)

Mel Stottlemyre (1964–74) ....Mel Stottlemyre Jr. (1990)

Todd Stottlemyre (1988–2002)

Dixie Walker (1909–12)..Dixie Walker (1931, 1933–49)

Harry Walker (1940–43, 1946–55)

*Still active.

Brother Double-Play Combinations

Garvin Hamner, second base, and Granny Hamner, shortstop, Phila. Phillies (NL), 1945
Eddie O'Brien, shortstop, and Johnny O'Brien, second base, Pitt. Pirates (NL), 1953, 1955–56
Billy Ripken, second base, and Cal Ripken Jr., shortstop, Balt. Orioles (AL), 1987–92

Most Home Runs, Brothers

Total	Brothers	Home Runs
768	Hank Aaron (1954–76)	755
	Tommie Aaron (1962–63, 1965, 1968–71)	13
573	Joe DiMaggio (1936–42, 1946–51)	361
	Vince DiMaggio (1937–46)	125
	Dom DiMaggio (1940–42, 1946–53)	87
508	Eddie Murray (1977–97)	504
	Rich Murray (1980,1983)	4
462	Jose Canseco (1985–2001)	462
	Ozzie Canseco (1990, 1992–93)	0
451	Cal Ripken, Jr. (1981–2001)	431
	Billy Ripken (1987–98)	20
444	Ken Boyer (1955–69)	282
	Clete Boyer (1955–71)	162
444	Lee May (1965–82)	354
	Carlos May (1968–77)	90
406	Graig Nettles (1967–88)	390
	Jim Nettles (1970–72, 1974, 1979, 1981)	16
378	Bret Boone (1992–2005)	252
	Aaron Boone (1997–2009)	126
358	Dick Allen (1963–77)	351
	Hank Allen (1966–70, 1972–73)	6
	Ron Allen (1972)	1
346	Bob Johnson (1933–45)	288
	Roy Johnson (1929–38)	58

Pitching Brothers Each Winning 20 Games in Same Season

1970	Gaylord Perry, S.F. Giants (NL)	23–13	1979	Joe Niekro, Hous. Astros (NL)	21–11
	Jim Perry, Minn. Twins (AL)	24–12		Phil Niekro, Atl. Braves (NL)	21–20

Hall of Famers' Brothers Who Played 10 or More Seasons in Majors (Post-1900)

Hall of Famer	Brother
Roberto Alomar (1988–2004)	Sandy Alomar, Jr. (1988–2007)
George Brett (1973–93)	Ken Brett (1967, 1969–81)
Ed Delahanty (1888–1903)	Jim Delahanty (1901–02, 1904–12, 1914–15)
Joe DiMaggio (1936–42, 1946–51)	Dom DiMaggio (1940–42, 1946–53)
Joe DiMaggio (1936–42, 1946–51)	Vince DiMaggio (1937–46)
Rick Ferrell (1929–45, 1947)	Wes Ferrell (1927–41)
Tony Gwynn (1982–2001)	Chris Gwynn (1987–96)
Phil Niekro (1964–87)	Joe Niekro (1967–88)
Gaylord Perry (1962–83)	Jim Perry (1959–75)
Cal Ripken Jr. (1981–2001)	Billy Ripken (1987–1998)
Joe Sewell (1920–33)	Luke Sewell (1921–39, 1942)
Lloyd Waner (1927–42, 1944–45)	Paul Waner (1926–45)
Paul Waner (1926–45)	Lloyd Waner (1927–42, 1944–45)

Father-Son Tandems Who Both Played for Same Manager

		Manager
Brucker	Earle Sr., Phila. A's (AL), 1937–40 and 1943	Connie Mack
	Earle Jr., Phila. A's (AL), 1948	
Collins	Eddie Sr., Phila. A's (AL), 1906–14	Connie Mack
	Eddie Jr., Phila. A's (AL), 1939 and 1941–42	
Hairston	Sam, Chi. White Sox (AL), 1951	Paul Richards
	Jerry, Chi. White Sox (AL), 1976	
Griffey	Ken Sr., Sea. Mariners (AL), 1990–91	Jim Lefebvre
	Ken Jr., Sea. Mariners (AL), 1989–91	
Raines	Tim Sr., Balt. Orioles (AL), 2001	Mike Hargrove
	Tim Jr., Balt. Orioles (AL), 2001	

Sons Who Played for Their Fathers

Son	Father-Manager
Moises Alou, Mont. Expos (NL), 1992–96; S.F. Giants (NL), 2005	Felipe Alou
Dale Berra, N.Y. Yankees (AL), 1985	Yogi Berra
Aaron Boone, Cin. Reds (NL), 2001–03	Bob Boone
Earle Mack, Phila. A's (AL), 1910–11 and 1914	Connie Mack
Brian McRae, K.C. Royals (AL), 1991–94	Hal McRae
Billy Ripken, Balt. Orioles (AL), 1987–88	Cal Ripken Sr.
Cal Ripken Jr., Balt. Orioles (AL), 1985 and 1987–88	Cal Ripken Sr.

Best Won-Lost Percentage for Pitching Brothers

Percentage	Brothers	Wins–Losses	Total
1.000	George Kelly (1917)	1–0	1–0
	Ren Kelly (1923)	0–0	
.800	Hick Hovlik (1918–19	2–1	4–1

	Joe Hovlik (1909–11)...	2–0	
.664	Christy Mathewson (1900–16)..............................	373–188	373–189
	Henry Mathewson (1906–07)	0–1	
.660	Larry Corcoran (1880–87)....................................	177–90	177–91
	Mike Corcoran (1884)	0–1	
.653	Pedro Martinez (1992–2009)................................	219–100	354–188
	Ramon Martinez (1988–2001).............................	135–88	
.639	Jim Hughes (1898–99, 1901–02)	83–41	122–69
	Mickey Hughes (1888–90)...................................	39–28	
.631	Dizzy Dean (1930, 1932–41, 1947)	150–83	200–117
	Paul Dean (1934–41, 1943)	50–34	
.623	Dad Clarkson (1891–96)......................................	39–39	383–232
	John Clarkson (1882, 1884–94)...........................	326–177	
	Walter Clarkson (1904–08)	18–16	
.616	George Radbourn (1883)	1–2	309–193
	Old Hoss Radbourn (1880–91).............................	301–191	
.600	Harry Coveleski (1907–10, 1014–18)...................	81–55	296–197
	Stan Coveleski (1912, 1916–28)	215–142	
.599	Greg Maddux (1986–2008)..................................	355–227	394–264
	Mike Maddux (1986–2000)	39–37	
.591	Dave Gregg (1913)...	0–0	91–63
	Vean Gregg (1911–16, 1918, 1925).....................	91–63	
.590	Greg Maddux (1986–2008)..................................	355–227	394–274
	Mike Maddux (1986–2000)	39–37	
.588	Cy Ferry (1904–05)..	0–1	10–7
	Jack Ferry (1910–13)...	10–6	
.583	Hooks Wiltse (1904–15).......................................	139–90	169–121
	Snake Wiltse (1901–03).......................................	30–31	
.580	Ed Pipgras (1932)	0–1	102–74
	George Pipgras (1923–24, 1927–35)...................	102–73	
.580	Deacon White (1876, 1890).................................	0–0	229–166
	Will White (1877–86)	229–166	
.576	Gene Ford (1905)..	0–1	98–72
	Russ Ford (1909–15)..	98–71	
.565	Erskine Mayer (1912–19).....................................	91–70	91–70
	Sam Mayer (1915)	0–0	
.563	Johnny Morrison (1920–27, 1929–30)..................	103–80	103–80
	Phil Morrison (1921)..	0–0	
.558	Harry Camnitz (1909, 1911)................................	1–0	134–106
	Howie Camnitz (1904, 1906–15)	133–106	
.556	Charlie Getting (1896–99)...................................	15–12	15–12
	Tom Gettinger (1895)..	0–0	
.556	Chet Johnson (1946)..	0–0	40–32
	Earl Johnson (1940–41, 1946–51)	40–32	
.554	Big Jeff Pfeffer (1905–08, 1910–11)...................	31–40	190–152
	Jeff Pfeffer (1911, 1913–24)...............................	158–112	
.546	Gaylord Perry (1962–83).....................................	314–265	529–439
	Jim Perry (1959–75)	215–174	
.544	Lindy McDaniel (1955–75)....................................	141–119	148–124
	Von McDaniel (1957–58)	7–5	
.542	Ad Gumbert (1888–96)..	122–101	129–109
	Billy Gumbert (1890, 1892–93)	7–8	
.538	Denny O'Toole (1969–73)	0–0	98–84

	Jim O'Toole (1958–67)	98–84	
.536	Lou Galvin (1884)	0–2	361–312
	Pud Galvin (1879–92)	361–310	
.535	Enrique Romo (1977–82)	44–33	76–66
	Vicente Romo (1968–74, 1982)	32–33	
.531	Bob Forsch (1974–89)	168–136	282–249
	Ken Forsch (1970–84, 1986)	114–113	
.531	Gus Weyhing (1887–96, 1898–1901)	264–232	267–236
	John Weyhing (1888–89)	3–4	
.530	Joe Niekro (1967–88)	221–204	539–478
	Phil Niekro (1964–87)	318–274	
.528	Jeff Weaver (1999–2007, 2009–10)	104–119	186–166
	Jered Weaver (2006–)	82–47	
.526	Paul Reuschel (1975–79)	16–16	230–207
	Rick Reuschel (1972–81, 1983–91)	214–191	
.522	Al Lary (1954–55)	0–1	128–117
	Frank Lary (1954–65)	128–116	
.514	Art Fowler (1954–57, 1959, 1961–64)	54–51	55–52
	Jesse Fowler (1924)	1–1	
.509	Matt Kilroy (1886–94, 1898)	142–134	142–137
	Mike Kilroy (1888, 1890)	0–3	
.507	Jesse Barnes (1915–27)	153–149	214–208
	Virgil Barnes (1919–20, 1922–28)	61–59	
.507	Brownie Foreman (1895–96)	11–13	109–106
	Frank Foreman (1884–85, 1889–93, 1895–96, 1901–02)	98–93	
.506	Camilo Pascual (1954–71)	174–170	175–171
	Carlos Pascual (1950)	1–1	
.500	Chi Chi Olivo (1961, 1964–66)	7–6	12–12
	Diomedes Olivo (1960, 1962–63)	5–6	

Most Total Combined Career Wins for Pitching Brothers

Total	Brothers	Wins
539	Phil Niekro (1964–87)	318
	Joe Niekro (1967–88)	221
529	Gaylord Perry (1962–83)	314
	Jim Perry (1959–75)	215
394	Greg Maddux (1986–2008)	355
	Mike Maddux (1986–2000)	39
383	John Clarkson (1882–94)	326
	Dad Clarkson (1891–96)	39
	Walter Clarkson (1904–08)	18
373	Christy Mathewson (1900–16)	373
	Henry Mathewson (1906–07)	0
361	Pud Galvin (1879–92)	361
	Lou Galvin (1884)	0
354	Pedro Martinez (1992–2009)	219
	Ramon Martinez (1988–2001)	135

296 ....Stan Coveleski (1912, 1916–28) 215
                                  Harry Coveleski (1907–10, 1914–18)..81
282 ....Bob Forsch (1974–89)...168
                                  Ken Forsch (1970–84, 1986) 114
230 ....Rick Reuschel (1972–89)..214
                                  Paul Reuschel (1975–79) 16
214 ....Jesse Barnes (1905–27)...153
                                  Virgil Barnes (1919–20, 1922–28)..61
200 ....Dizzy Dean (1930, 1932–41, 1947)...150
                                  Paul Dean (1934–41, 1947) 50

Pitching Brothers Facing Each Other, Regular Season

Frank Foreman, Cin. Reds (NL), vs. Brownie Foreman, Pitt. Pirates (NL), 1896*

Stan Coveleski, Cleve. Indians (AL), vs. Harry Coveleski, Det. Tigers (AL), 1916*

Virgil Barnes, N.Y. Giants (NL), vs. Jesse Barnes, Bost. Braves (NL), 1923

Virgil Barnes, N.Y. Giants (NL), vs. Jesse Barnes, Bklyn. Dodgers (NL), 1927

Phil Niekro, Atl. Braves (NL), vs. Joe Niekro, Chi. Cubs (NL), 1968

*Same game but not at same time.

**Interleague play.

Gaylord Perry, Cleve. Indians (AL), vs. Jim Perry, Det. Tigers (AL), 1973

Bob Forsch, St. L. Cardinals (NL), vs. Ken Forsch, Hous. Astros (NL), 1974

Tom Underwood, Tor. Blue Jays (AL), vs. Pat Underwood, Det. Tigers (AL), 1979

Greg Maddux, Chi. Cubs (NL), vs. Mike Maddux, Phila. Phillies (NL), 1986

Greg Maddux, Chi. Cubs (NL), vs. Mike Maddux, Phila. Phillies (NL), 1988

Jeff Weaver, L.A. Dodgers (NL), vs. Jered Weaver, L.A. Angels (AL), 2009**

Most Career Victories by Father-Son Combination (Post-1900)

Total	Father	Wins	Son	Wins
302	Mel Stottlemyre (1964–74)	164	Todd Stottlemyre (1988–2002)	138
258	Dizzy Trout (1939–52, 1957)	170	Steve Trout (1978–89)	88
224	Jim Bagby Sr. (1912, 1916–23)	127	Jim Bagby Jr. (1938–47)	97
206	Ed Walsh Sr. (1904–17)	195	Ed Walsh Jr. (1928–30, 1932)	11
194	Joe Coleman Sr. (1942, 1946–51, 1953–55)	52	Joe Coleman Jr. (1965–79)	142
171	Floyd Bannister (1977–89, 1991–92)	134	Brian Bannister (2006–10)	37
168	Clyde Wright (1966–75)	100	Jaret Wright (1997–2007)	68
159	Doug Drabek (1986–98)	155	Kyle Drabek (2010–)	4
157	Thorton Lee (1933–48)	117	Don Lee (1957–58, 1960–66)	40
124	Ross Grimsley Sr. (1951)	0	Ross Grimsley Jr. (1971–80, 1982)	124
123	Julio Navarro (1962–70)	7	Jaime Navarro (1989–2000)	116
117	Smokey Joe Wood (1908–15, 1917, 1919–20)	117	Joe Wood Jr. (1944)	0
116	Dick Ellsworth (1958, 1960–71)	115	Steve Ellsworth (1988)	1
73	Lew Krausse Sr. (1931–32)	5	Lew Krausse Jr. (1961, 1964–74)	68
72	Herman Pillette (1917, 1922–24)	34	Duane Pillette (1949–56)	38
58	Jeff Russell (1983–96)	56	James Russell (2010–)	2
47	Mel Queen Sr. (1942, 1944, 1946–49, 1951–52)	27	Mel Queen Jr. (1964–72)	20

Brothers Who Played Together on Three Major League Teams

Sandy Jr. and Roberto Alomar .....S.D. Padres (NL), 1988–89
Cleve. Indians (AI), 1999–2000
Chi. White Sox (AL), 2003–04
Arthur and John Irwin ......Worc. Brown Stockings (NL), 1882
Wash. Statesmen (NL), 1889
Bost. Reds (AA), 1891

Paul and Lloyd Waner ....Pitt. Pirates (NL), 1927–40
Bost. Braves (NL), 1941
Bklyn. Dodgers (NL), 1944

8

WORLD SERIES

Teams Never to Trail in a World Series

1963	L.A. Dodgers (NL) vs. N.Y. Yankees (AL)
1966	Balt. Orioles (AL) vs. L.A. Dodgers (NL)
1989	Oak. A's (AL) vs. S.F. Giants (NL)
2004	Bost. Red Sox (AL) vs. St. L. Cardinals (NL)

Highest Batting Average for a World Series Team

American League	National League

Batting Average		Batting Average	
.338	N.Y. Yankees, 1960*	.323	Pitt. Pirates, 1979
.333	Bost. Red Sox, 2007	.317	Cin. Reds, 1990
.316	Phila. Athletics, 1910	.313	Cin. Reds, 1990
.313	N.Y. Yankees, 1932	.309	N.Y. Giants, 1922
.311	Tor. Blue Jays, 1993	.300	Bklyn. Dodgers, 1953
.310	L.A. Angels, 2002		
.309	N.Y. Yankees, 1998		
.302	N.Y. Yankees, 1936		
.309	Oak. A's, 1989		

*Lost World Series.

Lowest Batting Average for a World Series Team

American League	National League

Batting Average		Batting Average	
.146	Balt. Orioles, 1969	.142	L.A. Dodgers, 1966
.161	Phila. Athletics, 1905	.175	N.Y. Giants 1911
.172	Phila. Athletics, 1914	.182	Phila. Phillies, 1915
.177	Oak. A's, 1988	.182	Bklyn. Dodgers, 1941
.179	Cleve. Indians, 1995	.185	St. L. Cardinals, 1985
.183	St. L. Browns, 1944	.190	St. L. Cardinals, 2004
.183	N.Y. Yankees, 2001	.195	Bklyn. Dodgers, 1956
.186	Bost. Red Sox, 1918*	.195	Phila. Phillies, 1983
.190	Cleve. Indians, 1954	.196	Chi. Cubs, 1906
.190	Tex. Rangers, 2010		

.197 ....Phila. Athletics, 1930*
.198 ....Chi. White Sox, 1906*
.199 ....Cleve. Indians, 1948*
.199...N.Y. Yankees, 1962*
.149 ....Det. Tigers, 2006

*World Series winners.

Most Regular Season Losses, Reaching World Series

American League

Losses

77	......................1987 Minn. Twins* (Record: 85–77)
75	......................1997 Cleve. Indians (Record: 86–75)
74	......................2000 N.Y. Yankees* (Record: 87–74)
72	......................1974 Oak. A's* (Record: 90–72)
72	......................2010 Tex. Rangers (Record: 90–72)
71	......................1985 K.C. Royals* (Record: 91–71)
70	......................1967 Bost. Red Sox (Record: 92–70)
70	......................1996 N.Y. Yankees* (Record: 92–70)
68	......................1973 Oak. A's* (Record: 94–68)
67	......................1982 Milw. Brewers (Record: 95–67)
67	......................1991 Minn. Twins* (Record: 95–67)
67	......................1993 Tor. Blue Jays* (Record: 95–67)

National League

Losses

79	......................1973 N.Y. Mets (Record: 82–79)
78	......................2006 St. L. Cardinals* (Record: 83–78)
73	......................2005 Hous. Astros (Record: 89–73)
73	......................2007 Colo. Rockies (Record: 90–73)
72	......................2011 St.L. Cardinals* (Record: 90–72)
71	......................1980 Phila. Phillies* (Record: 91–71)
71	......................1980 Phila. Phillies* (Record: 91–71)
71	......................1990 Cin. Reds* (Record: 91–71)
71	......................2003 Flor. Marlins* (Record: 91–71)
70	......................1982 St. L. Cardinals* (Record: 92–70)
70	......................1984 S.D. Padres (Record: 92–70)
70	......................1989 S.F. Giants (Record: 92–70)
70	......................1997 Florida Marlins* (Record: 92–70)
70	......................2001 Arizona D'backs* (Record: 92–70)
70	......................2008 Phila. Phillies* (Record 92–70)
70	......................2010 S.F.Giants* (Record: 92–70)
69	......................2009 Phila. Phillies (Record: 93–69)
69	......................1964 St. L. Cardinals (Record: 93–69)
68	......................1959 L.A. Dodgers* (Record: 88–68)
68	......................1991 Atl. Braves (Record: 94–68)
68	......................2000 N.Y. Mets (Record: 94–68)
68	......................1966 L.A. Dodgers (Record: 95–67)
68	......................1978 L.A. Dodgers (Record: 95–67)
68	......................1987 St. L. Cardinals (Record: 95–67)
68	......................1988 L.A. Dodgers* (Record: 95–67)

*Won World Series

Players Hitting .500 in World Series (Min. 10 At Bats)

Billy Hatcher, Cin. Reds (NL), 1990	9-for-12	.750
Babe Ruth, N.Y. Yankees (AL), 1928	10-for-16	.625
Hideki Matsui, N.Y. Yankees (AL), 2009	8-for-13	.615
Ricky Ledee, N.Y. Yankees (AL), 1998	6-for-10	.600
Chris Sabo, Cin. Reds (NL), 1990	9-for-16	.563
Hank Gowdy, Bost. Braves (NL), 1914	6-for-11	.545
Lou Gehrig, N.Y. Yankees (AL), 1928	6-for-11	.545
Bret Boone*, Atl. Braves (NL), 1999	7-for-13	.538
Johnny Bench, Cin. Reds (NL), 1976	8-for-15	.533
Lou Gehrig, N.Y. Yankees (AL), 1932	9-for-17	.529
Thurman Munson*, N.Y. Yankees (AL), 1976	9-for-17	.529
Dane Iorg, St. L. Cardinals (NL), 1982	9-for-17	.529
Larry McLean, N.Y. Giants (NL), 1913	6-for-12	.500

Dave Robertson, N.Y. Giants (NL), 1917 .... 11-for-22 .... .500
Mark Koenig, N.Y. Yankees (AL), 1927 .... 9-for-18 .... .500
Pepper Martin, St. L. Cardinals (NL), 1931 .... 12-for-24 .... .500
Joe Gordon, N.Y. Yankees (AL), 1941 .... 7-for-14 .... .500
Billy Martin, N.Y. Yankees (AL), 1953 .... 12-for-24 .... .500
Vic Wertz*, Cleve. Indians (AL), 1954 .... 8-for-16 .... .500
Phil Garner, Pitts. Pirates (NL), 1979 .... 12-for-24 .... .500
Paul Molitor, Tor. Blue Jays (AL), 1993 .... 12-for-24 .... .500
Tony Gwynn*, S.D. Padres (NL), 1998 .... 8-for-16 .... .500
*Member of losing team.

0-for-the Series (10 or More At Bats)

Dal Maxvill, St. L. Cardinals (NL), 1968 .... 0-for-22
Jimmy Sheckard, Chi. Cubs (NL), 1906 .... 0-for-21
Billy Sullivan, Chi. White Sox (AL), 1906 .... 0-for-21
Red Murray, N.Y. Giants (NL), 1911 .... 0-for-21
Gil Hodges, Bklyn. Dodgers (NL), 1952 .... 0-for-21
Lonny Frey, Cin. Reds (NL), 1939 .... 0-for-17
Flea Clifton, Det. Tigers (AL), 1935 .... 0-for-16
Mike Epstein, Oak. A's (AL), 1972 .... 0-for-16
Rafael Belliard, Atl. Braves (NL), 1995 .... 0-for-16
Bill Dahlen, N.Y. Giants (NL), 1905 .... 0-for-15
Wally Berger, Cin. Reds (NL), 1939 .... 0-for-15
Scott Rolen, St. L. Cardinals (NL), 2004 .... 0-for-15
Hal Wagner, Bost. Red Sox (AL), 1946 .... 0-for-13

Dick Green, Oak. A's (AL), 1974 .... 0-for-13
Pat Burrell, S.F. Giants (NL), 2010 .... 0 for 13
Carl Reynolds, Chi. Cubs (NL), 1938 .... 0-for-12
Joe Collins, N.Y. Yankees (AL), 1952 .... 0-for-12
Barbaro Garbey, Det. Tigers (AL), 1984 .... 0-for-12
Birdie Tebbetts, Det. Tigers (AL), 1940 .... 0-for-11
Davey Williams, N.Y. Giants (NL), 1954 .... 0-for-11
Jim Rivera, Chi. White Sox (AL), 1959 .... 0-for-11
Roy Howell, Milw. Brewers (AL), 1982 .... 0-for-11
Hippo Vaughn, Chi. Cubs (NL), 1918 .... 0-for-10
Lefty Grove, Phila. A's (AL), 1931 .... 0-for-10
Felix Mantilla, Milw. Braves (NL), 1957 .... 0-for-10
Jim Leyritz, S.D. Padres (NL), 1998 .... 0-for-10

Players on World Series–Winning Teams in Both Leagues

	American League	National League
Rick Aguilera	Minn. Twins, 1991	N.Y. Mets, 1986
Doug Bair	Det. Tigers, 1984	St. L. Cardinals, 1982
Josh Beckett	Bost. Red Sox, 2007	Flor. Marlins, 2003
Bert Blyleven	Minn. Twins, 1987	Pitt. Pirates, 1979
A.J. Burnett	N.Y. Yankees, 2009	Flor. Marlins, 2003*
Terry Crowley	Balt. Orioles, 1970	Cin. Reds, 1975
Mike Cuellar	Balt. Orioles, 1970	St. L. Cardinals, 1964*
Vic Davalillo	Oak. A's, 1973	Pitt. Pirates, 1971
Murray Dickson	N.Y. Yankees, 1958	St. L. Cardinals, 1942 and 1946
Mariano Duncan	N.Y. Yankees, 1996	Cin. Reds, 1990
Leo Durocher	N.Y. Yankees, 1928	St. L. Cardinals, 1934
David Eckstein	Ana. Angels, 2002	St. L. Cardinals, 2006
Lonny Frey	N.Y. Yankees, 1947	Cin. Reds, 1940
Billy Gardner	N.Y. Yankees, 1961	N.Y. Giants, 1954*
Kirk Gibson	Det. Tigers, 1984	L.A. Dodgers, 1988
Dwight Gooden	N.Y. Yankees, 1996*	N.Y. Mets, 1986
Alfredo Griffin	Tor. Blue Jays, 1992–93	L.A. Dodgers, 1988
Don Gullett	N.Y. Yankees, 1977	Cin. Reds, 1975–76
Mule Haas	Phila. A's, 1929–30	Pitt. Pirates, 1925*
Johnny Hopp	N.Y. Yankees, 1950–51	St. L. Cardinals, 1942 and 1944
Dane Iorg	K.C. Royals, 1985	St. L. Cardinals, 1982
Danny Jackson	K.C. Royals, 1985	Cin. Reds, 1990
Howard Johnson	Det. Tigers, 1984	N.Y. Mets, 1986
Jay Johnstone	N.Y. Yankees, 1978	L.A. Dodgers, 1981

continued on next page

David Justice ............N.Y. Yankees, 2000 ....Atl. Braves, 1995
Byung-Hyun Kim ....Bost. Red Sox, 2004* ....Ariz. D'backs, 2001
Al Leiter ....Tor. Blue Jays, 1993...Flor. Marlins, 1997
Javier Lopez ....Bost. Red Sox, 2007 ...............................S.F. Giants, 2010
Mike Lowell ....Bost. Red Sox, 2007 ....Flor. Marlins, 2003
Roger Maris .............N.Y. Yankees, 1960–61...........................St. L. Cardinals, 1967
Eddie Mathews ....Det. Tigers, 1968....................................Milw. Braves, 1957
Dal Maxvill...............Oak. A's, 1972* and 1974..St. L. Cardinals, 1964 and 1967
Stuffy McInnis...........Phila. A's, 1911 and 1913, and Bost. Red Sox, 1918......Pitt. Pirates, 1925
Don McMahon ....Det. Tigers, 1968....................................Milw. Braves, 1957
Paul O'Neill ............N.Y. Yankees, 1996 and 1998–2000............................Cin. Reds, 1990
Dave Parker ....Pitt. Pirates, 1979 ....Oak. A's, 1989
Paul Richards............Det. Tigers, 1945....................................N.Y. Giants, 1933*
Dutch Ruether ..........N.Y. Yankees, 1927*................................Cin. Reds, 1919
Rosy Ryan ...............N.Y. Yankees, 1928*................................N.Y. Giants, 1921* and 1923
Curt Schilling............Bost. Red Sox, 2004 and 2007 ....Ariz. D'backs, 2001
John Shelby..............Balt. Orioles, 1983 ................................L.A. Dodgers, 1988
Bill Skowron ............N.Y. Yankees, 1956, 1958, and 1961–62....L.A. Dodgers, 1963
Enos Slaughter..........N.Y. Yankees, 1956 and 1958..................St. L. Cardinals, 1942 and 1944
Lonnie Smith............K.C. Royals, 1985 ....Phila. Phillies, 1980, and St. L. Cardinals, 1982
Scott Spiezio ....Ana. Angels, 2002 ....St. L. Cardinals, 2006
Dave Stewart ....Oak. A's, 1989 ......................................L.A. Dodgers, 1981
Darryl Strawberry .....N.Y. Yankees, 1996 and 1999* ...............N.Y. Mets, 1986
Gene Tenace.............Oak. A's, 1972–74.................................St. L. Cardinals, 1982
Dick Tracewski ....Det. Tigers, 1968....................................L.A. Dodgers, 1963 and 1965
Bob Welch ....Oak. A's, 1989 ......................................L.A. Dodgers, 1981
Devon White ....Tor. Blue Jays, 1992–93 ....Flor. Marlins, 1997
*Did not play.

Pitchers in World Series with Highest Slugging Average

Slugging Avg.	Pitcher	Games	At Bats	Hits	Doubles	Triples	Home Runs	Batting Avg.
1.667*	Orel Hershiser	2	3	3	2	0	0	1.000*
.833	Ken Holtzman	8	12	4	3*	0	1	.333
.818	Dutch Ruether	7	11	4	1	2*	0	.364
.777	Pop Haines	6	9	4	0	0	2	.444
.750	Jack Bentley	10	12	5	1	0	1	.417
.667	Mike Moore	2	3	1	1	0	0	.333
.500	Dave McNally	9	16	2	0	0	2*	.125
.467	Dizzy Dean	6	15	5	2	0	0	.333
.375	Jack Coombs	6	24	8	1	0	0	.333
.375	Johnny Podres	7	16	5	1	0	0	.313
.357	Bob Gibson	9	28	4	0	0	2*	.143
.346	Allie Reynolds	15	26	8	1	0	0	.308
.316	Burleigh Grimes	9	19	6	0	0	0	.316
.281	Christy Mathewson	11	32	9*	0	0	0	.281
.206	Red Ruffing	14	34	6	1	0	0	.176
.082	Whitey Ford	22*	49*	4	0	0	0	.082

*Leader in category.

World Series–Ending Hits

1912 ....Bost. Red Sox (AL) Larry Gardner hits a deep sacrifice drive to N.Y. Giant (NL) right fielder Josh Devore to score Boston second baseman Steve Yerkes with the winning run in the eighth game of the Series (one had ended in a tie) as Boston scored two in the bottom of the 10th inning for a comeback 3–2 win to win Series 4 games to 3.

1924 ....Earl McNeeley's single over Freddie Lindstrom's head in the 12th inning of Game 7 drives in Muddy Ruel with the winning run as the Wash. Senators (AL) beat the N.Y. Giants (NL), 4 games to 3.

1929 ....Bing Miller's double in the 9th inning of Game 5 drives in Al Simmons with the winning run as the Philadelphia A's (AL) beat the Chi. Cubs (NL), 4 games to 1.

1935 ....Goose Goslin's single in the ninth inning drives in Charlie Gehringer with the winning run as the Det. Tigers (AL) beat the Chi. Cubs (NL), 4 games to 2.

1953 ....Billy Martin's 12th hit of the Series, a single, drives in Hank Bauer with the winning run as the N.Y. Yankees (AL) beat the Bklyn. Dodgers (NL), 4 games to 2.

1960 ....Bill Mazeroski's lead-off home run in the bottom of the 9th inning of Game 7 wins the Series for the Pittsburgh Pirates (NL) over the N.Y. Yankees (AL), 4 games to 3.

1993 ....Joe Carter's bottom-of-the-9th home run off pitcher Mitch Williams with Rickey Henderson and Paul Molitor aboard gives the Tor. Blue Jays (AL) an 8–6 victory over the Phila. Phillies (NL) (and their 2nd straight World Championship), 4 games to 2.

1997 ....Edgar Renteria's ground-ball single up the middle scored Craig Counsell as the Florida Marins (NL) rallied with two in the ninth against the Cleve. Indians (AL) to win game seven 3–.2

2001 ....Luis Gonzalez's bloop single over a drawn-in N.Y. Yankees (AL) infield in the bottom of the 9th inning of Game 7 wins the Series for the Ariz. D'backs (NL), 4 games to 3.

Pitchers in World Series with 300 Career Wins

	Wins		Wins
Cy Young, Bost. Red Sox (AL), 1903	378	Grover C. Alexander, St. L. Cardinals (NL), 1928	364
Christy Mathewson, N.Y. Giants (NL), 1912	312	Warren Spahn, Bos. Braves (NL), 1948	363
Christy Mathewson, N.Y. Giants (NL), 1913	337	Milw. Braves (NL), 1957	363
Eddie Plank, Phil. A's (AL), 1905	326	Milw. Braves (NL), 1958	363
Phil. A's (AL), 1911	326	Don Sutton, L.A. Dodgers (NL), 1974	329
Phil. A's (AL), 1913	326	L.A. Dodgers (NL), 1974	324
Phil. A's (AL), 1914	326	L.A. Dodgers (NL), 1977	324
Walter Johnson, Wash. Senators (AL), 1924	376	L.A. Dodgers (NL), 1978	324
Walter Johnson, Wash. Senators (AL), 1925	396	Milw. Brewers (AL), 1982	324
Grover C. Alexander, St. L. Cardinals (NL), 1926	327	Nolan Ryan, N.Y. Mets (NL), 1969	324
		Tom Seaver, N.Y. Mets (NL), 1969	311
		N.Y. Mets (NL), 1973	311
		Lefty Grove, Phil. A's (AL), 1929	300
		Phil. A's (AL), 1930	300
		Phil. A's (AL), 1931	300
		Early Wynn, Chi. White Sox (AL), 1959	300
		Steve Carlton, Phila. Phillies (NL), 1983	300
		Tom Glavine, Atl. Braves (NL), 1991–92, 1995–96	305
		Greg Maddux, Atl. Braves (NL), 1995–96, 1999	355
		Randy Johnson, Ariz. D'Backs (NL), 2001	303
		Roger Clemens, N.Y. Yankees (AL), 2003	310

Players on World Series Teams in Three Decades

Yogi Berra	N.Y. Yankees (AL)	1947 and 1949
	N.Y. Yankees (AL)	1950–53 and 1955–58
	N.Y. Yankees (AL)	1960–61 and 1963
Bill Dickey	N.Y. Yankees (AL)	1928*

continued on next page

N.Y. Yankees (AL)	1932 and 1936–39	
	N.Y. Yankees (AL)	1941–43
Joe DiMaggio	N.Y. Yankees (Al)	1936–39
	N.Y. Yankees (AL)	1941–42, 1947, and 1949
	N.Y. Yankees (AL)	1950–51
Leo Durocher	N.Y. Yankees (AL)	1928
	St. L. Cardinals (NL)	1934
	Bklyn. Dodgers (NL)	1941*
Willie Mays	N.Y. Giants (NL)	1951 and 1954
	S.F. Giants (NL)	1962
	N.Y. Mets (NL)	1973
Tug McGraw	N.Y. Mets (NL)	1969*
	N.Y. Mets (NL)	1973
	Phila. Phillies (NL)	1980
Jim Palmer	Balt. Orioles (AL)	1966 and 1969
	Balt. Orioles (AL)	1970–71 and 1979
	Balt. Orioles (AL)	1983
Herb Pennock	Phila. A's (AL)	1913* and 1914
	N.Y. Yankees (AL)	1923 and 1926–28*
	N.Y. Yankees (AL)	1932
Billy Pierce	Det. Tigers (AL)	1945*
	Chi. White Sox (AL)	1959
	S.F. Giants (NL)	1962
Babe Ruth	Bost. Red Sox (AL)	1915–16 and 1918
	N.Y. Yankees (AL)	1921–23 and 1926–28
	N.Y. Yankees (AL)	1932
Wally Schang	Phila. A's (AL); and Bost. Red Sox (AL)	1913–14 and 1918
	N.Y. Yankees (AL)	1921–23
	Phila. A's (AL)	1930*
Jimmy Wilson	St. L. Cardinals (NL)	1928
	St. L. Cardinals (NL)	1930–31
	Cin. Reds (NL)	1940

*Did not play.

Players with World Series Home Runs in Three Decades

Yogi Berra	N.Y. Yankees (AL)	1947
	N.Y. Yankees (AL)	1950, 1952–53, and 1955–57
	N.Y. Yankees (AL)	1960–61
Joe DiMaggio	N.Y. Yankees (AL)	1937–39
	N.Y. Yankees (AL)	1947 and 1949
	N.Y. Yankees (AL)	1950–51
Eddie Murray	Balt. Orioles (AL)	1979
	Balt. Orioles (AL)	1983
	Cleve. Indians (AL)	1995

Player-Managers on World Series–Winning Teams

Jimmy Collins............Bost. Red Sox (AL), 1903	Bucky Harris............Wash. Senators (AL), 1924
John McGraw..............N.Y. Giants (NL), 1905	Rogers Hornsby..........St. L. Cardinals (NL), 1926
Fielder Jones............Chi. White Sox (AL), 1906	Gabby Street............St. L. Cardinals (NL), 1931
Frank Chance............Chi. Cubs (NL), 1907, 1908	Bill Terry..............N.Y. Giants (NL), 1933

Fred Clarke ....Pitt. Pirates (NL), 1909
Jake Stahl...Bost. Red Sox (AL), 1912
John Carrigan ....Bost. Red Sox (AL), 1915, 1916
Tris Speaker ....Cleve. Indians (AL), 1920

Frankie Frisch ....St. L. Cardinals (NL), 1934
Mickey Cochrane...............................Det. Tigers (NL), 1935
Lou Boudreau ....Cleve. Indians (AL), 1948

World Series-Winning Managers Who Never Played in Majors

Ed Barrow.. Bost. Red Sox (AL) 1918
Johnny Keane .... St. Louis Cardinals (NL) 1964
Jim Leyland..Flor. Marlins (NL) 1997
Joe McCarthy .... N.Y. Yankees (AL) ....1932, 1936, 1937, 1938, 1939, 1941, and 1943
Jack McKeon .... Fl. Marlins (NL) 2003
Clarence "Pants" Rowland .... Chi. White Sox (AL) 1917
Earl Weaver... Balt. Orioles (AL) ....1966 and 1970

Leaders in Offensive Categories, Never Appearing in World Series (Post-1903)

Games...Rafael Palmeiro 2831
Base Hits ....Rod Carew 3053
Runs...Rafael Palmeiro 1663
Singles..Rod Carew 2404
Doubles ....Rafael Palmeiro 585
Triples ....George Sisler 164
Home Runs...Sammy Sosa 609
Grand Slams...Dave Kingman 16
Pinch-Hit Home Runs..........................Dave Hanson 15
Total Bases ....Rafael Palmeiro 5388
Extra-Base Hits ....Rafael Palmeiro 1192
RBIs...Rafael Palmeiro 1835
Walks..Frank Thomas 1667
Strikeouts ....Sammy Sosa 2306
Slugging Average (Min. 4000 Total Bases)..............Frank Thomas 555
Batting Average (Min. 10 Seasons)............Lefty O'Doul 349
.300 Seasons..Luke Appling 13
Stolen Bases ....Rod Carew, Clyde Milan..495

Most Seasons, Never Appearing in World Series (Post-1903)

24 ....Phil Niekro, pitcher (1964–87)
23 ....Julio Franco, first base (1982–94,
 1996–97,1999, 2001–07)
22 ....Harold Baines, outfield and designated hitter
 (1980–2001)
22 ....Gaylord Perry, pitcher (1962–83)
22 ....Ken Griffey Jr., outfield (1989–2010)
21 ....Ted Lyons, pitcher (1923–42, 1946)
21 ....Lindy McDaniel, pitcher (1955–75)
21 ....Danny Darwin, pitcher (1978–98)
21 ....Frank Tanana, pitcher (1973–93)
20 ....Johnny Cooney, outfield (1921–30, 1935–44)
20 ....Mel Harder, pitcher (1928–47)
20 ....Luke Appling, shortstop (1930–43, 1945–50)
20 ....Dutch Leonard, pitcher (1933–36, 1938–53)

20 ....Mickey Vernon, first base (1939–43, 1946–60)
20 ....Elmer Valo, outfield (1940–43, 1946–61)
20 ....Brian Downing, outfielder (1973–92)
20 ....Rafael Palmeiro, first base (1986–2005)
19 ....Cy Williams, outfield (1912–30)
19 ....Rube Bressler, outfield and pitcher (1914–32)
19 ....Al Lopez, catcher (1928, 1930–47)
19 ....Ernie Banks, shortstop and first base (1953–71)
19 ....Tony Taylor, second base (1958–76)
19 ....Ferguson Jenkins, pitcher (1965–83)
19 ....Rod Carew, infield (1967–85)
19 ....Gene Garber, pitcher (1969–70, 1972–88)
19 ....Jose Cruz, outfield (1970–88)
19 ....Andres Galarraga, first base (1985–2004)
19 ..............B.J. Surhoff, infield (1987–2005)
19 ....Frank Thomas, first base (1990–2008)

*Still active.

Playing Most Games, Never Appearing in World Series (Post-1903)

Rafael Palmeiro (1986–2005)	2831	Billy Williams (1959–76)	2488
Ken Griffey Jr. (1989–2010)	2671	Rod Carew (1967–85)	2469
Andre Dawson (1976–86)	2627	Luke Appling (1930–43, 1945–50)	2422
Ernie Banks (1953–71)	2528	Mickey Vernon (1939–43, 1946–60)	2409
Julio Franco (1982–94, 1996–97, 1999, 2001–07)	2527	Buddy Bell (1972–89)	2405

*Still active.

Players with the Most Home Runs, Never Appearing in World Series

Ken Griffey Jr. (1989–2010)	630	Andres Galarraga (1985–2004)	399
Sammy Sosa (1989–2005, 2007)	609	Dale Murphy (1976–93)	398
Rafael Palmeiro (1986–2005)	569	Harold Baines (1980–2000)	384
Frank Thomas (1990–2008)	521	Rocky Colavito (1955–68)	374
Ernie Banks (1953–71)	512	Ralph Kiner (1946–55)	369
Carlos Delgado (1193–2009)	473	Adam Dunn* (2001–)	365
Dave Kingman (1971–86)	442	Ellis Burks (1987–2004)	352
Andre Dawson (1976–96)	438	Dick Allen (1963–77)	351
Juan Gonzalez (1990–2005)	434	Ron Santo (1960–74)	342
Billy Williams (1959–76)	426	Bobby Bonds (1968–81)	332

*Still active.

Players with Highest Lifetime Batting Average, Never Appearing in World Series (Post-1903; Min. 10 Seasons)

Harry Heilmann (1914, 1916–30, 1932)	.342	Ken Williams (1915–29)	.319
George Sisler (1915–22, 1924–30)	.340	Bibb Falk (1920–31)	.314
Nap Lajoie (1903–16)	.328	Cecil Travis (1933–41, 1945–47)	.314
Rod Carew (1967–85)	.328	Jack Fournier (1912–18, 1920–27)	.313
Ichiro Suzuki (2001–)	.326	Nomar Garciaparra (1996–2009)	.313
Fats Fothergill (1922–33)	.325	Baby Doll Jacobson (1915, 1917, 1919–27)	.311
Babe Herman (1926–37, 1945)	.324	Rip Radcliff (1934–43)	.311

Players with Most Hits, Never Appearing in World Series (Post-1903)

Rod Carew (1967–85)	3053		
Rafael Palmeiro (1986–2005)	3020	Mickey Vernon (1939–43, 1946–60)	2495
Harold Baihes (1980–2001)	2866	Julio Franco (1982–94, 1996–97, 1999, 2001–07)	2586
George Sisler (1915–22, 1924–30)	2812	Frank Thomas (1990–2008)	2468
Ken Griffey Jr. (1989–2010)	2781	Ichiro Suzuki* (2001–)	2428
Andre Dawson (1976–96)	2774	Samma Sosa (1989–2007)	2408
Luke Appling (1930–43, 1945–50)	2749	Ryne Sandberg (1981–97)	2386
Al Oliver (1968–85)	2743	Brett Butler (1981–97)	2375
Billy Williams (1959–76)	2711	Lou Whitaker (1977–95)	2369
Harry Heilmann (1914, 1916–30, 1932)	2660	Alan Trammell (1977–94)	2365
Julio Franco (1982–94, 1996–97, 1999, 2001–07)	2586	Miguel Tejada* (1997–)	2362
Ernie Banks (1953–71)	2583	Joe Torre (1960–77)	2342
Buddy Bell (1972–89)	2514	Andres Galarraga (1985–2004)	2333

*Still active.

Leaders in Pitching Categories, Never Pitching in World Series (Post-1903)

Victories	Phil Niekro (1964–87)	318
Games Pitched	Dan Plesac (1986–2003)	1064
Games Started	Phil Niekro (1964–87)	716
Complete Games	Ted Lyons (1923–42, 1946)	356
Innings Pitched	Phil Niekro (1964–87)	5404
ERA (Min. 2000 Innings)	Addie Joss (1903–10)	1.89
Hits Allowed	Phil Niekro (1964–87)	5044
Runs Allowed	Phil Niekro (1964–87)	2337
Losses	Phil Niekro (1964–87)	274
Grand Slams Allowed	Ned Garver (1948–61)	9
	Milt Pappas (1957–73)	9
	Lee Smith (1980–97)	9
20-Win Seasons	Ferguson Jenkins (1965–83)	7
Saves	Lee Smith (1980–97)	478
Shutouts	Gaylord Perry (1962–83)	53
Walks	Phil Niekro (1964–87)	1809
Strikeouts	Gaylord Perry (1962–83)	3534

Pitchers with Most Wins, Never Appearing in World Series (Post-1903)

Phil Niekro (1964–87)	318	Joe Niekro (1967–88)	221
Gaylord Perry (1961–83)	314	Jerry Reuss (1969–90)	220
Ferguson Jenkins (1965–83)	284	Wilbur Cooper (1912–26)	216
Ted Lyons (1923–42, 1946)	260	Jim Perry (1959–75)	215
Frank Tanana (1973–93)	240	Milt Pappas (1957–73)	209
Jim Bunning (1955–71)	224	George Uhle (1919–34, 1936)	200
Mel Harder (1928–47)	223	Chuck Finley (1986–2003)	200
Hooks Dauss (1912–26)	223		

Pitchers with World Series Wins in Both Leagues

Hank Borowy	N.Y. Yankees (AL), 1943; Chi. Cubs (NL), 1945
Jack Coombs	Phila. Athletics (AL), 1910, 1911; Bklyn. Robins (NL), 1916
Don Larsen	N.Y. Yankees (AL), 1956, 1957, 1958; S.F. Giants (NL), 1962
Johnny Sain	Bost. Braves (NL), 1948; N.Y. Yankees (AL), 1953
Curt Schilling	Phila. Phillies (NL), 1993; Ariz. D'backs (NL), 2001; Bost. Red Sox (AL), 2004
Josh Beckett	Flor. Marlins (NL), 2003; Bost. Red Sox (AL), 2007

Pitchers with World Series Losses in Both Leagues

Al Downing	N.Y. Yankees (AL), 1963, 1964; L.A. Dodgers (NL), 1974
Dock Ellis	Pitt. Pirates (NL), 1971; N.Y. Yankees (AL), 1976
Don Gullett	Cin. Reds (NL), 1975; N.Y. Yankees (AL), 1976–77
Pat Malone	Chi. Cubs (NL), 1929; N.Y. Yankees (AL), 1936
Johnny Sain	Bost. Braves (NL), 1948; N.Y. Yankees (AL), 1952

Players Whose Home Run Won World Series Game 1–0

Casey Stengel, N.Y. Giants (NL), 1923, Game 3, 7th inning, off Sam Jones, N.Y. Yankees (AL)

Tommy Henrich, N.Y. Yankees (AL), 1949, Game 1, 9th inning, off Don Newcombe, Bklyn. Dodgers (NL)

Paul Blair, Balt. Orioles (AL), 1966, Game 3, 5th inning, off Claude Osteen, L.A. Dodgers (NL)

Frank Robinson, Balt. Orioles (AL), 1966, Game 4 (final game), 4th inning, off Don Drysdale, L.A. Dodgers (NL)

David Justice, Atl. Braves (NL), 1995, Game 6 (final game), 6th inning, off Jim Poole, Cleve. Indians (AL)

Brothers Who Were World Series Teammates

Felipe Alou, outfield, and Matty Alou, outfield, S.F. Giants (NL), 1962
Jesse Barnes, pitcher, and Virgil Barnes, pitcher, N.Y. Giants (NL), 1922
George Brett, third base, and Ken Brett, pitcher, K.C. Royals (AL), 1980
Mort Cooper, pitcher, and Walker Cooper, catcher, St. L. Cardinals (NL), 1942–44
Dizzy Dean, pitcher, and Paul Dean, pitcher, St. L. Cardinals (NL), 1934
Lloyd Waner, outfield, and Paul Waner, outfield, Pitt. Pirates (NL), 1927

Brothers Facing Each Other in World Series

Clete Boyer, third base, N.Y. Yankees (AL), and Ken Boyer, third base, St. L. Cardinals (NL), 1964
Doc Johnston, first base, Cleve. Indians (AL), and Jimmy Johnston, third base, Bklyn. Dodgers (NL), 1920
Bob Meusel, outfield, N.Y. Yankees (AL), and Irish Meusel, outfield, N.Y. Giants (NL), 1921–23

Fathers and Sons in World Series Competition

Father	Son
Jim Bagby Sr., pitcher, Cleve. Indians (AL), 1920	Jim Bagby Jr., pitcher, Bost. Red Sox (AL), 1946
Ray Boone, pinch hitter, Cleve. Indians (AL), 1948	Bob Boone, catcher, Phila. Phillies (NL), 1980
Bob Boone, catcher, Phila. Phillies (NL), 1980	Aaron Boone, third base, N.Y. Yankees (AL), 2003
Dave Duncan, Catcher, Oak. A's (AL), 1972	Chris Duncan, outfielder, St.L. Cardinals (NL), 2006
Jim Hegan, catcher, Cleve. Indians (AL), 1948 and 1954	Mike Hegan, pinch hitter and first base, N.Y. Yankees (AL), 1964, and Oak. A's (AL), 1972
Ernie Johnson, shortstop, N.Y. Yankees (AL), 1923	Don Johnson, second base, Chi. Cubs (NL), 1945
Bob Kennedy, outfield, Cleve. Indians (AL), 1948	Terry Kennedy, catcher, S.D. Padres (NL), 1984
Ed Spiezio, infielder, St.L. Cardinals, 1967–68	Scott Spiezio, infielder, L.A. Angels (AL) 2002, St.L. Cardinals (NL), 2006
Billy Sullivan Sr., catcher, Chi. White Sox (AL), 1906	Billy Sullivan Jr., catcher, Det. Tigers (AL), 1940

Batting Average of .400 Hitters in World Series Play

.345....Joe Jackson, 1919 World Series, Chi. White Sox .... .408 in 1910
.295....Bill Terry, 1924, 1933, and 1934 World Series, N.Y. Giants .... .401 in 1930
.262....Ty Cobb, 1907, 1908 and 1909 World Series, Det Tigers .... .420 in 1911, .410 in 1912, .401 in 1922
.245....Rogers Hornsby, 1926 World Series, St. L. Cardinals
              1929 World Series Chi. Cubs... .401 in 1922, .424 in 1924, .403 in 1925
.200....Ted Williams, 1946 World Series, Bost. Red Sox .... .406 in 1941

Batting Averages of .400 in World Series Play

Career Leaders			Single-Season Leaders			
	BA	PA		BA	PA	Series/Year
Phil Garner	.500	28	Billy Hatcher	.750	15	1990 World Series
Amos Otis	.478	26	Babe Ruth	.625	17	1928 World Series
Barry Bonds	.471	30	Hideki Matsui	.615	14	2009 World Series
Max Carey	.458	31	Ricky Ledee	.600	13	1998 World Series
Bobby Brown	.439	46	Danny Bautista	.583	13	2001 World Series
Jake Powell	.435	27	Ivey Wingo	.571	11	1919 World Series
Marty Barrett	.433	35	Chris Sabo	.562	18	1990 World Series
Paul Molitor	.418	61	Lou Gehrig	.545	17	1928 World Series
Pepper Martin	.418	60	Hank Gowdy	.545	16	1914 World Series
Robin Yount	.414	31	Bret Boone	.538	14	1999 World Series

Players Hitting World Series Home Runs in Each League

	American League	National League
Kirk Gibson	Det. Tigers, 1984	L.A. Dodgers, 1988
Roger Maris	N.Y. Yankees, 1960–62 and 1964	St. L. Cardinals, 1967
Frank Robinson	Balt. Orioles, 1966 and 1969–71	Cin. Reds, 1961
Bill Skowron	N.Y. Yankees, 1955–56, 1958, and 1960–61	L.A. Dodgers, 1963
Enos Slaughter	N.Y. Yankees, 1956	St. L. Cardinals, 1942 and 1946
Reggie Smith	Bost. Red Sox, 1967	St. L. Cardinals, 1977–78

World Series Inside-The-Park Home Runs

	HRs		Player's Team	Opponent's Team
1903	1	Jimmy Sebrig	Pitt. Pirates	Bost. Americans
1903	2	Patsy Dougherty	Bost. Americans	Pitt. Pirates
1915	5	Duffy Lewis	Bost. Red Sox	Phila. Phillies
1916	2	Hy Myers	Bklyn. Robins	Bost. Red Sox
1916	4	Larry Gardner	Bost. Red Sox	Bklyn. Robins
1923	1	Casey Stengel	N.Y. Giants	N.Y. Yankees
1926	2	Tommy Thevenow	St. L. Cardinals	N.Y. Yankees
1928	3	Lou Gehrig	N.Y. Yankees	St. L. Cardinals
1929	4	Mule Haas	Phila. Athletics	Chi. Cubs

World Series Teams Using Six Different Starting Pitchers

Bklyn. Dodgers (NL), 1947	Game 1	Ralph Branca (lost)
	Games 2 and 6	Vic Lombardi (lost and won)
	Game 3	Joe Hatten (won)
	Game 4	Harry Taylor (won)
	Game 5	Rex Barney (lost)
	Game 7	Hal Gregg (lost)
Bklyn. Dodgers (NL), 1955	Game 1	Don Newcombe (lost)
	Game 2	Billy Loes (lost)
	Games 3 and 7	Johnny Podres (won and won)
	Game 4	Carl Erskine (won)
	Game 5	Roger Craig (won)
	Game 6	Karl Spooner (lost)
Pitt. Pirates (NL), 1971	Game 1	Dock Ellis (lost)
	Game 2	Bob Johnson (lost)
	Games 3 and 7	Steve Blass (won and won)
	Game 4	Luke Walker (won)
	Game 5	Nelson Briles (won)
	Game 6	Bob Moose (lost)

Rookies Starting Seventh Game of World Series

Babe Adams, Pitt. Pirates (NL) (vs. Det. Tigers, AL), 1909 .... Pitched complete game and wins 8–0

Hugh Bedient, Bost. Red Sox (AL) (vs. N.Y. Giants, NL), 1912 .... Pitched 7 innings, no decision* (Bost. wins 3–2)

Spec Shea, N.Y. Yankees (AL) (vs. Bklyn. Dodgers, NL), 1947 .... Pitched 1⅓ innings, no decision (N.Y. wins 5–2)

Joe Black, Bklyn. Dodgers (NL) (vs. N.Y. Yankees, AL), 1952 .... Pitched 5⅓ innings and loses 4–2

Mel Stottlemyre, N.Y. Yankees (AL) (vs. St. L. Cardinals, NL), 1964 .... Pitched 4 innings and loses 7–5

Joe Magrane, St. L. Cardinals (NL) (vs. Minn. Twins, AL), 1987 .... Pitched 4⅓ innings, no decision (Minn. wins 4–2)

John Lackey, L.A. Angels (AL) (vs. S.F. Giants, NL), 2002 .... Pitched 5 innings and wins 4–1

*Started last game of eight-game Series.

Players Playing Four Different Positions in World Series Competition, Career

Elston Howard ....Left field, right field, first base, catcher

Tony Kubek ....Left field, third base, center field, shortstop

Jackie Robinson .First base, second base, left field, third base

Pete Rose...............Right field, left field, third base, first base

Babe Ruth ....Pitcher, left field, right field, first base

Players Stealing Home in World Series Game

Bill Dahlen, N.Y. Giants (NL) (vs. Phila. A's, AL), 1905, Game 3, 5th inning*

George Davis, Chi. White Sox (AL) (vs. Chi. Cubs, NL), 1906, Game 5, 3rd inning*

Jimmy Slagle, Chi. Cubs (NL) (vs. Det. Tigers, AL), 1907, Game 4, 7th inning*

Ty Cobb, Det. Tigers (AL) (vs. Pitt. Pirates, NL), 1909, Game 2, 3rd inning

Buck Herzog, N.Y. Giants (NL) (vs. Bost. Red Sox, AL), 1912, Game 6, 1st inning

Butch Schmidt, Bost. Braves (NL) (vs. Phila. A's, AL), 1914, Game 1, 8th inning*

Mike McNally, N.Y. Yankees (AL) (vs. N.Y. Giants, NL), 1921, Game 1, 5th inning

Bob Meusel, N.Y. Yankees (AL) (vs. N.Y. Giants, NL), 1921, Game 2, 8th inning

Bob Meusel, N.Y. Yankees (AL) (vs. St. L. Cardinals, NL), 1928, Game 3, 6th inning*

Hank Greenberg, Det. Tigers (AL) (vs. St. L. Cardinals, NL), 1934, Game 4, 8th inning*

Monte Irvin, N.Y. Giants (NL) (vs. N.Y. Yankees, AL), 1951, Game 1, 1st inning

Jackie Robinson, Bklyn. Dodgers (NL) (vs. N.Y. Yankees, AL), 1955, Game 1, 8th inning

Tim McCarver, St. L. Cardinals (NL) (vs. N.Y. Yankees, AL), 1964, Game 7, 4th inning*

Brad Fullmer, Ana. Angels (AL) (vs. S.F. Giants, NL), 2002, Games 2, 1st inning

*Front end of double steal.

Pitchers Hitting Home Runs in World Series Play

Jim Bagby Sr., Cleve. Indians (AL) (vs. Bklyn. Dodgers, NL), 1920, Game 5

Rosy Ryan, N.Y. Giants (NL) (vs. Wash. Senators, AL), 1924, Game 3

Jack Bentley, N.Y. Giants (NL) (vs. Wash. Senators, AL), 1924, Game 5

Jesse Haines, St. L. Cardinals (NL) (vs. N.Y. Yankees, AL), 1926, Game 3

Bucky Walters, Cin. Reds (NL) (vs. Det. Tigers, AL), 1940, Game 6

Lew Burdette, Milw. Braves (NL) (vs. N.Y. Yankees, AL), 1958, Game 2

*Hit home run in losing effort.

**Hit grand slam home run.

Jim "Mudcat" Grant, Minn. Twins (AL) (vs. L.A. Dodgers, NL), 1965, Game 6

Jose Santiago, Bost. Red Sox (AL) (vs. St. L. Cardinals, NL), 1967, Game 1*

Bob Gibson, St. L. Cardinals (NL) (vs. Bost. Red Sox, AL), 1967, Game 4

Mickey Lolich, Det. Tigers (AL) (vs. St. L. Cardinals, NL), 1968, Game 2

Dave McNally, Balt. Orioles (AL) (vs. N.Y. Mets, NL), 1969, Game 5*

Dave McNally**, Balt. Orioles (AL) (vs. Cin. Reds, NL), 1970, Game 3

Ken Holtzman, Oak. A's (AL) (vs. L.A. Dodgers, NL), 1974, Game 4

Cy Young Winners Facing Each Other in World Series Games

Denny McLain, Det. Tigers (AL), vs. Bob Gibson, St. L. Cardinals (NL), 1968, Games 1 and 4

Mike Cuellar, Balt. Orioles (AL), vs. Tom Seaver, N.Y. Mets (NL), 1969, Games 1 and 4

Catfish Hunter, Oak. A's (AL), vs. Mike Marshall, L.A. Dodgers (NL), 1974, Games 1 and 3

World Series in Which Neither Team Had a 20-Game Winner

Bost. Red Sox (AL) vs. Cin. Reds (NL), 1975

N.Y. Yankees (AL) vs. Cin. Reds (NL), 1976

N.Y. Yankees (AL) vs. L.A. Dodgers (NL), 1981

Milw. Brewers (AL) vs. St. L. Cardinals (NL), 1982

Balt. Orioles (AL) vs. Phila. Phillies (NL), 1983

Cleve. Indians (AL) vs. Atl. Braves (NL), 1995

Cleve. Indians (AL) vs. Flor. Marlins (NL), 1997

N.Y. Yankees (AL) vs. N.Y. Mets (NL), 2000

L.A. Angels (AL) vs. S.F. Giants (NL), 2002

Det. Tigers (AL) vs. St. L. Cardinals (NL), 2006

Continued on next page

Det. Tigers (AL) vs. S.D. Padres (NL), 1984
Minn. Twins (AL) vs. St. L. Cardinals (NL), 1987
Tor. Blue Jays (AL) vs. Phila. Phillies (NL), 1993

Bost. Red Sox (AL) vs. Colo. Rockies (NL), 2007
T.B. Rays (AL) vs. Phila. Phillies (NL), 2008
N.Y. Yankees (AL) vs. Phila. Phillies (NL), 2009
Tex. Rangers (AL) vs. S.F. Giants (NL), 2010
Tex. Rangers (AL)) vs. St.L. Cardinals (NL), 2011

Pitchers with Lowest ERA in Total World Series Play (Min. 25 Innings)

Career Leaders		
	ERA	IP
Jack Billingham	0.36	25.1
Harry Brecheen	0.83	32.2
Claude Osteen	0.86	21.0
Babe Ruth	0.87	31.0
Sherry Smith	0.89	30.1
Sandy Koufax	0.95	57.0
Christy Mathewson	0.97	101.2
Mariano Rivera	0.99	36.1
Hippo Vaughn	1.00	27.0
Monte Pearson	1.01	35.2

Single-Season Leaders			
	ERA	IP	Series/Year
Waite Hoyt	.00	27.0	1921 World Series
Christy Mathewson	.00	27.0	1905 World Series
Carl Hubbell	.00	20.0	1933 World Series
Whitey Ford	.00	18.0	1960 World Series
Joe McGinnity	.00	17.0	1905 World Series
Duster Mails	.00	15.2	1920 World Series
Rube Benton	.00	14.0	1917 World Series
Whitey Ford	.00	14.0	1961 World Series
Jack Billingham	.00	13.2	1972 World Series
Joe Dobson	.00	12.2	1946 World Series
Allie Reynolds	.00	12.1	1949 World Series
Clem Labine	.00	12.0	1956 World Series
Mordecai Brown	.00	11.0	1908 World Series
Bill James	.00	11.0	1914 World Series
Jack Kramer	.00	11.0	1944 World Series
Gene Bearden	.00	10.2	1948 World Series
Don Larsen	.00	10.2	1956 World Series

World Series Grand Slams

Elmer Smith, Cleve. Indians (AL), 1920, Game 5, 1st inning, off Burleigh Grimes, Bklyn. Dodgers (NL)

Tony Lazzeri, N.Y. Yankees (AL), 1936, Game 2, 3rd inning, off Dick Coffman, N.Y. Giants (NL)

Gil McDougald, N.Y. Yankees (AL), 1951, Game 5, 3rd inning, off Larry Jansen, N.Y. Giants (NL)

Mickey Mantle, N.Y. Yankees (AL), 1953, Game 5, 3rd inning, off Russ Meyer, Bklyn. Dodgers (NL)

Yogi Berra, N.Y. Yankees (AL), 1956, Game 2, 2nd inning, off Don Newcombe, Bklyn. Dodgers (NL)

Bill Skowron, N.Y. Yankees (AL), 1956, Game 7, 7th inning, off Roger Craig, Bklyn. Dodgers (NL)

Bobby Richardson, N.Y. Yankees (AL), 1960, Game 3, 1st inning, off Clem Labine, Pitt. Pirates (NL)

Chuck Hiller, S.F. Giants (NL), 1962, Game 4, 7th inning, off Marshall Bridges, N.Y. Yankees (AL)

Ken Boyer, St. L. Cardinals (NL), 1964, Game 4, 6th inning, off Al Downing, N.Y. Yankees (AL)

Joe Pepitone, N.Y. Yankees (AL), 1964, Game 6, 8th inning, off Gordie Richardson, St. L. Cardinals (NL)

Jim Northrup, Det. Tigers (AL), 1968, Game 6, 3rd inning, off Larry Jaster, St. L. Cardinals (NL)

Dave McNally, Balt. Orioles (AL), 1970, Game 3, 6th inning, off Wayne Granger, Cin. Reds (NL)

Dan Gladden, Minn. Twins (AL), 1987, Game 1, 4th inning, off Bob Forsch, St. L. Cardinals (NL)

Kent Hrbek, Minn. Twins (AL), 1987, Game 6, 6th inning, off Ken Dayley, St. L. Cardinals (NL)

Jose Canseco, Oak. A's (AL), 1988, Game 1, 2nd inning, off Tim Belcher, L.A. Dodgers (NL)

Lonnie Smith, Atl. Braves (NL), 1992, Game 5, 5th inning, off Jack Morris, Tor. Blue Jays (AL)

Tino Martinez, N.Y. Yankees (AL), 1998, Game 1, 7th inning, off Mark Langston, S.D. Padres (NL)

Paul Konerko, Chi. White Sox (AL), 2005, Game 2, 7th inning, off Chad Qualls, Hous. Astros (NL)

Players on Three Different World Series Clubs

Don Baylor....................................Bost. Red Sox (AL), 1986
Minn. Twins (AL), 1987
Oak. A's (AL), 1988
Joe Bush ....Phila. A's (AL), 1913–14
Bost. Red Sox (AL), 1918
N.Y. Yankees (AL), 1922–23
Bobby Byrne...................................Pitt. Pirates (NL), 1909
Phila. Phillies (NL), 1915
Chi. White Sox (AL), 1917*
Vic Davalillo ....Pitt. Pirates (NL), 1971
Oak. A's (AL), 1973
L.A. Dodgers (NL), 1977–78
Paul Derringer ....St. L. Cardinals (NL), 1931
Cin. Reds (NL), 1939–40
Chi. Cubs (NL), 1945
Leo Durocher.................................N.Y. Yankees (AL), 1928
St. L. Cardinals (NL), 1934
Bklyn. Dodgers (NL), 1941*
Mike Gonzalez ..............................N.Y. Giants (NL), 1921*
Chi. Cubs (NL), 1929
St. L. Cardinals (NL), 1931*
Burleigh Grimes.........................Bklyn. Dodgers (NL), 1920
St. L. Cardinals (NL), 1930–31
Chi. Cubs (NL), 1932
Heinie Groh..............N.Y. Giants (NL), 1912* and 1922–24
Cin. Reds (NL), 1919
Pitt. Pirates (NL), 1927
Pinky Higgins ....Phila. A's (AL), 1930*
Det. Tigers (AL), 1940
Bost. Red Sox (AL), 1946
Grant Jackson ....Balt. Orioles (AL), 1971
N.Y. Yankees (AL), 1976
Pitt. Pirates (NL), 1979
Mark Koenig............................N.Y. Yankees (AL), 1926–28
Chi. Cubs (NL), 1932
N.Y. Giants (NL), 1936

Mike McCormick ....Cin. Reds (NL), 1940
Bost. Braves (NL), 1948
Bklyn. Dodgers (NL), 1949
Stuffy McInnis .....Phila. A's (AL), 1910,* 1911, and 1913–14
Bost. Red Sox (AL), 1918
Pitt. Pirates (NL), 1925
Fred Merkle................................N.Y. Giants (NL), 1911–13
Bklyn. Dodgers (NL), 1916
Chi. Cubs (NL), 1918
N.Y. Yankees (AL), 1926*
Andy Pafko ....Chi. Cubs (NL), 1945
Bklyn. Dodgers (NL), 1952
Milw. Braves (NL), 1957–58
Billy Pierce.......................................Det. Tigers (AL), 1945*
Chi. White Sox (AL), 1959
S.F. Giants (NL), 1962
Edgar Renteria ....Flo. Marins (NL) 1997
St.L. Cardinals (NL), 2004
S.F. Giants (NL), 2010
Dutch Ruether ....Cin. Reds (NL), 1919
Wash. Senators (AL), 1925
N.Y. Yankees (AL), 1926 and 1927*
Wally Schang ....Phila. A's (AL), 1913–14 and 1930*
Bost. Red Sox (AL), 1918
N.Y. Yankees (AL), 1921–22
Everett Scott..............Bost. Red Sox (AL), 1915–16 and 1918
N.Y. Yankees (AL), 1922–23
Wash. Senators (AL), 1925*
Earl Smith ..................................N.Y. Giants (NL), 1921–22
Pitt. Pirates (NL), 1925 and 1927
St. L. Cardinals (NL), 1928
Lonnie Smith..................................Phila. Phillies (NL), 1980
St. L. Cardinals (NL), 1982
K.C. Royals (NL), 1985
Tuck Stainback ....Chi. Cubs (NL), 1935*
Det. Tigers (AL), 1940*
N.Y. Yankees (AL), 1942–43
Eddie Stanky..............................Bklyn. Dodgers (NL), 1947
Bost. Braves (NL), 1948
N.Y. Giants (NL), 1951

*Did not play in Series.

Players Playing for 2 Different World Series Champions in Successive Years

Allie Clark, outfield...1947 N.Y. Yankees; 1948 Cleve. Indians
Clem Labine, pitcher ....1959 L.A. Dodgers; 1960 Pitt. Pirates
Moose Skowron, first base ....1962 N.Y. Yankees; 1963 L.A. Dodgers
Don Gullett, pitcher..1976 Cin. Reds; 1977 N.Y. Yankees
Jack Morris, pitcher...1991 Minn. Twins; 1992 Tor. Blue Jays

Players with Same Lifetime Batting Average as Their World Series Overall Average

	Lifetime/World Series Batting Average	World Series Appearances
Duffy Lewis (1910–17, 1919–21)	.284	1912 and 1915–16
Phil Linz (1962–68)	.235	1963–64
Danny Murphy (1900–15)	.288	1905 and 1910–11
Paul Waner (1926–45)	.333	1927

Batting Champions Facing Each Other in World Series

Ty Cobb (.377), Det. Tigers (AL), and Honus Wagner (.339), Pitt. Pirates (NL), 1909
Al Simmons (.390), Phila. A's (AL), and Chick Hafey (.349), St. L. Cardinals (NL), 1931
Bobby Avila (.341), Cleve. Indians (AL), and Willie Mays (.345), N.Y. Giants (NL), 1954

Home Run Champions Facing Each Other in World Series

Babe Ruth (59), N.Y. Yankees (AL), and George Kelly (23), N.Y. Giants (NL), 1921
Babe Ruth (54), N.Y. Yankees (AL), and Jim Bottomley (31), St. L. Cardinals (NL), 1928
Lou Gehrig (49), N.Y. Yankees (AL), and Mel Ott (33), N.Y. Giants (NL), 1936
Joe DiMaggio (46), N.Y. Yankees (AL), and Mel Ott (31), N.Y. Giants (NL), 1937
Mickey Mantle (52), N.Y. Yankees (AL), and Duke Snider (43), Bklyn. Dodgers (NL), 1956

Players Hitting Home Run in First World Series At Bat

Joe Harris, Wash. Senators (AL), 1925
George Watkins, St. L. Cardinals (NL), 1930
Mel Ott, N.Y. Giants (NL), 1933
George Selkirk, N.Y. Yankees (AL), 1936
Dusty Rhodes, N.Y. Giants (NL), 1954
Elston Howard, N.Y. Yankees (AL), 1955
Roger Maris, N.Y. Yankees (AL), 1960
Don Mincher, Minn. Twins (AL), 1965
Brooks Robinson, Balt. Orioles (AL), 1966
Jose Santiago, Bost. Red Sox (AL), 1967
Mickey Lolich, Det. Tigers (AL), 1968
Don Buford, Balt. Orioles (AL), 1969
Gene Tenace*, Oak. A's (AL), 1972
Jim Mason, N.Y. Yankees (AL), 1976

Doug DeCinces, Balt. Orioles (AL), 1979
Amos Otis, K.C. Royals (AL), 1980
Bob Watson, N.Y. Yankees (AL), 1981
Jim Dwyer, Balt. Orioles (AL), 1983
Jose Canseco, Oak. A's (AL), 1988
Mickey Hatcher, L.A. Dodgers (NL), 1988
Bill Bathe, S.F. Giants (NL), 1989
Eric Davis, Cin. Reds (NL), 1990
Ed Sprague Jr., Tor. Blue Jays (AL), 1992
Fred McGriff, Atl. Braves (NL), 1995
Andruw Jones, Atl. Braves (NL), 1996
Barry Bonds, S.F. Giants (NL), 2002
David Ortiz, Bost. Red Sox (AL), 2004

*Hit home runs in first two times at bat in World Series.

World Series Pitchers with Most Losses, Season

American League		National League	
George Mullin, Det. Tigers, 1907	20	Larry French, Chi. Cubs, 1938	19
Ken Holtzman, Oak. A's, 1974	17	Pat Malone, Chi. Cubs, 1932	17
Dennis Martinez, Balt. Orioles, 1979	16	Don Drysdale, L.A. Dodgers, 1963	17
Dennis Martinez, Balt. Orioles, 1983	16	Don Drysdale, L.A. Dodgers, 1966	16
Jason Marquis, St. L. Cardinals, 2006	16	Jon Matlack, N.Y. Mets, 1973	16
Joe Bush, Bost. Red Sox, 1918	15	Steve Carlton, Phila. Phillies, 1983	16
Joe Bush, N.Y. Yankees, 1923	15	Livan Hernandez, S.F. Giants, 2002	16
Tom Zachary, Wash. Senators, 1925	15	Joe McGinnity, N.Y. Giants, 1905	15
General Crowder, Wash. Senators, 1933	15	Erskine Mayer, Phila. Phillies, 1915	15
Dizzy Trout, Det. Tigers, 1945	15	Harry Brecheen, St. L. Cardinals, 1946	15

continued on next page

Bob Feller, Cleve. Indians, 1948 15		Johnny Sain, Bost. Braves, 1948 15	
Billy Pierce, Chi. White Sox, 1959 15		Claude Osteen, L.A. Dodgers, 1965 15	
Ralph Terry, N.Y. Yankees, 1963 15		Jerry Koosman, N.Y. Mets, 1973 15	
Vida Blue, Oak. A's, 1974 15			
Catfish Hunter, N.Y. Yankees, 1976 15			
Bud Black, K.C. Royals, 1985 15			
Mike Moore, Oak. A's, 1990 15			

Teams Winning a World Series in First Year in New Ballpark

Team	Ballpark	Opponent	Series
Pittsburg* Pirates (NL) ....Forbes Field, 1909 ....Det Tigers (AL) ....4 games to 3			
Bost. Red Sox (AL) ....Fenway Park, 1912 ..........................N.Y. Giants (NL) ....4 games to 3			
N.Y. Yankees (AL) ....Yankee Stadium I, 1923 ..................N.Y. Giants (NL) ....4 games to 2			
St. L. Cardinals (NL) ....Busch Stadium III, 2006 ....Det. Tigers (AL) ....4 games to 2			
N.Y. Yankees (AL) ....Yankee Stadium II, 2009 ....Phila. Phillies (NL) ....4 games to 2			

*Then spelled without an "h."

Pitchers on World Series Winning Teams, Both Winning 20 Games and *All* of Their Team's Series Victories

American League

1903* Cy Young (28 season wins, 2 Series wins) and Bill Dineen (21 season wins, 3 Series wins), Bost. Americans
1910   Jack Coombs (31 season wins, 3 Series wins) and Chief Bender (23 season wins, 1 Series win), Phila. Athletics
1912   Smokey Joe Wood (34 season wins, 3 Series wins) amd Hugh Bedient (20 season wins, 1 Series win), Bost. Red Sox
1930   Lefty Grove (28 season wins, 2 Series wins), Phila. Athletics

National League

1905   Christy Mathewson (31 season wins, 3 Series wins) and Joe McGinnity (21 season wins, 1 Series win), N.Y. Giants
1914   Bill James (26 season wins, 2 Series wins) and Dick Rudolph (26 season wins, 2 Series wins), Bost. Braves
1940   Bucky Walters (22 season wins, 2 Series wins) and Paul Derringer (20 season wins, 2 Series wins), Cin. Reds
2001   Curt Schilling (22 season wins, 1 Series win) and Randy Johnson (21 season wins, 3 Series wins), Ariz. D'backs

Teams' Overall Won-Lost Percentage in World Series Games Played

American League

	Games Won–Lost	Percentage
Tor. Blue Jays (2 appearances, 2–0)	8–4	.667
Bost. Red Sox (11 appearances, 7–4)	41–26–1	.612
N.Y. Yankees (40 appearances, 27–13)	134–90–1	.598
Balt. Orioles (6 appearances, 3–3)	19–14	.576
L.A. Angels (1 appearance, 1–0)	4–3	.571
Chi. White Sox (5 appearances, 3–2)	17–13	.567
Phila. A's (8 appearances, 5–3)	24–19	.558
Oak. A's (6 appearances, 4–2)	17–15	.531
Minn. Twins (3 appearances, 2–1)	11–10	.524
Cleve. Indians (5 appearances, 2–3)	14–16	.467
K.C. Royals (2 appearances, 1–1)	6–7	.462
Det. Tigers (10 appearances, 4–6)	27–33–1	.450

American League

	Games Won–Lost	Percentage
Milw. Brewers (1 appearance, 0–1)	3–4	.429
Wash. Senators (3 appearances, 1–2)	8–11	.421
St. L. Browns (1 appearance, 0–1)	2–4	.333
Tex. Rangers (2 appearances, 0–2)	4–8	.333
T.B. Rays (1 appearance, 0–1)	1–4	.200

National League

	Games Won–Lost	Percentage
Flor. Marlins (2 appearances, 2–0)	8–5	.615
Bost. Braves (2 appearances, 1–1)	6–4	.600
Ariz. D'backs (1 appearance, 1–0)	4–3	.571
Cin. Reds (9 appearances, 5–4)	26–25	.510
L.A. Dodgers (9 appearances, 5–4)	25–24	.510
Milw. Braves (2 appearances, 1–1)	7–7	.500
N.Y. Mets (4 appearances, 2–2)	12–12	.500
St. L. Cardinals (18 appearances, 11–7)	56–56	.500
N.Y. Giants (13 appearances, 5–8)	36–37–2	.493
Pitt. Pirates (7 appearances, 5–2)	23–24	.489
S.F. Giants (4 appearances, 1–3)	10–13	.435
Atl. Braves (5 appearances, 1–4)	11–18	.379
Phila. Phillies (7 appearances, 2-5)	14–23	.378
Chi. Cubs (10 appearances, 2–8)	19–33–1	.365
Bklyn. Dodgers (9 appearances, 1–8)	20–36	.357
S.D. Padres (2 appearances, 0–2)	1–8	.111
Colo. Rockies (1 appearance, 0–1)	0–4	.000
Hous. Astros (1 appearance, 0–1)	0–4	.000

Oldest Players to Appear in World Series

47 years, 3 months	Jack Quinn, Phila. Athletics, 1929 pitcher
46 years, 10 months	Jamie Moyer, Phila. Phillies, 2009 pitcher
46 years, 3 months	Jack Quinn, Phila. Athletics, 1930 pitcher
45 years, 10 months	Jamie Moyer, Phila. Phillies, 2008 pitcher
42 years, 3 months	Satchel Paige, Cleve. Indians, 1948 pitcher
42 years, 1 month	Chuck Hostetler, Det. Tigers, 1945 pinch hit
41 years, 9 months	Grover C. Alexander, St. L. Cardinals, 1928 pitcher
40 years, 5 months	Rick Reuschel, S.F. Giants, 1989 pitcher
40 years, 3 months	Freddie Fitzsimmons, Bklyn. Dodgers, 1941 pitcher
40 years, 3 months	Bobo Newsom, N.Y. Yankees, 1947 pitcher

Players with 3000 Hits Playing in World Series

	Number of Hits at Time
Willie Mays (1973 N.Y. Mets)	3000
Pete Rose (1980 Phila. Phillies)	3557
Pete Rose (1983 Phila. Phillies)	3990
Eddie Murray (1995 Cleve. Indians)	3071

9

ALL-STAR GAME

Players Who Made All-Star Roster After Starting Season in Minors

Don Newcombe, Bklyn. Dodgers (NL), 1949 ....Started season with Mont. (IL)

Don Schwall, Bost. Red Sox (AL), 1961 ....Started season with Sea. (PCL)

Alvin Davis, Sea. Mariners (AL), 1984 ....Started season with Salt Lake City (PCL)

Evan Longoria, T.B. Rays (AL), 2008 ....Started season with Durham (IL)

Pitchers Winning All-Star Game and World Series Game, Same Season

Lefty Gomez, N.Y. Yankees (AL), 1937

Paul Derringer, Cin. Reds (NL), 1940

Frank "Spec" Shea, N.Y. Yankees (AL), 1947

Vern Law, Pitt. Pirates (NL), 1960

Sandy Koufax, L.A. Dodgers (NL), 1965

Don Sutton, L.A. Dodgers (NL), 1977

John Smoltz, Atl. Braves (NL), 1996

Josh Beckett, Bost. Red Sox (AL), 2007

Pitchers Who Pitched More Than Three Innings in One All-Star Game

Lefty Gomez (AL), 1935	6	Spud Chandler (AL), 1942	4
Mel Harder (AL), 1934	5	Johnny Antonelli (NL), 1956	4
Al Benton (AL), 1942	5	Lew Burdette (NL), 1957	4
Larry Jansen (NL), 1950	5	Bob Feller (AL), 1939	3⅔
Catfish Hunter (AL), 1967	5	Frank Sullivan (AL), 1955	3½
Lon Warneke (NL), 1933	4	Joe Nuxhall (NL), 1955	3½
Hal Schumacher (NL), 1935	4	Ray Narleski (AL), 1958	3½

All-Star Game Managers Who Never Managed in World Series

Paul Richards, Balt. Orioles (AL), 1961 ....Replaced Casey Stengel, N.Y. Yankees

Gene Mauch, Phila. Phillies (NL), 1965...Replaced Johnny Keane, St. L. Cardinals

Brothers Selected to Play in All-Star Game, Same Season

Sandy Alomar Jr., Cleve. Indians (AL), and Roberto Alomar, S.D. Padres (NL) and Balt. Orioles (AL), 1990, 1996–98

Felipe Alou, Atl. Braves (NL), and Matty Alou, Pitt. Pirates (NL), 1968

Aaron Boone, Cin. Reds (NL), and Bret Boone, Sea. Mariners (AL), 2003

Mort Cooper, St. L. Cardinals (NL), and Walker Cooper, St. L. Cardinals (NL), 1942–43

Joe DiMaggio, N.Y. Yankees (AL), and Dom DiMaggio, Bost. Red Sox (AL), 1941–42, 1946, and 1949–51

Carlos May, Chi. White Sox (AL), and Lee May, Cin. Reds (NL), 1969 and 1971

Gaylord Perry, S.F. Giants (NL), and Jim Perry, Minn. Twins (AL), 1970

Dixie Walker, Bklyn. Dodgers (NL), and Harry Walker, St. L. Cardinals and Phila. Phillies (NL), 1943 and 1947

Players Hitting Home Runs in All-Star Game and World Series, Same Season

Joe Medwick, St. L. Cardinals (NL), 1934

Lou Gehrig, N.Y. Yankees (AL), 1936

Lou Gehrig, N.Y. Yankees (AL), 1937

Joe DiMaggio, N.Y. Yankees (AL), 1939

Jackie Robinson, Bklyn. Dodgers (NL), 1952

Mickey Mantle, N.Y. Yankees (AL), 1955

Mickey Mantle, N.Y. Yankees (AL), 1956

Ken Boyer, St. L. Cardinals (NL), 1964

Harmon Killebrew, Minn. Twins (AL), 1965

Roberto Clemente, Pitt. Pirates (NL), 1971

Frank Robinson, Balt. Orioles (AL), 1971

Steve Garvey, L.A. Dodgers (NL), 1977

Sandy Alomar, Cleve. Indians (AL), 1997

Barry Bonds, S.F. Giants (NL), 2002

David Ortiz, Bost. Red Sox (AL), 2004

Manny Ramirez, Bost. Red Sox (AL), 2004

Fathers and Sons, Both of Whom Played in All-Star Games

Father	Son
Sandy Alomar Sr., Cal. Angels (AL), 1970	Roberto Alomar, S.D. Padres (NL), 1990; Tor. Blue Jays (AL), 1991–95; Balt. Orioles (AL), 1996–98; Cleve. Indians (AL), 1999–2001
	Sandy Alomar Jr., Cleve. Indians (AL), 1990–92, 1996–98
Felipe Alou, S.F. Giants (NL), 1962; Atl. Braves (NL), 1966 and 1968	Moises Alou, Mont. Expos (NL), 1994; Flor. Marlins (NL), 1997; Hous. Astros (NL), 1998 and 2001
Gus Bell, Cin. Reds (NL), 1953–54, 1956–57	Buddy Bell, Cleve. Indians (AL), 1973; Tex. Rangers (AL), 1980–82 and 1984
Bobby Bonds, S.F. Giants (NL), 1971 and 1973; N.Y. Yankees (AL), 1975	Barry Bonds, Pitt. Pirates (NL), 1990 and 1992; S.F. Giants (NL), 1993–98, 2000–04
Bob Boone, Phila. Phillies (NL), 1976 and 1978–79; Cal. Angels (AL), 1983	Aaron Boone, Cin. Reds (NL), 2003
	Bret Boone, Cin. Reds (NL), 1998; Sea. Mariners (AL), 2001 and 2003
Ray Boone, Det. Tigers (AL), 1954 and 1956	Bob Boone, Phila. Phillies (NL), 1976 and 1978–79; Cal. Angels (AL), 1983
Ken Griffey Sr., Cin. Reds (NL), 1976–77, 1980	Ken Griffey Jr., Sea. Mariners (AL), 1990–99; Cin. Reds (NL), 2000
Jim Hegan, Cleve. Indians (AL), 1947, 1949–52	Mike Hegan, Sea. Pilots (AL), 1969
Randy Hundley, Chi. Cubs (NL), 1969	Todd Hundley, N.Y. Mets (NL), 1996–97
Vern Law, Pitt. Pirates (NL), 1960	Vance Law, Chi. Cubs (NL), 1988

Pitchers with No Victories, Named to All-Star Team

Dave Laroche, Cleve. Indians (AL), 1976

Tom Henke, Tor. Blue Jays (AL), 1987

Oldest Players Named to All-Star Team

Satchel Paige, pitcher, Cleve. Indians (AL), 1952 ....46 years, 1 day

Roger Clemens, pitcher, Hous. Astros (NL), 2004...41 years, 344 days

Mariano Rivera, pitcher, N.Y. Yankees (NL), 2011 ....41 years, 225 days

Arthur Rhodes, pitcher, Cin. Reds (NL), 2010,2010 ....40 years, 263 days

Jamie Moyer, pitcher, Sea. Mariners (AL), 2003 ....40 years, 239 days

Mariano Rivera, pitcher, N.Y. Yankees (AL), 2010 ....40 years, 226 days

Connie Marrero, pitcher, Wash. Senators (AL), 1951 ....40 years, 70 days

10

TEAMS

Teams' Won-Lost Percentage by Decade

1901–1909

American League

	Wins	Losses	%
Phila. Athletics	734	568	.564
Chi. White Sox	744	575	.564
Cleve. Indians	609	632	.525
Bost. Red Sox	691	634	.522
Det. Tigers	683	632	.519
Balt. Orioles/N.Y. Yankees*	638	671	.487
Milw. Brewers/St. L. Browns**	599	721	.454
Wash. Senators	480	834	.365

*Baltimore franchise moved to New York in 1903.

**Milwaukee moved to St. Louis in 1902.

National League

	Wins	Losses	%
Pitt. Pirates	859	478	.642
Chi. Cubs	814	517	.612
N.Y. Giants	763	507	.574
Cin. Reds	642	691	.482
Phila. Phillies	634	689	.479
Bklyn. Dodgers	567	755	.429
Bost. Braves	521	805	.393
St. L. Cardinals	515	813	.388

1910–1920

American League

	Wins	Losses	%
Bost. Red Sox	857	624	.579
Chi. White Sox	796	692	.535
Det. Tigers	790	704	.529
Wash. Senators	755	737	.506
Cleve. Indians	742	749	.498
Phila. Athletics	710	774	.478
N.Y. Yankees	701	780	.473
St. L. Browns	597	892	.401

National League

	Wins	Losses	%
N.Y. Giants	889	597	.598
Chi. Cubs	826	668	.553
Phila. Phillies	762	717	.515
Pitt. Pirates	736	751	.495
Cin. Reds	717	779	.479
Bklyn. Dodgers	696	787	.469
Bost. Braves	666	815	.450
St. L. Cardinals	652	830	.440

continued on next page

1920–1929

American League

	Wins	Losses	%
N.Y. Yankees	933	602	.608
Wash. Senators	791	735	.518
Cleve. Indians	786	749	.512
Phila. Athletics	770	754	.505
St. L. Browns	762	769	.496
Det. Tigers	760	778	.494
Chi. White Sox	731	804	.476
Bost. Red Sox	595	938	.388

National League

	Wins	Losses	%
N.Y. Giants	890	639	.582
Pitt. Pirates	887	656	.572
St. L. Cardinals	822	712	.536
Chi. Cubs	807	728	.526
Cin. Reds	798	736	.520
Bklyn. Dodgers	765	768	.499
Bost. Braves	603	928	.394
Phila. Phillies	566	962	.370

1930–1939

American League

	Wins	Losses	%
N.Y. Yankees	970	554	.636
Cleve. Indians	824	708	.538
Det. Tigers	818	716	.533
Wash. Senators	806	722	.527
Phila. Athletics	723	795	.476
Bost. Red Sox	705	815	.464
Chi. White Sox	678	841	.446
St. L. Browns	578	951	.378

National League

	Wins	Losses	%
Chi. Cubs	889	646	.579
N.Y. Giants	868	657	.569
St. L. Cardinals	869	665	.566
Pitt. Pirates	812	718	.531
Bklyn. Dodgers	724	793	.477
Bost. Braves	700	829	.458
Cin. Reds	664	866	.434
Phila. Phillies	581	943	.381

1940–1949

American League

	Wins	Losses	%
N.Y. Yankees	929	609	.604
Bost. Red Sox	754	683	.556
Det. Tigers	834	705	.542
Cleve. Indians	800	731	.523
Chi. White Sox	707	820	.463
St. L. Browns	698	833	.456
Wash. Senators	677	858	.441
Phila. Athletics	638	898	.415

National League

	Wins	Losses	%
St. L. Cardinals	960	580	.623
Bklyn. Dodgers	894	646	.581
Cin. Reds	767	769	.499
Pitt. Pirates	756	776	.493
Chi. Cubs	736	802	.479
N.Y. Giants	724	808	.473
Bost. Braves	719	808	.470
Phila. Phillies	584	951	.380

1950–1959

American League

	Wins	Losses	%
N.Y. Yankees	955	582	.621
Cleve. Indians	904	634	.588
Chi. White Sox	847	693	.550
Bost. Red Sox	814	725	.529
Det. Tigers	738	802	.479
Wash. Senators	640	898	.416
St. L. Browns/Balt. Orioles*	632	905	.412
Phila. Athletics/K.C. Athletics	624	915	.405

*St. Louis franchise moved to Baltimore in 1954.

**Philadelphia franchise moved to Kansas City in 1955.

National League

	Wins	Losses	%
Bklyn./L.A. Dodgers*	913	630	.592
Bost. Braves/Milw. Braves**	854	687	.554
N.Y. Giants/S.F. Giants***	822	721	.531
St. L. Cardinals	776	763	.504
Phila. Phillies	767	773	.498
Cin. Reds	741	798	.481
Chi. Cubs	672	866	.437
Pitt. Pirates	616	923	.400

*Brooklyn franchise moved to Los Angeles in 1958.

**Boston franchise moved to Milwaukee in 1953.

***New York franchise moved to San Francisco in 1958.

1960–1969

American League

	Wins	Losses	%
Balt. Orioles	911	698	.566
N.Y. Yankees	887	720	.552
Det. Tigers	882	729	.547
Minn. Twins*	852	747	.536
Chi. White Sox	783	760	.529
Cleve. Indians	764	826	.487
Bost. Red Sox	685	845	.475
Cal. Angels/L.A. Angels**	685	770	.471
K.C. Athletics/Oak. A's***	686	922	.427
K.C. Royals***	69	93	.426
Wash. Senators*	607	844	.418
Sea. Pilots/Milw. Brewers****	64	98	.395

*Original Washington Senators franchise moved to Minnesota in 1961.

**New team awarded Washington by League in expansion in 1961 along with Los Angeles in 1961.

***Kansas City franchise moved to Oakland in 1968.

****Kansas City and Seattle (now Milwaukee) entered the league in 1961 as expansion teams.

National League

	Wins	Losses	%
N.Y. Giants	902	704	.562
St. L. Cardinals	884	718	.552
L.A. Dodgers	878	729	.546
Cin. Reds	860	742	.537
Milw. Braves/Atl. Braves*	851	753	.531
Pitt. Pirates	848	755	.529
Phila. Phillies	759	843	.474
Chi. Cubs	735	868	.459
Hous. Astros*	555	739	.429
N.Y. Mets**	494	799	.382
Mont. Expos***	52	110	.321
S.D. Padres***	52	110	.321

*Milwaukee franchise moved to Atlanta in 1966.

**Houston and New York joined League as expansion teams in 1962.

***San Diego and Montreal joined League as expansion teams in 1969.

1970–1979

American League

	Wins	Losses	%
Balt. Orioles	944	656	.590
Bost. Red Sox	895	714	.556
N.Y. Yankees	892	715	.555
K.C. Royals	851	760	.528
Oak. A's	838	772	.520
Minn. Twins	812	794	.506
Det. Tigers	789	820	.490
Cal. Angels	781	831	.484
Chi. White Sox	752	853	.469
Wash. Senators/Tex. Rangers	747	860	.465
Cleve. Indians	737	866	.460
Milw. Brewers	838	873	.458
Sea. Mariners**	187	297	.386
Tor. Blue Jays**	166	318	.343

*The second edition of the Washington Senators moved to Texas in 1972.

**The Seattle Mariners and Toronto Blue Jays entered the League as expansion teams in 1977.

National League

	Wins	Losses	%
Cin. Reds	953	657	.592
Pitt. Pirates	916	695	.569
L.A. Dodgers	910	701	.565
Phila. Phillies	812	801	.503
St. L. Cardinals	800	813	.496
S.F. Giants	794	818	.493
Hous. Astros	793	817	.493
Chi. Cubs	785	827	.487
N.Y. Mets	763	850	.473
Mont. Expos	748	862	.465
Atl. Braves	725	883	.451
S.D. Padres	667	942	.415

continued on next page

1980-1989

American League	Wins	Losses	%
N.Y. Yankees	854	708	.547
Det. Tigers	839	727	.536
K.C. Royals	826	734	.529
Bost. Red Sox	821	742	.525
Tor. Blue Jays	817	746	.523
Milw. Brewers	804	760	.514
Balt. Orioles	800	761	.512
Oak. Athletics	803	764	.512
Cal. Angels	783	783	.500
Chi. White Sox	758	802	.486
Minn. Twins	733	833	.468
Tex. Rangers	720	839	.462
Cleve. Indians	710	849	.455
Sea. Mariners	673	893	.430

National League	Wins	Losses	%
St. L. Cardinals	825	734	.529
L.A. Dodgers	825	741	.527
N.Y. Mets	816	743	.523
Hous. Astros	819	750	.522
Mont. Expos	811	752	.519
Phila. Phillies	783	780	.501
Cin. Reds	781	783	.499
S.F. Giants	773	795	.493
S.D. Padres	762	805	.486
Chi. Cubs	735	821	.472
Pitt. Pirates	732	825	.470
Atl. Braves	712	845	.457

1990-1999

American League	Wins	Losses	%
N.Y. Yankees	851	702	.548
Cleve. Indians	823	728	.531
Chi. White Sox	816	735	.526
Bost. Red Sox	814	741	.523
Tex. Rangers	807	747	.519
Tor. Blue Jays	801	754	.515
Balt. Orioles	794	757	.512
Oak. A's	773	781	.497
Sea. Mariners	764	787	.493
Milw. Brewers*	594	636	.483
Ana. Angels	738	817	.475
K.C. Royals	725	825	.468
Minn. Twins	718	833	.463
Det. Tigers	702	852	.452
T.B. Devil Rays**	132	192	.407

*Milwaukee Brewers switched to National League in 1998.

**Tampa Bay entered League as an expansion team in 1998.

National League	Wins	Losses	%
Atl. Braves	925	629	.595
Hous. Astros	813	742	.523
Cin. Reds	809	746	.520
L.A. Dodgers	797	757	.513
Ariz. D'backs*	165	159	.509
S.F. Giants	790	766	.508
Mont. Expos	776	777	.499
Pitt. Pirates	774	779	.498
N.Y. Mets	767	786	.494
St. L. Cardinals	758	794	.488
S.D. Padres	758	799	.486
Colo. Rockies*	512	559	.478
Chi. Cubs	739	813	.476
Phila. Phillies	732	823	.471
Milw. Brewers	148	175	.458
Florida Marlins**	472	596	.442

*Arizona entered League as an expansion team in 1998.

**Colorado and Florida entered League as expansion teams in 1993.

2000-2011

American League	Wins	Losses	%
N.Y. Yankees	1157	783	.596
Bost. Red Sox	1099	844	.566
L.A. Angels	1066	878	.548
Oak. A's	1045	897	.538
Chi. White Sox	1024	921	.526
Minn. Twins	1020	915	.524
Tor. Blue Jays	971	972	.505
Sea. Mariners	965	979	.495
Cleve. Indians	965	979	.495
Tex. Rangers	962	982	.495
Det. Tigers	905	1039	.466
T.B. Rays	881	1060	.454
Balt. Orioles	833	1109	.429
K.C. Royals	810	1134	.428

National League	Wins	Losses	%
St. L. Cardinals	1089	854	.563
Atl. Braves	1072	870	.555
Phila. Phillies	1049	894	.540
L.A. Dodgers	1024	919	.526
S.F. Giants	1033	908	.524
N.Y. Mets	971	971	.500
Hous. Astros	964	979	.495
Ariz. D'backs	964	980	.496
Flor. Marlins	963	979	.496
Chi. Cubs	953	989	.491
Colo. Rockies	925	1020	.493
S.D. Padres	930	1015	.478
Cin. Reds	921	1023	.474
Milw. Brewers	918	1029	.469
Mont. Expos/Wash. Nationals*	860	1082	.443
Pitt. Pirates	810	1131	.417

*Montreal franchise moved to Washington in 2005.

Clubs Winning 100 Games, Not Winning Pennant

American League

Wins

116 ....Sea. Mariners, 2001 (116–46, .716)
(Lost League Championship Series to N.Y. Yankees)

103 ............................N.Y. Yankees, 1954 (103–51, .667)
(Finished second to Cleve. Indians by 8 games)

103 ............................N.Y. Yankees, 1980 (103–59, .636)
(Lost League Championship Series to K.C. Royals)

103 ............................N.Y. Yankees, 2002 (103–58, .640)
(Lost Division Series to Ana. Angels)

103 ....Oak. A's, 2002 (103–59, .636)
(Lost Division Series to Minn. Twins)

102 ..............................K.C. Royals, 1977 (102–60, .630)
(Lost League Championship Series to N.Y. Yankees)

102 ....Oak. A's, 2001 (102–60, .630)
(Lost Division Series to N.Y. Yankees)

101 ....Det. Tigers, 1961 (101–61, .623)
(Finished second to N.Y. Yankees by 8 games)

101 ....Oak. A's, 1971 (101–60, .627)
(Lost League Championship Series to Balt. Orioles)

101 ..............................N.Y. Yankees, 2004 (101–61, .623)
(Lost League Championship Series to Bost. Red Sox)

100 ....Det. Tigers, 1915 (100–54, .649)
(Finished second to Bost. Red Sox by 2½ games)

100 ....Balt. Orioles, 1980 (100–62, .617)
(Finished second in AL East to N.Y. Yankees by 3 games)

100 ..............................L.A. Angels, 2008 (100–62, .617)
(Lost Division Series to Bost. Red Sox)

National League

Wins

106 ....Atl. Braves, 1998 (106–56, .654)
(Lost League Championship Series to S.D. Padres)

104 ....Chi. Cubs, 1909 (104–49, .680)
(Finished second to Pitt. Pirates by 6½ games)

104 ....Bklyn. Dodgers, 1942 (104–50, .675)
(Finished second to St. L. Cardinals by 2 games)

104 ....Atl. Braves, 1993 (104–58, .642)
(Lost League Championship Series to Phila. Phillies)

103 ..................................S.F. Giants, 1993 (103–59, .636)
(Finished second to Atl. Braves in NL West by 1 game)

102 ..............................L.A. Dodgers, 1962 (102–63, .618)
(Lost Pennant Playoff to S.F. Giants)

102 ....Hous. Astros, 1998 (102–60, .630)
(Lost Division Series to S.D. Padres)

101 ....Phila. Phillies, 1976 (101–61, .623)
(Lost League Championship Series to Cin. Reds)

101 ....Phila. Phillies, 1977 (101–61, .623)
(Lost League Championship Series to L.A. Dodgers)

101 ....Atl. Braves, 2002 (101–59, .631)
(Lost Division Series to S.F. Giants)

101 ....Atl. Braves, 2003 (101–61, .623)
(Lost Division Series to Chi. Cubs)

100 ..................................N.Y. Mets, 1988 (100–60, .625)
(Lost League Championship Series to L.A. Dodgers)

100 ....Ariz. D'backs, 1999 (100–62, .617)
(Lost Division Series to St. L. Cardinals)

100 ..................................S.F. Giants, 2003 (100–62, .617)
(Lost Division Series to Chi. Cubs)

100 ....St.L.Cardinals, 2005 (100–62, .617)
(Lost Division Series to Hous. Astros)

Pennant Winners One Year, Losing Record Next (Post-1900)

American League

Won Pennant		Losing Record	%
1914	Phila. Athletics	1915: 43–109	.283
1917	Chi. White Sox	1918: 57–67	.460
1918	Bost. Red Sox*	1919: 66–71	.482
1933	Wash. Senators	1934: 66–86	.434
1964	N.Y. Yankees	1965: 77–85	.475
1966	Balt. Orioles*	1967: 76–85	.472
1980	K.C. Royals	1981: 50–53	.485
1981	N.Y. Yankees	1982: 79–83	.488
1985	K.C. Royals*	1986: 76–86	.469
1986	Bost. Red Sox	1987: 78–84	.481
1993	Tor. Blue Jays*	1994: 55–60	.478
2002	Ana. Angels*	2003: 77–85	.475

National League

Won Pennant		Losing Record	%
1916	Bklyn. Dodgers	1917: 70–81	.464
1931	St. L. Cardinals	1932: 72–82	.468
1948	Bost. Braves	1949: 75–79	.487
1950	Phila. Phillies	1951: 73–81	.474
1960	Pitt. Pirates	1961: 75–79	.487
1963	L.A. Dodgers	1964: 80–82	.494
1964	St. L. Cardinals*	1965: 80–81	.497
1966	L.A. Dodgers	1967: 73–89	.451
1970	Cin. Reds	1971: 79–83	.488
1973	N.Y. Mets	1974: 71–91	.438
1978	L.A. Dodgers	1979: 79–83	.488
1982	St. L. Cardinals	1983: 79–83	.488
1985	St. L. Cardinals	1986: 79–83	.488
1987	St. L. Cardinals	1988: 76–86	.469
1990	Cin. Reds	1991: 74–88	.457
1993	Phila. Phillies	1994: 54–61	.470
1997	Flor. Marlins	1998: 54–108	.333
1998	S.D. Padres	1999: 74–88	.457
2007	Colo. Rockies	2008: 74–88	.457

*World Series winner.

Pennant-Winning Season After Losing Record Year Before

American League

Won Pennant		Losing Record	%
1907	Det. Tigers	1906: 71–78	.477
1919	Chi. White Sox	1918: 57–67	.460
1924	Wash. Senators*	1923: 75–78	.490
1926	N.Y. Yankees	1925: 69–85	.448
1934	Det. Tigers	1933: 75–79	.487
1944	St. L. Browns	1943: 72–80	.474
1946	Bost. Red Sox	1945: 71–83	.461
1965	Minn. Twins	1964: 79–83	.488
1967	Bost. Red Sox	1966: 72–90	.444
1987	Minn. Twins*	1986: 71–91	.438
1991	Minn. Twins*	1990: 74–88	.457
2002	Ana. Angels*	2001: 75–87	.463
2008	T.B. Rays	2007: 66–96	.407

National League

Won Pennant	Losing Record	%
1914 ....Bost. Braves*	1913: 69–82......................	.457
1915 ....Phila. Phillies	1914: 74–80......................	.481
1918 ....Chi. Cubs	1917: 74–80......................	.481
1920 ....Bkly. Dodgers.......................	1919: 69–71......................	.493
1933 .....................................N.Y. Giants*	1932: 72–82......................	.468
1945 ....Chi. Cubs	1944: 75–79......................	.487
1954 .....................................N.Y. Giants*	1953: 70–84......................	.455
1959 .....................................L.A. Dodgers*	1958: 71–83......................	.461
1961 ....Cin. Reds	1960: 67–87......................	.435
1965 .....................................L.A. Dodgers*	1964: 80–82......................	.494
1969 .... N.Y. Mets*...........................	1968: 73–89......................	.451
1972 ....Cin. Reds	1971: 77–83......................	.488
1987 ....St. L. Cardinals	1986: 76–82......................	.491
1988 .....................................L.A. Dodgers*	1987: 73–89......................	.451
1990 ....Cin. Reds*	1989: 75–87......................	.463
1991 ....Atl. Braves...........................	1990: 65–97......................	.401
1993 ....Phila. Phillies	1992: 70–92......................	.432
1997 ....Flor. Marlins*........................	1996: 80–82......................	.494
1998 .....................................S.D. Padres	1997: 76–86......................	.469
2003 ....Flor. Marlins*........................	2002: 79–83......................	.488
2007 ....Colo. Rockies	2006: 76–86......................	.469

*World Series winner.

Teams Winning 100 Games in a Season, 3 Years in a Row

American League		National League	
1929–1931 Phila. Athletics	1929: 104 wins	1942–1944 St. L. Cardinals........................	1942: 106 wins
	1930: 102 wins		1943: 106 wins
	1931: 107 wins		1944: 105 wins
1969–1971 Balt. Orioles	1969: 109 wins	1997–1999 Atl. Braves	1997: 101 wins
	1970: 108 wins		1998: 106 wins
	1971: 101 wins		1999: 103 wins
2002–2004 N.Y. Yankees	2002: 103 wins		
	2003: 101 wins		
	2004: 101 wins		

Largest Increase in Games Won by Team Next Season

American League	National League (Post-1900)
Wins	**Wins**
+34.....Cleve. Indians, 1995 (100 wins vs. 66 wins in 1994)*	+36...........N.Y. Giants, 1903 (84 wins vs. 48 wins in 1902)
+33 .....Bost. Red Sox, 1946 (104 wins vs. 71 wins in 1945)	+35......Ariz. D'backs, 1999 (100 wins vs. 65 wins in 1998)
+33.........Balt. Orioles, 1989 (87 wins vs. 54 wins in 1988)	+34.........Phila. Phillies, 1962 (81 wins vs. 47 wins in 1961)
+32.......Bost. Red Sox, 1995 (86 wins vs. 54 wins in 1994)*	+33 ....Bost. Braves, 1936 (71 wins vs. 38 wins in 1935)
+31 ....Cal. Angels, 1995 (78 wins vs. 47 wins in 1994)*	+32....St. L. Cardinals, 1904 (75 wins vs. 43 wins in 1903)
+31 .....Chi. White Sox, 1919 (88 wins vs. 57 wins in 1918)*	+31.........Phila. Phillies, 1905 (83 wins vs. 52 wins in 1904)
+31 ..............T.B. Rays, 2008 (97 wins vs. 66 wins in 2007)	+31 ..........S.F. Giants, 1993 (103 wins vs. 72 wins in 1992)
+30..........Det. Tigers, 1961 (101 wins vs. 71 wins in 1960)	+30......St. L. Cardinals, 1914 (81 wins vs. 51 wins in 1913)
+30.......Bost. Red Sox, 1967 (92 wins vs. 72 wins in 1966)	
+30.......Sea. Mariners, 1995 (79 wins vs. 49 wins in 1994)*	
+29 ....Det. Tigers, 2004 (72 wins vs. 43 wins in 2003)	

*1994 was a strike-shortened season; 1918 was shortened by WWI.

Largest Decrease in Games Won Next Season

American League

Wins

-56 ....Phila. A's, 1915 (43 wins vs. 99 wins in 1914)

-47 .........K.C. Royals, 1981 (50 wins vs. 97 wins in 1980)*

-44 .....N.Y. Yankees, 1981 (59 wins vs. 103 wins in 1980)*

-43 ..Chi. White Sox, 1918 (57 wins vs. 100 wins in 1917)

-41 ......Balt. Orioles, 1981 (59 wins vs. 100 wins in 1980)*

-40 ....Tor. Blue Jays, 1994 (55 wins vs. 95 wins in 1993)*

-36 ....Minn. Twins, 1981 (41 wins vs. 77 wins in 1980)*

-35 ....Cleve. Naps, 1914 (51 wins vs. 86 wins in 1913)

-34 ....Tex. Rangers, 1994 (52 wins vs. 86 wins in 1993)*

-34 ....Chi. White Sox, 1921 (62 wins vs. 96 wins in 1920)

-33 ...Wash. Senators, 1934 (66 wins vs. 99 wins in 1933)

-33 ......Sea. Mariners, 1994 (49 wins vs. 82 wins in 1993)*

-32 ....Det. Tigers, 1994 (53 wins vs. 85 wins in 1993)*

*1981 and 1994 were strike-shortened seasons; 1918 was shortened by WWI.

National League

Wins

-48 .......S.F. Giants, 1994 (55 wins vs. 103 wins in 1993)*

-43 ......Phila. Phillies, 1994 (54 wins vs. 97 wins in 1993)*

-40 ....Bost. Braves, 1935 (38 wins vs. 78 wins in 1934)

-38 ....Flor. Marlins, 1998 (54 wins vs. 92 wins in 1997)

-37 ....Pitt. Pirates, 1981 (46 wins vs. 83 wins in 1980)*

-36 ......Atl. Braves, 1994 (68 wins vs. 104 wins in 1993)*

-35 ....Chi. Cubs, 1994 (49 wins vs. 84 wins in 1993)*

-34 ...St. L. Cardinals, 1994 (53 wins vs. 87 wins in 1993)*

-33 .....Ariz. D'backs, 2004 (51 wins vs. 84 wins in 2003)

-32 .....Phila. Phillies, 1918 (55 wins vs. 87 wins in 1917)

-32 .....Hous. Astros, 1981 (61 wins vs. 93 wins in 1980)*

-32 .....Phila. Phillies, 1981 (59 wins vs. 91 wins in 1980)*

-32 ........S.D. Padres, 1981 (41 wins vs. 73 wins in 1980)*

Teams with Worst Won-Lost Percentage

American League

	Wins–Losses	Percentage
Phila. A's, 1916	36–117	.235
Wash. Senators, 1904	38–113	.252
Phila. A's, 1919	36–104	.257
Det. Tigers, 2003	43–119	.265
Wash. Senators, 1909	42–110	.276
Bost. Red Sox, 1932	43–111	.279
St. L. Browns, 1939	43–111	.279
Phila. A's, 1915	43–109	.283
St. L. Browns, 1911	45–107	.296
St. L. Browns, 1937	46–108	.299

National League (Post-1900)

	Wins–Losses	Percentage
Bost. Braves, 1935	38–115	.248
N.Y. Mets, 1962	40–120	.250
Pitt. Pirates, 1952	42–112	.273
Phila. Phillies, 1942	42–109	.278
Phila. Phillies, 1941	43–111	.279
Phila. Phillies, 1928	43–109	.283
Bost. Rustlers, 1911	44–107	.291
Bost. Rustlers, 1909	45–108	.294
Phila. Phillies, 1939	45–106	.298
Phila. Phillies, 1945	46–108	.299
Phila. Phillies, 1938	45–105	.300

Teams Hitting .300

American League

St. L. Browns, 1920	.308
Cleve. Indians, 1920	.303
Det. Tigers, 1921	.316
Cleve. Indians, 1921	.308
St. L. Browns, 1921	.304
N.Y. Yankees, 1921	.300
St. L. Browns, 1922	.313
Det. Tigers, 1922	.305
Cleve. Indians, 1923	.301
Det. Tigers, 1923	.300
Phila. A's, 1925	.307
Wash. Senators, 1925	.303
Det. Tigers, 1925	.302
N.Y. Yankees, 1927	.307
Phila. A's, 1927	.303
N.Y. Yankees, 1930	.309
Cleve. Indians, 1930	.304
Wash. Senators, 1930	.302
Det. Tigers, 1934	.300
Cleve. Indians, 1936	.304
Det. Tigers, 1936	.300
N.Y. Yankees, 1936	.300
Bost. Red Sox, 1950	.302

National League (Post-1900)

St. L. Cardinals, 1921	.308
Pitt. Pirates, 1922	.308
N.Y. Giants, 1922	.305
St. L. Cardinals, 1922	.301
N.Y. Giants, 1924	.300
Pitt. Pirates, 1925	.307
Pitt. Pirates, 1927	.305
Pitt. Pirates, 1928	.309
Phila. Phillies, 1929	.309
Chi. Cubs, 1929	.303
Pitt. Pirates, 1929	.303
N.Y. Giants, 1930	.319
Phila. Phillies, 1930	.315
St. L. Cardinals, 1930	.314
Chi. Cubs, 1930	.309
Bklyn. Dodgers, 1930	.304
Pitt. Pirates, 1930	.303

Teams with Three 20-Game Winners

American League

Bost. Americans, 1903	Cy Young (28), Bill Dineen (21), Long Tom Hughes (20)
Bost. Americans, 1904	Cy Young (27), Bill Dineen (23), Jesse Tannehill (21)
Cleve. Indians, 1906	Otto Hess (22), Addie Joss (21), Bob Rhoads (21)
Chi. White Sox, 1907	Doc White (27), Ed Walsh (25), Frank Smith (23)
Det. Tigers, 1907	Bill Donovan (25), Ed Killian (25), George Mullin (20)
Chi. White Sox, 1920*	Red Faber (23), Lefty Williams (22), Eddie Cicotte (21), Dickie Kerr (21)
Cleve. Indians, 1920	Jim Bagby Sr. (31), Stan Coveleski (24), Ray Caldwell (20)
Phila. A's, 1931	Lefty Grove (31), George Earnshaw (21), Rube Walberg (20)
Cleve. Indians, 1951	Bob Feller (22), Mike Garcia (20), Early Wynn (20)
Cleve. Indians, 1952	Early Wynn (23), Mike Garcia (22), Bob Lemon (22)
Cleve. Indians, 1956	Bob Lemon (20), Herb Score (20), Early Wynn (20)
Balt. Orioles, 1970	Mike Cuellar (24), Dave McNally (24), Jim Palmer (20)
Balt. Orioles, 1971*	Dave McNally (21), Mike Cuellar (20), Pat Dobson (20), Jim Palmer (20)
Oak. A's, 1973	Ken Holtzman (21), Catfish Hunter (21), Vida Blue (20)

continued on next page

National League

Pitt. Pirates, 1902 ....Jack Chesbro (28), Deacon Phillippe (20), Jesse Tannehill (20)

Chi. Cubs, 1903...Jack Taylor (21), Jake Weimer (21), Bob Wicker (20)**

N.Y. Giants, 1904...Joe McGinnity (35), Christy Mathewson (33), Dummy Taylor (21)

N.Y. Giants, 1905..Christy Mathewson (31), Red Ames (22), Joe McGinnity (21)

Chi. Cubs, 1906 ....Three Finger Brown (26), Ed Reulbach (20), Jack Taylor (20)***

N.Y. Giants, 1913 ....Christy Mathewson (25), Rube Marquard (23), Jeff Tesreau (22)

N.Y. Giants, 1920 ....Art Nehf (21), Fred Toney (21), Jesse Barnes (20)

Cin. Reds, 1923 ....Dolf Luque (27), Pete Donohue (21), Eppa Rixey (20)

*Four 20-game winners on staff.
**Wicker started 1903 season with St. L. Cardinals (1 game, 0–0).
***Taylor started 1906 season with St. L. Cardinals (17 games, 8–9).

Teams with 30-Game Winners, Not Winning Pennant

American League

Team	Pitcher	Finish
Bost. Americans, 1901	Cy Young (33)	2nd, 4 games behind Chi. White Sox
Bost. Americans, 1902	Cy Young (32)	3rd, 6½ games behind Phila. A's
N.Y. Highlanders, 1904	Jack Chesbro (41)	2nd, 1½ games behind Bost. Red Sox
Chi. White Sox, 1908	Ed Walsh (40)	3rd, 1½ games behind Det. Tigers
Wash. Senators, 1912	Walter Johnson (32)	2nd, 14 games behind Bost. Red Sox
Wash. Senators, 1913	Walter Johnson (36)	2nd, 6½ games behind Phila. A'sA's

National League

Team	Pitcher	Finish
N.Y. Giants, 1903	Joe McGinnity (31), Christy Mathewson (30)	2nd, 6½ games behind Pitt. Pirates
N.Y. Giants, 1908	Christy Mathewson (37)	2nd, 1 game behind Chi. Cubs
Phila. Phillies, 1916	Grover C. Alexander (33)	2nd, 2½ games behind Bklyn. Dodgers
Phila. Phillies, 1917	Grover C. Alexander (30)	2nd, 10 games behind N.Y. Giants

Teams Leading or Tied for First Place Entire Season

American League

1927	N.Y. Yankees (Record: 110–44)
1984	Det. Tigers (Record: 104–58)
1997	Balt.Orioles (Record: 98–64)
1998	Cleve. Indians (Record: 89–73)
2001	Sea. Mariners (Record: 116–46)

National League

1923	N.Y. Giants (Record: 95–58)
1955	Bklyn. Dodgers (Record: 98–55)
1990	Cin. Reds (Record: 91–71)
2003	S.F. Giants (Record: 100–61)

Teams Scoring in Every Inning

American League

Bost. Red Sox vs. Cleve. Indians, Sept. 16, 1903 ....Cleve. Indians ....0 4 3 0 0 0 0 0 0 – 7
      Bost. Red Sox.................2 2 3 1 1 3 1 1 X – 14

Cleve. Indians vs. Bost. Red Sox, July 7, 1923 (First Game) ....Bost. Red Sox.................0 0 0 2 0 0 0 0 1 – 3
      Cleve. Indians ....3 2 3 1 2(13)1 2 X – 27

N.Y. Yankees vs. St. L. Browns, July 26, 1939...St. L. Browns ....0 0 0 0 0 0 0 1 0 – 1
      N.Y. Yankees.................2 1 1 4 1 3 1 1 X – 14

Chi. White Sox vs. Bost. Red Sox, May 11, 1949 ....Bost. Red Sox.................0 0 0 5 0 1 0 2 0 – 8
      Chi. White Sox...............1 1 2 1 2 1 1 3 X – 12

K.C. Royals vs. Oak. A's, Sept. 14, 1998 .... Oak. A's 100050000–6
K.C. Royals 11311324X–16
N.Y. Yankees vs. Tor. Blue Jays, Apr. 29, 2006 .... Tor. Blue Jays 203010000–6
N.Y. Yankees..................41223131X–17

National League (Post-1900)

N.Y. Giants vs. Phila. Phillies, June 1, 1923 .... N.Y. Giants 421155121–22
Phila. Phillies..................140110010–8
St. L. Cardinals vs. Chi. Cubs, Sept. 13, 1964 .... St. L. Cardinals..............212221311–15
Chi. Cubs 100001000–2
Col. Rockies vs. Chi. Cubs, May 5, 1999 .... Col. Rockies 111121222–13
Chi. Cubs 023000010–6

Most Lopsided Shutouts

American League	National League
22–0 ....Cleve. Indians over N.Y. Yankees, Aug. 31, 2004	22–0 ....Pitt. Pirates over Chi. Cubs, Sept. 16, 1975
21–0.............Det. Tigers over Cleve. Indians, Sept. 15, 1901	20–0............Milw. Brewers over Pitt. Pirates, Apr. 22, 2010
21–0 ........N.Y. Yankees over Phila. Athletics, Aug. 13, 1939	

Players with Both Little League and Major League World Series Teams

Boog Powell	1954 (Lakeland, Florida)	1966 World Series
Jim Barbieri	1954 (Schenectady, New York)	1966 World Series
Rick Wise	1958 (Portland, Oregon)	1988 World Series
		1975 World Series
Carney Lansford	1969 (Santa Clara, California)	1990 World Series
Ed Vosberg	1973 (Tucson, Arizona)	1997 World Series
Charlie Hayes	1977 (Hattiesburg, Mississippi)	1996 World Series
Dwight Gooden	1979 (Tampa, Florida)	1986 World Series
	1980 (Tampa, Florida)	
Derek Bell	1981 (Tampa, Florida)	1992 World Series
Gary Sheffield	1980 (Tampa, Florida)	1997 World Series
Jason Marquis	1991 (Staten Island, New York)	2004 World Series
Jason Varitek	1984 (Altamonte Springs, Florida)	2004 World Series
		2007 World Series

Olympians (in Sports Other Than Baseball) Who Played Major League Baseball

Ed "Cotton" Minahan, pitcher, Cin. Reds (NL), 1907	Track and field, Paris, 1900
Al Spalding, pitcher, Chi. Cubs (NL), 1876–78	Shooting, Paris, 1900
Jim Thorpe, outfield, N.Y. Giants (NL), 1913–15 and 1917–18; Cin. Reds (NL), 1917; Bost. Braves (NL), 1919	Decathlon, Stockholm, 1912

Babe Ruth's Yearly Salary

Bost. Red Sox (AL), 1914	$1,900	N.Y. Yankees (AL), 1926	$52,000
Bost. Red Sox (AL), 1915	$3,500	N.Y. Yankees (AL), 1927	$70,000
Bost. Red Sox (AL), 1916	$3,500	N.Y. Yankees (AL), 1928	$70,000
Bost. Red Sox (AL), 1917	$5,000	N.Y. Yankees (AL), 1929	$70,000
Bost. Red Sox (AL), 1918	$7,000	N.Y. Yankees (AL), 1930	$80,000
Bost. Red Sox (AL), 1919	$10,000	N.Y. Yankees (AL), 1931	$80,000
N.Y. Yankees (AL), 1920	$20,000	N.Y. Yankees (AL), 1932	$75,000
N.Y. Yankees (AL), 1921	$30,000	N.Y. Yankees (AL), 1933	$17,000
N.Y. Yankees (AL), 1922	$52,000	N.Y. Yankees (AL), 1934	$37,500
N.Y. Yankees (AL), 1923	$52,000	Bost. Braves (NL), 1935	$25,000
N.Y. Yankees (AL), 1924	$52,000	22 Seasons Total	$900,400
N.Y. Yankees (AL), 1925	$52,000		

Players Leading N.Y. Yankees in Home Runs One Season, Playing Elsewhere Next Season

Danny Hoffman, 1907 .... 4 .... Traded to St. L. Browns (AL) with Jimmy Williams and Hobe Ferris for Fred Glade and Charlie Hemphill

Guy Zinn, 1912 .... 6 .... Sold to Bost. Braves (NL) for cash

Joe Pepitone, 1969 .... 27 .... Traded to Hous. Astros (NL) for Curt Blefary

Bobby Bonds, 1975 .... 32 .... Traded to Cal. Angels (AL) for Mickey Rivers and Ed Figueroa

Jack Clark, 1988 .... 27 .... Traded to S.D. Padres (NL) for Jimmy Jones, Lance McCullers, and Stan Jefferson

Tino Martinez, 2001 .... 34 .... Filed for free agency, signed with St. L. Cardinals (NL)

Billy Martin's Fights

May 1952 .... vs. Jimmy Piersall, Bost. Red Sox (AL)

July 14, 1952 .... vs. Clint Courtney, St. L. Browns (AL)

Apr. 30, 1953 .... vs. Clint Courtney, St. L. Browns (AL)

July 1953 .... vs. Matt Batts, Det. Tigers (AL)

May 16, 1957 .... with Hank Bauer, Whitey Ford, Yogi Berra, Mickey Mantle, and Johnny Kucks vs. patron at Copacabana nightclub, New York City

Aug. 4, 1960 .... vs. Jim Brewer, Chi. Cubs (NL)

July 12, 1966 .... vs. Howard Fox, traveling secretary, Minn. Twins (AL)

Aug. 6, 1969 .... vs. Jim Boswell, Minn. Twins (AL)

Apr. 20, 1972 .... vs. Det. Tigers (AL) fan

Mar. 8, 1973 .... vs. Lakeland, Florida, policeman

May 30, 1974 .... vs. Cleve. Indians (AL) team

Sept. 26, 1974 .... vs. Burt Hawkins, traveling secretary, Tex. Rangers (AL)

June 18, 1977 .... vs. Reggie Jackson, N.Y. Yankees (AL)

Nov. 10, 1978 .... vs. Ray Hagar, sportswriter, in Reno, Nevada

Oct. 25, 1979 .... vs. Joseph Cooper, marshmallow salesman, Minneapolis, Minnesota

May 25, 1983 .... vs. Robin Wayne Olson, nightclub patron, in Anaheim, California

Sept. 20, 1985 .... vs. patron at Cross Keys Inn, Baltimore, Maryland

Sept. 21, 1985 .... vs. Ed Whitson, N.Y. Yankees (AL), in Cross Keys Inn, Baltimore, Maryland

May 6, 1988 .... vs. unidentified assailant(s) in bathroom, Lace Nightclub, Arlington, Texas

Four-Decade Players

1870s–1900s

Dan Brouthers, first base (1879–96, 1904) Orator Jim O'Rourke, outfield (1876–93, 1904)

1880s–1910s

Kid Gleason, pitcher and second base (1888–1908, 1912) Jack O'Connor, catcher (1887–1904, 1906–07, 1910)

Deacon McGuire, catcher (1884–88, 1890–1908, 1910, 1912, 1912–13) John Ryan, catcher (1889–91, 1894–96, 1898–1903,

1890s–1920s

Nick Altrock, pitcher (1898, 1902–09, 1912–15, 1918–19, 1924, 1929, 1931, 1933)*

1900s–30s

Eddie Collins, second base (1906–30) John P. Quinn, pitcher (1909–15, 1918–33)

1910s–40s

[No player]

1920s–50s

Bobo Newsom, pitcher (1929–30, 1932, 1934–48, 1952–53)

1930s–60s

Elmer Valo, outfield (1939–43, 1946–61)**
Mickey Vernon, first base (1939–43, 1946–60)

Ted Williams, outfield (1939–42, 1946–60)
Early Wynn, pitcher (1939, 1941–44, 1946–63)

1940s–70s

Minnie Minoso, outfield (1949, 1951–64, 1976, 1980)*

1950s–80s

Jim Kaat, pitcher (1959–83)
Tim McCarver, catcher (1959–61, 1963–80)

Willie McCovey, first base (1959–80)

1960s–90s

Bill Buckner, outfield and first base (1969–90)
Rick Dempsey, catcher (1969–92)
Carlton Fisk, catcher (1969, 1971–90)

Jerry Reuss, pitcher (1969–90)
Nolan Ryan, pitcher (1966, 1968–93)

1970s–2000s

Rickey Henderson, outfield (1979–2003)
Mike Morgan, pitcher (1979, 1982–83, 1985–2002)

Jesse Orosco, pitcher (1979, 1981–2003)
Tim Raines, outfield (1979–99, 2001–02)

*Played five decades.
**Played in last game of 1939 season for Phila. A's (AL) but manager Connie Mack kept his name off the official line-up card.

1980s–2010s

Ken Griffey Jr., outfield (1989–2010)
Jamie Moyer, pitcher (1986–)

Omar Vizquel, shortstop (1989–)

First Players Chosen in Draft by Expansion Teams

American League	National League
K.C. Royals....................................Roger Nelson, pitcher	Ariz. D'backs....................................Brian Anderson, pitcher
L.A. Angels...Eli Grba, pitcher	Colo. Rockies..David Nied, pitcher
Sea. Pilots.................................Marv Staehle, second base	Flor. Marlins.......................................Nigel Wilson, outfield
Sea. Mariners..........................Dave Johnson, second base	Hous. Colt .45s................................Ed Bressoud, shortstop
T.B. Devil Rays...................................Tony Saunders, pitcher	Mont. Expos.......................................Manny Mota, outfield
Tor. Blue Jays.....................................Phil Roof, catcher	N.Y. Mets...Hobie Landrith, catcher
Wash. Senators II.................................John Gabler, pitcher	S.D. Padres..Ollie Brown, outfield

Last Active Player Once Playing for . . .

Casey Stengel...Tug McGraw (played for Stengel in 1965; active until 1984)	
Bklyn. Dodgers (NL)...Bob Aspromonte (played for Bklyn. Dodgers in 1956; active until 1971)	
N.Y. Giants (NL)...Willie Mays (played for N.Y. Giants in 1957; active until 1973)	
Bost. Braves (NL)..Eddie Mathews (played for Bost. Braves in 1952; active until 1968)	
Phila. A's (AL)..Vic Power (played for Phila. A's in 1954; active until 1965)	
St. L. Browns (AL)..Don Larsen (played for St. L. Browns in 1953; active until 1967)	
Milw. Braves (NL)...Phil Niekro (played for Milw. Braves in 1965; active until 1987)	
K.C. A's (AL)...Reggie Jackson (played for K.C. A's in 1967; active until 1987)	
Hous. Colt .45s (NL)..Rusty Staub (played for Hous. Astros in 1964; active until 1985)	
L.A. Angels (AL)...Jim Fregosi (played for L.A. Angels in 1964; active until 1978)	
Sea. Pilots (AL)...Fred Stanley (played for Sea. Pilots in 1969; active until 1982)	
Original Wash. Senators (AL)..Jim Kaat (played for Wash. Senators in 1960; active until 1983)	
Expansion Wash. Senators (AL)......................................Toby Harrah (played for Wash. Senators II in 1971; active until 1986)	

Last Players Born in Nineteenth Century to Play in Majors

American League

Fred Johnson, pitcher (b. Mar. 5, 1894) ....Played in 1939 with St. L. Browns

Jimmy Dykes, third base (b. Nov. 10, 1896)...Played in 1939 with Chi. White Sox

National League

Hod Lisenbee, pitcher (b. Sept. 23, 1898) ....Played in 1945 with Cin. Reds

Charlie Root, pitcher (b. Mar. 17, 1899)..Played in 1941 with Chi. Cubs

First Players Born in Twentieth Century to Play in Majors

American League

Ed Corey, pitcher (b. July 13, 1900)..Played in 1918 with Chi. White Sox

National League

John Cavanaugh, third base (b. June 5, 1900) ....Played in 1919 with Phila. Phillies

Second African American to Play for Each of
16 Original Major League Teams

American League

	Second African American	First African American
Bost. Red Sox	Earl Wilson, pitcher, 1959	Pumpsie Green, infield, 1959
Chi. White Sox	Sammy Hairston, catcher, 1951	Minnie Minoso, outfield, 1951
Cleve. Indians	Satchel Paige, pitcher, 1948	Larry Doby, outfield, 1947
Det. Tigers	Larry Doby, outfield, 1959	Ozzie Virgil, third base, 1958
N.Y. Yankees	Harry "Suitcase" Simpson, outfield, 1957	Elston Howard, catcher, 1955
Phila. A's	Vic Power, outfield and first base, 1954	Bob Trice, pitcher, 1953
St. L. Browns	Willard Brown, outfield, 1947	Hank Thompson, second base, 1947
Wash. Senators	Joe Black, pitcher, 1957	Carlos Paula, outfield, 1954

National League

	Second African American	First African American
Bost. Braves	Luis Marquez, outfield, 1951	Sam Jethroe, outfield, 1950
Bklyn. Dodgers	Dan Bankhead, pitcher, 1947	Jackie Robinson, first base, 1947
Chi. Cubs	Gene Baker, second base, 1953	Ernie Banks, shortstop, 1953
Cin. Reds	Chuck Harmon, infield, 1954	Nino Escalera, outfield, 1954
N.Y. Giants	Monte Irvin, outfield, 1949	Hank Thompson, second base, 1949
Phila. Phillies	Chuck Harmon, infield, 1957	John Kennedy, third base, 1957
Pitt. Pirates	Sam Jethroe, outfield, 1954	Curt Roberts, second base, 1954
St. L. Cardinals	Brooks Lawrence, pitcher, 1954	Tom Alston, first base, 1954

Players Having Same Number Retired on Two Different Clubs

Hank Aaron ....Atl. Braves (NL) and Milw. Brewers (AL)...44

Rod Carew...Cal. Angels (AL) and Minn. Twins (AL)..29

Rollie Fingers...Milw. Brewers (NL) and Oak. A's (AL)...34

Casey Stengel..N.Y. Mets (NL) and N.Y. Yankees (AL) 37

Major Leaguers Who Played Pro Football in Same Year(s)

	Baseball Team	Year(s)	Football Team
Red Badgro, outfield	St. L. Browns (AL)	1929–30	N.Y. Giants
Charlie Berry, catcher	Phila. A's (AL)	1925	Pottsville (PA) Maroons
Joe Berry, second base	N.Y. Giants (NL)	1921	Rochester (NY) Jeffs
Garland Buckeye, pitcher	Cleve. Indians (AL)	1926	Chi. Bulls
Bruce Caldwell, outfield	Cleve. Indians (AL)	1928	N.Y. Giants
Chuck Corgan, infield	Bklyn. Dodgers (NL)	1925	K.C. Cowboys
	Bklyn. Dodgers (NL)	1927	N.Y. Giants
Steve Filipowicz, outfield	N.Y. Giants (NL)	1945	N.Y. Giants
	Cin. Reds (NL)	1946	N.Y. Giants
Walter French, outfield	Phila. A's (AL)	1925	Pottsville (PA) Maroons
George Halas, outfield	N.Y. Yankees (AL)	1919	Decatur (IL) Staleys
Bo Jackson, outfield	K.C. Royals (AL)	1987–90	L.A. Raiders
Vic Janowicz, catcher	Pitt. Pirates (NL)	1954	Wash. Redskins
Bert Kuczynski, pitcher	Phila. A's (AL)	1943	Det. Lions
Pete Layden, outfield	St. L. Browns (AL)	1948	N.Y. Yankees
Christy Mathewson, pitcher	N.Y. Giants (NL)	1902	Pitt. Pros
John Mohardt, second base	Det. Tigers (AL)	1922	Chi. Cardinals
Ernie Nevers, pitcher	St. L. Browns (AL)	1926–27	Duluth Eskimos
Ace Parker, shortstop	Phila. A's (AL)	1937–38	Bklyn. Dodgers
Al Pierotti, pitcher	Bost. Braves (NL)	1920	Cleve. Tigers
	Bost. Braves (NL)	1921	N.Y. Giants
Pid Purdy, outfield	Cin. Reds (NL), Chi. White Sox (AL)	1926–27	G.B. Packers
Dick Reichle, outfield	Bost. Red Sox (AL)	1923	Milw. Badgers
Deion Sanders, outfield	N.Y. Yankees (AL)	1989–90	Atl. Falcons
	Atl. Braves (NL)	1991–94	Atl. Falcons (until 1993)
	Cin. Reds (NL)	1994–95, 1997	S.F. 49ers (1994)
	S.F. Giants (NL)	1995	Dallas Cowboys
John Scalzi, outfield	Bost. Braves (NL)	1931	Bklyn. Dodgers
Red Smith, catcher	N.Y. Giants (NL)	1927	G.B. Packers
Jim Thorpe, outfield	N.Y. Giants (NL)	1915, 1917	Canton Bulldogs
	Cin. Reds (NL)	1917	Canton Bulldogs
	Bost. Braves (NL)	1919	Canton Bulldogs
Ernie Vick, catcher	St. L. Cardinals (NL)	1925	Det. Panthers
Rube Waddell, pitcher	Phila. A's (AL)	1902	Pitt. Pros
Tom Whelan, first base	Bost. Braves (NL)	1920	Canton Bulldogs

Performances by Oldest Players

Pitched	Satchel Paige, K.C. A's (AL), Sept. 25, 1965	59 years, 2 months
Batted (0-for-1)	Satchel Paige, K.C. A's (AL), Sept. 25, 1965	59 years, 2 months
Caught	Orator Jim O'Rourke, N.Y. Giants (NL), Sept. 20, 1904	52 years, 1 month
At Bat	Nick Altrock, Wash. Senators (AL), Sept. 30, 1933	57 years, 0 months
Base Hit	Minnie Minoso, Chi. White Sox (AL), Sept. 12, 1976	53 years, 9 months
Double	Julio Franco, Atl. Braves (NL), July 27, 2007	48 years, 11 months
Triple	Nick Altrock, Wash. Senators (AL), Sept. 30, 1924	48 years, 0 months
Home Run	Julio Franco, N.Y. Mets (NL), May 4, 2007	48 years, 9 months
Grand Slam Home Run	Julio Franco, Atl. Braves (NL), June 3, 2004	45 years, 10 months
Run Scored	Charlie O'Leary, St. L. Browns (AL), Sept. 30, 1934	52 years, 11 months
RBI	John P. Quinn, Bklyn. Dodgers (NL), June 7, 1932	47 years, 11 months
Stolen Base	Arlie Latham, N.Y. Giants (NL), Aug. 18, 1909	50 years, 5 months

continued on next page

100 Games, Season ....Cap Anson, Chi. Colts (NL), 1897 ....45 years, 0 months
Game Won, Relief..............................John P. Quinn, Bklyn. Dodgers (NL), Aug. 14, 1932....................48 years, 1 month
Game Lost, Relief ....Hoyt Wilhelm, L.A. Dodgers (NL), June 24, 1972 ....48 years, 11 months
Complete Game ....Phil Niekro, N.Y. Yankees (AL), Oct. 6, 1985................................46 years, 6 months
Shutout..Phil Niekro, N.Y. Yankees (AL), Oct. 6, 1985................................46 years, 6 months
No-Hitter..Cy Young, Bost. Red Sox (AL), June 30, 1908 ....41 years, 3 months
Perfect Game ....Randy Johnson, Ariz. D'backs (NL), May 18, 2004 ....39 years, 8 months

Oldest Players, by Position

First Base ....Julio Franco, Atl. Braves (NL), 2007 48
Second Base ....Arlie Latham, N.Y. Giants (NL), 1909 49
Third Base ....Jimmy Austin, St. L. Browns (AL), 1929 49
Shortstop..Bobby Wallace, St. L. Cardinals (NL), 1918.......................................44
Outfield..Sam Thompson, Det. Tigers (AL), 1906...46
Catcher..Orator Jim O'Rourke, N.Y. Giants (NL), 1904....................................52
Pitcher..Satchel Paige, K.C. A's (AL), 1965...59
Designated Hitter............................Minnie Minoso, Chi. White Sox (AL), 1976 53
Pinch Hitter....................................Nick Altrock, Wash. Senators (AL), 1933 57

Youngest Players to Play in Majors

Fred Chapman, pitcher, Phila. Athletics (AA), July 22, 1887 ....14 years, 8 months
Joe Nuxhall, pitcher, Cin. Reds (NL), June 10, 1944...15 years, 10 months
Willie McGill, pitcher, Cleve. (P), May 8, 1890...16 years, 6 months
Joe Stanley, outfield, Balt. (U), Sept. 11, 1897..16 years, 6 months
Carl Scheib, pitcher, Phila. A's (AL), Sept. 6, 1943...16 years, 8 months
Tommy Brown, shortstop, Bklyn. Dodgers (NL) Aug. 3, 1944...............................16 years, 8 months
Milton Scott, first base, Chi. Cubs (NL), Sept. 30, 1882......................................16 years, 9 months
Putsy Caballero, third base, Phila. Phillies (NL), Sept. 14, 1944 ....16 years, 10 months
Jim Derrington, pitcher, Chi. White Sox (AL), Sept. 30, 1956 ....16 years, 10 months
Rogers McKee, pitcher, Phila. Phillies (NL), Aug. 18, 1943.................................16 years, 11 months
Alex George, shortstop, K.C. A's (AL), Sept. 16, 1955..16 years, 11 months
Merito Acosta, outfield, Wash. Senators (AL), June 5, 1913 ....17 years, 0 months

Youngest Players, by Position

First Base ....Milton Scott, Chi. Cubs (NL), 1882 16
Second Base ....Ted Sepkowski, Cleve. Indians (AL), 1942...18
Third Base ....Putsy Caballero, Phila. Phillies (NL), 1944 16
Shortstop..Tommy Brown, Bklyn. Dodgers (NL), 1944..16
Outfield..Merito Acosta, Wash. Senators (AL), 1913 17
....................................Mel Ott, N.Y. Giants (NL), 1926...17
....................................Willie Crawford, L.A. Dodgers (NL), 1964...17
Catcher..Jimmie Foxx, Phila. A's (AL), 1925...17
Right-Handed Pitcher......................Fred Chapman, Phila. Athletics (AA), 1887 14
Left-Handed Pitcher ....Joe Nuxhall, Cin. Reds (NL), 1944..15

Players Who Played During Most Presidential Administrations

Cap Anson (1876–97) ....8 ....Ulysses S. Grant (1876–77)
Rutherford B. Hayes (1887–81)
James A. Garfield (1881)
Chester A. Arthur (1881–85)
Grover Cleveland (1885–89)
Benjamin Harrison (1889–93)
Grover Cleveland (1893–97)
William McKinley (1897)
Orator Jim O'Rourke (1876–93, 1904) ....8 ....Ulysses S. Grant (1876–77)
Rutherford B. Hayes (1877–81)
James A. Garfield (1881)
Chester A. Arthur (1881–85)
Grover Cleveland (1885–89)
Benjamin Harrison (1889–93)
Grover Cleveland (1893–97)
Theodore Roosevelt (1904)
Nick Altrock (1898, 1902–09, 1912–15, 1918–19,
1924, 1929, 1931, 1933) ....7 ....William McKinley (1898)
Theodore Roosevelt (1902–09)
William Howard Taft (1909–13)
Woodrow Wilson (1913–19)
Calvin Coolidge (1924)
Herbert Hoover (1929, 1931)
Franklin D. Roosevelt (1933)
Jim Kaat (1959–83) ....7 ....Dwight D. Eisenhower (1959–61)
John F. Kennedy (1961–63)
Lyndon B. Johnson (1963–69)
Richard M. Nixon (1969–75)
Gerald Ford (1975–77)
Jimmy Carter (1977–81)
Ronald Reagan (1981–83)

Players Playing Most Seasons with One Address (One Club, One City in Majors)

23 ....Brooks Robinson, Balt. Orioles (AL), 1955–77
23 ....Carl Yastrzemski, Bost. Red Sox (AL), 1961–83
22 ....Cap Anson, Chi. Cubs (Colts) (NL), 1876–97
22 ....Al Kaline, Det. Tigers (AL), 1953–74
22 ....Stan Musial, St. L. Cardinals (NL), 1941–44 and 1946–63
22 ....Mel Ott, N.Y. Giants (NL), 1926–47
21 ....George Brett, K.C. Royals (AL), 1973–83
21 ....Walter Johnson, Wash. Senators (AL), 1907–27
21 ....Ted Lyons, Chi. White Sox (AL), 1923–42 and 1946
21 ....Cal Ripken Jr., Balt. Orioles (AL), 1981–2001
21 ....Willie Stargell, Pitt. Pirates (NL), 1962–82
20 ....Luke Appling, Chi. White Sox (AL), 1930–43 and 1945–50
20 ....Red Faber, Chi. White Sox (AL), 1914–33
20 ....Tony Gwynn, S.D. Padres (NL), 1982–2001
20 ....Mel Harder, Cleve. Indians (AL), 1928–47
20 ....Alan Trammell, Det. Tigers (AL), 1977–96
20 ....Robin Yount, Milw. Brewers (AL), 1974–93

Players Who Played 2500 Games in One Uniform (Post-1900)

3308...Carl Yastrzemski, Bost. Red Sox (AL), 1961–83
3026...Stan Musial, St. L. Cardinals (NI), 1941–44 and 1946–63
3001...Cal Ripken Jr., Balt. Orioles (AL), 1981–2001
2896...Brooks Robinson, Balt. Orioles (AL), 1955–77
2856...Robin Yount, Milw. Brewers (AL), 1974–93
2834..Al Kaline, Det. Tigers (AL), 1953–74
2732...Mel Ott, N.Y. Giants (NL), 1926–47
2707...George Brett, K.C. Royals (AL), 1973–93
2528...Ernie Banks, Chi. Cubs (NL), 1953–71

Players Playing Most Seasons in City of Birth

22...Phil Cavarretta, Chi. Cubs (NL), 1934–53, and Chi. White Sox (AL), 1954–55
19 ....Pete Rose, Cin. Reds (NL), 1963–78 and 1984–86
19 ....Barry Larkin, Cin. Reds (NL), 1986–2004
18 ....Ed Kranepool, N.Y. Mets (NL), 1962–79
17 ....Lou Gehrig, N.Y. Yankees (AL), 1923–39
16 ....Harry Davis, Phila. A's (AL), 1901–11 and 1913–17
16 ....Whitey Ford, N.Y. Yankees (AL), 1950 and 1953–67

Players with Same Surname as Town of Birth

Loren Bader, pitcher (1912, 1917–18), born in Bader, Illinois
Verne Clemons, catcher (1916, 1919–24), born in Clemons, Iowa
Estel Crabtree, outfield (1929, 1931–33, 1941–44), born in Crabtree, Ohio
Charlie Gassaway, pitcher, (1944–46), born in Gassaway, Tennessee
Elmer "Slim" Love, pitcher, (1913, 1916–20), born in Love, Missouri
Jack Ogden, pitcher, (1918, 1928–29, 1931–32), born in Ogden, Pennsylvania
Curly Ogden, pitcher, (1922–26), born in Ogden, Pennsylvania
Steve Phoenix, pitcher (1984–95), born in Phoenix, Arizona
Happy Townsend, pitcher (1901–06), born in Townsend, Delaware
George Turbeville, pitcher (1935–37), born in Turbeville, South Carolina

Players with Longest Given Names

Alan Mitchell Edward George Patrick Henry Gallagher ("Al"), third base (1970–73)..45 characters
Christian Frederick Albert John Henry David Betzel ("Bruno"), infield (1914–18)..44 characters
Calvin Coolidge Julius Caesar Tuskahoma McLish ("Cal"), pitcher, (1944, 1946–49, 1951, 1956–64).................41 characters

Players with Palindromic Surnames*

Truck Hannah, catcher (1918–20)   Robb Nen, pitcher (1993–2002)
Toby Harrah, infield (1969, 1971–86)   Dave Otto, pitcher (1987–94)
Eddie Kazak, shortstop (1948–52)   Johnny Reder, first base (1932)
Dick Nen, first base (1963, 1965–68, 1970)   Mark Salas, catcher (1984–91)
*Last name spelled the same forward and backward.

Most Common Last Names in Baseball History

Smith	145	Miller	84
Johnson	106	Williams	73
Jones	95	Wilson	70
Brown	85	Davis	66

Number of Major League Players by First Letter of Last Name*

A	498	N	303
B	1685	O	320
C	1376	P	816
D	848	Q	35
E	325	R	936
F	618	S	1711
G	922	T	568
H	1280	U	53
I	52	V	229
J	459	W	488
K	658	X	0
L	804	Y	102
M	1841	Z	84

*From 1871 through 2010.

Third Basemen on Tinker-to-Evers-to-Chance Chicago Cubs Teams*

Doc Casey	1903–05	388 games
Harry Steinfeldt	1906–10	729 games
Heinie Zimmerman	1908, 1910	23 games
Solly Hoffman	1905–08	20 games
Otto Williams	1903–04	7 games
John Kane	1909–10	7 games
Tommy Raub	1903	4 games
George Moriarty	1903–04	3 games
Bobby Lowe	1903	1 game
Broadway Aleck Smith	1904	1 game

*Famed Hall of Fame double-play combination for the Chicago Cubs, 1903–10.

First Designated Hitter for Each Major League Team

American League

Balt. Orioles	Terry Crowley (vs. Milw. Brewers), Apr. 6, 1973	2-for-4
Bost. Red Sox	Orlando Cepeda (vs. N.Y. Yankees), Apr. 6, 1973	0-for-6
Cal. Angels	Tom McCraw (vs. K.C. Royals), Apr. 6, 1973	1-for-4
Chi. White Sox	Mike Andrews (vs. Tex. Rangers), Apr. 7, 1973	1 for 3
Cleve. Indians	John Ellis (vs. Det. Tigers), Apr. 7, 1973	0-for-4
Det. Tigers	Gates Brown (vs. Clev. Indians), Apr. 7, 1973	0-for-4
K.C. Royals	Ed Kirkpatrick (vs. Cal. Angels), Apr. 6, 1973	0-for-3

Milw. Brewers ....Ollie Brown (vs. Balt. Orioles), Apr. 6, 1973 ....0-for-3

Minn. Twins ....Tony Oliva (vs. Oak. A's), Apr. 6, 1973 ....2-for-4

N.Y. Yankees ....Ron Blomberg* (vs. Bost. Red Sox), Apr. 6, 1973..1-for-3

Oak. A's...Bill North (vs. Minn. Twins), Apr. 6, 1973 ....2-for-5

Sea. Mariners ....Dave Collins (vs. Cal. Angels), Apr. 6, 1977 ....0-for-4

T.B. Devil Rays ....Paul Sorrento (vs. Det. Tigers), Mar. 31, 1998 ....1-for-5

Tex. Rangers ....Rico Carty (vs. Chi. White Sox), Apr. 7, 1973 ....1-for-4

Tor. Blue Jays.....................................Otto Velez (vs. Chi. White Sox), Apr. 7, 1977 ....2-for-4

National League

Ariz. D'backs...................................Kelly Stinnett (vs. Oak. A's, AL), June 5, 1998 ....1-for-3

Atl. Braves.......................................Keith Lockhart (vs. Tor. Blue Jays, AL), June 16, 1997 ....0-for-4

Chi. Cubs...Dave Clark (vs. Chi. White Sox, AL), June 16, 1997 ....1-for-4

Cin. Reds...Eddie Taubensee (vs. Cleve. Indians, AL), June 16, 1997 ....0-for-3

Colo. Rockies...................................Dante Bichette (vs. Sea. Mariners, AL), June 12, 1997 ....3-for-5

Flor. Marlins ....Jim Eisenreich (vs. Det. Tigers, AL), June 16, 1997...................................1-for-5

Hous. Astros ....Sean Berry (vs. K.C. Royals, AL), June 16, 1997 ....1-for-4

L.A. Dodgers ....Mike Piazza (vs. Oak. A's, AL), June 12, 1997 ....3-for-4

Mont. Expos ....Jose Vidro (vs. Balt. Orioles, AL), June 16, 1997 ....0-for-4

N.Y. Mets...Butch Huskey (vs. N.Y. Yankees, AL), June 16, 1997...............................2-for-4

Phila. Phillies ....Darren Daulton (vs. Bost. Red Sox, AL), June 16, 1997 ....1-for-5

Pitt. Pirates ....Mark Smith (vs. Minn. Twins, AL), June 16, 1997....................................1-for-4

St. L. Cardinals ....Dmitri Young (vs. Milw. Brewers, AL), June 16, 1997...............................1-for-4

S.D. Padres ....Rickey Henderson (vs. Ana. Angels, AL), June 12, 1997 ....2-for-5

S.F. Giants.......................................Glenallen Hill** (vs. Tex. Rangers, AL), June 12, 1997.............................0-for-3

*First AL designated hitter.

**First NL designated hitter.

Players Killed as Direct Result of Injuries Sustained in Major League Games

Maurice "Doc" Powers, catcher, Phila. A's (AL) ....Died Apr. 26, 1909, after 3 operations for "intestinal problems" after running into railing on Apr. 12, 1909, at Shibe Park inaugural game

Ray Chapman, shortstop, Cleve. Indians (AL)..................Died Aug. 17, 1920, after being hit by pitch thrown by N.Y. Yankees pitcher Carl Mays at the Polo Grounds on Aug. 16, 1920

Players Who Played for Three New York Teams

Dan Brouthers...Troy Trojans (NL), 1879–80

Buff. Bisons (NL), 1881–85

N.Y. Giants (NL), 1904

Jack Doyle ....N.Y. Giants (NL), 1893–95, 1898–1900, and 1902

Bklyn. Dodgers (NL), 1903–04

N.Y. Yankees (AL), 1905

Dude Esterbrook..Buff. Bisons (NL), 1880

N.Y. Metropolitans (AA), 1883–84 and 1887

N.Y. Gothams/Giants (NL), 1885–86 and 1890

Bklyn. Dodgers (NL), 1891

Burleigh Grimes...Bklyn. Dodgers (NL), 1918–26

N.Y. Giants (NL), 1927

N.Y. Yankees (AL), 1934

Benny Kauff ....N.Y. Yankees (AL), 1912

Bklyn. Brook-Feds (FL), 1915

N.Y. Giants (NL), 1916–20

Willie Keeler..N.Y. Giants (NL), 1892–93 and 1910
Bklyn. Dodgers (NL), 1893 and 1899–1902
N.Y. Yankees (AL), 1903–09
Tony Lazzeri..N.Y. Yankees (AL), 1926–37
Bklyn. Dodgers (NL), 1939
N.Y. Giants (NL), 1939
Sal Maglie..N.Y. Giants (NL), 1945 and 1950–55
Bklyn. Dodgers (NL), 1956–57
N.Y. Yankees (AL), 1957–58
Fred Merkle..N.Y. Giants (NL), 1907–16
Bklyn. Dodgers (NL), 1916–17
N.Y. Yankees (AL), 1925–26
Jack Nelson..Troy Trojans (NL), 1879
N.Y. Metropolitans (AA), 1883–87
N.Y. Giants (NL), 1887
Bklyn. Bridegrooms (AA), 1890
Lefty O'Doul..N.Y. Yankees (AL), 1919–20 and 1922
N.Y. Giants (NL), 1928 and 1933–34
Bklyn. Dodgers (NL), 1931–33
Dave Orr..N.Y. Gothams (NL), 1883
N.Y. Metropolitans (AA), 1884–87
Bklyn. Bridegrooms (AA), 1888
Bklyn. Wonders (PL), 1890
Jack Taylor..Bklyn. Dodgers (NL), 1920–25 and 1935
N.Y. Giants (NL), 1927
N.Y. Yankees (AL), 1934
Monte Ward..N.Y. Gothams/Giants (NL), 1883–89 and 1893–94
Bklyn. Wonders (PL), 1890
Bklyn. Bridegrooms (NL), 1891–92

Players Who Played for Both Original and Expansion Washington Senators

Rudy Hernandez, pitcher ....Original Senators, 1960...Expansion Senators, 1961
Hector Maestri, pitcher ....Original Senators, 1960...Expansion Senators, 1961
Pedro Pamos, pitcher ....Original Senators, 1955–60 ....Expansion Senators, 1970
Camilo Pascual, pitcher ....Original Senators, 1954–60.............................Expansion Senators, 1967–69
Zoilo Versalles, shortstop ....Original Senators, 1959–60 ....Expansion Senators, 1969

Players Who Played for Both K.C. A's and K.C. Royals

Moe Drabowsky, pitcher..............................K.C. A's, 1963–65 ....K.C. Royals, 1969–70
Aurelio Monteagudo, pitcher........................K.C. A's, 1963–66 ....K.C. Royals, 1970
Ken Sanders, pitcher ...............................K.C. A's, 1964, 1966 ....K.C. Royals, 1976
Dave Wickersham, pitcher ...........................K.C. A's, 1960–63 ....K.C. Royals, 1969

Players Who Played for Both Milwaukee Braves and Milwaukee Brewers

Hank Aaron, outfielder and DH..........................Milw. Braves, 1954–65.....................Milw. Brewers, 1975–76
Felipe Alou, outfielder ....Milw. Braves, 1964–65 ....Milw. Brewers, 1974
Phil Roof, catcher.......................................Milw. Braves, 1961 and 1964............Milw. Brewers, 1970–71

Pitchers Who Gave Up Most Hits to Pete Rose

Phil Niekro	.64	Claude Osteen	.38
Don Sutton	.60	Ron Reed	.38
Juan Marichal	.42	Bob Gibson	.36

Gaylord Perry 42   Ferguson Jenkins 36
Joe Niekro..39

Pitchers Who Gave Up Home Runs to Both Mark McGwire and Barry Bonds in Their Record-Breaking Seasons (1998 and 2001)

Scott Elarton ....Pitching for Hous. Astros (NL), gave up #40 to McGwire
                                                              Pitching for Colo. Rockies (NL), gave up #61 and #62 to Bonds
Bobby Jones ....Pitching for N.Y. Mets (NL), gave up #47 to McGwire
                                                              Pitching for S.D. Padres (NL), gave up #30 to Bonds
John Thomson ....Pitching for Colo. Rockies (NL), gave up #25 and #44 to McGwire
                                                              Pitching for Colo. Rockies (NL), gave up #25 and #57 to Bonds
Steve Trachsel ....Pitching for Chi. Cubs (NL), gave up #62 to McGwire
                                                              Pitching for N.Y. Mets (NL), gave up #15 to Bonds

Major League Shortstops from San Pedro de Macoris, Dominican Republic

Manny Alexander (1992–98)
Juan Bell (1989–95)
Robinson Cano (2005–)
Juan Castillo (1986–89)
Luis Castillo (1994–2010)
Pedro Ciriaco (2010–)
Mariano Duncan (1985–97)
Tony Fernandez (1983–2001)
Pepe Frias (1973–81)
Luis Garcia (1999)
Pedro Gonzalez (1963–97)
Jerry Gil (2004–07)
Diory Hernandez (2009–)
Julian Javier (1960–72)
Manuel Lee (1985–95)

Norberto Martin (1993–98)
Yamaico Navarro (2010–)
Nelson Norman (1978–82, 1987)
Jose Offerman (1990–2005)
Elvis Pena (2000–01)
Santiago Perez (2000–01)
Rafael Ramirez (1980–92)
Rafael Robles (1969–72)
Eddie Rogers (2002–06)
Amado Samuel (1962–64)
Andres Santana (1990)
Juan Sosa (1999–2001)
Fernando Tatis (1997–03, 2006, 2008-2010)

Players Born on Leap Year Day (February 29)

	Year of Birth		Year of Birth
Ed Appleton, pitcher (1913, 1916)	1892	Pepper Martin, outfield (1928, 1930–40, 1944)	1904
Al Autry, pitcher (1976)	1952	Ralph Miller, infield (1920–21, 1924)	1896
Jerry Fry, catcher (1978)	1956	Steve Mingori, pitcher (1970–79)	1944
Bill Long, pitcher (1985, 1987–91)	1960	Roy Parker, pitcher (1919)	1896
Terrence Long, outfield (1999–2006)	1976	Dickey Pearce, shortstop (1871–77)	1836
Al Rosen, third base (1947–56)	1924		

Players Who Played on Four of California's Five Major League Teams

Mike Aldrete ....................................S.F. Giants, 1986–88; S.D. Padres, 1991; Oak. A's, 1993–95; and Cal. Angels, 1995–96
John D'Acquisto ..................................S.F. Giants, 1973–76; S.D. Padres, 1977–80; Cal. Angels, 1981; and Oak. A's, 1982
Rickey Henderson ....Oak. A's, 1979–84, 1989–93, 1994–95, and 1998; S.D. Padres, 1996–97;
                                                              Ana. Angels, 1997; and L.A. Dodgers, 2003
Stan Javier ....Oak. A's, 1986–90 and 1994–95; L.A. Dodgers, 1990–92; Cal. Angels, 1993; and S.F. Giants, 1996–99
Jay Johnstone ....Cal. Angels, 1966–70; Oak. A's, 1973; S.D. Padres, 1979; L.A. Dodgers, 1980–82 and 1985
Dave Kingman ......................................S.F. Giants, 1971–74; S.D. Padres, 1977; Cal. Angels, 1977; and Oak. A's, 1984–86
Elias Sosa..S.F. Giants, 1972–74; L.A. Dodgers, 1976–77; Oak. A's, 1978; and S.D. Padres, 1983
Derrel Thomas ..........S.D. Padres, 1972–74 and 1978; S.F. Giants, 1975–77; L.A. Dodgers, 1979–83; and Cal. Angels, 1984

Tallest Players in Major League History

6'10" .... Eric Hillman, pitcher (1992–94)
Randy Johnson, pitcher (1988–2009)
Jon Rauch*, pitcher (2002, 2004–)
Andy Sisco, Pitcher (2005–07)
Chris Young*, pitcher (2004–)

6'9" .... Terry Bross, pitcher (1991, 1993)
Johnny Gee, pitcher (1939, 1941, 1943–46)
Mark Hendrickson*, pitcher (2002–)
Kam Mickolio*, pitcher (2008–)
Jeff Niemann*, pitcher (2008–)

6'8" .... Mark Acre, pitcher (1994–97)
Tony Clark, first baseman (1995–2009)
Darren Clarke, pitcher (2007)
Gene Conley, pitcher (1952, 1954–63)
Steve Ellsworth, pitcher (1988)
Doug Fister*, pitcher (2009–)
Lee Guetterman, pitcher (1984, 1986–93, 1995–96)
Jason Hirsh, pitcher (2006–08)
Graeme Lloyd pitcher (1993–2003)
Kameron Loe*, pitcher (2004–)
Nate Minchey, pitcher (1993–97)
Mike Naymick, pitcher (1939–40, 1943–44)
Logan Ondrusek*, pitcher (2010–)
J. R. Richard, pitcher (1971–80)
Adam Russell*, pitcher (2008–)
Michael Schwimer*, pitcher (2011–)
Mike Smithson, pitcher (1982–89)
Kyle Snyder, pitcher (2003–2008)
Phil Stockman, pitcher (2006–2008)
Billy Taylor, pitcher (1994, 1996–98)
Joe Vitko, pitcher (1992)
Chris Volstad*, pitcher (2008–)
Sean West, pitcher (2009–10)
Stefan Wever, pitcher (1982)

*Still active.

Shortest Players in Major League History

3'7" .... Eddie Gaedel, pinch hitter (1951)
5'3" .... Jess Cortazzo, pinch hitter (1923)
Yo-Yo Davalillo, shortstop (1953)
Bob Emmerich, outfield (1923)
Bill Finley, outfield/catcher (1886)
Stubby Magner, infield (1911)
Mike McCormick, third base (1904)
Tom Morrison, infield (1895–96)
Yale Murphy, shortstop/outfield (1894–95, 1897)
Dickey Pearce, shortstop (1871–77)
Frank Shannon, infield (1892, 1896)
Cub Stricker, second base (1882–85, 1887–93)

Teammates the Longest

18 years	Joe Judge (first base) and Sam Rice (outfield), Wash. Senators, 1915–32
18 years	Alan Trammell (third base) and Lou Whitaker (second base), Det. Tigers, 1977–95
15 years	Jeff Bagwell (first base) and Craig Biggio (second base/outfield), Hous. Astros, 1991–2005
14 years	Duke Snider (outfield) and Carl Furillo (outfield), Bklyn./L.A. Dodgers, 1947–60
13 years	Joe Judge (first base) and Walter Johnson (pitcher), Wash. Senators, 1915–27

Teammates with 300 Wins and 500 Home Runs

Lefty Grove (pitcher) and Jimmie Foxx (batter) ....1941 Bost. Red Sox (AL)

Warren Spahn (pitcher) and Willie Mays (batter) ....1965 S.F. Giants (NL)

Don Sutton (pitcher) and Reggie Jackson (batter) ....1985 Cal. Angels (AL)

Greg Maddux (pitcher) and Sammy Sosa (batter) ....2004 Chi. Cubs (NL)

New Baseball Stadiums Built Since 2005

Team	Stadium	Opened	Capacity	Surface	Approximate Cost (in millions)	Center Field Distance
Minn. Twins	Target Field	2010	40,000	Grass	$522	404' (124 m)
N.Y. Mets	Citi Field	2009	41,800	Grass	$850	408' (124 m)
N.Y. Yankees	Yankee Stadium	2009	52,325	Grass	$1300	408' (124.3 m)
Wash. Nationals	Nationals Park	2008	41,888	Grass	$611	402' (122.5 m)
St. L. Cardinals	Busch Stadium	2006	46,861	Grass	$346	400' (122 m)

Players Traded for Themselves

Harry Chiti (Apr. 26, 1962 and June 15, 1962)

Archie Cobin (Nov. 20, 1992 and Feb. 5, 1993)

Clint Courtney (Jan. 24, 1961 and Mar. 14, 1961)

John MacDonald (July 22, 2005 and Nov. 10, 2005)

Dickie Noles (Sept. 22, 1987 and Oct. 23, 1987)

Mark Ross (Dec. 9, 1985 and Mar. 31, 1986)

Players Wearing Numbers "0" and "00"

"0"

Oscar Gamble, Chi. White Sox

Oddibe McDowell, Tex. Rangers

Al Oliver, L.A. Dodgers, S.F. Giants, Mont. Expos, Phila. Phillies, Tex. Rangers, Tor. Blue Jays

Junior Ortiz, Clev. Indians, Tex. Rangers

George Scott, K.C. Royals

"00"

Bobby Bonds, St. L. Cardinals

Jack Clark, S.D. Padres

Paul Dade, Cleve. Indians

Jerry Hairston, Chi. White Sox

Cliff Johnson, Tor. Blue Jays

Jeff Leonard, Milw. Brewers, S.F. Giants, Sea. Mariners

Bobo Newsom, Wash. Senators

Omar Olivares, St.L. Cardinals

Joe Page, Pitt. Pirates

Brandon Watson, Cin. Reds, Wash. Nationals

PART 2
Team-by-Team Histories

Baltimore Orioles

Dates of Operation: 1954–present (58 years)
Overall Record: 4686 wins, 4498 losses (.510)
Stadiums: Memorial Stadium, 1954–91; Oriole Park at Camden Yards, 1992–present (capacity: 45,438)

Year-by-Year Finishes

Year	Finish	Wins	Losses	Percentage	Games Behind	Manager	Attendance
1954	7th	54	100	.351	57.0	Jimmy Dykes	1,060,910
1955	7th	57	97	.370	39.0	Paul Richards	852,039
1956	6th	69	85	.448	28.0	Paul Richards	901,201
1957	5th	76	76	.500	21.0	Paul Richards	1,029,581
1958	6th	74	79	.484	17.5	Paul Richards	829,991
1959	6th	74	80	.481	20.0	Paul Richards	891,926
1960	2nd	89	65	.578	8.0	Paul Richards	1,187,849
1961	3rd	95	67	.586	14.0	Paul Richards, Luman Harris	951,089
1962	7th	77	85	.475	19.0	Billy Hitchcock	790,254
1963	4th	86	76	.531	18.5	Billy Hitchcock	774,343
1964	3rd	97	65	.599	2.0	Hank Bauer	1,116,215
1965	3rd	94	68	.580	8.0	Hank Bauer	781,649
1966	1st	97	63	.606	+9.0	Hank Bauer	1,203,366
1967	6th (Tie)	76	85	.472	15.5	Hank Bauer	955,053
1968	2nd	91	71	.562	12.0	Hank Bauer, Earl Weaver	943,977
East Division							
1969	1st	109	53	.673	+19.0	Earl Weaver	1,058,168
1970	1st	108	54	.667	+15.0	Earl Weaver	1,057,069
1971	1st	101	57	.639	+12.0	Earl Weaver	1,023,037
1972	3rd	80	74	.519	5.0	Earl Weaver	899,950
1973	1st	97	65	.599	+8.0	Earl Weaver	958,667
1974	1st	91	71	.562	+2.0	Earl Weaver	962,572
1975	2nd	90	69	.566	4.5	Earl Weaver	1,002,157
1976	2nd	88	74	.543	10.5	Earl Weaver	1,058,609
1977	2nd (Tie)	97	64	.602	2.5	Earl Weaver	1,195,769
1978	4th	90	71	.559	9.0	Earl Weaver	1,051,724
1979	1st	102	57	.642	+8.0	Earl Weaver	1,681,009
1980	2nd	100	62	.617	3.0	Earl Weaver	1,797,438
1981*	2nd/4th	59	46	.562	2.0/2.0	Earl Weaver	1,024,652

1982	2nd	94	68	.580	1.0	Earl Weaver	1,613,031
1983	1st	98	64	.605	+6.0	Joe Altobelli	2,042,071
1984	5th	85	77	.525	19.0	Joe Altobelli	2,045,784
1985	4th	83	78	.516	16.0	Joe Altobelli, Earl Weaver	2,132,387
1986	7th	73	89	.451	22.5	Earl Weaver	1,973,176
1987	6tt	67	95	.414	31.0	Cal Ripken Sr.	1,835,692
1988	7th	54	107	.335	34.5	Cal Ripken Sr., Frank Robinson	1,660,738
1989	2nd	87	75	.537	2.0	Frank Robinson	2,535,208
1990	5th	76	85	.472	11.5	Frank Robinson	2,415,189
1991	6th	67	95	.414	24.0	Frank Robinson, Johnny Oates	2,552,753
1992	3rd	89	73	.549	7.0	Johnny Oates	3,567,819
1993	3rd (Tie)	85	77	.525	10.0	Johnny Oates	3,644,965
1994	2nd	63	49	.563	6.5	Johnny Oates	2,535,359
1995	3rd	71	73	.493	15.0	Phil Regan	3,098,475
1996	2nd	88	74	.543	4.0	Davey Johnson	3,646,950
1997	1st	98	64	.605	+2.0	Davey Johnson	3,711,132
1998	4th	79	83	.488	35.0	Ray Miller	3,685,194
1999	4th	78	84	.481	20.0	Ray Miller	3,433,150
2000	4th	74	88	.457	13.5	Mike Hargrove	3,295,128
2001	4th	63	98	.391	32.5	Mike Hargrove	3,094,841
2002	4th	67	95	.414	36.5	Mike Hargrove	2,682,917
2003	4th	71	91	.438	30.0	Mike Hargrove	2,454,523
2004	3rd	78	84	.481	23.0	Lee Mazzilli	2,747,573
2005	4th	74	88	.457	21.0	Lee Mazzilli, Sam Perlozzo	2,624,740
2006	4th	70	92	.432	27.0	Sam Perlozzo	2,153,139
2007	4th	69	93	.426	27.0	Sam Perlozzo, Dave Trembley	2,164,822
2008	5th	68	93	.422	28.5	Dave Trembley	1,950,075
2009	5th	64	98	.395	39.0	Dave Trembley	1,907,163
2010	5th	66	96	.407	30.0	Dave Trembley, Juan Samuel and Buck Showalter	1,733,019
2011	5th	69	93	.425	28.0	Buck Showalter	1755,461

*Split season.

Awards

Most Valuable Player
Brooks Robinson, third base, 1964
Frank Robinson, outfield, 1966
Boog Powell, first base, 1970
Cal Ripken Jr., shortstop, 1983
Cal Ripken Jr., shortstop, 1991

Rookie of the Year
Ron Hansen, shortstop, 1960
Curt Blefary, outfield, 1965
Al Bumbry, outfield, 1973
Eddie Murray, first base, 1977
Cal Ripken Jr., shortstop and third base, 1982
Gregg Olson, pitcher, 1989

Cy Young
Mike Cuellar (co-winner), 1969
Jim Palmer, 1973
Jim Palmer, 1975

Jim Palmer, 1976
Mike Flanagan, 1979
Steve Stone, 1980

Hall of Famers Who Played for the Orioles
Luis Aparicio, shortstop, 1963–67
Reggie Jackson, outfield, 1976
George Kell, third base, 1956–57
Eddie Murray, first base and designated hitter, 1977–88 and 1996
Jim Palmer, pitcher, 1965–84
Cal Ripken Jr., shortstop and third base, 1981–2001
Robin Roberts, pitcher, 1962–65
Brooks Robinson, third base, 1955–77
Frank Robinson, outfield, 1966–71
Hoyt Wilhelm, pitcher, 1958–62

Retired Numbers
4....................................Earl Weaver

5..............................Brooks Robinson
8....................................Cal Ripken Jr.
20 ....Frank Robinson
22......................................Jim Palmer
33..................................Eddie Murray

League Leaders, Batting

Batting Average, Season
Frank Robinson, 1966................. .316

Home Runs, Season
Frank Robinson, 1966....................49
Eddie Murray, 1981 ....22 (Tie)

RBIs, Season
Brooks Robinson, 1964 118
Frank Robinson, 1966...................122
Lee May, 1976 109
Eddie Murray, 1981 78
Miguel Tejada, 2004....................150

Stolen Bases, Season
Luis Aparicio, 1963 40
Luis Aparicio, 1964 57
Brady Anderson, 1992....................53
Brian Roberts, 2008........................50

Total Bases, Season
Frank Robinson, 1966....................367
Cal Ripken Jr., 1991 368

Most Hits, Season
Cal Ripken Jr., 1983 211

Most Runs, Season
Frank Robinson, 1966....................122
Don Buford, 1971 99
Cal Ripken Jr., 1983 121

Batting Feats

Triple Crown Winners
Frank Robinson, 1966 (.316 BA, 49
    HRs, 122 RBIs)

Hitting for the Cycle
Brooks Robinson, July 15, 1960
Cal Ripken Jr., May 6, 1984
Aubrey Huff, June 29, 2007
Felix Pie, Aug. 14, 2009

Six Hits in a Game
Cal Ripken Jr., June 13, 1999

40 or More Home Runs, Season
50....................Brady Anderson, 1996
49.....................Frank Robinson, 1966
46............................Jim Gentile, 1961
43 ....Rafael Palmeiro, 1998

League Leaders, Pitching

Most Wins, Season
Chuck Estrada, 1960 ....18 (Tie)
Mike Cuellar, 1970..................24 (Tie)
Dave McNally, 1970................24 (Tie)
Jim Palmer, 1975 ....23 (Tie)
Jim Palmer, 1976 22
Jim Palmer, 1977 ....20 (Tie)
Mike Flanagan, 1979 23
Steve Stone, 1980 25
Dennis Martinez, 1981 ....14 (Tie)
Mike Boddicker, 1984....................20
Mike Mussina, 1995.......................19

Most Strikeouts, Season
Bob Turley, 1954 185

Lowest ERA, Season
Hoyt Wilhelm, 1959 ....2.19
Jim Palmer, 1973........................2.40
Jim Palmer, 1975........................2.09
Mike Boddicker, 1984 ....2.79

Most Saves, Season
Lee Smith, 1994 33
Randy Myers, 1997 45

Best Won-Lost Percentage, Season
Wally Bunker, 1964.....19–5........ .792
Jim Palmer, 1969 ....16–4....... .800
Mike Cuellar, 1970 .....24–8........ .750
Dave McNally, 1971 ...21–5........ .808
Mike Cuellar, 1974....22–10........ .688
Mike Torrez, 1975......20–9........ .690
Steve Stone, 1980 ....25–7........ .781
Mike Mussina, 1992....18–5........ .783

Pitching Feats

20 Wins, Season
Steve Barber, 1963 20–13
Dave McNally, 1968 22–10
Mike Cuellar, 1969 23–11
Dave McNally, 1969 20–7
Mike Cuellar, 1970 24–8
Dave McNally, 1970 24–9
Jim Palmer, 1970 20–10
Dave McNally, 1971 21–5
Pat Dobson, 1971 20–8
Mike Cuellar, 1971 20–9
Jim Palmer, 1971 20–9
Jim Palmer, 1972 21–10
Jim Palmer, 1973 22–9
Mike Cuellar, 1974 22–10
Jim Palmer, 1975 23–11
Mike Torrez, 1975 20–9
Jim Palmer, 1976 22–13
Wayne Garland, 1976 20–7
Jim Palmer, 1977 20–11
Jim Palmer, 1978 21–12
Mike Flanagan, 1979...................23–9
Steve Stone, 1980......................25–7
Scott McGregor, 1980 20–8
Mike Boddicker, 1984 20–11

No-Hitters
Hoyt Wilhelm (vs. N.Y. Yankees),
    Sept. 2, 1958 (final: 1–0)
Steve Barber and Stu Miller (vs. Det.
    Tigers), Apr. 30, 1967 (final: 1–2)
Tom Phoebus (vs. Bost. Red Sox),
    Apr. 27, 1968 (final: 6–0)
Jim Palmer (vs. Oak. A's), Aug. 13,
    1969 (final: 8–0)
Bob Milacki, Mike Flanagan, Mark
    Williamson, and Gregg Olson (vs.
    Oak. A's), July 13, 1991 (final: 2–0)

No-Hitters Pitched Against
Bo Belinsky, L.A. Angels, May 5,
    1962 (final: 2–0)
Nolan Ryan, Cal. Angels, June 1,
    1975 (final: 1–0)
Juan Nieves, Milw. Brewers (AL), Apr.
    15, 1987 (final: 7–0)
Wilson Alvarez, Chi. White Sox, Aug.
    11, 1991 (final: 7–0)
Hideo Nomo, Bost. Red Sox, Apr.
    4, 2001 (final: 3–0)
Clay Buchholz, Bost. Red Sox, Sept.
    1, 2007 (final: 10–0)

Postseason Play

1966 World Series vs. L.A. Dodgers
        (NL), won 4 games to 0
1969 League Championship Series vs.
        Minn. Twins, won 3 games to 0
        World Series vs. N.Y. Mets (NL),
        lost 4 games to 1
1970 League Championship Series vs.
        Minn. Twins, won 3 games to 0
        World Series vs. Cin. Reds (NL),
        won 4 games to 1
1971 League Championship Series vs.
        Oak. A's, won 3 games to 0
        World Series vs. Pitt. Pirates (NL),
        lost 4 games to 3
1973 League Championship Series vs.
        Oak. A's, lost 3 games to 2
1974 League Championship Series vs.
        Oak. A's, lost 3 games to 1
1979 League Championship Series vs.
        Cal. Angels, won 3 games to 1
        World Series vs. Pitt. Pirates (NL),
        lost 4 games to 3

1983 League Championship Series vs.
      Chi. White Sox, won 3
      games to 1
      World Series vs. Phila. Phillies
      (NL), won 4 games to 1

1996 Division Series vs. Cleve. Indians,
      won 3 games to 1
      League Championship Series vs.
      N.Y. Yankees, lost 4 games to 1

1997 Division Series vs. Sea. Mariners,
      won 3 games to 1
      League Championship Series vs.
      Cleve. Indians, lost 4 games
      to 2

Boston Red Sox

Dates of Operation: 1901–present (111 years)

Overall Record: 8909 wins, 8305 losses (.517)

Stadiums: Huntington Avenue Baseball Grounds, 1901–11; Braves Field, 1915–16 World Series and 1929–32 (Sundays only); Fenway Park, 1912–present (capacity: 37,493)

Other Names: Americans, Puritans, Pilgrims, Plymouth Rocks, Somersets

Year-by-Year Finishes

Year	Finish	Wins	Losses	Percentage	Games Behind	Manager	Attendance
1901	2nd	79	57	.581	4.0	Jimmy Collins	289,448
1902	3rd	77	60	.562	6.5	Jimmy Collins	348,567
1903	1st	91	47	.659	+14.5	Jimmy Collins	379,338
1904	1st	95	59	.617	+1.5	Jimmy Collins	623,295
1905	4th	78	74	.513	16.0	Jimmy Collins	468,828
1906	8th	49	105	.318	45.5	Jimmy Collins, Chick Stahl	410,209
1907	7th	59	90	.396	32.5	George Huff, Bob Unglaub, Deacon McGuire	436,777
1908	5th	75	79	.487	15.5	Deacon McGuire, Fred Lake	473,048
1909	3rd	88	63	.583	9.5	Fred Lake	668,965
1910	4th	81	72	.529	22.5	Patsy Donovan	584,619
1911	5th	78	75	.510	24.0	Patsy Donovan	503,961
1912	1st	105	47	.691	+14.0	Jake Stahl	597,096
1913	4th	79	71	.527	15.5	Jake Stahl, Bill Carrigan	437,194
1914	2nd	91	62	.595	8.5	Bill Carrigan	481,359
1915	1st	101	50	.669	+2.5	Bill Carrigan	539,885
1916	1st	91	63	.591	+2.0	Bill Carrigan	496,397
1917	2nd	90	62	.592	9.0	Jack Barry	387,856
1918	1st	75	51	.595	+2.5	Ed Barrow	249,513
1919	6th	66	71	.482	20.5	Ed Barrow	417,291
1920	5th	72	81	.471	25.5	Ed Barrow	402,445
1921	5th	75	79	.487	23.5	Hugh Duffy	279,273
1922	8th	61	93	.396	33.0	Hugh Duffy	259,184
1923	8th	61	91	.401	37.0	Frank Chance	229,668
1924	7th	67	87	.435	25.0	Lee Fohl	448,556
1925	8th	47	105	.309	49.5	Lee Fohl	267,782
1926	8th	46	107	.301	44.5	Lee Fohl	285,155
1927	8th	51	103	.331	59.0	Bill Carrigan	305,275
1928	8th	57	96	.373	43.5	Bill Carrigan	396,920
1929	8th	58	96	.377	48.0	Bill Carrigan	394,620
1930	8th	52	102	.338	50.0	Heinie Wagner	444,045
1931	6th	62	90	.408	45.0	Shano Collins	350,975
1932	8th	43	111	.279	64.0	Shano Collins, Marty McManus	182,150
1933	7th	63	86	.423	34.5	Marty McManus	268,715
1934	4th	76	76	.500	24.0	Bucky Harris	610,640
1935	4th	78	75	.510	16.0	Joe Cronin	558,568
1936	6th	74	80	.481	28.5	Joe Cronin	626,895
1937	5th	80	72	.526	21.0	Joe Cronin	559,659
1938	2nd	88	61	.591	9.5	Joe Cronin	646,459
1939	2nd	89	62	.589	17.0	Joe Cronin	573,070

1940	4th (Tie)	82	72	.532	8.0	Joe Cronin	716,234
1941	2nd	84	70	.545	17.0	Joe Cronin	718,497
1942	2nd	93	59	.612	9.0	Joe Cronin	730,340
1943	7th	68	84	.447	29.0	Joe Cronin	358,275
1944	4th	77	77	.500	12.0	Joe Cronin	506,975
1945	7th	71	83	.461	17.5	Joe Cronin	603,794
1946	1st	104	50	.675	+12.0	Joe Cronin	1,416,944
1947	3rd	83	71	.539	14.0	Joe Cronin	1,427,315
1948	2nd	96	59	.619	1.0	Joe McCarthy	1,558,798
1949	2nd	96	58	.623	1.0	Joe McCarthy	1,596,650
1950	3rd	94	60	.610	4.0	Joe McCarthy, Steve O'Neill	1,344,080
1951	3rd	87	67	.565	11.0	Steve O'Neill	1,312,282
1952	6th	76	78	.494	19.0	Lou Boudreau	1,115,750
1953	4th	84	69	.549	16.0	Lou Boudreau	1,026,133
1954	4th	69	85	.448	42.0	Lou Boudreau	931,127
1955	4th	84	70	.545	12.0	Pinky Higgins	1,203,200
1956	4th	84	70	.545	13.0	Pinky Higgins	1,137,158
1957	3rd	82	72	.532	16.0	Pinky Higgins	1,181,087
1958	3rd	79	75	.513	13.0	Pinky Higgins	1,077,047
1959	5th	75	79	.487	19.0	Pinky Higgins, Billy Jurges	984,102
1960	7th	65	89	.422	32.0	Billy Jurges, Pinky Higgins	1,129,866
1961	6th	76	86	.469	33.0	Pinky Higgins	850,589
1962	8th	76	84	.475	19.0	Pinky Higgins	733,080
1963	7th	76	85	.472	28.0	Johnny Pesky	942,642
1964	8th	72	90	.444	27.0	Johnny Pesky, Billy Herman	883,276
1965	9th	62	100	.383	40.0	Billy Herman	652,201
1966	9th	72	90	.444	26.0	Billy Herman, Pete Runnels	811,172
1967	1st	92	70	.568	+1.0	Dick Williams	1,727,832
1968	4th	86	76	.531	17.0	Dick Williams	1,940,788

East Division

1969	3rd	87	75	.537	22.0	Dick Williams, Eddie Popowski	1,833,246
1970	3rd	87	75	.537	21.0	Eddie Kasko	1,595,278
1971	3rd	85	77	.525	18.0	Eddie Kasko	1,678,732
1972	2nd	85	70	.548	0.5	Eddie Kasko	1,441,718
1973	2nd	89	73	.549	8.0	Eddie Kasko	1,481,002
1974	3rd	84	78	.519	7.0	Darrell Johnson	1,556,411
1975	1st	95	65	.594	+4.5	Darrell Johnson	1,748,587
1976	3rd	83	79	.512	15.5	Darrell Johnson, Don Zimmer	1,895,846
1977	2nd (Tie)	97	64	.602	2.5	Don Zimmer	2,074,549
1978	2nd	99	64	.607	1.0	Don Zimmer	2,320,643
1979	3rd	91	69	.569	11.5	Don Zimmer	2,353,114
1980	4th	83	77	.519	19.0	Don Zimmer, Johnny Pesky	1,956,092
1981*	5th/ 2nd (Tie)	59	49	.546	4.0/1.5	Ralph Houk	1,060,379
1982	3rd	89	73	.549	6.0	Ralph Houk	1,950,124
1983	6th	78	84	.481	20.0	Ralph Houk	1,782,285
1984	4th	86	76	.531	18.0	Ralph Houk	1,661,618
1985	5th	81	81	.500	18.5	John McNamara	1,786,633
1986	1st	95	66	.590	+5.5	John McNamara	2,147,641
1987	5th	78	84	.481	20.0	John McNamara	2,231,551

1988	1st	89	73	.549	+1.0	John McNamara, Joe Morgan	2,464,851
1989	3rd	83	79	.512	6.0	Joe Morgan	2,510,012
1990	1st	88	74	.543	+2.0	Joe Morgan	2,528,986
1991	2nd (Tie)	84	78	.519	7.0	Joe Morgan	2,562,435
1992	7th	73	89	.451	23.0	Butch Hobson	2,468,574
1993	5th	80	82	.494	15.0	Butch Hobson	2,422,021
1994	4th	54	61	.470	17.0	Butch Hobson	1,775,818
1995	1st	86	58	.597	+7.0	Kevin Kennedy	2,164,410
1996	3rd	85	77	.525	7.0	Kevin Kennedy	2,315,231
1997	4th	78	84	.481	20.0	Jimy Williams	2,226,136
1998	2nd	92	70	.568	22.0	Jimy Williams	2,343,947
1999	2nd	94	68	.580	4.0	Jimy Williams	2,446,162
2000	2nd	85	77	.525	2.5	Jimy Williams	2,586,032
2001	2nd	82	79	.509	13.5	Jimy Williams, Joe Kerrigan	2,625,333
2002	2nd	93	69	.574	10.5	Grady Little	2,650,063
2003	2nd	95	67	.586	6.0	Grady Little	2,724,165
2004	2nd	98	64	.605	3.0	Terry Francona	2,837,304
2005	1st (Tie)	95	67	.586	—	Terry Francona	2,847,888
2006	3rd	86	76	.531	11.0	Terry Francona	2,967,508
2007	1st	96	66	.593	+2.0	Terry Francona	2,971,025
2008	2nd	95	67	.586	2.0	Terry Francona	3,048,250
2009	2nd	95	67	.586	8.0	Terry Francona	3,062,699
2010	3rd	89	73	.549	7.0	Terry Francona	3,046,445
2011	3rd	90	72	.556	7.0	Terry Francona	3,054,001

*Split season.

Awards

Most Valuable Player

Tris Speaker, outfield, 1912
Jimmie Foxx, first base, 1938
Ted Williams, outfield, 1946
Ted Williams, outfield, 1949
Jackie Jensen, outfield, 1958
Carl Yastrzemski, outfield, 1967
Fred Lynn, outfield, 1975
Jim Rice, outfield, 1978
Roger Clemens, pitcher, 1986
Mo Vaughn, first base, 1995
Dustin Pedroia, second base, 2008

Rookie of the Year

Walt Dropo, first base, 1950
Don Schwall, pitcher, 1961
Carlton Fisk, catcher, 1972
Fred Lynn, outfield, 1975
Nomar Garciaparra, shortstop, 1997
Dustin Pedroia, second base, 2007

Cy Young

Jim Lonborg, 1967
Roger Clemens, 1986
Roger Clemens, 1987

Roger Clemens, 1991
Pedro Martinez, 1999
Pedro Martinez, 2000

Hall of Famers Who Played for the Red Sox

Luis Aparicio, shortstop, 1971–73
Wade Boggs, third base, 1982–92
Lou Boudreau, shortstop, 1951–52
Jesse Burkett, outfield, 1905
Orlando Cepeda, designated hitter, 1973
Jack Chesbro, pitcher, 1909
Jimmy Collins, third base, 1901–07
Joe Cronin, shortstop, 1935–45
Andre Dawson, outfielder, designated hitter, 1993-94
Bobby Doerr, second base, 1937–44 and 1946–51
Dennis Eckersley, pitcher, 1978–84 and 1998
Rick Ferrell, catcher, 1933–37
Carlton Fisk, catcher, 1969–80
Jimmie Foxx, first base, 1936–42
Lefty Grove, pitcher, 1934–41
Rickey Henderson, outfielder, 2002
Harry Hooper, outfield, 1909–20
Waite Hoyt, pitcher, 1919–20

Ferguson Jenkins, pitcher, 1976–77
George Kell, third base, 1952–54
Heinie Manush, outfield, 1936
Juan Marichal, pitcher, 1974
Herb Pennock, pitcher, 1915–22
Tony Perez, first base, 1980–82
Jim Rice, outfielder, 1974-89
Red Ruffing, pitcher, 1924–30
Babe Ruth, pitcher and outfield, 1914–19
Tom Seaver, pitcher, 1986
Al Simmons, outfield, 1943
Tris Speaker, outfield, 1907–15
Ted Williams, outfield, 1939–42 and 1946–60
Carl Yastrzemski, outfield, 1961–83
Cy Young, pitcher, 1901–08

Retired Numbers

1	Bobby Doerr
4	Joe Cronin
6	Johnny Pesky
8	Carl Yastrzemski
9	Ted Williams
14	Jim Rice
27	Carlton Fisk

League Leaders, Batting

Batting Average, Season

Dale Alexander*, 1932	.367
Jimmie Foxx, 1938	.349
Ted Williams, 1941	.406
Ted Williams, 1942	.356
Ted Williams, 1947	.343
Ted Williams, 1948	.369
Billy Goodman, 1950	.354
Ted Williams, 1957	.388
Ted Williams, 1958	.328
Pete Runnels, 1960	.320
Pete Runnels, 1962	.326
Carl Yastrzemski, 1963	.321
Carl Yastrzemski, 1967	.326
Carl Yastrzemski, 1968	.301
Fred Lynn, 1979	.333
Carney Lansford, 1981	.336
Wade Boggs, 1983	.361
Wade Boggs, 1985	.368
Wade Boggs, 1986	.357
Wade Boggs, 1987	.363
Wade Boggs, 1988	.366
Nomar Garciaparra, 1999	.357
Nomar Garciaparra, 2000	.372
Manny Ramirez, 2002	.349
Bill Mueller, 2003	.326

*Played part of season with Det. Tigers.

Home Runs, Season

Buck Freeman, 1903	13
Jake Stahl, 1910	10
Tris Speaker, 1912	10 (Tie)
Babe Ruth, 1918	11 (Tie)
Babe Ruth, 1919	29
Jimmie Foxx, 1939	35
Ted Williams, 1941	37
Ted Williams, 1942	36
Ted Williams, 1947	32
Ted Williams, 1949	43
Tony Conigliaro, 1965	32
Carl Yastrzemski, 1967	44 (Tie)
Jim Rice, 1977	39
Jim Rice, 1978	46
Dwight Evans, 1981	22 (Tie)
Jim Rice, 1983	39
Tony Armas, 1984	43
Manny Ramirez, 2004	43
David Ortiz, 2006	54

RBIs, Season

Babe Ruth, 1919	112
Jimmie Foxx, 1938	175
Ted Williams, 1939	145
Ted Williams, 1942	137
Ted Williams, 1947	114
Vern Stephens, 1949	159 (Tie)
Ted Williams, 1949	159 (Tie)
Walt Dropo, 1950	144 (Tie)
Vern Stephens, 1950	144 (Tie)
Jackie Jensen, 1955	116 (Tie)
Jackie Jensen, 1958	122
Jackie Jensen, 1959	112
Dick Stuart, 1963	118
Carl Yastrzemski, 1967	121
Ken Harrelson, 1968	109
Jim Rice, 1978	139
Jim Rice, 1983	126 (Tie)
Tony Armas, 1984	123
Mo Vaughn, 1995	126 (Tie)
David Ortiz, 2005	148
David Ortiz, 2006	137

Stolen Bases, Season

Buddy Myer, 1928	30
Billy Werber, 1934	40
Billy Werber, 1935	29
Ben Chapman*, 1937	35 (Tie)
Dom DiMaggio, 1950	15
Jackie Jensen, 1954	22
Tommy Harper, 1973	54
Jacoby Ellsbury, 2008	50
Jacoby Ellsbury, 2009	70

*Played part of season with Wash. Senators.

Total Bases, Season

Buck Freeman, 1902	287
Buck Freeman, 1903	281
Tris Speaker, 1914	287
Babe Ruth, 1919	284
Jimmie Foxx, 1938	398
Ted Williams, 1939	344
Ted Williams, 1942	338
Ted Williams, 1946	343
Ted Williams, 1947	335
Ted Williams, 1949	368
Walt Dropo, 1950	326
Ted Williams, 1951	295
Dick Stuart, 1963	319
Carl Yastrzemski, 1967	360
Carl Yastrzemski, 1970	335
Reggie Smith, 1971	302
Jim Rice, 1977	382
Jim Rice, 1978	406

Jim Rice, 1979	369
Dwight Evans, 1981	215
Jim Rice, 1983	344
Tony Armas, 1984	339
David Ortiz, 2006	355
Jacoby Ellsburg, 2011	364

Most Hits, Season

Patsy Dougherty, 1903	195
Tris Speaker, 1914	193
Joe Vosmik, 1938	201
Doc Cramer, 1940	200 (Tie)
Johnny Pesky, 1942	205
Johnny Pesky, 1946	208
Johnny Pesky, 1947	207
Carl Yastrzemski, 1963	183
Carl Yastrzemski, 1967	189
Jim Rice, 1978	213
Wade Boggs, 1985	240
Nomar Garciaparra, 1997	209
Dustin Pedroia, 2008	213 (Tie)
Adrian Gonzalez, 2011	213 (tie)

Most Runs, Season

Patsy Dougherty, 1903	108
Babe Ruth, 1919	103
Ted Williams, 1940	134
Ted Williams, 1941	135
Ted Williams, 1942	141
Ted Williams, 1946	142
Ted Williams, 1947	125
Ted Williams, 1949	150
Dom DiMaggio, 1950	131
Dom DiMaggio, 1951	113
Carl Yastrzemski, 1967	112
Carl Yastrzemski, 1970	125
Carl Yastrzemski, 1974	93
Fred Lynn, 1975	103
Dwight Evans, 1984	121
Wade Boggs, 1988	128
Wade Boggs, 1989	113 (Tie)
Dustin Pedroia, 2008	118
Dustin Pedroia, 2009	115

Batting Feats

Triple Crown Winners

Ted Williams, 1942 (.356 BA, 35 HRs, 137 RBIs)

Ted Williams, 1947 (.343 BA, 32 HRs, 114 RBIs)

Carl Yastrzemski, 1967 (.326 BA, 44 HRs (Tie), 121 RBIs)

Hitting for the Cycle

Buck Freeman, July 21, 1903
Patsy Dougherty, July 29, 1903
Tris Speaker, June 9, 1912
Roy Carlyle, July 21, 1925
Moose Solters, Aug. 19, 1934
Joe Cronin, Aug. 2, 1940
Leon Culberson, July 3, 1943
Bobby Doerr, May 17, 1944
Bob Johnson, July 6, 1944
Ted Williams, July 21, 1946
Bobby Doerr, May 13, 1947
Lou Clinton, July 13, 1962
Carl Yastrzemski, May 14, 1965
Bob Watson, Sept. 15, 1979
Fred Lynn, May 13, 1980
Dwight Evans, June 28, 1984
Rich Gedman, Sept. 18, 1985
Mike Greenwell, Sept. 14, 1988
Scott Cooper, Apr. 12, 1994
John Valentin, June 6, 1996

Six Hits in a Game

Jimmy Piersall, June 10, 1953
Pete Runnels, Aug. 30, 1960*
Jerry Remy, Sept. 3, 1981*
Nomar Garciaparra, June 21, 2003*
*Extra-inning game.

40 or More Home Runs, Season

54	..........................David Ortiz, 2006
50	..........................Jimmie Foxx, 1938
47	..........................David Ortiz, 2005
46	..............................Jim Rice, 1978
45	..............Manny Ramirez, 2005
44	...............Carl Yastrzemski, 1967
	Mo Vaughn, 1996
43	.........................Ted Williams, 1949
	Tony Armas, 1984
	Manny Ramirez, 2004
42	..........................Dick Stuart, 1963
41	.........................Jimmie Foxx, 1936
	Manny Ramirez, 2001
	David Ortiz, 2004
40	.....................Rico Petrocelli, 1969
	Carl Yastrzemski, 1969
	Carl Yastrzemski, 1970
	Mo Vaughn, 1998

League Leaders, Pitching

Most Wins, Season

Cy Young, 1901	33
Cy Young, 1902	32
Cy Young, 1903	28
Smokey Joe Wood, 1912	34
Wes Ferrell, 1935	25
Tex Hughson, 1942	22
Mel Parnell, 1949	25
Frank Sullivan, 1955	18
Jim Lonborg, 1967	.................22 (Tie)
Roger Clemens, 1986	24
Roger Clemens, 1987	.............20 (Tie)
Curt Schilling, 2004	21
Josh Beckett, 2007	20

Most Strikeouts, Season

Cy Young, 1901	158
Tex Hughson, 1942	...............113 (Tie)
Jim Lonborg, 1967	246
Roger Clemens, 1988	291
Roger Clemens, 1991	241
Roger Clemens, 1996	257
Pedro Martinez, 1999	313
Pedro Martinez, 2000	284
Hideo Nomo, 2001	220
Pedro Martinez, 2002	239

Lowest ERA, Season

Dutch Leonard, 1914	...................1.00
Smokey Joe Wood, 1915	...........1.49
Babe Ruth, 1916	.........................1.75
Lefty Grove, 1935	.......................2.70
Lefty Grove, 1936	.......................2.81
Lefty Grove, 1938	.......................3.07
Lefty Grove, 1939	.......................2.54
Mel Parnell, 1949	.......................2.78
Luis Tiant, 1972	..........................1.91
Roger Clemens, 1986	..................2.48
Roger Clemens, 1990	..................1.93
Roger Clemens, 1991	..................2.62
Roger Clemens, 1992	..................2.41
Pedro Martinez, 1999	.................2.07
Pedro Martinez, 2000	.................1.74
Pedro Martinez, 2002	.................2.26
Pedro Martinez, 2003	.................2.22

Most Saves, Season

Bill Campbell, 1977	31
Tom Gordon, 1998	46
Derek Lowe, 2000	..................42 (Tie)

Best Won–Lost Percentage, Season

Cy Young, 1903	..............28–9..	.757
Jesse Tannehill, 1905	.......22–9..	.710
Smokey Joe Wood, 1912..34–5..		.872
Smokey Joe Wood, 1915..15–5..		.750
Sad Sam Jones, 1918.......16–5..		.762
Lefty Grove, 1939	.............15–4..	.789
Tex Hughson, 1944	..........18–5..	.783
Boo Ferriss, 1946	............25–6..	.806
Jack Kramer, 1948	...........18–5..	.783
Ellis Kinder, 1949	............23–6..	.793
Roger Clemens, 1986.......24–4..		.857
Roger Clemens, 1987.......20–9..		.690
Pedro Martinez, 1999	......23–4..	.852
Pedro Martinez, 2002	......20–4..	.833
Curt Schilling, 2004	.........21–6..	.778

Pitching Feats

20 Wins, Season

Cy Young, 1901	33–10
Cy Young, 1902	32–11
Bill Dineen, 1902	21–21
Cy Young, 1903	28–9
Bill Dineen, 1903	21–13
Tom Hughes, 1903	20–7
Cy Young, 1904	26–16
Bill Dineen, 1904	23–14
Jesse Tannehill, 1904	21–11
Jesse Tannehill, 1905	22–9
Cy Young, 1907	22–15
Cy Young, 1908	21–11
Smokey Joe Wood, 1911...........23–17
Smokey Joe Wood, 1912.............34–5
Hugh Bedient, 1912	20–9
Buck O'Brien, 1912	20–13
Ray Collins, 1914	20–13
Babe Ruth, 1916	23–12
Babe Ruth, 1917	24–13
Carl Mays, 1917	22–9
Carl Mays, 1918	21–13
Sad Sam Jones, 1921	23–16
Howard Ehmke, 1923	20–17
Wes Ferrell, 1935	25–14
Lefty Grove, 1935	20–12
Wes Ferrell, 1936	20–15
Tex Hughson, 1942	22–6
Boo Ferriss, 1945	21–10
Boo Ferriss, 1946	25–6
Tex Hughson, 1946	20–11
Mel Parnell, 1949	25–7
Ellis Kinder, 1949	23–6
Mel Parnell, 1953	21–8

Bill Monbouquette, 1963............20–10
Jim Lonborg, 1967.....................22–9
Luis Tiant, 1973........................20–13
Luis Tiant, 1974........................22–13
Luis Tiant, 1976........................21–12
Dennis Eckersley, 1978...............20–8
Roger Clemens, 1986.................24–4
Roger Clemens, 1987.................20–9
Roger Clemens, 1990.................21–6
Pedro Martinez, 1999................23–4
Derek Lowe, 2002......................21–8
Pedro Martinez, 2002................20–4
Curt Schilling, 2004...................21–6
Josh Beckett, 2007.....................20–7

No-Hitters

Cy Young (vs. Phila. A's), May 5, 1904
(final: 3–0) (perfect game)
Jesse Tannehill (vs. Chi. White Sox), Aug.
17, 1904 (final: 6–0)
Bill Dineen (vs. Chi. White Sox), Sept.
27, 1905 (final: 2–0)
Cy Young (vs. N.Y. Yankees), June 30,
1908 (final: 8–0)
Smokey Joe Wood (vs. St. L. Browns),
July 29, 1911 (final: 5–0)
George Foster (vs. N.Y. Yankees), June
21, 1916 (final: 2–0)
Hub Leonard (vs. St. L. Browns), Aug.
30, 1916 (final: 4–0)
Ernie Shore (vs. Wash. Senators),
June 23, 1917 (final: 4–0) (perfect
game)
Hub Leonard (vs. Det. Tigers), June 3,
1918 (final: 5–0)
Ray Caldwell (vs. N.Y. Yankees), Sept.
10, 1919 (final: 3–0)
Howard Ehmke (vs. Phila. A's), Sept.
7, 1923 (final: 4–0)
Mel Parnell (vs. Chi. White Sox), July
14, 1956 (final: 4–0)
Earl Wilson (vs. L.A. Angels), June
26, 1962 (final: 2–0)
Bill Monbouquette (vs. Chi. White Sox),
Aug. 1, 1962 (final: 1–0)
Dave Morehead (vs. Cleve. Indians),
Sept. 16, 1965 (final: 2–0)
Matt Young (vs. Cleve. Indians), Apr.
12, 1992 (final: 1–2) (8 innings, lost)

Hideo Nomo (vs. Balt. Orioles), Apr. 4,
2001 (final: 3–0)
Derek Lowe (vs. T.B. Devil Rays), Apr.
27, 2002 (final: 10–0)
Clay Buchholz (vs. Balt. Orioles),
Sept. 1, 2007 (final: 10–0)
Jon Lester (vs. K.C. Royals), May 19,
2008 (final 7–0)

No-Hitters Pitched Against

Ed Walsh, Chi. White Sox, Aug. 27,
1911 (final: 5–0)
George Mogridge, N.Y. Yankees,
Apr. 24, 1917 (final: 2–1)
Walter Johnson, Wash. Senators,
July 1, 1920 (final: 1–0)
Ted Lyons, Chi. White Sox, Aug.
21, 1926 (final: 6–0)
Bob Burke, Wash. Senators, Aug.
8, 1931 (final: 5–0)
Bobo Newsom, St. L. Browns, Sept. 18,
1934 (final: 1–2) (lost in 10th)
Allie Reynolds, N.Y. Yankees, Sept. 28,
1951 (final: 8–0)
Jim Bunning, Det. Tigers, July 20,
1958 (final: 3–0)
Tom Phoebus, Balt. Orioles, Apr. 27,
1968 (final: 6–0)
Dave Righetti, N.Y. Yankees, July 4,
1983 (final: 4–0)
Chris Bosio, Sea. Mariners, Apr. 22,
1993 (final: 7–0)

Postseason Play

1903   World Series vs. Pitt. Pirates (NL),
won 5 games to 3
1912   World Series vs. N.Y. Giants (NL),
won 4 games to 3
1915   World Series vs. Phila. Phillies
(NL), won 4 games to 1
1916   World Series vs. Bklyn. Dodgers
(NL), won 4 games to 1
1918   World Series vs. Chi. Cubs (NL),
won 4 games to 2
1946   World Series vs. St. L. Cardinals
(NL), lost 4 games to 3
1948   Pennant Playoff Game vs. Cleve.
Indians, lost

1967   World Series vs. St. L. Cardinals
(NL), lost 4 games to 3
1975   League Championship Series vs.
Oak. A's, won 3 games to 0
World Series vs. Cin. Reds (NL),
lost 4 games to 3
1978   East Division Playoff Game vs.
N.Y. Yankees, lost
1986   League Championship Series vs.
Cal. Angels, won 4 games to 3
World Series vs. N.Y. Mets (NL),
lost 4 games to 3
1988   League Championship Series vs.
Oak. A's, lost 4 games to 0
1990   League Championship Series vs.
Oak. A's, lost 4 games to 0
1995   Division Series vs. Cleve. Indians,
lost 3 games to 0
1998   Division Series vs. Cleve. Indians,
lost 3 games to 1
1999   Division Series vs. Cleve. Indians,
won 3 games to 2
League Championship Series vs.
N.Y. Yankees, lost 4 games to 1
2003   Division Series vs. Oak. A's, won
3 games to 2
League Championship Series vs.
N.Y. Yankees, lost 4 games to 3
2004   Division Series vs. Ana. Angels,
won 3 games to 0
League Championship Series vs.
N.Y. Yankees, won 4 games to 3
World Series vs. St. L. Cardinals
(NL), won 4 games to 0
2005   Division Series vs. Chi. White Sox,
lost 3 games to 0
2007   Division Series vs. L.A. Angels, won
3 games to 0
League Championship Series vs.
Cleve. Indians, won 4 games to 3
World Series vs. Col. Rockies,
won 4 games to 0
2008   Division Series vs. L.A. Angels, won
3 games to 1
League Championship Series vs.
T.B. Rays, lost 4 games to 3
2009   Division Series vs. L.A. Angels, lost
3 games to 0

Chicago White Sox

Dates of Operation: 1901–present (111 years)

Overall Record: 8707 wins, 8446 losses (.506) (AL)

Stadiums: South Side Park (also known as White Stocking Park, 1901–03; White Sox Park, 1904–10), 1901–10; Comiskey Park (also known as White Sox Park, 1910–12, 1962–75), 1910–90; Milwaukee County Stadium, 1968–69; New Comiskey Park, 1991–2002; now U.S. Cellular Field, 2003–present (capacity: 40,615)

Other Name: White Stockings

Year-by-Year Finishes

Year	Finish	Wins	Losses	Percentage	Games Behind	Manager	Attendance
1901	1st	83	53	.610	+4.0	Clark Griffith	354,350
1902	4th	74	60	.552	8.0	Clark Griffith	337,898
1903	7th	60	77	.438	30.5	Nixey Callahan	286,183
1904	3rd	89	65	.578	6.0	Nixey Callahan, Fielder Jones	557,123
1905	2nd	92	60	.605	2.0	Fielder Jones	687,419
1906	1st	93	58	.616	+3.0	Fielder Jones	585,202
1907	3rd	87	64	.576	5.5	Fielder Jones	666,307
1908	3rd	88	64	.579	1.5	Fielder Jones	636,096
1909	4th	78	74	.513	20.0	Billy Sullivan	478,400
1910	6th	68	85	.444	35.5	Hugh Duffy	552,084
1911	4th	77	74	.510	24.0	Hugh Duffy	583,208
1912	4th	78	76	.506	28.0	Nixey Callahan	602,241
1913	5th	78	74	.513	17.5	Nixey Callahan	644,501
1914	6th (Tie)	70	84	.455	30.0	Nixey Callahan	469,290
1915	3rd	93	61	.604	9.5	Pants Rowland	539,461
1916	2nd	89	65	.578	2.0	Pants Rowland	679,923
1917	1st	100	54	.649	+9.0	Pants Rowland	684,521
1918	6th	57	67	.460	17.0	Pants Rowland	195,081
1919	1st	88	52	.629	+3.5	Kid Gleason	627,186
1920	2nd	96	58	.623	2.0	Kid Gleason	833,492
1921	7th	62	92	.403	36.5	Kid Gleason	543,650
1922	5th	77	77	.500	17.0	Kid Gleason	602,860
1923	7th	69	85	.448	30.0	Kid Gleason	573,778
1924	8th	66	87	.431	25.5	Johnny Evers	606,658
1925	5th	79	75	.513	18.5	Eddie Collins	832,231
1926	5th	81	72	.529	9.5	Eddie Collins	710,339
1927	5th	70	83	.458	29.5	Ray Schalk	614,423
1928	5th	72	82	.468	29.0	Ray Schalk, Lena Blackburne	494,152
1929	7th	59	93	.388	46.0	Lena Blackburne	426,795
1930	7th	62	92	.403	40.0	Donie Bush	406,123
1931	8th	56	97	.366	51.0	Donie Bush	403,550
1932	7th	49	102	.325	56.5	Lew Fonseca	233,198
1933	6th	67	83	.447	31.0	Lew Fonseca	397,789
1934	8th	53	99	.349	47.0	Lew Fonseca, Jimmy Dykes	236,559
1935	5th	74	78	.487	19.5	Jimmy Dykes	470,281
1936	3rd	81	70	.536	20.0	Jimmy Dykes	440,810
1937	3rd	86	68	.558	16.0	Jimmy Dykes	589,245
1938	6th	65	83	.439	32.0	Jimmy Dykes	338,278

1939	4th	85	69	.552	22.5	Jimmy Dykes	594,104
1940	4th (Tie)	82	72	.532	8.0	Jimmy Dykes	660,336
1941	3rd	77	77	.500	24.0	Jimmy Dykes	677,077
1942	6th	66	82	.446	34.0	Jimmy Dykes	425,734
1943	4th	82	72	.532	16.0	Jimmy Dykes	508,962
1944	7th	71	83	.461	18.0	Jimmy Dykes	563,539
1945	6th	71	78	.477	15.0	Jimmy Dykes	657,981
1946	5th	74	80	.481	30.0	Jimmy Dykes, Ted Lyons	983,403
1947	6th	70	84	.455	27.0	Ted Lyons	876,948
1948	8th	51	101	.336	44.5	Ted Lyons	777,844
1949	6th	63	91	.409	34.0	Jack Onslow	937,151
1950	6th	60	94	.390	38.0	Jack Onslow, Red Corriden	781,330
1951	4th	81	73	.526	17.0	Paul Richards	1,328,234
1952	3rd	81	73	.526	14.0	Paul Richards	1,231,675
1953	3rd	89	65	.578	11.5	Paul Richards	1,191,353
1954	3rd	94	60	.610	17.0	Paul Richards, Marty Marion	1,231,629
1955	3rd	91	63	.591	5.0	Marty Marion	1,175,684
1956	3rd	85	69	.552	12.0	Marty Marion	1,000,090
1957	2nd	90	64	.584	8.0	Al Lopez	1,135,668
1958	2nd	82	72	.532	10.0	Al Lopez	797,451
1959	1st	94	60	.610	+5.0	Al Lopez	1,423,144
1960	3rd	87	67	.565	10.0	Al Lopez	1,644,460
1961	4th	86	76	.531	23.0	Al Lopez	1,146,019
1962	5th	85	77	.525	11.0	Al Lopez	1,131,562
1963	2nd	94	68	.580	10.5	Al Lopez	1,158,848
1964	2nd	98	64	.605	1.0	Al Lopez	1,250,053
1965	2nd	95	67	.586	7.0	Al Lopez	1,130,519
1966	4th	83	79	.512	15.0	Eddie Stanky	990,016
1967	4th	89	73	.549	3.0	Eddie Stanky	985,634
1968	8th (Tie)	67	95	.414	36.0	Eddie Stanky, Al Lopez	803,775

West Division

1969	5th	68	94	.420	29.0	Al Lopez, Don Gutteridge	589,546
1970	6th	56	106	.346	42.0	Don Gutteridge, Chuck Tanner	495,355
1971	3rd	79	83	.488	22.5	Chuck Tanner	833,891
1972	2nd	87	67	.565	5.5	Chuck Tanner	1,177,318
1973	5th	77	85	.475	17.0	Chuck Tanner	1,302,527
1974	4th	80	80	.500	9.0	Chuck Tanner	1,149,596
1975	5th	75	86	.466	22.5	Chuck Tanner	750,802
1976	6th	64	97	.398	25.5	Paul Richards	914,945
1977	3rd	90	72	.556	12.0	Bob Lemon	1,657,135
1978	5th	71	90	.441	20.5	Bob Lemon, Larry Doby	1,491,100
1979	5th	73	87	.456	14.0	Don Kessinger, Tony LaRussa	1,280,702
1980	5th	70	90	.438	26.0	Tony La Russa	1,200,365
1981*	3rd/6th	54	52	.509	2.5/7.0	Tony La Russa	946,651
1982	3rd	87	75	.537	6.0	Tony La Russa	1,567,787
1983	1st	99	63	.611	+20.0	Tony La Russa	2,132,821
1984	5th (Tie)	74	88	.457	10.0	Tony La Russa	2,136,988
1985	3rd	85	77	.525	6.0	Tony La Russa	1,669,888
1986	5th	72	90	.444	20.0	Tony La Russa, Jim Fregosi	1,424,313
1987	5th	77	85	.475	8.0	Jim Fregosi	1,208,060

Year	Finish	W	L	Pct.	GB	Manager	Attendance
1988	5th	71	90	.441	32.5	Jim Fregosi	1,115,749
1989	7th	69	92	.429	29.5	Jeff Torborg	1,045,651
1990	2nd	94	68	.580	9.0	Jeff Torborg	2,002,357
1991	2nd	87	75	.537	8.0	Jeff Torborg	2,934,154
1992	3rd	86	76	.531	10.0	Gene Lamont	2,681,156
1993	1st	94	68	.580	+8.0	Gene Lamont	2,581,091

Central Division

Year	Finish	W	L	Pct.	GB	Manager	Attendance
1994	1st	67	46	.593	+1.0	Gene Lamont	1,697,398
1995	3rd	68	76	.472	32.0	Gene Lamont, Terry Bevington	1,609,773
1996	2nd	85	77	.525	14.5	Terry Bevington	1,676,403
1997	2nd	80	81	.497	6.0	Terry Bevington	1,864,782
1998	2nd	80	82	.494	9.0	Jerry Manuel	1,391,146x
1999	2nd	75	86	.466	21.5	Jerry Manuel	1,338,851
2000	1st	95	67	.586	+5.0	Jerry Manuel	1,947,799
2001	3rd	83	79	.512	8.0	Jerry Manuel	1,766,172
2002	2nd	81	81	.500	13.5	Jerry Manuel	1,676,804
2003	2nd	86	76	.531	4.0	Jerry Manuel	1,939,524
2004	2nd	83	79	.512	9.0	Ozzie Guillen	1,930,537
2005	1st	99	63	.611	+6.0	Ozzie Guillen	2,342,833
2006	3rd	90	72	.556	6.0	Ozzie Guillen	2,057,411
2007	4th	72	90	.444	24.5	Ozzie Guillen	2,684,395
2008	1st	89	74	.546	+1.0	Ozzie Guillen	2,501,103
2009	3rd	79	83	.488	7.5	Ozzie Guillen	2,284,164
2010	2nd	88	74	.543	6.0	Ozzie Guillen	2,194,378
2011	3rd	79	83	.488	16.0	Ozzie Guillen	2,001,117

*Split season.

Awards

Most Valuable Player

Nellie Fox, second base, 1959
Dick Allen, first base, 1972
Frank Thomas, first base, 1993
Frank Thomas, first base, 1994

Rookie of the Year

Luis Aparicio, shortstop, 1956
Gary Peters, pitcher, 1963
Tommie Agee, outfield, 1966
Ron Kittle, outfield, 1983
Ozzie Guillen, shortstop, 1985

Cy Young

Early Wynn, 1959
LaMarr Hoyt, 1983
Jack McDowell, 1993

Hall of Famers Who Played for the White Sox

Roberto Alomar, second base, 2003–04
Luis Aparicio, shortstop, 1956–62
Luke Appling, shortstop, 1930–43 and 1945–50

Chief Bender, pitcher, 1925
Steve Carlton, pitcher, 1986
Eddie Collins, second base, 1915–26
Jocko Conlan, outfield, 1934–35
George Davis, shortstop, 1902 and 1904–09
Larry Doby, outfield, 1956–57 and 1959
Johnny Evers, second base, 1922
Red Faber, pitcher, 1914–33
Carlton Fisk, catcher, 1981–93
Nellie Fox, second base, 1950–63
Goose Gossage, pitcher, 1972–76
Clark Griffith, pitcher, 1901–02
Harry Hooper, outfield, 1921–25
George Kell, third base, 1954–56
Ted Lyons, pitcher, 1923–42 and 1946
Edd Roush, outfield, 1913
Red Ruffing, pitcher, 1947
Ray Schalk, catcher, 1912–28
Tom Seaver, pitcher, 1984–86
Al Simmons, outfield, 1933–35
Ed Walsh, pitcher, 1904–16
Hoyt Wilhelm, pitcher, 1963–68
Early Wynn, pitcher, 1958–62

Retired Numbers

2 .... Nellie Fox
3 .... Harold Baines
4 .... Luke Appling
9 .... Minnie Minoso
11 .... Luis Aparicio
16 .... Ted Lyons
19 .... Billy Pierce
35 .... Frank Thomas
72 .... Carlton Fisk

League Leaders, Batting

Batting Average, Season

Luke Appling, 1936 .... .388
Luke Appling, 1943 .... .328
Frank Thomas, 1997 .... .347

Home Runs, Season

Braggo Roth*, 1915 7
Gus Zernial**, 1951 33
Bill Melton, 1971 33
Dick Allen, 1972 37
Dick Allen, 1974 32

*Played part of season with Cleve. Indians.
**Played part of season with Phila. A's.

RBIs, Season
Gus Zernial*, 1951 129
Dick Allen, 1972.........................113
*Played part of season with Phila. A's.

Stolen Bases, Season
Frank Isbell, 1901 48
Patsy Dougherty, 1908...................47
Eddie Collins, 1919 33
Eddie Collins, 1923 49
Eddie Collins, 1924 42
Johnny Mostil, 1925 43
Johnny Mostil, 1926 35
Minnie Minoso*, 1951 31
Minnie Minoso, 1952 22
Minnie Minoso, 1953 25
Jim Rivera, 1955...........................25
Luis Aparicio, 1956 21
Luis Aparicio, 1957 28
Luis Aparicio, 1958 29
Luis Aparicio, 1959 56
Luis Aparicio, 1960 51
Luis Aparicio, 1961 53
Luis Aparicio, 1962 31
Juan Pierre, 2010..........................68
*Played part of season with Cleve. Indians.

Total Bases, Season
Joe Jackson, 1916 293
Minnie Minoso, 1954...................304
Albert Belle, 1998 399

Most Hits, Season
Nellie Fox, 1952 192
Nellie Fox, 1954 ....201 (Tie)
Nellie Fox, 1957 196
Nellie Fox, 1958 187
Minnie Minoso, 1960...................184
Lance Johnson, 1995 186

Most Runs, Season
Johnny Mostil, 1925 135
Frank Thomas, 1994.....................106

Batting Feats

Triple Crown Winners
[No player]

Hitting for the Cycle
Ray Schalk, June 27, 1922
Jack Brohamer, Sept. 24, 1977

Carlton Fisk, May 16, 1984
Chris Singleton, July 6, 1999
Jose Valentin, Apr. 27, 2000

Six Hits in a Game
Ray Radcliffe, July 18, 1936
Hank Steinbacher, June 22, 1938
Floyd Robinson, July 22, 1962
Lance Johnson, Sept. 23, 1995

40 or More Home Runs, Season
49 ....Albert Belle, 1998
44 ....Jermaine Dye, 2006
43......................Frank Thomas, 2000
42......................Frank Thomas, 2003
                            Jim Thome, 2006
41 ....Frank Thomas, 1993
                            Paul Konerko, 2004
40 ....Frank Thomas, 1995
                            Frank Thomas, 1996
                            Paul Konerko, 2005

League Leaders, Pitching

Most Wins, Season
Doc White, 1907 ....27 (Tie)
Ed Walsh, 1908 40
Eddie Cicotte, 1917 28
Eddie Cicotte, 1919 29
Ted Lyons, 1925 ....21 (Tie)
Ted Lyons, 1927 ....22 (Tie)
Billy Pierce, 1957 ....20 (Tie)
Early Wynn, 1959.........................22
Gary Peters, 1964...................20 (Tie)
Wilbur Wood, 1972 ....24 (Tie)
Wilbur Wood, 1973 24
La Marr Hoyt, 1982.......................19
La Marr Hoyt, 1983.......................24
Jack McDowell, 1993......................22

Most Strikeouts, Season
Ed Walsh, 1908 269
Frank Smith, 1909........................177
Ed Walsh, 1911 255
Billy Pierce, 1953 186
Early Wynn, 1958 179
Esteban Loaiza, 2003 207

Lowest ERA, Season
Eddie Cicotte, 1917 ....1.53
Red Faber, 1921 ....2.47
Red Faber, 1922 ....2.80

Thornton Lee, 1941.......................2.37
Ted Lyons, 1942...........................2.10
Saul Rogovin*, 1951....................2.78
Billy Pierce, 1955 ....1.97
Frank Baumann, 1960 ....2.68
Gary Peters, 1963.........................2.33
Gary Peters, 1966.........................1.98
Joel Horlen, 1967.........................2.06
*Pitched part of season with Det. Tigers.

Most Saves, Season
Terry Forster, 1974 24
Goose Gossage, 1975 26
Bobby Thigpen, 1990 57

Best Won–Lost Percentage, Season
Clark Griffith, 1901 ....24–7........ .774
Ed Walsh, 1908 ....40–15....... .727
Eddie Cicotte, 1916....15–7........ .682
Reb Russell, 1917....15–5........ .750
Eddie Cicotte, 1919....29–7........ .806
Sandy Consuegra,
  1954 ....16–3........ .842
Dick Donovan, 1957.........16–6.. .727 (Tie)
Bob Shaw, 1959 ....18–6........ .750
Ray Herbert, 1962 ......20–9........ .690
Joe Horlen, 1967 ....19–7........ .731
Rich Dotson, 1983.......22–7........ .759
Jason Bere, 1994........12–2........ .857

Pitching Feats

20 Wins, Season
Clark Griffith, 1901 24–7
Roy Patterson, 1902.................20–12
Frank Owen, 1904....................21–15
Nick Altrock, 1905 24–12
Frank Owen, 1905....................21–13
Frank Owen, 1906....................22–13
Nick Altrock, 1906 20–13
Doc White, 1907 27–13
Ed Walsh, 1907.......................24–18
Frank Smith, 1907 23–10
Ed Walsh, 1908.......................40–15
Frank Smith, 1909....................25–17
Ed Walsh, 1911.......................27–18
Ed Walsh, 1912.......................27–17
Reb Russell, 1913 22–16
Jim Scott, 1913.........................20–20
Jim Scott, 1915.........................24–11
Red Faber, 1915.......................24–14
Eddie Cicotte, 1917 28–12

Eddie Cicotte, 1919 29–7
Lefty Williams, 1919 23–11
Red Faber, 1920 23–13
Lefty Williams, 1920 22–14
Dickie Kerr, 1920.......................21–9
Eddie Cicotte, 1920 21–10
Red Faber, 1921 25–15
Red Faber, 1922 21–17
Sloppy Thurston, 1924 20–14
Ted Lyons, 1925.......................21–11
Ted Lyons, 1927.......................22–14
Ted Lyons, 1930........................22–15
Vern Kennedy, 1936 21–9
Thornton Lee, 1941 22–11
Virgil Trucks, 1953 ....20–10*
Billy Pierce, 1956 20–9
Billy Pierce, 1957.....................20–12
Early Wynn, 1959 22–10
Ray Herbert, 1962 20–9
Gary Peters, 1964 20–8
Wilbur Wood, 1971.................22–13
Wilbur Wood, 1972 24–17
Stan Bahnsen, 1972.................21–16
Wilbur Wood, 1973.................24–20
Jim Kaat, 1974..........................21–13
Wilbur Wood, 1974.................20–19
Jim Kaat, 1975..........................20–14
La Marr Hoyt, 1983 24–10
Rich Dotson, 1983 22–7
Jack McDowell, 1992 20–10
Jack McDowell, 1993 22–10
Esteban Loaiza, 2003.................21–9
*15–6 with Chi. White Sox and 5–4 with
St. L. Browns.

No-Hitters

Jimmy Callahan (vs. Det. Tigers),
   Sept. 20, 1902 (final: 3–0)
Frank Smith (vs. Det. Tigers), Sept.
   6, 1905 (final: 15–0)
Frank Smith (vs. Phila. A's), Sept. 20,
   1908 (final: 1–0)
Ed Walsh (vs. Bost. Red Sox), Aug.
   27, 1911 (final: 5–0)

Jim Scott (vs. Wash. Senators), May
   14, 1914 (final: 0–1) (allowed hit
   and lost in 10th)
Joe Benz (vs. Cleve. Indians), May 31,
   1914 (final: 6–1)
Eddie Cicotte (vs. St. L. Browns), Apr.
   14, 1917 (final: 11–0)
Charlie Robertson (vs. Det. Tigers),
   Apr. 30, 1922 (final: 2–0) (perfect
   game)
Ted Lyons (vs. Bost. Red Sox), Aug.
   21, 1926 (final: 6–0)
Vern Kennedy (vs. St. L. Browns),
   Aug. 31, 1935 (final: 5–0)
Bill Dietrich (vs. St. L. Browns), June
   1, 1937 (final: 8–0)
Bob Keegan (vs. Wash. Senators),
   Aug. 20, 1957 (final: 6–0)
Joe Horlen (vs. Det. Tigers), Sept.
   10, 1967 (final: 6–0)
Blue Moon Odom and Francisco
   Barrios (vs. Oak. A's), July 28, 1976
   (final: 6–0)
Joe Cowley (vs. Cal. Angels), Sept. 19,
   1986 (final: 7–1)
Wilson Alvarez (vs. Balt. Orioles),
   Aug. 11, 1991 (final: 7–0)
Mark Buehrle (vs. Tex. Rangers), Apr.
   18, 2007 (final: 6–0)
Mark Buehrle (vs. T.B. Rays), July 23,
   2009 (final: 5–0) (perfect game)

No-Hitters Pitched Against

Earl Moore, Cleve. Indians, May 9, 1901
   (final: 2–4) (lost in 10th)
Jesse Tannehill, Bost. Red Sox, Aug.
   17, 1904 (final: 6–0)
Bill Dineen, Bost. Red Sox, Sept. 27,
   1905 (final: 2–0)
Bob Rhoads, Cleve. Indians, Sept. 18,
   1908 (final: 2–0)
Addie Joss, Cleve. Indians, Oct. 2,
   1908 (final: 1–0) (perfect game)
Addie Joss, Cleve. Indians, Apr. 20,

1910 (final: 1–0)
Ernie Koob, St. L. Browns, May 5,
   1917 (final: 1–0)
Bob Groom, St. L. Browns, May 6,
   1917 (final: 3–0)
Bob Feller, Cleve. Indians, Apr. 16,
   1940 (final: 1–0)
Mel Parnell, Bost. Red Sox, July 14,
   1956 (final: 4–0)
Bill Monbouquette, Bost. Red Sox,
   Aug. 1, 1962 (final: 1–0)
Mike Warren, Oak. A's, Sept. 29, 1983
   (final: 3–0)
Jack Morris, Det. Tigers, Apr. 7, 1984
   (final: 4–0)
Andy Hawkins, N.Y. Yankees, July 1,
   1990 (final: 0–4) (8 innings, lost)
Bret Saberhagen, K.C. Royals, Aug.
   26, 1991 (final: 7–0)
Francisco Liriano, Minn. Twins, May
   3, 2011 (final 1–0)

Postseason Play

1906   World Series vs. Chi. Cubs (NL),
      won 4 games to 2
1917   World Series vs. N.Y. Giants (NL),
      won 4 games to 2
1919   World Series vs. Cin. Reds (NL),
      lost 5 games to 3
1959   World Series vs. L.A. Dodgers
      (NL), lost 4 games to 2
1983   League Championship Series vs.
      Balt. Orioles, lost 3 games to 1
1993   League Championship Series vs.
      Tor. Blue Jays, lost 4 games
      to 2
2000   Division Series vs. Sea. Mariners,
      lost 3 games to 0
2005   Division Series vs. Bost. Red Sox,
      won 3 games to 0
      League Championship Series vs.
      L.A. Angels, won 4 games to 1
      World Series vs. Hous. Astros,
      won 4 games to 0
2008   Division Series vs. T.B. Rays, lost 3
      games to 1

Cleveland Indians

Dates of Operation: 1901–present (111 years)

Overall Record: 8771 wins, 8449 losses (.509)

Stadiums: League Park, 1901–09; League Park II (also called Dunn Field, 1916–27), 1910–32 and 1934–36; Cleveland Stadium (also known as Lakefront Stadium and Municipal Stadium, 1932–33, 1936–93), 1932–93; Jacobs Field (also called The Jake), 1994–2007; now Progressive Field, 2008–present (capacity: 43,515)

Other Names: Blues, Broncos (or Bronchos), Molly Maguires, Naps

Year-by-Year Finishes

Year	Finish	Wins	Losses	Percentage	Games Behind	Manager	Attendance
1901	7th	54	82	.397	29.0	Jimmy McAleer	131,380
1902	5th	69	67	.507	14.0	Bill Armour	275,395
1903	3rd	77	63	.550	15.0	Bill Armour	311,280
1904	4th	86	65	.570	7.5	Bill Armour	264,749
1905	5th	76	78	.494	19.0	Nap Lajoie	316,306
1906	3rd	89	64	.582	5.0	Nap Lajoie	325,733
1907	4th	85	67	.559	8.0	Nap Lajoie	382,046
1908	2nd	90	64	.584	0.5	Nap Lajoie	422,242
1909	6th	71	82	.464	27.5	Nap Lajoie, Deacon McGuire	354,627
1910	5th	71	81	.467	32.0	Deacon McGuire	293,456
1911	3rd	80	73	.523	22.0	Deacon McGuire, George Stovall	406,296
1912	5th	75	78	.490	30.5	Harry Davis, Joe Birmingham	336,844
1913	3rd	86	66	.566	9.5	Joe Birmingham	541,000
1914	8th	51	102	.333	48.5	Joe Birmingham	185,997
1915	7th	57	95	.375	44.5	Joe Birmingham, Lee Fohl	159,285
1916	6th	77	77	.500	14.0	Lee Fohl	492,106
1917	3rd	88	66	.571	12.0	Lee Fohl	477,298
1918	2nd	73	54	.575	2.5	Lee Fohl	295,515
1919	2nd	84	55	.604	3.5	Lee Fohl, Tris Speaker	538,135
1920	1st	98	56	.636	+2.0	Tris Speaker	912,832
1921	2nd	94	60	.610	4.5	Tris Speaker	748,705
1922	4th	78	76	.506	16.0	Tris Speaker	528,145
1923	3rd	82	71	.536	16.5	Tris Speaker	558,856
1924	6th	67	86	.438	24.5	Tris Speaker	481,905
1925	6th	70	84	.455	27.5	Tris Speaker	419,005
1926	2nd	88	66	.571	3.0	Tris Speaker	627,426
1927	6th	66	87	.431	43.5	Jack McAllister	373,138
1928	7th	62	92	.403	39.0	Roger Peckinpaugh	375,907
1929	3rd	81	71	.533	24.0	Roger Peckinpaugh	536,210
1930	4th	81	73	.526	21.0	Roger Peckinpaugh	528,657
1931	4th	78	76	.506	30.0	Roger Peckinpaugh	483,027
1932	4th	87	65	.572	19.0	Roger Peckinpaugh	468,953
1933	4th	75	76	.497	23.5	Roger Peckinpaugh, Walter Johnson	387,936
1934	3rd	85	69	.552	16.0	Walter Johnson	391,338
1935	3rd	82	71	.536	12.0	Walter Johnson, Steve O'Neill	397,615
1936	5th	80	74	.519	22.5	Steve O'Neill	500,391
1937	4th	83	71	.539	19.0	Steve O'Neill	564,849
1938	3rd	86	66	.566	13.0	Ossie Vitt	652,006

1939	3rd	87	67	.565	20.5	Ossie Vitt	563,928
1940	2nd	89	65	.578	1.0	Ossie Vitt	902,576
1941	4th (Tie)	75	79	.487	26.0	Roger Peckinpaugh	745,948
1942	4th	75	79	.487	28.0	Lou Boudreau	459,447
1943	3rd	82	71	.536	15.5	Lou Boudreau	438,894
1944	5th (Tie)	72	82	.468	17.0	Lou Boudreau	475,272
1945	5th	73	72	.503	11.0	Lou Boudreau	558,182
1946	6th	68	86	.442	36.0	Lou Boudreau	1,057,289
1947	4th	80	74	.519	17.0	Lou Boudreau	1,521,978
1948	1st	97	58	.626	+1.0	Lou Boudreau	2,620,627
1949	3rd	89	65	.578	8.0	Lou Boudreau	2,233,771
1950	4th	92	62	.597	6.0	Lou Boudreau	1,727,464
1951	2nd	93	61	.604	5.0	Al Lopez	1,704,984
1952	2nd	93	61	.604	2.0	Al Lopez	1,444,607
1953	2nd	92	62	.597	8.5	Al Lopez	1,069,176
1954	1st	111	43	.721	+8.0	Al Lopez	1,335,472
1955	2nd	93	61	.604	3.0	Al Lopez	1,221,780
1956	2nd	88	66	.571	9.0	Al Lopez	865,467
1957	6th	76	77	.497	21.5	Kerby Farrell	722,256
1958	4th	77	76	.503	14.5	Bobby Bragan, Joe Gordon	663,805
1959	2nd	89	65	.578	5.0	Joe Gordon	1,497,976
1960	4th	76	78	.494	21.0	Joe Gordon, Jimmy Dykes	950,985
1961	5th	78	83	.484	30.5	Jimmy Dykes	725,547
1962	6th	80	82	.494	16.0	Mel McGaha	716,076
1963	5th (Tie)	79	83	.488	25.5	Birdie Tebbetts	562,507
1964	6th (Tie)	79	83	.488	20.0	Birdie Tebbetts	653,293
1965	5th	87	75	.537	15.0	Birdie Tebbetts	934,786
1966	5th	81	81	.500	17.0	Birdie Tebbetts, George Strickland	903,359
1967	8th	75	87	.463	17.0	Joe Adcock	662,980
1968	3rd	86	75	.534	16.5	Alvin Dark	857,994

East Division

1969	6th	62	99	.385	46.5	Alvin Dark	619,970
1970	5th	76	86	.469	32.0	Alvin Dark	729,752
1971	6th	60	102	.370	43.0	Alvin Dark, Johnny Lipon	591,361
1972	5th	72	84	.462	14.0	Ken Aspromonte	626,354
1973	6th	71	91	.438	26.0	Ken Aspromonte	615,107
1974	4th	77	85	.475	14.0	Ken Aspromonte	1,114,262
1975	4th	79	80	.497	15.5	Frank Robinson	977,039
1976	4th	81	78	.509	16.0	Frank Robinson	948,776
1977	5th	71	90	.441	28.5	Frank Robinson, Jeff Torborg	900,365
1978	6th	69	90	.434	29.0	Jeff Torborg	800,584
1979	6th	81	80	.503	22.0	Jeff Torborg, Dave Garcia	1,011,644
1980	6th	79	81	.494	23.0	Dave Garcia	1,033,827
1981*	6th/5th	52	51	.505	5.0/5.0	Dave Garcia	661,026
1982	6th (Tie)	78	84	.481	17.0	Dave Garcia	1,044,021
1983	7th	70	92	.432	28.0	Mike Ferraro, Pat Corrales	768,941
1984	6th	75	87	.463	29.0	Pat Corrales	734,079
1985	7th	60	102	.370	39.5	Pat Corrales	655,181
1986	5th	84	78	.519	11.5	Pat Corrales	1,471,805
1987	7th	61	101	.377	37.0	Pat Corrales, Doc Edwards	1,077,898

1988	6th	78	84	.481	11.0	Doc Edwards	1,411,610
1989	6th	73	89	.451	16.0	Doc Edwards, John Hart	1,285,542
1990	4th	77	85	.475	11.0	John McNamara	1,225,240
1991	7th	57	105	.352	34.0	John McNamara, Mike Hargrove	1,051,863
1992	4th (Tie)	76	86	.469	20.0	Mike Hargrove	1,224,274
1993	6th	76	86	.469	19.0	Mike Hargrove	2,177,908

Central Division

1994	2nd	66	47	.584	1.0	Mike Hargrove	1,995,174
1995	1st	100	44	.694	+30.0	Mike Hargrove	2,842,745
1996	1st	99	62	.615	+14.5	Mike Hargrove	3,318,174
1997	1st	86	75	.534	+6.0	Mike Hargrove	3,404,750
1998	1st	89	73	.549	+9.0	Mike Hargrove	3,467,299
1999	1st	97	65	.599	+21.5	Mike Hargrove	3,468,456
2000	2nd	90	72	.556	5.0	Charlie Manuel	3,456,278
2001	1st	91	71	.562	+6.0	Charlie Manuel	3,175,523
2002	3rd	74	88	.457	20.5	Charlie Manuel, Joel Skinner	2,616,940
2003	4th	68	94	.420	22.0	Eric Wedge	1,730,002
2004	3rd	80	82	.494	12.0	Eric Wedge	1,814,401
2005	2nd	93	69	.574	6.0	Eric Wedge	2,013,763
2006	4th	78	84	.481	18.0	Eric Wedge	1,997,995
2007	1st	96	66	.593	+8.5	Eric Wedge	2,275,916
2008	3rd	81	81	.500	7.5	Eric Wedge	2,169,760
2009	4th	65	97	.401	21.5	Eric Wedge	1,766,242
2010	4th	69	93	.416	25.0	Manny Acta	1,391,644
2011	2nd	80	82	.494	15.0	Manny Acta	1,840,835

*Split season.

Awards

Most Valuable Player
George H. Burns, first base, 1926
Lou Boudreau, shortstop, 1948
Al Rosen, third base, 1953

Rookie of the Year
Herb Score, pitcher, 1955
Chris Chambliss, first base, 1971
Joe Charboneau, outfield, 1980
Sandy Alomar Jr., catcher, 1990

Cy Young
Gaylord Perry, 1972
C. C. Sabathia, 2007
Cliff Lee, 2008

Hall of Famers Who Played for the Indians
Roberto Alomar, 1999–2001
Earl Averill, outfield, 1929–39
Lou Boudreau, shortstop, 1938–50
Steve Carlton, pitcher, 1987
Stan Coveleski, pitcher, 1916–24

Larry Doby, outfield, 1947–55 and 1958
Dennis Eckersley, pitcher, 1975–77
Bob Feller, pitcher, 1936–41 and 1945–56
Elmer Flick, outfield, 1902–10
Joe Gordon, second base, 1947–50
Addie Joss, pitcher, 1902–10
Ralph Kiner, outfield, 1955
Nap Lajoie, second base, 1902–14
Bob Lemon, pitcher, 1941–42 and 1946–58
Al Lopez, catcher, 1947
Eddie Murray, designated hitter, 1994–96
Hal Newhouser, pitcher, 1954–55
Phil Niekro, pitcher, 1986–87
Satchel Paige, pitcher, 1948–49
Gaylord Perry, pitcher, 1972–75
Sam Rice, outfield, 1934
Frank Robinson, designated hitter, 1974–76
Joe Sewell, shortstop, 1920–30

Billy Southworth, outfield, 1913 and 1915
Tris Speaker, outfield, 1916–26
Hoyt Wilhelm, pitcher, 1957–58
Dave Winfield, designated hitter, 1995
Early Wynn, pitcher, 1949–57
Cy Young, pitcher, 1890–98 and 1909–11

Retired Numbers
3 ....Earl Averill
5....................................Lou Boudreau
14 ....Larry Doby
18 ....Mel Harder
19 ....Bob Feller
21 ....Bob Lemon
455........The Fans (consecutive sellouts)

League Leaders, Batting

Batting Average, Season
Nap Lajoie, 1903 .... .355
Nap Lajoie, 1904 .... .381
Elmer Flick, 1905 .... .308
Tris Speaker, 1916 .... .386

Lew Fonseca, 1929 .... .369
Lou Boudreau, 1944 .... .327
Roberto Avila, 1954 .... .341

Home Runs, Season
Braggo Roth*, 1915 7
Al Rosen, 1950 37
Larry Doby, 1952 32
Al Rosen, 1953 43
Larry Doby, 1954 32
Rocky Colavito, 1959 .... 42 (Tie)
Albert Belle, 1995 50
*Played part of season with Chi. White Sox.

RBIs, Season
Hal Trosky, 1936 162
Al Rosen, 1952 105
Al Rosen, 1953 145
Larry Doby, 1954 126
Rocky Colavito, 1965 108
Joe Carter, 1986 121
Albert Belle, 1993 129
Albert Belle, 1995 .... 126 (Tie)
Albert Belle, 1996 148
Manny Ramirez, 1999 165

Stolen Bases, Season
Harry Bay, 1903 46
Harry Bay, 1904 .... 42 (Tie)
Elmer Flick, 1904 .... 42 (Tie)
Elmer Flick, 1906 .... 39 (Tie)
George Case, 1946 28
Minnie Minoso*, 1951 31
Kenny Lofton, 1992 66
Kenny Lofton, 1993 70
Kenny Lofton, 1994 60
Kenny Lofton, 1995 54
Kenny Lofton, 1996 75
*Played part of season with Chi. White Sox.

Total Bases, Season
Nap Lajoie, 1904 304
Nap Lajoie, 1910 304
Joe Jackson, 1912 331
Hal Trosky, 1936 405
Al Rosen, 1952 297
Al Rosen, 1953 367
Rocky Colavito, 1959 301
Albert Belle, 1994 294
Albert Belle, 1995 377

Most Hits, Season
Piano Legs Hickman*, 1902 194
Nap Lajoie, 1904 211
Nap Lajoie, 1906 214
Nap Lajoie, 1910 227
Joe Jackson, 1913 197
Tris Speaker, 1916 211
Charlie Jamieson, 1923 222
George Burns, 1926 .... 216 (Tie)
Johnny Hodapp, 1930 225
Joe Vosmik, 1935 216
Earl Averill, 1936 232
Dale Mitchell, 1949 203
Kenny Lofton, 1994 160
*Played part of season with Bost. Red Sox.

Most Runs, Season
Elmer Flick, 1906 98
Ray Chapman, 1918 84
Larry Doby, 1952 104
Al Rosen, 1953 115
Al Smith, 1955 123
Albert Belle, 1995 .... 121 (Tie)
Roberto Alomar, 1999 138
Grady Sizemore, 2006 134

Batting Feats

Triple Crown Winners
[No player]

Hitting for the Cycle
Bill Bradley, Sept. 24, 1903
Earl Averill, Aug. 17, 1933
Odell Hale, July 12, 1938
Larry Doby, June 4, 1952
Tony Horton, July 2, 1970
Andre Thornton, Apr. 22, 1978
Travis Hafner, Aug. 14, 2003

Six Hits in a Game
Zaza Harvey, Apr. 25, 1902
Frank Brower, Aug. 7, 1923
George H. Burns, June 19, 1924
Johnny Burnett, July 10, 1932*
 (9 hits in game)
Bruce Campbell, July 2, 1936
Jim Fridley, Apr. 29, 1952
Jorge Orta, June 15, 1980
Carlos Baerga, Apr. 11, 1992*
Omar Vizquel, Aug. 31, 2004
*Extra-inning game.

40 or More Home Runs, Season
52 .... Jim Thome, 2002
50 .... Albert Belle, 1995
49 .... Jim Thome, 2001
48 .... Albert Belle, 1996
45 .... Manny Ramirez, 1998
44 .... Manny Ramirez, 1999
43 .... Al Rosen, 1953
42 .... Hal Trosky, 1936
                         Rocky Colavito, 1959
                          Travis Hafner, 2006
41 .... Rocky Colavito, 1958
                          David Justice, 2000*
40 .... Jim Thome, 1997
*20 with N.Y. Yankees and 21 with Cleve.
Indians.

League Leaders, Pitching

Most Wins, Season
Addie Joss, 1907 .... 27 (Tie)
Jim Bagby Sr., 1920 31
George Uhle, 1923 26
George Uhle, 1926 27
Bob Feller, 1939 24
Bob Feller, 1940 27
Bob Feller, 1941 25
Bob Feller, 1946 .... 26 (Tie)
Bob Feller, 1947 20
Bob Lemon, 1950 23
Bob Feller, 1951 22
Bob Lemon, 1954 .... 23 (Tie)
Early Wynn, 1954 .... 23 (Tie)
Bob Lemon, 1955 .... 18 (Tie)
Jim Perry, 1960 .... 18 (Tie)
Cliff Lee, 2008 22

Most Strikeouts, Season
Stan Coveleski, 1920 133
Bob Feller, 1938 240
Bob Feller, 1939 246
Bob Feller, 1940 261
Bob Feller, 1941 260
Allie Reynolds, 1943 151
Bob Feller, 1946 348
Bob Feller, 1947 196
Bob Feller, 1948 164
Bob Lemon, 1950 170
Herb Score, 1955 245
Herb Score, 1956 263
Early Wynn, 1957 184
Sam McDowell, 1965 325
Sam McDowell, 1966 225

Sam McDowell, 1968....................283
Sam McDowell, 1969....................279
Sam McDowell, 1970....................304
Len Barker, 1980 187
Len Barker, 1981 127
Bert Blyleven*, 1985 206
*Pitched part of season with Minn. Twins.

Lowest ERA, Season

Stan Coveleski, 1923 ....2.76
Monte Pearson, 1933...................2.33
Bob Feller, 1940 ....2.62
Gene Bearden, 1948 ....2.43
Early Wynn, 1950 ....3.20
Mike Garcia, 1954.......................2.64
Sam McDowell, 1965....................2.18
Luis Tiant, 1968...........................1.60
Rick Sutcliffe, 1982......................2.96
Kevin Millwood, 2005...................2.64
Cliff Lee, 2008 ....2.54

Most Saves, Season

Jose Mesa, 1995 46
Bob Wickman, 2005...............45 (Tie)
Joe Borowski, 2007 45

Best Won–Lost Percentage, Season

Bill Bernhard*, 1902 ......18–5.... .783
Jim Bagby, 1920..........31–12.... .721
George Uhle, 1926 ......27–11.... .711
Johnny Allen, 1937........15–1.... .938
Bob Feller, 1951 ....22–8.... .733
Jim Perry, 1960 ....18–10.... .643
Sonny Siebert, 1966 ......16–8.... .667
Charles Nagy, 1996.......17–5.... .773
Cliff Lee, 2005 ....18–5.... .783
Cliff Lee, 2008 ....22–3.... .880
*Pitched part of season with Phila. A's.

Pitching Feats

20 Wins, Season

Bill Bernhard, 1904...................23–13
Addie Joss, 1905.......................20–12
Bob Rhoads, 1906 22–10
Addie Joss, 1906.........................21–9
Otto Hess, 1906 20–17
Addie Joss, 1907......................27–10
Addie Joss, 1908......................24–11
Vean Gregg, 1911.......................23–7
Vean Gregg, 1912....................20–13
Cy Falkenberg, 1913.................23–10
Vean Gregg, 1913....................20–13

Jim Bagby, 1917.......................23–13
Stan Coveleski, 1918 22–13
Stan Coveleski, 1919 23–12
Jim Bagby, 1920.......................31–12
Stan Coveleski, 1920 24–14
Ray Caldwell, 1920 20–10
Stan Coveleski, 1921 23–13
George Uhle, 1922 22–16
George Uhle, 1923 26–16
Joe Shaute, 1924.......................20–17
George Uhle, 1926 27–11
Wes Ferrell, 1929 21–10
Wes Ferrell, 1930 25–13
Wes Ferrell, 1931 22–12
Wes Ferrell, 1932 23–13
Mel Harder, 1934 20–12
Mel Harder, 1935 22–11
Johnny Allen, 1936....................20–10
Bob Feller, 1937 24–9
Bob Feller, 1940 27–11
Bob Feller, 1941 25–13
Bob Feller, 1946 26–15
Bob Feller, 1947 20–11
Gene Bearden, 1948...................20–7
Bob Lemon, 1948......................20–14
Bob Lemon, 1949......................22–10
Bob Lemon, 1950......................23–11
Bob Feller, 1951 22–8
Mike Garcia, 1951 20–13
Early Wynn, 1951 20–13
Early Wynn, 1952 23–12
Mike Garcia, 1952 22–11
Bob Lemon, 1952......................22–11
Bob Lemon, 1953......................21–15
Bob Lemon, 1954 23–7
Early Wynn, 1954 23–11
Herb Score, 1956 20–9
Early Wynn, 1956 20–9
Bob Lemon, 1956......................20–14
Dick Donovan, 1962 20–10
Luis Tiant, 1968...........................21–9
Sam McDowell, 1970 20–12
Gaylord Perry, 1972 24–16
Gaylord Perry, 1974 21–13
Cliff Lee, 2008 22–3

No-Hitters

Earl Moore (vs. Chi. White Sox), May 9,
1901 (final: 2–4) (lost in 10th)
Bob Rhoads (vs. Chi. White Sox), Sept.
18, 1908 (final: 2–0)
Addie Joss (vs. Chi. White Sox), Oct. 2,
1908 (final: 1–0) (perfect game)

Addie Joss (vs. Chi. White Sox), Apr.
20, 1910 (final: 1–0)
Wes Ferrell (vs. St. L. Browns), Apr. 29,
1931 (final: 9–0)
Bob Feller (vs. Chi. White Sox), Apr.
16, 1940 (final: 1–0)
Bob Feller (vs. N.Y. Yankees), Apr. 30,
1946 (final: 1–0)
Don Black (vs. Phila. A's), July 10,
1947 (final: 3–0)
Bob Lemon (vs. Det. Tigers), June 30,
1948 (final: 2–0)
Bob Feller (vs. Det. Tigers), July 1,
1951 (final: 2–1)
Sonny Siebert (vs. Wash. Senators II),
June 10, 1966 (final: 2–0)
Dick Bosman (vs. Oak. A's), July 19,
1974 (final: 4–0)
Dennis Eckersley (vs. Cal. Angels), May
30, 1977 (final: 1–0)
Len Barker (vs. Tor. Blue Jays), May 15,
1981 (final: 3–0) (perfect game)

No-Hitters Pitched Against

Chief Bender, Phila. A's, May 12, 1910
(final: 4–0)
Tom Hughes, N.Y. Yankees, Aug. 30,
1910 (final: 0–5) (lost in 11th)
Joe Benz, Chi. White Sox, May 31,
1914 (final: 6–1)
Joe Bush, Phila. A's, Aug. 26, 1916
(final: 5–0)
Monte Pearson, N.Y. Yankees, Aug. 27,
1938 (final: 13–0)
Allie Reynolds, N.Y. Yankees, July 12,
1951 (final: 1–0)
Dave Morehead, Bost. Red Sox, Sept.
16, 1965 (final: 2–0)
Dean Chance, Minn. Twins, Aug. 25,
1967 (final: 2–1)
Matt Young, Bost. Red Sox, Apr. 12,
1992 (final: 1–2) (8 innings, lost)
Jim Abbott, N.Y. Yankees, Sept. 4,
1993 (final: 4–0)
Ervin Santana, L.A. Angels, July 27,
2011 (final: 3–1)

Postseason Play

1920 World Series vs. Bklyn. Dodgers
(NL), won 5 games to 2
1948 Pennant Playoff Game vs. Bost.
Red Sox, won
World Series vs. Bost. Braves
(NL), won 4 games to 2

1954 World Series vs. N.Y. Giants (NL),
      lost 4 games to 0
1995 Division Series vs. Bost. Red Sox,
      won 3 games to 0
      League Championship Series vs.
      Sea. Mariners, won 4 games
      to 2
      World Series vs. Atl. Braves (NL),
      lost 4 games to 2

1996 Division Series vs. Balt. Orioles,
      lost 3 games to 1
1997 Division Series vs. N.Y. Yankees,
      won 3 games to 2
      League Championship Series vs.
      Balt. Orioles, won 4 games to 2
      World Series vs. Flor. Marlins
      (NL), lost 4 games to 3
1998 Division Series vs. Bost. Red Sox,
      won 3 games to 1

      League Championship Series vs.
      N.Y. Yankees, lost 4 games
      to 2
1999 Division Series vs. Bost. Red Sox,
      lost 3 games to 2
2001 Division Series vs. Sea. Mariners,
      lost 3 games to 2
2007 Division Series vs. N.Y. Yankees,
      won 3 games to 1
      League Championship vs. Bost.
      Red Sox, lost 4 games to 3

Detroit Tigers

Dates of Operation: 1901–present (111 years)
Overall Record: 8740 wins, 8504 losses (.507)
Stadiums: Bennett Park, 1901–11; Burns Park, 1901–02 (Sundays only); Tiger Stadium, 1912–1999
(also known as Navin Field, 1912–37, and Briggs Stadium, 1938–60); Comerica Park,
2000–present (capacity: 41,782)

Year-by-Year Finishes

Year	Finish	Wins	Losses	Percentage	Games Behind	Manager	Attendance
1901	3rd	74	61	.548	8.5	George Stallings	259,430
1902	7th	52	83	.385	30.5	Frank Dwyer	189,469
1903	5th	65	71	.478	25.0	Ed Barrow	224,523
1904	7th	62	90	.408	32.0	Ed Barrow, Bobby Lowe	177,796
1905	3rd	79	74	.516	15.5	Bill Armour	193,384
1906	6th	71	78	.477	21.0	Bill Armour	174,043
1907	1st	92	58	.613	+1.5	Hughie Jennings	297,079
1908	1st	90	63	.588	+0.5	Hughie Jennings	436,199
1909	1st	98	54	.645	+3.5	Hughie Jennings	490,490
1910	3rd	86	68	.558	18.0	Hughie Jennings	391,288
1911	2nd	89	65	.578	13.5	Hughie Jennings	484,988
1912	6th	69	84	.451	36.5	Hughie Jennings	402,870
1913	6th	66	87	.431	30.0	Hughie Jennings	398,502
1914	4th	80	73	.523	19.5	Hughie Jennings	416,225
1915	2nd	100	54	.649	2.5	Hughie Jennings	476,105
1916	3rd	87	67	.565	4.0	Hughie Jennings	616,772
1917	4th	78	75	.510	21.5	Hughie Jennings	457,289
1918	7th	55	71	.437	20.0	Hughie Jennings	203,719
1919	4th	80	60	.571	8.0	Hughie Jennings	643,805
1920	7th	61	93	.396	37.0	Hughie Jennings	579,650
1921	6th	71	82	.464	27.0	Ty Cobb	661,527
1922	3rd	79	75	.513	15.0	Ty Cobb	861,206
1923	2nd	83	71	.539	16.0	Ty Cobb	911,377
1924	3rd	86	68	.558	6.0	Ty Cobb	1,015,136
1925	4th	81	73	.526	16.5	Ty Cobb	820,766
1926	6th	79	75	.513	12.0	Ty Cobb	711,914
1927	4th	82	71	.536	27.5	George Moriarty	773,716
1928	6th	68	86	.442	33.0	George Moriarty	474,323
1929	6th	70	84	.455	36.0	Bucky Harris	869,318
1930	5th	75	79	.487	27.0	Bucky Harris	649,450
1931	7th	61	93	.396	47.0	Bucky Harris	434,056
1932	5th	76	75	.503	29.5	Bucky Harris	397,157
1933	5th	75	79	.487	25.0	Del Baker	320,972
1934	1st	101	53	.656	+7.0	Mickey Cochrane	919,161
1935	1st	93	58	.616	+3.0	Mickey Cochrane	1,034,929
1936	2nd	83	71	.539	19.5	Mickey Cochrane	875,948
1937	2nd	89	65	.578	13.0	Mickey Cochrane	1,072,276
1938	4th	84	70	.545	16.0	Mickey Cochrane, Del Baker	799,557
1939	5th	81	73	.526	26.5	Del Baker	836,279
1940	1st	90	64	.584	+1.0	Del Baker	1,112,693

1941	4th (Tie)	75	79	.487	26.0	Del Baker	684,915
1942	5th	73	81	.474	30.0	Del Baker	580,087
1943	5th	78	76	.506	20.0	Steve O'Neill	606,287
1944	2nd	88	66	.571	1.0	Steve O'Neill	923,176
1945	1st	88	65	.575	+1.5	Steve O'Neill	1,280,341
1946	2nd	92	62	.597	12.0	Steve O'Neill	1,722,590
1947	2nd	85	69	.552	12.0	Steve O'Neill	1,398,093
1948	5th	78	76	.506	18.5	Steve O'Neill	1,743,035
1949	4th	87	67	.565	10.0	Red Rolfe	1,821,204
1950	2nd	95	59	.617	3.0	Red Rolfe	1,951,474
1951	5th	73	81	.474	25.0	Red Rolfe	1,132,641
1952	8th	50	104	.325	45.0	Red Rolfe, Fred Hutchinson	1,026,846
1953	6th	60	94	.390	40.5	Fred Hutchinson	884,658
1954	5th	68	86	.442	43.0	Fred Hutchinson	1,079,847
1955	5th	79	75	.513	17.0	Bucky Harris	1,181,838
1956	5th	82	72	.532	15.0	Bucky Harris	1,051,182
1957	4th	78	76	.506	20.0	Jack Tighe	1,272,346
1958	5th	77	77	.500	15.0	Jack Tighe, Bill Norman	1,098,924
1959	4th	76	78	.494	18.0	Bill Norman, Jimmy Dykes	1,221,221
1960	6th	71	83	.461	26.0	Jimmy Dykes, Billy Hitchcock, Joe Gordon	1,167,669
1961	2nd	101	61	.623	8.0	Bob Scheffing	1,600,710
1962	4th	85	76	.528	10.5	Bob Scheffing	1,207,881
1963	5th (Tie)	79	83	.488	25.5	Bob Scheffing, Chuck Dressen	821,952
1964	4th	85	77	.525	14.0	Chuck Dressen	816,139
1965	4th	89	73	.549	13.0	Chuck Dressen, Bob Swift	1,029,645
1966	3rd	88	74	.543	10.0	Chuck Dressen, Bob Swift, Frank Skaff	1,124,293
1967	2nd (Tie)	91	71	.562	1.0	Mayo Smith	1,447,143
1968	1st	103	59	.636	+12.0	Mayo Smith	2,031,847

East Division

1969	2nd	90	72	.556	19.0	Mayo Smith	1,577,481
1970	4th	79	83	.488	29.0	Mayo Smith	1,501,293
1971	2nd	91	71	.562	12.0	Billy Martin	1,591,073
1972	1st	86	70	.551	+0.5	Billy Martin	1,892,386
1973	3rd	85	77	.525	12.0	Billy Martin, Joe Schultz	1,724,146
1974	6th	72	90	.444	19.0	Ralph Houk	1,243,080
1975	6th	57	102	.358	37.5	Ralph Houk	1,058,836
1976	5th	74	87	.460	24.0	Ralph Houk	1,467,020
1977	4th	74	88	.457	26.0	Ralph Houk	1,359,856
1978	5th	86	76	.531	13.5	Ralph Houk	1,714,893
1979	5th	85	76	.528	18.0	Les Moss, Dick Tracewski, Sparky Anderson	1,630,929
1980	5th	84	78	.519	19.0	Sparky Anderson	1,785,293
1981	4th/2nd (Tie)	60	49	.550	3.5/1.5	Sparky Anderson	1,149,144
1982	4th	83	79	.512	12.0	Sparky Anderson	1,636,058
1983	2nd	92	70	.568	6.0	Sparky Anderson	1,829,636
1984	1st	104	58	.642	+15.0	Sparky Anderson	2,704,794
1985	3rd	84	77	.522	15.0	Sparky Anderson	2,286,609

1986	3rd	87	75	.537	8.5	Sparky Anderson	1,899,437
1987	1st	98	64	.605	+2.0	Sparky Anderson	2,061,830
1988	2nd	88	74	.543	1.0	Sparky Anderson	2,081,162
1989	7th	59	103	.364	30.0	Sparky Anderson	1,543,656
1990	3rd	79	83	.488	9.0	Sparky Anderson	1,495,785
1991	2nd	84	78	.519	7.0	Sparky Anderson	1,641,661
1992	6th	75	87	.463	21.0	Sparky Anderson	1,423,963
1993	3rd (Tie)	85	77	.525	10.0	Sparky Anderson	1,971,421

Central Division

1994	5th	53	62	.461	18.0	Sparky Anderson	1,184,783
1995	4th	60	84	.417	26.0	Sparky Anderson	1,180,979
1996	5th	53	109	.327	39.0	Buddy Bell	1,168,610
1997	3rd	79	83	.488	19.0	Buddy Bell	1,365,157
1998	5th	65	97	.401	24.0	Buddy Bell, Larry Parrish	1,409,391
1999	3rd	69	92	.429	27.5	Larry Parrish	2,026,441
2000	3rd	79	83	.488	16.0	Phil Garner	2,533,752
2001	4th	66	96	.407	25.0	Phil Garner	1,921,305
2002	4th	55	106	.342	39.0	Phil Garner, Luis Pujols	1,503,623
2003	5th	43	119	.265	47.0	Alan Trammell	1,368,245
2004	4th	72	90	.444	20.0	Alan Trammell	1,917,004
2005	4th	71	91	.438	28.0	Alan Trammell	2,024,485
2006	2nd	95	67	.586	1.0	Jim Leyland	2,595,937
2007	2nd	88	74	.543	8.5	Jim Leyland	3,047,139
2008	5th	74	88	.457	14.5	Jim Leyland	3,202,645
2009	2nd	86	77	.528	1.0	Jim Leyland	2,567,185
2010	3rd	81	81	.500	13.0	Jim Leyland	2,461,237
2011	1st	95	67	.586	+15.0	Jim Leyland	2,642,045

*Split season.

Awards

Most Valuable Player

Ty Cobb, outfield, 1911
Mickey Cochrane, catcher, 1934
Hank Greenberg, first base, 1935
Charley Gehringer, second base, 1937
Hank Greenberg, outfield, 1940
Hal Newhouser, pitcher, 1944
Hal Newhouser, pitcher, 1945
Denny McLain, pitcher, 1968
Willie Hernandez, pitcher, 1984
Justin Verlander, pitcher, 2011

Rookie of the Year

Harvey Kuenn, shortstop, 1953
Mark Fidrych, pitcher, 1976
Lou Whitaker, second base, 1978
Justin Verlander, pitcher, 2006

Cy Young

Denny McLain, 1968
Denny McLain (co-winner), 1969
Willie Hernandez, 1984
Justin Verlander, pitcher, 2011

Hall of Famers Who Played for the Tigers

Earl Averill, outfield, 1939–40
Jim Bunning, pitcher, 1955–63
Ty Cobb, outfield, 1905–26
Mickey Cochrane, catcher, 1934–37
Sam Crawford, outfield, 1903–17
Larry Doby, outfield, 1959
Charlie Gehringer, second base, 1924–42
Goose Goslin, outfield, 1934–37
Hank Greenberg, first base and outfield, 1930, 1933–41, and 1945–46
Bucky Harris, second base, 1929 and 1931
Harry Heilmann, outfield, 1914 and 1916–29
Waite Hoyt, pitcher, 1930–31
Hughie Jennings, infield, 1907, 1909, 1912, and 1918
Al Kaline, outfield, 1953–74
George Kell, third base, 1946–52
Heinie Manush, outfield, 1923–27

Eddie Mathews, third base, 1967–68
Hal Newhouser, pitcher, 1939–53
Al Simmons, outfield, 1936

Retired Numbers

—	Ty Cobb
—	Ernie Harwell
2	Charlie Gehringer
5	Hank Greenberg
6	Al Kaline
11	Sparky Anderson
16	Hal Newhouser
23	Willie Horton

League Leaders, Batting

Batting Average, Season

Ty Cobb, 1907	.350
Ty Cobb, 1908	.324
Ty Cobb, 1909	.377
Ty Cobb, 1910	.385
Ty Cobb, 1911	.420
Ty Cobb, 1912	.410
Ty Cobb, 1913	.390
Ty Cobb, 1914	.368

Ty Cobb, 1915............................369
Ty Cobb, 1917............................383
Ty Cobb, 1918............................382
Ty Cobb, 1919............................384
Harry Heilmann, 1921 394
Harry Heilmann, 1923 403
Harry Heilmann, 1925 393
Heinie Manush, 1926 378
Harry Heilmann, 1927 398
Dale Alexander*, 1932 367
Charlie Gehringer, 1937 371
George Kell, 1949.......................343
Al Kaline, 1955 340
Harvey Kuenn, 1959....................353
Norm Cash, 1961 361
Maglio Ordonez, 2007 363
Miguel Cabrera, 2011 344
*Played part of season with Bost. Red Sox.

Home Runs, Season

Sam Crawford, 1908........................7
Ty Cobb, 1909.................................9
Hank Greenberg, 1935............36 (Tie)
Hank Greenberg, 1938...................58
Hank Greenberg, 1940...................41
Rudy York, 1943 34
Hank Greenberg, 1946...................44
Darrell Evans, 1985.......................40
Cecil Fielder, 1990 51
Cecil Fielder, 1991 44
Miguel Cabrera, 2008 ....37 (Tie)

RBIs, Season

Ty Cobb, 1907 116
Ty Cobb, 1908 101
Ty Cobb, 1909 115
Sam Crawford, 1910 115
Ty Cobb, 1911 144
Sam Crawford, 1914 112
Sam Crawford, 1915 116
Bobby Veach, 1917 115
Bobby Veach, 1918........................74 (Tie)
Hank Greenberg, 1935....................170
Hank Greenberg, 1937.....................183
Hank Greenberg, 1940....................150
Rudy York, 1943 118
Hank Greenberg, 1946....................127
Ray Boone, 1955 ....116 (Tie)
Cecil Fielder, 1990 132
Cecil Fielder, 1991 133
Cecil Fielder, 1992 124
Miguel Cabrera, 2010 126

Stolen Bases, Season

Ty Cobb, 1907 49
Ty Cobb, 1909 76
Ty Cobb, 1911 83
Ty Cobb, 1915 96
Ty Cobb, 1916 68
Ty Cobb, 1917 55
Charlie Gehringer, 1929 27
Marty McManus, 1930 23
Ron LeFlore, 1978 68
Brian Hunter, 1997 74
Brian Hunter*, 1999 44
*Played part of season with Sea. Mariners.

Total Bases, Season

Ty Cobb, 1907 286
Ty Cobb, 1908 276
Ty Cobb, 1909 296
Ty Cobb, 1911 367
Sam Crawford, 1913 298
Ty Cobb, 1915 274
Ty Cobb, 1917 336
Hank Greenberg, 1935....................389
Hank Greenberg, 1940....................384
Rudy York, 1943 301
Al Kaline, 1955..............................321
Rocky Colavito, 1962......................309
Cecil Fielder, 1990 339
Miguel Cabrera, 2008 ....331 (Tie)

Most Hits, Season

Ty Cobb, 1907 212
Ty Cobb, 1908 188
Ty Cobb, 1909 216
Ty Cobb, 1911 248
Ty Cobb, 1912 227
Ty Cobb, 1915 208
Ty Cobb, 1917 225
Ty Cobb, 1919......................191 (Tie)
Bobby Veach, 1919 ....191 (Tie)
Harry Heilmann, 1921 237
Dale Alexander, 1929.............215 (Tie)
Charlie Gehringer, 1929 ....215 (Tie)
Charlie Gehringer, 1934 214
Barney McCosky, 1940 ....200 (Tie)
Dick Wakefield, 1943 200
George Kell, 1950..........................218
George Kell, 1951..........................191
Harvey Kuenn, 1953.......................209
Harvey Kuenn, 1954 ....201 (Tie)
Al Kaline, 1955..............................200
Harvey Kuenn, 1956.......................196

Harvey Kuenn, 1959 198
Norm Cash, 1961 193

Most Runs, Season

Sam Crawford, 1907 102
Matty McIntyre, 1908 105
Ty Cobb, 1909 116
Ty Cobb, 1910 106
Ty Cobb, 1911 147
Ty Cobb, 1915 144
Ty Cobb, 1916 113
Donie Bush, 1917..........................112
Charlie Gehringer, 1929 131
Charlie Gehringer, 1935 134
Hank Greenberg, 1938 144
Eddie Yost, 1959 115
Dick McAuliffe, 1968......................95
Ron LeFlore, 1978 126
Tony Phillips, 1992 114

Batting Feats

Triple Crown Winners

Ty Cobb, 1909 (.377 BA, 9 HRs, 115
  RBIs)

Hitting for the Cycle

Bobby Veach, Sept. 17, 1920
Fats Fothergill, Sept. 26, 1926
Gee Walker, Apr. 20, 1937
Charlie Gehringer, May 27, 1939
Vic Wertz, Sept. 14, 1947
George Kell, June 2, 1950
Hoot Evers, Sept. 7, 1950
Travis Fryman, July 28, 1993
Damion Easley, June 8, 2001
Carlos Guillen, Aug. 1, 2006

Six Hits in a Game

Doc Nance, July 13, 1901
Bobby Veach, Sept. 17, 1920*
Ty Cobb, May 5, 1925
George Kell, Sept. 20, 1946
Rocky Colavito, June 24, 1962*
  (7 hits in game)
Jim Northrup, Aug. 28, 1969*
Cesar Gutierrez, June 21, 1970*
  (7 hits in game)
Damion Easley, Aug. 8, 2001
Carlos Pena, May 27, 2004
*Extra-inning game.

40 or More Home Runs, Season

58	Hank Greenberg, 1938
51	Cecil Fielder, 1990
45	Rocky Colavito, 1961
44	Hank Greenberg, 1946
	Cecil Fielder, 1991
41	Hank Greenberg 1940
	Norm Cash 1961
40	Hank Greenberg 1937
	Darrell Evans, 1985

League Leaders, Pitching

Most Wins, Season

George Mullin, 1909	29
Tommy Bridges, 1936	23
Dizzy Trout, 1943	20 (Tie)
Hal Newhouser, 1944	29
Hal Newhouser, 1945	25
Hal Newhouser, 1946	26 (Tie)
Hal Newhouser, 1948	21
Frank Lary, 1956	21
Jim Bunning, 1957	20 (Tie)
Earl Wilson, 1967	22 (Tie)
Denny McLain, 1968	31
Denny McLain, 1969	24
Mickey Lolich, 1971	25
Jack Morris, 1981	14 (Tie)
Bill Gullickson, 1991	20 (Tie)
Justin Verlander, 2009	19 (Tie)
Justin Verlander, 2011	24

Most Strikeouts, Season

Tommy Bridges, 1935	163
Tommy Bridges, 1936	175
Hal Newhouser, 1944	187
Hal Newhouser, 1945	212
Virgil Trucks, 1949	153
Jim Bunning, 1959	201
Jim Bunning, 1960	201
Mickey Lolich, 1971	308
Jack Morris, 1983	232
Justin Verlander, 2009	269
Justin Verlander, 2011	250

Lowest ERA, Season

Dizzy Trout, 1944	2.12
Hal Newhouser, 1945	1.81
Hal Newhouser, 1946	1.94
Hank Aguirre, 1962	2.21
Mark Fidrych, 1976	2.34
Justin Verlander, 2011	2.40

Most Saves, Season

John Hiller, 1973	38
Todd Jones, 2000	42 (Tie)
Jose Valverde, 2011	49

Best Won–Lost Percentage, Season

Bill Donovan, 1907	25–4	.862
George Mullin, 1909	29–8	.784
Eldon Auker, 1935	18–7	.720
Schoolboy Rowe, 1940	16–3	.842
Hal Newhouser, 1945	25–9	.735
Denny McLain, 1968	31–6	.838
Justin Verlander, 2009	18–6	.750
Justin Verlander, 2011	24–5	.828

Pitching Feats

20 Wins, Season

Roscoe Miller, 1901	23–13
Ed Killian, 1905	23–13
George Mullin, 1905	21–20
George Mullin, 1906	21–18
Bill Donovan, 1907	25–4
Ed Killian, 1907	25–13
George Mullin, 1907	20–20
Ed Summers, 1908	24–12
George Mullin, 1909	29–8
Ed Willett, 1909	21–10
George Mullin, 1910	21–12
Harry Coveleski, 1914	22–12
Hooks Dauss, 1915	24–13
Harry Coveleski, 1915	22–13
Harry Coveleski, 1916	21–11
Hooks Dauss, 1919	21–9
Hooks Dauss, 1923	21–13
Schoolboy Rowe, 1934	24–8
Tommy Bridges, 1934	22–11
Tommy Bridges, 1935	21–10
Tommy Bridges, 1936	23–11
Bobo Newsom, 1939	20–11*
Bobo Newsom, 1940	21–5
Dizzy Trout, 1943	20–12
Hal Newhouser, 1944	29–9
Dizzy Trout, 1944	27–14
Hal Newhouser, 1945	25–9
Hal Newhouser, 1946	26–9
Hal Newhouser, 1948	21–12
Frank Lary, 1956	21–13
Billy Hoeft, 1956	20–14
Jim Bunning, 1957	20–8
Frank Lary, 1961	23–9
Denny McLain, 1966	20–14
Earl Wilson, 1967	22–11
Denny McLain, 1968	31–6
Denny McLain, 1969	24–9
Mickey Lolich, 1971	25–14
Joe Coleman, 1971	20–9
Mickey Lolich, 1972	22–14
Joe Coleman, 1973	23–15
Jack Morris, 1983	20–13
Jack Morris, 1986	21–8

Bill Gullickson, 1991	20–9
Justin Verlander, 2009	20
Justin Verlander, 2011	24

*17–10 with Det. Tigers and 3–1 with St. L. Browns.

No-Hitters

George Mullin (vs. St. L. Browns), July 4, 1912 (final: 7–0)

Virgil Trucks (vs. Wash. Senators), May 15, 1952 (final: 1–0)

Virgil Trucks (vs. N.Y. Yankees), Aug. 25, 1952 (final: 1–0)

Jim Bunning (vs. Bost. Red Sox), July 20, 1958 (final: 3–0)

Jack Morris (vs. Chi. White Sox), Apr. 7, 1984 (final: 4–0)

Justin Verlander (vs. Milw. Brewers), June 12, 2007 (final: 4–0)

Justin Verlander (vs. Toronto Blue Jays), May 7, 2011 (final: 9–0)

No-Hitters Pitched Against

Jimmy Callahan, Chi. White Sox, Sept. 20, 1902 (final: 3–0)

Frank Smith, Chi. White Sox, Sept. 6, 1905 (final: 15–0)

Earl Hamilton, St. L. Browns, Aug. 30, 1912 (final: 5–1)

Hub Leonard, Bost. Red Sox, June 3, 1918 (final: 5–0)

Charlie Robertson, Chi. White Sox, Apr. 30, 1922 (final: 2–0) (perfect game)

Bob Lemon, Cleve. Indians, June 30, 1948 (final: 2–0)

Bob Feller, Cleve. Indians, July 1, 1951 (final: 2–1)

Steve Barber and Stu Miller, Balt. Orioles, Apr. 30, 1967 (final: 1–2)

Joel Horlen, Chi. White Sox, Sept. 10, 1967 (final: 6–0)

Steve Busby, K.C. Royals, Apr. 27, 1973 (final: 3–0)

Nolan Ryan, Cal. Angels, July 15, 1973 (final: 6–0)

Randy Johnson, Sea. Mariners, June 2, 1990 (final: 2–0)

Dave Stieb, Tor. Blue Jays, Sept. 2, 1990 (final: 3–0)

Matt Garza, T.B. Rays, July 26, 2010 (final: 5–0)

Postseason Play

1907   World Series vs. Chi. Cubs (NL), lost 4 games to 0, 1 tie

1908 World Series vs. Chi. Cubs (NL), lost 4 games to 1

1909 World Series vs. Pitt. Pirates (NL), lost 4 games to 3

1934 World Series vs. St. L. Cardinals (NL), lost 4 games to 3

1935 World Series vs. Chi. Cubs (NL), won 4 games to 2

1940 World Series vs. Cin. Reds (NL), lost 4 games to 3

1945 World Series vs. Chi. Cubs (NL), won 4 games to 3

1968 World Series vs. St. L. Cardinals (NL), won 4 games to 3

1972 League Championship Series vs. Oak. A's, lost 3 games to 2

1984 League Championship Series vs. K.C. Royals, won 3 games to 0

World Series vs. S.D. Padres (NL), won 4 games to 1

1987 League Championship Series vs. Minn. Twins, lost 4 games to 1

2006 Division Series vs. N.Y. Yankees, won 3 games to 1

League Championship Series vs. Oak. A's, won 4 games to 0

World Series vs. St. L. Cardinals, lost 4 games to 1

2009 Division Playoff Game vs. Minn. Twins, lost

2011 Division Series vs. N.Y. Yankees, won 3 games to 2

2011 League Championship Series vs. Tex. Rangers, lost 4 games to 2

Kansas City Royals

Dates of Operation: 1969–present (43 years)
Overall Record: 3281 wins, 3546 losses (.481)
Stadiums: Municipal Stadium, 1969–72; Royals Stadium (also called Kauffman Stadium), 1973–present (capacity: 37,903)

Year-by-Year Finishes

Year	Finish	Wins	Losses	Percentage	Games Behind	Manager	Attendance
					West Division		
1969	4th	69	93	.426	28.0	Joe Gordon	902,414
1970	4th (Tie)	65	97	.401	33.0	Charlie Metro, Bob Lemon	693,047
1971	2nd	85	76	.528	16.0	Bob Lemon	910,784
1972	4th	76	78	.494	16.5	Bob Lemon	707,656
1973	2nd	88	74	.543	6.0	Jack McKeon	1,345,341
1974	5th	77	85	.475	13.0	Jack McKeon	1,173,292
1975	2nd	91	71	.562	7.0	Jack McKeon, Whitey Herzog	1,151,836
1976	1st	90	72	.556	+2.5	Whitey Herzog	1,680,265
1977	1st	102	60	.630	+8.0	Whitey Herzog	1,852,603
1978	1st	92	70	.568	+5.0	Whitey Herzog	2,255,493
1979	2nd	85	77	.525	3.0	Whitey Herzog	2,261,845
1980	1st	97	65	.599	+14.0	Jim Frey	2,288,714
1981*	5th/1st	50	53	.485	12.0/+1.0	Jim Frey, Dick Howser	1,279,403
1982	2nd	90	72	.556	3.0	Dick Howser	2,284,464
1983	2nd	79	83	.488	20.0	Dick Howser	1,963,875
1984	1st	84	78	.519	+3.0	Dick Howser	1,810,018
1985	1st	91	71	.562	+1.0	Dick Howser	2,162,717
1986	3rd (Tie)	76	86	.469	16.0	Dick Howser, Mike Ferraro	2,320,794
1987	2nd	83	79	.512	2.0	Billy Gardner, John Wathan	2,392,471
1988	3rd	84	77	.522	19.5	John Wathan	2,350,181
1989	2nd	92	70	.568	7.0	John Wathan	2,477,700
1990	6th	75	86	.466	27.5	John Wathan	2,244,956
1991	6th	82	80	.506	13.0	John Wathan, Hal McRae	2,161,537
1992	5th (Tie)	72	90	.444	24.0	Hal McRae	1,867,689
1993	3rd	84	78	.519	10.0	Hal McRae	1,934,578
					Central Division		
1994	3rd	64	51	.557	4.0	Hal McRae	1,400,494
1995	2nd	70	74	.486	30.0	Bob Boone	1,233,530
1996	5th	75	86	.466	24.0	Bob Boone	1,435,997
1997	5th	67	94	.416	19.0	Bob Boone, Tony Muser	1,517,638
1998	3rd	72	89	.447	16.5	Tony Muser	1,494,875
1999	4th	64	97	.398	32.5	Tony Muser	1,506,068
2000	4th	77	85	.475	18.0	Tony Muser	1,677,915
2001	5th	65	97	.401	26.0	Tony Muser	1,536,371
2002	4th	62	100	.383	32.5	Tony Muser, Tony Pena	1,323,034
2003	3rd	83	79	.512	7.0	Tony Pena	1,779,895
2004	5th	58	104	.358	34.0	Tony Pena	1,661,478
2005	5th	56	106	.346	43.0	Tony Pena, Bob Schaefer, Buddy Bell	1,371,181

2006	5th	62	100	.383	34.0	Buddy Bell	1,372,638
2007	5th	69	93	.426	27.5	Buddy Bell	1,616,867
2008	4th	75	87	.463	13.5	Trey Hillman	1,578,922
2009	4th	65	97	.401	21.5	Trey Hillman	1,797,887
2010	5th	67	95	.414	27.0	Trey Hillman, Ned Yost	1,615,327
2011	4th	71	91	.438	24.0	Ned Yost	1,724,450

*Split season.

Awards

Most Valuable Player
George Brett, third base, 1980

Rookie of the Year
Lou Piniella, outfield, 1969
Bob Hamelin, designated hitter, 1994
Carlos Beltran, outfield, 1999
Angel Berroa, shortstop, 2003

Cy Young
Bret Saberhagen, 1985
Bret Saberhagen, 1909
David Cone, 1994
Zack Greinke, 2009

Hall of Famers Who Played for the Royals
George Brett, infield, 1973–93
Orlando Cepeda, designated hitter, 1974
Harmon Killebrew, designated hitter, 1975
Gaylord Perry, pitcher, 1983

Retired Numbers
5 ....George Brett
10.................................Dick Howser
20...................................Frank White

League Leaders, Batting

Batting Average, Season
George Brett, 1976 .... .333
George Brett, 1980 .... .390
Willie Wilson, 1982 .... .332
George Brett, 1990 .... .329

Home Runs, Season
[No player]

RBIs, Season
Hal McRae, 1982 133

Stolen Bases, Season
Amos Otis, 1971............................52
Freddie Patek, 1977 53

Willie Wilson, 1979 83
Johnny Damon, 2000 46

Total Bases, Season
George Brett, 1976......................298

Most Hits, Season
George Brett, 1975......................195
George Brett, 1976......................215
George Brett, 1979......................212
Willie Wilson, 1980 230
Kevin Seitzer, 1987 ....207 (Tie)

Most Runs, Season
Willie Wilson, 1980 133
Johnny Damon, 2000....................136

Batting Feats

Triple Crown Winners
[No player]

Hitting for the Cycle
Freddie Patek, July 9, 1971
John Mayberry, Aug. 5, 1977
George Brett, May 28, 1979
Frank White, Sept. 26, 1979
Frank White, Aug. 3, 1982
George Brett, July 25, 1990

Six Hits in a Game
Bob Oliver, May 4, 1969
Kevin Seitzer, Aug. 2, 1987
Joe Randa, Sept. 9, 2004

40 or More Home Runs, Season
[No player]

League Leaders, Pitching

Most Wins, Season
Dennis Leonard, 1977 ....20 (Tie)
Bret Saberhagen, 1989...................23

Most Strikeouts, Season
[No pitcher]

Lowest ERA, Season
Bret Saberhagen, 1989 ....2.16
Kevin Appier, 1993 ....2.56
Zack Greinke, 2009.....................2.16

Most Saves, Season
Dan Quisenberry, 1980 ....33 (Tie)
Dan Quisenberry, 1982 35
Dan Quisenberry, 1983 45
Dan Quisenberry, 1984 44
Dan Quisenberry, 1985 37
Jeff Montgomery, 1993............45 (Tie)

Best Won–Lost Percentage, Season
Paul Splittorff, 1977 ....16–6 .... .727
Bret Saberhagen, 1981....23–6........ .793

Pitching Feats

20 Wins, Season
Paul Splittorff, 1973 20–11
Steve Busby, 1974......................22–14
Dennis Leonard, 1977 20–12
Dennis Leonard, 1978 21–17
Dennis Leonard, 1980 20–11
Bret Saberhagen, 1985 20–6
Mark Gubicza, 1988...................20–8
Bret Saberhagen, 1989 23–6

No-Hitters
Steve Busby (vs. Det. Tigers), Apr. 27,
    1973 (final: 3–0)
Steve Busby (vs. Milw. Brewers), June
    19, 1974 (final: 2–0)
Jim Colburn (vs. Tex. Rangers), May
    14, 1977 (final: 6–0)
Bret Saberhagen (vs. Chi. White Sox),
    Aug. 26, 1991 (final: 7–0)

No-Hitters Pitched Against
Nolan Ryan, Cal. Angels, May 15, 1973
    (final: 3–0)
Jon Lester, Bost. Red Sox, May 19,
    2008 (final: 7–10)

Postseason Play

1976 League Championship Series vs.
N.Y. Yankees, lost 3 games to 2

1977 League Championship Series vs.
N.Y. Yankees, lost 3 games to 2

1978 League Championship Series vs.
N.Y. Yankees, lost 3 games to 1

1980 League Championship Series vs.
N.Y. Yankees, won 3 games
to 0
World Series vs. Phila. Phillies
(NL), lost 4 games to 2

1981 First-Half Division Playoff vs. Oak.
A's, lost 3 games to 0

1984 League Championship Series vs.
Det. Tigers, lost 3 games to 0

1985 League Championship Series vs.
Tor. Blue Jays, won 4 games
to 3
World Series vs. St. L. Cardinals
(NL), won 4 games to 3

Los Angeles Angels of Anaheim

Dates of Operation: 1961–present (51 years)
Overall Record: 4053 wins, 4079 losses (.498)
Stadiums: Wrigley Field, 1961; Chavez Ravine (a.k.a. Dodger Stadium), 1962–65; Angel Stadium of Anaheim (formerly Edison International Field), 1966–present (capacity: 45,050)
Other Names: Los Angeles Angels (1961–64), California Angels (1965–96), Anaheim Angels (1996–2004)

Year-by-Year Finishes

Year	Finish	Wins	Losses	Percentage	Games Behind	Manager	Attendance
1961	8th	70	91	.435	38.5	Bill Rigney	603,510
1962	3rd	86	76	.531	10.0	Bill Rigney	1,144,063
1963	9th	70	91	.435	34.0	Bill Rigney	821,015
1964	5th	82	80	.506	17.0	Bill Rigney	760,439
1965	7th	75	87	.463	27.0	Bill Rigney	566,727
1966	6th	80	82	.494	18.0	Bill Rigney	1,400,321
1967	5th	84	77	.522	7.5	Bill Rigney	1,317,713
1968	8th	67	95	.414	36.0	Bill Rigney	1,025,956
				West Division			
1969	3rd	71	91	.438	26.0	Bill Rigney, Lefty Phillips	758,388
1970	3rd	86	76	.531	12.0	Lefty Phillips	1,077,741
1971	4th	76	86	.469	25.5	Lefty Phillips	926,373
1972	5th	75	80	.484	18.0	Del Rice	744,190
1973	4th	79	83	.488	15.0	Bobby Winkles	1,058,206
1974	6th	68	94	.420	22.0	Bobby Winkles, Dick Williams	917,269
1975	6th	72	89	.447	25.5	Dick Williams	1,058,163
1976	4th (Tie)	76	86	.469	14.0	Dick Williams, Norm Sherry	1,006,774
1977	5th	74	88	.457	28.0	Norm Sherry, Dave Garcia	1,432,633
1978	2nd (Tie)	87	75	.537	5.0	Dave Garcia, Jim Fregosi	1,755,386
1979	1st	88	74	.543	+3.0	Jim Fregosi	2,523,575
1980	6th	65	95	.406	31.0	Jim Fregosi	2,297,327
1981*	4th/7th	51	59	.464	6.0/8.5	Jim Fregosi, Gene Mauch	1,441,545
1982	1st	93	69	.574	+3.0	Gene Mauch	2,807,360
1983	5th (Tie)	70	92	.432	29.0	John McNamara	2,555,016
1984	2nd (Tie)	81	81	.500	3.0	John McNamara	2,402,997
1985	2nd	90	72	.556	1.0	Gene Mauch	2,567,427
1986	1st	92	70	.568	+5.0	Gene Mauch	2,655,872
1987	6th (Tie)	75	87	.463	10.0	Gene Mauch	2,696,299
1988	4th	75	87	.463	29.0	Cookie Rojas	2,340,925
1989	3rd	91	71	.562	8.0	Doug Rader	2,647,291
1990	4th	80	82	.494	23.0	Doug Rader	2,555,688
1991	7th	81	81	.500	14.0	Doug Rader, Buck Rodgers	2,416,236
1992	5th (Tie)	72	90	.444	24.0	Buck Rodgers	2,065,444
1993	5th (Tie)	71	91	.438	23.0	Buck Rodgers	2,057,460
1994	4th	47	68	.409	5.5	Buck Rodgers, Marcel Lachemann	1,512,622
1995	2nd	78	67	.538	1.0	Marcel Lachemann	1,748,680
1996	4th	70	91	.435	19.5	Marcel Lachemann, John McNamara, Joe Maddon	1,820,521
1997	2nd	84	78	.519	6.0	Terry Collins	1,767,330

1998	2nd	85	77	.525	3.0	Terry Collins	2,519,210
1999	4th	70	92	.432	25.0	Terry Collins, Joe Maddon	2,253,123
2000	3rd	82	80	.506	9.5	Mike Scioscia	2,066,977
2001	3rd	75	87	.463	41.0	Mike Scioscia	2,000,917
2002	2nd	99	63	.611	4.0	Mike Scioscia	2,305,565
2003	3rd	77	85	.475	19.0	Mike Scioscia	3,061,094
2004	1st	92	70	.568	+1.0	Mike Scioscia	3,375,677
2005	1st	95	67	.586	+7.0	Mike Scioscia	3,404,686
2006	2nd	89	73	.649	4.0	Mike Scioscia	3,406,790
2007	1st	94	68	.580	+6.5	Mike Scioscia	3,365,632
2008	1st	100	62	.617	+21.0	Mike Scioscia	3,336,744
2009	1st	97	65	.599	+10.0	Mike Scioscia	3,240,386
2010	3rd	80	82	.494	10.0	Mike Scioscia	3,250,814
2011	2nd	86	76	.531	10.0	Mike Scioscia	3,166,321

*Split season.

Awards

Most Valuable Player
Don Baylor, outfield, 1979
Vladimir Guererro, outfield, 2004

Rookie of the Year
Tim Salmon, outfield, 1993

Cy Young
Dean Chance, 1964
Bartolo Colon, 2005

Hall of Famers Who Played for the Angels
Rod Carew, infield, 1979–85
Rickey Henderson, outfield, 1997
Reggie Jackson, designated hitter and outfield, 1982–86
Eddie Murray, designated hitter, 1997
Frank Robinson, designated hitter, 1973–74
Nolan Ryan, pitcher, 1972–79
Don Sutton, pitcher, 1985–87
Hoyt Wilhelm, pitcher, 1969
Dave Winfield, outfield and designated hitter, 1990–91

Retired Numbers
11 ....Jim Fregosi
GA ....Gene Autry
29 ....Rod Carew
30 ....Nolan Ryan
50 ....Jimmy Reese

League Leaders, Batting

Batting Average, Season
Alex Johnson, 1970 .... .329

Home Runs, Season
Bobby Grinch, 1981 ....22 (Tie)
Reggie Jackson, 1982..............39 (Tie)
Troy Glaus, 2000 47

RBIs, Season
Don Baylor, 1979 139

Stolen Bases, Season
Mickey Rivers, 1975 70
Chone Figgins, 2005 62

Total Bases, Season
Vladimir Guerrero, 2004...............366

Most Hits, Season
Darin Erstad, 2000 240

Most Runs, Season
Albie Pearson, 1962....................115
Don Baylor, 1979 120
Vladimir Guerrero, 2004...............124

Batting Feats

Royal Crown Winners
[No player]

Hitting for the Cycle
Jim Fregosi, July 28, 1964
Jim Fregosi, May 20, 1968
Dan Ford, Aug. 10, 1979
Dave Winfield, June 24, 1991

Jeff DaVanon, Aug. 25, 2004
Chone Figgins, Sept. 16, 2006

Six Hits in a Game
Garret Anderson, Sept. 27, 1996*
*Extra-inning game.

40 or More Home Runs, Season
47 ....Troy Glaus, 2000
41 ....Troy Glaus, 2001

League Leaders, Pitching

Most Wins, Season
Dean Chance, 1964 ....20 (Tie)
Bartolo Colon, 2005 21

Most Strikeouts, Season
Nolan Ryan, 1972........................329
Nolan Ryan, 1973........................383
Nolan Ryan, 1974........................367
Frank Tanana, 1975 269
Nolan Ryan, 1976........................327
Nolan Ryan, 1977........................341
Nolan Ryan, 1978........................260
Nolan Ryan, 1979........................223
Jered Weaver, 2010 233

Lowest ERA, Season
Dean Chance, 1964....................1.65
Frank Tanana, 1977 ....2.54
John Lackey, 2007 ....3.01

Most Saves, Season
Bryan Harvey, 1991 46
Francisco Rodriguez, 2005........45 (Tie)
Francisco Rodriguez, 2006..............47

Francisco Rodriguez, 2007.............62
Brian Fuentes, 2008.......................48

Best Won–Lost Percentage, Season
[No pitcher]

Pitching Feats

20 Wins, Season
Dean Chance, 1964....................20–9
Clyde Wright, 1970 22–12
Andy Messersmith, 1971 20–13
Nolan Ryan, 1973 21–16
Bill Singer, 1973 20–14
Nolan Ryan, 1974 22–16
Bartolo Colon, 2005 21–8

No-Hitters
Bo Belinsky (vs. Balt. Orioles), May 5,
 1962 (final: 2–0)
Clyde Wright (vs. Oak. A's), July 3,
 1970 (final: 4–0)
Nolan Ryan (vs. K.C. Royals), May 15,
 1973 (final: 3–0)
Nolan Ryan (vs. Det. Tigers), July 15,
 1973 (final: 6–0)

Nolan Ryan (vs. Minn. Twins), Sept. 28,
 1974 (final: 4–0)
Nolan Ryan (vs. Balt. Orioles), June 1,
 1975 (final: 1–0)
Mike Witt (vs. Tex. Rangers), Sept. 30,
 1984 (perfect game) (final: 1–0)
Mark Langston and Mike Witt (vs. Sea.
 Mariners), Apr. 11, 1990 (final: 1–0)

No-Hitters Pitched Against
Earl Wilson, Bost. Red Sox, June 26,
 1962 (final: 2–0)
Vida Blue, Glenn Abbott, Paul Lindblad,
 and Rollie Fingers, Oak. A's, Sept.
 28, 1975 (final: 5–0)
Dennis Eckersley, Cleve. Indians, May
 30, 1977 (final: 1–0)
Bert Blyleven, Tex. Rangers, Sept. 22,
 1977 (final: 6–0)
Joe Cowley, Chi. White Sox, Sept. 19,
 1986 (final: 7–1)
Kenny Rogers, Tex. Rangers, July 28,
 1994 (final: 4–0) (perfect game)
Eric Milton, Minn. Twins, Sept. 11,
 1999 (final: 7–0)

Postseason

1979 League Championship Series vs.
   Balt. Orioles, lost 3 games to 1
1982 League Championship Series vs.
   Milw. Brewers, lost 3 games to 2
1986 League Championship Series vs.
   Bost. Red Sox, lost 4 games to 3
1995 AL West Playoff Game vs. Sea.
   Mariners, lost
2002 Division Series vs. N.Y. Yankees,
   won 3 games to 1
   League Championship Series vs.
   Minn. Twins, won 4 games to 1
   World Series vs. S.F. Giants (NL),
   won 4 games to 3
2004 Division Series vs. Bost. Red Sox,
   lost 3 games to 0
2005 Division Series vs. N.Y. Yankees,
   won 3 games to 2
   League Championship Series vs.
   Chi. White Sox, lost 4 games to 1
2007 Division Series vs. Bost. Red Sox,
   lost 3 games to 0
2008 Division Series vs. Bost. Red Sox,
   lost 3 games to 1
2009 Division Series vs. Bost. Red Sox,
   won 3 games to 0
   League Championship Series vs.
   N.Y. Yankees, lost 4 games to 2

Minnesota Twins

Dates of Operation: 1961–present (51 years)
Overall Record: 4072 wins, 4051 losses (.501)
Stadiums: Metropolitan Stadium, 1961–81; Hubert H. Humphrey Metrodome (also known as The Metrodome), 1982–2009; Target Field, 2010 (capacity: 39,500)

Year-by-Year Finishes

Year	Finish	Wins	Losses	Percentage	Games Behind	Manager	Attendance
1961	7th	70	90	.438	38.0	Cookie Lavagetto, Sam Mele	1,256,723
1962	2nd	91	71	.562	5.0	Sam Mele	1,433,116
1963	3rd	91	70	.565	13.0	Sam Mele	1,406,652
1964	6th (Tie)	79	83	.488	20.0	Sam Mele	1,207,514
1965	1st	102	60	.630	+7.0	Sam Mele	1,463,258
1966	2nd	89	73	.549	9.0	Sam Mele	1,259,374
1967	2nd (Tie)	91	71	.562	1.0	Sam Mele, Cal Ermer	1,483,547
1968	7th	79	83	.488	24.0	Cal Ermer	1,143,257

West Division

Year	Finish	Wins	Losses	Percentage	Games Behind	Manager	Attendance
1969	1st	97	65	.599	+9.0	Billy Martin	1,349,328
1970	1st	98	64	.605	+9.0	Bill Rigney	1,261,887
1971	5th	74	86	.463	26.5	Bill Rigney	940,858
1972	3rd	77	77	.500	15.5	Bill Rigney, Frank Quilici	797,901
1973	3rd	81	81	.500	13.0	Frank Quilici	907,499
1974	3rd	82	80	.506	8.0	Frank Quilici	662,401
1975	4th	76	83	.478	20.5	Frank Quilici	737,156
1976	3rd	85	77	.525	5.0	Gene Mauch	715,394
1977	4th	84	77	.522	17.5	Gene Mauch	1,162,727
1978	4th	73	89	.451	19.0	Gene Mauch	787,878
1979	4th	82	80	.506	6.0	Gene Mauch	1,070,521
1980	3rd	77	84	.478	19.5	Gene Mauch, Johnny Goryl	769,206
1981*	7th/4th	41	68	.376	18.0/6.0	Johnny Goryl, Billy Gardner	469,090
1982	7th	60	102	.370	33.0	Billy Gardner	921,186
1983	5th (Tie)	70	92	.432	29.0	Billy Gardner	858,939
1984	2nd (Tie)	81	81	.500	3.0	Billy Gardner	1,598,422
1985	4th (Tie)	77	85	.475	14.0	Billy Gardner, Ray Miller	1,651,814
1986	6th	71	91	.438	21.0	Ray Miller, Tom Kelly	1,255,453
1987	1st	85	77	.525	+2.0	Tom Kelly	2,081,976
1988	2nd	91	71	.562	13.0	Tom Kelly	3,030,672
1989	5th	80	82	.494	19.0	Tom Kelly	2,277,438
1990	7th	74	88	.457	29.0	Tom Kelly	1,751,584
1991	1st	95	67	.586	+8.0	Tom Kelly	2,293,842
1992	2nd	90	72	.556	6.0	Tom Kelly	2,482,428
1993	5th (Tie)	71	91	.438	23.0	Tom Kelly	2,048,673

Central Division

Year	Finish	Wins	Losses	Percentage	Games Behind	Manager	Attendance
1994	4th	53	60	.469	14.0	Tom Kelly	1,398,565
1995	5th	56	88	.389	44.0	Tom Kelly	1,057,667
1996	4th	78	84	.481	21.5	Tom Kelly	1,437,352
1997	4th	68	94	.420	18.5	Tom Kelly	1,411,064
1998	4th	70	92	.432	19.0	Tom Kelly	1,165,980

1999	5th	63	97	.394	33.0	Tom Kelly	1,202,829
2000	5th	69	93	.426	26.0	Tom Kelly	1,059,715
2001	2nd	85	77	.525	6.0	Tom Kelly	1,782,926
2002	1st	94	67	.584	+13.5	Ron Gardenhire	1,924,473
2003	1st	90	72	.556	+4.0	Ron Gardenhire	1,946,011
2004	1st	92	70	.568	+9.0	Ron Gardenhire	1,911,418
2005	3rd	83	79	.512	16.0	Ron Gardenhire	2,034,243
2006	1st	96	66	.593	+1.0	Ron Gardenhire	2,285,018
2007	3rd	79	83	.488	17.5	Ron Gardenhire	2,296,347
2008	2nd	88	75	.540	1.0	Ron Gardenhire	2,302,431
2009	1st	87	76	.534	+1.0	Ron Gardenhire	2,416,237
2010	1st	94	68	.580	+6.0	Ron Gardenhire	3,223,640
2011	5th	63	99	.389	32.0	Ron Gardenhire	3,168,116

*Split season.

Awards

Most Valuable Player
Zoilo Versalles, shortstop, 1965
Harmon Killebrew, infield, 1969
Rod Carew, first base, 1977
Justin Morneau, first base, 2006
Joe Mauer, catcher, 2009

Rookie of the Year
Tony Oliva, outfield, 1964
Rod Carew, second base, 1967
John Castino (co-winner), third base, 1979
Chuck Knoblauch, second base, 1991
Marty Cordova, outfield, 1995

Cy Young
Jim Perry, 1970
Pete Vuckovich, 1982
Frank Viola, 1988
Johan Santana, 2004
Johan Santana, 2006

Hall of Famers Who Played for the Twins
Rod Carew, infield, 1967–78
Steve Carlton, pitcher, 1987–88
Harmon Killebrew, infield and outfield, 1961–74
Paul Molitor, shortstop, second base, designated hitter, 1996–98
Kirby Puckett, outfield, 1984–95
Dave Winfield, designated hitter, 1993–94

Retired Numbers
3............................Harmon Killebrew
6..Tony Oliva
14......................................Kent Hrbek
29..Rod Carew
34................................Kirby Puckett

League Leaders, Batting

Batting Average, Season
Tony Oliva, 1964 .... .323
Tony Oliva, 1965 .... .321
Rod Carew, 1969 .... .332
Tony Oliva, 1971 .... .337
Rod Carew, 1972 .... .318
Rod Carew, 1973 .... .350
Rod Carew, 1974 .... .364
Rod Carew, 1975 .... .359
Rod Carew, 1977 .... .388
Rod Carew, 1978 .... .333
Kirby Puckett, 1989 .... .339
Joe Mauer, 2006 .... .347
Joe Mauer, 2008 .... .328
Joe Mauer, 2009 .... .365

Home Runs, Season
Harmon Killebrew, 1962 48
Harmon Killebrew, 1963 45
Harmon Killebrew, 1964 49
Harmon Killebrew, 1967 ....44 (Tie)
Harmon Killebrew, 1969 49

RBIs, Season
Harmon Killebrew, 1962 126
Harmon Killebrew, 1969 140
Harmon Killebrew, 1971 119
Larry Hisle, 1977 119
Kirby Puckett, 1994 112

Stolen Bases, Season
[No player]

Total Bases, Season
Tony Oliva, 1964 374
Zoilo Versalles, 1965 308
Kirby Puckett, 1988 358
Kirby Puckett, 1992 313

Most Hits, Season
Tony Oliva, 1964 217
Tony Oliva, 1965 185
Tony Oliva, 1966 191
Tony Oliva, 1969 197
Tony Oliva, 1970 204
Cesar Tovar, 1971 204
Rod Carew, 1973 203
Rod Carew, 1974 218
Rod Carew, 1977 239
Kirby Puckett, 1987 ....207 (Tie)
Kirby Puckett, 1988 234
Kirby Puckett, 1989 215
Kirby Puckett, 1992 210
Paul Molitor, 1996......................225

Most Runs, Season
Bob Allison, 1963 99
Tony Oliva, 1964 109
Zoilo Versalles, 1965 126
Rod Carew, 1977 128

Batting Feats

Triple Crown Winners
[No player]

Hitting for the Cycle
Rod Carew, May 20, 1970
Cesar Tovar, Sept. 19, 1972
Larry Hisle, June 4, 1976
Lyman Bostock, July 24, 1976

Mike Cubbage, July 27, 1978
Gary Ward, Sept. 18, 1980
Kirby Puckett, Aug. 1, 1986
Carlos Gomez, May 7, 2008
Jason Kubel, Apr. 17, 2009
Michael Cuddyer, May 22, 2009

Six Hits in a Game
Kirby Puckett, Aug. 30, 1987
Kirby Puckett, May 23, 1991*
*Extra-inning game.

40 or More Home Runs, Season
49 ....Harmon Killebrew, 1964
      Harmon Killebrew, 1969
48 ....Harmon Killebrew, 1962
46 ....Harmon Killebrew, 1961
45 ....Harmon Killebrew, 1963
44 ....Harmon Killebrew, 1967
41 ....Harmon Killebrew, 1970

League Leaders, Pitching

Most Wins, Season
Mudcat Grant, 1965.......................21
Jim Kaat, 1966 25
Jim Perry, 1970 24
Gaylord Perry, 1972................24 (Tie)
Frank Viola, 1988 24
Scott Erickson, 1991 ....20 (Tie)
Johan Santana, 2006 ....19 (Tie)

Most Strikeouts, Season
Camilo Pascual, 1961 221
Camilo Pascual, 1962...................206
Camilo Pascual, 1963...................202
Bert Blyleven*, 1985 206
Johan Santana, 2004...................265
Johan Santana, 2005...................238
Johan Santana, 2006...................245
*Pitched part of season with Cleve. Indians.

Lowest ERA, Season
Allan Anderson, 1988 ....2.45
Johan Santana, 2004...................2.61
Johan Santana, 2006...................2.77

Most Saves, Season
Ron Perranoski, 1969 31
Ron Perranoski, 1970 34
Mike Marshall, 1979 32
Eddie Guardado, 2002...................45

Best Won–Lost Percentage, Season
Mudcat Grant, 1965.....21–7 .... .750
Bill Campbell, 1976......17–5 .... .773
Frank Viola, 1988 ....24–7 .... .774
Scott Erickson, 1991 .....20–8 .... .714
Johan Santana, 2003....12–3 .... .800
Francisco Liriano, 2006 ..12–3 .... .800

Pitching Feats

20 Wins, Season
Camilo Pascual, 1962 20–11
Camilo Pascual, 1963 21–9
Mudcat Grant, 1965 21–7
Jim Kaat, 1966.........................25–13
Dean Chance, 1967 20–14
Jim Perry, 1969 20–6
Dave Boswell, 1969 20–12
Jim Perry, 1970 24–12
Bert Blyleven, 1973 20–17
Dave Goltz, 1977 20–11
Jerry Koosman, 1979 20–13
Frank Viola, 1988......................24–7
Scott Erickson, 1991 20–8
Brad Radke, 1997....................20–10
Johan Santana, 2004.................20–6

No-Hitters
Jack Kralick (vs. K.C. A's), Aug. 26,
   1962 (final: 1–0)
Dean Chance (vs. Cleve. Indians), Aug.
   25, 1967 (final: 2–1)

Scott Erickson (vs. Milw. Brewers), Apr.
   27, 1994 (final: 6–0)
Eric Milton (vs. Ana. Angels), Sept. 11,
   1999 (final: 7–0)
Francisco Liriano (vs. Cleve. Indians),
   May 3, 2011 (final 1–0)

No-Hitters Pitched Against
Catfish Hunter, Oak. A's, May 8, 1968
   (final: 4–0) (perfect game)
Vida Blue, Oak. A's, Sept. 21, 1970
   (final: 6–0)
Nolan Ryan, Cal. Angels, Sept. 28, 1974
   (final: 4–0)
David Wells, N.Y. Yankees, May 17, 1998
   (final: 4–0) (perfect game)

Postseason Play

1965   World Series vs. L.A. Dodgers
       (NL), lost 4 games to 3
1969   Championship Series vs. Balt.
       Orioles, lost 3 games to 0
1970   Championship Series vs. Balt.
       Orioles, lost 3 games to 0
1987   Championship Series vs. Det.
       Tigers, won 3 games to 1
       World Series vs. St. L. Cardinals
       (NL), won 4 games to 3
1991   Championship Series vs. Tor. Blue
       Jays, won 4 games to 1
       World Series vs. Atl. Braves (NL),
       won 4 games to 3
2002   Division Series vs. Oak. A's, won
       3 games to 2
       Championship Series vs. Ana.
       Angels, lost 4 games to 1
2003   Division Series vs. N.Y. Yankees,
       lost 3 games to 1
2004   Division Series vs. N.Y. Yankees,
       lost 3 games to 1
2006   Division Series vs. Oak. A's, lost
       3 games to 0
2009   Division Playoff Game vs. Det.
       Tigers, won
       Division Series vs. N.Y. Yankees,
       lost 3 games to 0
2010   Division Series vs. N.Y. Yankees,
       lost 3 games to 0

New York Yankees

Dates of Operation: (as the Baltimore Orioles) 1901–02 (2 years)
Overall Record: 118 wins, 153 losses (.435)
Stadium: Oriole Park, Baltimore, 1901–02

Dates of Operation: (as the New York Yankees) 1903–present (109 years)
Overall Record: 9649 wins, 7273 losses (.570)
Stadiums: Hilltop Park, 1903–12; Polo Grounds, 1912, 1913–22; Harrison Field, 1918 (Sundays only); Yankee Stadium, 1923–73, 1976–2008; Shea Stadium, 1974–75; Yankee Stadium II, 2009–present (capacity: 52,325)
Other Name: Hilltoppers, Highlanders

Year-by-Year Finishes

Year	Finish	Wins	Losses	Percentage	Games Behind	Manager	Attendance
					Balt. Orioles		
1901	5th	68	65	.511	13.5	John McGraw	141,952
1902	8th	50	88	.362	34.0	John McGraw, Wilbert Robinson	174,606
					N.Y. Yankees		
1903	4th	72	62	.537	17.0	Clark Griffith	211,808
1904	2nd	92	59	.609	1.5	Clark Griffith	438,919
1905	6th	71	78	.477	21.5	Clark Griffith	309,100
1906	2nd	90	61	.596	3.0	Clark Griffith	434,709
1907	5th	70	78	.473	21.0	Clark Griffith	350,020
1908	8th	51	103	.331	39.5	Clark Griffith, Kid Elberfeld	305,500
1909	5th	74	77	.490	23.5	George Stallings	501,000
1910	2nd	88	63	.583	14.5	George Stallings, Hal Chase	355,857
1911	6th	76	76	.500	25.5	Hal Chase	302,444
1912	8th	50	102	.329	55.0	Harry Wolverton	242,194
1913	7th	57	94	.377	38.0	Frank Chance	357,551
1914	6th (Tie)	70	84	.455	30.0	Frank Chance, Roger Peckinpaugh	359,477
1915	5th	69	83	.454	32.5	Bill Donovan	256,035
1916	4th	80	74	.519	11.0	Bill Donovan	469,211
1917	6th	71	82	.464	28.5	Bill Donovan	330,294
1918	4th	60	63	.488	13.5	Miller Huggins	282,047
1919	3rd	80	59	.576	7.5	Miller Huggins	619,164
1920	3rd	95	59	.617	3.0	Miller Huggins	1,289,422
1921	1st	98	55	.641	+4.5	Miller Huggins	1,230,696
1922	1st	94	60	.610	+1.0	Miller Huggins	1,026,134
1923	1st	98	54	.645	+16.0	Miller Huggins	1,007,066
1924	2nd	89	63	.586	2.0	Miller Huggins	1,053,533
1925	7th	69	85	.448	30.0	Miller Huggins	697,267
1926	1st	91	63	.591	+3.0	Miller Huggins	1,027,095
1927	1st	110	44	.714	+19.0	Miller Huggins	1,164,015
1928	1st	101	53	.656	+2.5	Miller Huggins	1,072,132
1929	2nd	88	66	.571	18.0	Miller Huggins, Art Fletcher	960,148
1930	3rd	86	68	.558	16.0	Bob Shawkey	1,169,230
1931	2nd	94	59	.614	13.5	Joe McCarthy	912,437
1932	1st	107	47	.695	+13.0	Joe McCarthy	962,320

1933	2nd	91	59	.607	7.0	Joe McCarthy	728,014
1934	2nd	94	60	.610	7.0	Joe McCarthy	854,682
1935	2nd	89	60	.597	3.0	Joe McCarthy	657,508
1936	1st	102	51	.667	+19.5	Joe McCarthy	976,913
1937	1st	102	52	.662	+13.0	Joe McCarthy	998,148
1938	1st	99	53	.651	+9.5	Joe McCarthy	970,916
1939	1st	106	45	.702	+17.0	Joe McCarthy	859,785
1940	3rd	88	66	.571	2.0	Joe McCarthy	988,975
1941	1st	101	53	.656	+17.0	Joe McCarthy	964,722
1942	1st	103	51	.669	+9.0	Joe McCarthy	988,251
1943	1st	98	56	.636	+13.5	Joe McCarthy	645,006
1944	3rd	83	71	.539	6.0	Joe McCarthy	822,864
1945	4th	81	71	.533	6.5	Joe McCarthy	881,846
1946	3rd	87	67	.565	17.0	Joe McCarthy, Bill Dickey, Johnny Neun	2,265,512
1947	1st	97	57	.630	+12.0	Bucky Harris	2,178,937
1948	3rd	94	60	.610	2.5	Bucky Harris	2,373,901
1949	1st	97	57	.630	+1.0	Casey Stengel	2,281,676
1950	1st	98	56	.636	+3.0	Casey Stengel	2,081,380
1951	1st	98	56	.636	+5.0	Casey Stengel	1,950,107
1952	1st	95	59	.617	+2.0	Casey Stengel	1,629,665
1953	1st	99	52	.656	+8.5	Casey Stengel	1,537,811
1954	2nd	103	51	.669	8.0	Casey Stengel	1,475,171
1955	1st	96	58	.623	+3.0	Casey Stengel	1,490,138
1956	1st	97	57	.630	+9.0	Casey Stengel	1,491,784
1957	1st	98	56	.636	+8.0	Casey Stengel	1,497,134
1958	1st	92	62	.597	+10.0	Casey Stengel	1,428,438
1959	3rd	79	75	.513	15.0	Casey Stengel	1,552,030
1960	1st	97	57	.630	+8.0	Casey Stengel	1,627,349
1961	1st	109	53	.673	+8.0	Ralph Houk	1,747,725
1962	1st	96	66	.593	+5.0	Ralph Houk	1,493,574
1963	1st	104	57	.646	+10.5	Ralph Houk	1,308,920
1964	1st	99	63	.611	+1.0	Yogi Berra	1,305,638
1965	6th	77	85	.475	25.0	Johnny Keane	1,213,552
1966	10th	70	89	.440	26.5	Johnny Keane, Ralph Houk	1,124,648
1967	9th	72	90	.444	20.0	Ralph Houk	1,259,514
1968	5th	83	79	.512	20.0	Ralph Houk	1,185,666

East Division

1969	5th	80	81	.497	28.5	Ralph Houk	1,067,996
1970	2nd	93	69	.574	15.0	Ralph Houk	1,136,879
1971	4th	82	80	.506	21.0	Ralph Houk	1,070,771
1972	4th	79	76	.510	6.5	Ralph Houk	966,328
1973	4th	80	82	.494	17.0	Ralph Houk	1,262,103
1974	2nd	89	73	.549	2.0	Bill Virdon	1,273,075
1975	3rd	83	77	.519	12.0	Bill Virdon, Billy Martin	1,288,048
1976	1st	97	62	.610	+10.5	Billy Martin	2,012,434
1977	1st	100	62	.617	+2.5	Billy Martin	2,103,092
1978	1st	100	63	.613	+1.0	Billy Martin, Dick Howser, Bob Lemon	2,335,871
1979	4th	89	71	.556	13.5	Bob Lemon, Billy Martin	2,537,765
1980	1st	103	59	.636	+3.0	Dick Howser	2,627,417

1981*	1st/6th	59	48	.551	+2.0/5.0	Gene Michael, Bob Lemon	1,614,533
1982	5th	79	83	.488	16.0	Bob Lemon, Gene Michael, Clyde King	2,041,219
1983	3rd	91	71	.562	7.0	Billy Martin	2,257,976
1984	3rd	87	75	.537	17.0	Yogi Berra	1,821,815
1985	2nd	97	64	.602	2.0	Yogi Berra, Billy Martin	2,214,587
1986	2nd	90	72	.556	5.5	Lou Piniella	2,268,030
1987	4th	89	73	.549	9.0	Lou Piniella	2,427,672
1988	5th	85	76	.528	3.5	Billy Martin, Lou Piniella	2,633,701
1989	5th	74	87	.460	14.5	Dallas Green, Bucky Dent	2,170,485
1990	7th	67	95	.414	21.0	Bucky Dent, Stump Merrill	2,006,436
1991	5th	71	91	.438	20.0	Stump Merrill	1,863,733
1992	4th (Tie)	76	86	.469	20.0	Buck Showalter	1,748,733
1993	2nd	88	74	.543	7.0	Buck Showalter	2,416,965
1994	1st	70	43	.619	+6.5	Buck Showalter	1,675,556
1995	2nd	79	65	.549	7.0	Buck Showalter	1,705,263
1996	1st	92	70	.568	+4.0	Joe Torre	2,250,877
1997	2nd	96	66	.593	2.0	Joe Torre	2,580,325
1998	1st	114	48	.704	+22.0	Joe Torre	2,949,734
1999	1st	98	64	.605	+4.0	Joe Torre	3,292,736
2000	1st	87	74	.540	+2.5	Joe Torre	3,227,657
2001	1st	95	65	.594	+13.5	Joe Torre	3,264,777
2002	1st	103	58	.640	+10.5	Joe Torre	3,461,644
2003	1st	101	61	.623	+6.0	Joe Torre	3,465,600
2004	1st	101	61	.623	+3.0	Joe Torre	3,775,292
2005	1st (Tie)	95	67	.585	—	Joe Torre	4,090,692
2006	1st	97	65	.599	+10.0	Joe Torre	4,243,780
2007	2nd	94	68	.580	2.0	Joe Torre	4,271,083
2008	3rd	89	73	.549	8.0	Joe Girardi	4,298,655
2009	1st	103	59	.636	+8.0	Joe Girardi	3,719,358
2010	2nd	95	67	.586	1.0	Joe Girardi	3,765,807
2011	1st	97	65	.599	+6.0	Joe Girardi	3,653,680

*Split season.

Awards

Most Valuable Player

Babe Ruth, outfield, 1923
Lou Gehrig, first base, 1927
Lou Gehrig, first base, 1936
Joe DiMaggio, outfield, 1939
Joe DiMaggio, outfield, 1941
Joe Gordon, second base, 1942
Spud Chandler, pitcher, 1943
Joe DiMaggio, outfield, 1947
Phil Rizzuto, shortstop, 1950
Yogi Berra, catcher, 1951
Yogi Berra, catcher, 1954
Yogi Berra, catcher, 1955
Mickey Mantle, outfield, 1956
Mickey Mantle, outfield, 1957
Roger Maris, outfield, 1960
Roger Maris, outfield, 1961

Mickey Mantle, outfield, 1962
Elston Howard, catcher, 1963
Thurman Munson, catcher, 1976
Don Mattingly, first base, 1985
Alex Rodriguez, third base, 2005
Alex Rodriguez, third base, 2007

Rookie of the Year

Gil McDougald, infield, 1951
Bob Grim, pitcher, 1954
Tony Kubek, infield, 1957
Tom Tresh, shortstop and outfield, 1962
Stan Bahnsen, pitcher, 1968
Thurman Munson, catcher, 1970
Dave Righetti, pitcher, 1981
Derek Jeter, shortstop, 1996

Cy Young

Bob Turley, 1958
Whitey Ford, 1961
Sparky Lyle, 1977
Ron Guidry, 1978
Roger Clemens, 2001

Hall of Famers Who Played for the Yankees

Home Run Baker, third base, 1916–19 and 1921–22
Yogi Berra, catcher and outfield, 1946–63 and 1965
Wade Boggs, third base, 1993–97
Frank Chance, first base, 1913–14
Jack Chesbro, pitcher, 1903–09
Earle Combs, outfield, 1924–35
Stan Coveleski, pitcher, 1928

Bill Dickey, catcher, 1928–43 and 1946
Joe DiMaggio, outfield, 1936–42 and
  1946–51
Leo Durocher, shortstop, 1925 and
  1928–29
Whitey Ford, pitcher, 1950 and
  1953–67
Lou Gehrig, first base, 1923–39
Lefty Gomez, pitcher, 1930–42
Joe Gordon, second base, 1938–43 and
  1946
Goose Gossage, pitcher, 1978–83 and
  1989
Clark Griffith, pitcher, 1903–07
Burleigh Grimes, pitcher, 1934
Rickey Henderson, outfield, 1985–89
Waite Hoyt, pitcher, 1921–30
Catfish Hunter, pitcher, 1975–79
Reggie Jackson, outfield, 1977–81
Wee Willie Keeler, outfield, 1903–09
Tony Lazzeri, second base, 1926–37
Mickey Mantle, outfield, 1951–68
Bill McKechnie, infield, 1913
Johnny Mize, first base and pinch hitter,
  1949–53
Phil Niekro, pitcher, 1984–85
Herb Pennock, pitcher, 1923–33
Gaylord Perry, pitcher, 1980
Branch Rickey, outfield and catcher, 1907
Phil Rizzuto, shortstop, 1941–42 and
  1946–56
Red Ruffing, pitcher, 1930–42 and
  1945–46
Babe Ruth, outfield, 1920–34
Joe Sewell, third base, 1931–33
Enos Slaughter, outfield, 1954–55
  and 1956–59
Dazzy Vance, pitcher, 1915
Paul Waner, pinch hitter, 1944–45
Dave Winfield, outfield, 1981–90

Retired Numbers

1 ....Billy Martin
3 ....Babe Ruth
4 ....Lou Gehrig
5 ....Joe DiMaggio
7 ....Mickey Mantle
8 ....Bill Dickey and Yogi Berra
9 ....Roger Maris
10 ....Phil Rizzuto
15 ....Thurman Munson
16 ....Whitey Ford

23 ....Don Mattingly
32 ....Elston Howard
37 ....Casey Stengel
44 ....Reggie Jackson
49 ....Ron Guidry

League Leaders, Batting

Batting Average, Season

Babe Ruth, 1924 378
Lou Gehrig, 1934 363
Joe DiMaggio, 1939 381
Joe DiMaggio, 1940 352
Snuffy Stirnweiss, 1945 309
Mickey Mantle, 1956 353
Don Mattingly, 1984 343
Paul O'Neill, 1994 359
Bernie Williams, 1998 339

Home Runs, Season

Wally Pipp, 1916 12
Wally Pipp, 1917 9
Babe Ruth, 1920 54
Babe Ruth, 1921 59
Babe Ruth, 1923 41
Babe Ruth, 1924 46
Bob Meusel, 1925 33
Babe Ruth, 1926 47
Babe Ruth, 1927 60
Babe Ruth, 1928 54
Babe Ruth, 1929 46
Babe Ruth, 1930 49
Babe Ruth, 1931 ....46 (Tie)
Lou Gehrig, 1931 ....46 (Tie)
Lou Gehrig, 1934 49
Lou Gehrig, 1936 49
Joe DiMaggio, 1937 46
Nick Etten, 1944 22
Joe DiMaggio, 1948 39
Mickey Mantle, 1955 37
Mickey Mantle, 1956 52
Mickey Mantle, 1958 42
Mickey Mantle, 1960 40
Roger Maris, 1961 61
Graig Nettles, 1976 32
Reggie Jackson, 1980 ....41 (Tie)
Alex Rodriguez, 2005 48
Alex Rodriguez, 2007 54
Mark Teixeira, 2009 ....39 (Tie)

RBIs, Season

Wally Pipp, 1916 99
Babe Ruth, 1920 137

Babe Ruth, 1921 171
Babe Ruth, 1923 131
Bob Meusel, 1925 138
Babe Ruth, 1926 145
Lou Gehrig, 1927 175
Lou Gehrig, 1928 ....142 (Tie)
Babe Ruth, 1928 ....142 (Tie)
Lou Gehrig, 1930 174
Lou Gehrig, 1931 184
Lou Gehrig, 1934 165
Joe DiMaggio, 1941 125
Nick Etten, 1945 111
Joe DiMaggio, 1948 155
Mickey Mantle, 1956 130
Roger Maris, 1960 112
Roger Maris, 1961 142
Reggie Jackson, 1973 117
Don Mattingly, 1985 145
Alex Rodriguez, 2007 156
Mark Teixeira, 2009 122
Curtis Granderson, 2011 119

Stolen Bases, Season

Fritz Maisel, 1914 74
Ben Chapman, 1931 61
Ben Chapman, 1932 38
Ben Chapman, 1933 27
Frankie Crosetti, 1938 27
Snuffy Stirnweiss, 1944 55
Snuffy Stirnweiss, 1945 33
Rickey Henderson, 1985 80
Rickey Henderson, 1986 87
Rickey Henderson, 1988 93
Rickey Henderson*, 1989 77
Alfonso Soriano, 2002 41
*Played part of season with Oak. A's.

Total Bases, Season

Babe Ruth, 1921 457
Babe Ruth, 1923 399
Babe Ruth, 1924 391
Babe Ruth, 1926 365
Lou Gehrig, 1927 447
Babe Ruth, 1928 380
Lou Gehrig, 1930 419
Lou Gehrig, 1931 410
Lou Gehrig, 1934 409
Joe DiMaggio, 1937 418
Joe DiMaggio, 1941 348
Johnny Lindell, 1944 297
Snuffy Stirnweiss, 1945 301
Joe DiMaggio, 1948 355
Mickey Mantle, 1956 376

Mickey Mantle, 1958 307
Mickey Mantle, 1960 294
Roger Maris, 1961 366
Bobby Murcer, 1972 314
Don Mattingly, 1985 370
Don Mattingly, 1986 388
Alex Rodriguez, 2007 376
Mark Teixeira, 2009 344

Most Hits, Season
Earle Combs, 1927 231
Lou Gehrig, 1931 211
Red Rolfe, 1939 213
Snuffy Stirnweiss, 1944 205
Snuffy Stirnweiss, 1945 195
Bobby Richardson, 1962 209
Don Mattingly, 1984 207
Don Mattingly, 1986 238
Derek Jeter, 1999 219
Alfonso Soriano, 2002 209

Most Runs, Season
Patsy Dougherty*, 1904 113
Babe Ruth, 1920 158
Babe Ruth, 1921 177
Babe Ruth, 1923 151
Babe Ruth, 1924 143
Babe Ruth, 1926 139
Babe Ruth, 1927 158
Babe Ruth, 1928 163
Lou Gehrig, 1931 163
Lou Gehrig, 1933 138
Lou Gehrig, 1935 125
Lou Gehrig, 1936 167
Joe DiMaggio, 1937 151
Red Rolfe, 1939 139
Snuffy Stirnweiss, 1944 125
Snuffy Stirnweiss, 1945 107
Tommy Henrich, 1948 138
Mickey Mantle, 1954 129
Mickey Mantle, 1956 132
Mickey Mantle, 1957 121
Mickey Mantle, 1958 127
Mickey Mantle, 1960 119
Mickey Mantle, 1961 .... 132 (Tie)
Roger Maris, 1961 .... 132 (Tie)
Bobby Murcer, 1972 102
Roy White, 1976 104
Rickey Henderson, 1985 146
Rickey Henderson, 1986 130
Derek Jeter, 1998 127
Alfonso Soriano, 2002 128
Alex Rodriguez, 2005 124

Alex Rodriguez, 2007 143
Curtis Granderson, 2011 136
Mark Teixeira, 2010 113
Curtis Granderson, 2011 136
*Played part of season with Bost. Red Sox.

Batting Feats

Triple Crown Winners
Lou Gehrig, 1934 (.363 BA, 49 HRs, 165 RBIs)
Mickey Mantle, 1956 (.353 BA, 52 HRs, 130 RBIs)

Hitting for the Cycle
Bert Daniels, July 25, 1912
Bob Meusel, May 7, 1921
Bob Meusel, July 3, 1922
Bob Meusel, July 26, 1928
Tony Lazzeri, June 3, 1932
Lou Gehrig, June 25, 1934
Joe DiMaggio, July 9, 1937
Lou Gehrig, Aug. 1, 1937
Buddy Rosar, July 19, 1940
Joe Gordon, Sept. 8, 1940
Joe DiMaggio, May 20, 1948
Mickey Mantle, July 23, 1957
Bobby Murcer, Aug. 29, 1972
Tony Hernandez, Sept. 3, 1995
Johnny Damon, June 7, 2008
Melky Cabrera, Aug. 2, 2009

Six Hits in a Game
Mike Donlin, June 24, 1901 (Balt. Orioles)
Jimmy Williams, Aug. 25, 1902 (Balt. Orioles)
Myril Hoag, June 6, 1934
Gerald Williams, May 1, 1996*
*Extra-inning game.

40 or More Home Runs, Season
61 .... Roger Maris, 1961
60 .... Babe Ruth, 1927
59 .... Babe Ruth, 1921
54 .... Babe Ruth, 1920
          Babe Ruth, 1928
          Mickey Mantle, 1961
          Alex Rodriguez, 2005
52 .... Mickey Mantle, 1956
49 .... Babe Ruth, 1930
          Lou Gehrig, 1934
          Lou Gehrig, 1936
48 .... Alex Rodriguez, 2007
47 .... Babe Ruth, 1926

          Lou Gehrig, 1927
46 .... Babe Ruth, 1924
          Babe Ruth, 1929
          Lou Gehrig, 1931
          Babe Ruth, 1931
          Joe DiMaggio, 1937
44 .... Tino Martinez, 1997
42 .... Mickey Mantle, 1958
41 .... Babe Ruth, 1923
          Lou Gehrig, 1930
          Babe Ruth, 1932
          Reggie Jackson, 1980
          David Justice, 2000*
          Jason Giambi, 2002
          Jason Giambi, 2003
          Curtis Granderson, 2011
40 .... Mickey Mantle, 1960
*21 with N.Y. Yankees and 20 with Cleve. Indians.

League Leaders, Pitching

Most Wins, Season
Jack Chesbro, 1904 41
Al Orth, 1906 27
Carl Mays, 1921 .... 27 (Tie)
Waite Hoyt, 1927 .... 22 (Tie)
George Pipgras, 1928 .... 24 (Tie)
Lefty Gomez, 1934 26
Lefty Gomez, 1937 21
Red Ruffing, 1938 21
Spud Chandler, 1943 .... 20 (Tie)
Whitey Ford, 1958 .... 18 (Tie)
Bob Turley, 1958 21
Whitey Ford, 1961 25
Ralph Terry, 1962 23
Whitey Ford, 1963 24
Ron Guidry, 1978 25
Ron Guidry, 1985 22
Jimmy Key, 1994 17
Andy Pettitte, 1996 21
David Cone, 1998 .... 20 (Tie)
Chien-Ming Wang, 2006 19
C. C. Sabathia, 2009 .... 19 (Tie)
C. C. Sabathia, 2010 21

Most Strikeouts, Season
Red Ruffing, 1932 190
Lefty Gomez, 1933 163
Lefty Gomez, 1934 158
Lefty Gomez, 1937 194
Vic Raschi, 1951 164
Allie Reynolds, 1952 160
Al Downing, 1964 217

Lowest ERA, Season

Bob Shawkey, 1920		2.45
Wiley Moore, 1927		2.28
Lefty Gomez, 1934		2.33
Lefty Gomez, 1937		2.33
Spud Chandler, 1943		1.64
Spud Chandler, 1947		2.46
Allie Reynolds, 1952		2.07
Eddie Lopat, 1953		2.43
Whitey Ford, 1956		2.47
Bobby Shantz, 1957		2.45
Whitey Ford, 1958		2.01
Ron Guidry, 1978		1.74
Ron Guidry, 1979		2.78
Rudy May, 1980		2.47

Most Saves, Season

Sparky Lyle, 1972	35
Sparky Lyle, 1976	23
Goose Gossage, 1978	27
Goose Gossage, 1980	33 (Tie)
Dave Righetti, 1986	46
John Wetteland, 1996	43
Mariano Rivera, 1999	45
Mariano Rivera, 2001	50
Mariano Rivera, 2004	53

Best Won–Lost Percentage, Season

Jack Chesbro, 1904	41–13	.759
Carl Mays, 1921	27–9	.750
Joe Bush, 1922	26–7	.788
Herb Pennock, 1923	19–6	.760
Waite Hoyt, 1927	22–7	.759
Johnny Allen, 1932	17–4	.810
Lefty Gomez, 1934	26–5	.839
Monte Pearson, 1936	19–7	.731
Red Ruffing, 1938	21–7	.750
Lefty Gomez, 1941	15–5	.750
Tiny Bonham, 1942	21–5	.808
Spud Chandler, 1943	20–4	.833
Allie Reynolds, 1947	19–8	.704
Vic Rashi, 1950	21–8	.724
Eddie Lopat, 1953	16–4	.800
Tommy Byrne, 1955	16–5	.762
Whitey Ford, 1956	19–6	.760
Tom Sturdivant, 1957	16–6	.727
		(Tie)
Bob Turley, 1958	21–7	.750
Whitey Ford, 1961	25–4	.862
Whitey Ford, 1963	24–7	.774
Ron Guidry, 1978	25–3	.893
Ron Guidry, 1985	22–6	.786

Jimmy Key, 1993	18–6	.750
David Wells, 1998	18–4	.818
Roger Clemens, 2001	20–3	.870

Pitching Feats

20 Wins, Season

Joe McGinnity, 1901		26–21
		(Balt. Orioles)
Jack Chesbro, 1903		21–15
Jack Chesbro, 1904		41–13
Jack Powell, 1904		23–19
Al Orth, 1906		27–17
Jack Chesbro, 1906		24–16
Russ Ford, 1910		26–6
Russ Ford, 1911		22–11
Bob Shawkey, 1916		24–14
Bob Shawkey, 1919		20–13
Carl Mays, 1920		26–11
Bob Shawkey, 1920		20–13
Carl Mays, 1921		27–9
Joe Bush, 1922		26–7
Bob Shawkey, 1922		20–12
Sad Sam Jones, 1923		21–8
Herb Pennock, 1924		21–9
Herb Pennock, 1927		23–11
Waite Hoyt, 1927		22–7
George Pipgras, 1928		24–13
Waite Hoyt, 1928		23–7
Lefty Gomez, 1931		21–9
Lefty Gomez, 1932		24–7
Lefty Gomez, 1934		26–5
Red Ruffing, 1936		20–12
Lefty Gomez, 1937		21–11
Red Ruffing, 1937		20–7
Red Ruffing, 1938		21–7
Red Ruffing, 1939		21–7
Tiny Bonham, 1942		21–5
Spud Chandler, 1943		20–4
Spud Chandler, 1946		20–8
Vic Raschi, 1949		21–10
Vic Raschi, 1950		21–8
Ed Lopat, 1951		21–9
Vic Raschi, 1951		21–10
Allie Reynolds, 1952		20–8
Bob Grim, 1954		20–6
Bob Turley, 1958		21–7
Whitey Ford, 1961		25–4
Ralph Terry, 1962		23–12
Whitey Ford, 1963		24–7
Jim Bouton, 1963		21–7
Mel Stottlemyre, 1965		20–9
Mel Stottlemyre, 1968		21–12
Mel Stottlemyre, 1969		20–14

Fritz Peterson, 1970		20–11
Catfish Hunter, 1975		23–14
Ron Guidry, 1978		25–3
Ed Figueroa, 1978		20–9
Tommy John, 1979		21–9
Tommy John, 1980		22–9
Ron Guidry, 1983		21–9
Ron Guidry, 1985		22–6
Andy Pettitte, 1996		21–8
David Cone, 1998		20–7
Roger Clemens, 2001		20–3
Andy Pettitte, 2003		21–8
Mike Mussina, 2008		20–9
C.C. Sabathia, 2010		21–7

No-Hitters

Tom Hughes (vs. Cleve. Indians), Aug. 30, 1910 (final: 0–5) (lost in 11th)

George Mogridge (vs. Bost. Red Sox), Apr. 24, 1917 (final: 2–1)

Sam Jones (vs. Phila. A's), Sept. 4, 1923 (final: 4–0)

Monte Pearson (vs. Cleve. Indians), Aug. 27, 1938 (final: 13–0)

Allie Reynolds (vs. Cleve. Indians), July 12, 1951 (final: 1–0)

Allie Reynolds (vs. Bost. Red Sox), Sept. 28, 1951 (final: 8–0)

Don Larsen (vs. Bklyn. Dodgers, NL), Oct. 8, 1956 (final: 2–0) (World Series, perfect game)

Dave Righetti (vs. Bost. Red Sox), July 4, 1983 (final: 4–0)

Andy Hawkins (vs. Chi. White Sox), July 1, 1990 (final: 0–4) (8 innings, lost)

Jim Abbott (vs. Cleve. Indians), Sept. 4, 1993 (final: 4–0)

Dwight Gooden (vs. Sea. Mariners), May 14, 1996 (final: 2–0)

David Wells (vs. Minn. Twins), May 17, 1998 (final: 4–0) (perfect game)

David Cone (vs. Mont. Expos, NL), July 18, 1999 (final: 6–0) (perfect game)

No-Hitters Pitched Against

Cy Young, Bost. Red Sox, June 30, 1908 (final: 8–0)

George Foster, Bost. Red Sox, June 21, 1916 (final: 2–0)

Ray Caldwell, Bost. Red Sox, Sept. 10, 1919 (final: 3–0)

Bob Feller, Cleve. Indians, Apr. 30, 1946 (final: 1–0)

Virgil Trucks, Det. Tigers, Aug. 25, 1952 (final: 1–0)

Hoyt Wilhelm, Balt. Orioles, Sept. 2, 1958 (final: 1–0)

Roy Oswalt, Pete Munro, Kirk Saarloos, Brad Lidge, Octavio Dotel, and Billy Wagner, Hous. Astros, June 11, 2003 (final: 8–0)

Postseason Play

1921 World Series vs. N.Y. Giants (NL), lost 5 games to 3

1922 World Series vs. N.Y. Giants (NL), lost 4 games to 0, 1 tie

1923 World Series vs. N.Y. Giants (NL), won 4 games to 2

1926 World Series vs. St. L. Cardinals (NL), lost 4 games to 3

1927 World Series vs. Pitt. Pirates (NL), won 4 games to 0

1928 World Series vs. St. L. Cardinals (NL), won 4 games to 0

1932 World Series vs. Chi. Cubs (NL), won 4 games to 0

1936 World Series vs. N.Y. Giants (NL), won 4 games to 2

1937 World Series vs. N.Y. Giants (NL), won 4 games to 1

1938 World Series vs. Chi. Cubs (NL), won 4 games to 0

1939 World Series vs. Cin. Reds (NL), won 4 games to 0

1941 World Series vs. Bklyn. Dodgers (NL), won 4 games to 1

1942 World Series vs. St. L. Cardinals (NL), lost 4 games to 1

1943 World Series vs. St. L. Cardinals (NL), won 4 games to 1

1947 World Series vs. Bklyn. Dodgers (NL), won 4 games to 3

1949 World Series vs. Bklyn. Dodgers (NL), won 4 games to 1

1950 World Series vs. Phila. Phillies (NL), won 4 games to 0

1951 World Series vs. N.Y. Giants (NL), won 4 games to 2

1952 World Series vs. Bklyn. Dodgers (NL), won 4 games to 3

1953 World Series vs. Bklyn. Dodgers (NL), won 4 games to 2

1955 World Series vs. Bklyn. Dodgers (NL), lost 4 games to 3

1956 World Series vs. Bklyn. Dodgers (NL), won 4 games to 3

1957 World Series vs. Milw. Braves (NL), lost 4 games to 3

1958 World Series vs. Milw. Braves (NL), won 4 games to 3

1960 World Series vs. Pitt. Pirates (NL), lost 4 games to 3

1961 World Series vs. Cin. Reds (NL), won 4 games to 1

1962 World Series vs. S.F. Giants (NL), won 4 games to 3

1963 World Series vs. L.A. Dodgers (NL), lost 4 games to 0

1964 World Series vs. St. L. Cardinals (NL), lost 4 games to 3

1976 League Championship Series vs. K.C. Royals, won 3 games to 2
World Series vs. Cin. Reds (NL), lost 4 games to 0

1977 League Championship Series vs. K.C. Royals, won 3 games to 2
World Series vs. L.A. Dodgers (NL), won 4 games to 2

1978 Pennant Playoff Game vs. Bost. Red Sox, won League Championship Series vs. K.C. Royals, won 3 games to 1
World Series vs. L.A. Dodgers (NL), won 4 games to 2

1980 League Championship Series vs. K.C. Royals, lost 3 games to 0

1981 Second-Half Division Playoff vs. Milw. Brewers, won 3 games to 2
League Championship Series vs. Oak. A's, won 3 games to 0
World Series vs. L.A. Dodgers (NL), lost 4 games to 2

1995 Division Series vs. Sea. Mariners, lost 3 games to 2

1996 Division Series vs. Tex. Rangers, won 3 games to 1
League Championship Series vs. Balt. Orioles, won 4 games to 1
World Series vs. Atl. Braves (NL), won 4 games to 2

1997 Division Series vs. Clev. Indians, lost 3 games to 2

1998 Division Series vs. Tex. Rangers, won 3 games to 0
League Championship Series vs. Cleve. Indians, won 4 games to 2
World Series vs. S.D. Padres (NL), won 4 games to 0

1999 Division Series vs. Tex. Rangers, won 3 games to 0
League Championship Series vs. Bost. Red Sox, won 4 games to 1
World Series vs. Atl. Braves (NL), won 4 games to 0

2000 Division Series vs. Oak. A's, won 3 games to 2
League Championship Series vs. Sea. Mariners, won 4 games to 2
World Series vs. N.Y. Mets (NL), won 4 games to 1

2001 Division Series vs. Oak. A's, won 3 games to 2
League Championship Series vs. Sea. Mariners, won 4 games to 1
World Series vs. Ariz. D'backs (NL), lost 4 games to 3

2002 Division Series vs. Ana. Angels, lost 3 games to 1

2003 Division Series vs. Minn. Twins, won 3 games to 1
League Championship Series vs. Bost. Red Sox, won 4 games to 3
World Series vs. Flor. Marlins (NL), lost 4 games to 2

2004 Division Series vs. Minn. Twins, won 3 games to 1
League Championship Series vs. Bost. Red Sox, lost 4 games to 3

2005 Division Series vs. L.A. Angels, lost 3 games to 2

2006 Division Series vs. Det. Tigers, lost 3 games to 1

2007 Division Series vs. Cleve. Indians, lost 3 games to 1

2009 Division Series vs. Minn. Twins, won 3 games to 0
League Championship Series vs. L.A. Angels, won 4 games to 2
World Series vs. Phila. Phillies, won 4 games to 2

2010 Division Series vs. Minn. Twins, won 3 games to 0
League Championship Series vs. Tex. Rangers, lost 4 games to 2

2011 Division Series vs. Det. Tigers, lost 3 games to 2

Oakland A's (formerly the Kansas City A's)

Dates of Operation: (as the philadelphia A's) 1901–1954
Overall Record: 3886 wins, 4248 losses
Stadium: Columbia Park (1901–1908), Shibe Park, Park (1909–1954)
Other Name: Althetics

Dates of Operation: (as the Kansas City A's) 1955–67 (13 years)
Overall Record: 829 wins, 1224 losses (.404)
Stadium: Municipal Stadium, 1955–67
Other Name: Athletics

Dates of Operation: (as the Oakland A's) 1968–present (44 years)
Overall Record: 3629 wins, 3368 losses (.519)
Stadium: Oakland–Alameda County Coliseum (formerly UMax Coliseum, 1997–98, Network Associates Coliseum, 1998–2004, and McAfee Coliseum, 2004–08), 1968–present (capacity: 35,067)
Other Name: Athletics

Year-by-Year Finishes

Year	Finish	Wins	Losses	Percentage	Games Behind	Manager	Attendance
					K.C. A's		
1955	6th	63	91	.409	33.0	Lou Boudreau	1,393,054
1956	8th	52	102	.338	45.0	Lou Boudreau	1,015,154
1957	7th	59	94	.386	38.5	Lou Boudreau, Harry Craft	901,067
1958	7th	73	81	.474	19.0	Harry Craft	925,090
1959	7th	66	88	.429	28.0	Harry Craft	963,683
1960	8th	58	96	.377	39.0	Bob Elliot	774,944
1961	9th (Tie)	61	100	.379	47.5	Joe Gordon, Hank Bauer	683,817
1962	9th	72	90	.444	24.0	Hank Bauer	635,675
1963	8th	73	89	.451	31.5	Ed Lopat	762,364
1964	10th	57	105	.352	42.0	Ed Lopat, Mel McGaha	642,478
1965	10th	59	103	.364	43.0	Mel McGaha, Haywood Sullivan	528,344
1966	7th	74	86	.463	23.0	Alvin Dark	773,929
1967	10th	62	99	.385	29.5	Alvin Dark, Luke Appling	726,639
					Oak. A's		
1968	6th	82	80	.506	21.0	Bob Kennedy	837,466
					West Division		
1969	2nd	88	74	.543	9.0	Hank Bauer, John McNamara	778,232
1970	2nd	89	73	.549	9.0	John McNamara	778,355
1971	1st	101	60	.627	+16.0	Dick Williams	914,993
1972	1st	93	62	.600	+5.5	Dick Williams	921,323
1973	1st	94	68	.580	+6.0	Dick Williams	1,000,763
1974	1st	90	72	.556	+5.0	Alvin Dark	845,693
1975	1st	98	64	.605	+7.0	Alvin Dark	1,075,518
1976	2nd	87	74	.540	2.5	Chuck Tanner	780,593
1977	7th	63	98	.391	38.5	Jack McKeon, Bobby Winkles	495,599
1978	6th	69	93	.426	23.0	Bobby Winkles, Jack McKeon	526,999
1979	7th	54	108	.333	34.0	Jim Marshall	306,763
1980	2nd	83	79	.512	14.0	Billy Martin	842,259
1981*	1st/2nd	64	45	.587	+1.5/1.0	Billy Martin	1,304,054

1982	5th	68	94	.420	25.0	Billy Martin	1,735,489
1983	4th	74	88	.457	25.0	Steve Boros	1,294,941
1984	4th	77	85	.475	7.0	Steve Boros, Jackie Moore	1,353,281
1985	4th (Tie)	77	85	.475	14.0	Jackie Moore	1,334,599
1986	3rd (Tie)	76	86	.469	16.0	Jackie Moore, Tony La Russa	1,314,646
1987	3rd	81	81	.500	4.0	Tony La Russa	1,678,921
1988	1st	104	58	.642	+13.0	Tony La Russa	2,287,335
1989	1st	99	63	.611	+7.0	Tony La Russa	2,667,225
1990	1st	103	59	.636	+9.0	Tony La Russa	2,900,217
1991	4th	84	78	.519	11.0	Tony La Russa	2,713,493
1992	1st	96	66	.593	+6.0	Tony La Russa	2,494,160
1993	7th	68	94	.420	26.0	Tony La Russa	2,035,025
1994	2nd	51	63	.447	1.0	Tony La Russa	1,242,692
1995	4th	67	77	.465	11.5	Tony La Russa	1,174,310
1996	3rd	78	84	.481	12.0	Art Howe	1,148,380
1997	4th	65	97	.401	25.0	Art Howe	1,264,218
1998	4th	74	88	.457	14.0	Art Howe	1,232,339
1999	2nd	87	75	.537	8.0	Art Howe	1,434,610
2000	1st	91	70	.565	+0.5	Art Howe	1,728,888
2001	2nd	102	60	.630	14.0	Art Howe	2,133,277
2002	1st	103	59	.636	+4.0	Art Howe	2,169,811
2003	1st	96	66	.593	+3.0	Ken Macha	2,216,596
2004	2nd	91	71	.562	1.0	Ken Macha	2,201,516
2005	2nd	88	74	.543	7.0	Ken Macha	2,109,118
2006	1st	93	69	.574	+4.0	Ken Macha	1,976,625
2007	3rd	76	86	.469	18.0	Bob Geren	1,921,834
2008	3rd	75	86	.466	24.5	Bob Geren	1,665,256
2009	4th	75	87	.463	22.0	Bob Geren	1,408,783
2010	2nd	81	81	.500	9.0	Bob Geren	1,418,391
2011	3rd	74	88	.457	22.0	Bob Geren, Bob Melvin	1,476,791

*Split season.

Awards

Most Valuable Player
Vida Blue, pitcher, 1971
Reggie Jackson, outfield, 1973
Jose Canseco, outfield, 1988
Rickey Henderson, outfield, 1990
Dennis Eckersley, pitcher, 1992
Jason Giambi, first base, 2000
Miguel Tejada, shortstop, 2002

Rookie of the Year
Jose Canseco, outfield, 1986
Mark McGwire, first base, 1987
Walt Weiss, shortstop, 1988
Ben Grieve, outfield, 1998
Bobby Crosby, shortstop, 2004
Huston Street, pitcher, 2005
Andrew Bailey, pitcher, 2009

Cy Young
Vida Blue, 1971
Catfish Hunter, 1974
Bob Welch, 1990

Dennis Eckersley, 1992
Barry Zito, 2002

**Hall of Famers Who Played for
the A's**
Dennis Eckersley, pitcher, 1987–95
Rollie Fingers, pitcher, 1968–76
Goose Gossage, pitcher, 1992–93
Rickey Henderson, outfield, 1979–84,
1989–93, 1994–95, and 1998
Catfish Hunter, pitcher, 1965–74
Reggie Jackson, outfield, 1967–75
and 1987
Willie McCovey, designated hitter, 1976
Joe Morgan, second base, 1984
Satchel Paige, pitcher, 1965 (K.C.)
Enos Slaughter, outfield, 1955–56 (K.C.)
Don Sutton, pitcher, 1985

Retired Numbers
9 ....Reggie Jackson
24 ....Rickey Henderson
27 ....Catfish Hunter

34 ....Rollie Fingers
43 ....Dennis Eckersley

League Leaders, Batting

Batting Average, Season
[No player]

Home Runs, Season
Reggie Jackson, 1973.....................32
Reggie Jackson, 1975..............36 (Tie)
Tony Armas, 1981...................22 (Tie)
Mark McGwire, 1987 49
Jose Canseco, 1988.........................42
Jose Canseco, 1991 ....44 (Tie)
Mark McGwire, 1996 52

RBIs, Season
Jose Canseco, 1988......................124

Stolen Bases, Season
Bert Campaneris, 1965 (K.C.)..........51
Bert Campaneris, 1966 (K.C.)..........52
Bert Campaneris, 1967 (K.C.)..........55

Bert Campaneris, 1968 62
Bert Campaneris, 1970 42
Bert Campaneris, 1972 52
Billy North, 1974 54
Billy North, 1976 75
Rickey Henderson, 1980 100
Rickey Henderson, 1981 56
Rickey Henderson, 1982 130
Rickey Henderson, 1983 108
Rickey Henderson, 1984 66
Rickey Henderson*, 1989 77
Rickey Henderson, 1990 65
Rickey Henderson, 1991 58
Rickey Henderson, 1998 66
Coco Crisp, 2011 ....49(tie)
*Played part of season with N.Y. Yankees.

Total Bases, Season
Sal Bando, 1973 ....295 (Tie)
Joe Rudi, 1974 287

Most Hits, Season
Bert Campaneris, 1968 177
Joe Rudi, 1972 181
Rickey Henderson, 1981 135

Most Runs, Season
Reggie Jackson, 1969 123
Reggie Jackson, 1973 99
Rickey Henderson, 1981 89
Rickey Henderson*, 1989 ....113 (Tie)
Rickey Henderson, 1990 119
*Played part of season with N.Y. Yankees.

Batting Feats

Triple Crown Winners
[No player]

Hitting for the Cycle
Tony Phillips, May 16, 1986
Mike Blowers, May 18, 1998
Eric Chavez, June 21, 2000
Miguel Tejada, Sept. 29, 2001
Eric Byrnes, June 29, 2003
Mark Ellis, June 4, 2007

Six Hits in a Game
Joe DeMaestri, July 8, 1955* (K.C.)
*Extra-inning game.

40 or More Home Runs, Season
52 ....Mark McGwire, 1996
49 ....Mark McGwire, 1987

47 ....Reggie Jackson, 1969
44 ....Jose Canseco, 1991
43 ....Jason Giambi, 2000
42 ....Jose Canseco, 1988
        Mark McGwire, 1992

League Leaders, Pitching

Most Wins, Season
Catfish Hunter, 1974 ....25 (Tie)
Catfish Hunter, 1975 ....23 (Tie)
Steve McCatty, 1981 ....14 (Tie)
Dave Stewart, 1987 ....20 (Tie)
Bob Welch, 1990 27

Most Strikeouts, Season
[No pitcher]

Lowest ERA, Season
Diego Segui, 1970 ....2.56
Vida Blue, 1971 ....1.82
Catfish Hunter, 1974 ....2.49
Steve McCatty, 1981 ....2.32
Steve Ontiveros, 1994 ....2.65

Most Saves, Season
Dennis Eckersley, 1988 45
Dennis Eckersley, 1992 51
Keith Foulke, 2003 43

Best Won–Lost Percentage, Season
Catfish Hunter, 1972 .....21–7 ..... .750
Catfish Hunter, 1973 .....21–5 ..... .808
Bob Welch, 1982 ....27–6 ..... .818
Tim Hudson, 2000 ....20–6 ..... .769

Pitching Feats

20 Wins, Season
Vida Blue, 1971 24–8
Catfish Hunter, 1971 21–11
Catfish Hunter, 1972 21–7
Catfish Hunter, 1973 21–5
Ken Holtzman, 1973 21–13
Vida Blue, 1973 20–9
Catfish Hunter, 1974 25–12
Vida Blue, 1975 22–11
Mike Norris, 1980 22–9
Dave Stewart, 1987 20–13
Dave Stewart, 1988 21–12
Dave Stewart, 1989 21–9
Bob Welch, 1990 27–6
Dave Stewart, 1990 22–11
Tim Hudson, 2000 20–6

Mark Mulder, 2001 21–8
Barry Zito, 2002 23–5

No-Hitters
Catfish Hunter (vs. Minn. Twins), May
    8, 1968 (final: 4–0) (perfect game)
Vida Blue (vs. Minn. Twins), Sept. 21,
    1970 (final: 6–0)
Vida Blue, Glenn Abbott, Paul Lindblad,
    and Rollie Fingers (vs. Cal. Angels),
    Sept. 28, 1975 (final: 5–0)
Mike Warren (vs. Chi. White Sox), Sept.
    29, 1983 (final: 3–0)
Dave Stewart (vs. Tor. Blue Jays), June
    29, 1990 (final: 5–0)
Dallas Braden (v.s. T.B. Rays), May 9,
    2010 (final: 4–0) (perfect game)

No-Hitters Pitched Against
Jack Kralick, Minn. Twins (vs. K.C.), Aug.
    26, 1962 (final: 1–0)
Jim Palmer, Balt. Orioles, Aug. 13,
    1969 (final: 8–0)
Clyde Wright, Cal. Angels, July 3, 1970
    (final: 4–0)
Jim Bibby, Tex. Rangers, July 30, 1973
    (final: 6–0)
Dick Bosman, Cleve. Indians, July 19,
    1974 (final: 4–0)
Blue Moon Odom and Francisco Barrios,
    Chi. White Sox, July 28, 1976
(final: 6–0)
Nolan Ryan, Tex. Rangers, June 11,
    1990 (final: 5–0)
Bob Milacki, Mike Flanagan, Mark
    Williamson, and Gregg Olson, Balt.
    Orioles, July 13, 1991 (final: 2–0)

Postseason Play

1971   League Championship Series vs.
        Balt. Orioles, lost 3 games to 0
1972   League Championship Series vs.
        Det. Tigers, won 3 games to 2
        World Series vs. Cin. Reds (NL),
        won 4 games to 3
1973   League Championship Series vs.
        Balt. Orioles, won 3 games
        to 2
        World Series vs. N.Y. Mets (NL),
        won 4 games to 3
1974   League Championship Series vs.
        Balt. Orioles, won 3 games to 1

World Series vs. L.A. Dodgers (NL), won 4 games to 1

1975 League Championship Series vs. Bost. Red Sox, lost 3 games to 0

1981 First-Half Pennant Playoff vs. K.C. Royals, won 3 games to 0
League Championship Series vs. N.Y. Yankees, lost 3 games to 0

1988 League Championship Series vs. Bost. Red Sox, won 4 games to 0
World Series vs. L.A. Dodgers (NL), lost 4 games to 1

1989 League Championship Series vs. Tor. Blue Jays, won 4 games to 1
World Series vs. S.F. Giants (NL), won 4 games to 0

1990 League Championship Series vs. Bost. Red Sox, won 4 games to 0
World Series vs. Cin. Reds (NL), lost 4 games to 0

1992 League Championship Series vs. Tor. Blue Jays, lost 4 games to 2

2000 Division Series vs. N.Y. Yankees, lost 3 games to 2

2001 Division Series vs. N.Y. Yankees, lost 3 games to 2

2002 Division Series vs. Minn. Twins, lost 3 games to 2

2003 Division Series vs. Bost. Red Sox, lost 3 games to 2

2006 Division Series vs. Minn. Twins, won 3 games to 0
League Championship Series vs. Det. Tigers, lost 4 games to 0

Seattle Mariners

Dates of Operation: 1977–present (35 years)
Overall Record: 2589 wins, 2956 losses (.467)
Stadiums: Kingdome, 1977–99; Safeco Field (also known as King County Stadium), 1999–present
(capacity: 47,116)

Year-by-Year Finishes

Year	Finish	Wins	Losses	Percentage	Games Behind	Manager	Attendance
					West Division		
1977	6th	64	98	.395	38.0	Darrell Johnson	1,338,511
1978	7th	56	104	.350	35.0	Darrell Johnson	877,440
1979	6th	67	95	.414	21.0	Darrell Johnson	844,447
1980	7th	59	103	.364	38.0	Darrell Johnson, Maury Wills	836,204
1981*	6th/5th	44	65	.404	14.5/6.5	Maury Wills, Rene Lachemann	636,276
1982	4th	76	86	.469	17.0	Rene Lachemann	1,070,404
1983	7th	60	102	.370	39.0	Rene Lachemann, Del Crandall	813,537
1984	5th (Tie)	74	88	.457	10.0	Del Crandall, Chuck Cottier	870,372
1985	6th	74	88	.457	17.0	Chuck Cottier	1,128,696
1986	7th	67	95	.414	25.0	Chuck Cottier, Marty Martinez, Dick Williams	1,029,045
1987	4th	78	84	.481	7.0	Dick Williams	1,134,255
1988	7th	68	93	.422	35.5	Dick Williams, Jim Snyder	1,022,398
1989	6th	73	89	.451	26.0	Jim Lefebvre	1,298,443
1990	5th	77	85	.475	26.0	Jim Lefebvre	1,509,727
1991	5th	83	79	.512	12.0	Jim Lefebvre	2,147,905
1992	7th	64	98	.395	32.0	Bill Plummer	1,651,398
1993	4th	82	80	.506	12.0	Lou Piniella	2,051,853
1994	3rd	49	63	.438	2.0	Lou Piniella	1,104,206
1995	1st	79	66	.545	+1.0	Lou Piniella	1,643,203
1996	2nd	85	76	.528	4.5	Lou Piniella	2,732,850
1997	1st	90	72	.556	+6.0	Lou Piniella	3,192,237
1998	3rd	76	85	.472	11.5	Lou Piniella	2,644,166
1999	3rd	79	83	.488	16.0	Lou Piniella	2,916,346
2000	2nd	91	71	.562	0.5	Lou Piniella	3,148,317
2001	1st	116	46	.716	+14.0	Lou Piniella	3,507,975
2002	3rd	93	69	.574	10.0	Lou Piniella	3,540,482
2003	2nd	93	69	.574	3.0	Bob Melvin	3,268,509
2004	4th	63	99	.389	29.0	Bob Melvin	2,940,731
2005	4th	69	93	.426	26.0	Mike Hargrove	2,725,549
2006	4th	78	84	.481	15.0	Mike Hargrove	2,481,375
2007	2nd	88	75	.540	6.5	Mike Hargrove, John McLaren	2,672,485
2008	4th	61	101	.377	39.0	John McLaren, Jim Riggleman	2,329,702
2009	3rd	85	77	.525	12.0	Don Wakamatsu	2,195,284
2010	4th	61	101	.377	29.0	Don Wakamatsu, Darren Brown	2,085,630
2011	4th	67	95	.414	29.0	Eric Wedge	1,939,421

*Split season.

Awards

Most Valuable Player
Ken Griffey Jr., outfield, 1997
Ichiro Suzuki, outfield, 2001
Ichiro Suzuki, outfield, 2002

Rookie of the Year
Alvin Davis, first base, 1984
Kazuhiro Sasaki, pitcher, 2000
Ichiro Suzuki, outfield, 2001

Cy Young
Randy Johnson, 1995
Felix Hernandez, 2010

**Hall of Famers Who Played for
the Mariners**
Goose Gossage, pitcher, 1994
Gaylord Perry, pitcher, 1982–83

Retired Numbers
[No player]

League Leaders, Batting

Batting Average, Season
Edgar Martinez, 1992 .... .343
Edgar Martinez, 1995 .... .356
Alex Rodriguez, 1996................ .358
Ichiro Suzuki, 2001 .... .350
Ichiro Suzuki, 2004 .... .372

Home Runs, Season
Ken Griffey Jr., 1994 40
Ken Griffey Jr., 1997 56
Ken Griffey Jr., 1998 56
Ken Griffey Jr., 1999 48

RBIs, Season
Ken Griffey Jr., 1997 147
Edgar Martinez, 2000 145
Bret Boone, 2001 141

Stolen Bases, Season
Harold Reynolds, 1987 60
Brian Hunter*, 1999 44
Ichiro Suzuki, 2001 56
*Played part of season with Det. Tigers.

Total Bases, Season
Ken Griffey Jr., 1993 359
Alex Rodriguez, 1996.................... 379
Ken Griffey Jr., 1997 393

Most Hits, Season
Alex Rodriguez, 1998.................... 213
Ichiro Suzuki, 2001 242
Ichiro Suzuki, 2004 262
Ichiro Suzuki, 2006 224
Ichiro Suzuki, 2007 238
Ichiro Suzuki, 2008 .... 213 (Tie)
Ichiro Suzuki, 2009 225
Ichiro Suzuki, 2010 214

Most Runs, Season
Edgar Martinez, 1995 .... 121 (Tie)
Alex Rodriguez, 1996.................... 141
Ken Griffey Jr., 1997 125

Batting Feats

Triple Crown Winners
[No player]

Hitting for the Cycle
Jay Buhner, July 23, 1993
Alex Rodriguez, June 5, 1997
John Olerud, June 16, 2001
Adrian Beltre, Sept. 1, 2008

Six Hits in a Game
Raul Ibanez, Sept. 22, 2004

40 or More Home Runs, Season
56 ....Ken Griffey Jr., 1997
Ken Griffey Jr., 1998
49 ....Ken Griffey Jr., 1996
48 ....Ken Griffey Jr., 1999
45 ....Ken Griffey Jr., 1993
44 ....Jay Buhner, 1996
42......................Alex Rodriguez, 1998
Alex Rodriguez, 1999
41......................Alex Rodriguez, 2000
40 ....Ken Griffey Jr., 1994
Jay Buhner, 1995
Jay Buhner, 1997

League Leaders, Pitching

Most Wins, Season
Felix Hernandez, 2009 ....19 (Tie)

Most Strikeouts, Season
Floyd Bannister, 1982 209
Mark Langston, 1984.................... 204
Mark Langston, 1986.................... 245
Mark Langston, 1987.................... 262
Randy Johnson, 1992 241
Randy Johnson, 1993 308
Randy Johnson, 1994 204

Randy Johnson, 1995 294

Lowest ERA, Season
Randy Johnson, 1995 .... 2.48
Freddy Garcia, 2001 .... 3.05
Felix Hernandez, 2010 .... 2.27

Most Saves, Season
[No pitcher]

Best Won–Lost Percentage, Season
Randy Johnson, 1995 .....18–2 ... .900
Randy Johnson, 1997 .....20–4 ... .833
Felix Hernandez, 2009 ...19–5 ... .792

Pitching Feats

20 Wins, Season
Randy Johnson, 1997.................... 20–4
Jamie Moyer, 2001 20–6
Jamie Moyer, 2003 21–7

No-Hitters
Randy Johnson (vs. Det. Tigers), June 2,
1990 (final: 2–0)
Chris Bosio (vs. Bost. Red Sox), Apr. 22,
1993 (final: 7–0)

No-Hitters Pitched Against
Mark Langston and Mike Witt, Cal.
Angels, Apr. 11, 1990 (final: 1–0)
Dwight Gooden, N.Y. Yankees (AL),
May 14, 1996 (final: 2–0)

Postseason Play

1995 Division Playoff Game vs. Cal.
Angels, won
Division Series vs. N.Y.
Yankees, won 3 games to 2
League Championship Series vs.
Cleve. Indians, lost 4 games
to 2
1997 Division Series vs. Balt. Orioles,
lost 3 games to 1
2000 Division Series vs. Chi. White
Sox, won 3 games to 0
League Championship Series vs.
N.Y. Yankees, lost 4 games
to 2
2001 Division Series vs. Cleve.
Indians, won 3 games to 2
League Championship Series vs.
N.Y. Yankees, lost 4 games
to 1

Tampa Bay Rays

Dates of Operation: 1998–present (14 years)
Overall Record: 1013 wins, 1252 losses (.447)
Stadium: Sun Coast Dome, Tropicana Field, 1998–present (capacity: 36,970)
Other Name: Devil Rays

Year-by-Year Finishes

Year	Finish	Wins	Losses	Percentage	Games Behind	Manager	Attendance
					East Division		
1998	5th	63	99	.389	51.0	Larry Rothschild	2,261,158
1999	5th	69	93	.426	29.0	Larry Rothschild	1,562,827
2000	5th	69	92	.429	18.0	Larry Rothschild	1,549,052
2001	5th	62	100	.383	34.0	Larry Rothschild, Hal McRae	1,227,673
2002	5th	55	106	.342	48.0	Hal McRae	1,065,762
2003	5th	63	99	.389	38.0	Lou Piniella	1,058,695
2004	4th	70	91	.435	30.0	Lou Piniella	1,275,011
2005	5th	67	95	.414	28.0	Lou Piniella	1,152,793
2006	5th	61	101	.377	36.0	Joe Maddon	1,370,963
2007	5th	66	96	.407	30.0	Joe Maddon	1,387,603
2008	1st	97	65	.599	+2.0	Joe Maddon	1,780,791
2009	3rd	84	78	.519	19.0	Joe Maddon	1,874,962
2010	1st	96	66	.593	+1.0	Joe Maddon	1,864,999
2011	2nd	91	71	.562	6.0	Joe Maddon	1,529,188

Awards

Most Valuable Player
[No player]

Rookie of the Year
Evan Longoria, third base, 2008
Jeremy Hellickson, pitcher, 2011

Cy Young
[No player]

Hall of Famer Who Played for the Rays
Wade Boggs, third base, 1998–99

Retired Numbers
12 ....Wade Boggs

League Leaders, Batting

Batting Average, Season
[No player]

Home Runs, Season
Carlos Pena, 2009 ....39 (Tie)

RBIs, Season
[No player]

Stolen Bases, Season
Carl Crawford, 2003 55
Carl Crawford, 2004 59
Carl Crawford, 2006 58
Carl Crawford, 2007 ....50 (Tie)

Total Bases, Season
[No player]

Most Hits, Season
[No player]

Most Runs, Season
[No player]

Batting Feats

Triple Crown Winners
[No player]

Hitting for the Cycle
B.J. Upton, Oct. 2, 2009

Six Hits in a Game
[No player]

40 or More Home Runs, Season
46 ....Carlos Pena, 2007

League Leaders, Pitching

Most Wins, Season
[No pitcher]

Most Strikeouts, Season
Scott Kazmir, 2007 239

Lowest ERA, Season
[No pitcher]

Most Saves, Season
Rafael Soriano, 2010.....................45

Pitching Feats

Best Won–Lost Percentage, Season
[No pitcher]

20 Wins, Season
[No pitcher]

No-Hitters

Matt Garza (vs. Detroit Tigers) July 26, 2010 (final 5–0)

No-Hitter Pitched Against

Derek Lowe, Bost. Red Sox, Apr. 27, 2002 (final: 10–0)

Mark Buehrle, Chi. White Sox, July 23, 2009 (final: 5–0) (perfect game)

Dallas Braden, Oak. A's, May 9, 2010 (final: 4–0) (perfect game)

Edwin Jackson, Ariz. Diamondbacks (NL), June 25, 2010 (final 1–0)

Postseason Play

2008	Division Series vs. Chi. White Sox, won 3 games to 1
	League Championship Series vs. Bost. Red Sox, won 4 games to 3
	World Series vs. Phila. Phillies, lost 4 games to 1
2010	Division Series vs. Texas Rangers, lost 3 games to 2
2011	Division Series vs. Tex. Ranges, lost 3 games to 1

Texas Rangers

Dates of Operation: 1972–present (40 years)
Overall Record: 3103 wins, 3240 losses (.489)
Stadiums: Arlington Stadium, 1972–93; Rangers Ballpark at Arlington (previously The Ballpark in Arlington, 1994–2004, and Ameriquest Field in Arlington, 2004–06), 1994–present (capacity: 49,115)

Year-by-Year Finishes

Year	Finish	Wins	Losses	Percentage	Games Behind	Manager	Attendance
					West Division		
1972	6th	54	100	.351	38.5	Ted Williams	662,974
1973	6th	57	105	.352	37.0	Whitey Herzog, Del Wilber, Billy Martin	686,085
1974	2nd	84	76	.525	5.0	Billy Martin	1,193,902
1975	3rd	79	83	.488	19.0	Billy Martin, Frank Lucchesi	1,127,924
1976	4th (Tie)	76	86	.469	14.0	Frank Lucchesi	1,164,982
1977	2nd	94	68	.580	8.0	Frank Lucchesi, Eddie Stanky, Connie Ryan, Billy Hunter	1,250,722
1978	2nd (Tie)	87	75	.537	5.0	Billy Hunter, Pat Corrales	1,447,963
1979	3rd	83	79	.512	5.0	Pat Corrales	1,519,671
1980	4th (Tie)	76	85	.472	20.5	Pat Corrales	1,198,175
1981*	2nd/3rd	57	48	.543	1.5/4.5	Don Zimmer	850,076
1982	6th	64	98	.395	29.0	Don Zimmer, Darrell Johnson	1,154,432
1983	3rd	77	85	.475	22.0	Doug Rader	1,363,469
1984	7th	69	92	.429	14.5	Doug Rader	1,102,471
1985	7th	62	99	.385	28.5	Doug Rader, Bobby Valentine	1,112,497
1986	2nd	87	75	.537	5.0	Bobby Valentine	1,692,002
1987	6th (Tie)	75	87	.463	10.0	Bobby Valentine	1,763,053
1988	6th	70	91	.435	33.5	Bobby Valentine	1,581,901
1989	4th (Tie)	83	79	.512	16.0	Bobby Valentine	2,043,993
1990	3rd	83	79	.512	20.0	Bobby Valentine	2,057,911
1991	3rd	85	77	.525	10.0	Bobby Valentine	2,297,720
1992	4th (Tie)	77	85	.475	19.0	Bobby Valentine, Toby Harrah	2,198,231
1993	2nd	86	76	.531	8.0	Kevin Kennedy	2,244,616
1994	1st	52	62	.456	+1.0	Kevin Kennedy	2,503,198
1995	3rd	74	70	.514	4.5	Johnny Oates	1,985,910
1996	1st	90	72	.556	+4.5	Johnny Oates	2,889,020
1997	3rd	77	85	.475	13.0	Johnny Oates	2,945,228
1998	1st	88	74	.543	+3.0	Johnny Oates	2,927,409
1999	1st	95	67	.586	+8.0	Johnny Oates	2,771,469
2000	4th (Tie)	71	91	.438	20.5	Johnny Oates	2,800,147
2001	4th (Tie)	73	89	.451	43.0	Johnny Oates, Jerry Narron	2,831,111
2002	4th (Tie)	72	90	.444	31.0	Jerry Narron	2,352,447
2003	4th	71	91	.438	25.0	Buck Showalter	2,094,394
2004	3rd	89	73	.549	3.0	Buck Showalter	2,513,685
2005	3rd	79	83	.488	16.0	Buck Showalter	2,525,221
2006	3rd	80	82	.494	13.0	Buck Showalter	2,388,757
2007	4th	75	87	.463	19.0	Ron Washington	2,353,862
2008	2nd	79	83	.488	21.0	Ron Washington	1,945,677
2009	2nd	87	75	.537	10.0	Ron Washington	2,156,016
2010	1st	90	72	.556	+9.0	Ron Washington	2,505,171
2011	1st	96	65	.593	+10.0	Ron Washington	2,946,949

*Split season.

Awards

Most Valuable Player

Jeff Burroughs, outfield, 1974

Juan Gonzalez, outfield, 1996

Juan Gonzalez, outfield, 1998

Ivan Rodriguez, catcher, 1999

Alex Rodriguez, shortstop, 2003

Josh Hamilton, outfield, 2010

Rookie of the Year

Mike Hargrove, first base, 1974

Neftali Feliz, pitcher, 2010

Cy Young

[No pitcher]

Hall of Famers Who Played for the Rangers

Goose Gossage, picher, 1993

Ferguson Jenkins, pitcher, 1974–75 and 1978–81

Gaylord Perry, pitcher, 1975–77 and 1980

Nolan Ryan, pitcher, 1989–93

Retired Numbers

26 ....Johnny Oates

34 ....Nolan Ryan

League Leaders, Batting

Batting Average, Season

Julio Franco, 1991 .... .341

Michael Young, 2005.................. .331

Josh Hamilton, 2010................... .359

Home Runs, Season

Juan Gonzalez, 1992 43

Juan Gonzalez, 1993 46

Alex Rodriguez, 2001......................52

Alex Rodriguez, 2002.....................57

Alex Rodriguez, 2003.....................47

RBIs, Season

Jeff Burroughs, 1974 118

Ruben Sierra, 1989 119

Juan Gonzalez, 1998 157

Alex Rodriguez, 2002...................142

Josh Hamilton, 2008......................130

Stolen Bases, Season

[No player]

Total Bases, Season

Ruben Sierra, 1989 344

Alex Rodriguez, 2001 393

Alex Rodriguez, 2002...................389

Mark Teixeira, 2005 370

Josh Hamilton, 2008..............331 (Tie)

Most Hits, Season

Rafael Palmeiro, 1990 191

Michael Young, 2005....................221

Michael Young, 2011..............213 (Tie)

Most Runs, Season

Rafael Palmeiro, 1993 124

Alex Rodriguez, 2001 133

Alex Rodriguez, 2003...................124

Batting Feats

Triple Crown Winners

[No player]

Hitting for the Cycle

Oddibe McDowell, July 23, 1985

Mark Teixeira, Aug. 17, 2004

Gary Matthews Jr., Sept. 13, 2006

Ian Kinsler, Apr. 15, 2005

Bengie Molina, July 16, 2010

Six Hits in a Game

Alfonso Soriano, May 8, 2004

Ian Kinsler, Apr. 15, 2005

40 or More Home Runs, Season

57......................Alex Rodriguez, 2002

52......................Alex Rodriguez, 2001

47 ....Juan Gonzalez, 1996

Rafael Palmeiro, 1999

Rafael Palmeiro, 2001

Alex Rodriguez, 2003

46 ....Juan Gonzalez, 1993

45 ....Juan Gonzalez, 1998

43 ....Juan Gonzalez, 1992

Rafael Palmeiro, 2002

Mark Teixeira, 2005

42 ....Juan Gonzalez, 1997

League Leaders, Pitching

Most Wins, Season

Ferguson Jenkins, 1974 ....25 (Tie)

Kevin Brown, 1992..................21 (Tie)

Rich Helling, 1998..................20 (Tie)

Most Strikeouts, Season

Nolan Ryan, 1989.......................301

Nolan Ryan, 1990.......................232

Lowest ERA, Season

Rick Honeycutt, 1983..................2.42

Most Saves, Season

Jeff Russell, 1989 38

Best Won–Lost Percentage, Season

Tommy Hunter, 2010................... .765

Pitching Feats

20 Wins, Season

Ferguson Jenkins, 1974 25–12

Kevin Brown, 1992 21–11

Rich Helling, 1998 20–7

No-Hitters

Jim Bibby (vs. Oak. A's), July 30, 1973 (final: 6–0)

Bert Blyleven (vs. Cal. Angels), Sept. 22, 1977 (final: 6–0)

Nolan Ryan (vs. Oak. A's), June 11, 1990 (final: 5–0)

Nolan Ryan (vs. Tor. Blue Jays), May 1, 1991 (final: 3–0)

Kenny Rogers (vs. Cal. Angels), July 28, 1994 (final: 4–0) (perfect game)

No-Hitters Pitched Against

Jim Colburn, K.C. Royals, May 14, 1977 (final: 6–0)

Mike Witt, Cal. Angels, Sept. 30, 1984 (final: 1–0) (perfect game)

Mark Buehrle, Chi. White Sox, Apr. 18, 2007 (final: 6–0)

Postseason Play

1996 Division Series vs. N.Y. Yankees, lost 3 games to 1

1999 Division Series vs. N.Y. Yankees, lost 3 games to 0

1998 Division Series vs. N.Y. Yankees, lost 3 games to 0

2010 Division Series vs. T. B. Rays, won 3 games to 2

League Championship Series vs. N.Y. Yankees, won 4 games to 2

World Series vs. S. F. Giants (NL), lost 4 games to 1

2011 Division Series vs. T. B. Rays, won 3 games to 1

League Championship Series vs. Det. Tigers, won 4 games to 2

World Series vs. St.L. Cardinals (NL) lost 4 games to 3

Toronto Blue Jays

Dates of Operation: 1977–present (35 years)
Overall Record: 2755 wins, 2790 losses (.497)
Stadiums: Exhibition Stadium (also known as Prohibition Stadium, 1977–82), 1977–89; Skydome, 1989–2004; now Rogers Centre, 2005–present (capacity: 49,539)

Year-by-Year Finishes

Year	Finish	Wins	Losses	Percentage	Games Behind	Manager	Attendance
					East Division		
1977	7th	54	107	.335	45.5	Roy Hartsfield	1,701,052
1978	7th	59	102	.366	40.0	Roy Hartsfield	1,562,585
1979	7th	53	109	.327	50.5	Roy Hartsfield	1,431,651
1980	7th	67	95	.414	36.0	Bobby Mattick	1,400,327
1981*	7th/7th	37	69	.349	19.0/7.5	Bobby Mattick	755,083
1982	6th (Tie)	78	84	.481	17.0	Bobby Cox	1,275,978
1983	4th	89	73	.549	9.0	Bobby Cox	1,930,415
1984	2nd	89	73	.549	15.0	Bobby Cox	2,110,009
1985	1st	99	62	.615	+2.0	Bobby Cox	2,468,925
1986	4th	86	76	.531	9.5	Jimy Williams	2,455,477
1987	2nd	96	66	.593	2.0	Jimy Williams	2,778,429
1988	3rd (Tie)	87	75	.537	2.0	Jimy Williams	2,595,175
1989	1st	89	73	.549	+2.0	Jimy Williams, Cito Gaston	3,375,883
1990	2nd	86	76	.531	2.0	Cito Gaston	3,885,284
1991	1st	91	71	.562	+7.0	Cito Gaston	4,001,527
1992	1st	96	66	.593	+4.0	Cito Gaston	4,028,318
1993	1st	95	67	.586	+7.0	Cito Gaston	4,057,947
1994	3rd	55	60	.478	16.0	Cito Gaston	2,907,933
1995	5th	56	88	.389	30.0	Cito Gaston	2,826,483
1996	4th	74	88	.457	18.0	Cito Gaston	2,559,573
1997	5th	76	86	.469	22.0	Cito Gaston, Mel Queen	2,589,297
1998	3rd	88	74	.543	26.0	Tim Johnson	2,454,183
1999	3rd	84	78	.519	14.0	Jim Fregosi	2,163,464
2000	3rd	83	79	.512	4.5	Jim Fregosi	1,819,886
2001	3rd	80	82	.494	16.0	Buck Martinez	1,915,438
2002	3rd	78	84	.481	25.5	Buck Martinez, Carlos Tosca	1,636,904
2003	3rd	86	76	.531	15.0	Carlos Tosca	1,799,458
2004	5th	67	94	.416	33.5	Carlos Tosca, John Gibbons	1,900,041
2005	3rd	80	82	.494	15.0	John Gibbons	2,014,987
2006	2nd	87	75	.537	10.0	John Gibbons	2,302,212
2007	3rd	83	79	.512	13.0	John Gibbons	2,360,648
2008	4th	86	76	.531	11.0	John Gibbons, Cito Gaston	2,399,786
2009	4th	75	87	.463	28.0	Cito Gaston	1,876,129
2010	4th	85	77	.525	11.0	Cito Gaston	1,495,482
2011	4th	81	81	.500	16.0	John Farrell	1,818,103

*Split season.

Awards

Most Valuable Player
George Bell, outfield, 1987

Rookie of the Year
Alfredo Griffin (co-winner), shortstop, 1979
Eric Hinske, third base, 2002

Cy Young
Pat Hentgen, 1996
Roger Clemens, 1997
Roger Clemens, 1998
Roy Halladay, 2003

Hall of Famers Who Played for the Blue Jays
Rickey Henderson, outfield, 1993
Paul Molitor, designated hitter, 1993–95
Phil Niekro, pitcher, 1987
Dave Winfield, designated hitter, 1992
Roberto Alomar, 1991–95

Retired Numbers
12..............................Roberto Alomar

League Leaders, Batting

Batting Average, Season
John Olerud, 1993......................363

Home Runs, Season
Jesse Barfield, 1986 40
Fred McGriff, 1989 36
Jose Bautista, 2010 54
Jose Bautista, 2011 43

RBIs, Season
George Bell, 1987.........................134
Carlos Delgado, 2003 145

Stolen Bases, Season
[No player]

Total Bases, Season
George Bell, 1987 369
Shawn Green, 1999 361
Carlos Delgado, 2000 378
Vernon Wells, 2003......................373
Jose Bautista, 2010.......................351

Most Hits, Season
Paul Molitor, 1993.......................211
Vernon Wells, 2003......................215

Most Runs, Season
[No player]

Batting Feats

Triple Crown Winners
[No player]

Hitting for the Cycle
Kelly Gruber, Apr. 16, 1989
Jeff Frye, Aug. 17, 2001

Six Hits in a Game
Frank Catalanotto, May 1, 2004

40 or More Home Runs, Season
54 ....Jose Bautista, 2010
47..........................George Bell, 1987
46......................Jose Canseco, 1998
44 ....Carlos Delgado, 1999
43 ....Jose Bautista, 2011
42 ....Shawn Green, 1999
Carlos Delgado, 2003
41 ....Tony Batista, 2000
Carlos Delgado, 2000
40 ....Jesse Barfield, 1986

League Leaders, Pitching

Most Wins, Season
Jack Morris, 1992 ....21 (Tie)
Roger Clemens, 1997 21
Roger Clemens, 1998 ....20 (Tie)

Most Strikeouts, Season
Roger Clemens, 1997 292
Roger Clemens, 1998 271
A.J. Burnett, 2008 231

Lowest ERA, Season
Dave Stieb, 1985 ....2.48
Jimmy Key, 1987.........................2.76
Juan Guzman, 1996 ....2.93

Roger Clemens, 1997 ....2.05
Roger Clemens, 1998 ....2.65

Most Saves, Season
Tom Heinke, 1987 34
Duane Ward, 1993 ....45 (Tie)

Best Won–Lost Percentage, Season
Doyle Alexander, 1984.....17–6.. .739
Roy Halladay, 2003 ....22–7.. .759

Pitching Feats

20 Wins, Season
Jack Morris, 1992.......................21–6
Pat Hentgen, 1996 20–10
Roger Clemens, 1997..................21–7
Roger Clemens, 1998 20–6
David Wells, 2000 20–8
Roy Halladay, 2003 22–7
Roy Halladay, 2008 20–11

No-Hitters
Dave Stieb (vs. Det. Tigers), Sept. 2, 1990 (final: 3–0)

No-Hitters Pitched Against
Len Barker, Cleve. Indians, May 15, 1981 (final: 3–0) (perfect game)
Dave Stewart, Oak. A's, June 29, 1990 (final: 5–0)
Nolan Ryan, Tex. Rangers, May 1, 1991 (final: 3–0)
Justin Verlander, Det. Tigers, May 7, 2011 (final: 9–0)

Postseason Play

1985 League Championship Series vs. K.C. Royals, lost 4 games to 3
1989 League Championship Series vs. Oak. A's, lost 4 games to 1
1991 League Championship Series vs. Minn. Twins, lost 4 games to 1
1992 League Championship Series vs. Oak. A's, won 4 games to 2
World Series vs. Atl. Braves (NL), won 4 games to 2
1993 League Championship Series vs. Chi. White Sox, won 4 games to 2
World Series vs. Phila. Phillies (NL), won 4 games to 2

Arizona Diamondbacks

Dates of Operation: 1998–present (14 years)
Overall Record: 1129 wins, 1139 losses (.498)
Stadium: Chase Field (formerly Bank One Ballpark (The BOB), 1998–2005) 1998–present (capacity: 49,033)

Year-by-Year Finishes

Year	Finish	Wins	Losses	Percentage	Games Behind	Manager	Attendance
				West Division			
1998	5th	65	97	.401	33.0	Buck Showalter	3,600,412
1999	1st	100	62	.617	+14.0	Buck Showalter	3,019,654
2000	3rd	85	77	.525	12.0	Buck Showalter	2,942,516
2001	1st	92	70	.556	+2.0	Bob Brenly	2,740,554
2002	1st	98	64	.605	+2.5	Bob Brenly	3,200,725
2003	3rd	84	78	.519	16.5	Bob Brenly	2,805,542
2004	5th	51	111	.315	42.0	Bob Brenly, Al Pedrique	2,519,560
2005	2nd	77	85	.465	5.0	Bob Melvin	2,058,718
2006	4th	76	86	.469	12.0	Bob Melvin	2,092,189
2007	1st	90	72	.556	+0.5	Bob Melvin	2,325,414
2008	2nd	82	80	.506	2.0	Bob Melvin	2,509,924
2009	5th	70	92	.432	25.0	Bob Melvin, A. J. Hinch	2,129,183
2010	5th	65	97	.401	27.0	A.J. Hinch, Kirk Gibson	2,056,697
2011	1st	94	68	.580	+8.0	Kirk Gibson	2,105,432

Awards

Most Valuable Player
[No player]

Rookie of the Year
[No player]

Cy Young
Randy Johnson, 1999
Randy Johnson, 2000
Randy Johnson, 2001
Randy Johnson, 2002
Brandon Webb, 2006

Hall of Famers Who Played for the Diamondbacks

Roberto Alomar, 2004

Retired Numbers
[None]

League Leaders, Batting

Batting Average, Season
[No player]

Home Runs, Season
[No player]

RBIs, Season
[No player]

Stolen Bases, Season
Tony Womack, 1999......................72

Total Bases, Season
[No player]

Most Hits, Season
Luis Gonzalez, 1999....................206

Most Runs, Season
[No player]

Batting Feats

Triple Crown Winners
[No player]

Hitting for the Cycle
Luis Gonzalez, July 5, 2000
Greg Colbrunn, Sept. 18, 2002
Stephen Drew, Sept. 1, 2008
Kelly Johnson, July 13, 2010

Six Hits in a Game
[No player]

40 or More Home Runs, Season
57......................Luis Gonzalez, 2001
44......................Mark Reynolds, 2009
40 ....Adam Dunn, 2008*
*Ariz.-Cin.

League Leaders, Pitching

Most Wins, Season
Brandon Webb, 2006..............16 (Tie)
Brandon Webb, 2008 22
Ian Kennedy, 2011 ....21 (Tie)

Most Strikeouts, Season
Randy Johnson, 1999 364
Randy Johnson, 2000 347
Randy Johnson, 2001 372

Randy Johnson, 2002 334
Randy Johnson, 2004 290

Lowest ERA, Season
Randy Johnson, 1999 ....2.48
Randy Johnson, 2001 ....2.49
Randy Johnson, 2002 ....2.32

Most Saves, Season
Jose Valverde, 2007 47

Best Won–Lost Percentage, Season
Randy Johnson, 2000.....19–7.....731
Curt Schilling, 2001.......22–6.....786
Randy Johnson, 2002.....24–5.....828
Ian Kennedy, 2011 ....21–4.....840

Pitching Feats

20 Wins, Season
Curt Schilling, 2001 22–6
Randy Johnson, 2001 21–6
Randy Johnson, 2002 24–5
Curt Schilling, 2002 23–7
Brandon Webb, 2008 22–7
Ian Kennedy, 2011......................21–4

No-Hitters
Randy Johnson (vs. Atl. Braves), May
18, 2004 (final: 2–0) (perfect game)
Edwin Jackson (vs. Tampa Bay Rays),
June 25, 2010 (final: 1–0)

No-Hitter Pitched Against
Jose Jimenez, St. L. Cardinals, June 25,
1999 (final: 1–0)
Anibal Sanchez, Fla. Marlins, Sept. 6,
2006 (final: 2–0)

Postseason Play

1999   Division Series vs. N.Y. Mets,
lost 3 games to 1
2001   Division Series vs. St. L.
Cardinals, won 3 games to 2
League Championship Series vs.
Atl. Braves, won 4 games
to 1
World Series vs. N.Y. Yankees
(AL), won 4 games to 3
2002   Division Series vs. St. L.
Cardinals, lost 3 games to 2
2007   Division Series vs. Chi. Cubs,
won 3 games to 0
League Championship Series vs.
Colo. Rockies, lost 4 games
to 0
2011   Division Series vs. Milw.
Brewers, lost 3 games to 2

Atlanta Braves (formerly the Milwaukee Braves)

Dates of Operation: (as the Milwaukee Braves) 1953–65 (13 years)
Overall Record: 1146 wins, 890 losses (.563)
Stadium: Milwaukee County Stadium, 1953–65 (capacity: 44,091)

Dates of Operation: (as the Atlanta Braves) 1966–present (46 years)
Overall Record: 3770 wins, 3539 losses (.516)
Stadiums: Atlanta–Fulton County Stadium, 1966–96; Turner Field, 1997–present (capacity: 50,096)

Year-by-Year Finishes

Year	Finish	Wins	Losses	Percentage	Games Behind	Manager	Attendance
				Milw. Braves			
1953	2nd	92	62	.597	13.0	Charlie Grimm	1,826,397
1954	3rd	89	65	.578	8.0	Charlie Grimm	2,131,388
1955	2nd	85	69	.552	13.5	Charlie Grimm	2,005,836
1956	2nd	92	62	.597	1.0	Charlie Grimm, Fred Haney	2,046,331
1957	1st	95	59	.617	+8.0	Fred Haney	2,215,404
1958	1st	92	62	.597	+8.0	Fred Haney	1,971,101
1959	2nd	86	70	.551	2.0	Fred Haney	1,749,112
1960	2nd	88	66	.571	7.0	Chuck Dressen	1,497,799
1961	4th	83	71	.539	10.0	Chuck Dressen, Birdie Tebbetts	1,101,441
1962	5th	86	76	.531	15.5	Birdie Tebbetts	766,921
1963	6th	84	78	.519	15.0	Bobby Bragan	773,018
1964	5th	88	74	.543	5.0	Bobby Bragan	910,911
1965	5th	86	76	.531	11.0	Bobby Bragan	555,584
				Atl. Braves			
1966	5th	85	77	.525	10.0	Bobby Bragan, Billy Hitchcock	1,539,801
1967	7th	77	85	.475	24.5	Billy Hitchcock, Ken Silvestri	1,389,222
1968	5th	81	81	.500	16.0	Lum Harris	1,126,540
				West Division			
1969	1st	93	69	.574	+3.0	Lum Harris	1,458,320
1970	5th	76	86	.469	26.0	Lum Harris	1,078,848
1971	3rd	82	80	.506	8.0	Lum Harris	1,006,320
1972	4th	70	84	.455	25.0	Lum Harris, Eddie Mathews	752,973
1973	5th	76	85	.472	22.5	Eddie Mathews	800,655
1974	3rd	88	74	.543	14.0	Eddie Mathews, Clyde King	981,085
1975	5th	67	94	.416	40.5	Clyde King, Connie Ryan	534,672
1976	6th	70	92	.432	32.0	Dave Bristol	818,179
1977	6th	61	101	.377	37.0	Dave Bristol, Ted Turner	872,464
1978	6th	69	93	.426	26.0	Bobby Cox	904,494
1979	6th	66	94	.413	23.5	Bobby Cox	769,465
1980	4th	81	80	.503	11.0	Bobby Cox	1,048,411
1981*	4th/5th	50	56	.472	9.5/7.5	Bobby Cox	535,418
1982	1st	89	73	.549	+1.0	Joe Torre	1,801,985
1983	2nd	88	74	.543	3.0	Joe Torre	2,119,935
1984	2nd (Tie)	80	82	.494	12.0	Joe Torre	1,724,892
1985	5th	66	96	.407	29.0	Eddie Haas, Bobby Wine	1,350,137

1986	6th	72	89	.447	23.5	Chuck Tanner	1,387,181
1987	5th	69	92	.429	20.5	Chuck Tanner	1,217,402
1988	6th	54	106	.338	39.5	Chuck Tanner, Russ Nixon	848,089
1989	6th	63	97	.394	28.0	Russ Nixon	984,930
1990	6th	65	97	.401	26.0	Russ Nixon, Bobby Cox	980,129
1991	1st	94	68	.580	+1.0	Bobby Cox	2,140,217
1992	1st	98	64	.605	+8.0	Bobby Cox	3,077,400
1993	1st	104	58	.642	+1.0	Bobby Cox	3,884,725
				East Division			
1994	2nd	68	46	.596	6.0	Bobby Cox	2,539,240
1995	1st	90	54	.625	+21.0	Bobby Cox	2,561,831
1996	1st	96	66	.593	+8.0	Bobby Cox	2,901,242
1997	1st	101	61	.623	+9.0	Bobby Cox	3,464,488
1998	1st	106	56	.654	+18.0	Bobby Cox	3,361,350
1999	1st	103	59	.636	+6.5	Bobby Cox	3,284,897
2000	1st	95	67	.586	+1.0	Bobby Cox	3,234,301
2001	1st	88	74	.543	+2.0	Bobby Cox	2,823,494
2002	1st	101	59	.631	+19.0	Bobby Cox	2,603,482
2003	1st	101	61	.623	+10.0	Bobby Cox	2,401,104
2004	1st	96	66	.593	+10.0	Bobby Cox	2,322,565
2005	1st	90	72	.556	+2.0	Bobby Cox	2,521,167
2006	3rd	79	83	.488	18.0	Bobby Cox	2,550,524
2007	3rd	84	78	.519	5.0	Bobby Cox	2,745,210
2008	4th	72	90	.444	20.0	Bobby Cox	2,532,834
2009	3rd	86	76	.531	7.0	Bobby Cox	2,373,631
2010	2nd	91	71	.562	6.0	Bobby Cox	2,510,119
2011	2nd	89	73	.549	13.0	Fredi Gonzalez	2,372,940

*Split season.

Awards

Most Valuable Player
Dale Murphy, outfield, 1982
Dale Murphy, outfield, 1983
Terry Pendleton, third base, 1991
Chipper Jones, third base, 1999

Rookie of the Year
Bob Horner, third base, 1978
David Justice, outfield, 1990
Rafael Furcal, second base and shortstop, 2000
Craig Kimbrel, pitcher, 2011

Cy Young
Tom Glavine, 1991
Greg Maddux, 1993
Greg Maddux, 1994
Greg Maddux, 1995
John Smoltz, 1996
Tom Glavine, 1998

Hall of Famers Who Played for the Braves
Hank Aaron, outfield, 1954–65 (Milw.) and 1966–74 (Atl.)
Orlando Cepeda, first base, 1969–72
Eddie Mathews, third base, 1953–65 (Milw.) and 1966 (Atl.)
Phil Niekro, pitcher, 1964–65 (Milw.) and 1966–83 (Atl.)
Gaylord Perry, pitcher, 1981
Red Schoendienst, infield, 1957–60 (Milw.)
Enos Slaughter, outfield, 1959 (Milw.)
Warren Spahn, pitcher, 1953–64 (Milw.)
Bruce Sutter, pitcher, 1958–88
Hoyt Wilhelm, pitcher, 1969–70 and 1971

Retired Numbers
3 .... Dale Murphy
6 .... Bobby Cox
21 .... Warren Spahn
31 .... Greg Maddux
35 .... Phil Niekro
41 .... Eddie Mathews
44 .... Hank Aaron
47 .... Tom Glavine

League Leaders, Batting

Batting Average, Season
Hank Aaron, 1956 (Milw.) .... .328
Hank Aaron, 1959 (Milw.) .... .355
Rico Carty, 1970 .... .366
Ralph Garr, 1974 .... .353
Terry Pendleton, 1991 .... .319
Chipper Jones, 2008 .... .364

Home Runs, Season
Eddie Mathews, 1953 (Milw.) 47
Hank Aaron, 1957 (Milw.) 44
Eddie Mathews, 1959 (Milw.) 46
Hank Aaron, 1963 (Milw.) 44
Hank Aaron, 1966 44
Hank Aaron, 1967 39
Dale Murphy, 1984 .... 36 (Tie)

Dale Murphy, 1985 37
Andruw Jones, 2005........................51

RBIs, Season
Hank Aaron, 1957 (Milw.).............132
Hank Aaron, 1960 (Milw.).............126
Hank Aaron, 1963 (Milw.).............130
Hank Aaron, 1966 127
Dale Murphy, 1982 ....109 (Tie)
Dale Murphy, 1983 121
Andruw Jones, 2005.....................128

Stolen Bases, Season
Bill Bruton, 1953 (Milw.) 26
Bill Bruton, 1954 (Milw.) 34
Bill Bruton, 1955 (Milw.) 25
Michael Bourn, 2011*......................61
*Played part of Season with Hous. Astros

Total Bases, Season
Hank Aaron, 1956 (Milw.).............340
Hank Aaron, 1957 (Milw.).............369
Hank Aaron, 1959 (Milw.).............400
Hank Aaron, 1960 (Milw.).............334
Hank Aaron, 1961 (Milw.).............358
Hank Aaron, 1963 (Milw.).............370
Felipe Alou, 1966.........................355
Hank Aaron, 1967 344
Hank Aaron, 1969 332
Dale Murphy, 1984 332
Terry Pendleton, 1991.............303 (Tie)

Most Hits, Season
Hank Aaron, 1956 (Milw.).............200
Red Schoendienst*, 1957 (Milw.)....200
Hank Aaron, 1959 (Milw.).............223
Felipe Alou, 1966..........................218
Felipe Alou, 1968 ....210 (Tie)
Ralph Garr, 1974 214
Terry Pendleton, 1991 187
Terry Pendleton, 1992............199 (Tie)
*Played part of season with N.Y. Giants.

Most Runs, Season
Hank Aaron, 1957 (Milw.).............118
Bill Bruton, 1960 (Milw.) 112
Hank Aaron, 1963 (Milw.) 121
Felipe Alou, 1966..........................122
Hank Aaron, 1967 ....113 (Tie)
Dale Murphy, 1985 118

Batting Feats

Triple Crown Winners
[No player]

Hitting for the Cycle
Albert Hall, Sept. 23, 1987
Mark Kotsay, Aug. 14, 2008

Six Hits in a Game
Felix Milan, July 6, 1970
Willie Harris, July 21, 2007

40 or More Home Runs, Season
51.......................Andruw Jones, 2005
47 ....Eddie Mathews, 1953 (Milw.)
                     Hank Aaron, 1971
46 ....Eddie Mathews, 1959 (Milw.)
45 ....Hank Aaron, 1962 (Milw.)
                     Chipper Jones, 1999
44 ....Hank Aaron, 1957 (Milw.)
                Hank Aaron, 1963 (Milw.)
                     Hank Aaron, 1966
                     Hank Aaron, 1969
                     Dale Murphy, 1987
                 Andres Galarraga, 1998
43 ....Davey Johnson, 1973
                     Javy Lopez, 2003
41 ....Eddie Mathews, 1955 (Milw.)
                     Darrell Evans, 1973
                     Jeff Burroughs, 1977
                     Andruw Jones, 2006
40 ....Eddie Mathews, 1954 (Milw.)
                     Hank Aaron, 1960 (Milw.)
                     Hank Aaron, 1973
                     David Justice, 1993

League Leaders, Pitching

Most Wins, Season
Warren Spahn, 1957 (Milw.)............21
Warren Spahn, 1958 (Milw.)....22 (Tie)
Lew Burdette, 1959 (Milw.).......21 (Tie)
Warren Spahn, 1959 (Milw.)....21 (Tie)
Warren Spahn, 1960 (Milw.)....21 (Tie)
Warren Spahn, 1961 (Milw.)....21 (Tie)
Phil Niekro, 1974....................20 (Tie)
Phil Niekro, 1979....................21 (Tie)
Tom Glavine, 1991 ....20 (Tie)
Tom Glavine, 1992.................20 (Tie)
Tom Glavine, 1993.................22 (Tie)
Greg Maddux, 1994 ....16 (Tie)
Greg Maddux, 1995.......................19
John Smoltz, 1996..........................24
Denny Neagle, 1997 20
Tom Glavine, 1998 20
John Smoltz, 2006 ....16 (Tie)

Most Strikeouts, Season
Phil Niekro, 1977.........................262
John Smoltz, 1992........................215
John Smoltz, 1996........................276

Lowest ERA, Season
Warren Spahn, 1953 (Milw.) 2.10
Lew Burdette, 1956 (Milw.)............2.71
Warren Spahn, 1961 (Milw.) 3.01
Phil Niekro, 1967.........................1.87
Buzz Capra, 1974.........................2.28
Greg Maddux, 1993....................2.36
Greg Maddux, 1994....................1.56
Greg Maddux, 1995....................1.63
Greg Maddux, 1998....................2.22

Most Saves, Season
John Smoltz, 2002..........................55
Craig Kimbrel, 2011 ....46 (tie)

Best Won-Lost Percentage, Season
Bob Buhl, 1957 (Milw.)...18-7 .... .720
Warren Spahn, 1958
     (Milw.) ....22-11 .... .667
                                         (Tie)
Lew Burdette, 1958
     (Milw.) ....20-10 .... .667
                                         (Tie)
Phil Niekro, 1982 ....17-4 .... .810
Greg Maddux, 1995 ....19-2 .... .905
John Smoltz, 1996.........24-8 .... .750
Greg Maddux, 1997 ......19-4 .... .826
John Smoltz, 1998.........17-3 .... .850
Russ Ortiz, 2003 ....21-7 .... .750
Jorge Sosa, 2005 ....13-3 .... .813
Chuck James, 2006........11-4 .... .733

Pitching Feats

20 Wins, Season
Warren Spahn, 1953 (Milw.) 23-7
Warren Spahn, 1954 (Milw.).......21-12
Warren Spahn, 1956 (Milw.)......20-11
Warren Spahn, 1957 (Milw.)......21-11
Warren Spahn, 1958 (Milw.)......22-11
Lew Burdette, 1958 (Milw.) 20-10
Lew Burdette, 1959 (Milw.) 21-15
Warren Spahn, 1959 (Milw.)......21-15
Warren Spahn, 1960 (Milw.)......21-10
Warren Spahn, 1961 (Milw.)......21-13
Warren Spahn, 1963 (Milw.) 23-7
Tony Cloninger, 1965 (Milw.) 24-11
Phil Niekro, 1969 23-13

Phil Niekro, 1974 20–13
Phil Niekro, 1979 21–20
Tom Glavine, 1991 20–11
Tom Glavine, 1992 20–8
Tom Glavine, 1993 22–6
Greg Maddux, 1993 20–10
John Smoltz, 1996 24–8
Denny Neagle, 1997...................20–5
Tom Glavine, 1998 20–6
Tom Glavine, 2000 21–9
Russ Ortiz, 2003 21–7

No-Hitters

Jim Wilson (vs. Phila. Phillies), June 12,
    1954 (final: 2–0) (Milw.)
Lew Burdette (vs. Phila. Phillies), Aug. 18,
    1960 (final: 1–0) (Milw.)
Warren Spahn (vs. Phila. Phillies), Sept.
    15, 1960 (final: 4–0) (Milw.)
Warren Spahn (vs. S.F. Giants), Apr. 28,
    1961 (final: 1–0) (Milw.)
Phil Niekro (vs. S.D. Padres), Aug. 5, 1973
    (final: 9–0)
Kent Mercker, Mark Wohlers, and
    Alejandro Pena (vs. S.D. Padres), Sept.
    11, 1991 (final: 1–0)
Kent Mercker (vs. L.A. Dodgers), Apr. 8,
    1994 (final: 6–0)

No-Hitters Pitched Against

Harvey Haddix, Pitt. Pirates, May 26,
    1959 (final: 0–1) (lost perfect game
    in 13th) (vs. Milw.)
Don Wilson, Hous. Astros, June 18,
    1967 (final: 2–0)
Ken Holtzman, Chi. Cubs, Aug. 19,
    1969 (final: 3–0)

John Montefusco, S.F. Giants, Sept. 29,
    1976 (final: 9–0)
Ken Forsch, Hous. Astros, Apr. 7, 1979
    (final: 6–0)
Randy Johnson, Ariz. D'backs, May 18,
    2004 (final: 2–0) (perfect game)
Ubaldo Jimenez, Colo. Rockies, Apr. 17,
    2010 (final: 4–0)

Postseason Play

1957   World Series vs. N.Y. Yankees (AL),
       won 4 games to 3 (Milw.)
1958   World Series vs. N.Y. Yankees (AL),
       lost 4 games to 3 (Milw.)
1959   Pennant Playoff Game vs. L.A.
       Dodgers, lost (Milw.)
1969   League Championship Series vs.
       N.Y. Mets, lost 3 games to 0
1982   League Championship Series vs.
       St. L. Cardinals, lost 3 games to 0
1991   League Championship Series vs.
       Pitt. Pirates, won 4 games to 3
       World Series vs. Minn. Twins (AL),
       lost 4 games to 3
1992   League Championship Series vs.
       Pitt. Pirates, won 4 games to 3
       World Series vs. Tor. Blue Jays
       (AL), lost 4 games to 2
1993   League Championship Series vs.
       Phila. Phillies, lost 4 games to 2
1995   Division Series vs. Colo. Rockies,
       won 3 games to 1
       League Championship Series vs.
       Cin. Reds, won 4 games to 0
       World Series vs. Cleve. Indians
       (AL), won 4 games to 2

1996   Division Series vs. L.A. Dodgers,
       won 3 games to 0
       League Championship Series vs.
       St. L. Cardinals, won 4 games
       to 3
       World Series vs. N.Y. Yankees
       (AL), lost 4 games to 2
1997   Division Series vs. Hous. Astros,
       won 3 games to 0
       League Championship Series vs.
       Flor. Marlins, lost 4 games to 2
1998   Division Series vs. Chi. Cubs, won
       3 games to 0
       League Championship Series vs.
       S.D. Padres, lost 4 games to 2
1999   Division Series vs. Hous. Astros,
       won 3 games to 1
       League Championship Series vs.
       N.Y. Mets, won 4 games to 2
       World Series vs. N.Y. Yankees
       (AL), lost 4 games to 0
2000   Division Series vs. St. L.
       Cardinals, lost 3 games to 0
2001   Division Series vs. Hous. Astros,
       won 3 games to 0
       League Championship Series vs.
       Ariz. D'backs, lost 4 games
       to 1
2002   Division Series vs. S.F. Giants, lost
       3 games to 1
2003   Division Series vs. Chi. Cubs, lost
       3 games to 2
2004   Division Series vs. Hous. Astros,
       lost 3 games to 2
2005   Division Series vs. Hous. Astros,
       lost 3 games to 1
2010   Division Series vs. S. F. Giants,
       lost 3 games to 1

Chicago Cubs

Dates of Operation: 1876–present (136 years)
Overall Record: 10,311 wins, 9779 losses (.513)
Stadiums: 23rd Street Grounds, 1876–77; Lakefront Park, 1878–84; West Side Park, 1885–92;
    South Side Park, 1891–93 and 1897; New West Side Park (also called West Side Grounds),
    1893–1915; Comiskey Park, 1918 (World Series only); Wrigley Field (formerly Weeghman Field),
    1916–present (capacity: 41,118)
Other Names: Broncos, Colts, Cowboys, Orphans, White Stockings

Year-by-Year Finishes

Year	Finish	Wins	Losses	Percentage	Games Behind	Manager	Attendance
1876	1st	52	14	.788	+6.0	A. G. Spalding	not available
1877	5th	26	33	.441	15.5	A. G. Spalding	not available
1878	4th	30	30	.500	11.0	Robert Ferguson	not available
1879	3rd (Tie)	44	32	.579	10.0	Cap Anson	not available
1880	1st	67	17	.798	+15.0	Cap Anson	not available
1881	1st	56	28	.667	+9.0	Cap Anson	not available
1882	1st	55	29	.655	+3.0	Cap Anson	not available
1883	2nd	59	29	.602	4.0	Cap Anson	not available
1884	4th (Tie)	62	50	.554	22.0	Cap Anson	not available
1885	1st	87	25	.776	+2.0	Cap Anson	not available
1886	1st	90	34	.725	+2.5	Cap Anson	not available
1887	3rd	71	50	.587	6.5	Cap Anson	not available
1888	2nd	77	58	.578	9.0	Cap Anson	not available
1889	3rd	67	65	.508	19.0	Cap Anson	not available
1890	2nd	83	53	.610	6.5	Cap Anson	not available
1891	2nd	82	53	.607	3.5	Cap Anson	not available
1892	7th	70	76	.479	40.0	Cap Anson	not available
1893	9th	57	71	.445	28.0	Cap Anson	not available
1894	8th	57	75	.432	34.0	Cap Anson	not available
1895	4th	72	58	.554	15.0	Cap Anson	not available
1896	5th	71	57	.555	18.5	Cap Anson	not available
1897	9th	59	73	.447	34.0	Cap Anson	not available
1898	4th	85	65	.567	17.5	Tom Burns	not available
1899	8th	75	73	.507	22.0	Tom Burns	not available
1900	5th (Tie)	65	75	.464	19.0	Tom Loftus	not available
1901	6th	53	86	.381	37.0	Tom Loftus	205,071
1902	5th	68	69	.496	34.0	Frank Selee	263,700
1903	3rd	82	56	.594	8.0	Frank Selee	386,205
1904	2nd	93	60	.608	13.0	Frank Selee	439,100
1905	3rd	92	61	.601	13.0	Frank Selee, Frank Chance	509,900
1906	1st	116	36	.763	+20.0	Frank Chance	654,000
1907	1st	107	45	.704	+17.0	Frank Chance	422,550
1908	1st	99	55	.643	+1.0	Frank Chance	665,325
1909	2nd	104	49	.680	6.5	Frank Chance	633,480
1910	1st	104	50	.675	+13.0	Frank Chance	526,152
1911	2nd	92	62	.597	7.5	Frank Chance	576,000
1912	3rd	91	59	.607	11.5	Frank Chance	514,000

1913	3rd	88	65	.575	13.5	Johnny Evers	419,000
1914	4th	78	76	.506	16.5	Hank O'Day	202,516
1915	4th	73	80	.477	17.5	Roger Bresnahan	217,058
1916	5th	67	86	.438	26.5	Joe Tinker	453,685
1917	5th	74	80	.481	24.0	Fred Mitchell	360,218
1918	1st	84	45	.651	+10.5	Fred Mitchell	337,256
1919	3rd	75	65	.536	21.0	Fred Mitchell	424,430
1920	5th (Tie)	75	79	.487	18.0	Fred Mitchell	480,783
1921	7th	64	89	.418	30.0	Johnny Evers, Bill Killefer	410,107
1922	5th	80	74	.519	13.0	Bill Killefer	542,283
1923	4th	83	71	.539	12.5	Bill Killefer	703,705
1924	5th	81	72	.529	12.0	Bill Killefer	716,922
1925	8th	68	86	.442	27.5	Bill Killefer, Rabbit Maranville, George Gibson	622,610
1926	4th	82	72	.532	7.0	Joe McCarthy	885,063
1927	4th	85	68	.556	8.5	Joe McCarthy	1,159,168
1928	3rd	91	63	.591	4.0	Joe McCarthy	1,143,740
1929	1st	98	54	.645	+10.5	Joe McCarthy	1,485,166
1930	2nd	90	64	.584	2.0	Joe McCarthy, Rogers Hornsby	1,463,624
1931	3rd	84	70	.545	17.0	Rogers Hornsby	1,086,422
1932	1st	90	64	.584	+4.0	Rogers Hornsby, Charlie Grimm	974,688
1933	3rd	86	68	.558	6.0	Charlie Grimm	594,112
1934	3rd	86	65	.570	8.0	Charlie Grimm	707,525
1935	1st	100	54	.649	+4.0	Charlie Grimm	692,604
1936	2nd (Tie)	87	67	.565	5.0	Charlie Grimm	699,370
1937	2nd	93	61	.604	3.0	Charlie Grimm	895,020
1938	1st	89	63	.586	+2.0	Charlie Grimm, Gabby Hartnett	951,640
1939	4th	84	70	.545	13.0	Gabby Hartnett	726,663
1940	5th	75	79	.487	25.5	Gabby Hartnett	534,878
1941	6th	70	84	.455	30.0	Jimmy Wilson	545,159
1942	6th	68	86	.442	38.0	Jimmy Wilson	590,872
1943	5th	74	79	.484	30.5	Jimmy Wilson	508,247
1944	4th	75	79	.487	30.0	Jimmy Wilson, Charlie Grimm	640,110
1945	1st	98	56	.636	+3.0	Charlie Grimm	1,036,386
1946	3rd	82	71	.536	14.5	Charlie Grimm	1,342,970
1947	6th	69	85	.448	25.0	Charlie Grimm	1,364,039
1948	8th	64	90	.416	27.5	Charlie Grimm	1,237,792
1949	8th	61	93	.396	36.0	Charlie Grimm, Frankie Frisch	1,143,139
1950	7th	64	89	.418	26.5	Frankie Frisch	1,165,944
1951	8th	62	92	.403	34.5	Frankie Frisch, Phil Cavarretta	894,415
1952	5th	77	77	.500	19.5	Phil Cavarretta	1,024,826
1953	7th	65	89	.422	40.0	Phil Cavarretta	763,658
1954	7th	64	90	.416	33.0	Stan Hack	748,183
1955	6th	72	81	.471	26.0	Stan Hack	875,800
1956	8th	60	94	.390	33.0	Stan Hack	720,118
1957	7th (Tie)	62	92	.403	33.0	Bob Scheffing	670,629
1958	5th (Tie)	72	82	.468	20.0	Bob Scheffing	979,904
1959	5th (Tie)	74	80	.481	13.0	Bob Scheffing	858,255
1960	7th	60	94	.390	35.0	Charlie Grimm, Lou Boudreau	809,770
1961	7th	64	90	.416	29.0	Vedie Himsl, Harry Craft, Elvin Tappe, Lou Klein	673,057
1962	9th	59	103	.364	42.5	Charlie Metro, Elvin Tappe, Lou Klein	609,802
1963	7th	82	80	.506	17.0	Bob Kennedy	979,551

1964	8th	76	86	.469	17.0	Bob Kennedy	751,647
1965	8th	72	90	.444	25.0	Bob Kennedy, Lou Klein	641,361
1966	10th	59	103	.364	36.0	Leo Durocher	635,891
1967	3rd	87	74	.540	14.0	Leo Durocher	977,226
1968	3rd	84	78	.519	13.0	Leo Durocher	1,043,409

East Division

1969	2nd	92	70	.568	8.0	Leo Durocher	1,674,993
1970	2nd	84	78	.519	5.0	Leo Durocher	1,642,705
1971	3rd (Tie)	83	79	.512	14.0	Leo Durocher	1,653,007
1972	2nd	85	70	.548	11.0	Leo Durocher, Whitey Lockman	1,299,163
1973	5th	77	84	.478	5.0	Whitey Lockman	1,351,705
1974	6th	66	96	.407	22.0	Whitey Lockman, Jim Marshall	1,015,378
1975	5th (Tie)	75	87	.463	17.5	Jim Marshall	1,034,819
1976	4th	75	87	.463	26.0	Jim Marshall	1,026,217
1977	4th	81	81	.500	20.0	Herman Franks	1,439,834
1978	3rd	79	83	.488	11.0	Herman Franks	1,525,311
1979	5th	80	82	.494	18.0	Herman Franks, Joe Amalfitano	1,648,587
1980	6th	64	98	.395	27.0	Preston Gomez, Joe Amalfitano	1,206,776
1981*	6th/5th	38	65	.369	17.5/6.0	Joe Amalfitano	565,637
1982	5th	73	89	.451	19.0	Lee Elia	1,249,270
1983	5th	71	91	.438	19.0	Lee Elia, Charlie Fox	1,479,717
1984	1st	96	65	.596	+6.5	Jim Frey	2,107,655
1985	4th	77	84	.478	23.5	Jim Frey	2,161,534
1986	5th	70	90	.438	37.0	Jim Frey, John Vukovich, Gene Michael	1,859,102
1987	6th	76	85	.472	18.5	Gene Michael, Frank Lucchesi	2,035,130
1988	4th	77	85	.475	24.0	Don Zimmer	2,089,034
1989	1st	93	69	.574	+6.0	Don Zimmer	2,491,942
1990	4th	77	85	.475	18.0	Don Zimmer	2,243,791
1991	4th	77	83	.481	20.0	Don Zimmer, Joe Altobelli, Jim Essian	2,314,250
1992	4th	78	84	.481	18.0	Jim Lefebvre	2,126,720
1993	4th	84	78	.519	13.0	Jim Lefebvre	2,653,763

Central Division

1994	5th	49	64	.434	16.5	Tom Trebelhorn	1,845,208
1995	3rd	73	71	.570	12.0	Jim Riggleman	1,918,265
1996	4th	76	86	.469	12.0	Jim Riggleman	2,219,110
1997	5th	68	94	.420	16.0	Jim Riggleman	2,190,308
1998	2nd	90	73	.552	12.5	Jim Riggleman	2,623,000
1999	6th	67	95	.414	30.0	Jim Riggleman	2,813,854
2000	6th	65	97	.401	30.0	Don Baylor	2,789,511
2001	3rd	88	74	.543	5.0	Don Baylor	2,779,456
2002	5th	67	95	.414	30.0	Don Baylor, Bruce Kimm	2,693,071
2003	1st	88	74	.543	+1.0	Dusty Baker	2,962,630
2004	3rd	89	73	.549	16.0	Dusty Baker	3,170,184
2005	4th	79	83	.488	21.0	Dusty Baker	3,099,992
2006	6th	66	96	.407	17.5	Dusty Baker	3,123,215
2007	1st	85	77	.525	+2.0	Lou Piniella	3,123,215
2008	1st	97	64	.602	+7.5	Lou Piniella	3,300,200
2009	2nd	83	78	.516	7.5	Lou Piniella	3,168,859
2010	5th	75	87	.463	16.0	Lou Piniella, Mike Quade	3,062,973
2011	5th	71	91	.438	25.0	Mike Quade	3,017,966

*Split season.

Awards

Most Valuable Player

Wildfire Schulte, outfield, 1911
Rogers Hornsby, second base, 1929
Gabby Hartnett, catcher, 1935
Phil Cavarretta, first base, 1945
Hank Sauer, outfield, 1952
Ernie Banks, shortstop, 1958
Ernie Banks, shortstop, 1959
Ryne Sandberg, second base, 1984
Andre Dawson, outfield, 1987
Sammy Sosa, outfield, 1998

Rookie of the Year

Billy Williams, outfield, 1961
Ken Hubbs, second base, 1962
Jerome Walton, outfield, 1989
Kerry Wood, pitcher, 1998
Geovany Soto, catcher, 2008

Cy Young

Ferguson Jenkins, 1971
Bruce Sutter, 1979
Rick Sutcliffe, 1984
Greg Maddux, 1992

Hall of Famers Who Played for the Cubs

Grover C. Alexander, pitcher, 1918–26
Cap Anson, first base, 1876–97
Richie Ashburn, outfield, 1960–61
Ernie Banks, shortstop, 1953–71
Roger Bresnahan, catcher, 1900 and 1913–15
Lou Brock, outfield, 1961–64
Three Finger Brown, pitcher, 1904–12 and 1916
Frank Chance, first base, 1898–1912
John Clarkson, pitcher, 1884–87
Kiki Cuyler, outfield, 1928–35
Andre Dawson, outfield, 1987–92
Dizzy Dean, pitcher, 1938–41
Hugh Duffy, outfield, 1888–89
Dennis Eckersley, pitcher, 1984–86
Johnny Evers, second base, 1902–13
Jimmie Foxx, first base, 1942 and 1944
Goose Gossage, pitcher, 1988
Clark Griffith, pitcher, 1893–1900
Burleigh Grimes, pitcher, 1932–33
Gabby Hartnett, catcher, 1922–40
Billy Herman, second base, 1931–41
Rogers Hornsby, second base, 1929–32

Monte Irvin, outfield, 1956
Ferguson Jenkins, pitcher, 1966–73 and 1982–83
George Kelly, first base, 1930
King Kelly, outfield, 1880–86
Ralph Kiner, outfield, 1953–54
Chuck Klein, outfield, 1934–36
Tony Lazzeri, second base, 1938
Fred Lindstrom, outfield, 1935
Rabbit Maranville, shortstop, 1925
Robin Roberts, pitcher, 1966
Ryne Sandberg, second base, 1982–94, 1996–97
Al Spalding, pitcher, 1876–78
Bruce Sutter, pitcher, 1976–88
Joe Tinker, shortstop, 1902–12 and 1916
Rube Waddell, pitcher, 1901
Hoyt Wilhelm, pitcher, 1970
Billy Williams, outfield, 1959–74
Hack Wilson, outfield, 1926–31

Retired Numbers

10.......................................Ron Santo
14.....................................Ernie Banks
23..............................Ryne Sandberg
26..............................Billy Williams
31 ...Ferguson Jenkins and Greg Maddux

League Leaders, Batting (Post-1900)

Batting Average, Season

Heinie Zimmerman, 1912............ .372
Phil Cavarretta, 1945 .... .355
Billy Williams, 1972 .... .333
Bill Madlock, 1975 .... .354
Bill Madlock, 1976 .... .339
Bill Buckner, 1980 .... .324
Derrek Lee, 2005 .... .335

Home Runs, Season

Wildfire Schulte, 1910.............10 (Tie)
Wildfire Schulte, 1911 21
Heinie Zimmerman, 1912...............14
Cy Williams, 1916 ....12 (Tie)
Hack Wilson, 1926 21
Hack Wilson, 1927 ....30 (Tie)
Hack Wilson, 1928 ....31 (Tie)
Hack Wilson, 1930 56
Bill Nicholson, 1943 29
Bill Nicholson, 1944 33

Hank Sauer, 1952 ....37 (Tie)
Ernie Banks, 1958 47
Ernie Banks, 1960 41
Dave Kingman, 1979......................48
Andre Dawson, 1987 49
Ryne Sandberg, 1990.....................40
Sammy Sosa, 2000 50
Sammy Sosa, 2002 49

RBIs, Season

Wildfire Schulte, 1911 121
Heinie Zimmerman, 1912...............98
Heinie Zimmerman*, 1916 83
Fred Merkle, 1918..........................71
Hack Wilson, 1929 159
Hack Wilson, 1930 191
Bill Nicholson, 1943 128
Bill Nicholson, 1944 122
Hank Sauer, 1952 121
Ernie Banks, 1958 129
Ernie Banks, 1959 143
Andre Dawson, 1987.....................137
Sammy Sosa, 1998........................158
Sammy Sosa, 2001........................160

*Played part of season with N.Y. Giants.

Stolen Bases, Season

Frank Chance, 1903................67 (Tie)
Billy Maloney, 1905............59 (Tie)
Frank Chance, 1906 57
Kiki Cuyler, 1928 37
Kiki Cuyler, 1929 43
Kiki Cuyler, 1930 37
Augie Galan, 1935 22
Augie Galan, 1937 23
Stan Hack, 1938 16
Stan Hack, 1939 ....17 (Tie)

Total Bases, Season

Wildfire Schulte, 1911 308
Heinie Zimmerman, 1912..............318
Charlie Hollocher, 1918 202
Rogers Hornsby, 1929 409
Bill Nicholson, 1944 317
Ernie Banks, 1958 379
Billy Williams, 1968 321
Billy Williams, 1970 373
Billy Williams, 1972 348
Andre Dawson, 1987.....................353
Ryne Sandberg, 1990....................344
Sammy Sosa, 1998........................416
Sammy Sosa, 1999........................397

Sammy Sosa, 2001........................425

Most Hits, Season

Harry Steinfeldt, 1906 176
Heinie Zimmerman, 1912..............207
Charlie Hollocher, 1918 161
Billy Herman, 1935 227
Stan Hack, 1940 ....191 (Tie)
Stan Hack, 1941 186
Phil Cavarretta, 1944 ....197 (Tie)
Billy Williams, 1970 ....205 (Tie)
Derrek Lee, 2005...........................199
Juan Pierre, 2006..........................204
Starlin Castro, 2011 207

Most Runs, Season

Frank Chance, 1906..............103 (Tie)
Jimmy Sheckard, 1911...................121
Tommy Leach, 1913.................99 (Tie)
Rogers Hornsby, 1929 156
Augie Galan, 1935 133
Bill Nicholson, 1944 116
Glenn Beckert, 1968.......................98
Billy Williams, 1970 137
Ivan DeJesus, 1978........................104
Ryne Sandberg, 1984 114
Ryne Sandberg, 1989 ....104 (Tie)
Ryne Sandberg, 1990 116
Sammy Sosa, 1998........................134
Sammy Sosa, 2001........................146
Sammy Sosa, 2002........................122

Batting Feats

Triple Crown Winners

Heinie Zimmerman, 1912 (.372 BA, 14
    HRs, 98 RBIs)

Hitting for the Cycle

Jimmy Ryan, July 28, 1888
Jimmy Ryan, July 1, 1891
Hack Wilson, June 23, 1930
Babe Herman, Sept. 30, 1933
Roy Smalley, June 28, 1950
Lee Walls, July 2, 1957
Billy Williams, July 17, 1966
Randy Hundley, Aug. 11, 1966
Ivan DeJesus, Apr. 22, 1980
Andre Dawson, Apr. 29, 1987
Mark Grace, May 9, 1993

Six Hits in a Game (Post-1900)

Frank Demaree, July 5, 1937*

Don Kessinger, July 17, 1971*
Bill Madlock, July 26, 1975*
Jose Cardenal, May 2, 1976*
Sammy Sosa, July 2, 1993
*Extra-inning game.

40 or More Home Runs, Season

66 ....Sammy Sosa, 1998
64 ....Sammy Sosa, 2001
63 ....Sammy Sosa, 1999
56 ....Hack Wilson, 1930
50 ....Sammy Sosa, 2000
49 ....Andre Dawson, 1987
                        Sammy Sosa, 2002
48 ....Dave Kingman, 1979
47 ....Ernie Banks, 1958
46 ....Derrek Lee, 2005
45 ....Ernie Banks, 1959
44 ....Ernie Banks, 1955
43 ....Ernie Banks, 1957
42 ....Billy Williams, 1970
41 ....Hank Sauer, 1954
                        Ernie Banks, 1960
40 ....Ryne Sandberg, 1990
                        Sammy Sosa, 1996
                        Sammy Sosa, 2003

League Leaders, Pitching (Post-1900)

Most Wins, Season

Three Finger Brown, 1909 27
Larry Cheney, 1912.................26 (Tie)
Hippo Vaughn, 1918 22
Grover C. Alexander, 1920 27
Charlie Root, 1927 26
Pat Malone, 1929...........................22
Pat Malone, 1930 ....20 (Tie)
Lon Warneke, 1932........................22
Bill Lee, 1938................................22
Larry Jackson, 1964 24
Ferguson Jenkins, 1971..................24
Rick Sutcliffe, 1987........................18
Greg Maddux, 1992 ....20 (Tie)
Carlos Zambrano, 2006...........16 (Tie)

Most Strikeouts, Season

Fred Beebe*, 1906 171
Orval Overall, 1909 205
Hippo Vaughn, 1918 148
Hippo Vaughn, 1919 141
Grover C. Alexander, 1920 173
Pat Malone, 1929.........................166

Clay Bryant, 1938 135
Claude Passeau**, 1939 ....137 (Tie)
Johnny Schmitz, 1946...................135
Sam Jones, 1955...........................198
Sam Jones, 1956...........................176
Ferguson Jenkins, 1969.................273
Kerry Wood, 2003 266
*Pitched part of season with St. L. Cardinals.
**Pitched part of season with Phila. Phillies.

Lowest ERA, Season

Hippo Vaughn, 1918 ....1.74
Grover C. Alexander, 1919 ....1.72
Grover C. Alexander, 1920 ....1.91
Lon Warneke, 1932......................2.37
Bill Lee, 1938...............................2.66
Hank Borowy*, 1945 ....2.14
*Pitched part of season with N.Y. Yankees (AL).

Most Saves, Season

Bruce Sutter, 1979.........................37
Bruce Sutter, 1980.........................28
Lee Smith, 1983.............................29
Randy Myers, 1993........................53
Randy Myers, 1995........................38

Best Won–Lost Percentage, Season

Ed Reulbach, 1906 ....19–4.....826
Ed Reulbach, 1907 ....17–4.....810
Ed Reulbach, 1908 ....24–7.....774
King Cole, 1910.............20–4.....833
Bert Humphries, 1913 ...16–4.....800
Claude Hendrix, 1918...20–7.....741
Charlie Root, 1929 ....19–6.....760
Lon Warneke, 1932.......22–6.....786
Bill Lee, 1935................20–6.....769
Bill Lee, 1938................22–9.....710
Rick Sutcliffe, 1984........16–1.....941
Mike Bielecki, 1989 ....18–7.....720

Pitching Feats

20 Wins, Season

Jack Taylor, 1902.....................22–10
Jack Taylor, 1903.....................21–14
Jake Weimer, 1903......................20–8
Jake Weimer, 1904......................20–14
Three Finger Brown, 1906 26–6
Jack Pfiester, 1906.......................20–8
Jack Taylor, 1906 ....20–12*
Orval Overall, 1907 23–8
Three Finger Brown, 1907 20–6
Three Finger Brown, 1908 29–9

Ed Reulbach, 1908 24–7
Three Finger Brown, 1909 27–9
Orval Overall, 1909 20–11
Three Finger Brown, 1910 25–14
King Cole, 1910 20–4
Three Finger Brown, 1911 21–11
Larry Cheney, 1912 26–10
Larry Cheney, 1913 21–14
Hippo Vaughn, 1914.................21–13
Larry Cheney, 1914 20–18
Hippo Vaughn, 1915.................20–12
Hippo Vaughn, 1917.................23–13
Hippo Vaughn, 1918.................22–10
Claude Hendrix, 1918.................20–7
Hippo Vaughn, 1919.................21–14
Grover C. Alexander, 1920........27–14
Grover C. Alexander, 1923........22–12
Charlie Root, 1927 26–15
Pat Malone, 1929 22–10
Pat Malone, 1930 20–9
Lon Warneke, 1932 22–6
Guy Bush, 1933.........................20–12
Lon Warneke, 1934 22–10
Bill Lee, 1935 20–6
Lon Warneke, 1935 20–13
Bill Lee, 1938 22–9
Claude Passeau, 1940...............20–13
Hank Wyse, 1945......................22–10
Hank Borowy, 1945 ....21–7**
Dick Ellsworth, 1953 22–10
Larry Jackson, 1964..................24–11
Ferguson Jenkins, 1967 20–13
Ferguson Jenkins, 1968 20–15
Ferguson Jenkins, 1969 21–15
Bill Hands, 1969.......................20–14
Ferguson Jenkins, 1970 22–16
Ferguson Jenkins, 1971 24–13
Ferguson Jenkins, 1972 20–12
Rick Reuschel, 1977 20–10
Rick Sutcliffe, 1984..................20–6***
Greg Maddux, 1992 20–11
Jon Lieber, 2001 20–6

*8–9 with St. L. Cardinals and 12–3 with Chi. Cubs.
**10–5 with N.Y. Yankees (AL) and 11–2 with Chi. Cubs.
***4–5 with Cleve. Indians (AL) and 16–1 with Chi. Cubs.

No-Hitters

Bob Wicker (vs. N.Y. Giants), June 11, 1904 (final: 1–0) (hit in 10th and won in 12th)

Jimmy Lavender (vs. N.Y. Giants), Aug. 31, 1915 (final: 2–0)

Hippo Vaughn (vs. Cin. Reds), May 2, 1917 (final: 0–1) (lost in 10)

Sam Jones (vs. Pitt. Pirates), May 12, 1955 (final: 4–0)

Don Cardwell (vs. St. L. Cardinals), May 15, 1960 (final: 4–0)

Ken Holtzman (vs. Atl. Braves), Aug. 19, 1969 (final: 3–0)

Ken Holtzman (vs. Cin. Reds), June 3, 1971 (final: 1–0)

Burt Hooton (vs. Phila. Phillies), Apr. 16, 1972 (final: 4–0)

Milt Pappas (vs. S.D. Padres), Sept. 2, 1972 (final: 8–0)

Carlos Zambrano (vs. Hous. Astros), Sept. 14, 2008 (final: 5–0)

No-Hitters Pitched Against

Chick Fraser, Phila. Phillies, Sept. 18, 1903 (final: 10–0)

Christy Mathewson, N.Y. Giants, June 13, 1905 (final: 1–0)

Jim Toney, Cin. Reds, May 2, 1917 (final: 1–0) (10 innings)

Carl Erskine, Bklyn. Dodgers, June 19, 1952 (final: 5–0)

Jim Maloney, Cin. Reds, Aug. 9, 1965 (final: 1–0) (10 innings)

Sandy Koufax, L.A. Dodgers, Sept. 9, 1965 (final: 1–0) (perfect game)

Postseason Play

1906   World Series vs. Chi. White Sox (AL), lost 4 games to 2
1907   World Series vs. Det. Tigers (AL), won 4 games to 0, 1 tie
1908   Pennant Playoff Game vs. N.Y. Giants, won
       World Series vs. Det. Tigers (AL), won 4 games to 1
1910   World Series vs. Phila. A's (AL), lost 4 games to 1
1918   World Series vs. Bost. Red Sox (AL), lost 4 games to 2
1929   World Series vs. Phila. A's (AL), lost 4 games to 1
1932   World Series vs. N.Y. Yankees (AL), lost 4 games to 0
1935   World Series vs. Det. Tigers (AL), lost 4 games to 2
1938   World Series vs. N.Y. Yankees (AL), lost 4 games to 0
1945   World Series vs. Det. Tigers (AL), lost 4 games to 3
1984   League Championship Series vs. S.D. Padres, lost 3 games to 2
1989   League Championship Series vs. S.F. Giants, lost 4 games to 1
1998   NL Wild Card Playoff Game vs. S.F. Giants, won
       Division Series vs. Atl. Braves, lost 3 games to 0
2003   Division Series vs. Atl. Braves, won 3 games to 2
       League Championship Series vs. Flor. Marlins, lost 4 games to 3
2007   Division Series vs. Ariz. D'backs, lost 3 games to 0
2008   Division Series vs. L.A. Dodgers, lost 3 games to 0

Cincinnati Reds

Dates of Operation: 1876–80; 1890–present (127 years)
Overall Record: 9445 wins, 9306 losses (.504)
Stadiums: Avenue Grounds, 1876–79; Bank Street Grounds, 1880; League Park, 1890–92; Redland Field, 1892–1901; Palace of the Fans, 1902–11; Redland Field (also known as Crosley Field), 1912–70; Riverfront Stadium (also known as Cinergy Field, 1996–2002), 1970–2002; Great American Ball Park, 2003–present (capacity: 42,059)
Other Names: Red Stockings, Redlegs

Year-by-Year Finishes

Year	Finish	Wins	Losses	Percentage	Games Behind	Manager	Attendance
1876	8th	9	56	.138	42.5	Charlie Gould	not available
1877	6th	15	42	.263	25.5	Lip Pike, Bob Addy	not available
1878	2nd	37	23	.617	4.0	Cal McVey	not available
1879	5th	43	37	.538	14.0	Deacon White, Cal McVey	not available
1880	8th	21	59	.263	44.0	John Clapp	not available
1890	4th	78	55	.586	10.0	Tom Loftus	not available
1891	7th	56	81	.409	30.5	Tom Loftus	not available
1892	5th	82	68	.547	20.0	Charles Comiskey	not available
1893	6th	65	63	.508	20.0	Charles Comiskey	not available
1894	10th	54	75	.419	35.5	Charles Comiskey	not available
1895	8th	66	64	.508	21.0	Buck Ewing	not available
1896	3rd	77	50	.606	12.0	Buck Ewing	not available
1897	4th	76	56	.576	17.0	Buck Ewing	not available
1898	3rd	92	60	.605	11.5	Buck Ewing	not available
1899	6th	83	67	.553	15.0	Buck Ewing	not available
1900	7th	62	77	.446	21.5	Robert Allen	not available
1901	8th	52	87	.374	38.0	Bid McPhee	205,728
1902	4th	70	70	.500	33.5	Bid McPhee, Frank Bancroft, Joe Kelley	217,300
1903	4th	74	65	.532	16.5	Joe Kelley	351,680
1904	3rd	88	65	.575	18.0	Joe Kelley	391,915
1905	5th	79	74	.516	26.0	Joe Kelley	313,927
1906	6th	64	87	.424	51.5	Ned Hanlon	330,056
1907	6th	66	87	.431	41.5	Ned Hanlon	317,500
1908	5th	73	81	.474	26.0	John Ganzel	399,200
1909	4th	77	76	.503	33.5	Clark Griffith	424,643
1910	5th	75	79	.487	29.0	Clark Griffith	380,622
1911	6th	70	83	.458	29.0	Clark Griffith	300,000
1912	4th	75	78	.490	29.0	Hank O'Day	344,000
1913	7th	64	89	.418	37.5	Joe Tinker	258,000
1914	8th	60	94	.390	34.5	Buck Herzog	100,791
1915	7th	71	83	.461	20.0	Buck Herzog	218,878
1916	7th (Tie)	60	93	.392	33.5	Buck Herzog, Christy Mathewson	255,846
1917	4th	78	76	.506	20.0	Christy Mathewson	269,056
1918	3rd	68	60	.531	15.5	Christy Mathewson, Heinie Groh	163,009
1919	1st	96	44	.686	+9.0	Pat Moran	532,501
1920	3rd	82	71	.536	10.5	Pat Moran	568,107
1921	6th	70	83	.458	24.0	Pat Moran	311,227

1922	2nd	86	68	.558	7.0	Pat Moran	493,754
1923	2nd	91	63	.591	4.5	Pat Moran	575,063
1924	4th	83	70	.542	10.0	Jack Hendricks	437,707
1925	3rd	80	73	.523	15.0	Jack Hendricks	464,920
1926	2nd	87	67	.565	2.0	Jack Hendricks	672,987
1927	5th	75	78	.490	18.5	Jack Hendricks	442,164
1928	5th	78	74	.513	16.0	Jack Hendricks	490,490
1929	7th	66	88	.429	33.0	Jack Hendricks	295,040
1930	7th	59	95	.383	33.0	Dan Howley	386,727
1931	8th	58	96	.377	43.0	Dan Howley	263,316
1932	8th	60	94	.390	30.0	Dan Howley	356,950
1933	8th	58	94	.382	33.0	Donie Bush	218,281
1934	8th	52	99	.344	42.0	Bob O'Farrell, Chuck Dressen	206,773
1935	6th	68	85	.444	31.5	Chuck Dressen	448,247
1936	5th	74	80	.481	18.0	Chuck Dressen	466,245
1937	8th	56	98	.364	40.0	Chuck Dressen, Bobby Wallace	411,221
1938	4th	82	68	.547	6.0	Bill McKechnie	706,756
1939	1st	97	57	.630	+4.5	Bill McKechnie	981,443
1940	1st	100	53	.654	+12.0	Bill McKechnie	850,180
1941	3rd	88	66	.571	12.0	Bill McKechnie	643,513
1942	4th	76	76	.500	29.0	Bill McKechnie	427,031
1943	2nd	87	67	.565	18.0	Bill McKechnie	379,122
1944	3rd	89	65	.578	16.0	Bill McKechnie	409,567
1945	7th	61	93	.396	37.0	Bill McKechnie	290,070
1946	6th	67	87	.435	30.0	Bill McKechnie	715,751
1947	5th	73	81	.474	21.0	Johnny Neun	899,975
1948	7th	64	89	.418	27.0	Johnny Neun, Bucky Walters	823,386
1949	7th	62	92	.403	35.0	Bucky Walters	707,782
1950	6th	66	87	.431	24.5	Luke Sewell	538,794
1951	6th	68	86	.442	28.5	Luke Sewell	588,268
1952	6th	69	85	.448	27.5	Luke Sewell, Rogers Hornsby	604,197
1953	6th	68	86	.442	37.0	Rogers Hornsby, Buster Mills	548,086
1954	5th	74	80	.481	23.0	Birdie Tebbetts	704,167
1955	5th	75	79	.487	23.5	Birdie Tebbetts	693,662
1956	3rd	91	63	.591	2.0	Birdie Tebbetts	1,125,928
1957	4th	80	74	.519	15.0	Birdie Tebbetts	1,070,850
1958	4th	76	78	.494	16.0	Birdie Tebbetts, Jimmy Dykes	788,582
1959	5th (Tie)	74	80	.481	13.0	Mayo Smith, Fred Hutchinson	801,289
1960	6th	67	87	.435	28.0	Fred Hutchinson	663,486
1961	1st	93	61	.604	+4.0	Fred Hutchinson	1,117,603
1962	3rd	98	64	.605	3.5	Fred Hutchinson	982,085
1963	5th	86	76	.531	13.0	Fred Hutchinson	858,805
1964	2nd (Tie)	92	70	.568	1.0	Fred Hutchinson, Dick Sisler	862,466
1965	4th	89	73	.549	8.0	Dick Sisler	1,047,824
1966	7th	76	84	.475	18.0	Don Heffner, Dave Bristol	742,958
1967	4th	87	75	.537	14.5	Dave Bristol	958,300
1968	4th	83	79	.512	14.0	Dave Bristol	733,354

West Division

1969	3rd	89	73	.549	4.0	Dave Bristol	987,991
1970	1st	102	60	.630	+14.5	Sparky Anderson	1,803,568

1971	4th (Tie)	79	83	.488	11.0	Sparky Anderson	1,501,122
1972	1st	95	59	.617	+10.5	Sparky Anderson	1,611,459
1973	1st	99	63	.611	+3.5	Sparky Anderson	2,017,601
1974	2nd	98	64	.605	4.0	Sparky Anderson	2,164,307
1975	1st	108	54	.667	+20.0	Sparky Anderson	2,315,603
1976	1st	102	60	.630	+10.0	Sparky Anderson	2,629,708
1977	2nd	88	74	.543	10.0	Sparky Anderson	2,519,670
1978	2nd	92	69	.571	2.5	Sparky Anderson	2,532,497
1979	1st	90	71	.559	+1.5	John McNamara	2,356,933
1980	3rd	89	73	.549	3.5	John McNamara	2,022,450
1981*	2nd/2nd	66	42	.611	0.5/1.5	John McNamara	1,093,730
1982	6th	61	101	.377	28.0	John McNamara, Russ Nixon	1,326,528
1983	6th	74	88	.457	17.0	Russ Nixon	1,190,419
1984	5th	70	92	.432	22.0	Vern Rapp, Pete Rose	1,275,887
1985	2nd	89	72	.553	5.5	Pete Rose	1,834,619
1986	2nd	86	76	.531	10.0	Pete Rose	1,692,432
1987	2nd	84	78	.519	6.0	Pete Rose	2,185,205
1988	2nd	87	74	.540	7.0	Pete Rose	2,072,528
1989	5th	75	87	.463	17.0	Pete Rose, Tommy Helms	1,979,320
1990	1st	91	71	.562	+5.0	Lou Piniella	2,400,892
1991	5th	74	88	.457	20.0	Lou Piniella	2,372,377
1992	2nd	90	72	.556	8.0	Lou Piniella	2,315,946
1993	5th	73	89	.451	31.0	Tony Perez, Davey Johnson	2,453,232

Central Division

1994	1st	66	48	.579	+0.5	Davey Johnson	1,897,681
1995	1st	85	59	.590	+9.0	Davey Johnson	1,837,649
1996	3rd	81	81	.500	7.0	Ray Knight	1,861,428
1997	3rd	76	86	.469	8.0	Ray Knight, Jack McKeon	1,785,788
1998	4th	77	85	.475	25.0	Jack McKeon	1,793,679
1999	2nd	96	67	.589	1.5	Jack McKeon	2,061,222
2000	2nd	85	77	.525	10.0	Jack McKeon	2,577,351
2001	5th	66	96	.407	27.0	Bob Boone	1,882,732
2002	3rd	78	84	.481	19.0	Bob Boone	1,855,973
2003	5th	69	93	.426	19.0	Bob Boone, Dave Miley	2,355,259
2004	4th	76	86	.469	29.0	Dave Miley	2,287,250
2005	5th	73	89	.451	27.0	Dave Miley, Jerry Narron	1,943,068
2006	3rd	80	82	.494	3.5	Jerry Narron	2,134,633
2007	5th	72	90	.444	13.0	Jerry Narron, Pete Mackanin	2,058,632
2008	5th	74	88	.457	23.5	Dusty Baker	2,058,632
2009	4th	78	84	.481	13.0	Dusty Baker	1,747,919
2010	1st	91	71	.562	+5.0	Dusty Baker	2,060,550
2011	3rd	79	83	.488	17.0	Dusty Baker	2,213,588

*Split season.

Awards

Most Valuable Player

Ernie Lombardi, catcher, 1938
Bucky Walters, pitcher, 1939
Frank McCormick, first base, 1940
Frank Robinson, outfield, 1961
Johnny Bench, catcher, 1970
Johnny Bench, catcher, 1972
Pete Rose, outfield, 1973
Joe Morgan, second base, 1975
Joe Morgan, second base, 1976
George Foster, outfield, 1977
Barry Larkin, shortstop, 1995
Joey Votto, first baseman, 2010

Rookie of the Year

Frank Robinson, outfield, 1956
Pete Rose, second base, 1963
Tommy Helms, third base, 1966
Johnny Bench, catcher, 1968
Pat Zachry, pitcher, 1976
Chris Sabo, third base, 1988
Scott Williamson, pitcher, 1999

Cy Young
[No pitcher]

Hall of Famers Who Played for the Reds

Jake Beckley, first base, 1897–1903
Johnny Bench, catcher, 1967–83
Jim Bottomley, first base, 1933–35
Three Finger Brown, pitcher, 1913
Sam Crawford, outfield, 1899–1902
Candy Cummings, pitcher, 1877
Kiki Cuyler, outfield, 1935–37
Leo Durocher, shortstop, 1930–33
Clark Griffith, pitcher, 1909–10
Chick Hafey, outfield, 1932–35 and 1937
Jesse Haines, pitcher, 1918
Harry Heilmann, outfield, 1930–31
Miller Huggins, second base, 1904–09
Joe Kelley, outfield, 1902–06
George Kelly, first base, 1927–30
King Kelly, outfield, 1878–79
Ernie Lombardi, catcher, 1932–41
Rube Marquard, pitcher, 1921
Christy Mathewson, pitcher, 1916
Bill McKechnie, second base, 1916–17
Joe Morgan, second base, 1972–79
Tony Perez, first base, 1964–76 and
   1984–86
Old Hoss Radbourn, pitcher, 1891
Eppa Rixey, pitcher, 1921–33
Frank Robinson, outfield, 1956–65
Edd Roush, outfield, 1916–26, 1931
Amos Rusie, pitcher, 1901
Tom Seaver, pitcher, 1977–82
Al Simmons, outfield, 1939
Joe Tinker, shortstop, 1913
Dazzy Vance, pitcher, 1934
Lloyd Waner, outfield, 1941

Retired Numbers

1 ....Fred Hutchinson
5 ....Willard Hershberger and
                  Johnny Bench
8 ....Joe Morgan
10............................Sparky Anderson
13 ....Dave Concepcion
18 ....Ted Kluszewski
20 ....Frank Robinson
24 ....Tony Perez

League Leaders, Batting (Post-1900)

Batting Average, Season

Cy Seymour, 1905.......................377
Hal Chase, 1916.........................339
Edd Roush, 1917.........................341
Edd Roush, 1919.........................321
Bubbles Hargrave, 1926 353
Ernie Lombardi, 1938 342
Pete Rose, 1968 335
Pete Rose, 1969 348
Pete Rose, 1973 338

Home Runs, Season

Sam Crawford, 1901 16
Fred Odwell, 1905............................9
Ted Kluszewski, 1954.....................49
Johnny Bench, 1970 45
Johnny Bench, 1972 40
George Foster, 1977......................52
George Foster, 1978......................40

RBIs, Season

Frank McCormick, 1939.................128
Ted Kluszewski, 1954....................141
Deron Johnson, 1965.....................130
Johnny Bench, 1970 148
Johnny Bench, 1972 125
Johnny Bench, 1974 129
George Foster, 1976......................121
George Foster, 1977......................149
George Foster, 1978......................120
Dave Parker, 1985........................125

Stolen Bases, Season

Jimmy Barrett, 1900 46
Bob Bescher, 1909...........................54
Bob Bescher, 1910...........................70
Bob Bescher, 1911...........................81
Bob Bescher, 1912...........................67
Lonny Frey, 1940 22
Bobby Tolan, 1970 57

Total Bases, Season

Sam Crawford, 1902 256
Cy Seymour, 1905.........................325
Johnny Bench, 1974 315
George Foster, 1977......................388
Dave Parker, 1985........................350
Dave Parker, 1986........................304

Most Hits, Season

Cy Seymour, 1905.......................219
Hal Chase, 1916 184
Heinie Groh, 1917 182
Frank McCormick, 1938................209
Frank McCormick, 1939................209
Frank McCormick, 1940.........191 (Tie)
Ted Kluszewski, 1955....................192
Vada Pinson, 1961 208
Vada Pinson, 1963 204
Pete Rose, 1965 209
Pete Rose, 1968 ....210 (Tie)
Pete Rose, 1970 205
Pete Rose, 1972 198
Pete Rose, 1973 230
Pete Rose, 1976 215

Most Runs, Season

Bob Bescher, 1912.......................120
Heinie Groh, 1918 88
Billy Werber, 1939 115
Frank Robinson, 1956...................122
Vada Pinson, 1959 131
Frank Robinson, 1962...................134
Tommy Harper, 1965.....................126
Pete Rose, 1969 ....120 (Tie)
Joe Morgan, 1972.........................122
Pete Rose, 1974 110
Pete Rose, 1975 112
Pete Rose, 1976 130
George Foster, 1977.....................124

Batting Feats

Triple Crown Winners
[No player]

Hitting for the Cycle

John Reilly, Aug. 6, 1890
Tom Parrott, Sept. 28, 1894
Mike Mitchell, Aug. 19, 1911
Heinie Groh, July 5, 1915
Harry Craft, June 8, 1940
Frank Robinson, May 2, 1959
Eric Davis, June 2, 1989

Six Hits in a Game (Post-1900)

Tony Cuccinello, Aug. 13, 1931
Ernie Lombardi, May 9, 1937
Walker Cooper, July 6, 1949

40 or More Home Runs, Season

52	George Foster, 1977
49	Ted Kluszewski, 1954
47	Ted Kluszewski, 1955
46	Adam Dunn, 2004
45	Johnny Bench, 1970
	Greg Vaughn, 1999
40	Ted Kluszewski, 1953
	Wally Post, 1955
	Tony Perez, 1970
	Johnny Bench, 1972
	George Foster, 1978
	Ken Griffey Jr., 2000
	Adam Dunn, 2005
	Adam Dunn, 2006
	Adam Dunn, 2007
	Adam Dunn, 2008

League Leaders, Pitching (Post-1900)

Most Wins, Season

Eppa Rixey, 1922	25
Dolf Luque, 1923	27
Pete Donohue, 1926	20 (Tie)
Bucky Walters, 1939	27
Bucky Walters, 1940	22
Elmer Riddle, 1943	21 (Tie)
Bucky Walters, 1944	23
Ewell Blackwell, 1947	22
Joey Jay, 1961	21 (Tie)
Tom Seaver, 1981	14
Danny Jackson, 1988	23 (Tie)
Aaron Harang, 2006	16 (Tie)

Most Strikeouts, Season

Noodles Hahn, 1901	233
Bucky Walters, 1939	137 (Tie)
Johnny Vander Meer, 1941	202
Johnny Vander Meer, 1942	186
Johnny Vander Meer, 1943	174
Ewell Blackwell, 1947	193
Jose Rijo, 1993	227
Aaron Harang, 2006	216

Lowest ERA, Season

Dolf Luque, 1923	1.93
Dolf Luque, 1925	2.63
Bucky Walters, 1939	2.29
Bucky Walters, 1940	2.48
Elmer Riddle, 1941	2.24
Ed Heusser, 1944	2.38

Most Saves, Season

Wayne Granger, 1970	35
Clay Carroll, 1972	37
Rawly Eastwick, 1975	22 (Tie)
Rawly Eastwick, 1977	26
John Franco, 1988	39
Jeff Brantley, 1996	44
Jeff Shaw, 1997	42

Best Won–Lost Percentage, Season

Dutch Ruether, 1919	19–6	.760
Pete Donohue, 1922	18–9	.667
Dolf Luque, 1923	27–8	.771
Paul Derringer, 1939	25–7	.781
Elmer Riddle, 1941	19–4	.826
Bob Purkey, 1962	23–5	.821
Don Gullett, 1971	16–6	.727
Gary Nolan, 1972	15–5	.750
Don Gullett, 1975	15–4	.789
Tom Seaver, 1979	16–6	.727
Tom Seaver, 1981	14–2	.875
Jose Rijo, 1991	15–6	.714

Pitching Feats

20 Wins, Season

Noodles Hahn, 1901	22–19
Noodles Hahn, 1902	22–12
Noodles Hahn, 1903	22–12
Jack Harper, 1904	23–9
Bob Ewing, 1905	20–11
Jake Weimer, 1906	20–14
George Suggs, 1910	20–12
Fred Toney, 1917	24–16
Pete Schneider, 1917	20–19
Slim Sallee, 1919	21–7
Eppa Rixey, 1922	25–13
Dolf Luque, 1923	27–8
Pete Donohue, 1923	21–15
Eppa Rixey, 1923	20–15
Carl Mays, 1924	20–9
Eppa Rixey, 1925	21–11
Pete Donohue, 1925	21–14
Pete Donohue, 1926	20–14
Paul Derringer, 1935	22–13
Paul Derringer, 1938	21–14
Bucky Walters, 1939	27–11
Paul Derringer, 1939	25–7
Bucky Walters, 1940	22–10
Paul Derringer, 1940	20–12
Elmer Riddle, 1943	21–11
Bucky Walters, 1944	23–8

Ewell Blackwell, 1947	22–8
Joey Jay, 1961	21–10
Bob Purkey, 1962	23–5
Joey Jay, 1962	21–14
Jim Maloney, 1963	23–7
Sammy Ellis, 1965	22–10
Jim Maloney, 1965	20–9
Jeff Merritt, 1970	20–12
Tom Seaver, 1977	21–6*
Tom Browning, 1985	20–9
Danny Jackson, 1988	23–8

*7–3 with N.Y. Mets and 14–3 with Cin. Reds.

No-Hitters

Jim Toney (vs. Chi. Cubs), May 2, 1917 (final: 1–0) (10 innings)

Hod Eller (vs. St. L. Cardinals), May 11, 1919 (final: 6–0)

Johnny Vander Meer (vs. Bost. Braves), June 11, 1938 (final: 3–0)

Johnny Vander Meer (vs. Bklyn. Dodgers), June 15, 1938 (final: 6–0)

Clyde Shoun (vs. Bost. Braves), May 15, 1944 (final: 1–0)

Ewell Blackwell (vs. Bost. Braves), June 18, 1947 (final: 6–0)

Jim Maloney (vs. N.Y. Mets), June 14, 1965 (final: 0–1) (lost in 10th)

Jim Maloney (vs. Chi. Cubs), Aug. 9, 1965 (final: 1–0) (10 innings)

George Culver (vs. Phila. Phillies), July 29, 1968 (final: 6–1)

Jim Maloney (vs. Hous. Astros), Apr. 30, 1969 (final: 1–0)

Tom Seaver (vs. St. L. Cardinals), June 16, 1978 (final: 4–0)

Tom Browning (vs. L.A. Dodgers), Sept. 16, 1988 (final: 1–0) (perfect game)

No-Hitters Pitched Against

Fred Pfeffer, Bost. Braves, May 8, 1907 (final: 6–0)

Hippo Vaughn, Chi. Cubs, May 2, 1917 (final: 0–1) (lost in 10)

Tex Carleton, Bklyn. Dodgers, Apr. 30, 1940 (final: 3–0)

Lon Warneke, St. L. Cardinals, Aug. 30, 1941 (final: 2–0)

Ken Johnson, Hous. Astros, Apr. 23, 1964 (final: 0–1)

Don Wilson, Hous. Astros, May 1, 1969 (final: 4–0)

Ken Holtzman, Chi. Cubs, June 3, 1971
(final: 1–0)

Rick Wise, Phila. Phillies, June 23, 1971
(final. 4–0)

Roy Halladay, Phila. Phillies, Oct. 6,
2010 (final: 4–0) (Post season game)

Postseason Play

1919   World Series vs. Chi. White Sox
(AL), won 5 games to 3

1939   World Series vs. N.Y. Yankees (AL),
lost 4 games to 0

1940   World Series vs. Det. Tigers (AL),
won 4 games to 3

1961   World Series vs. N.Y. Yankees (AL),
lost 4 games to 1

1970   League Championship Series vs.
Pitt. Pirates, won 3 games to 0
World Series vs. Balt. Orioles (AL),
lost 4 games to 1

1972   League Championship Series vs.
Pitt. Pirates, won 3 games to 2
World Series vs. Oak. A's (AL), lost
4 games to 3

1973   League Championship Series vs.
N.Y. Mets, lost 3 games to 2

1975   League Championship Series vs.
Pitt. Pirates, won 3 games to 0
World Series vs. Bost. Red Sox
(AL), won 4 games to 3

1976   League Championship Series vs.
Phila. Phillies, won 3 games
to 0
World Series vs. N.Y. Yankees
(AL), won 4 games to 0

1979   League Championship Series vs.
Pitt. Pirates, lost 3 games to 0

1990   League Championship Series vs.
Pitt. Pirates, won 4 games to 2
World Series vs. Oak. A's (AL),
won 4 games to 0

1995   Division Series vs. L.A. Dodgers,
won 3 games to 0
League Championship Series vs.
Atl. Braves, lost 4 games to 0

1999   NL Wild Card Playoff Game vs.
N.Y. Mets, lost

2010   Division Series vs. Phila. Phillies,
lost 3 games to 0

Colorado Rockies

Dates of Operation: 1993–present (19 years)
Overall Record: 1437 wins, 1579 losses (.476)
Stadiums: Mile High Stadium, 1993–94; Coors Field, 1995–present (capacity: 50,445)

Year-by-Year Finishes

Year	Finish	Wins	Losses	Percentage	Games Behind	Manager	Attendance
					West Division		
1993	6th	67	95	.414	37.0	Don Baylor	4,483,350
1994	3rd	53	64	.453	6.5	Don Baylor	3,281,511
1995	2nd	77	67	.535	1.0	Don Baylor	3,390,037
1996	3rd	83	79	.512	8.0	Don Baylor	3,891,014
1997	3rd	83	79	.512	7.0	Don Baylor	3,888,453
1998	4th	77	85	.475	21.0	Don Baylor	3,789,347
1999	5th	72	90	.444	28.0	Jim Leyland	3,481,065
2000	4th	82	80	.506	15.0	Buddy Bell	3,285,710
2001	5th	73	89	.451	19.0	Buddy Bell	3,159,385
2002	4th	70	89	.451	25.0	Buddy Bell, Clint Hurdle	2,737,918
2003	4th	74	88	.457	26.5	Clint Hurdle	2,334,085
2004	4th	68	94	.420	25.0	Clint Hurdle	2,338,069
2005	5th	67	95	.414	15.0	Clint Hurdle	1,914,389
2006	4th	76	86	.469	12.0	Clint Hurdle	2,104,362
2007	2nd	90	73	.552	5.5	Clint Hurdle	2,376,250
2008	3rd	74	88	.457	10.0	Clint Hurdle	2,650,218
2009	2nd	92	70	.568	3.0	Clint Hurdle, Jim Tracy	2,665,080
2010	3rd	83	79	.512	9.0	Jim Tracy	2,875,245
2011	4th	73	84	.451	21.0	Jim Tracy	2,909,777

Awards

Most Valuable Player
Larry Walker, outfield, 1997

Rookie of the Year
Jason Jennings, pitcher, 2002

Cy Young
[No pitcher]

Hall of Famers Who Played for the Rockies
[No player]

Retired Numbers
[None]

League Leaders, Batting

Batting Average, Season
Andres Galarraga, 1993 .... .370
Larry Walker, 1998 .... .363
Larry Walker, 1999 .... .379
Todd Helton, 2000...................... .372
Larry Walker, 2001 .... .350
Matt Holliday, 2007.................... .340
Carlos Gonzalez, 2010.............. .336

Home Runs, Season
Dante Bichette, 1995 40
Andres Galarraga, 1996 47
Larry Walker, 1997 49

RBIs, Season
Dante Bichette, 1995 128
Andres Galarraga, 1996............... 150
Andres Galarraga, 1997............... 140
Todd Helton, 2000 147
Preston Wilson, 2003................... 141
Vinny Castilla, 2004 131
Matt Holliday, 2007..................... 137

Stolen Bases, Season
Eric Young, 1996 53
Juan Pierre, 2001................... 46 (Tie)
Willy Taveras, 2007 68

Total Bases, Season
Dante Bichette, 1995 359
Ellis Burks, 1996 392
Larry Walker, 1997 409
Todd Helton, 2000........................ 405
Matt Holliday, 2007...................... 386
Carlos Gonzalez, 2010................ 351

Most Hits, Season
Dante Bichette, 1995 .... 197 (Tie)
Dante Bichette, 1998 219
Todd Helton, 2000........................ 216
Matt Holliday, 2007...................... 216
Carlos Gonzalez, 2010................ 197

Most Runs, Season
Ellis Burks, 1996 142

Batting Feats

Triple Crown Winners
[No player]

Hitting for the Cycle
Dante Bichette, June 10, 1998
Neifi Perez, July 25, 1998
Todd Helton, June 19, 1999
Mike Lansing, June 18, 2000
Troy Tulowitzki, Aug. 10, 2009
Carlos Gonzalez, July 31, 2010

Six Hits in a Game
Andres Galarraga, July 3, 1995

40 or More Home Runs, Season
49 ....Larry Walker, 1997
                Todd Helton, 2001
47 ....Andres Galarraga, 1996
46 ....Vinny Castilla, 1998
42..........................Todd Helton, 2000
41 ....Andres Galarraga, 1997

40 ....Dante Bichette, 1995
                   Ellis Burks, 1996
             Vinny Castilla, 1996
             Vinny Castilla, 1997

League Leaders, Pitching

Most Wins, Season
[No pitcher]

Most Strikeouts, Season
[No pitcher]

Lowest ERA, Season
[No pitcher]

Most Saves, Season
[No pitcher]

Best Won–Lost Percentage, Season
Marvin Freeman, 1994...10–2.... .833
Ubaldo Jimenez, 2010...19–8.... .704

Pitching Feats

20 Wins, Season
[No pitcher]

No-Hitters
Ubaldo Jimenez (vs. Atl. Braves), Apr.
   17, 2010 (final: 4–0)

No-Hitters Pitched Against
Al Leiter, Flor. Marlins, May 11, 1996
   (final: 11–0)
Hideo Nomo, L.A. Dodgers, Sept. 17,
   1996 (final: 9–0)

Postseason Play

1995 Division Series vs. Atl. Braves, lost
       3 games to 1
2007 Division Series vs. Phila. Phillies,
       won 3 games to 0
       League Championship Series vs.
       Ariz. D'backs, won 4 games to 0
       World Series vs. Bost. Red Sox, lost
       4 games to 0
2009 Division Series vs. Phila. Phillies, lost
       3 games to 0

Florida Marlins

Dates of Operation: 1993–present (19 years)
Overall Record: 1435 wins, 1575 losses (.477)
Stadium: Sun Life Stadium (formerly Joe Robbie Stadium, 1993–96; Pro Player Stadium,
   1996–2004; Dolphins Stadium, 2005–06; Dolphin Stadium, 2006–08; and Land Shark Stadium,
   2009), 1993–2011 (capacity: 36,331)

Year-by-Year Finishes

Year	Finish	Wins	Losses	Percentage	Games Behind	Manager	Attendance
					East Division		
1993	6th	64	98	.395	33.0	Rene Lachemann	3,064,847
1994	5th	51	64	.443	23.5	Rene Lachemann	1,937,467
1995	4th	67	76	.469	22.5	Rene Lachemann	1,700,466
1996	3rd	80	82	.494	16.0	Rene Lachemann, John Boles	1,746,767
1997	2nd	92	70	.586	9.0	Jim Leyland	2,364,387
1998	5th	54	108	.333	52.0	Jim Leyland	1,750,395
1999	5th	64	98	.395	39.0	John Boles	1,369,421
2000	3rd	79	82	.491	15.5	John Boles	1,218,326
2001	4th	76	86	.469	12.0	John Boles, Tony Perez	1,261,220
2002	4th	79	83	.488	23.0	Jeff Torborg	813,111
2003	2nd	91	71	.562	10.0	Jeff Torborg, Jack McKeon	1,303,215
2004	3rd	83	79	.512	13.0	Jack McKeon	1,723,105
2005	3rd (Tie)	83	79	.512	7.0	Jack McKeon	1,852,608
2006	4th	78	84	.481	19.0	Joe Girardi	1,164,134
2007	5th	71	91	.438	18.0	Fredi Gonzalez	1,370,511
2008	3rd	84	77	.522	7.5	Fredi Gonzalez	1,335,075
2009	2nd	87	75	.537	6.0	Fredi Gonzalez	1,464,109
2010	3rd	80	82	.494	17.0	Fredi Gonzalez, Edwin Rodriguez	1,524,894
2011	5th	72	90	.444	30.0	Edwin Rodriguez, Brandon Hyde, and Jack McKeon	1,477,462

Awards

Most Valuable Player
[No player]

Rookie of the Year
Dontrell Willis, pitcher, 2003
Hanley Ramirez, shortstop, 2006
Chris Coghlan, outfield, 2009

Cy Young
[No pitcher]

Hall of Famers Who Played for the Marlins
Andre Dawson, outfield, 1995–1996

Retired Numbers
5......................................Carl Barger

League Leaders, Batting

Batting Average, Season
Hanley Ramirez, 2009 .... .342

Home Runs, Season
[No player]

RBIs, Season
[No player]

Stolen Bases, Season
Chuck Carr, 1993...........................58
Quilvio Veras, 1995 56
Luis Castillo, 2000...........................62
Luis Castillo, 2002...........................48
Juan Pierre, 2003...........................65

Total Bases, Season
[No player]

Most Hits, Season
Juan Pierre, 2004.........................221

Most Runs, Season
Hanley Ramirez, 2008 125

Batting Feats

Triple Crown Winners
[No player]

Hitting for the Cycle
[No player]

Six Hits in a Game
[No player]

40 or More Home Runs, Season
42......................Gary Sheffield, 1996

League Leaders, Pitching

Most Wins, Season
Dontrelle Willis, 2005.....................22

Most Strikeouts, Season
[No pitcher]

Lowest ERA, Season
Kevin Brown, 1996......................1.89
Josh Johnson, 2010 ....2.30

Most Saves, Season
Antonio Alfonseca, 2000 45
Armando Benitez, 2004...........47 (Tie)

Best Won–Lost Percentage, Season
[No pitcher]

Pitching Feats

20 Wins, Season
Dontrelle Willis, 2005 22–10

No-Hitters
Al Leiter (vs. Colo. Rockies), May 11,
  1996 (final: 11–0)
Kevin Brown (vs. S.F. Giants), June 10,
  1997 (final: 9–0)
A. J. Burnett (vs. S.D. Padres), May 12,
  2001 (final: 3–0)
Anibal Sanchez (vs. Ariz. D'backs),
  Sept. 6, 2006 (final: 2–0)

No-Hitters Pitched Against
Ramon Martinez, L.A. Dodgers, July
  14, 1995 (final: 7–0)
Roy Halladay, Phila. Phillies, May 29,
  2010 (final: 1–0)

Postseason Play

1997 Division Series vs. S.F. Giants, won
  3 games to 0
  League Championship Series vs.
    Atl. Braves, won 4 games to 2
  World Series vs. Cleve. Indians
    (AL), won 4 games to 3
2003 Division Series vs. S.F. Giants, won
  3 games to 1
  League Championship Series vs.
    Chi. Cubs, won 4 games to 3
  World Series vs. N.Y. Yankees
    (AL), won 4 games to 2

Houston Astros

Dates of Operation: 1962–present (50 years)
Overall Record: 3944 wins, 4027 losses (.495)
Stadiums: Colt Stadium, 1962–64; The Astrodome, 1965–99; Minute Maid Park (formerly Enron Field, 2000–02, and Astros Field, 2002), 2000–present (capacity: 40,950)
Other Name: Colt .45s

Year-by-Year Finishes

Year	Finish	Wins	Losses	Percentage	Games Behind	Manager	Attendance
1962	8th	64	96	.400	36.5	Harry Craft	924,456
1963	9th	66	96	.407	33.0	Harry Craft	719,502
1964	9th	66	96	.407	27.0	Harry Craft, Luman Harris	725,773
1965	9th	65	97	.401	32.0	Luman Harris	2,151,470
1966	8th	72	90	.444	23.0	Grady Hatton	1,872,108
1967	9th	69	93	.426	32.5	Grady Hatton	1,348,303
1968	10th	72	90	.444	25.0	Grady Hatton, Harry Walker	1,312,887
West Division							
1969	5th	81	81	.500	12.0	Harry Walker	1,442,995
1970	4th	79	83	.488	23.0	Harry Walker	1,253,444
1971	4th (Tie)	79	83	.488	11.0	Harry Walker	1,261,589
1972	2nd	84	69	.549	10.5	Harry Walker, Salty Parker, Leo Durocher	1,469,247
1973	4th	82	80	.506	17.0	Leo Durocher, Preston Gomez	1,394,004
1974	4th	81	81	.500	21.0	Preston Gomez	1,090,728
1975	6th	64	97	.398	43.5	Preston Gomez, Bill Virdon	858,002
1976	3rd	80	82	.494	22.0	Bill Virdon	886,146
1977	3rd	81	81	.500	17.0	Bill Virdon	1,109,560
1978	5th	74	88	.457	21.0	Bill Virdon	1,126,145
1979	2nd	89	73	.549	1.5	Bill Virdon	1,900,312
1980	1st	93	70	.571	+1.0	Bill Virdon	2,278,217
1981*	3rd/1st	61	49	.555	8.0/+1.5	Bill Virdon	1,321,282
1982	5th	77	85	.475	12.0	Bill Virdon, Bob Lillis	1,558,555
1983	3rd	85	77	.525	6.0	Bob Lillis	1,351,962
1984	2nd (Tie)	80	82	.494	12.0	Bob Lillis	1,229,862
1985	3rd (Tie)	83	79	.512	12.0	Bob Lillis	1,184,314
1986	1st	96	66	.593	+10.0	Hal Lanier	1,734,276
1987	3rd	76	86	.469	14.0	Hal Lanier	1,909,902
1988	5th	82	80	.506	12.5	Hal Lanier	1,933,505
1989	3rd	86	76	.531	6.0	Art Howe	1,834,908
1990	4th (Tie)	75	87	.463	16.0	Art Howe	1,310,927
1991	6th	65	97	.401	29.0	Art Howe	1,196,152
1992	4th	81	81	.500	17.0	Art Howe	1,211,412
1993	3rd	85	77	.525	19.0	Art Howe	2,084,546
Central Division							
1994	2nd	66	49	.574	0.5	Terry Collins	1,561,136
1995	2nd	76	68	.528	9.0	Terry Collins	1,363,801
1996	2nd	82	80	.506	6.0	Terry Collins	1,975,888
1997	1st	84	78	.519	+5.0	Larry Dierker	2,046,781

1998	1st	102	60	.630	+12.5	Larry Dierker	2,450,451
1999	1st	97	65	.599	+1.5	Larry Dierker	2,706,017
2000	4th (Tie)	72	90	.444	23.0	Larry Dierker	3,056,139
2001	1st (Tie)	93	69	.574	0.0	Larry Dierker	2,904,280
2002	2nd	84	78	.519	13.0	Jimy Williams	2,517,407
2003	2nd	87	75	.537	1.0	Jimy Williams	2,454,241
2004	2nd	92	70	.568	13.0	Jimy Williams, Phil Garner	3,087,872
2005	2nd	89	73	.552	11.0	Phil Garner	2,804,760
2006	2nd	82	80	.506	1.5	Phil Garner	3,022,763
2007	4th	73	89	.451	12.0	Phil Garner, Cecil Cooper	3,020,405
2008	3rd	86	75	.534	11.0	Cecil Cooper	2,779,287
2009	5th	74	88	.457	17.0	Cecil Cooper, Dave Clark	2,521,076
2010	4th	76	86	.469	15.0	Brad Mills	2,331,490
2011	6th	56	106	.345	40.0	Brad Mills	2,067,016

*Split season.

Awards

Most Valuable Player
Jeff Bagwell, first base, 1994

Rookie of the Year
Jeff Bagwell, first base, 1991

Cy Young
Mike Scott, 1986
Roger Clemens, 2004

Hall of Famers Who Played for the Astros
Nellie Fox, second base, 1964–65
Eddie Mathews, third base, 1967
Joe Morgan, second base, 1963–71 and 1980
Robin Roberts, pitcher, 1965–66
Nolan Ryan, pitcher, 1980–88
Don Sutton, pitcher, 1981–82

Retired Numbers
5 ....Jeff Bagwell
7 ....Craig Biggio
24 ....Jimmy Wynn
25 ....Jose Cruz
32 ....Jim Umbricht
33 ....Mike Scott
34 ....Nolan Ryan
40 ....Don Wilson
49 ....Larry Dierker

League Leaders, Batting

Batting Average, Season
[No player]

Home Runs, Season
[No player]

RBIs, Season
Jeff Bagwell, 1994 116
Lance Berkman, 2002 128

Stolen Bases, Season
Craig Biggio, 1994 39
Michael Bourn, 2009 61
Michael Bourn, 2010 52

Total Bases, Season
Jeff Bagwell, 1994 300

Most Hits, Season
Jose Cruz, 1983 ....189 (Tie)

Most Runs, Season
Jeff Bagwell, 1994 104
Craig Biggio, 1995 123
Craig Biggio, 1997 146
Jeff Bagwell, 1999 143
Jeff Bagwell, 2000 152

Batting Feats

Triple Crown Winners
[No player]

Hitting for the Cycle
Cesar Cedeno, Aug. 2, 1972
Cesar Cedeno, Aug. 9, 1976
Bob Watson, June 24, 1977
Andujar Cedeno, Aug. 25, 1992
Jeff Bagwell, July 18, 2001
Craig Biggio, Apr. 8, 2002
Luke Scott, July 28, 2006

Six Hits in a Game
Joe Morgan, July 8, 1965*
*Extra-inning game.

40 or More Home Runs, Season
47 ....Jeff Bagwell, 2000
45 ....Lance Berkman, 2006
44 ....Richard Hidalgo, 2000
43 ....Jeff Bagwell, 1997
42 ....Jeff Bagwell, 1999
Lance Berkman, 2002

League Leaders, Pitching

Most Wins, Season
Joe Niekro, 1979 ....21 (Tie)
Mike Scott, 1989 20
Roy Oswalt, 2004 20

Most Strikeouts, Season
J. R. Richard, 1978 303
J. R. Richard, 1979 313
Mike Scott, 1986 306
Nolan Ryan, 1987 270
Nolan Ryan, 1988 228

Lowest ERA, Season
J. R. Richard, 1979 ....2.71
Nolan Ryan, 1981 ....1.69
Mike Scott, 1986 ....2.22
Nolan Ryan, 1987 ....2.76
Danny Darwin, 1990 ....2.21
Roger Clemens, 2005 ....1.87
Roy Oswalt, 2006 ....2.98

Most Saves, Season

Fred Gladding, 1969 29

Jose Valverde, 2008 44

Best Won–Lost Percentage, Season

Mark Portugal, 1993 ...... 18–4 .... .818

Mike Hampton, 1999 ..... 22–4 .... .846

Roger Clemens, 2004 ..... 18–4 .... .818

Pitching Feats

20 Wins, Season

Larry Dierker, 1969 20–13

J. R. Richard, 1976 20–15

Joe Niekro, 1979 21–11

Joe Niekro, 1980 20–12

Mike Scott, 1989 20–10

Mike Hampton, 1999 22–4

Jose Lima, 1999 21–10

Roy Oswalt, 2004 20–10

Roy Oswalt, 2005 20–12

No-Hitters

Don Nottebart (vs. Phila. Phillies), May 17, 1963 (final: 4–1)

Ken Johnson (vs. Cin. Reds), Apr. 23, 1964 (final: 0–1)

Don Wilson (vs. Atl. Braves), June 18, 1967 (final: 2–0)

Don Wilson (vs. Cin. Reds), May 1, 1969 (final: 4–0)

Larry Dierker (vs. Mont. Expos), July 9, 1976 (final: 6–0)

Ken Forsch (vs. Atl. Braves), Apr. 7, 1979 (final: 6–0)

Nolan Ryan (vs. L.A. Dodgers), Sept. 26, 1981 (final: 5–0)

Mike Scott (vs. S.F. Giants), Sept. 25, 1986 (final: 2–0)

Darryl Kile (vs. N.Y. Mets), Sept. 8, 1993 (final: 7–1)

Roy Oswalt, Pete Munro, Kirk Saarloos, Brad Lidge, Octavio Dotel, and Billy Wagner (vs. N.Y. Yankees, AL), June 11, 2003 (final: 8–0)

No-Hitters Pitched Against

Juan Marichal, S.F. Giants, June 15, 1963 (final: 1–0)

Jim Maloney, Cin. Reds, Apr. 30, 1969 (final: 1–0)

Francisco Cordova and Ricardo Rincon, Pitt. Pirates, July 12, 1997 (final: 3–0)

Carlos Zambrano, Chi. Cubs, Sept. 14, 2008 (final: 5–0)

Postseason Play

1980   NL West Playoff Game vs. L.A. Dodgers, won

League Championship Series vs. Phila. Phillies, lost 3 games to 2

1981   First-Half Division Playoff Series vs. L.A. Dodgers, lost 3 games to 2

1986   League Championship Series vs. N.Y. Mets, lost 4 games to 2

1997   Division Series vs. Atl. Braves, lost 3 games to 0

1998   Division Series vs. S.D. Padres, lost 3 games to 1

1999   Division Series vs. Atl. Braves, lost 3 games to 1

2001   Division Series vs. Atl. Braves, lost 3 games to 0

2004   Division Series vs. Atl. Braves, won 3 games to 2

League Championship Series vs. St. L. Cardinals, lost 4 games to 3

2005   Division Series vs. Atl. Braves, won 3 games to 1

League Championship Series vs. St. L. Cardinals, won 4 games to 2

World Series vs. Chi. White Sox, lost 4 games to 0

Los Angeles Dodgers

Dates of Operation: 1958–present (54 years)
Overall Record: 4593 wins, 3998 losses (.535)
Stadiums: L.A. Memorial Coliseum, 1958–61; Dodger Stadium (also known as Chavez Ravine),
 1962–present (capacity: 56,000)

Year-by-Year Finishes

Year	Finish	Wins	Losses	Percentage	Games Behind	Manager	Attendance
1958	7th	71	83	.461	21.0	Walter Alston	1,845,556
1959	1st	88	68	.564	+2.0	Walter Alston	2,071,045
1960	4th	82	72	.532	13.0	Walter Alston	2,253,887
1961	2nd	89	65	.578	4.0	Walter Alston	1,804,250
1962	2nd	102	63	.618	1.0	Walter Alston	2,755,184
1963	1st	99	63	.611	+6.0	Walter Alston	2,538,602
1964	6th (Tie)	80	82	.494	13.0	Walter Alston	2,228,751
1965	1st	97	65	.599	+2.0	Walter Alston	2,553,577
1966	1st	95	67	.586	+1.5	Walter Alston	2,617,029
1967	8th	73	89	.451	28.5	Walter Alston	1,664,362
1968	7th	76	86	.469	21.0	Walter Alston	1,581,093

West Division

Year	Finish	Wins	Losses	Percentage	Games Behind	Manager	Attendance
1969	4th	85	77	.525	8.0	Walter Alston	1,784,527
1970	2nd	87	74	.540	14.5	Walter Alston	1,697,142
1971	2nd	89	73	.549	1.0	Walter Alston	2,064,594
1972	3rd	85	70	.548	10.5	Walter Alston	1,860,858
1973	2nd	95	66	.590	3.5	Walter Alston	2,136,192
1974	1st	102	60	.630	+4.0	Walter Alston	2,632,474
1975	2nd	88	74	.543	20.0	Walter Alston	2,539,349
1976	2nd	92	70	.568	10.0	Walter Alston, Tommy Lasorda	2,386,301
1977	1st	98	64	.605	+10.0	Tommy Lasorda	2,955,087
1978	1st	95	67	.586	+2.5	Tommy Lasorda	3,347,845
1979	3rd	79	83	.488	11.5	Tommy Lasorda	2,860,954
1980	2nd	92	71	.564	1.0	Tommy Lasorda	3,249,287
1981*	1st/4th	63	47	.573	+0.5/6.0	Tommy Lasorda	2,381,292
1982	2nd	88	74	.543	1.0	Tommy Lasorda	3,608,881
1983	1st	91	71	.562	+3.0	Tommy Lasorda	3,510,313
1984	4th	79	83	.488	13.0	Tommy Lasorda	3,134,824
1985	1st	95	67	.586	+5.5	Tommy Lasorda	3,264,593
1986	5th	73	89	.451	23.0	Tommy Lasorda	3,023,208
1987	4th	73	89	.451	17.0	Tommy Lasorda	2,797,409
1988	1st	94	67	.584	+7.0	Tommy Lasorda	2,980,262
1989	4th	77	83	.481	14.0	Tommy Lasorda	2,944,653
1990	2nd	86	76	.531	5.0	Tommy Lasorda	3,002,396
1991	2nd	93	69	.574	1.0	Tommy Lasorda	3,348,170
1992	6th	63	99	.389	35.0	Tommy Lasorda	2,473,266
1993	4th	81	81	.500	23.0	Tommy Lasorda	3,170,392
1994	1st	58	56	.509	+3.5	Tommy Lasorda	2,279,355
1995	1st	78	66	.542	+1.0	Tommy Lasorda	2,766,251
1996	2nd	90	72	.556	1.0	Tommy Lasorda, Bill Russell	3,188,454
1997	2nd	88	74	.543	2.0	Bill Russell	3,319,504

1998	3rd	83	79	.512	15.0	Bill Russell, Glenn Hoffman	3,089,201
1999	3rd	77	85	.475	23.0	Davey Johnson	3,095,346
2000	2nd	86	76	.531	11.0	Davey Johnson	3,010,819
2001	3rd	86	76	.531	6.0	Jim Tracy	3,017,502
2002	3rd	92	70	.568	6.0	Jim Tracy	3,131,077
2003	2nd	85	77	.525	10.5	Jim Tracy	3,138,626
2004	1st	93	69	.574	+2.0	Jim Tracy	3,488,283
2005	4th	71	91	.438	11.0	Jim Tracy	3,603,646
2006	1st	88	74	.543	+11.5	Grady Little	3,758,545
2007	4th	82	80	.506	8.0	Grady Little	3,857,036
2008	1st	84	78	.519	+2.0	Joe Torre	3,730,553
2009	1st	95	67	.586	+3.0	Joe Torre	3,761,669
2010	4th	80	82	.494	12.0	Joe Torre	3,562,310
2011	3rd	82	79	.509	11.5	Don Mattingly	2,935,139

*Split season.

Awards

Most Valuable Player
Maury Wills, shortstop, 1962
Sandy Koufax, pitcher, 1963
Steve Garvey, first base, 1974
Kirk Gibson, outfield, 1988

Rookie of the Year
Frank Howard, outfield, 1960
Jim Lefebvre, second base, 1965
Ted Sizemore, second base, 1969
Rick Sutcliffe, pitcher, 1979
Steve Howe, pitcher, 1980
Fernando Valenzuela, pitcher, 1981
Steve Sax, second base, 1982
Eric Karros, first base, 1992
Mike Piazza, catcher, 1993
Raul Mondesi, outfield, 1994
Hideo Nomo, pitcher, 1995
Todd Hollandsworth, outfield, 1996

Cy Young
Don Drysdale, 1962
Sandy Koufax, 1963
Sandy Koufax, 1965
Sandy Koufax, 1966
Mike Marshall, 1974
Fernando Valenzuela, 1981
Orel Hershiser, 1988
Eric Gagne, 2003
Clayton Kershaw, 2011

Hall of Famers Who Played for the Los Angeles Dodgers
Jim Bunning, pitcher, 1969
Gary Carter, catcher, 1991

Don Drysdale, pitcher, 1958–69
Rickey Henderson, outfield, 2003
Sandy Koufax, pitcher, 1958–66
Juan Marichal, pitcher, 1975
Eddie Murray, first base, 1989–91 and 1997
Pee Wee Reese, shortstop, 1958
Frank Robinson, outfield, 1972
Duke Snider, outfield, 1958–62
Don Sutton, pitcher, 1966–80 and 1988
Hoyt Wilhelm, pitcher, 1971–72

Retired Numbers
1	Pee Wee Reese
2	Tommy Lasorda
4	Duke Snider
19	Jim Gilliam
20	Don Sutton
24	Walter Alston
32	Sandy Koufax
39	Roy Campanella
42	Jackie Robinson
53	Don Drysdale

League Leaders, Batting

Batting Average, Season
Tommy Davis, 1962 .... .346
Tommy Davis, 1963 .... .326

Home Runs, Season
Adrian Beltre, 2004 48
Matt Kemp, 2011 39

RBIs, Season
Tommy Davis, 1962 153
Matt Kemp, 2011 125

Stolen Bases, Season
Maury Wills, 1960 50
Maury Wills, 1961 35
Maury Wills, 1962 104
Maury Wills, 1963 40
Maury Wills, 1964 53
Maury Wills, 1965 94
Davey Lopes, 1975 77
Davey Lopes, 1976 63

Total Bases, Season
Matt Kemp, 2011 353

Most Hits, Season
Tommy Davis, 1962 230
Steve Garvey, 1978 202
Steve Garvey, 1980 200

Most Runs, Season
Brett Butler, 1990 112
Matt Kemp, 2011 115

Batting Feats

Triple Crown Winners
[No player]

Hitting for the Cycle
Wes Parker, May 7, 1970
Orlando Hudson, Apr. 13, 2009

Six Hits in a Game
Willie Davis, May 24, 1973*
Paul LoDuca, May 28, 2001*
Shawn Green, May 23, 2002

*Extra-inning game.

40 or More Home Runs, Season

49	Shawn Green, 2001
48	Adrian Beltre, 2004
43	Gary Sheffield, 2000
42	Shawn Green, 2002
40	Mike Piazza, 1997

League Leaders, Pitching

Most Wins, Season

Don Drysdale, 1962	25
Sandy Koufax, 1963	25 (Tie)
Sandy Koufax, 1965	26
Sandy Koufax, 1966	27
Andy Messersmith, 1974	20 (Tie)
Fernando Valenzuela, 1986	21
Orel Hershiser, 1988	23 (Tie)
Derek Lowe, 2006	16 (Tie)
Clayton Kershaw, 2011	21 (Tie)

Most Strikeouts, Season

Don Drysdale, 1959	242
Don Drysdale, 1960	246
Sandy Koufax, 1961	269
Don Drysdale, 1962	232
Sandy Koufax, 1963	306
Sandy Koufax, 1965	382
Sandy Koufax, 1966	317
Fernando Valenzuela, 1981	180
Hideo Nomo, 1995	236
Clayton Kershaw, 2011	248

Lowest ERA, Season

Sandy Koufax, 1962	2.54
Sandy Koufax, 1963	1.88
Sandy Koufax, 1964	1.74
Sandy Koufax, 1965	2.04
Sandy Koufax, 1966	1.73
Don Sutton, 1980	2.21
Alejandro Pena, 1984	2.48
Kevin Brown, 2000	2.58
Clayton Kershaw, 2011	2.28

Most Saves, Season

Mike Marshall, 1974	21
Todd Worrell, 1996	44 (Tie)
Eric Gagne, 2003	55

Best Won–Lost Percentage, Season

Johnny Podres, 1961	18–5	.783
Ron Perranoski, 1963	17–3	.842
Sandy Koufax, 1964	19–5	.792

Sandy Koufax, 1965	26–8	.765
Tommy John, 1973	16–7	.696
Andy Messersmith, 1974	20–6	.769
Orel Hershiser, 1985	19–3	.864
Brad Penny, 2007	16–4	.800

Pitching Feats

20 Wins, Season

Don Drysdale, 1962	25–9
Sandy Koufax, 1963	25–5
Sandy Koufax, 1965	26–8
Don Drysdale, 1965	23–12
Sandy Koufax, 1966	27–9
Bill Singer, 1969	20–12
Claude Osteen, 1969	20–15
Al Downing, 1971	20–9
Claude Osteen, 1972	20–11
Andy Messersmith, 1974	20–6
Don Sutton, 1976	21–10
Tommy John, 1977	20–7
Fernando Valenzuela, 1986	21–11
Orel Hershiser, 1988	23–8
Ramon Martinez, 1990	20–6
Clayton Kershaw, 2011	21–5

No-Hitters

Sandy Koufax (vs. N.Y. Mets), June 30, 1962 (final: 5–0)

Sandy Koufax (vs. S.F. Giants), May 11, 1963 (final: 8–0)

Sandy Koufax (vs. Phila. Phillies), June 4, 1964 (final: 3–0)

Sandy Koufax (vs. Chi. Cubs), Sept. 9, 1965 (final: 1–0) (perfect game)

Bill Singer (vs. Phila. Phillies), July 20, 1970 (final: 5–0)

Jerry Reuss (vs. S.F. Giants), June 27, 1980 (final: 8–0)

Fernando Valenzuela (vs. St. L. Cardinals), June 29, 1990 (final: 6–0)

Kevin Gross (vs. S.F. Giants), Aug. 17, 1992 (final: 2–0)

Ramon Martinez (vs. Flor. Marlins), July 14, 1995 (final: 7–0)

Hideo Nomo (vs. Colo. Rockies), Sept. 17, 1996 (final: 9–0)

No-Hitters Pitched Against

John Candelaria, Pitt. Pirates, Aug. 9, 1976 (final: 2–0)

Nolan Ryan, Hous. Astros, Sept. 26, 1981 (final: 5–0)

Tom Browning, Cin. Reds, Sept. 16, 1988 (final: 1–0) (perfect game)

Mark Gardner, Mont. Expos, July 26, 1991 (final: 0–1) (lost in 10th)

Dennis Martinez, Mont. Expos, July 28, 1991 (final: 2–0) (perfect game)

Kent Mercker, Atl. Braves, Apr. 8, 1994 (final: 6–0)

Postseason Play

1959	Pennant Playoff Game vs. Milw. Braves, won
	World Series vs. Chi. White Sox (AL), won 4 games to 2
1962	Pennant Playoff Series vs. S.F. Giants, lost 2 games to 1
1963	World Series vs. N.Y. Yankees (AL), won 4 games to 0
1965	World Series vs. Minn. Twins (AL), won 4 games to 3
1966	World Series vs. Balt. Orioles (AL), lost 4 games to 0
1974	League Championship Series vs. Pitt. Pirates, won 3 games to 1
	World Series vs. Oak. A's (AL) lost 4 games to 1
1977	League Championship Series vs. Phila. Phillies, won 3 games to 1
	World Series vs. N.Y. Yankees (AL), lost 4 games to 2
1978	League Championship Series vs. Phila. Phillies, won 3 games to 1
	World Series vs. N.Y. Yankees (AL), lost 4 games to 2
1980	NL West Playoff Game vs. Hous. Astros, lost
1981	First-Half Division Playoff Series vs. Hous. Astros, won 3 games to 2
	League Championship Series vs. Mont. Expos, won 3 games to 2
	World Series vs. N.Y. Yankees (AL), won 4 games to 2
1983	League Championship Series vs. Phila. Phillies, lost 3 games to 1
1985	League Championship Series vs. St. L. Cardinals, lost 4 games to 2

1988 League Championship Series vs. N.Y. Mets, won 4 games to 3

World Series vs. Oak. A's (AL), won 4 games to 1

1995 Division Series vs. Cin. Reds, lost 3 games to 0

1996 Division Series vs. Atl. Braves, lost 3 games to 0

2004 Division Series vs. St. L. Cardinals, lost 3 games to 1

2006 Division Series vs. N.Y. Mets, lost 3 games to 0

2008 Division Series vs. Chi. Cubs, won 3 games to 0

League Championship Series vs. Phila. Phillies lost 4 games to 1

2009 Division Series vs. St. L. Cardinals, won 3 games to 0

League Championship Series vs. Phila. Phillies, lost 4 games to 1

Milwaukee Brewers (formerly the Seattle Pilots)

Dates of Operation: (as the Seattle Pilots) 1969 (1 year)
Overall Record: 64 wins, 98 losses (.395)
Stadium: Sick's Stadium, 1969

Dates of Operation: (as the Milwaukee Brewers) AL: 1970–97 (28 years); NL: 1998–present
(12 years)
Overall Record: AL: 2136 wins, 2269 losses (.485); NL: 889 wins, 1053 losses (.458); combined:
3198 wins, 3473 losses (.479)
Stadiums: County Stadium, 1970–2000; Miller Park, 2001–present (capacity: 41,900)

Year-by-Year Finishes

Year	Finish	Wins	Losses	Percentage	Games Behind	Manager	Attendance
American League West Division							
Sea. Pilots							
1969	6th	64	98	.395	33.0	Joe Schultz	677,944
Milw. Brewers							
1970	4th	65	97	.401	33.0	Dave Bristol	933,690
1971	6th	69	92	.429	32.0	Dave Bristol	731,531
American League East Division							
1972	6th	65	91	.417	21.0	Dave Bristol, Del Crandall	600,440
1973	5th	74	88	.457	23.0	Del Crandall	1,092,158
1974	5th	76	86	.469	15.0	Del Crandall	955,741
1975	5th	68	94	.420	28.0	Del Crandall	1,213,357
1976	6th	66	95	.410	32.0	Alex Grammas	1,012,164
1977	6th	67	95	.414	33.0	Alex Grammas	1,114,938
1978	3rd	93	69	.574	6.5	George Bamberger	1,601,406
1979	2nd	95	66	.590	8.0	George Bamberger	1,918,343
1980	3rd	86	76	.531	17.0	George Bamberger, Buck Rodgers	1,857,408
1981*	3rd/1st	62	47	.569	3.0/+1.5	Buck Rodgers	878,432
1982	1st	95	67	.586	+1.0	Buck Rodgers, Harvey Kuenn	1,978,896
1983	5th	87	75	.537	11.0	Harvey Kuenn	2,397,131
1984	7th	67	94	.416	36.5	Rene Lachemann	1,608,509
1985	6th	71	90	.441	28.0	George Bamberger	1,360,265
1986	6th	77	84	.478	18.0	George Bamberger, Tom Trebelhorn	1,265,041
1987	3rd	91	71	.562	7.0	Tom Trebelhorn	1,909,244
1988	3rd (Tie)	87	75	.537	2.0	Tom Trebelhorn	1,923,238
1989	4th	81	81	.500	8.0	Tom Trebelhorn	1,970,735
1990	6th	74	88	.457	14.0	Tom Trebelhorn	1,752,900
1991	4th	83	79	.512	8.0	Tom Trebelhorn	1,478,729
1992	2nd	92	70	.568	4.0	Phil Garner	1,857,314
1993	7th	69	93	.426	26.0	Phil Garner	1,688,080
American League Central Division							
1994	5th	53	62	.461	15.0	Phil Garner	1,268,399
1995	4th	65	79	.451	35.0	Phil Garner	1,087,560
1996	3rd	80	82	.494	19.5	Phil Garner	1,327,155
1997	3rd	78	83	.484	8.0	Phil Garner	1,444,027

National League Central Division

1998	5th	74	88	.457	28.0	Phil Garner	1,811,548
1999	5th	74	87	.460	22.5	Phil Garner, Jim Lefebvre	1,701,796
2000	3rd	73	89	.451	22.0	Davey Lopes	1,573,621
2001	4th	68	94	.420	25.0	Davey Lopes	2,811,041
2002	6th	56	106	.346	41.0	Davey Lopes, Jerry Royster	1,969,693
2003	6th	68	94	.420	20.0	Ned Yost	1,700,354
2004	6th	67	94	.416	37.5	Ned Yost	2,062,382
2005	3rd	81	81	.500	19.0	Ned Yost	2,211,023
2006	4th	75	87	.463	8.5	Ned Yost	2,335,643
2007	2nd	83	79	.512	2.0	Ned Yost	2,869,144
2008	2nd	90	72	.556	7.5	Ned Yost, Dave Sveum	3,068,458
2009	3rd	80	82	.494	11.0	Ken Macha	3,037,451
2010	3rd	77	85	.475	14.0	Ken Macha	2,776,531
2011	1st	96	66	.593	+6.0	Ron Roenicke	3,071,373

*Split season.

Awards

Most Valuable Player
Rollie Fingers, pitcher, 1981
Robin Yount, shortstop, 1982
Robin Yount, outfield, 1989
Ryan Braun, outfield, 2011

Rookie of the Year
Pat Listach, shortstop, 1992
Ryan Braun, third base, 2007

Cy Young
Rollie Fingers, 1981
Pete Vuckovich, 1982

Hall of Famers Who Played for the Brewers
Hank Aaron, designated hitter, 1975–76
Rollie Fingers, pitcher, 1981–82 and 1984–85
Paul Molitor, infield and designated hitter, 1978–92
Don Sutton, pitcher, 1982–84
Robin Yount, shortstop and outfield, 1974–93

Retired Numbers
4 ....Paul Molitor
19 ....Robin Yount
34 ....Rollie Fingers
44..................................Hank Aaron

League Leaders, Batting

Batting Average, Season
[No player]

Home Runs, Season
George Scott, 1975 (AL) ....36 (Tie)
Gorman Thomas, 1979 (AL) 45
Ben Oglivie, 1980 (AL) ....41 (Tie)
Gorman Thomas, 1982 (AL) .....39 (Tie)
Prince Fielder, 2007 (NL).................50

RBIs, Season
George Scott, 1975 (AL) 109
Cecil Cooper, 1980 (AL)................122
Cecil Cooper, 1983 (AL)................126
Prince Fielder, 2009 (NL)........141 (Tie)

Stolen Bases, Season
Tommy Harper, 1969 (Sea. Pilots) 73
Scott Podsednik, 2004 (NL) 70

Total Bases, Season
Dave May, 1973 (AL)..............295 (Tie)
George Scott, 1973 (AL) ....295 (Tie)
George Scott, 1975 (AL) 318
Cecil Cooper, 1980 (AL)................335
Robin Yount, 1982 (AL) 367

Most Hits, Season
Robin Yount, 1982 (AL) 210
Paul Molitor, 1991 (AL) 216
Ryan Braun, 2009 (NL) 203

Most Runs, Season
Paul Molitor, 1982 (AL) 136
Paul Molitor, 1987 (AL) 114
Paul Molitor, 1991 (AL) 133

Batting Feats

Triple Crown Winners
[No player]

Hitting for the Cycle
Mike Hegan, Sept. 3 1976 (AL)
Charlie Moore, Oct. 1, 1980 (AL)
Robin Yount, June 12, 1988 (AL)
Paul Molitor, May 15, 1991 (AL)
Chad Moeller, Apr. 27, 2004 (NL)
Jody Gerut, May 8, 2010 (NL)
George Kottaras, Sept. 3, 2011 (NL)

Six Hits in a Game
Johnny Briggs, Aug. 4, 1973 (AL)
Kevin Reimer, Aug. 24, 1993 (AL)

40 or More Home Runs, Season
50.................Prince Fielder, 2009 (NL)
46.................Prince Fielder, 2007 (NL)
45 ....Gorman Thomas, 1979 (AL)
            Richie Sexson, 2001 (NL)
            Richie Sexson, 2003 (NL)
41 ....Ben Oglivie, 1980 (AL)

League Leaders, Pitching

Most Wins, Season
Pete Vuckovich, 1981 (AL)........14 (Tie)

Most Strikeouts, Season
[No pitcher]

Lowest ERA, Season
[No pitcher]

Most Saves, Season

Ken Sanders, 1971 (AL) 31
Rollie Fingers, 1981 (AL) 28
Jon Axford, 2011 (NL) ....46 (Tie)

Best Won–Lost Percentage, Season

Mike Caldwell, 1979 (AL) ......16–6.. .727
Pete Vuckovich, 1981 (AL) .....14–4.. .778
Pete Vuckovich, 1982 (AL) .....18–6.. .750

Pitching Feats

20 Wins, Season

Jim Colborn, 1973 (AL) 20–12
Mike Caldwell, 1978 (AL) 22–9
Ted Higuera, 1986 (AL) 20–11

No-Hitters

Juan Nieves (AL) (vs. Balt. Orioles, AL),
Apr. 15, 1987 (final: 7–0)

No-Hitters Pitched Against

Steve Busby, K.C. Royals (AL), June 19,
1974 (final: 2–0)
Scott Erickson, Minn. Twins (AL), Apr.
27, 1994 (final: 6–0)
Justin Verlander, Det. Tigers (AL),
June 12, 2007 (final: 6–0)

Postseason Play

1981 (AL) Second-Half Pennant Playoff
Series vs. N.Y. Yankees, lost 3
games to 2
1982 (AL) League Championship Series
vs. Calif. Angels, won 3 games
to 2
World Series vs. St. L. Cardinals
(NL), lost 4 games to 3

2006 (NL) Division Series vs. N.Y. Mets,
lost 3 games to 0
2008 (NL) Division Series vs. Phila.
Phillies, lost 3 games to 1
2009 (NL) Division Series vs. St. L.
Cardinals, won 3 games to 0
(NL) League Championship Series
vs. Phila. Phillies, lost 4 games
to 1
2011 (NL) Division Series vs. Ariz.
Diamondbacks, won 3 games
to 2
(NL) League Championship Series
vs. St. L. Cardinals, lost 4
games to 2

New York Mets

Dates of Operation: 1962–present (50 years)
Overall Record: 3811 wins, 4149 losses (.479)
Stadiums: Polo Grounds, 1962–63; Shea Stadium, 1964–2008; Citi Field, 2009–present (capacity: 41,800)

Year-by-Year Finishes

Year	Finish	Wins	Losses	Percentage	Games Behind	Manager	Attendance
1962	10th	40	120	.250	60.5	Casey Stengel	922,530
1963	10th	51	111	.315	48.0	Casey Stengel	1,080,108
1964	10th	53	109	.327	40.0	Casey Stengel	1,732,597
1965	10th	50	112	.309	47.0	Casey Stengel, Wes Westrum	1,768,389
1966	9th	66	95	.410	28.5	Wes Westrum	1,932,693
1967	10th	61	101	.377	40.5	Wes Westrum, Salty Parker	1,565,492
1968	9th	73	89	.451	24.0	Gil Hodges	1,781,657
East Division							
1969	1st	100	62	.617	+8.0	Gil Hodges	2,175,373
1970	3rd	83	79	.512	6.0	Gil Hodges	2,697,479
1971	3rd (Tie)	83	79	.512	14.0	Gil Hodges	2,266,680
1972	3rd	83	73	.532	13.5	Yogi Berra	2,134,185
1973	1st	82	79	.509	+1.5	Yogi Berra	1,912,390
1974	5th	71	91	.438	17.0	Yogi Berra	1,722,209
1975	3rd (Tie)	82	80	.506	10.5	Yogi Berra, Roy McMillan	1,730,566
1976	3rd	86	76	.531	15.0	Joe Frazier	1,468,754
1977	6th	64	98	.395	37.0	Joe Frazier, Joe Torre	1,066,825
1978	6th	66	96	.407	24.0	Joe Torre	1,007,328
1979	6th	63	99	.389	35.0	Joe Torre	788,905
1980	5th	67	95	.414	24.0	Joe Torre	1,192,073
1981*	5th/4th	41	62	.398	15.0/5.5	Joe Torre	704,244
1982	6th	65	97	.401	27.0	George Bamberger	1,323,036
1983	6th	68	94	.420	22.0	George Bamberger, Frank Howard	1,112,774
1984	2nd	90	72	.556	6.5	Davey Johnson	1,842,695
1985	2nd	98	64	.605	3.0	Davey Johnson	2,761,601
1986	1st	108	54	.667	+21.5	Davey Johnson	2,767,601
1987	2nd	92	70	.568	3.0	Davey Johnson	3,034,129
1988	1st	100	60	.625	+15.0	Davey Johnson	3,055,445
1989	2nd	87	75	.537	6.0	Davey Johnson	2,918,710
1990	2nd	91	71	.562	4.0	Davey Johnson, Bud Harrelson	2,732,745
1991	5th	77	84	.478	20.5	Bud Harrelson, Mike Cubbage	2,284,484
1992	5th	72	90	.444	24.0	Jeff Torborg	1,779,534
1993	7th	59	103	.364	38.0	Jeff Torborg, Dallas Green	1,873,183
1994	3rd	55	58	.487	18.5	Dallas Green	1,151,471
1995	2nd (Tie)	69	75	.479	21.0	Dallas Green	1,273,183
1996	4th	71	91	.438	25.0	Dallas Green, Bobby Valentine	1,588,323
1997	3rd	88	74	.543	13.0	Bobby Valentine	1,766,174
1998	2nd	88	74	.543	18.0	Bobby Valentine	2,287,942
1999	2nd	97	66	.595	6.5	Bobby Valentine	2,725,668
2000	2nd	94	68	.580	1.0	Bobby Valentine	2,800,221

2001	3rd	82	80	.506	6.0	Bobby Valentine	2,658,279
2002	5th	75	86	.466	26.5	Bobby Valentine	2,804,838
2003	5th	66	95	.410	34.5	Art Howe	2,140,599
2004	4th	71	91	.438	25.0	Art Howe	2,318,321
2005	3rd	83	79	.512	7.0	Willie Randolph	2,829,931
2006	1st	97	65	.599	+12.0	Willie Randolph	3,379,535
2007	2nd	88	74	.543	1.0	Willie Randolph	3,853,949
2008	2nd	89	73	.549	3.0	Willie Randolph, Jerry Manuel	4,042,047
2009	4th	70	92	.432	23.0	Jerry Manuel	3,154,262
2010	4th	79	83	.488	18.0	Jerry Manuel	2,559,738
2011	4th	77	85	.475	25.0	Terry Collins	2,352,596

*Split season.

Awards

Most Valuable Player
[No player]

Rookie of the Year
Tom Seaver, pitcher, 1967
Jon Matlack, pitcher, 1972
Darryl Strawberry, outfield, 1983
Dwight Gooden, pitcher, 1984

Cy Young
Tom Seaver, 1969
Tom Seaver, 1973
Tom Seaver, 1975
Dwight Gooden, 1985

Hall of Famers Who Played for the Mets
Roberto Alomar, second base, 2002–03
Richie Ashburn, outfield, 1962
Yogi Berra, catcher, 1963 and 1965
Gary Carter, catcher, 1985–89
Rickey Henderson, outfield, 1999–2000
Willie Mays, outfield, 1972–73
Eddie Murray, first base, 1992–93
Nolan Ryan, pitcher, 1966 and 1968–71
Tom Seaver, pitcher, 1967–77 and 1983
Duke Snider, outfield, 1963
Warren Spahn, pitcher, 1965

Retired Numbers
14 ....Gil Hodges
37 ....Casey Stengel
41 ....Tom Seaver

League Leaders, Batting

Batting Average, Season
Jose Reyes, 2011 .... .337

Home Runs, Season
Dave Kingman, 1982......................37
Darryl Strawberry, 1988 39
Howard Johnson, 1991 38

RBIs, Season
Howard Johnson, 1991 117

Stolen Bases, Season
Jose Reyes, 2005 60
Jose Reyes, 2006 64
Jose Reyes, 2007 78

Total Bases, Season
[No player]

Most Hits, Season
Lance Johnson, 1996 227
Jose Reyes, 2008.........................204

Most Runs, Season
Howard Johnson, 1989..........104 (Tie)

Batting Feats

Triple Crown Winners
[No player]

Hitting for the Cycle
Jim Hickman, Aug. 7, 1963
Tommie Agee, July 6, 1970
Mike Phillips, June 25, 1976
Keith Hernandez, July 4, 1985
Kevin McReynolds, Aug. 1, 1989
Alex Ochoa, July 3, 1996
John Olerud, Sept. 11, 1997
Eric Valent, July 29, 2004
Jose Reyes, June 21, 2006

Six Hits in a Game
Edgardo Alfonzo, Aug. 30, 1999

40 or More Home Runs, Season
41 ....Todd Hundley, 1996
               Carlos Beltran, 2006
40 ....Mike Piazza, 1999

League Leaders, Pitching

Most Wins, Season
Tom Seaver, 1969...........................25
Tom Seaver, 1975...........................22
Dwight Gooden, 1985 24

Most Strikeouts, Season
Tom Seaver, 1970.........................283
Tom Seaver, 1971.........................289
Tom Seaver, 1973.........................251
Tom Seaver, 1975.........................243
Tom Seaver, 1976.........................235
Dwight Gooden, 1984 276
Dwight Gooden, 1985 268
David Cone, 1990 233
David Cone, 1991 241

Lowest ERA, Season
Tom Seaver, 1970.........................2.81
Tom Seaver, 1971.........................1.76
Tom Seaver, 1973.........................2.08
Craig Swan, 1978 ....2.43
Dwight Gooden, 1985 ....1.53
Johan Santana, 2008...................2.53

Most Saves, Season
John Franco, 1990 33
John Franco, 1994 30

Best Won–Lost Percentage, Season

Tom Seaver, 1969..........25–7.... .781
Bob Ojeda, 1986 ....18–5.... .783
Dwight Gooden, 1987....15–7.... .682
David Cone, 1988 ....20–3.... .870

Pitching Feats

20 Wins, Season

Tom Seaver, 1969 25–7
Tom Seaver, 1971 20–10
Tom Seaver, 1972 21–12
Tom Seaver, 1975 22–9
Jerry Koosman, 1976 21–10
Dwight Gooden, 1985.................24–4
David Cone, 1988 20–3
Frank Viola, 1990.....................20–12

No-Hitters

[No pitcher]

No-Hitters Pitched Against

Sandy Koufax, L.A. Dodgers, June 30,
1962 (final: 5–0)

Jim Bunning, Phila. Phillies, June 21,
1964 (final: 6–0) (perfect game)
Jim Maloney, Cin. Reds, June 14, 1965
(final: 0–1) (lost in 10th)
Bob Moose, Pitt. Pirates, Sept. 20, 1969
(final: 4–0)
Bill Stoneman, Mont. Expos, Oct. 2,
1972 (final: 7–0)
Ed Halicki, S.F. Giants, Aug. 24, 1975
(final: 6–0)
Darryl Kile, Hous. Astros, Sept. 8, 1993
(final: 7–1)

Postseason Play

1969   League Championship Series vs.
       Atl. Braves, won 3 games to 0
       World Series vs. Balt. Orioles (AL),
       won 4 games to 1
1973   League Championship Series vs.
       Cin. Reds, won 3 games to 2
       World Series vs. Oak. A's (AL), lost
       4 games to 3

1986   League Championship Series vs.
       Hous. Astros, won 4 games
       to 2
       World Series vs. Bost. Red Sox
       (AL), won 4 games to 3
1988   League Championship Series vs.
       L.A. Dodgers, lost 4 games
       to 3
1999   NL Wild Card Playoff Game vs.
       Cin. Reds, won
       Division Series vs. Ariz. D'backs,
       won 3 games to 1
       League Championship Series vs.
       Atl. Braves, lost 4 games to 2
2000   Division Series vs. S.F. Giants,
       won 3 games to 1
       League Championship Series vs.
       St. L. Cardinals, won 4 games
       to 1
       World Series vs. N.Y. Yankees
       (AL), lost 4 games to 1
2006   Division Series vs. L.A. Dodgers,
       won 3 games to 0
       League Championship Series vs.
       St. L. Cardinals, lost 4 games
       to 3

Philadelphia Phillies

Dates of Operation: 1876, 1883–present (130 years)
Overall Record: 9251 wins, 10,338 losses (.472)
Stadiums: Jefferson Street Grounds, 1876; Recreation Park, 1883–86; Huntington Grounds, 1887–94; University of Pennsylvania Athletic Field, 1894; Baker Bowl, 1895–1938; Columbia Park, 1903; Shibe Park (also known as Connie Mack Stadium), 1927; 1938–70; Veterans Stadium, 1971–2003; Citizens Bank Park, 2004–present (capacity: 43,647)
Other Names: Quakers, Live Wires, Blue Jays

Year-by-Year Finishes

Year	Finish	Wins	Losses	Percentage	Games Behind	Manager	Attendance
1876	7th	14	45	.237	34.5	Al Wright	not available
1883	8th	17	81	.173	46.0	Robert Ferguson	not available
1884	6th	39	73	.348	45.0	Harry Wright	not available
1885	3rd	56	54	.509	30.0	Harry Wright	not available
1886	4th	71	43	.622	19.0	Harry Wright	not available
1887	2nd	75	48	.610	3.5	Harry Wright	not available
1888	3rd	69	61	.531	15.5	Harry Wright	not available
1889	4th	63	64	.496	20.5	Harry Wright	not available
1890	3rd	78	54	.591	9.5	Harry Wright	not available
1891	4th	68	69	.496	18.5	Harry Wright	not available
1892	4th	87	66	.569	16.5	Harry Wright	not available
1893	4th	72	57	.558	13.5	Harry Wright	not available
1894	4th	71	56	.559	17.5	Arthur Irwin	not available
1895	3rd	78	53	.595	9.5	Arthur Irwin	not available
1896	8th	62	68	.477	28.5	William Nash	not available
1897	10th	55	77	.417	38.0	George Stallings	not available
1898	6th	78	71	.523	24.0	George Stallings, Bill Shettsline	not available
1899	3rd	94	58	.618	5.0	Bill Shettsline	not available
1900	3rd	75	63	.543	8.0	Bill Shettsline	not available
1901	2nd	83	57	.593	7.5	Bill Shettsline	234,937
1902	7th	56	81	.409	46.0	Bill Shettsline	112,066
1903	7th	49	86	.363	39.5	Chief Zimmer	151,729
1904	8th	52	100	.342	53.5	Hugh Duffy	140,771
1905	4th	83	69	.546	21.5	Hugh Duffy	317,932
1906	4th	71	82	.464	45.5	Hugh Duffy	294,680
1907	3rd	83	64	.565	21.5	Bill Murray	341,216
1908	4th	83	71	.539	16.0	Bill Murray	420,660
1909	5th	74	79	.484	36.5	Bill Murray	303,177
1910	4th	78	75	.510	25.5	Red Dooin	296,597
1911	4th	79	73	.520	19.5	Red Dooin	416,000
1912	5th	73	79	.480	30.5	Red Dooin	250,000
1913	2nd	88	63	.583	12.5	Red Dooin	470,000
1914	6th	74	80	.481	20.5	Red Dooin	138,474
1915	1st	90	62	.592	+7.0	Pat Moran	449,898
1916	2nd	91	62	.595	2.5	Pat Moran	515,365
1917	2nd	87	65	.572	10.0	Pat Moran	354,428
1918	6th	55	68	.447	26.0	Pat Moran	122,266
1919	8th	47	90	.343	47.5	Jack Coombs, Gavvy Cravath	240,424

1920	8th	62	91	.405	30.5	Gavvy Cravath	330,998
1921	8th	51	103	.331	43.5	Bill Donovan, Kaiser Wilhelm	273,961
1922	7th	57	96	.373	35.5	Kaiser Wilhelm	232,471
1923	8th	50	104	.325	45.5	Art Fletcher	228,168
1924	7th	55	96	.364	37.0	Art Fletcher	299,818
1925	6th (Tie)	68	85	.444	27.0	Art Fletcher	304,905
1926	8th	58	93	.384	29.5	Art Fletcher	240,600
1927	8th	51	103	.331	43.0	Stuffy McInnis	305,420
1928	8th	43	109	.283	51.0	Burt Shotton	182,168
1929	5th	71	82	.464	27.5	Burt Shotton	281,200
1930	8th	52	102	.338	40.0	Burt Shotton	299,007
1931	6th	66	88	.429	35.0	Burt Shotton	284,849
1932	4th	78	76	.506	12.0	Burt Shotton	268,914
1933	7th	60	92	.395	31.0	Burt Shotton	156,421
1934	7th	56	93	.376	37.0	Jimmie Wilson	169,885
1935	7th	64	89	.418	35.5	Jimmie Wilson	205,470
1936	8th	54	100	.351	38.0	Jimmie Wilson	249,219
1937	7th	61	92	.399	34.5	Jimmie Wilson	212,790
1938	8th	45	105	.300	43.0	Jimmie Wilson, Hans Lobert	166,111
1939	8th	45	106	.298	50.5	Doc Prothro	277,973
1940	8th	50	103	.327	50.0	Doc Prothro	207,177
1941	8th	43	111	.279	57.0	Doc Prothro	231,401
1942	8th	42	109	.278	62.5	Hans Lobert	230,183
1943	7th	64	90	.416	41.0	Bucky Harris, Fred Fitzsimmons	466,975
1944	8th	61	92	.399	43.5	Fred Fitzsimmons	369,586
1945	8th	46	108	.299	52.0	Fred Fitzsimmons, Ben Chapman	285,057
1946	5th	69	85	.448	28.0	Ben Chapman	1,045,247
1947	7th (Tie)	62	92	.403	32.0	Ben Chapman	907,332
1948	6th	66	88	.429	25.5	Ben Chapman, Dusty Cooke, Eddie Sawyer	767,429
1949	3rd	81	73	.526	16.0	Eddie Sawyer	819,698
1950	1st	91	63	.591	+2.0	Eddie Sawyer	1,217,035
1951	5th	73	81	.474	23.5	Eddie Sawyer	937,658
1952	4th	87	67	.565	9.5	Eddie Sawyer, Steve O'Neill	775,417
1953	3rd (Tie)	83	71	.539	22.0	Steve O'Neill	853,644
1954	4th	75	79	.487	22.0	Steve O'Neill, Terry Moore	738,991
1955	4th	77	77	.500	21.5	Mayo Smith	922,886
1956	5th	71	83	.461	22.0	Mayo Smith	934,798
1957	5th	77	77	.500	19.0	Mayo Smith	1,146,230
1958	8th	69	85	.448	23.0	Mayo Smith, Eddie Sawyer	931,110
1959	8th	64	90	.416	23.0	Eddie Sawyer	802,815
1960	8th	59	95	.383	36.0	Eddie Sawyer, Andy Cohen, Gene Mauch	862,205
1961	8th	47	107	.305	46.0	Gene Mauch	590,039
1962	7th	81	80	.503	20.0	Gene Mauch	762,034
1963	4th	87	75	.537	12.0	Gene Mauch	907,141
1964	2nd (Tie)	92	70	.568	1.0	Gene Mauch	1,425,891
1965	6th	85	76	.528	11.5	Gene Mauch	1,166,376
1966	4th	87	75	.537	8.0	Gene Mauch	1,108,201
1967	5th	82	80	.506	19.5	Gene Mauch	828,888
1968	7th (Tie)	76	86	.469	21.0	Gene Mauch, George Myatt, Bob Skinner	664,546

East Division

1969	5th	63	99	.389	37.0	Bob Skinner, George Myatt	519,414
1970	5th	73	88	.453	15.5	Frank Lucchesi	708,247
1971	6th	67	95	.414	30.0	Frank Lucchesi	1,511,223
1972	6th	59	97	.378	37.5	Frank Lucchesi, Paul Owens	1,343,329
1973	6th	71	91	.438	11.5	Danny Ozark	1,475,934
1974	3rd	80	82	.494	8.0	Danny Ozark	1,808,648
1975	2nd	86	76	.531	6.5	Danny Ozark	1,909,233
1976	1st	101	61	.623	+9.0	Danny Ozark	2,480,150
1977	1st	101	61	.623	+5.0	Danny Ozark	2,700,070
1978	1st	90	72	.556	+1.5	Danny Ozark	2,583,389
1979	4th	84	78	.519	14.0	Danny Ozark, Dallas Green	2,775,011
1980	1st	91	71	.562	+1.0	Dallas Green	2,651,650
1981*	1st/3rd	59	48	.551	+1.5/4.5	Dallas Green	1,638,752
1982	2nd	89	73	.549	3.0	Pat Corrales	2,376,394
1983	1st	90	72	.556	+6.0	Pat Corrales, Paul Owens	2,128,339
1984	4th	81	81	.500	15.5	Paul Owens	2,062,693
1985	5th	75	87	.463	26.0	John Felske	1,830,350
1986	2nd	86	75	.534	21.5	John Felske	1,933,335
1987	4th (Tie)	80	82	.494	15.0	John Felske, Lee Elia	2,100,110
1988	6th	65	96	.404	35.5	Lee Elia, John Vukovich	1,990,041
1989	6th	67	95	.414	26.0	Nick Leyva	1,861,985
1990	4th (Tie)	77	85	.475	18.0	Nick Leyva	1,992,484
1991	3rd	78	84	.481	20.0	Nick Leyva, Jim Fregosi	2,050,012
1992	6th	70	92	.432	26.0	Jim Fregosi	1,927,448
1993	1st	97	65	.599	+3.0	Jim Fregosi	3,137,674
1994	4th	54	61	.470	20.5	Jim Fregosi	2,290,971
1995	2nd (Tie)	69	75	.479	21.0	Jim Fregosi	2,043,598
1996	5th	67	95	.414	29.0	Jim Fregosi	1,801,677
1997	5th	68	94	.420	33.0	Terry Francona	1,490,638
1998	3rd	75	87	.463	31.0	Terry Francona	1,715,702
1999	3rd	77	85	.475	26.0	Terry Francona	1,825,337
2000	5th	65	97	.401	30.0	Terry Francona	1,612,769
2001	2nd	86	76	.531	2.0	Larry Bowa	1,782,460
2002	3rd	80	81	.497	21.5	Larry Bowa	1,618,141
2003	3rd	86	76	.531	15.0	Larry Bowa	2,259,940
2004	2nd	86	76	.531	10.0	Larry Bowa, Gary Varsho	3,250,092
2005	2nd	88	74	.543	2.0	Charlie Manuel	2,665,304
2006	2nd	85	77	.525	12.0	Charlie Manuel	2,701,815
2007	1st	89	73	.549	+1.0	Charlie Manuel	3,108,325
2008	1st	92	70	.568	+3.0	Charlie Manuel	3,422,583
2009	1st	93	69	.574	+6.0	Charlie Manuel	3,600,693
2010	1st	97	65	.599	+6.0	Charlie Manuel	3,377,322
2011	1st	102	60	.630	+13.0	Charlie Manuel	3,680,718

*Split season.

Awards

Most Valuable Player
Chuck Klein, outfield, 1932
Jim Konstanty, pitcher, 1950
Mike Schmidt, third base, 1980
Mike Schmidt, third base, 1981

Mike Schmidt, third base, 1986
Ryan Howard, first base, 2006
Jimmy Rollins, shortstop, 2007

Rookie of the Year
Jack Sanford, pitcher, 1957

Dick Allen, third base, 1964
Scott Rolen, third base, 1997
Ryan Howard, first base, 2005

Cy Young
Steve Carlton, 1972

Steve Carlton, 1977
Steve Carlton, 1980
Steve Carlton, 1982
John Denny, 1983
Steve Bedrosian, 1987
Roy Halladay, 2010

Hall of Famers Who Played for the Phillies

Grover C. Alexander, pitcher, 1911–17 and 1930
Richie Ashburn, outfield, 1948–59
Dave Bancroft, shortstop, 1915–20
Chief Bender, pitcher, 1916–17
Dan Brouthers, first base, 1896
Jim Bunning, pitcher, 1964–67 and 1970–71
Steve Carlton, pitcher, 1972–86
Roger Connor, first base, 1892
Ed Delahanty, outfield, 1888–89 and 1891–1901
Hugh Duffy, outfield, 1904–06
Johnny Evers, second base, 1917
Elmer Flick, outfield, 1898–1901
Jimmie Foxx, first base, 1945
Billy Hamilton, outfield, 1890–95
Ferguson Jenkins, pitcher, 1965–66
Hughie Jennings, infield, 1901–02
Tim Keefe, pitcher, 1891–93
Chuck Klein, outfield, 1928–33, 1936–39, and 1940–44
Nap Lajoie, second base and first base, 1896–1900
Tommy McCarthy, outfield, 1886–87
Joe Morgan, second base, 1983
Kid Nichols, pitcher, 1905–06
Tony Perez, first base, 1983
Eppa Rixey, pitcher, 1912–17 and 1919–20
Robin Roberts, pitcher, 1948–61
Ryne Sandberg, shortstop, 1981
Mike Schmidt, third base, 1972–89
Casey Stengel, outfield, 1920–21
Sam Thompson, outfield, 1889–98
Lloyd Waner, outfield, 1942
Hack Wilson, outfield, 1934

Retired Numbers

PA......................Grover C. Alexander
HK..................................Harry Kalas
CK ....Chuck Klein
1 ....Richie Ashburn
14 ....Jim Bunning

20	Mike Schmidt
32	Steve Carlton
36	Robin Roberts

League Leaders, Batting (Post-1900)

Batting Average, Season

Sherry Magee, 1910	.331
Lefty O'Doul, 1929	.398
Chuck Klein, 1933	.368
Harry Walker*, 1947	.363
Richie Ashburn, 1955	.338
Richie Ashburn, 1958	.350

*Played part of season with St. L. Cardinals.

Home Runs, Season

Gavvy Cravath, 1913	19
Gavvy Cravath, 1914	19
Gavvy Cravath, 1915	24
Gavvy Cravath, 1917	12 (Tie)
Gavvy Cravath, 1918	8
Gavvy Cravath, 1919	12
Cy Williams, 1920	15
Cy Williams, 1923	41
Cy Williams, 1927	30 (Tie)
Chuck Klein, 1929	43
Chuck Klein, 1931	31
Chuck Klein, 1932	38 (Tie)
Chuck Klein, 1933	28
Mike Schmidt, 1974	36
Mike Schmidt, 1975	38
Mike Schmidt, 1976	38
Mike Schmidt, 1980	48
Mike Schmidt, 1981	31
Mike Schmidt, 1983	40
Mike Schmidt, 1984	36 (Tie)
Mike Schmidt, 1986	37
Jim Thome, 2003	47
Ryan Howard, 2006	58
Ryan Howard, 2008	48

RBIs, Season

Sherry Magee, 1910	116
Gavvy Cravath, 1913	118
Sherry Magee, 1914	101
Gavvy Cravath, 1915	110
Chuck Klein, 1931	121
Don Hurst, 1932	143
Chuck Klein, 1933	120
Del Ennis, 1950	126
Greg Luzinski, 1975	120
Mike Schmidt, 1980	121
Mike Schmidt, 1981	91

Mike Schmidt, 1984	106 (Tie)
Mike Schmidt, 1986	119
Darren Daulton, 1992	109
Ryan Howard, 2006	149
Ryan Howard, 2008	146
Ryan Howard, 2009	141 (Tie)

Stolen Bases, Season

Chuck Klein, 1932	20
Danny Murtaugh, 1941	18
Richie Ashburn, 1948	32
Jimmy Rollins, 2001	46 (Tie)

Total Bases, Season

Elmer Flick, 1900	305
Sherry Magee, 1910	263
Gavvy Cravath, 1913	298
Sherry Magee, 1914	277
Gavvy Cravath, 1915	266
Chuck Klein, 1930	445
Chuck Klein, 1931	347
Chuck Klein, 1932	420
Chuck Klein, 1933	365
Dick Allen, 1964	352
Greg Luzinski, 1975	322
Mike Schmidt, 1976	306
Mike Schmidt, 1980	342
Mike Schmidt, 1981	228
Ryan Howard, 2006	383

Most Hits, Season

Gavvy Cravath, 1913	179
Sherry Magee, 1914	171
Lefty O'Doul, 1929	254
Chuck Klein, 1932	226
Chuck Klein, 1933	223
Richie Ashburn, 1951	221
Richie Ashburn, 1953	205
Richie Ashburn, 1958	215
Dave Cash, 1975	213
Pete Rose, 1981	140
Lenny Dykstra, 1990	192 (Tie)
Lenny Dykstra, 1993	194

Most Runs, Season

Roy Thomas, 1900	131
Sherry Magee, 1910	110
Gavvy Cravath, 1915	89
Chuck Klein, 1930	158
Chuck Klein, 1931	121 (Tie)
Chuck Klein, 1932	152
Dick Allen, 1964	125

Mike Schmidt, 1981 78
Van Hayes, 1986 ....107 (Tie)
Lenny Dykstra, 1993 143
Chase Utley, 2006 131
Jimmy Rollins, 2007 139

Batting Feats

Triple Crown Winners
Chuck Klein, 1933 (.368 BA, 28 HRs,
120 RBIs)

Hitting for the Cycle
Lave Cross, Apr. 24, 1894
Sam Thompson, Aug. 17, 1894
Cy Williams, Aug. 5, 1927
Chuck Klein, July 1, 1931
Chuck Klein, May 26, 1933
Johnny Callison, June 27, 1963
Gregg Jefferies, Aug. 25, 1995
David Bell, June 28, 2004

Six Hits in a Game (Post-1900)
Connie Ryan, Apr. 16, 1953

40 or More Home Runs, Season
58 ....Ryan Howard, 2006
48 ....Mike Schmidt, 1980
........................Ryan Howard, 2008
47............................Jim Thome, 2003
........................Ryan Howard, 2007
45 ....Mike Schmidt, 1979
........................Ryan Howard, 2009
43............................Chuck Klein, 1929
42............................Jim Thome, 2004
41 ....Cy Williams, 1923
40..........................Chuck Klein, 1930
........................Dick Allen, 1966
........................Mike Schmidt, 1983

League Leaders, Pitching (Post-1900)

Most Wins, Season
Grover C. Alexander, 1911 28
Tom Seaton, 1913 27
Grover C. Alexander, 1914......27 (Tie)
Grover C. Alexander, 1915..............31
Grover C. Alexander, 1916..............33
Grover C. Alexander, 1917..............30
Jumbo Elliott, 1931..................19 (Tie)
Robin Roberts, 1952 28
Robin Roberts, 1953................23 (Tie)
Robin Roberts, 1954 23

Robin Roberts, 1955.....................23
Steve Carlton, 1972.......................27
Steve Carlton, 1977.......................23
Steve Carlton, 1980.......................24
Steve Carlton, 1982.......................23
John Denny, 1983 19
Roy Halladay, 2011.......................19

Most Strikeouts, Season
Grover C. Alexander, 1912 195
Tom Seaton, 1913 165
Grover C. Alexander, 1914 214
Grover C. Alexander, 1915 241
Grover C. Alexander, 1916 167
Grover C. Alexander, 1917 200
Kirby Higbe, 1940.......................137
Robin Roberts, 1953 198
Robin Roberts, 1954 185
Jack Sanford, 1957 188
Jim Bunning, 1967 253
Steve Carlton, 1972......................310
Steve Carlton, 1974......................240
Steve Carlton, 1980......................286
Steve Carlton, 1982......................286
Steve Carlton, 1983......................275
Curt Schilling, 1997......................319
Curt Schilling, 1998......................300

Lowest ERA, Season
Grover C. Alexander, 1915 ....1.22
Grover C. Alexander, 1916 ....1.55
Grover C. Alexander, 1917 ....1.83
Steve Carlton, 1972......................1.98

Most Saves, Season
Steve Bedrosian, 1987 40

Best Won–Lost Percentage, Season
Grover C. Alexander,
    1915 ....31–10 .... .756
Steve Carlton, 1976 ....20–7 .... .741
John Denny, 1983..........19–6 .... .760

Pitching Feats

20 Wins, Season
Al Orth, 1901 20–12
Frank Donahue, 1901 20–13
Togie Pittinger, 1905 23–14
Tully Sparks, 1907 22–8
George McQuillan, 1908...........23–17
Earl Moore, 1910 22–15
Grover C. Alexander, 1911........28–13

Tom Seaton, 1913....................27–12
Grover C. Alexander, 1913 22–8
Grover C. Alexander, 1914........27–15
Erskine Mayer, 1914 21–19
Grover C. Alexander, 1915........31–10
Erskine Mayer, 1915 21–15
Grover C. Alexander, 1916........33–12
Eppa Rixey, 1916 22–10
Grover C. Alexander, 1917........30–13
Robin Roberts, 1950 20–11
Robin Roberts, 1951 21–15
Robin Roberts, 1952 28–7
Robin Roberts, 1953 23–16
Robin Roberts, 1954 23–15
Robin Roberts, 1955 23–14
Chris Short, 1966 20–10
Steve Carlton, 1972 27–10
Steve Carlton, 1976 20–7
Steve Carlton, 1977 23–10
Steve Carlton, 1980 24–9
Steve Carlton, 1982 23–11
Roy Halladay, 2010 21–10

No-Hitters
Chick Fraser (vs. Chi. Cubs), Sept. 18,
    1903 (final: 10–0)
John Lush (vs. Bklyn. Dodgers), May 1,
    1906 (final: 1–0)
Jim Bunning (vs. N.Y. Mets), June 21,
    1964 (final: 6–0) (perfect game)
Rick Wise (vs. Cin. Reds), June 23,
    1971 (final: 4–0)
Terry Mulholland (vs. S.F. Giants),
    Aug. 15, 1990 (final: 6–0)
Tommy Greene (vs. Mont. Expos),
    May 23, 1991 (final: 2–0)
Kevin Millwood (vs. S.F. Giants),
    Apr. 27, 2003 (final: 1–0)
Roy Halladay (vs. Fla. Marins), May 29,
    2010 (final: 1–0) (Perfect Game)
Roy Halladay (vs. Cin. Reds), Oct. 6, 2010
    (final: 4–0) (Post-season Game)

No-Hitters Pitched Against
Hooks Wiltse, N.Y. Giants, Sept. 5,
    1908 (final: 1–0) (10 innings)
Jeff Tesereau, N.Y. Giants, Sept. 6,
    1912 (final: 3–0)
George Davis, Bost. Braves, Sept. 9,
    1914 (final: 7–0)
Jesse Barnes, N.Y. Giants, May 7, 1922
    (final: 6–0)

Dazzy Vance, Bklyn. Dodgers, Sept. 13, 1925 (final: 10–1)

Jim Wilson, Milw. Braves, June 12, 1954 (final: 2–0)

Sal Maglie, Bklyn. Dodgers, Sept. 25, 1956 (final: 5–0)

Lew Burdette, Milw. Braves, Aug. 18, 1960 (final: 1–0)

Warren Spahn, Milw. Braves, Sept. 15, 1960 (final: 4–0)

Don Nottebart, Hous. Astros, May 17, 1963 (final: 4–1)

Sandy Koufax, L.A. Dodgers, June 4, 1964 (final: 3–0)

George Culver, Cin. Reds, July 29, 1968 (final: 6–1)

Bill Stoneman, Mont. Expos, Apr. 17, 1969 (final: 7–0)

Bill Singer, L.A. Dodgers, July 20, 1970 (final: 5–0)

Burt Hooton, Chi. Cubs, Apr. 16, 1972 (final: 4–0)

Bob Forsch, St. L. Cardinals, Apr. 16, 1978 (final: 5–0)

Postseason Play

1915 World Series vs. Bost. Red Sox (AL), lost 4 games to 1

1950 World Series vs. N.Y. Yankees (AL), lost 4 games to 0

1976 League Championship Series vs. Cin. Reds, lost 3 games to 0

1977 League Championship Series vs. L.A. Dodgers, lost 3 games to 1

1978 League Championship Series vs. L.A. Dodgers, lost 3 games to 1

1980 League Championship Series vs. Hous. Astros, won 3 games to 2
World Series vs. K.C. Royals (AL), won 4 games to 2

1981 First-Half Division Playoff Series vs. Mont. Expos, lost 3 games to 2

1983 League Championship Series vs. L.A. Dodgers, won 3 games to 1
World Series vs. Balt. Orioles (AL), lost 4 games to 1

1993 League Championship Series vs. Atl. Braves, won 4 games to 2
World Series vs. Tor. Blue Jays

(AL), lost 4 games to 2

2007 Division Series vs. Colo. Rockies, lost 3 games to 0

2008 Division Series vs. Milwaukee Brewers, won 3 games to 1
League Championship vs. L.A. Dodgers, won 4 games to 1
World Series vs. T.B. Rays, won 4 games to 1

2009 Division Series vs. Colo. Rockies, won 3 games to 1
League Championship Series vs. L.A. Dodgers, won 4 games to 1
World Series vs. N.Y. Yankees, lost 4 games to 2

2010 Division Series vs. Cin. Reds, won 3 games to 0
League Championship Series vs. S.F. Giants, lost 4 games to 2

2011 Division Series vs. St. L. Cardinals, lost 3 games to 2

Pittsburgh Pirates

Dates of Operation: 1887–present (125 years)
Overall Record: 9646 wins, 9478 losses (.504)
Stadiums: Recreation Park, 1887–90; Exposition Park, 1891–1909; Forbes Field, 1909–70; Three
   Rivers Stadium, 1970–2000; PNC Park, 2001–present (capacity: 38,496)
Other Names: Alleghenys, Innocents

Year-by-Year Finishes

Year	Finish	Wins	Losses	Percentage	Games Behind	Manager	Attendance
1887	6th	55	69	.444	24.0	Horace Phillips	not available
1888	6th	66	68	.493	19.5	Horace Phillips	not available
1889	5th	61	71	.462	25.0	Horace Phillips, Fred Dunlap, Ned Hanlon	not available
1890	8th	23	113	.169	66.5	Guy Hecker	not available
1891	8th	55	80	.407	30.5	Ned Hanlon, Bill McGunnigle	not available
1892	6th	80	73	.523	23.5	Tom Burns, Al Buckenberger	not available
1893	2nd	81	48	.628	4.5	Al Buckenberger	not available
1894	7th	65	65	.500	25.0	Al Buckenberger, Connie Mack	not available
1895	7th	71	61	.538	17.0	Connie Mack	not available
1896	6th	66	63	.512	24.0	Connie Mack	not available
1897	8th	60	71	.458	32.5	Patrick Donovan	not available
1898	8th	72	76	.486	29.5	Bill Watkins	not available
1899	7th	76	73	.510	15.5	Bill Watkins, Patsy Donovan	not available
1900	2nd	79	60	.568	4.5	Fred Clarke	not available
1901	1st	90	49	.647	+7.5	Fred Clarke	251,955
1902	1st	103	36	.741	+27.5	Fred Clarke	243,826
1903	1st	91	49	.650	+6.5	Fred Clarke	326,855
1904	4th	87	66	.569	19.0	Fred Clarke	340,615
1905	2nd	96	57	.627	9.0	Fred Clarke	369,124
1906	3rd	93	60	.608	23.5	Fred Clarke	394,877
1907	2nd	91	63	.591	17.0	Fred Clarke	319,506
1908	2nd (Tie)	98	56	.636	1.0	Fred Clarke	382,444
1909	1st	110	42	.724	+6.5	Fred Clarke	534,950
1910	3rd	86	67	.562	17.5	Fred Clarke	436,586
1911	3rd	85	69	.552	14.5	Fred Clarke	432,000
1912	2nd	93	58	.616	10.0	Fred Clarke	384,000
1913	4th	78	71	.523	21.5	Fred Clarke	296,000
1914	7th	69	85	.448	25.5	Fred Clarke	139,620
1915	5th	73	81	.474	18.0	Fred Clarke	225,743
1916	6th	65	89	.422	29.0	Jimmy Callahan	289,132
1917	8th	51	103	.331	47.0	Jimmy Callahan, Honus Wagner, Hugo Bezdek	192,807
1918	4th	65	60	.520	17.0	Hugo Bezdek	213,610
1919	4th	71	68	.511	24.5	Hugo Bezdek	276,810
1920	4th	79	75	.513	14.0	George Gibson	429,037
1921	2nd	90	63	.588	4.0	George Gibson	701,567
1922	3rd (Tie)	85	69	.552	8.0	George Gibson, Bill McKechnie	523,675
1923	3rd	87	67	.565	8.5	Bill McKechnie	611,082
1924	3rd	90	63	.588	3.0	Bill McKechnie	736,883

1925	1st	95	58	.621	+8.5	Bill McKechnie	804,354
1926	3rd	84	69	.549	4.5	Bill McKechnie	798,542
1927	1st	94	60	.610	+1.5	Donie Bush	869,720
1928	4th	85	67	.559	9.0	Donie Bush	495,070
1929	2nd	88	65	.575	10.5	Donie Bush, Jewel Ens	491,377
1930	5th	80	74	.519	12.0	Jewel Ens	357,795
1931	5th	75	79	.487	26.0	Jewel Ens	260,392
1932	2nd	86	68	.558	4.0	George Gibson	287,262
1933	2nd	87	67	.565	5.0	George Gibson	288,747
1934	5th	74	76	.493	19.5	George Gibson, Pie Traynor	322,622
1935	4th	86	67	.562	13.5	Pie Traynor	352,885
1936	4th	84	70	.545	8.0	Pie Traynor	372,524
1937	3rd	86	68	.558	10.0	Pie Traynor	459,679
1938	2nd	86	64	.573	2.0	Pie Traynor	641,033
1939	6th	68	85	.444	28.5	Pie Traynor	376,734
1940	4th	78	76	.506	22.5	Frankie Frisch	507,934
1941	4th	81	73	.526	19.0	Frankie Frisch	482,241
1942	5th	66	81	.449	36.5	Frankie Frisch	448,897
1943	4th	80	74	.519	25.0	Frankie Frisch	604,278
1944	2nd	90	63	.588	14.5	Frankie Frisch	498,740
1945	4th	82	72	.532	16.0	Frankie Frisch	604,694
1946	7th	63	91	.409	34.0	Frankie Frisch, Spud Davis	749,962
1947	7th (Tie)	62	92	.403	32.0	Billy Herman, Bill Burwell	1,283,531
1948	4th	83	71	.539	8.5	Billy Meyer	1,517,021
1949	6th	71	83	.461	26.0	Billy Meyer	1,499,435
1950	8th	57	96	.373	33.5	Billy Meyer	1,166,267
1951	7th	64	90	.416	32.5	Billy Meyer	980,590
1952	8th	42	112	.273	54.5	Billy Meyer	686,673
1953	8th	50	104	.325	55.0	Fred Haney	572,757
1954	8th	53	101	.344	44.0	Fred Haney	475,494
1955	8th	60	94	.390	38.5	Fred Haney	469,397
1956	7th	66	88	.429	27.0	Bobby Bragan	949,878
1957	7th (Tie)	62	92	.403	33.0	Bobby Bragan, Danny Murtaugh	850,732
1958	2nd	84	70	.545	8.0	Danny Murtaugh	1,311,988
1959	4th	78	76	.506	9.0	Danny Murtaugh	1,359,917
1960	1st	95	59	.617	+7.0	Danny Murtaugh	1,705,828
1961	6th	75	79	.487	18.0	Danny Murtaugh	1,199,128
1962	4th	93	68	.578	8.0	Danny Murtaugh	1,090,648
1963	8th	74	88	.457	25.0	Danny Murtaugh	783,648
1964	6th (Tie)	80	82	.494	13.0	Danny Murtaugh	759,496
1965	3rd	90	72	.556	7.0	Harry Walker	909,279
1966	3rd	92	70	.568	3.0	Harry Walker	1,196,618
1967	6th	81	81	.500	20.5	Harry Walker, Danny Murtaugh	907,012
1968	6th	80	82	.494	17.0	Larry Shepard	693,485

EAST DIVISION

1969	3rd	88	74	.543	12.0	Larry Shepard, Alex Grammas	769,369
1970	1st	89	73	.549	+5.0	Danny Murtaugh	1,341,947
1971	1st	97	65	.599	+7.0	Danny Murtaugh	1,501,132
1972	1st	96	59	.619	+11.0	Bill Virdon	1,427,460
1973	3rd	80	82	.494	2.5	Bill Virdon, Danny Murtaugh	1,319,913

1974	1st	88	74	.543	+1.5	Danny Murtaugh	1,110,552
1975	1st	92	69	.571	+6.5	Danny Murtaugh	1,270,018
1976	2nd	92	70	.568	9.0	Danny Murtaugh	1,025,945
1977	2nd	96	66	.593	5.0	Chuck Tanner	1,237,349
1978	2nd	88	73	.547	1.5	Chuck Tanner	964,106
1979	1st	98	64	.605	+2.0	Chuck Tanner	1,435,454
1980	3rd	83	79	.512	8.0	Chuck Tanner	1,646,757
1981*	4th/6th	46	56	.451	5.5/9.5	Chuck Tanner	541,789
1982	4th	84	78	.519	8.0	Chuck Tanner	1,024,106
1983	2nd	84	78	.519	6.0	Chuck Tanner	1,225,916
1984	6th	75	87	.463	21.5	Chuck Tanner	773,500
1985	6th	57	104	.354	43.5	Chuck Tanner	735,900
1986	6th	64	98	.395	44.0	Jim Leyland	1,000,917
1987	4th (Tie)	80	82	.494	15.0	Jim Leyland	1,161,193
1988	2nd	85	75	.531	15.0	Jim Leyland	1,866,713
1989	5th	74	88	.457	19.0	Jim Leyland	1,374,141
1990	1st	95	67	.586	+4.0	Jim Leyland	2,049,908
1991	1st	98	64	.605	+14.0	Jim Leyland	2,065,302
1992	1st	96	66	.593	+9.0	Jim Leyland	1,829,395
1993	5th	75	87	.463	22.0	Jim Leyland	1,650,593

Central Division

1994	3rd (Tie)	53	61	.465	13.0	Jim Leyland	1,222,520
1995	5th	58	86	.403	27.0	Jim Leyland	905,517
1996	5th	73	89	.451	15.0	Jim Leyland	1,332,150
1997	2nd	79	83	.488	5.0	Gene Lamont	1,657,022
1998	6th	69	93	.426	33.0	Gene Lamont	1,560,950
1999	3rd	78	83	.484	18.5	Gene Lamont	1,638,023
2000	5th	69	93	.426	26.0	Gene Lamont	1,748,908
2001	6th	62	100	.383	31.0	Lloyd McClendon	2,436,126
2002	4th	72	89	.447	24.5	Lloyd McClendon	1,784,993
2003	4th	75	87	.463	13.0	Lloyd McClendon	1,636,751
2004	5th	72	89	.447	32.5	Lloyd McClendon	1,583,031
2005	6th	67	95	.414	33.0	Lloyd McClendon, Pete Mackanin	1,817, 245
2006	5th	67	95	.414	16.5	Jim Tracy	1,861,549
2007	6th	68	94	.420	17.0	Jim Tracy	1,749,142
2008	6th	67	95	.414	30.5	John Russell	1,609,076
2009	6th	62	99	.385	28.5	John Russell	1,577,853
2010	6th	57	105	.352	34.0	John Russell	1,613,399
2011	4th	72	90	.444	24.0	Clint Hurdle	1,940,429

*Split season.

Awards

Most Valuable Player
Paul Waner, outfield, 1927
Dick Groat, shortstop, 1960
Roberto Clemente, outfield, 1966
Dave Parker, outfield, 1978
Willie Stargell (co-winner), first base, 1979
Barry Bonds, outfield, 1990
Barry Bonds, outfield, 1992

Rookie of the Year
Jason Bay, outfield, 2004

Cy Young
Vernon Law, 1960
Doug Drabek, 1990

Hall of Famers Who Played for the Pirates
Jake Beckley, first base, 1888–89 and 1891–96

Jim Bunning, pitcher, 1968–69
Max Carey, outfield, 1910–26
Jack Chesbro, pitcher, 1899–1902
Fred Clarke, outfield, 1900–11 and 1913–15
Roberto Clemente, outfield, 1955–72
Joe Cronin, infield, 1926–27
Kiki Cuyler, outfield, 1921–27
Pud Galvin, pitcher, 1887–89 and 1891–92

Goose Gossage, pitcher, 1977
Hank Greenberg, first base, 1947
Burleigh Grimes, pitcher, 1916–17,
    1928–29, and 1934
Billy Herman, second base, 1947
Waite Hoyt, pitcher, 1933–37
Joe Kelley, outfield, 1891–92
George Kelly, first base, 1917
Ralph Kiner, outfield, 1946–53
Chuck Klein, outfield, 1939
Fred Lindstrom, outfield, 1933–34
Al Lopez, catcher, 1940–46
Connie Mack, catcher, 1891–96
Heinie Manush, outfield, 1938–39
Rabbit Maranville, shortstop, 1921–24
Bill Mazeroski, second base, 1956–72
Bill McKechnie, infield, 1907, 1910–12,
    1918, and 1920
Billy Southworth, outfield, 1918–20
Willie Stargell, outfield and first base,
    1962–82
Casey Stengel, outfield, 1918–19
Pie Traynor, third base, 1920–35 and
    1937
Dazzy Vance, pitcher, 1915
Arky Vaughan, shortstop, 1932–41
Rube Waddell, pitcher, 1900–01
Honus Wagner, shortstop, 1900–17
Lloyd Waner, outfield, 1927–41 and
    1944–45
Paul Waner, outfield, 1926–40
Vic Willis, pitcher, 1906–09

Retired Numbers

1	Billy Meyer
4	Ralph Kiner
8	Willie Stargell
9	Bill Mazeroski
11	Paul Waner
20	Pie Traynor
21	Roberto Clemente
33	Honus Wagner
40	Danny Murtaugh

League Leaders, Batting
(Post 1900)

Batting Average, Season

Honus Wagner, 1900	.381
Ginger Beaumont, 1902	.357
Honus Wagner, 1903	.355
Honus Wagner, 1904	.349
Honus Wagner, 1906	.339
Honus Wagner, 1907	.350
Honus Wagner, 1908	.354
Honus Wagner, 1909	.339
Honus Wagner, 1911	.334
Paul Waner, 1927	.380
Paul Waner, 1934	.362
Arky Vaughan, 1935	.385
Paul Waner, 1936	.373
Debs Garms, 1940	.355
Dick Groat, 1960	.325
Roberto Clemente, 1961	.351
Roberto Clemente, 1964	.339
Roberto Clemente, 1965	.329
Matty Alou, 1966	.342
Roberto Clemente, 1967	.357
Dave Parker, 1977	.338
Dave Parker, 1978	.334
Bill Madlock, 1981	.341
Bill Madlock, 1983	.323
Freddy Sanchez, 2006	.344

Home Runs, Season

Tommy Leach, 1902	6
Ralph Kiner, 1946	23
Ralph Kiner, 1947	51 (Tie)
Ralph Kiner, 1948	40 (Tie)
Ralph Kiner, 1949	54
Ralph Kiner, 1950	47
Ralph Kiner, 1951	42
Ralph Kiner, 1952	37 (Tie)
Willie Stargell, 1971	48
Willie Stargell, 1973	44

RBIs, Season

Honus Wagner, 1907	91
Honus Wagner, 1908	106
Honus Wagner, 1909	102
Paul Waner, 1927	131
Ralph Kiner, 1949	127
Willie Stargell, 1973	119

Stolen Bases, Season

Honus Wagner, 1901	48
Honus Wagner, 1902	43
Honus Wagner, 1904	53
Honus Wagner, 1907	61
Honus Wagner, 1908	53
Max Carey, 1913	61
Max Carey, 1915	36
Max Carey, 1916	63
Max Carey, 1917	46
Max Carey, 1918	58
Max Carey, 1920	52
Max Carey, 1922	51
Max Carey, 1923	51
Max Carey, 1924	49
Max Carey, 1925	46
Kiki Cuyler, 1926	35
Lee Handley, 1939	17 (Tie)
Johnny Barrett, 1944	28
Frank Tavaras, 1977	70
Omar Moreno, 1978	71
Omar Moreno, 1979	77
Tony Womack, 1997	60
Tony Womack, 1998	58

Total Bases, Season

Ginger Beaumont, 1903	272
Honus Wagner, 1904	255
Honus Wagner, 1906	237
Honus Wagner, 1907	264
Honus Wagner, 1908	308
Honus Wagner, 1909	242
Paul Waner, 1927	342
Ralph Kiner, 1947	361
Dave Parker, 1978	340

Most Hits, Season

Ginger Beaumont, 1902	194
Ginger Beaumont, 1903	209
Ginger Beaumont, 1904	185
Honus Wagner, 1908	201
Bobby Byrne, 1910	178 (Tie)
Honus Wagner, 1910	178 (Tie)
Paul Waner, 1927	237
Lloyd Waner, 1931	214
Paul Waner, 1934	217
Roberto Clemente, 1964	211 (Tie)
Roberto Clemente, 1967	209
Matty Alou, 1969	231
Dave Parker, 1977	215
Andy Van Slyke, 1992	199 (Tie)

Most Runs, Season

Honus Wagner, 1902	105
Ginger Beaumont, 1903	137
Honus Wagner, 1906	103 (Tie)
Tommy Leach, 1909	126
Max Carey, 1913	99 (Tie)
Kiki Cuyler, 1925	144
Kiki Cuyler, 1926	113
Lloyd Waner, 1927	133 (Tie)
Paul Waner, 1928	142
Paul Waner, 1934	122

Arky Vaughan, 1936 122
Arky Vaughan, 1940 113
Ralph Kiner, 1951 ....124 (Tie)
Barry Bonds, 1992 109

Batting Feats

Triple Crown Winners
[No player]

Hitting for the Cycle
Fred Carroll, May 2, 1887
Fred Clarke, July 23, 1901
Fred Clarke, May 7, 1903
Chief Wilson, July 3, 1910
Honus Wagner, Aug. 22, 1912
Dave Robertson, Aug. 30, 1921
Pie Traynor, July 7, 1923
Kiki Cuyler, June 4, 1925
Max Carey, June 20, 1925
Arky Vaughan, June 24, 1933
Arky Vaughan, July 19, 1939
Bob Elliott, July 15, 1945
Bill Salkeld, Aug. 4, 1945
Wally Westlake, July 30, 1948
Wally Westlake, June 14, 1949
Ralph Kiner, June 25, 1950
Gus Bell, June 4, 1951
Willie Stargell, July 22, 1964
Richie Zisk, June 9, 1974
Mike Easler, June 12, 1980
Gary Redus, Aug. 25, 1989
Jason Kendall, May 19, 2000
Daryle Ward, May 27, 2004

Six Hits in a Game (Post-1900)
Carson Bigbee, Aug. 22, 1917*
Max Carey, July 7, 1922*
Johnny Gooch, July 7, 1922*
Kiki Cuyler, Aug. 9, 1924
Paul Waner, Aug. 26, 1926
Lloyd Waner, June 15, 1929
Johnny Hopp, May 14, 1950
Dick Groat, May 13, 1960
Rennie Stennett, Sept. 16, 1975
    (7 hits in game)
Wally Backman, Apr. 27, 1990
Freddy Sanchez, May 25, 2009
*Extra-inning game.

40 or More Home Runs, Season
54 ....Ralph Kiner, 1949
51 ....Ralph Kiner, 1947

48 ....Willie Stargell, 1971
47 ....Ralph Kiner, 1950
44 ....Willie Stargell, 1973
42 ....Ralph Kiner, 1951
40 ....Ralph Kiner, 1948

League Leaders, Pitching (Post-1900)

Most Wins, Season
Jack Chesbro, 1902.......................28
Wilbur Cooper, 1921 ....22 (Tie)
Roy Kremer, 1926 ....20 (Tie)
Lee Meadows, 1926 ....20 (Tie)
Burleigh Grimes, 1928.............25 (Tie)
Ray Kremer, 1930 ....20 (Tie)
Heinie Meine, 1931..................19 (Tie)
Rip Sewell, 1943.....................21 (Tie)
Bob Friend, 1958 ....22 (Tie)
Doug Drabek, 1990.......................22
John Smiley, 1991 ....20 (Tie)

Most Strikeouts, Season
Rube Waddell, 1900.....................133
Preacher Roe, 1945 148
Bob Veale, 1964 250

Lowest ERA, Season
Ray Kremer, 1926 ....2.61
Ray Kremer, 1927 ....2.47
Cy Blanton, 1935 ....2.59
Bob Friend, 1955 ....2.84
John Candelaria, 1977 ....2.34

Most Saves, Season
Dave Giusti, 1971 30

Best Won–Lost Percentage, Season
Jack Chesbro, 1901 ....21–9 .... .700
Jack Chesbro, 1902 ....28–6 .... .824
Sam Leever, 1903 ....25–7 .... .781
Sam Leever, 1905 ....20–5 .... .800
Howie Camnitz, 1909 ....25–6 .... .806
                                   (Tie)
Claude Hendrix, 1912....24–9 .... .727
Emil Yde, 1924 ....16–3 .... .842
Ray Kremer, 1926..........20–6 .... .769
Roy Face, 1959 ....18–1 .... .947
Steve Blass, 1968 ....18–6 .... .750
John Candelaria, 1977 ..20–5 .... .800
Jim Bibby, 1980 ....19–6 .... .760
Doug Drabek, 1990 ....22–6 .... .786
John Smiley, 1991 ....20–8 .... .714
                                   (Tie)

Pitching Feats

20 Wins, Season
Jesse Tannehill, 1900 20–7
Deacon Phillippe, 1901 22–12
Jack Chesbro, 1901 21–9
Jack Chesbro, 1902 28–6
Jesse Tannehill, 1902 20–6
Deacon Phillippe, 1902 20–9
Sam Leever, 1903 25–7
Deacon Phillippe, 1903 25–9
Patsy Flaherty, 1904 ....21–11*
Sam Leever, 1905 20–5
Deacon Phillippe, 1905 20–13
Vic Willis, 1906........................23–13
Sam Leever, 1906 22–7
Vic Willis, 1907........................21–11
Lefty Leifield, 1907....................20–16
Nick Maddox, 1908 23–8
Vic Willis, 1908........................23–11
Howie Camnitz, 1909 25–6
Vic Willis, 1909........................22–11
Babe Adams, 1911 22–12
Howie Camnitz, 1911 20–15
Claude Hendrix, 1912 24–9
Howie Camnitz, 1912 22–12
Babe Adams, 1913 21–10
Al Mamaux, 1915 21–8
Al Mamaux, 1916 21–15
Wilbur Cooper, 1920 24–15
Wilbur Cooper, 1921 22–14
Wilbur Cooper, 1922 23–14
Johnny Morrison, 1923 25–13
Wilbur Cooper, 1924 20–14
Ray Kremer, 1926......................20–6
Lee Meadows, 1926 20–9
Carmen Hill, 1927 22–11
Burleigh Grimes, 1928 25–14
Ray Kremer, 1930....................20–12
Rip Sewell, 1943 21–9
Rip Sewell, 1944 21–12
Murray Dickson, 1951 20–16
Bob Friend, 1958......................22–14
Vernon Law, 1960......................20–9
John Candelaria, 1977................20–5
Doug Drabek, 1990 22–6
John Smiley, 1991 20–8
*2–2 with Chi. White Sox (AL) and 19–9 with
Pitt. Pirates.

No-Hitters
Nick Maddox (vs. Bklyn. Dodgers),
    Sept. 29, 1907 (final: 2–1)

Cliff Chambers (vs. Bost. Braves), May 6, 1951 (final: 3–0)

Harvey Haddix (vs. Milw. Braves), May 26, 1959 (final: 0–1) (lost perfect game in 13th)

Bob Moose (vs. N.Y. Mets), Sept. 20, 1969 (final: 4–0)

Dock Ellis (vs. S.D. Padres), June 12, 1970 (final: 2–0)

John Candelaria (vs. L.A. Dodgers), Aug. 9, 1976 (final: 2–0)

Francisco Cordova and Ricardo Rincon (vs. Hous. Astros), July 12, 1997 (final: 3–0)

No-Hitters Pitched Against

Harry McIntyre, Bklyn. Dodgers, Aug. 1, 1906 (final: 0–1) (hit in 11th and lost in 13th)

Tom Hughes, Bost. Braves, June 16, 1916 (final: 2–0)

Carl Hubbell, N.Y. Giants, May 8, 1929 (final: 11–0)

Sam Jones, Chi. Cubs, May 12, 1955 (final: 4–0)

Bob Gibson, St. L. Cardinals, Aug. 14, 1971 (final: 11–0)

Postseason Play

1903 World Series vs. Bost. Red Sox (AL), lost 5 games to 3

1909 World Series vs. Det. Tigers (AL), won 4 games to 3

1925 World Series vs. Wash. Senators (AL), won 4 games to 3

1927 World Series vs. N.Y. Yankees (AL), lost 4 games to 0

1960 World Series vs. N.Y. Yankees (AL), won 4 games to 3

1970 League Championship Series vs. Cin. Reds, lost 3 games to 0

1971 League Championship Series vs. S.F. Giants, won 3 games to 1
World Series vs. Balt. Orioles (AL), won 4 games to 3

1972 League Championship Series vs. Cin. Reds, lost 3 games to 2

1974 League Championship Series vs. L.A. Dodgers, lost 3 games to 1

1975 League Championship Series vs. Cin. Reds, lost 3 games to 0

1979 League Championship Series vs. Cin. Reds, won 3 games to 0
World Series vs. Balt. Orioles (AL), won 4 games to 3

1990 League Championship Series vs. Cin. Reds, lost 4 games to 2

1991 League Championship Series vs. Atl. Braves, lost 4 games to 3

1992 League Championship Series vs. Atl. Braves, lost 4 games to 3

St. Louis Cardinals

Dates of Operation: 1876–77, 1885–86, 1892–present (124 years)

Overall Record: 9567 wins, 9260 losses (.508)

Stadiums: Lucas Park, 1876; Sportsman's Park, 1876–77; Palace Park of America and Vandeventer Lot, 1885–86; Sportsman's Park II (also known as Robison Field and League Park, 1899–1911; Cardinal Field, 1918–20), 1892–1920; Sportsman's Park V (also known as Busch Stadium, 1954–66), 1920–66; Busch Memorial Stadium II, 1966–2005; Busch Stadium III, 2006–present (capacity: 46,861)

Other Names: Browns, Perfectos

Year-by-Year Finishes

Year	Finish	Wins	Losses	Percentage	Games Behind	Manager	Attendance
1876	2nd	45	19	.703	6.0	Herman Hehlman	not available
1877	4th	28	32	.467	32.0	John Lucas, George McManus	not available
1885	8th	36	72	.333	49.0	Henry Lucas	not available
1886	6th	43	79	.352	46.0	Gus Schmelz	not available
1892	11th	56	94	.373	46.0	Chris Von der Ahe	not available
1893	10th	57	75	.432	29.0	Bill Watkins	not available
1894	9th	56	76	.424	35.0	George Miller	not available
1895	11th	39	92	.298	48.5	Al Buckenberger, Joe Quinn, Lew Phelan, Chris Von der Ahe	not available
1896	11th	40	90	.308	50.5	Harry Diddledock, Arlie Latham, Chris Von der Ahe, Roger Conner, Tommy Dowd	not available
1897	12th	29	102	.221	63.5	Tommy Dowd, Hugh Nicol, Bill Hallman, Chris Von der Ahe	not available
1898	12th	39	111	.260	63.5	Tim Hurst	not available
1899	5th	83	66	.557	9.5	Patsy Tebeau	not available
1900	5th (Tie)	65	75	.464	19.0	Patsy Tebeau, Louie Heilbroner	not available
1901	4th	76	64	.543	14.5	Patsy Donovan	379,988
1902	6th	56	78	.418	44.5	Patsy Donovan	226,417
1903	8th	43	94	.314	46.5	Patsy Donovan	226,538
1904	5th	75	79	.487	31.5	Kid Nichols	386,750
1905	6th	58	96	.377	47.5	Kid Nichols, Jimmy Burke, Matt Robison	292,800
1906	7th	52	98	.347	63.0	John McCloskey	283,770
1907	8th	52	101	.340	55.5	John McCloskey	185,377
1908	8th	49	105	.318	50.0	John McCloskey	205,129
1909	7th	54	98	.355	56.0	Roger Bresnahan	299,982
1910	7th	63	90	.412	40.5	Roger Bresnahan	355,668
1911	5th	75	74	.503	22.0	Roger Bresnahan	447,768
1912	6th	63	90	.412	41.0	Roger Bresnahan	241,759
1913	8th	51	99	.340	49.0	Miller Huggins	203,531
1914	3rd	81	72	.529	13.0	Miller Huggins	256,099
1915	6th	72	81	.471	18.5	Miller Huggins	252,666
1916	7th (Tie)	60	93	.392	33.5	Miller Huggins	224,308
1917	3rd	82	70	.539	15.0	Miller Huggins	288,491
1918	8th	51	78	.395	33.0	Jack Hendricks	110,599

1919	7th	54	83	.394	40.5	Branch Rickey	167,059
1920	5th (Tie)	75	79	.487	18.0	Branch Rickey	326,836
1921	3rd	87	66	.569	7.0	Branch Rickey	384,773
1922	3rd (Tie)	85	69	.552	8.0	Branch Rickey	536,998
1923	5th	79	74	.516	16.0	Branch Rickey	338,551
1924	6th	65	89	.422	28.5	Branch Rickey	272,885
1925	4th	77	76	.503	18.0	Branch Rickey, Rogers Hornsby	404,959
1926	1st	89	65	.578	+2.0	Rogers Hornsby	668,428
1927	2nd	92	61	.601	1.5	Bob O'Farrell	749,340
1928	1st	95	59	.617	+2.0	Bill McKechnie	761,574
1929	4th	78	74	.513	20.0	Bill McKechnie, Billy Southworth	399,887
1930	1st	92	62	.597	+2.0	Gabby Street	508,501
1931	1st	101	53	.656	+13.0	Gabby Street	608,535
1932	6th (Tie)	72	82	.468	18.0	Gabby Street	279,219
1933	5th	82	71	.536	9.5	Gabby Street, Frankie Frisch	256,171
1934	1st	95	58	.621	+2.0	Frankie Frisch	325,056
1935	2nd	96	58	.623	4.0	Frankie Frisch	506,084
1936	2nd (Tie)	87	67	.565	5.0	Frankie Frisch	448,078
1937	4th	81	73	.526	15.0	Frankie Frisch	430,811
1938	6th	71	80	.470	17.5	Frankie Frisch, Mike Gonzalez	291,418
1939	2nd	92	61	.601	4.5	Ray Blades	400,245
1940	3rd	84	69	.549	16.0	Ray Blades, Mike Gonzalez, Billy Southworth	324,078
1941	2nd	97	56	.634	2.5	Billy Southworth	633,645
1942	1st	106	48	.688	+2.0	Billy Southworth	553,552
1943	1st	105	49	.682	+18.0	Billy Southworth	517,135
1944	1st	105	49	.682	+14.5	Billy Southworth	461,968
1945	2nd	95	59	.617	3.0	Billy Southworth	594,630
1946	1st	98	58	.628	+2.0	Eddie Dyer	1,061,807
1947	2nd	89	65	.578	5.0	Eddie Dyer	1,247,913
1948	2nd	85	69	.552	6.5	Eddie Dyer	1,111,440
1949	2nd	96	58	.623	1.0	Eddie Dyer	1,430,676
1950	5th	78	75	.510	12.5	Eddie Dyer	1,093,411
1951	3rd	81	73	.526	15.5	Marty Marion	1,013,429
1952	3rd	88	66	.571	8.5	Eddie Stanky	913,113
1953	3rd (Tie)	83	71	.539	22.0	Eddie Stanky	880,242
1954	6th	72	82	.468	25.0	Eddie Stanky	1,039,698
1955	7th	68	86	.442	30.5	Eddie Stanky, Harry Walker	849,130
1956	4th	76	78	.494	17.0	Fred Hutchinson	1,029,773
1957	2nd	87	67	.565	8.0	Fred Hutchinson	1,183,575
1958	5th (Tie)	72	82	.468	20.0	Fred Hutchinson, Stan Hack	1,063,730
1959	7th	71	83	.461	16.0	Solly Hemus	929,953
1960	3rd	86	68	.558	9.0	Solly Hemus	1,096,632
1961	5th	80	74	.519	13.0	Solly Hemus, Johnny Keane	855,305
1962	6th	84	78	.519	17.5	Johnny Keane	960,095
1963	2nd	93	69	.574	6.0	Johnny Keane	1,170,546
1964	1st	93	69	.574	+1.0	Johnny Keane	1,143,294
1965	7th	80	81	.497	16.5	Red Schoendienst	1,241,201
1966	6th	83	79	.512	12.0	Red Schoendienst	1,712,980
1967	1st	101	60	.627	+10.5	Red Schoendienst	2,090,145
1968	1st	97	65	.599	+9.0	Red Schoendienst	2,011,167

East Division

1969	4th	87	75	.537	13.0	Red Schoendienst	1,682,783
1970	4th	76	86	.469	13.0	Red Schoendienst	1,629,736
1971	2nd	90	72	.556	7.0	Red Schoendienst	1,604,671
1972	4th	75	81	.481	21.5	Red Schoendienst	1,196,894
1973	2nd	81	81	.500	1.5	Red Schoendienst	1,574,046
1974	2nd	86	75	.534	1.5	Red Schoendienst	1,838,413
1975	3rd (Tie)	82	80	.506	10.5	Red Schoendienst	1,695,270
1976	5th	72	90	.444	29.0	Red Schoendienst	1,207,079
1977	3rd	83	79	.512	18.0	Vern Rapp	1,659,287
1978	5th	69	93	.426	21.0	Vern Rapp, Jack Krol, Ken Boyer	1,278,215
1979	3rd	86	76	.531	12.0	Ken Boyer	1,627,256
1980	4th	74	88	.457	17.0	Ken Boyer, Jack Krol, Whitey Herzog, Red Schoendienst	1,385,147
1981*	2nd/2nd	59	43	.578	1.5/0.5	Whitey Herzog	1,010,247
1982	1st	92	70	.568	+3.0	Whitey Herzog	2,111,906
1983	4th	79	83	.488	11.0	Whitey Herzog	2,317,914
1984	3rd	84	78	.519	12.5	Whitey Herzog	2,037,448
1985	1st	101	61	.623	+3.0	Whitey Herzog	2,637,563
1986	3rd	79	82	.491	28.5	Whitey Herzog	2,471,974
1987	1st	95	67	.586	+3.0	Whitey Herzog	3,072,122
1988	5th	76	86	.469	25.0	Whitey Herzog	2,892,799
1989	3rd	86	76	.531	7.0	Whitey Herzog	3,080,980
1990	6th	70	92	.432	25.0	Whitey Herzog, Red Schoendienst, Joe Torre	2,573,225
1991	2nd	84	78	.519	14.0	Joe Torre	2,448,699
1992	3rd	83	79	.512	13.0	Joe Torre	2,418,483
1993	3rd	87	75	.537	10.0	Joe Torre	2,844,328

Central Division

1994	3rd (Tie)	53	61	.465	13.0	Joe Torre	1,866,544
1995	4th	62	81	.434	22.5	Joe Torre, Mike Jorgensen	1,756,727
1996	1st	88	74	.543	+6.0	Tony La Russa	2,654,718
1997	4th	73	89	.451	11.0	Tony La Russa	2,634,014
1998	3rd	83	79	.512	19.0	Tony La Russa	3,194,092
1999	4th	75	86	.466	21.5	Tony La Russa	3,225,334
2000	1st	95	67	.586	+10.0	Tony La Russa	3,336,493
2001	1st (Tie)	93	69	.574	0.0	Tony La Russa	3,113,091
2002	1st	97	65	.599	+13.0	Tony La Russa	3,011,756
2003	3rd	85	77	.525	3.0	Tony La Russa	2,910,386
2004	1st	105	57	.648	+13.0	Tony La Russa	3,048,427
2005	1st	100	62	.617	+11.0	Tony La Russa	3,538,988
2006	1st	83	78	.516	+1.5	Tony La Russa	3,407,114
2007	3rd	78	84	.481	7.0	Tony La Russa	3,552,180
2008	4th	86	76	.531	11.5	Tony La Russa	3,430,660
2009	1st	91	71	.562	+7.5	Tony La Russa	3,343,252
2010	2nd	86	76	.531	5.0	Tony La Russa	3,301,218
2011	2nd	90	72	.556	6.0	Tony La Russa	3,093,954

*Split season.

Awards

Most Valuable Player

Rogers Hornsby, second base, 1925
Bob O'Farrell, catcher, 1926
Jim Bottomley, first base, 1928
Frankie Frisch, second base, 1931
Dizzy Dean, pitcher, 1934
Joe Medwick, outfield, 1937
Mort Cooper, pitcher, 1942
Stan Musial, outfield, 1943
Marty Marion, shortstop, 1944
Stan Musial, first base and outfield, 1946
Stan Musial, outfield, 1948
Ken Boyer, third base, 1964
Orlando Cepeda, first base, 1967
Bob Gibson, pitcher, 1968
Joe Torre, third base, 1971
Keith Hernandez (co-winner), first base, 1979
Willie McGee, outfield, 1985
Albert Pujols, first base, 2005
Albert Pujols, first base, 2008
Albert Pujols, first base, 2009

Rookie of the Year

Wally Moon, outfield, 1954
Bill Virdon, outfield, 1955
Bake McBride, outfield, 1974
Vince Coleman, outfield, 1985
Todd Worrell, pitcher, 1986
Albert Pujols, outfield, 2001

Cy Young

Bob Gibson, 1968
Bob Gibson, 1970
Chris Carpenter, 2005

Hall of Famers Who Played for the Cardinals

Grover C. Alexander, pitcher, 1926–29
Walter Alston, first base, 1936
Jake Beckley, first base, 1904–07
Jim Bottomley, first base, 1922–32
Roger Bresnahan, catcher, 1909–12
Lou Brock, outfield, 1964–79
Three Finger Brown, pitcher, 1903
Jesse Burkett, outfield, 1899–1901
Steve Carlton, pitcher, 1965–71
Orlando Cepeda, first base, 1966–68
Roger Connor, first base, 1894–97

Dizzy Dean, pitcher, 1930 and 1932–37
Leo Durocher, shortstop, 1933–37
Dennis Eckersley, pitcher, 1996–97
Frankie Frisch, second base, 1927–37
Pud Galvin, pitcher, 1892
Bob Gibson, pitcher, 1959–75
Burleigh Grimes, pitcher, 1930–31 and 1933–34
Chick Hafey, outfield, 1924–31
Jesse Haines, pitcher, 1920–37
Rogers Hornsby, second base, 1915–26 and 1933
Miller Huggins, second base, 1910–16
Rabbit Maranville, shortstop, 1927–28
John McGraw, third base, 1900
Joe Medwick, outfield, 1932–40 and 1947–48
Johnny Mize, first base, 1936–41
Stan Musial, outfield and first base, 1941–44 and 1946–63
Kid Nichols, pitcher, 1904–05
Wilbert Robinson, catcher, 1900
Red Schoendienst, second base, 1945–56 and 1961–63
Enos Slaughter, outfield, 1938–42 and 1946–53
Ozzie Smith, shortstop, 1982–96
Billy Southworth, outfield, 1926–27, 1929
Bruce Sutter, pitcher, 1981–84
Dazzy Vance, pitcher, 1933–34
Bobby Wallace, shortstop, 1899–1901 and 1917–18
Hoyt Wilhelm, pitcher, 1957
Vic Willis, pitcher, 1910
Cy Young, pitcher, 1899–1900

Retired Numbers

JB ....Jack Buck
RH...........................Rogers Hornsby
1......................................Ozzie Smith
2 ....Red Schoendienst
6.......................................Stan Musial
9 ....Enos Slaughter
14 ....Ken Boyer
17.......................................Dizzy Dean
20...Lou Brock
42 ....Bruce Sutter
45......................................Bob Gibson
85 ....August Busch Jr.

League Leaders, Batting (Post-1900)

Batting Average, Season

Jesse Burkett, 1901 382
Rogers Hornsby, 1920 370
Rogers Hornsby, 1921 397
Rogers Hornsby, 1922 401
Rogers Hornsby, 1923 384
Rogers Hornsby, 1924 424
Rogers Hornsby, 1925 403
Chick Hafey, 1931......................349
Joe Medwick, 1937.....................374
Johnny Mize, 1939.....................349
Stan Musial, 1943.......................357
Stan Musial, 1946.......................365
Harry Walker*, 1947...................363
Stan Musial, 1948.......................376
Stan Musial, 1950.......................346
Stan Musial, 1951.......................355
Stan Musial, 1952.......................336
Stan Musial, 1957.......................351
Joe Torre, 1971 363
Keith Hernandez, 1979..............344
Willie McGee, 1985 353
Willie McGee**, 1990 335
Albert Pujols, 2003.....................359

*Played part of season with Phila. Phillies.
**Played part of season with Oak. A's.

Home Runs, Season

Rogers Hornsby, 1922 42
Rogers Hornsby, 1925 39
Jim Bottomley, 1928 31
Rip Collins, 1934 ....35 (Tie)
Joe Medwick, 1937 ....31 (Tie)
Johnny Mize, 1939.........................28
Johnny Mize, 1940.........................43
Mark McGwire, 1988 70
Mark McGwire, 1999 65
Albert Pujols, 2009 47
Albert Pujols, 2010 42

RBIs, Season

Rogers Hornsby, 1920 ....94 (Tie)
Rogers Hornsby, 1921 126
Rogers Hornsby, 1922 152
Rogers Hornsby, 1925 143
Jim Bottomley, 1926.....................120
Jim Bottomley, 1928......................136
Joe Medwick, 1936.......................138
Joe Medwick, 1937.......................154
Joe Medwick, 1938.......................122
Johnny Mize, 1940.......................137

Enos Slaughter, 1946 130
Stan Musial, 1948 131
Stan Musial, 1956 109
Ken Boyer, 1964 119
Joe Torre, 1971 137
Mark McGwire, 1999 147
Albert Pujols, 2010 118

Stolen Bases, Season

Frankie Frisch, 1927 48
Frankie Frisch, 1931 28
Pepper Martin, 1933 26
Pepper Martin, 1934 23
Pepper Martin, 1936 23
Red Schoendienst, 1945 26
Lou Brock, 1966 74
Lou Brock, 1967 52
Lou Brock, 1968 62
Lou Brock, 1969 53
Lou Brock, 1971 64
Lou Brock, 1972 63
Lou Brock, 1973 70
Lou Brock, 1974 118
Vince Coleman, 1985 110
Vince Coleman, 1986 107
Vince Coleman, 1987 109
Vince Coleman, 1988 81
Vince Coleman, 1989 65
Vince Coleman, 1990 77

Total Bases, Season

Jesse Burkett, 1901 313
Rogers Hornsby, 1917 253
Rogers Hornsby, 1920 329
Rogers Hornsby, 1921 378
Rogers Hornsby, 1922 450
Rogers Hornsby, 1924 373
Rogers Hornsby, 1925 381
Jim Bottomley, 1926 305
Jim Bottomley, 1928 362
Rip Collins, 1934 369
Joe Medwick, 1935 365
Joe Medwick, 1936 367
Joe Medwick, 1937 406
Johnny Mize, 1938 326
Johnny Mize, 1939 353
Johnny Mize, 1940 368
Enos Slaughter, 1942 292
Stan Musial, 1943 347
Stan Musial, 1946 366
Stan Musial, 1948 429
Stan Musial, 1949 382

Stan Musial, 1951 355
Stan Musial, 1952 311
Joe Torre, 1971 352
Albert Pujols, 2003 394
Albert Pujols, 2004 389
Albert Pujols, 2008 342
Albert Pujols, 2009 374

Most Hits, Season

Jesse Burkett, 1901 228
Rogers Hornsby, 1920 218
Rogers Hornsby, 1921 235
Rogers Hornsby, 1922 250
Rogers Hornsby, 1924 227
Jim Bottomley, 1925 227
Joe Medwick, 1936 223
Joe Medwick, 1937 237
Enos Slaughter, 1942 188
Stan Musial, 1943 220
Stan Musial, 1944 .... 197 (Tie)
Stan Musial, 1946 228
Stan Musial, 1948 230
Stan Musial, 1949 207
Stan Musial, 1952 194
Curt Flood, 1964 .... 211 (Tie)
Joe Torre, 1971 230
Garry Templeton, 1979 211
Willie McGee, 1985 216
Albert Pujols, 2003 212

Most Runs, Season

Jesse Burkett, 1901 139
Rogers Hornsby, 1921 131
Rogers Hornsby, 1922 141
Rogers Hornsby, 1924 .... 121 (Tie)
Pepper Martin, 1933 122
Joe Medwick, 1937 111
Stan Musial, 1946 124
Stan Musial, 1948 135
Stan Musial, 1951 .... 124 (Tie)
Stan Musial, 1952 .... 105 (Tie)
Solly Hemus, 1952 .... 105 (Tie)
Stan Musial, 1954 .... 120 (Tie)
Lou Brock, 1967 .... 113 (Tie)
Lou Brock, 1971 126
Keith Hernandez, 1979 116
Keith Hernandez, 1980 111
Lonnie Smith, 1982 120
Albert Pujols, 2003 137
Albert Pujols, 2004 133
Albert Pujols, 2005 129
Albert Pujols, 2009 124
Albert Pujols, 2010 115

Batting Feats

Triple Crown Winners

Rogers Hornsby, 1922 (.401 BA, 42
HRs, 152 RBIs)
Rogers Hornsby, 1925 (.403 BA, 39
HRs, 143 RBIs)
Joe Medwick, 1937 (.374 BA, 31 HRs,
153 RBIs)

Hitting for the Cycle

Fred Dunlap, May 24, 1886
Tip O'Neil, Apr. 30, 1887
Tip O'Neil, May 7, 1887
Tommy Dowd, Aug. 16, 1895
Cliff Heathcote, July 13, 1918
Jim Bottomley, July 15, 1927
Chick Hafey, Aug. 21, 1930
Pepper Martin, May 5, 1933
Joe Medwick, June 29, 1935
Johnny Mize, July 13, 1940
Stan Musial, July 24, 1949
Bill White, Aug. 14, 1960
Ken Boyer, Sept. 14, 1961
Ken Boyer, June 16, 1964
Joe Torre, June 27, 1973
Lou Brock, May 27, 1975
Willie McGee, June 23, 1984
Ray Lankford, Sept. 15, 1991
John Mabry, May 18, 1996
Mark Grudzielanek, Apr. 27, 2005

Six Hits in a Game (Post-1900)

Jim Bottomley, Sept. 16, 1924
Jim Bottomley, Aug. 5, 1931
Terry Moore, Sept. 5, 1935

40 or More Home Runs, Season

70 .... Mark McGwire, 1998
65 .... Mark McGwire, 1999
49 .... Albert Pujols, 2006
47 .... Albert Pujols, 2009
46 .... Albert Pujols, 2004
43 .... Johnny Mize, 1940
Albert Pujols, 2003
42 .... Rogers Hornsby, 1922
Jim Edmonds, 2000
Jim Edmonds, 2004
Albert Pujols, 2010
41 .... Albert Pujols, 2005

League Leaders, Pitching (Post-1900)

Most Wins, Season

Flint Rhem, 1926	20 (Tie)
Bill Hallahan, 1931	19 (Tie)
Dizzy Dean, 1934	30
Dizzy Dean, 1935	28
Mort Cooper, 1942	22
Mort Cooper, 1943	21 (Tie)
Red Barrett*, 1945	23
Howie Pollet, 1946	21
Ernie Broglio, 1960	21 (Tie)
Bob Gibson, 1970	23 (Tie)
Joaquin Andujar, 1984	20
Adam Wainwright, 2009	19

*Pitched part of season with Bost. Braves.

Most Strikeouts, Season

Fred Beebe*, 1906	171
Bill Hallahan, 1930	177
Bill Hallahan, 1931	159
Dizzy Dean, 1932	191
Dizzy Dean, 1933	199
Dizzy Dean, 1934	195
Dizzy Dean, 1935	182
Harry Brecheen, 1948	149
Sam Jones, 1958	225
Bob Gibson, 1968	268
Jose DeLeon, 1989	201

*Pitched part of season with Chi. Cubs.

Lowest ERA, Season

Bill Doak, 1914	1.72
Bill Doak, 1921	2.58
Mort Cooper, 1942	1.77
Howie Pollet, 1943	1.75
Howie Pollet, 1946	2.10
Harry Brecheen, 1948	2.24
Bob Gibson, 1968	1.12
John Denny, 1976	2.52
Joe Magrane, 1988	2.18
Chris Carpenter, 2009	2.24

Most Saves, Season

Al Hrabosky, 1976	22 (Tie)
Bruce Sutter, 1981	25
Bruce Sutter, 1982	36
Bruce Sutter, 1984	45
Todd Worrell, 1986	36
Lee Smith, 1991	47
Lee Smith, 1992	43
Jason Isringhausen, 2004	47 (Tie)

Best Won–Lost Percentage, Season

Bill Doak, 1921	15–6	.714
Willie Sherdel, 1925	15–6	.714
Paul Derringer, 1931	18–8	.692
Dizzy Dean, 1934	30–7	.811
Mort Cooper, 1943	21–8	.724
Ted Wilks, 1944	17–4	.870
Harry Brecheen, 1945	15–4	.789
Murray Dickson, 1946	15–6	.714
Harry Brecheen, 1948	20–7	.741
Ernie Broglio, 1960	21–9	.700
Dick Hughes, 1967	16–6	.727
Bob Gibson, 1970	23–7	.767
Bob Tewksbury, 1992	16–5	.762
Chris Carpenter, 2009	17–4	.810

Pitching Feats

20 Wins, Season

Cy Young, 1900	20–18
Jack Harper, 1901	20–12
Bob Wicker, 1903	20–9*
Kid Nichols, 1904	21–13
Jack Taylor, 1904	20–19
Bob Harmon, 1911	23–16
Bill Doak, 1920	20–12
Jesse Haines, 1923	20–13
Flint Rhem, 1926	20–7
Jesse Haines, 1927	24–10
Grover C. Alexander, 1927	21–10
Bill Sherdel, 1928	21–10
Jesse Haines, 1928	20–8
Dizzy Dean, 1933	20–18
Dizzy Dean, 1934	30–7
Dizzy Dean, 1935	28–12
Dizzy Dean, 1936	24–13
Curt Davis, 1939	22–16
Mort Cooper, 1942	22–7
Johnny Beazley, 1942	21–6
Mort Cooper, 1943	21–8
Mort Cooper, 1944	22–7
Red Barrett, 1945	23–12**
Howie Pollet, 1946	21–10
Howie Pollet, 1949	20–9
Harvey Haddix, 1953	20–9
Ernie Broglio, 1960	21–9
Ray Sadecki, 1964	20–11
Bob Gibson, 1965	20–12
Bob Gibson, 1966	21–12
Bob Gibson, 1968	22–9
Bob Gibson, 1969	20–13
Bob Gibson, 1970	23–7
Steve Carlton, 1971	20–9

Bob Forsch, 1977	20–7
Joaquin Andujar, 1984	20–14
John Tudor, 1985	21–8
Joaquin Andujar, 1985	21–12
Darryl Kile, 2000	20–9
Matt Morris, 2001	22–8
Chris Carpenter, 2005	21–5
Adam Wainwright, 2010	20–11

*0–0 with Chi. Cubs and 20–9 with St. L. Cardinals.
**2–3 with Bost. Braves and 21–9 with St. L. Cardinals.

No-Hitters

Jesse Haines (vs. Bost. Braves), July 17, 1924 (final: 5–0)

Paul Dean (vs. Bklyn. Dodgers), Sept. 21, 1934 (final: 3–0)

Lon Warneke (vs. Cin. Reds), Aug. 30, 1941 (final: 2–0)

Ray Washburn (vs. S.F. Giants), Sept. 18, 1968 (final: 2–0)

Bob Gibson (vs. Pitt. Pirates), Aug. 14, 1971 (final: 11–0)

Bob Forsch (vs. Phila. Phillies), Apr. 16, 1978 (final: 5–0)

Bob Forsch (vs. Mont. Expos), Sept. 26, 1983 (final: 3–0)

Jose Jimenez (vs. Ariz. D'backs), June 25, 1999 (final: 1–0)

Bud Smith (vs. S.D. Padres), Sept. 3, 2001 (final: 4–0)

No-Hitters Pitched Against

Christy Mathewson, N.Y. Giants, July 15, 1901 (final: 4–0)

Mal Eason, Bklyn. Dodgers, July 20, 1906 (final: 2–0)

Hod Eller, Cin. Reds, May 11, 1919 (final: 6–0)

Don Cardwell, Chi. Cubs, May 15, 1960 (final: 4–0)

Gaylord Perry, S.F. Giants, Sept. 17, 1968 (final: 1–0)

Tom Seaver, Cin. Reds, June 16, 1978 (final: 4–0)

Fernando Valenzuela, L.A. Dodgers, June 29, 1990 (final: 6–0)

Postseason Play

1926	World Series vs. N.Y. Yankees (AL), won 4 games to 3
1928	World Series vs. N.Y. Yankees (AL), lost 4 games to 0

1930   World Series vs. Phila. A's (AL),
        lost 4 games to 2
1931   World Series vs. Phila. A's (AL),
        won 4 games to 3
1934   World Series vs. Det. Tigers (AL),
        won 4 games to 3
1942   World Series vs. N.Y. Yankees
        (AL), won 4 games to 1
1943   World Series vs. N.Y. Yankees
        (AL), lost 4 games to 1
1944   World Series vs. St. L. Browns (AL),
        won 4 games to 2
1946   Pennant Playoff Series vs. Bklyn.
        Dodgers, won 2 games to 0
        World Series vs. Bost. Red Sox
        (AL), won 4 games to 3
1964   World Series vs. N.Y. Yankees
        (AL), won 4 games to 3
1967   World Series vs. Bost. Red Sox
        (AL), won 4 games to 3
1968   World Series vs. Det. Tigers (AL),
        lost 4 games to 3
1982   League Championship Series vs.
        Atl. Braves, won 3 games to 0
        World Series vs. Milw. Brewers
        (AL), won 4 games to 3

1985   League Championship Series vs.
        L.A. Dodgers, won 4 games
        to 2
        World Series vs. K.C. Royals (AL),
        lost 4 games to 3
1987   League Championship Series vs.
        S.F. Giants, won 4 games to 3
        World Series vs. Minn. Twins (AL),
        lost 4 games to 3
1996   Division Series vs. S.D. Padres,
        won 3 games to 0
        League Championship Series vs.
        Atl. Braves, lost 4 games to 3
2000   Division Series vs. Atl. Braves, won
        3 games to 0
        League Championship Series vs.
        N.Y. Mets, lost 4 games to 1
2001   Division Series vs. Ariz. D'backs,
        lost 3 games to 2
2002   Division Series vs. Ariz. D'backs,
        won 3 games to 0
        League Championship Series vs.
        S.F. Giants, lost 4 games to 1

2004   Division Series vs. L.A. Dodgers,
        won 3 games to 1
        League Championship Series vs.
        Hous. Astros, won 4 games
        to 3
        World Series vs. Bost. Red Sox
        (AL), lost 4 games to 0
2005   Division Series vs. S.D. Padres,
        won 3 games to 0
        League Championship Series vs.
        Hous. Astros, lost 4 games to 2
2006   Division Series vs. S.D. Padres,
        won 3 games to 1
        League Championship Series vs.
        N.Y. Mets, won 4 games to 3
        World Series vs. Det. Tigers (AL),
        won 4 games to 1
2009   Division Series vs. L.A. Dodgers,
        lost 3 games to 0
2011   Division Series vs. Phila. Phillies,
        won 3 games to 2
        League Championship Series vs.
        Milw. Brewers, won 4 games
        to 2
        World Series vs. Tex. Rangers
        (AL), won 4 games to 3

San Diego Padres

Dates of Operation: 1969–present (43 years)
Overall Record: 3169 wins, 3671 losses (.463)
Stadiums: Qualcomm Stadium at Jack Murphy Field (also known as San Diego Stadium, 1967–79; San Diego–Jack Murphy Stadium, 1980; Jack Murphy Stadium, 1981–97), 1969–2003; PETCO Park, 2004–present (capacity: 42,445)

Year-by-Year Finishes

Year	Finish	Wins	Losses	Percentage	Games Behind	Manager	Attendance
					West Division		
1969	6th	52	110	.321	41.0	Preston Gomez	512,970
1970	6th	63	99	.389	39.0	Preston Gomez	643,679
1971	6th	61	100	.379	28.5	Preston Gomez	557,513
1972	6th	58	95	.379	36.5	Preston Gomez, Don Zimmer	644,273
1973	6th	60	102	.370	39.0	Don Zimmer	611,826
1974	6th	60	102	.370	42.0	John McNamara	1,075,399
1975	4th	71	91	.438	37.0	John McNamara	1,281,747
1976	5th	73	89	.451	29.0	John McNamara	1,458,478
1977	5th	69	93	.426	29.0	John McNamara, Bob Skinner, Alvin Dark	1,376,269
1978	4th	84	78	.519	11.0	Roger Craig	1,670,107
1979	5th	68	93	.422	22.0	Roger Craig	1,456,967
1980	6th	73	89	.451	19.5	Jerry Coleman	1,139,026
1981*	6th/6th	41	69	.373	12.5/15.5	Frank Howard	519,161
1982	4th	81	81	.500	8.0	Dick Williams	1,607,516
1983	4th	81	81	.500	10.0	Dick Williams	1,539,815
1984	1st	92	70	.568	+12.0	Dick Williams	1,983,904
1985	3rd (Tie)	83	79	.512	12.0	Dick Williams	2,210,352
1986	4th	74	88	.457	22.0	Steve Boros	1,805,716
1987	6th	65	97	.401	25.0	Larry Bowa	1,454,061
1988	3rd	83	78	.516	11.0	Larry Bowa, Jack McKeon	1,506,896
1989	2nd	89	73	.549	3.0	Jack McKeon	2,009,031
1990	4th (Tie)	75	87	.463	16.0	Jack McKeon, Greg Riddoch	1,856,396
1991	3rd	84	78	.519	10.0	Greg Riddoch	1,804,289
1992	3rd	82	80	.506	16.0	Greg Riddoch, Jim Riggleman	1,722,102
1993	7th	61	101	.377	43.0	Jim Riggleman	1,375,432
1994	4th	47	70	.402	12.5	Jim Riggleman	953,857
1995	3rd	70	74	.486	8.0	Bruce Bochy	1,041,805
1996	1st	91	71	.562	+1.0	Bruce Bochy	2,187,886
1997	4th	76	86	.469	14.0	Bruce Bochy	2,089,333
1998	1st	98	64	.605	+9.5	Bruce Bochy	2,555,901
1999	4th	74	88	.457	26.0	Bruce Bochy	2,523,538
2000	5th	76	86	.469	21.0	Bruce Bochy	2,423,149
2001	4th	79	83	.488	13.0	Bruce Bochy	2,377,969
2002	5th	66	96	.407	32.0	Bruce Bochy	2,220,416
2003	5th	64	98	.395	36.5	Bruce Bochy	2,030,084
2004	3rd	87	75	.537	6.0	Bruce Bochy	3,016,752
2005	1st	82	80	.506	+5.0	Bruce Bochy	2,869,787
2006	1st (Tie)	88	74	.543	—	Bruce Bochy	2,659,754

2007	3rd	89	74	.546	1.5	Bud Black	2,790,074
2008	5th	63	99	.389	21.0	Bud Black	2,427,535
2009	4th	75	87	.463	20.0	Bud Black	1,922,603
2010	2nd	90	72	.556	2.0	Bud Black	2,131,774
2011	5th	71	91	.438	23.0	Bud Black	2,143,018

*Split season.

Awards

Most Valuable Player
Ken Caminiti, third base, 1996

Rookie of the Year
Butch Metzger (cowinner), pitcher, 1976
Benito Santiago, catcher, 1987

Cy Young
Randy Jones, 1976
Gaylord Perry, 1978
Mark Davis, 1989
Jake Peavy, 2007

Hall of Famers Who Played for the Padres
Rollie Fingers, pitcher, 1977–80
Goose Gossage, pitcher, 1984–87
Tony Gwynn, outfield, 1982–2001
Rickey Henderson, outfield, 1996–2001
Willie McCovey, first base, 1974–76
Gaylord Perry, pitcher, 1978–79
Ozzie Smith, shortstop, 1978–81
Dave Winfield, outfield, 1973–80

Retired Numbers
JC ....Jerry Coleman
RK ....Ray Kroc
6 ....Steve Garvey
19 ....Tony Gwynn
31 ....Dave Winfield
35...................................Randy Jones
51...............................Trevor Hoffman

League Leaders, Batting

Batting Average, Season
Tony Gwynn, 1984 351
Tony Gwynn, 1987 370
Tony Gwynn, 1988 313
Tony Gwynn, 1989 336
Gary Sheffield, 1992...................330
Tony Gwynn, 1994 394
Tony Gwynn, 1995 368
Tony Gwynn, 1996 353
Tony Gwynn, 1997 372

Home Runs, Season
Fred McGriff, 1992 35

RBIs, Season
Dave Winfield, 1979 118

Stolen Bases, Season
[No player]

Total Bases, Season
Dave Winfield, 1979 333
Gary Sheffield, 1992...................323

Most Hits, Season
Tony Gwynn, 1984 213
Tony Gwynn, 1986 211
Tony Gwynn, 1987 218
Tony Gwynn, 1989 203
Tony Gwynn, 1994 165
Tony Gwynn, 1995 ....197 (Tie)
Tony Gwynn, 1997 220

Most Runs, Season
Tony Gwynn, 1986 ....107 (Tie)

Batting Feats

Triple Crown Winners
[No player]

Hitting for the Cycle
[No player]

Six Hits in a Game
Gene Richards, July 26, 1977*
Jim Lefebvre, Sept. 13, 1982*
Tony Gwynn, Aug. 4, 1993*
Adrian Gonzalez, Aug. 11, 2009
*Extra-inning game.

40 or More Home Runs, Season
50 ....Greg Vaughn, 1998
41 ....Phil Nevin, 2001
40 ....Ken Caminiti, 1996
    Adrian Gonzalez, 2009

League Leaders, Pitching

Most Wins, Season
Randy Jones, 1976.........................22
Gaylord Perry, 1978......................21
Jake Peavy, 2007 19

Most Strikeouts, Season
Andy Benes, 1994 189
Jake Peavy, 2005 216
Jake Peavy, 2007 240

Lowest ERA, Season
Randy Jones, 1975 ....2.24
Jake Peavy, 2004 ....2.27
Jake Peavy, 2007 ....2.54

Most Saves, Season
Rollie Fingers, 1977.......................35
Rollie Fingers, 1978.......................37
Mark Davis, 1989 44
Trevor Hoffman, 1998....................53
Trevor Hoffman, 2006....................46
Heath Bell, 2009 42

Best Won–Lost Percentage, Season
Gaylord Perry, 1978 ......21–6.... .778

Pitching Feats

20 Wins, Season
Randy Jones, 1975 20–12
Randy Jones, 1976 22–14
Gaylord Perry, 1978 21–6

No-Hitters
[No pitcher]

No-Hitters Pitched Against
Dock Ellis, Pitt. Pirates, June 12, 1970
    (final: 2–0)
Milt Pappas, Chi. Cubs, Sept. 2, 1972
    (final: 8–0)
Phil Niekro, Atl. Braves, Aug. 5, 1973
    (final: 9–0)

Kent Mercker, Mark Wohlers, and Alejandro Pena, Atl. Braves, Sept. 11, 1991 (final: 1–0)

Pedro Martinez and Mel Rojas, Mont. Expos, June 3, 1995 (final: 1–0) (allowed hit in 10th inning)

A. J. Burnett, Flor. Marlins, May 12, 2001 (final: 3–0)

Bud Smith, St. L. Cardinals, Sept. 3, 2001 (final: 4–0)

Jonathan Sanchez, S.F. Giants, July 10, 2009 (final: 8–0)

Postseason Play

1984 League Championship Series vs. Chi. Cubs, won 3 games to 2
      World Series vs. Det. Tigers (AL), lost 4 games to 1

1996 Division Series vs. St. L. Cardinals, lost 3 games to 0

1998 Division Series vs. Hous. Astros, won 3 games to 1
      League Championship Series vs. Atl. Braves, won 4 games to 2
      World Series vs. N.Y. Yankees (AL), lost 4 games to 0

2005 Division Series vs. St. L. Cardinals, lost 3 games to 0

2006 Division Series vs. St. L. Cardinals, lost 3 games to 1

San Francisco Giants

Dates of Operation: 1958–present (54 years)
Overall Record: 4455 wins, 4136 losses (.519)
Stadiums: Seals Stadium, 1958–59; Candlestick Park (also known as 3Com Park, 1996–99),
1960–2000; AT&T Park (formerly Pacific Bell Park, or Pac Bell, 2000–02; and SBC Park,
2003–05), 2000–present (capacity: 41,503)

Year-by-Year Finishes

Year	Finish	Wins	Losses	Percentage	Games Behind	Manager	Attendance
1958	3rd	80	74	.519	12.0	Bill Rigney	1,272,625
1959	3rd	83	71	.539	4.0	Bill Rigney	1,422,130
1960	5th	79	75	.513	16.0	Bill Rigney, Tom Sheehan	1,795,356
1961	3rd	85	69	.552	8.0	Alvin Dark	1,390,679
1962	1st	103	62	.624	+1.0	Alvin Dark	1,592,594
1963	3rd	88	74	.543	11.0	Alvin Dark	1,571,306
1964	4th	90	72	.556	3.0	Alvin Dark	1,504,364
1965	2nd	95	67	.586	2.0	Herman Franks	1,546,075
1966	2nd	93	68	.578	1.5	Herman Franks	1,657,192
1967	2nd	91	71	.562	10.5	Herman Franks	1,242,480
1968	2nd	88	74	.543	9.0	Herman Franks	837,220
West Division							
1969	2nd	90	72	.556	3.0	Clyde King	873,603
1970	3rd	86	76	.531	16.0	Clyde King, Charlie Fox	740,720
1971	1st	90	72	.556	+1.0	Charlie Fox	1,106,043
1972	5th	69	86	.445	26.5	Charlie Fox	647,744
1973	3rd	88	74	.543	11.0	Charlie Fox	834,193
1974	5th	72	90	.444	30.0	Charlie Fox, Wes Westrum	519,987
1975	3rd	80	81	.497	27.5	Wes Westrum	522,919
1976	4th	74	88	.457	28.0	Bill Rigney	626,868
1977	4th	75	87	.463	23.0	Joe Altobelli	700,056
1978	3rd	89	73	.549	6.0	Joe Altobelli	1,740,477
1979	4th	71	91	.438	19.5	Joe Altobelli, Dave Bristol	1,456,402
1980	5th	75	86	.466	17.0	Dave Bristol	1,096,115
1981*	5th/3rd	56	55	.505	10.0/3.5	Frank Robinson	632,274
1982	3rd	87	75	.537	2.0	Frank Robinson	1,200,948
1983	5th	79	83	.488	12.0	Frank Robinson	1,251,530
1984	6th	66	96	.407	26.0	Frank Robinson, Danny Ozark	1,001,545
1985	6th	62	100	.383	33.0	Jim Davenport, Roger Craig	818,697
1986	3rd	83	79	.512	13.0	Roger Craig	1,528,748
1987	1st	90	72	.556	+6.0	Roger Craig	1,917,168
1988	4th	83	79	.512	11.5	Roger Craig	1,785,297
1989	1st	92	70	.568	+3.0	Roger Craig	2,059,701
1990	3rd	85	77	.525	6.0	Roger Craig	1,975,528
1991	4th	75	87	.463	19.0	Roger Craig	1,737,478
1992	5th	72	90	.444	26.0	Roger Craig	1,561,987
1993	2nd	103	59	.636	1.0	Dusty Baker	2,606,354
1994	2nd	55	60	.478	3.5	Dusty Baker	1,704,608
1995	4th	67	77	.465	11.0	Dusty Baker	1,241,500
1996	4th	68	94	.420	23.0	Dusty Baker	1,413,922

1997	1st	90	72	.556	+2.0	Dusty Baker	1,690,869
1998	2nd	89	74	.546	9.5	Dusty Baker	1,925,634
1999	2nd	86	76	.531	14.0	Dusty Baker	2,078,399
2000	1st	97	65	.599	+11.0	Dusty Baker	3,315,330
2001	2nd	90	72	.556	2.0	Dusty Baker	3,277,244
2002	2nd	95	66	.590	2.5	Dusty Baker	3,253,205
2003	1st	100	61	.621	+15.5	Felipe Alou	3,264,898
2004	2nd	91	71	.562	2.0	Felipe Alou	3,256,858
2005	3rd	75	87	.463	7.0	Felipe Alou	3,223,217
2006	3rd	76	85	.472	11.5	Felipe Alou	3,129,785
2007	5th	71	91	.438	19.0	Bruce Bochy	3,223,217
2008	4th	72	90	.444	12.0	Bruce Bochy	2,863,837
2009	3rd	88	74	.543	7.0	Bruce Bochy	2,861,113
2010	1st	92	70	.568	+2.0	Bruce Bochy	3,037,443
2011	2nd	86	76	.531	8.0	Bruce Bochy	3,387,303

*Split season.

Awards

Most Valuable Player

Willie McCovey, first base, 1969
Kevin Mitchell, outfield, 1989
Barry Bonds, outfield, 1993
Jeff Kent, second base, 2000
Barry Bonds, outfield, 2001
Barry Bonds, outfield, 2002
Barry Bonds, outfield, 2003
Barry Bonds, outfield, 2004

Rookie of the Year

Orlando Cepeda, first base, 1958
Willie McCovey, first base, 1959
Gary Matthews, outfield, 1973
John Montefusco, pitcher, 1975
Buster Posey, catcher, 2010

Cy Young

Mike McCormick, 1967
Tim Lincecum, 2008
Tim Lincecum, 2009

Hall of Famers Who Played for the San Francisco Giants

Steve Carlton, pitcher, 1986
Gary Carter, catcher, 1990
Orlando Cepeda, first base, 1958–66
Goose Gossage, pitcher, 1989
Juan Marichal, pitcher, 1960–73
Willie Mays, outfield, 1958–72
Willie McCovey, first base and outfield, 1959–73 and 1977–80
Joe Morgan, second base, 1981–82
Gaylord Perry, pitcher, 1962–71

Duke Snider, outfield, 1964
Warren Spahn, pitcher, 1965

Retired Numbers

	Christy Mathewson
	John McGraw
	Russ Hodges
	Lon Simmons
3	Bill Terry
4	Mel Ott
11	Carl Hubbell
20	Monte Irvin
24	Willie Mays
27	Juan Marichal
30	Orlando Cepeda
36	Gaylord Perry
44	Willie McCovey

League Leaders, Batting

Batting Average, Season

Barry Bonds, 2002 .... .370
Barry Bonds, 2004 .... .363

Home Runs, Season

Orlando Cepeda, 1961 46
Willie Mays, 1962 49
Willie McCovey, 1963 .... 44 (Tie)
Willie Mays, 1964 47
Willie Mays, 1965 52
Willie McCovey, 1968 36
Willie McCovey, 1969 45
Kevin Mitchell, 1989 47
Barry Bonds, 1993 46
Matt Williams, 1994 43
Barry Bonds, 2001 73

RBIs, Season

Orlando Cepeda, 1961 142
Orlando Cepeda, 1967 111
Willie McCovey, 1968 105
Willie McCovey, 1969 126
Will Clark, 1988 109
Kevin Mitchell, 1989 125
Matt Williams, 1990 122
Barry Bonds, 1993 123

Stolen Bases, Season

Willie Mays, 1958 31
Willie Mays, 1959 27

Total Bases, Season

Willie Mays, 1962 382
Willie Mays, 1965 360
Bobby Bonds, 1973 341
Kevin Mitchell, 1989 345
Will Clark, 1991 .... 303 (Tie)
Barry Bonds, 1993 365

Most Hits, Season

Willie Mays, 1960 190
Brett Butler, 1990 .... 192 (Tie)
Rich Aurilia, 2001 206

Most Runs, Season

Willie Mays, 1958 121
Willie Mays, 1961 129
Bobby Bonds, 1969 .... 120 (Tie)
Bobby Bonds, 1973 131
Brett Butler, 1988 109
Will Clark, 1989 .... 104 (Tie)

Batting Feats

Triple Crown Winners
[No player]

Hitting for the Cycle
Jim Ray Hart, July 8, 1970
Dave Kingman, Apr. 16, 1972
Jeffrey Leonard, June 27, 1985
Candy Maldonado, May 4, 1987
Chris Speier, July 9, 1988
Robby Thompson, Apr. 22, 1991
Jeff Kent, May 3, 1999
Randy winn, August 15, 2005
Fred Lewis, May 13, 2007
Pablo Sandoval, Sept. 15, 2011

Six Hits in a Game
Jesus Alou, July 10, 1964
Mike Benjamin, June 14, 1995*
Randy Winn, Aug. 15, 2005
Fred Lewis, May 13, 2007
*Extra-inning game.

40 or More Home Runs, Season

73	Barry Bonds, 2001
52	Willie Mays, 1965
49	Willie Mays, 1962
	Barry Bonds, 2000
47	Willie Mays, 1964
	Kevin Mitchell, 1989
46	Orlando Cepeda, 1961
	Barry Bonds, 1993
	Barry Bonds, 2002
45	Willie McCovey, 1969
	Barry Bonds, 2003
	Barry Bonds, 2004
44	Willie McCovey, 1963
43	Matt Williams, 1994
42	Barry Bonds, 1996
40	Willie Mays, 1961
	Barry Bonds, 1997

League Leaders, Pitching

Most Wins, Season
Sam Jones, 1959 .... 21 (Tie)
Juan Marichal, 1963 .... 25 (Tie)
Mike McCormick, 1967 22
Juan Marichal, 1968 26
Gaylord Perry, 1970 .... 23 (Tie)
Ron Bryant, 1973 24
John Burnett, 1993 .... 22 (Tie)

Most Strikeouts, Season
Tim Lincecum, 2008 265
Tim Lincecum, 2009 261

Tim Lincecum, 2010 231

Lowest ERA, Season
Stu Miller, 1958 .... 2.47
Sam Jones, 1959 .... 2.82
Mike McCormick, 1960 .... 2.70
Juan Marichal, 1969 .... 2.10
Atlee Hammaker, 1983 .... 2.25
Scott Garrelts, 1989 .... 2.28
Bill Swift, 1992 .... 2.08
Jason Schmidt, 2003 .... 2.34

Most Saves, Season
Rob Nen, 2001 45
Brian Wilson, 2010 48

Best Won-Lost Percentage, Season
Juan Marichal, 1966 ...... 25–6 .... .806
Jason Schmidt, 2003 ...... 17–5 .... .773
Tim Lincecum, 2008 .... 18–5 .... .783

Pitching Feats

20 Wins, Season
Sam Jones, 1959 21–15
Jack Sanford, 1962 24–7
Juan Marichal, 1963 25–8
Juan Marichal, 1964 21–8
Juan Marichal, 1965 22–13
Juan Marichal, 1966 25–6
Gaylord Perry, 1966 21–8
Mike McCormick, 1967 22–10
Juan Marichal, 1968 26–9
Juan Marichal, 1969 21–11
Gaylord Perry, 1970 23–13
Ron Bryant, 1973 24–12
Mike Krukow, 1986 20–9
John Burkett, 1993 22–7
Bill Swift, 1993 21–8

No-Hitters
Juan Marichal (vs. Hous. Astros), June 15, 1963 (final: 1–0)
Gaylord Perry (vs. St. L. Cardinals), Sept. 17, 1968 (final: 1–0)
Ed Halicki (vs. N.Y. Mets), Aug. 24, 1975 (final: 6–0)
John Montefusco (vs. Atl. Braves), Sept. 29, 1976 (final: 9–0)
Jonathan Sanchez (vs. S.D. Padres), July 10, 2009 (final 8–0)

No-Hitters Pitched Against
Warren Spahn, Milw. Braves, Apr. 28, 1961 (final: 1–0)
Sandy Koufax, L.A. Dodgers, May 11,

1963 (final: 8–0)
Ray Washburn, St. L. Cardinals, Sept. 18, 1968 (final: 2–0)
Jerry Reuss, L.A. Dodgers, June 27, 1980 (final: 8–0)
Charlie Lea, Mont. Expos, May 10, 1981 (final: 4–0)
Mike Scott, Hous. Astros, Sept. 25, 1986 (final: 2–0)
Terry Mulholland, Phila. Phillies, Aug. 15, 1990 (final: 6–0)
Kevin Gross, L.A. Dodgers, Aug. 17, 1992 (final: 2–0)
Kevin Brown, Flor. Marlins, June 10, 1997 (final: 9–0)
Kevin Millwood, Phila. Phillies, Apr. 27, 2003 (final: 1–0)

Postseason Play

1962 Pennant Playoff Series vs. L.A. Dodgers, won 2 games to 1
World Series vs. N.Y. Yankees (AL), lost 4 games to 3

1971 League Championship Series vs. Pitt. Pirates, lost 3 games to 1

1987 League Championship Series vs. St. L. Cardinals, lost 4 games to 3

1989 League Championship Series vs. Chi. Cubs, won 4 games to 1
World Series vs. Oak. A's (AL), lost 4 games to 0

1997 Division Series vs. Flor. Marlins, lost 3 games to 0

1998 NL Wild Card Playoff Game vs. Chi. Cubs, lost

2000 Division Series vs. N.Y. Mets, lost 3 games to 1

2002 Division Series vs. Atl. Braves, won 3 games to 1
League Championship Series vs. St. L. Cardinals, won 4 games to 1
World Series vs. Ana. Angels (AL), lost 4 games to 3

2003 Division Series vs. Flor. Marlins, lost 3 games to 1

2010 Division Series vs. Atl. Braves, won 3 games to 1
League Championship Series vs. Phila. Phillies, won 4 games to 2
World Series vs. Tex. Rangers (AL), won 4 games to 1

Washington Nationals (formerly the Montreal Expos)

Dates of Operation: (as the Montreal Expos) 1969–2004 (36 years)
Overall Record: 2755 wins, 2943 losses (.484)
Stadiums: Jerry Park, 1969–76; Olympic Stadium, 1977–2004 (capacity: 46,500); Estadio Hiram
   Bithorn, San Juan, Puerto Rico (part of 2003 and 2004 seasons) (capacity: 18,000)

Dates of Operation: (as the Washington Nationals) 2005–present (7 years)
Overall Record: 492 wins, 640 losses (.435)
Stadiums: RFK Stadium, 2005–2007; Nationals Park, 2008–present (capacity: 41, 888)

Year-by-Year Finishes

Year	Finish	Wins	Losses	Percentage	Games Behind	Manager	Attendance
					East Division		
1969	6th	52	110	.321	48.0	Gene Mauch	1,212,608
1970	6th	73	89	.451	16.0	Gene Mauch	1,424,683
1971	5th	71	90	.441	25.5	Gene Mauch	1,290,963
1972	5th	70	86	.449	26.5	Gene Mauch	1,142,145
1973	4th	79	83	.488	3.5	Gene Mauch	1,246,863
1974	4th	79	82	.491	0.5	Gene Mauch	1,019,134
1975	5th (Tie)	75	87	.463	17.5	Gene Mauch	908,292
1976	6th	55	107	.340	46.0	Karl Kuehl, Charlie Fox	646,704
1977	5th	75	87	.463	26.0	Dick Williams	1,433,757
1978	4th	76	86	.469	14.0	Dick Williams	1,427,007
1979	2nd	95	65	.594	2.0	Dick Williams	2,102,173
1980	2nd	90	72	.556	1.0	Dick Williams	2,208,175
1981*	3rd/1st	60	48	.556	4.0/+0.5	Dick Williams, Jim Fanning	1,534,564
1982	3rd	86	76	.531	6.0	Jim Fanning	2,318,292
1983	3rd	82	80	.506	8.0	Bill Virdon	2,320,651
1984	5th	78	83	.484	18.0	Bill Virdon, Jim Fanning	1,606,531
1985	3rd	84	77	.522	16.5	Buck Rodgers	1,502,494
1986	4th	78	83	.484	29.5	Buck Rodgers	1,128,981
1987	3rd	91	71	.562	4.0	Buck Rodgers	1,850,324
1988	3rd	81	81	.500	20.0	Buck Rodgers	1,478,659
1989	4th	81	81	.500	12.0	Buck Rodgers	1,783,533
1990	3rd	85	77	.525	10.0	Buck Rodgers	1,373,087
1991	6th	71	90	.441	26.5	Buck Rodgers, Tom Runnells	934,742
1992	2nd	87	75	.537	9.0	Tom Runnells, Felipe Alou	1,669,077
1993	2nd	94	68	.580	3.0	Felipe Alou	1,641,437
1994	1st	74	40	.649	+6.0	Felipe Alou	1,276,250
1995	5th	66	78	.458	24.0	Felipe Alou	1,309,618
1996	2nd	88	74	.543	8.0	Felipe Alou	1,616,709
1997	4th	78	84	.481	23.0	Felipe Alou	1,497,609
1998	4th	65	97	.401	41.0	Felipe Alou	914,717
1999	4th	68	94	.420	35.0	Felipe Alou	773,277
2000	4th	67	95	.414	28.0	Felipe Alou	926,263
2001	5th	68	94	.420	20.0	Felipe Alou, Jeff Torborg	609,473
2002	2nd	83	79	.512	19.0	Frank Robinson	732,901
2003	4th	83	79	.512	18.0	Frank Robinson	1,025,639
2004	5th	67	95	.414	29.0	Frank Robinson	748,550

Wash. Nationals

2005	5th	81	81	.500	9.0	Frank Robinson	2,731,993
2006	5th	71	91	.438	26.0	Frank Robinson	2,153,058
2007	4th	73	89	.451	16.0	Manny Acta	1,961,606
2008	5th	59	102	.366	32.5	Manny Acta	2,320,400
2009	5th	59	103	.364	34.0	Manny Acta, Jim Riggleman	1,817,226
2010	5th	69	93	.425	28.0	Jim Riggleman	1,828,065
2011	3rd	80	81	.497	21.5	Jim Riggleman, Davey Johnson	1,940,478

*Split season.

Awards

Most Valuable Player
[No player]

Rookie of the Year
Carl Morton, pitcher, 1970
Andre Dawson, outfield, 1977

Cy Young
Pedro Martinez, 1997

Hall of Famers Who Played for the Expos
Gary Carter, catcher, 1974–84 and 1992
Andre Dawson, outfield, 1976–86
Tony Perez, first base, 1977–79

Retired Numbers (Mont.)
CB...........................Charles Bronfman
8.......................................Gary Carter
10 ....Andre Dawson and Rusty Staub
30 ....Tim Raines

League Leaders, Batting

Batting Average, Season
Al Oliver, 1982........................... .331
Tim Raines, 1986 .... .334

Home Runs, Season
[No player]

RBIs, Season
Al Oliver, 1982....................109 (Tie)
Gary Carter, 1984 ....106 (Tie)

Stolen Bases, Season
Ron LeFlore, 1980 97
Tim Raines, 1981 71
Tim Raines, 1982 78

Tim Raines, 1983 90
Tim Raines, 1984 75
Marquis Grissom, 1991 76
Marquis Grissom, 1992 78

Total Bases, Season
Al Oliver, 1982.............................317
Andre Dawson, 1983....................341
Andres Galarraga, 1988...............329
Vladimir Guerrero, 2002...............364

Most Hits, Season
Al Oliver, 1982.............................204
Andre Dawson, 1983 ....189 (Tie)
Andres Galarraga, 1988...............184
Vladimir Guerrero, 2002...............206

Most Runs, Season
Tim Raines, 1983 133
Tim Raines, 1987 123

Batting Feats

Triple Crown Winners
[No player]

Hitting for the Cycle
Tim Foli, Apr. 22, 1976
Chris Speier, July 20, 1978
Tim Raines, Aug. 16, 1987
Rondell White, June 11, 1995
Brad Wilkerson, June 24, 2003
Vladimir Guerrero, Sept. 14, 2003

Six Hits in a Game
Rondell White, June 11, 1995* (Mont.)
Brad Wilkerson, Apr. 6, 2005 (Wash.)
Cristian Guzman, Aug. 28, 2008 (Wash.)
*Extra-inning game.

40 or More Home Runs, Season

46........Alfonso Soriano, 2006 (Wash.)
44 ....Vladimir Guerrero, 2000
42 ....Vladimir Guerrero, 1999

League Leaders, Pitching

Most Wins, Season
Ken Hill, 1994 ....16 (Tie)

Most Strikeouts, Season
[No pitcher]

Lowest ERA, Season
Steve Rogers, 1982.....................2.40
Dennis Martinez, 1991 ....2.39
Pedro Martinez, 1997.................1.90

Most Saves, Season
Mike Marshall, 1973 31
Jeff Reardon, 1985.........................41
Ugueth Urbina, 1999.....................41
Chad Cordero, 2005 47

Best Won–Lost Percentage, Season
[No pitcher]

Pitching Feats

20 Wins, Season
Ross Grimsley, 1978.................20–11
Bartolo Colon, 2002 ....20–8*
*10–4 with Cleve. Indians (AL) and 10–4 with Mont. Expos.

No-Hitters
Bill Stoneman (vs. Phila. Phillies), Apr. 17, 1969 (final: 7–0)
Bill Stoneman (vs. N.Y. Mets), Oct. 2, 1972 (final: 7–0)
Charlie Lea (vs. S.F. Giants), May 10, 1981 (final: 4–0)
Mark Gardner (vs. L.A. Dodgers), July

26, 1991 (final: 0–1) (lost in 10th)

Dennis Martinez (Mont.) (vs. L.A. Dodgers), July 28, 1991 (final: 2–0) (perfect game)

Pedro Martinez and Mel Rojas (Mont.) (vs. S.D. Padres), June 3, 1995 (final: 1–0) (allowed hit in 10th)

No-Hitters Pitched Against

Larry Dierker, Hous. Astros, July 9, 1976 (final: 6–0)

Bob Forsch, St. L. Cardinals, Sept. 26, 1983 (final: 3–0)

Tommy Greene, Phila. Phillies, May 23, 1991 (final: 2–0)

David Cone, N.Y. Yankees (AL), July 18, 1999 (final: 6–0) (perfect game)

Postseason Play

1981 Second-Half Division Playoff Series vs. Phila. Phillies, won 3 games to 2

League Championship Series vs. L.A. Dodgers, lost 3 games to 2

Boston Braves

Dates of Operation: 1876–1952 (77 years)

Overall Record: 5118 wins, 5598 losses (.478)

Stadiums: South End Grounds, 1876–93 and 1895–1914; Congress Street Grounds, 1894; Fenway Park, 1914–15 and 1946; Braves Field, 1915–52 (capacity: 44,500)

Other Names: Red Stockings, Red Caps, Beaneaters, Nationals, Doves, Rustlers, Bees

Year-by-Year Finishes

Year	Finish	Wins	Losses	Percentage	Games Behind	Manager	Attendance
1876	4th	39	31	.557	15.0	Harry Wright	not available
1877	1st	42	18	.700	+7.0	Harry Wright	not available
1878	1st	41	19	.683	+4.0	Harry Wright	not available
1879	2nd	49	29	.628	6.0	Harry Wright	not available
1880	6th	40	44	.476	27.0	Harry Wright	not available
1881	6th	38	45	.458	17.5	Harry Wright	not available
1882	3rd (Tie)	45	39	.536	10.0	John Morrill	not available
1883	1st	63	35	.643	+4.0	Jack Burdock, John Morrill	not available
1884	2nd	73	38	.658	10.5	John Morrill	not available
1885	5th	48	66	.410	31.0	John Morrill	not available
1886	5th	56	61	.478	30.5	John Morrill	not available
1887	5th	61	60	.504	16.5	John Morrill	not available
1888	4th	70	64	.522	15.5	John Morrill	not available
1889	2nd	83	45	.648	1.0	Jim Hart	not available
1890	5th	76	57	.571	12.0	Frank Selee	not available
1891	1st	87	51	.630	+3.5	Frank Selee	not available
1892	1st	102	48	.680	+9.5	Frank Selee	not available
1893	1st	86	44	.662	+4.5	Frank Selee	not available
1894	3rd	83	49	.629	8.0	Frank Selee	not available
1895	5th (Tie)	71	60	.542	16.5	Frank Selee	not available
1896	4th	74	57	.565	17.0	Frank Selee	not available
1897	1st	90	39	.705	+2.0	Frank Selee	not available
1898	1st	102	47	.685	+6.0	Frank Selee	not available
1899	2nd	95	57	.625	4.0	Frank Selee	not available
1900	4th	66	72	.478	17.0	Frank Selee	not available
1901	5th	69	69	.500	20.5	Frank Selee	146,502
1902	3rd	73	64	.533	29.0	Al Buckenberger	116,960
1903	6th	58	80	.420	32.0	Al Buckenberger	143,155
1904	7th	55	98	.359	51.0	Al Buckenberger	140,694
1905	7th	51	103	.331	54.5	Fred Tenney	150,003

1906	8th	49	102	.325	66.5	Fred Tenney	143,280
1907	7th	58	90	.392	47.0	Fred Tenney	203,221
1908	6th	63	91	.409	36.0	Joe Kelley	253,750
1909	8th	45	108	.294	65.5	Fred Bowerman, Harry Smith	195,188
1910	8th	53	100	.346	50.5	Fred Lake	149,027
1911	8th	44	107	.291	54.0	Fred Tenney	96,000
1912	8th	52	101	.340	52.0	Johnny Kling	121,000
1913	5th	69	82	.457	31.5	George Stallings	208,000
1914	1st	94	59	.614	+10.5	George Stallings	382,913
1915	2nd	83	69	.546	7.0	George Stallings	376,283
1916	3rd	89	63	.586	4.0	George Stallings	313,495
1917	6th	72	81	.471	25.5	George Stallings	174,253
1918	7th	53	71	.427	28.5	George Stallings	84,938
1919	6th	57	82	.410	38.5	George Stallings	167,401
1920	7th	62	90	.408	30.0	George Stallings	162,483
1921	4th	79	74	.516	15.0	Fred Mitchell	318,627
1922	8th	53	100	.346	39.5	Fred Mitchell	167,965
1923	7th	54	100	.351	41.5	Fred Mitchell	227,802
1924	8th	53	100	.346	40.0	Dave Bancroft	177,478
1925	5th	70	83	.458	25.0	Dave Bancroft	313,528
1926	7th	66	86	.434	22.0	Dave Bancroft	303,598
1927	7th	60	94	.390	34.0	Dave Bancroft	288,685
1928	7th	50	103	.327	44.5	Jack Slattery, Rogers Hornsby	227,001
1929	8th	56	98	.364	43.0	Judge Fuchs	372,351
1930	6th	70	84	.455	22.0	Bill McKechnie	464,835
1931	7th	64	90	.416	37.0	Bill McKechnie	515,005
1932	5th	77	77	.500	13.0	Bill McKechnie	507,606
1933	4th	83	71	.539	9.0	Bill McKechnie	517,803
1934	4th	78	73	.517	16.0	Bill McKechnie	303,205
1935	8th	38	115	.248	61.5	Bill McKechnie	232,754
1936	6th	71	83	.461	21.0	Bill McKechnie	340,585
1937	5th	79	73	.520	16.0	Bill McKechnie	385,339
1938	5th	77	75	.507	12.0	Casey Stengel	341,149
1939	7th	63	88	.417	32.5	Casey Stengel	285,994
1940	7th	65	87	.428	34.5	Casey Stengel	241,616
1941	7th	62	92	.403	38.0	Casey Stengel	263,680
1942	7th	59	89	.399	44.0	Casey Stengel	285,322
1943	6th	68	85	.444	36.5	Casey Stengel	271,289
1944	6th	65	89	.422	40.0	Bob Coleman	208,691
1945	6th	67	85	.441	30.0	Bob Coleman, Del Bissonette	374,178
1946	4th	81	72	.529	15.5	Billy Southworth	969,673
1947	3rd	86	68	.558	8.0	Billy Southworth	1,277,361
1948	1st	91	62	.595	+6.5	Billy Southworth	1,455,439
1949	4th	75	79	.487	22.0	Billy Southworth	1,081,795
1950	4th	83	71	.539	8.0	Billy Southworth	944,391
1951	4th	76	78	.494	20.5	Billy Southworth, Tommy Holmes	487,475
1952	7th	64	89	.418	32.0	Tommy Holmes, Charlie Grimm	281,278

Awards

Most Valuable Player
Johnny Evers, second base, 1914
Bob Elliott, third base, 1947

Rookie of the Year
Alvin Dark, shortstop, 1948
Sam Jethroe, outfield, 1950

Cy Young
[No pitcher]

Hall of Famers Who Played for the Boston Braves
Earl Averill, outfield, 1941
Dave Bancroft, shortstop, 1924–27
Dan Brouthers, first base, 1889
John Clarkson, pitcher, 1888–92
Hugh Duffy, outfield, 1892–1900
Johnny Evers, second base, 1914–17
Burleigh Grimes, pitcher, 1930
Billy Hamilton, outfield, 1896–1901
Billy Herman, second base, 1946
Rogers Hornsby, second base, 1928
Joe Kelley, outfield, 1891 and 1908
King Kelly, outfield and catcher, 1887–90
Ernie Lombardi, catcher, 1942
Al Lopez, catcher, 1936–40
Rabbit Maranville, shortstop, 1912–20 and 1929–35
Rube Marquard, pitcher, 1922–25
Eddie Mathews, third base, 1952
Tommy McCarthy, outfield and infield, 1885 and 1892–95
Bill McKechnie, infield, 1913
Joe Medwick, outfield, 1945
Kid Nichols, pitcher, 1890–1901
Jim O'Rourke, outfield and infield, 1876–78
Old Hoss Radbourn, pitcher, 1886–89
Babe Ruth, outfield, 1935
Al Simmons, outfield, 1939
George Sisler, first base, 1928–30
Billy Southworth, outfield, 1921–23
Warren Spahn, pitcher, 1942 and 1946–52
Casey Stengel, outfield, 1924–25
Ed Walsh, pitcher, 1917
Lloyd Waner, outfield, 1941
Paul Waner, outfield, 1941–42
Vic Willis, pitcher, 1898–1905
Cy Young, pitcher, 1911

Retired Numbers
[None]

League Leaders, Batting (Post-1900)

Batting Average, Season
Rogers Hornsby, 1928 .... .387
Ernie Lombardi, 1942 .... .330

Home Runs, Season
Herman Long, 1900 12
Dave Brain, 1907 10
Fred Beck, 1910 .... 10 (Tie)
Wally Berger, 1935 34
Tommy Holmes, 1945 28

RBIs, Season
Wally Berger, 1935 130

Stolen Bases, Season
Sam Jethroe, 1950 35
Sam Jethroe, 1951 33

Total Bases, Season
Tommy Holmes, 1945 367

Most Hits, Season
Ginger Beaumont, 1907 187
Doc Miller, 1911 192
Eddie Brown, 1926 201
Tommy Holmes, 1945 224
Tommy Holmes, 1947 191

Most Runs, Season
Earl Torgeson, 1950 120

Batting Feats

Triple Crown Winners
[No player]

Hitting for the Cycle
Herman Long, May 9, 1896
Duff Cooley, June 20, 1904
John Bates, Apr. 26, 1907
Bill Collins, Oct. 6, 1910

Six Hits in a Game
Sam Wise, June 20, 1883
King Kelly, Aug. 27, 1887
Bobby Lowe, June 11, 1891
Fred Tenney, May 31, 1897
Chick Stahl, May 31, 1899

40 or More Home Runs, Season

[No player]

League Leaders, Pitching (Post-1900)

Most Wins, Season
Dick Rudolph, 1914 .... 27 (Tie)
Johnny Sain, 1948 24
Warren Spahn, 1949 21
Warren Spahn, 1950 21
Warren Spahn, 1953 .... 23 (Tie)

Most Strikeouts, Season
Vic Willis, 1902 226
Warren Spahn, 1949 151
Warren Spahn, 1950 191
Warren Spahn, 1951 .... 164 (Tie)
Warren Spahn, 1952 183

Lowest ERA, Season
Jim Turner, 1937 .... 2.38
Warren Spahn, 1947 .... 2.33
Chet Nichols, 1951 .... 2.88

Most Saves, Season
[No pitcher]

Best Won–Lost Percentage, Season
Bill James, 1914 .... 26–7 .... .788
Tom Hughes, 1916 .... 16–3 .... .842
Ben Cantwell, 1933 ...... 20–10 .... .667

Pitching Feats

20 Wins, Season (1900–52)
Bill Dineen, 1900 21–15
Vic Willis, 1901 20–17
Togie Pittinger, 1902 27–16
Vic Willis, 1902 27–20
Irv Young, 1905 20–21
Bill James, 1914 26–7
Dick Rudolph, 1914 26–10
Dick Rudolph, 1915 22–19
Joe Oeschger, 1921 20–14
Ben Cantwell, 1933 20–10
Lou Fette, 1937 20–10
Jim Turner, 1937 20–11
Johnny Sain, 1946 20–14
Warren Spahn, 1947 21–10
Johnny Sain, 1947 21–12
Johnny Sain, 1948 24–15
Warren Spahn, 1948 20–7
Warren Spahn, 1949 21–14
Warren Spahn, 1950 21–17

Johnny Sain, 1950 20–13
Warren Spahn, 1951 22–14

No-Hitters

Fred Pfeffer (vs. Cin. Reds), May 8,
1907 (final: 6–0)
George Davis (vs. Phila. Phillies), Sept.
9, 1914 (final: 7–0)
Tom Hughes (vs. Pitt. Pirates), June 16,
1916 (final: 2–0)
Jim Tobin (vs. Bklyn. Dodgers), Apr. 27,
1944 (final: 2–0)
Vern Bickford (vs. Bklyn. Dodgers), Aug.

11, 1950 (final: 7–0)

No-Hitters Pitched Against

Nap Rucker, Bklyn. Dodgers, Sept. 5,
1908 (final: 6–0)
Jesse Haines, St. L. Cardinals, July 17,
1924 (final: 5–0)
Johnny Vander Meer, Cin. Reds, June
11, 1938 (final: 3–0)
Clyde Shoun, Cin. Reds, May 15, 1944
(final: 1–0)
Ed Head, Bklyn. Dodgers, Apr. 23,

1946 (final: 5–0)
Ewell Blackwell, Cin. Reds, June 18,
1947 (final: 6–0)
Cliff Chambers, Pitt. Pirates, May 6,
1951 (final: 3–0)

Postseason Play

1914   World Series vs. Phila. A's (AL),
won 4 games to 0
1948   World Series vs. Cleve. Indians
(AL), lost 4 games to 2

Brooklyn Dodgers

Dates of Operation: 1890–1957 (68 years)
Overall Record: 5214 wins, 4926 losses (.514)
Stadiums: Washington Park II, 1890; Eastern Park, 1891–97; West N.Y. Field Club Grounds, 1898;
    Washington Park III, 1898–1912; Ebbets Field, 1913–57; Roosevelt Stadium (Jersey City, NJ)
    1956–57 (capacity: 31,903)
Other Names: Bridegrooms, Superbas, Trolley Dodgers, Robins

Year-by-Year Finishes

Year	Finish	Wins	Losses	Percentage	Games Behind	Manager	Attendance
1890	1st	86	43	.667	+6.5	Bill McGunnigle	not available
1891	6th	61	76	.445	25.5	Monte Ward	not available
1892	3rd	95	59	.617	9.0	Monte Ward	not available
1893	6th	65	63	.508	20.0	Dave Foutz	not available
1894	5th	70	61	.534	25.5	Dave Foutz	not available
1895	5th	71	60	.542	16.5	Dave Foutz	not available
1896	9th	57	73	.443	33.0	Dave Foutz	not available
1897	6th	61	71	.462	32.0	Billy Barnie	not available
1898	10th	54	91	.372	46.0	Billy Barnie, Mike Griffin, Charlie Ebbets	not available
1899	1st	88	42	.677	+4.0	Ned Hanlon	not available
1900	1st	82	54	.603	+4.5	Ned Hanlon	not available
1901	3rd	79	57	.581	9.5	Ned Hanlon	198,200
1902	2nd	75	63	.543	27.5	Ned Hanlon	199,868
1903	5th	70	66	.515	19.0	Ned Hanlon	224,670
1904	6th	56	97	.366	50.0	Ned Hanlon	214,600
1905	8th	48	104	.316	56.5	Ned Hanlon	227,924
1906	5th	66	86	.434	50.0	Patsy Donovan	277,400
1907	5th	65	83	.439	40.0	Patsy Donovan	312,500
1908	7th	53	101	.344	46.0	Patsy Donovan	275,600
1909	6th	55	98	.359	55.5	Harry Lumley	321,300
1910	6th	64	90	.416	40.0	Bill Dahlen	279,321
1911	7th	64	86	.427	33.5	Bill Dahlen	269,000
1912	7th	58	95	.379	46.0	Bill Dahlen	243,000
1913	6th	65	84	.436	34.5	Bill Dahlen	347,000
1914	5th	75	79	.487	19.5	Wilbert Robinson	122,671
1915	3rd	80	72	.526	10.0	Wilbert Robinson	279,766
1916	1st	94	60	.610	+2.5	Wilbert Robinson	447,747
1917	7th	70	81	.464	26.5	Wilbert Robinson	221,619
1918	5th	57	69	.452	25.5	Wilbert Robinson	83,831
1919	5th	69	71	.493	27.0	Wilbert Robinson	360,721
1920	1st	93	61	.604	+7.0	Wilbert Robinson	808,722
1921	5th	77	75	.507	16.5	Wilbert Robinson	613,245
1922	6th	76	78	.494	17.0	Wilbert Robinson	498,865
1923	6th	76	78	.494	19.5	Wilbert Robinson	564,666
1924	2nd	92	62	.597	1.5	Wilbert Robinson	818,883
1925	6th (Tie)	68	85	.444	27.0	Wilbert Robinson	659,435
1926	6th	71	82	.464	17.5	Wilbert Robinson	650,819
1927	6th	65	88	.425	28.5	Wilbert Robinson	637,230

1928	6th	77	76	.503	17.5	Wilbert Robinson	664,863
1929	6th	70	83	.458	28.5	Wilbert Robinson	731,886
1930	4th	86	68	.558	6.0	Wilbert Robinson	1,097,339
1931	4th	79	73	.520	21.0	Wilbert Robinson	753,133
1932	3rd	81	73	.526	9.0	Max Carey	681,827
1933	6th	65	88	.425	26.5	Max Carey	526,815
1934	6th	71	81	.467	23.5	Casey Stengel	434,188
1935	5th	70	83	.458	29.5	Casey Stengel	470,517
1936	7th	67	87	.435	25.0	Casey Stengel	489,618
1937	6th	62	91	.405	33.5	Burleigh Grimes	482,481
1938	7th	69	80	.463	18.5	Burleigh Grimes	663,087
1939	3rd	84	69	.549	12.5	Leo Durocher	955,668
1940	2nd	88	65	.575	12.0	Leo Durocher	975,978
1941	1st	100	54	.649	+2.5	Leo Durocher	1,214,910
1942	2nd	104	50	.675	2.0	Leo Durocher	1,037,765
1943	3rd	81	72	.529	23.5	Leo Durocher	661,739
1944	7th	63	91	.409	42.0	Leo Durocher	605,905
1945	3rd	87	67	.565	11.0	Leo Durocher	1,059,220
1946	2nd	96	60	.616	2.0	Leo Durocher	1,796,824
1947	1st	94	60	.610	+5.0	Burt Shotton	1,807,526
1948	3rd	84	70	.545	7.5	Leo Durocher, Burt Shotton	1,398,967
1949	1st	97	57	.630	+1.0	Burt Shotton	1,633,747
1950	2nd	89	65	.578	2.0	Burt Shotton	1,185,896
1951	2nd	97	60	.618	1.0	Chuck Dressen	1,282,628
1952	1st	96	57	.627	+4.5	Chuck Dressen	1,088,704
1953	1st	105	49	.682	+13.0	Chuck Dressen	1,163,419
1954	2nd	92	62	.597	5.0	Walter Alston	1,020,531
1955	1st	98	55	.641	+13.5	Walter Alston	1,033,589
1956	1st	93	61	.604	+1.0	Walter Alston	1,213,562
1957	3rd	84	70	.545	11.0	Walter Alston	1,028,258

Awards

Most Valuable Player

Jake Daubert, first base, 1913
Dazzy Vance, pitcher, 1924
Dolph Camilli, first base, 1941
Jackie Robinson, second base, 1949
Roy Campanella, catcher, 1953
Roy Campanella, catcher, 1955
Don Newcombe, pitcher, 1956

Rookie of the Year

Jackie Robinson, first base, 1947
Don Newcombe, pitcher, 1949
Joe Black, pitcher, 1952
Junior Gilliam, second base, 1953

Cy Young

Don Newcombe, 1956

Hall of Famers Who Played for the Brooklyn Dodgers

Dave Bancroft, shortstop, 1928–29
Dan Brouthers, first base, 1892–93
Roy Campanella, catcher, 1948–57
Max Carey, outfield, 1926–29
Kiki Cuyler, outfield, 1938
Don Drysdale, pitcher, 1956–57
Leo Durocher, shortstop, 1938–41, 1943, and 1945
Burleigh Grimes, pitcher, 1918–26
Billy Herman, second base, 1941–43 and 1946
Waite Hoyt, pitcher, 1932 and 1937–38
Hughie Jennings, infield, 1899–1900
Willie Keeler, outfield, 1893 and 1899–1902
Joe Kelley, outfield, 1899–1901

George Kelly, first base, 1932
Sandy Koufax, pitcher, 1955–57
Tony Lazzeri, second base, 1939
Fred Lindstrom, third base, 1936
Ernie Lombardi, catcher, 1931
Al Lopez, catcher, 1928 and 1930–35
Heinie Manush, outfield, 1937–38
Rabbit Maranville, shortstop, 1926
Rube Marquard, pitcher, 1915–20
Tommy McCarthy, outfield and infield, 1896
Joe McGinnity, pitcher, 1900
Joe Medwick, outfield, 1940–43 and 1946
Pee Wee Reese, shortstop, 1940–42 and 1946–57
Jackie Robinson, infield, 1947–56
Duke Snider, outfield, 1947–57
Casey Stengel, outfield, 1912–17

Dazzy Vance, pitcher, 1922–32 and 1935

Arky Vaughan, infield, 1942–43 and 1947–48

Paul Waner, outfield, 1941 and 1943–44

John Montgomery Ward, infield and pitcher, 1890–92

Zack Wheat, outfield, 1909–26

Hack Wilson, outfield, 1932–34

Retired Numbers

[None]

League Leaders, Batting (Post-1900)

Batting Average, Season

Jake Daubert, 1913	.350
Jake Daubert, 1914	.329
Zack Wheat, 1918	.335
Lefty O'Doul, 1932	.368
Pete Reiser, 1941	.343
Dixie Walker, 1944	.357
Jackie Robinson, 1949	.342
Carl Furillo, 1953	.344

Home Runs, Season

Jimmy Sheckard, 1903	9
Harry Lumley, 1904	9
Tim Jordan, 1906	12
Tim Jordan, 1908	12
Jack Fournier, 1924	27
Dolph Camilli, 1941	34
Duke Snider, 1956	43

RBIs, Season

Hy Myers, 1919	72
Dolph Camilli, 1941	120
Dixie Walker, 1945	124
Roy Campanella, 1953	142
Duke Snider, 1955	136

Stolen Bases, Season

Jimmy Sheckard, 1903	67
Pete Reiser, 1942	20
Arky Vaughan, 1943	20
Pete Reiser, 1946	34
Jackie Robinson, 1947	29
Jackie Robinson, 1949	37
Pee Wee Reese, 1952	30

Total Bases, Season

Zack Wheat, 1916	262
Hy Myers, 1919	223
Pete Reiser, 1941	299
Duke Snider, 1950	343
Duke Snider, 1953	370
Duke Snider, 1954	378

Most Hits, Season

Willie Keeler, 1900	208
Ivy Olson, 1919	164
Duke Snider, 1950	199

Most Runs, Season

Pete Reiser, 1941	117
Arky Vaughan, 1943	112
Eddie Stanky, 1945	128
Pee Wee Reese, 1949	132
Duke Snider, 1953	132
Duke Snider, 1954	120 (Tie)
Duke Snider, 1955	126

Batting Feats

Triple Crown Winners

[No player]

Hitting for the Cycle

Tom Burns, Aug. 1, 1890

Jimmy Johnston, May 25, 1922

Babe Herman, May 18, 1931

Babe Herman, July 24, 1931

Dixie Walker, Sept. 2, 1944

Jackie Robinson, Aug. 29, 1948

Gil Hodges, June 25, 1949

Six Hits in a Game

George Cutshaw, Aug. 9, 1915

Jack Fournier, June 29, 1923

Hank DeBerry, June 23, 1929*

Wally Gilbert, May 30, 1931

Cookie Lavagetto, Sept. 23, 1939

*Extra-inning game.

40 or More Home Runs, Season

43	Duke Snider, 1956	
42	Duke Snider, 1953	
	Gil Hodges, 1954	
	Duke Snider, 1955	
41	Roy Campanella, 1953	
40	Gil Hodges, 1951	
	Duke Snider, 1954	
	Duke Snider, 1957	

League Leaders, Pitching (Post-1900)

Most Wins, Season

Bill Donovan, 1901	25
Burleigh Grimes, 1921	22 (Tie)
Dazzy Vance, 1924	28
Dazzy Vance, 1925	22
Kirby Higbe, 1941	22 (Tie)
Whit Wyatt, 1941	22 (Tie)
Don Newcombe, 1956	27

Most Strikeouts, Season

Burleigh Grimes, 1921	136
Dazzy Vance, 1922	134
Dazzy Vance, 1923	197
Dazzy Vance, 1924	262
Dazzy Vance, 1925	221
Dazzy Vance, 1926	140
Dazzy Vance, 1927	184
Dazzy Vance, 1928	200
Van Lingle Mungo, 1936	238
Don Newcombe, 1951	164 (Tie)

Lowest ERA, Season

Dazzy Vance, 1924	2.16
Dazzy Vance, 1928	2.09
Dazzy Vance, 1930	2.61
Johnny Podres, 1957	2.66

Most Saves, Season

[No pitcher]

Best Won–Lost Percentage, Season

Joe McGinnity, 1900	29–9	.763
Burleigh Grimes, 1920	23–11	.676
Freddie Fitzsimmons, 1940	16–2	.889
Larry French, 1942	15–4	.789
Preacher Roe, 1949	15–6	.714
Preacher Roe, 1951	22–3	.880
Carl Erskine, 1953	20–6	.769
Don Newcombe, 1955	20–5	.800
Don Newcombe, 1956	27–7	.794

Pitching Feats

20 Wins, Season (1900–57)

Joe McGinnity, 1900	29–9
William Kennedy, 1900	22–15
Bill Dineen, 1901	25–15
Henry Schmidt, 1903	22–13
Nap Rucker, 1911	22–18
Jeff Pfeffer, 1914	23–12
Jeff Pfeffer, 1916	25–11

Burleigh Grimes, 1920 23–11
Burleigh Grimes, 1921 22–13
Dutch Ruether, 1922..................21–12
Burleigh Grimes, 1923 21–10
Dazzy Vance, 1924 28–6
Burleigh Grimes, 1924 22–13
Dazzy Vance, 1925 22–9
Dazzy Vance, 1928 22–10
Watty Clark, 1932 20–12
Luke Hamlin, 1939....................20–13
Kirby Higbe, 1941 22–9
Whit Wyatt, 1941......................22–10
Ralph Branca, 1947 21–12
Preacher Roe, 1951 22–3
Don Newcombe, 1951 20–9
Carl Erskine, 1953......................20–6
Don Newcombe, 1955 20–5
Don Newcombe, 1956 27–7

No-Hitters

Mal Eason (vs. St. L. Cardinals), July 20,
    1906 (final: 2–0)
Harry McIntyre (vs. Pitt. Pirates), Aug. 1,
    1906 (final: 0–1) (allowed hit in 11th
    and lost in 13th)
Nap Rucker (vs. Bost. Braves), Sept. 5,
    1908 (final: 6–0)

Dazzy Vance (vs. Phila. Phillies), Sept. 13,
    1925 (final: 10–1)
Tex Carleton (vs. Cin. Reds), Apr. 30,
    1940 (final: 3–0)
Ed Head (vs. Bost. Braves), Apr. 23, 1946
    (final: 5–0)
Rex Barney (vs. N.Y. Giants), Sept. 9,
    1948 (final: 2–0)
Carl Erskine (vs. Chi. Cubs), June 19,
    1952 (final: 5–0)
Carl Erskine (vs. N.Y. Giants), May 12,
    1956 (final: 3–0)
Sal Maglie (vs. Phila. Phillies), Sept. 25,
    1956 (final: 5–0)

No-Hitters Pitched Against

John Lush, Phila. Phillies, May 1, 1906
    (final: 1–0)
Nick Maddox, Pitt. Pirates, Sept. 29,
    1907 (final: 2–1)
Red Ames, N.Y. Giants, Apr. 15, 1909
    (final: 0–3) (hit in 10th and lost
    in 13th)
Rube Marquard, N.Y. Giants, Apr. 15,
    1915 (final: 2–0)
Paul Dean, St. L. Cardinals, Sept. 21,
    1934 (final: 3–0)

Johnny Vander Meer, Cin. Reds, June
    15, 1938 (final: 6–0)
Jim Tobin, Bost. Braves, Apr. 27, 1944
    (final: 2–0)
Vern Bickford, Bost. Braves, Aug. 11,
    1950 (final: 7–0)

Postseason Play

1916   World Series vs. Bost. Red Sox
        (AL), lost 4 games to 1
1920   World Series vs. Cleve. Indians
        (AL), lost 5 games to 2
1941   World Series vs. N.Y. Yankees
        (AL), lost 4 games to 1
1946   Pennant Playoff Series vs. St. L.
        Cardinals, lost 2 games to 0
1947   World Series vs. N.Y. Yankees
        (AL), lost 4 games to 3
1949   World Series vs. N.Y. Yankees
        (AL), lost 4 games to 1
1951   Pennant Playoff Series vs. N.Y.
        Giants, lost 2 games to 1
1952   World Series vs. N.Y. Yankees
        (AL), lost 4 games to 3
1953   World Series vs. N.Y. Yankees
        (AL), lost 4 games to 2
1955   World Series vs. N.Y. Yankees
        (AL), won 4 games to 3
1956   World Series vs. N.Y. Yankees
        (AL), lost 4 games to 3

New York Giants

Dates of Operation: 1876, 1883–1957 (76 years)
Overall Record: 6088 wins, 4933 losses (.552)
Stadiums: Polo Grounds I, 1876, 1883–88; Oakland Park, 1889; St. George Cricket Grounds, 1889; Polo Grounds III, 1889–90; Harrison Field, 1890–99 and 1918 (Sundays only); Polo Grounds IV, 1891–1911; Hilltop Park, 1911; Polo Grounds V, 1911–57 (capacity: 55,137)
Other Names: Maroons, Gothams

Year-by-Year Finishes

Year	Finish	Wins	Losses	Percentage	Games Behind	Manager	Attendance
1876	6th	21	35	.375	26.0	Bill Cammeyer	not available
1883	6th	46	50	.479	16.0	John Clapp	not available
1884	4th (Tie)	62	50	.544	22.0	James Price, Monte Ward	not available
1885	2nd	85	27	.758	2.0	Jim Mutrie	not available
1886	3rd	75	44	.630	12.5	Jim Mutrie	not available
1887	4th	68	55	.553	10.5	Jim Mutrie	not available
1888	1st	84	47	.641	+9.0	Jim Mutrie	not available
1889	1st	83	43	.659	+1.0	Jim Mutrie	not available
1890	6th	63	68	.481	24.0	Jim Mutrie	not available
1891	3rd	71	61	.538	13.0	Jim Mutrie	not available
1892	8th	71	80	.470	31.5	Pat Powers	not available
1893	5th	68	64	.515	19.0	Monte Ward	not available
1894	2nd	88	44	.667	3.0	Monte Ward	not available
1895	9th	66	65	.504	21.5	George Davis, Jack Doyle, Harvey Watkins	not available
1896	7th	64	67	.489	37.0	Arthur Irwin, Bill Joyce	not available
1897	3rd	83	48	.634	9.5	Bill Joyce	not available
1898	7th	77	73	.513	25.5	Bill Joyce, Cap Anson	not available
1899	10th	60	86	.411	26.0	John Day, Fred Hoey	not available
1900	8th	60	78	.435	23.0	Buck Ewing, George Davis	not available
1901	7th	52	85	.380	37.0	George Davis	297,650
1902	8th	48	88	.353	53.5	Horace Fogel, Heinie Smith, John McGraw	302,875
1903	2nd	84	55	.604	6.5	John McGraw	579,530
1904	1st	106	47	.693	+13.0	John McGraw	609,826
1905	1st	105	48	.686	+9.0	John McGraw	552,700
1906	2nd	96	56	.632	20.0	John McGraw	402,850
1907	4th	82	71	.536	25.5	John McGraw	538,350
1908	2nd (Tie)	98	56	.636	1.0	John McGraw	910,000
1909	3rd	92	61	.601	18.5	John McGraw	783,700
1910	2nd	91	63	.591	13.0	John McGraw	511,785
1911	1st	99	54	.647	+7.5	John McGraw	675,000
1912	1st	103	48	.682	+10.0	John McGraw	638,000
1913	1st	101	51	.664	+12.5	John McGraw	630,000
1914	2nd	84	70	.545	10.5	John McGraw	364,313
1915	8th	69	83	.454	21.0	John McGraw	391,850
1916	4th	86	66	.566	7.0	John McGraw	552,056
1917	1st	98	56	.636	+10.0	John McGraw	500,264
1918	2nd	71	53	.573	10.5	John McGraw	256,618

1919	2nd	87	53	.621	9.0	John McGraw	708,857
1920	2nd	86	68	.558	7.0	John McGraw	929,609
1921	1st	94	59	.614	+4.0	John McGraw	773,477
1922	1st	93	61	.604	+7.0	John McGraw	945,809
1923	1st	95	58	.621	+4.5	John McGraw	820,780
1924	1st	93	60	.608	+1.5	John McGraw	844,068
1925	2nd	86	66	.566	8.5	John McGraw	778,993
1926	5th	74	77	.490	13.5	John McGraw	700,362
1927	3rd	92	62	.597	2.0	John McGraw	858,190
1928	2nd	93	61	.604	2.0	John McGraw	916,191
1929	3rd	84	67	.556	13.5	John McGraw	868,806
1930	3rd	87	67	.565	5.0	John McGraw	868,714
1931	2nd	87	65	.572	13.0	John McGraw	812,163
1932	6th (Tie)	72	82	.468	18.0	John McGraw, Bill Terry	484,868
1933	1st	91	61	.599	+5.0	Bill Terry	604,471
1934	2nd	93	60	.608	2.0	Bill Terry	730,851
1935	3rd	91	62	.595	8.5	Bill Terry	748,748
1936	1st	92	62	.597	+5.0	Bill Terry	837,952
1937	1st	95	57	.625	+3.0	Bill Terry	926,887
1938	3rd	83	67	.553	5.0	Bill Terry	799,633
1939	5th	77	74	.510	18.5	Bill Terry	702,457
1940	6th (Tie)	72	80	.474	27.5	Bill Terry	747,852
1941	5th	74	79	.484	25.5	Bill Terry	763,098
1942	3rd	85	67	.559	20.0	Mel Ott	779,621
1943	8th	55	98	.359	49.5	Mel Ott	466,095
1944	5th	67	87	.435	38.0	Mel Ott	674,083
1945	5th	78	74	.513	19.0	Mel Ott	1,016,468
1946	8th	61	93	.396	36.0	Mel Ott	1,219,873
1947	4th	81	73	.526	13.0	Mel Ott	1,600,793
1948	5th	78	76	.506	13.5	Mel Ott, Leo Durocher	1,459,269
1949	5th	73	81	.474	24.0	Leo Durocher	1,218,446
1950	3rd	86	68	.558	5.0	Leo Durocher	1,008,876
1951	1st	98	59	.624	+1.0	Leo Durocher	1,059,539
1952	2nd	92	62	.597	4.5	Leo Durocher	984,940
1953	5th	70	84	.455	35.0	Leo Durocher	811,518
1954	1st	97	57	.630	+5.0	Leo Durocher	1,155,067
1955	3rd	80	74	.519	18.5	Leo Durocher	824,112
1956	6th	67	87	.435	26.0	Bill Rigney	629,179
1957	6th	69	85	.448	26.0	Bill Rigney	653,923

Awards

Most Valuable Player
Larry Doyle, second base, 1912
Carl Hubbell, pitcher, 1933
Carl Hubbell, pitcher, 1936
Willie Mays, outfield, 1954

Rookie of the Year
Willie Mays, outfield, 1951

Cy Young
[No pitcher]

**Hall of Famers Who Played for the
New York Giants**
Dave Bancroft, shortstop, 1920–23 and
1930
Jake Beckley, first base, 1896–97
Roger Bresnahan, catcher, 1902–08
Dan Brouthers, first base, 1904

Jesse Burkett, outfield, 1890
Roger Connor, first base, 1883–89,
1891, and 1893–94
George Davis, outfield and infield,
1893–1901 and 1903
Buck Ewing, catcher and infield,
1883–89 and 1891–92
Frankie Frisch, second base, 1919–26
Burleigh Grimes, pitcher, 1927
Gabby Hartnett, catcher, 1941

Waite Hoyt, pitcher, 1918 and 1932
Monte Irvin, outfield, 1949–55
Travis Jackson, shortstop, 1922–36
Tim Keefe, pitcher, 1885–91
Willie Keeler, outfield, 1892–93 and
    1910
George Kelly, first base, 1915–17 and
    1919–26
King Kelly, catcher and infield, 1893
Tony Lazzeri, second base, 1939
Fred Lindstrom, third base, 1924–32
Ernie Lombardi, catcher, 1943–47
Rube Marquard, pitcher, 1908–15
Christy Mathewson, pitcher, 1900–16
Willie Mays, outfield, 1951–52 and
    1954–57
Joe McGinnity, pitcher, 1902–08
John McGraw, infield, 1902–06
Bill McKechnie, third base, 1916
Joe Medwick, outfield, 1943–45
Johnny Mize, first base, 1942 and
    1948–49
Orator Jim O'Rourke, catcher, outfield,
    and infield, 1885–89, 1904
Mel Ott, outfield, 1926–47
Edd Roush, outfield, 1916 and 1927–29
Amos Rusie, pitcher, 1890–95 and
    1897–98
Ray Schalk, catcher, 1929
Red Schoendienst, second base, 1956–57
Billy Southworth, outfield, 1924–26
Casey Stengel, outfield, 1921–23
Bill Terry, first base, 1923–36
Monte Ward, infield and pitcher,
    1883–89
Mickey Welch, pitcher, 1883–92
Hoyt Wilhelm, pitcher, 1952–56
Hack Wilson, outfield, 1923–25
Ross Youngs, outfield, 1917–26

Retired Numbers
[None]

League Leaders, Batting
(Post-1900)

Batting Average, Season
Larry Doyle, 1915 .... .320
Bill Terry, 1930 .... .401
Willie Mays, 1954 .... .345

Home Runs, Season
Red Murray, 1909 7
Dave Robertson, 1916 ....12 (Tie)
Dave Robertson, 1917 ....12 (Tie)
George Kelly, 1921 23
Mel Ott, 1932 ....38 (Tie)
Mel Ott, 1934 ....35 (Tie)
Mel Ott, 1936 33
Mel Ott, 1937 ....31 (Tie)
Mel Ott, 1938 ....36 (Tie)
Mel Ott, 1942 30
Johnny Mize, 1947 ....51 (Tie)
Johnny Mize, 1948 ....40 (Tie)
Willie Mays, 1955 51

RBIs, Season
Heinie Zimmerman*, 1916 83
Heinie Zimmerman, 1917 102
George Kelly, 1920 ....94 (Tie)
Irish Meusel, 1923 125
George Kelly, 1924 136
Mel Ott, 1934 135
Johnny Mize, 1942 110
Johnny Mize, 1947 138
Monte Irvin, 1951 121
*Played part of season with Chi. Cubs.

Stolen Bases, Season
Art Devlin, 1905 ....59 (Tie)
George J. Burns, 1914....................62
George J. Burns, 1919....................40
Frankie Frisch, 1921 49
Willie Mays, 1956..........................40
Willie Mays, 1957..........................38

Total Bases, Season
Frankie Frisch, 1923.....................311
Willie Mays, 1955........................382

Most Hits, Season
Larry Doyle, 1909 172
Larry Doyle, 1915 189
Frankie Frisch, 1923 223
Fred Lindstrom, 1928 231
Bill Terry, 1930...........................254
Don Mueller, 1954 212

Most Runs, Season
George Browne, 1904 99
Mike Donlin, 1905........................124
Spike Shannon, 1907 104
Fred Tenney, 1908 101

George J. Burns, 1914..................100
George J. Burns, 1916..................105
George J. Burns, 1917..................103
George J. Burns, 1919....................86
George J. Burns, 1920..................115
Ross Youngs, 1923 121
Frankie Frisch, 1924..............121 (Tie)
Rogers Hornsby, 1927 ....133 (Tie)
Bill Terry, 1931 ....121 (Tie)
Mel Ott, 1938 116
Mel Ott, 1942 118
Johnny Mize, 1947.......................137

Batting Feats

Triple Crown Winners
[No player]

Hitting for the Cycle
Dave Orr, June 12, 1885
Dave Orr, Aug. 10, 1887
Mike Tiernan, Aug. 25, 1888
Mike Tiernan, Aug. 28, 1890
Sam Mertes, Oct. 4, 1904
Chief Meyers, June 10, 1912
George J. Burns, Sept. 17, 1920
Dave Bancroft, June 1, 1921
Ross Youngs, Apr. 29, 1922
Bill Terry, May 29, 1928
Mel Ott, May 16, 1929
Fred Lindstrom, May 8, 1930
Sam Leslie, May 24, 1936
Harry Danning, June 15, 1940
Don Mueller, July 11, 1954

Six Hits in a Game
Kip Selbach, June 9, 1901
Dave Bancroft, June 28, 1920
Frankie Frisch, Sept. 10, 1924

40 or More Home Runs, Season
51..........................Johnny Mize, 1947
                          Willie Mays, 1955
42................................Mel Ott, 1929
41..........................Willie Mays, 1954
40..........................Johnny Mize, 1948

League Leaders, Pitching
(Post-1900)

Most Wins, Season
Joe McGinnity, 1900 29
Joe McGinnity, 1903 31

Joe McGinnity, 1904 35
Christy Mathewson, 1905................31
Joe McGinnity, 1906 27
Christy Mathewson, 1907................24
Christy Mathewson, 1908................37
Christy Mathewson, 1910................27
Rube Marquard, 1912 ....26 (Tie)
Jesse Barnes, 1919 25
Larry Benton, 1928..................25 (Tie)
Carl Hubbell, 1933.........................23
Carl Hubbell, 1936.........................26
Carl Hubbell, 1937.........................22
Larry Jansen, 1951 ....23 (Tie)
Sal Maglie, 1951 ....23 (Tie)

Most Strikeouts, Season

Christy Mathewson, 1903..............267
Christy Mathewson, 1904..............212
Christy Mathewson, 1905..............206
Christy Mathewson, 1907..............178
Christy Mathewson, 1908..............259
Christy Mathewson, 1910..............190
Rube Marquard, 1911 237
Carl Hubbell, 1937.......................159
Bill Voiselle, 1944..........................161

Lowest ERA, Season

Jeff Tesreau, 1912 ....1.96
Christy Mathewson, 1913..............2.06
Rosy Ryan, 1922 ....3.00
Bill Walker, 1929 ....3.08
Bill Walker, 1931 ....2.26
Carl Hubbell, 1933.......................1.66
Carl Hubbell, 1934.......................2.30
Carl Hubbell, 1936.......................2.31
Dave Koslo, 1949.........................2.50
Jim Hearn*, 1950.........................2.49
Hoyt Wilhelm, 1952 ....2.43
Johnny Antonelli, 1954 ....2.29
*Pitched part of season with St. L. Cardinals.

Most Saves, Season
[No pitcher]

Best Won–Lost Percentage, Season

Joe McGinnity, 1904......35–8 .... .814
Christy Mathewson, 1909
.................................25–6 .... .806
....(Tie)
Rube Marquard, 1911....24–7 .... .774
Ferdie Schupp, 1917......21–7 .... .750
Larry Benton*, 1927 ......17–7 .... .708

Larry Benton, 1928........25–9 .... .735
Freddie Fitzsimmons, 1930
................................19–7 .... .731
Carl Hubbell, 1936........26–6 .... .813
Carl Hubbell, 1937........22–8 .... .733
Larry Jansen, 1947 ....21–5 .... .808
Sal Maglie, 1950...........18–4 .... .818
Hoyt Wilhelm, 1952.......15–3 .... .833
Johnny Antonelli, 1954 ..21–7 .... .750
*Played part of season with Boston.

Pitching Feats

20 Wins, Season (1900–57)

Christy Mathewson, 1901 20–17
Joe McGinnity, 1902.................21–18*
Joe McGinnity, 1903 31–20
Christy Mathewson, 1903 30–13
Joe McGinnity, 1904 35–8
Christy Mathewson, 1904 33–12
Dummy Taylor, 1904 21–15
Christy Mathewson, 1905 31–9
Red Ames, 1905 22–8
Joe McGinnity, 1905 21–15
Joe McGinnity, 1906 27–12
Christy Mathewson, 1906 22–12
Christy Mathewson, 1907 24–12
Christy Mathewson, 1908 37–11
Hooks Wiltse, 1908 23–14
Christy Mathewson, 1909 25–6
Hooks Wiltse, 1909 20–11
Christy Mathewson, 1910 27–9
Christy Mathewson, 1911 26–13
Rube Marquard, 1911.................24–7
Rube Marquard, 1912...............26–11
Christy Mathewson, 1912 23–12
Christy Mathewson, 1913 25–11
Rube Marquard, 1913...............23–10
Jeff Tesreau, 1913.....................22–13
Jeff Tesreau, 1914.....................26–10
Christy Mathewson, 1914 24–13
Ferdie Schupp, 1917...................21–7
Jesse Barnes, 1919 25–9
Fred Toney, 1920.......................21–11
Art Nehf, 1920..........................21–12
Jesse Barnes, 1920 20–15
Art Nehf, 1921 20–10
Larry Benton, 1928.....................25–9
Freddie Fitzsimmons, 1928 20–9
Carl Hubbell, 1933....................23–12
Hal Schumacher, 1934 23–10
Carl Hubbell, 1934 21–12
Carl Hubbell, 1935 23–12

Carl Hubbell, 1936....................26–6
Carl Hubbell, 1937....................22–8
Cliff Melton, 1937 20–9
Bill Voiselle, 1944.......................21 16
Larry Jansen, 1947 21–5
Sal Maglie, 1951.......................23–6
Larry Jansen, 1951 23–11
Johnny Antonelli, 1954 21–7
Johnny Antonelli, 1956.............20–13
*13–10 with Balt. Orioles (AL) and 8–8 with N.Y. Giants.

No-Hitters

Christy Mathewson (vs. St. L. Cardinals), July 15, 1901 (final: 4–0)
Christy Mathewson (vs. Chi. Cubs), June 13, 1905 (final: 1–0)
Hooks Wiltse (vs. Phila. Phillies), Sept. 5, 1908 (final: 1–0) (10 innings)
Red Ames (vs. Bklyn. Dodgers), Apr. 15, 1909 (final: 0–3) (allowed hit in 10th and lost in 13th)
Jeff Tesreau (vs. Phila. Phillies), Sept. 6, 1912 (final: 3–0)
Rube Marquard (vs. Bklyn. Dodgers), Apr. 15, 1915 (final: 2–0)
Jesse Barnes (vs. Phila. Phillies), May 7, 1922 (final: 6–0)
Carl Hubbell (vs. Pitt. Pirates), May 8, 1929 (final: 11–0)

No-Hitters Pitched Against

Bob Wicker, Chi. Cubs, June 11, 1904 (final: 1–0) (allowed hit in 10th and won in 12th)
Jimmy Lavender, Chi. Cubs, Aug. 31, 1915 (final: 2–0)
Rex Barney, Bklyn. Dodgers, Sept. 9, 1948 (final: 2–0)
Carl Erskine, Bklyn. Dodgers, May 12, 1956 (final: 3–0)

Postseason Play

1905   World Series vs. Phila. A's (AL), won 4 games to 1
1908   Pennant Playoff Game vs. Chi. Cubs (NL), lost
1911   World Series vs. Phila. A's (AL), lost 4 games to 2
1912   World Series vs. Bost. Red Sox (AL), lost 4 games to 3

1913 World Series vs. Phila. A's (AL),
lost 4 games to 1

1917 World Series vs. Chi. White Sox
(AL), lost 4 games to 2

1921 World Series vs. N.Y. Yankees
(AL), won 5 games to 3

1922 World Series vs. N.Y. Yankees
(AL), won 4 games to 0 to 1

1923 World Series vs. N.Y. Yankees (AL),
lost 4 games to 2

1924 World Series vs. Wash. Senators
(AL), lost 4 games to 3

1933 World Series vs. Wash. Senators
(AL), won 4 games to 1

1936 World Series vs. N.Y. Yankees (AL),
lost 4 games to 2

1937 World Series vs. N.Y. Yankees (AL),
lost 4 games to 1

1951 Pennant Playoff Series vs. Bklyn.
Dodgers (NL), won 2 games
to 1

World Series vs. N.Y. Yankees (AL),
lost 4 games to 2

1954 World Series vs. Cleve. Indians
(AL), won 4 games to 0

Philadelphia Athletics

Dates of Operation: 1901–54 (54 years)
Overall Record: 3886 wins, 4248 losses (.478)
Stadiums: Columbia Park, 1901–08; Shibe Park (also known as Connie Mack Stadium), 1909–54
(capacity: 33,000)
Other Name: A's

Year-by-Year Finishes

Year	Finish	Wins	Losses	Percentage	Games Behind	Manager	Attendance
1901	4th	74	62	.544	9.0	Connie Mack	206,329
1902	1st	83	53	.610	+5.0	Connie Mack	442,473
1903	2nd	75	60	.556	14.5	Connie Mack	420,078
1904	5th	81	70	.536	12.5	Connie Mack	512,294
1905	1st	92	56	.622	+2.0	Connie Mack	554,576
1906	4th	78	67	.538	12.0	Connie Mack	489,129
1907	2nd	88	57	.607	1.5	Connie Mack	625,581
1908	6th	68	85	.444	22.0	Connie Mack	455,062
1909	2nd	95	58	.621	3.5	Connie Mack	674,915
1910	1st	102	48	.680	+14.5	Connie Mack	588,905
1911	1st	101	50	.669	+13.5	Connie Mack	605,749
1912	3rd	90	62	.592	15.0	Connie Mack	517,653
1913	1st	96	57	.627	+6.5	Connie Mack	571,896
1914	1st	99	53	.651	+8.5	Connie Mack	346,641
1915	8th	43	109	.283	58.5	Connie Mack	146,223
1916	8th	36	117	.235	54.5	Connie Mack	184,471
1917	8th	55	98	.359	44.5	Connie Mack	221,432
1918	8th	52	76	.406	24.0	Connie Mack	177,926
1919	8th	36	104	.257	52.0	Connie Mack	225,209
1920	8th	48	106	.312	50.0	Connie Mack	287,888
1921	8th	53	100	.346	45.0	Connie Mack	344,430
1922	7th	65	89	.422	29.0	Connie Mack	425,356
1923	6th	69	83	.454	29.0	Connie Mack	534,122
1924	5th	71	81	.467	20.0	Connie Mack	531,992
1925	2nd	88	64	.579	8.5	Connie Mack	869,703
1926	3rd	83	67	.553	6.0	Connie Mack	714,308
1927	2nd	91	63	.591	19.0	Connie Mack	605,529
1928	2nd	98	55	.641	2.5	Connie Mack	689,756
1929	1st	104	46	.693	+18.0	Connie Mack	839,176
1930	1st	102	52	.662	+8.0	Connie Mack	721,663
1931	1st	107	45	.704	+13.5	Connie Mack	627,464
1932	2nd	94	60	.610	13.0	Connie Mack	405,500
1933	3rd	79	72	.523	19.5	Connie Mack	297,138
1934	5th	68	82	.453	31.0	Connie Mack	305,847
1935	8th	58	91	.389	34.0	Connie Mack	233,173
1936	8th	53	100	.346	49.0	Connie Mack	285,173
1937	7th	54	97	.358	46.5	Connie Mack	430,733
1938	8th	53	99	.349	46.0	Connie Mack	385,357
1939	7th	55	97	.362	51.5	Connie Mack	395,022
1940	8th	54	100	.351	36.0	Connie Mack	432,145

1941	8th	64	90	.416	37.0	Connie Mack	528,894
1942	8th	55	99	.357	48.0	Connie Mack	423,487
1943	8th	49	105	.318	49.0	Connie Mack	376,735
1944	5th (Tie)	72	82	.468	17.0	Connie Mack	505,322
1945	8th	52	98	.347	34.5	Connie Mack	462,631
1946	8th	49	105	.318	55.0	Connie Mack	621,793
1947	5th	78	76	.506	19.0	Connie Mack	911,566
1948	4th	84	70	.545	12.5	Connie Mack	945,076
1949	5th	81	73	.526	16.0	Connie Mack	816,514
1950	8th	52	102	.338	46.0	Connie Mack	309,805
1951	6th	70	84	.455	28.0	Jimmy Dykes	465,469
1952	4th	79	75	.513	16.0	Jimmy Dykes	627,100
1953	7th	59	95	.383	41.5	Jimmy Dykes	362,113
1954	8th	51	103	.331	60.0	Eddie Joost	304,666

Awards

Most Valuable Player
Eddie Collins, second base, 1914
Mickey Cochrane, catcher, 1928
Lefty Grove, pitcher, 1931
Jimmie Foxx, first base, 1932
Jimmie Foxx, first base, 1933
Bobby Shantz, pitcher, 1952

Rookie of the Year
Harry Byrd, pitcher, 1952

Cy Young
[No pitcher]

Hall of Famers Who Played for the Philadelphia A's
Home Run Baker, third base, 1908–14
Chief Bender, pitcher, 1903–14
Ty Cobb, outfield, 1927–28
Mickey Cochrane, catcher, 1925–33
Eddie Collins, second base, 1906–14 and 1927–30
Jimmy Collins, third base, 1907–08
Stan Coveleski, pitcher, 1912
Jimmie Foxx, catcher, third base, and first base, 1925–35
Waite Hoyt, pitcher, 1931
George Kell, third base, 1943–46
Nap Lajoie, second base, 1901–02, 1915–16
Herb Pennock, pitcher, 1912–15
Eddie Plank, pitcher, 1901–14
Al Simmons, outfield, 1924–32, 1940–41, and 1944

Tris Speaker, outfield, 1928
Rube Waddell, pitcher, 1902–07
Zack Wheat, outfield, 1927

Retired Numbers
[None]

League Leaders, Batting

Batting Average, Season
Nap Lajoie, 1901 .... .426
Al Simmons, 1930 .... .381
Al Simmons, 1931 .... .390
Jimmie Foxx, 1933 .... .356
Ferris Fain, 1951 .... .344
Ferris Fain, 1952 .... .327

Home Runs, Season
Nap Lajoie, 1901 14
Socks Seybold, 1902 16
Harry Davis, 1904 10
Harry Davis, 1905 8
Harry Davis, 1906 12
Harry Davis, 1907 8
Home Run Baker, 1911 11
Home Run Baker, 1912 .... 10 (Tie)
Home Run Baker, 1913 12
Home Run Baker, 1914 9
Tilly Walker, 1918 .... 11 (Tie)
Jimmie Foxx, 1932 58
Jimmie Foxx, 1933 48
Jimmie Foxx, 1935 .... 36 (Tie)
Gus Zernial*, 1951 33
*Played part of season with Chi. White Sox.

RBIs, Season
Home Run Baker, 1912 133
Home Run Baker, 1913 126
George H. Burns, 1918 .... 74 (Tie)
Al Simmons, 1929 157
Jimmie Foxx, 1932 169
Jimmie Foxx, 1933 163
Gus Zernial*, 1951 129
*Played part of season with Chi. White Sox.

Stolen Bases, Season
Topsy Hartsel, 1902 54
Danny Hoffman, 1905 46
Eddie Collins, 1910 81
Billy Werber, 1937 .... 35 (Tie)

Total Bases, Season
Nap Lajoie, 1901 345
George H. Burns, 1918 236
Al Simmons, 1925 392
Al Simmons, 1929 373
Jimmie Foxx, 1932 438
Jimmie Foxx, 1933 403

Most Hits, Season
Nap Lajoie, 1901 229
George H. Burns, 1918 178
Al Simmons, 1925 253
Al Simmons, 1932 216

Most Runs, Season
Nap Lajoie, 1901 145
Dave Fultz, 1902 110
Harry Davis, 1905 92
Eddie Collins, 1912 137

Eddie Collins, 1913 125
Eddie Collins, 1914 122
Al Simmons, 1930 152
Jimmie Foxx, 1932 151

Batting Feats

Triple Crown Winners

Nap Lajoie, 1901 (.426 BA, 14 HRs,
125 RBIs)

Hitting for the Cycle

Harry Davis, July 10, 1901
Nap Lajoie, July 30, 1901
Danny Murphy, Aug. 25, 1910
Home Run Baker, July 3, 1911
Mickey Cochrane, July 22, 1932
Mickey Cochrane, Aug. 2, 1933
Pinky Higgins, Aug. 6, 1933
Jimmie Foxx, Aug. 14, 1933
Doc Cramer, June 10, 1934
Sam Chapman, May 5, 1939
Elmer Valo, Aug. 2, 1950

Six Hits in a Game

Danny Murphy, July 8, 1902
Jimmie Foxx, May 30, 1930*
Doc Cramer, June 20, 1932
Jimmie Foxx, July 10, 1932*
Bob Johnson, June 16, 1934*
Doc Cramer, July 13, 1935
*Extra-inning game.

40 or More Home Runs, Season

58 ....Jimmie Foxx, 1932
48 ....Jimmie Foxx, 1933
44 ....Jimmie Foxx, 1934
42 ....Gus Zernial, 1953

League Leaders, Pitching

Most Wins, Season

Rube Waddell, 1905........................27
Jack Coombs, 1910 31
Jack Coombs, 1911 28
Ed Rommel, 1922...........................27
Ed Rommel, 1925....................21 (Tie)
Lefty Grove, 1928 ....24 (Tie)
George Earnshaw, 1929 24
Lefty Grove, 1930 28
Lefty Grove, 1931 31
Lefty Grove, 1933 ....24 (Tie)
Bobby Shantz, 1952 24

Most Strikeouts, Season

Rube Waddell, 1902.....................210
Rube Waddell, 1903.....................301
Rube Waddell, 1904.....................349
Rube Waddell, 1905.....................286
Rube Waddell, 1906.....................203
Rube Waddell, 1907.....................226
Lefty Grove, 1925 116
Lefty Grove, 1926 194
Lefty Grove, 1927 174
Lefty Grove, 1928 183
Lefty Grove, 1929 170
Lefty Grove, 1930 209
Lefty Grove, 1931 175

Lowest ERA, Season

Lefty Grove, 1926 ....2.51
Lefty Grove, 1929 ....2.81
Lefty Grove, 1930 ....2.54
Lefty Grove, 1931 ....2.06
Lefty Grove, 1932 ....2.84

Most Saves, Season

[No pitcher]

Best Won–Lost Percentage, Season

Eddie Plank, 1906 ....19–8 .... .760
Chief Bender, 1910........23–5 .... .821
Chief Bender, 1911........17–9 .... .773
Chief Bender, 1914........17–3 .... .850
Lefty Grove, 1929...........20–6 .... .769
Lefty Grove, 1930...........28–5 .... .848
Lefty Grove, 1931...........31–4 .... .886
Lefty Grove, 1933...........24–8 .... .750
Bobby Shantz, 1952 ......24–7 .... .774

Pitching Feats

20 Wins, Season

Chick Fraser, 1901 22–16
Rube Waddell, 1902 23–7
Eddie Plank, 1902 20–15
Eddie Plank, 1903 23–16
Rube Waddell, 1903 21–16
Eddie Plank, 1904 26–17
Rube Waddell, 1904 25–19
Rube Waddell, 1905 26–11
Eddie Plank, 1905 25–12
Eddie Plank, 1907 24–16
Jimmy Dygert, 1907....................20–9
Jack Coombs, 1910 31–9
Chief Bender, 1910......................23–5
Jack Coombs, 1911 28–12

Eddie Plank, 1911 22–8
Eddie Plank, 1912 26–6
Jack Coombs, 1912 21–10
Chief Bender, 1913......................21–10
Scott Perry, 1918 21–19
Eddie Rommel, 1922 27–13
Eddie Rommel, 1925 21–10
Lefty Grove, 1927 20–13
Lefty Grove, 1928.......................24–8
George Earnshaw, 1929.............24–8
Lefty Grove, 1929 20–6
Lefty Grove, 1930.......................28–5
George Earnshaw, 1930.............22–13
Lefty Grove, 1931.......................31–4
George Earnshaw, 1931.............21–7
Rube Walberg, 1931.................20–12
Lefty Grove, 1932.....................25–10
Lefty Grove, 1933.......................24–8
Alex Kellner, 1949 20–12
Bobby Shantz, 1952 24–7

No-Hitters

Weldon Henley (vs. St. L. Browns),
July 22, 1905 (final: 6–0)
Chief Bender (vs. Cleve. Indians), May
12, 1910 (final: 4–0)
Joe Bush (vs. Cleve. Indians), Aug. 26,
1916 (final: 5–0)
Dick Fowler (vs. St. L. Browns), Sept. 9,
1945 (final: 1–0)
Bill McCahan (vs. Wash. Senators),
Sept. 3, 1947 (final: 3–0)

No-Hitters Pitched Against

Cy Young, Bost. Red Sox, May 5, 1904
(final: 3–0) (perfect game)
Frank Smith, Chi. White Sox, Sept. 20,
1908 (final: 1–0)
Sam Jones, N.Y. Yankees, Sept. 4,
1923 (final: 4–0)
Howard Ehmke, Bost. Red Sox, Sept. 7,
1923 (final: 4–0)
Don Black, Cleve. Indians, July 10,
1947 (final: 3–0)
Bobo Holloman, St. L. Browns, May 6,
1953 (final: 6–0)

Postseason Play

1905 World Series vs. N.Y. Giants (NL),
       lost 4 games to 1
1910 World Series vs. Chi. Cubs (NL),
       won 4 games to 1

1911 World Series vs. N.Y. Giants (NL), won 4 games to 2

1913 World Series vs. N.Y. Giants (NL), won 4 games to 1

1914 World Series vs. Bost. Braves (NL), lost 4 games to 0

1929 World Series vs. Chi. Cubs (NL), won 4 games to 1

1930 World Series vs. St. L. Cardinals (NL), won 4 games to 3

1931 World Series vs. St. L. Cardinals (NL), lost 4 games to 2

St. Louis Browns

Date of Operation: (as the Milwaukee Brewers) 1901 (1 year)
Overall Record: 48 wins, 89 losses (.350)
Stadium: Lloyd Street Park, 1901

Dates of Operation: (as the St. Louis Browns) 1902–53 (52 years)
Overall Record: 3414 wins, 4465 losses (.433)
Stadiums: Sportsman's Park IV, 1902–08; Sportsman's Park V, 1909–53 (capacity: 30,500)

Year-by-Year Finishes

Year	Finish	Wins	Losses	Percentage	Games Behind	Manager	Attendance
					Milw. Brewers		
1901	8th	48	89	.350	35.5	Hugh Duffy	139,034
					St. L. Browns		
1902	2nd	78	58	.574	5.0	Jimmy McAleer	272,283
1903	6th	65	74	.468	26.5	Jimmy McAleer	380,405
1904	6th	65	87	.428	29.0	Jimmy McAleer	318,108
1905	8th	54	99	.353	40.5	Jimmy McAleer	339,112
1906	5th	76	73	.510	16.0	Jimmy McAleer	389,157
1907	6th	69	83	.454	24.0	Jimmy McAleer	419,025
1908	4th	83	69	.546	6.5	Jimmy McAleer	618,947
1909	7th	61	89	.407	36.0	Jimmy McAleer	366,274
1910	8th	47	107	.305	57.0	Jack O'Connor	249,889
1911	8th	45	107	.296	56.5	Bobby Wallace	207,984
1912	7th	53	101	.344	53.0	Bobby Wallace, George Stovall	214,070
1913	8th	57	96	.373	39.0	George Stovall, Branch Rickey	250,330
1914	5th	71	82	.464	28.5	Branch Rickey	244,714
1915	6th	63	91	.409	39.5	Branch Rickey	150,358
1916	5th	79	75	.513	12.0	Fielder Jones	335,740
1917	7th	57	97	.370	43.0	Fielder Jones	210,486
1918	5th	58	64	.475	15.0	Fielder Jones, Jimmy Austin, Jimmy Burke	122,076
1919	5th	67	72	.482	20.5	Jimmy Burke	349,350
1920	4th	76	77	.497	21.5	Jimmy Burke	419,311
1921	3rd	81	73	.526	17.5	Lee Fohl	355,978
1922	2nd	93	61	.604	1.0	Lee Fohl	712,918
1923	5th	74	78	.487	24.0	Lee Fohl, Jimmy Austin	430,296
1924	4th	74	78	.487	17.0	George Sisler	533,349
1925	3rd	82	71	.536	15.0	George Sisler	462,898
1926	7th	62	92	.403	29.0	George Sisler	283,986
1927	7th	59	94	.386	50.5	Dan Howley	247,879
1928	3rd	82	72	.532	19.0	Dan Howley	339,497
1929	4th	79	73	.520	26.0	Dan Howley	280,697
1930	6th	64	90	.416	38.0	Bill Killefer	152,088
1931	5th	63	91	.409	45.0	Bill Killefer	179,126
1932	6th	63	91	.409	44.0	Bill Killefer	112,558
1933	8th	55	96	.364	43.5	Bill Killefer, Allen Sothoron, Rogers Hornsby	88,113

1934	6th	67	85	.441	33.0	Rogers Hornsby	115,305
1935	7th	65	87	.428	28.5	Rogers Hornsby	80,922
1936	7th	57	95	.375	44.5	Rogers Hornsby	93,267
1937	8th	46	108	.299	56.0	Rogers Hornsby, Jim Bottomley	123,121
1938	7th	55	97	.362	44.0	Gabby Street	130,417
1939	8th	43	111	.279	64.5	Fred Haney	109,159
1940	6th	67	87	.435	23.0	Fred Haney	239,591
1941	6th (Tie)	70	84	.455	31.0	Fred Haney, Luke Sewell	176,240
1942	3rd	82	69	.543	19.5	Luke Sewell	255,617
1943	6th	72	80	.474	25.0	Luke Sewell	214,392
1944	1st	89	65	.578	+1.0	Luke Sewell	508,644
1945	3rd	81	70	.536	6.0	Luke Sewell	482,986
1946	7th	66	88	.429	38.0	Luke Sewell, Zack Taylor	526,435
1947	8th	59	95	.383	38.0	Muddy Ruel	320,474
1948	6th	59	94	.386	37.0	Zack Taylor	335,546
1949	7th	53	101	.344	44.0	Zack Taylor	270,936
1950	7th	58	96	.377	40.0	Zack Taylor	247,131
1951	8th	52	102	.338	46.0	Zack Taylor	293,790
1952	7th	64	90	.416	31.0	Rogers Hornsby, Marty Marion	518,796
1953	8th	54	100	.351	46.5	Marty Marion	297,238

Awards

Most Valuable Player
George Sisler, first base, 1922

Rookie of the Year
Roy Sievers, outfield, 1949

Cy Young
[No pitcher]

Hall of Famers Who Played for the St. Louis Browns
Jim Bottomley, first base, 1936–37
Jesse Burkett, outfield, 1902–04
Rick Ferrell, catcher, 1929–33 and
    1941–43
Goose Goslin, outfield, 1930–32
Heinie Manush, outfield, 1928–30
Satchel Paige, pitcher, 1951–53
Eddie Plank, pitcher, 1916–17
Branch Rickey, catcher, 1905–06 and
    1914
George Sisler, first base, 1915–22 and
    1924–27
Rube Waddell, pitcher, 1908–10
Bobby Wallace, shortstop, 1902–16

Retired Numbers
[None]

League Leaders, Batting

Batting Average, Season
George Stone, 1906 .... .358
George Sisler, 1920 .... .407
George Sisler, 1922 .... .420

Home Runs, Season
Ken Williams, 1922 39
Vern Stephens, 1945 24

RBIs, Season
Ken Williams, 1922 155
Vern Stephens, 1944 109

Stolen Bases, Season
George Sisler, 1918 45
George Sisler, 1921 35
George Sisler, 1922 51
George Sisler, 1927 27
Lyn Lary, 1936 37
Bob Dillinger, 1947 34
Bob Dillinger, 1948 28
Bob Dillinger, 1949 20

Total Bases, Season
George Stone, 1905 260
George Stone, 1906 288
George Stone, 1920 399
Ken Williams, 1922 367

Most Hits, Season
George Stone, 1905 187
George Sisler, 1920 257
George Sisler, 1922 246
Heinie Manush, 1928 241
Beau Bell, 1937 218
Rip Radcliff, 1940 .... 200 (Tie)
Bob Dillinger, 1948 207

Most Runs, Season
George Sisler, 1922 134

Batting Feats

Triple Crown Winners
[No player]

Hitting for the Cycle
George Sisler, Aug. 8, 1920
George Sisler, Aug. 13, 1921
Baby Doll Jacobson, Apr. 17, 1924
Oscar Melillo, May 23, 1929
George McQuinn, July 19, 1941

Six Hits in a Game
George Sisler, Aug. 9, 1921*
Sammy West, Apr. 13, 1933*
*Extra-inning game.

40 or More Home Runs, Season
[No player]

League Leaders, Pitching

Most Wins, Season
Urban Shocker, 1921..............27 (Tie)

Most Strikeouts, Season
Urban Shocker, 1922.....................149

Lowest ERA, Season
[No pitcher]

Most Saves, Season
[No pitcher]

Best Won–Lost Percentage, Season
General Crowder, 1928....21–5......808

Pitching Feats

20 Wins, Season (1901–53)
Frank Donahue, 1902 22–11
Jack Powell, 1902.....................22–17

Willie Sudhoff, 1903.................21–15
Allen Sothoron, 1919................21–11
Urban Shocker, 1920 20–10
Urban Shocker, 1921 27–12
Urban Shocker, 1922 24–17
Urban Shocker, 1923 20–12
General Crowder, 1928...............21–5
Sam Gray, 1928........................20–12
Lefty Stewart, 1930 20–12
Bobo Newsom, 1938.................20–16
Ned Garver, 1951 20–12

No-Hitters
Earl Hamilton (vs. Det. Tigers), Aug.
30, 1912 (final: 5–1)
Ernie Koob (vs. Chi. White Sox), May
5, 1917 (final: 1–0)
Bob Groom (vs. Chi. White Sox), May
6, 1917 (final: 3–0)
Bobo Newsom (vs. Bost. Red Sox), Sept.
18, 1934 (final: 1–2) (lost in 10th)
Bobo Holloman (vs. Phila. A's), May 6,
1953 (final: 6–0)

No-Hitters Pitched Against
Weldon Henley, Phila. A's, July 22,
1905 (final: 6–0)
Smokey Joe Wood, Bost. Red Sox, July
29, 1911 (final: 5–0)
George Mullin, Det. Tigers, July 4, 1912
(final: 7–0)
Hub Leonard, Bost. Red Sox, Aug. 30,
1916 (final: 4–0)
Eddie Cicotte, Chi. White Sox, Apr. 14,
1917 (final: 11–0)
Wes Ferrell, Cleve. Indians, Apr. 29,
1931 (final: 9–0)
Vern Kennedy, Chi. White Sox, Aug. 31,
1935 (final: 5–0)
Bill Dietrich, Chi. White Sox, June 1,
1937 (final: 8–0)
Dick Fowler, Phila. A's, Sept. 9, 1945
(final: 1–0)

Postseason Play

1944   World Series vs. St. L. Cardinals
(NL), lost 4 games to 2

Washington Senators

Dates of Operation: (as the Washington Senators) 1901–60 (60 years)
Overall Record: 4223 wins, 4864 losses (.465)
Stadiums: American League Park I, 1901–03; American League Park II, 1904–10; Griffith Stadium
(also known as National Park, 1911–21; Clark Griffith Park, 1922), 1911–60
Other Name: Nationals

Dates of Operation: (as the Washington Senators II) 1961–71 (11 years)
Overall Record: 740 wins, 1032 losses (.418)
Stadiums: Griffith Stadium, 1961; Robert F. Kennedy (RFK) Stadium, 1962–71
Other Name: Nats

Year-by-Year Finishes

Year	Finish	Wins	Losses	Percentage	Games Behind	Manager	Attendance
					Wash. Senators		
1901	6th	61	72	.459	20.5	Jimmy Manning	161,661
1902	6th	61	75	.449	22.0	Tom Loftus	188,158
1903	8th	43	94	.314	47.5	Tom Loftus	128,878
1904	8th	38	113	.252	55.5	Patsy Donovan	101,744
1905	7th	64	87	.424	29.5	Jake Stahl	252,027
1906	7th	55	95	.367	37.5	Jake Stahl	129,903
1907	8th	49	102	.325	43.5	Joe Cantillon	221,929
1908	7th	67	85	.441	22.5	Joe Cantillon	264,252
1909	8th	42	110	.276	56.0	Joe Cantillon	205,199
1910	7th	66	85	.437	36.5	Jimmy McAleer	254,591
1911	7th	64	90	.416	38.5	Jimmy McAleer	244,884
1912	2nd	91	61	.599	14.0	Clark Griffith	350,663
1913	2nd	90	64	.584	6.5	Clark Griffith	325,831
1914	3rd	81	73	.526	19.0	Clark Griffith	243,888
1915	4th	85	68	.556	17.0	Clark Griffith	167,332
1916	7th	76	77	.497	14.5	Clark Griffith	177,265
1917	5th	74	79	.484	25.5	Clark Griffith	89,682
1918	3rd	72	56	.563	4.0	Clark Griffith	182,122
1919	7th	56	84	.400	32.0	Clark Griffith	234,096
1920	6th	68	84	.447	29.0	Clark Griffith	359,260
1921	4th	80	73	.523	18.0	George McBride	456,069
1922	6th	69	85	.448	25.0	Clyde Milan	458,552
1923	4th	75	78	.490	23.5	Donie Bush	357,406
1924	1st	92	62	.597	+2.0	Bucky Harris	534,310
1925	1st	96	55	.636	+8.5	Bucky Harris	817,199
1926	4th	81	69	.540	8.0	Bucky Harris	551,580
1927	3rd	85	69	.552	25.0	Bucky Harris	528,976
1928	4th	75	79	.487	26.0	Bucky Harris	378,501
1929	5th	71	81	.467	34.0	Walter Johnson	355,506
1930	2nd	94	60	.610	8.0	Walter Johnson	614,474
1931	3rd	92	62	.597	16.0	Walter Johnson	492,657
1932	3rd	93	61	.604	14.0	Walter Johnson	371,396
1933	1st	99	53	.651	+7.0	Joe Cronin	437,533
1934	7th	66	86	.434	34.0	Joe Cronin	330,374

1935	6th	67	86	.438	27.0	Bucky Harris	255,011
1936	4th	82	71	.536	20.0	Bucky Harris	379,525
1937	6th	73	80	.477	28.5	Bucky Harris	397,799
1938	5th	75	76	.497	23.5	Bucky Harris	522,694
1939	6th	65	87	.428	41.5	Bucky Harris	339,257
1940	7th	64	90	.416	26.0	Bucky Harris	381,241
1941	6th (Tie)	70	84	.455	31.0	Bucky Harris	415,663
1942	7th	62	89	.411	39.5	Bucky Harris	403,493
1943	2nd	84	69	.549	13.5	Ossie Bluege	574,694
1944	8th	64	90	.416	25.0	Ossie Bluege	525,235
1945	2nd	87	67	.565	1.5	Ossie Bluege	652,660
1946	4th	76	78	.494	28.0	Ossie Bluege	1,027,216
1947	7th	64	90	.416	33.0	Ossie Bluege	850,758
1948	7th	56	97	.366	40.0	Joe Kuhel	795,254
1949	8th	50	104	.325	47.0	Joe Kuhel	770,745
1950	5th	67	87	.435	31.0	Bucky Harris	699,697
1951	7th	62	92	.403	36.0	Bucky Harris	695,167
1952	5th	78	76	.506	17.0	Bucky Harris	699,457
1953	5th	76	76	.500	23.5	Bucky Harris	595,594
1954	6th	66	88	.429	45.0	Bucky Harris	503,542
1955	8th	53	101	.344	43.0	Chuck Dressen	425,238
1956	7th	59	95	.383	38.0	Chuck Dressen	431,647
1957	8th	55	99	.357	43.0	Chuck Dressen, Cookie Lavagetto	457,079
1958	8th	61	93	.396	31.0	Cookie Lavagetto	475,288
1959	8th	63	91	.409	31.0	Cookie Lavagetto	615,372
1960	5th	73	81	.474	24.0	Cookie Lavagetto	743,404

Wash. Senators II

1961	9th (Tie)	61	100	.379	47.5	Mickey Vernon	597,287
1962	10th	60	101	.373	35.5	Mickey Vernon	729,775
1963	10th	56	106	.346	48.5	Mickey Vernon, Gil Hodges	535,604
1964	9th	62	100	.383	37.0	Gil Hodges	600,106
1965	8th	70	92	.432	32.0	Gil Hodges	560,083
1966	8th	71	88	.447	25.5	Gil Hodges	576,260
1967	6th (Tie)	76	85	.472	15.5	Gil Hodges	770,863
1968	10th	65	96	.404	37.5	Jim Lemon	546,661

East Division

1969	4th	86	76	.531	23.0	Ted Williams	918,106
1970	6th	70	92	.432	38.0	Ted Williams	824,789
1971	5th	63	96	.396	38.5	Ted Williams	655,156

Awards

Most Valuable Player
Walter Johnson, pitcher, 1913
Walter Johnson, pitcher, 1924
Roger Peckinpaugh, shortstop, 1925

Rookie of the Year
Albie Pearson, outfield, 1958
Bob Allison, outfield, 1959

Cy Young
[No pitcher]

Hall of Famers Who Played for the Senators
Stan Coveleski, pitcher, 1925–27
Joe Cronin, shortstop, 1928–34
Ed Delahanty, first base and outfield, 1902–03

Rick Ferrell, catcher, 1937–41, 1944–45, and 1947
Lefty Gomez, pitcher, 1943
Goose Goslin, outfield, 1921–30, 1933, and 1938
Bucky Harris, second base, 1919–28
Walter Johnson, pitcher, 1907–27
Harmon Killebrew, third base and first base, 1956–60

Heinie Manush, outfield, 1930–35
Sam Rice, outfield, 1915–33
Al Simmons, outfield, 1937–38
Early Wynn, pitcher, 1939, 1941–44,
   and 1946–48

Retired Numbers
[None]

League Leaders, Batting

Batting Average, Season
Ed Delahanty, 1902 .... .376
Goose Goslin, 1928 .... .379
Buddy Myer, 1935 .... .349
Mickey Vernon, 1946 .... .353
Mickey Vernon, 1953 .... .337

Home Runs, Season
Roy Sievers, 1957 42
Harmon Killebrew, 1959 .... 42 (Tie)
Frank Howard, 1968 (Senators II) 44
Frank Howard, 1970 (Senators II) 44

RBIs, Season
Goose Goslin, 1924 129
Roy Sievers, 1957 114
Frank Howard, 1970 (Senators II) ..126

Stolen Bases, Season
John Anderson, 1906 .... 39 (Tie)
Clyde Milan, 1912 88
Clyde Milan, 1913 75
Sam Rice, 1920 63
Ben Chapman*, 1937 .... 35 (Tie)
George Case, 1939 51
George Case, 1940 35
George Case, 1941 33
George Case, 1942 44
George Case, 1943 61
*Played part of season with Bost. Red Sox.

Total Bases, Season
Roy Sievers, 1957 331
Frank Howard, 1968 (Senators II) ..330
Frank Howard, 1969 (Senators II) ..340

Most Hits, Season
Sam Rice, 1924 216
Sam Rice, 1926 .... 216 (Tie)
Heinie Manush, 1933 221
Cecil Travis, 1941 218

Most Runs, Season
George Case, 1943 102

Batting Feats

Triple Crown Winners
[No player]

Hitting for the Cycle
Otis Clymer, Oct. 2, 1908
Goose Goslin, Aug. 28, 1924
Joe Cronin, Sept. 2, 1929
Mickey Vernon, May 19, 1946
Jim King, May 26, 1964 (Senators II)

Six Hits in a Game
George Myatt, May 1, 1944
Stan Spence, June 1, 1944

40 or More Home Runs, Season
48 ....Frank Howard, 1969 (Senators II)
44 ....Frank Howard, 1968 (Senators II)
      Frank Howard, 1970 (Senators II)
42 .... Roy Sievers, 1957
           Harmon Killebrew, 1959

League Leaders, Pitching

Most Wins, Season
Walter Johnson, 1913 36
Walter Johnson, 1914 28
Walter Johnson, 1915 27
Walter Johnson, 1916 25
Walter Johnson, 1918 23
Walter Johnson, 1924 23
General Crowder, 1932 26
General Crowder, 1933 .... 24 (Tie)
Bob Porterfield, 1953 22

Most Strikeouts, Season
Walter Johnson, 1910 313
Walter Johnson, 1912 303
Walter Johnson, 1913 243
Walter Johnson, 1914 225
Walter Johnson, 1915 203
Walter Johnson, 1916 228
Walter Johnson, 1917 188
Walter Johnson, 1918 162
Walter Johnson, 1919 147
Walter Johnson, 1921 143
Walter Johnson, 1923 130
Walter Johnson, 1924 158
Bobo Newsom, 1942 .... 113 (Tie)

Lowest ERA, Season
Walter Johnson, 1913 .... 1.14
Walter Johnson, 1918 .... 1.27
Walter Johnson, 1919 .... 1.49
Walter Johnson, 1924 .... 2.72
Stan Coveleski, 1925 .... 2.84
Garland Braxton, 1928 .... 2.52
Dick Donovan, 1961 (Senators II)....2.40
Dick Bosman, 1969 (Senators II) ...2.19

Most Saves, Season
[No pitcher]

Best Won–Lost Percentage, Season
Walter Johnson, 1913 ....36–7 .... .837
Walter Johnson, 1924 ....23–7 .... .767
Stan Coveleski, 1925 .....20–5 .... .800

Pitching Feats

20 Wins, Season
Walter Johnson, 1910 25–17
Walter Johnson, 1911 25–13
Walter Johnson, 1912 33–12
Bob Groom, 1912 24–13
Walter Johnson, 1913 36–7
Walter Johnson, 1914 28–18
Walter Johnson, 1915 27–13
Walter Johnson, 1916 25–20
Walter Johnson, 1917 23–16
Walter Johnson, 1918 23–13
Walter Johnson, 1919 20–14
Walter Johnson, 1924 23–7
Stan Coveleski, 1925 20–5
Walter Johnson, 1925 20–7
General Crowder, 1932 26–13
Monte Weaver, 1932 22–10
General Crowder, 1933 24–15
Earl Whitehill, 1933 22–8
Dutch Leonard, 1939 20–8
Roger Wolff, 1945 20–10
Bob Porterfield, 1953 22–10

No-Hitters
Walter Johnson (vs. Bost. Red Sox),
   July 1, 1920 (final: 1–0)
Bob Burke (vs. Bost. Red Sox), Aug.
   8, 1931 (final: 5–0)

No-Hitters Pitched Against
Jim Scott, Chi. White Sox, May 14,
   1914 (final: 0–1) (lost in 10th)
Ernie Shore, Bost. Red Sox, June 23,

1917 (final: 4–0) (perfect game)
Bill McCahan, Phila. A's, Sept. 3,
1947 (final: 3–0)
Virgil Trucks, Det. Tigers, May 15,
1952 (final: 1–0)
Bob Keegan, Chi. White Sox, Aug.

20, 1957 (final: 6–0)
Sonny Siebert, Cleve. Indians, June
10, 1966 (final: 2–0) (Senators II)

Postseason Play

1924 World Series vs. N.Y. Giants

(NL), won 4 games to 3
1925 World Series vs. Pitt. Pirates
(NL), lost 4 games to 3
1933 World Series vs. N.Y. Giants
(NL), lost 4 games to 1

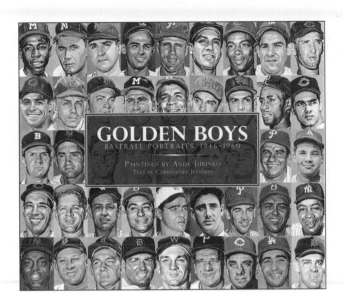

Golden Boys

Baseball Portraits, 1946–1960

by Andy Jurinko and Christopher Jennison

Renowned artist Andy Jurinko believed the golden age of baseball was 1946–1960, an era that, not coincidentally, coincided with his childhood. It was a time that welcomed such legendary stars as Willie Mays, Mickey Mantle, Jackie Robinson, Ted Williams, and Henry Aaron into the national consciousness, a fifteen-year stretch marked by Robinson's breaking of the color barrier in 1947 and by ten Yankee championships. Jurinko spent twenty years creating more than 600 portraits of the colorful characters and stadiums that typify this era, all collected here for the first time in *Golden Boys*. With illuminating text by sportswriter Christopher Jennison, *Golden Boys* is the definitive artistic portrait of a remarkable time in American sports history.

$50.00 Hardcover

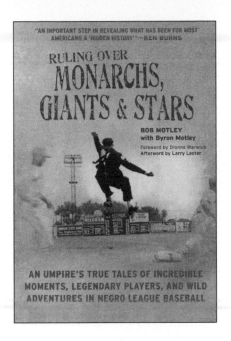

Ruling Over Monarchs, Giants & Stars

An Umpire's True Tales of Incredible Moments, Legendary Players, and Wild Adventures in Negro League Baseball

by Bob Motley with Byron Motley

Foreword by Dionne Warwick

Afterword by Larry Lester

The Kansas City Monarchs, the Chicago American Giants, the St. Louis Stars, the Birmingham Black Barons, the Homestead Grays, and the Indianapolis Clowns; for over fifty years, they were the Yankees, Cardinals, and Red Sox of black baseball in America. And for over a decade beginning in the late 1940s, umpire Bob Motley called balls and strikes for many of their games, working alongside such legends as Satchel Paige, Hank Aaron, Ernie Banks, and Willie Mays.

Today, Motley is the only living arbiter from the Negro Leagues. His personal account of the Negro Leagues is a revealing, humorous, and unforgettable memoir celebrating a long-lost league and a remarkable group of baseball players. In *Ruling Over Monarchs, Giants & Stars* Motley and his son Byron share the characters, adventures, and challenges faced by these amazing men as they enthusiastically embraced America's pastime and made it their own. Filled with stories of talented heroes, small miracles, and downright fun, this unique memoir is a must-read for any baseball fan.

$24.95 Hardcover

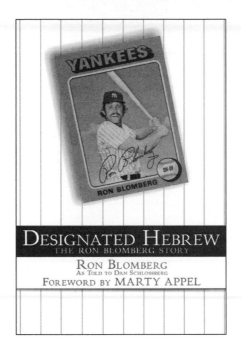

Designated Hebrew

The Ron Blomberg Story

by Ron Blomberg with Dan Schlossberg

Foreword by Marty Appel

On April 6, 1973, Ron Blomberg took a swing at home plate that changed baseball history. Through a quirk of fate the young Jewish Yankee became the first designated hitter to play an MLB game. At the time, George Steinbrenner had just taken control of the Bronx Bombers, the National League was still refusing to adopt the DH rule, and New Yorkers were pinning their hopes on a new generation of players. In this heart-warming autobiography, Blomberg relives the moment that made his career and the countless experiences before and after that helped boost him to legendary heights.

In *Designated Hebrew*, Blomberg recounts a time when baseball, and America itself, were changing. Before Blomberg arrived in New York, the Yankees only employed three Jews in the entire organization. Though his career goals were eventually thwarted by injury, Blomberg still represented hope and pride to millions of Americans across the country. This unforgettable story is the journey of one man as he learns to balance life, religion, and ultimately, baseball.

$19.95 Hardcover

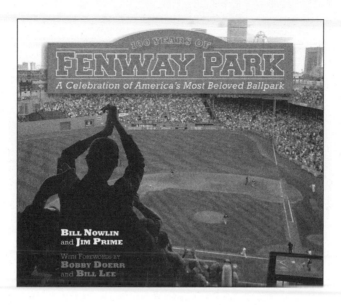

100 Years of Fenway Park

A Celebration of America's Most Beloved Ballpark

by Bill Nowlin and Jim Prime

Forewords by Bobby Doerr and Bill Lee

On April 20, 1912, The Boston Red Sox played their first official game at Fenway Park. Twenty-seven thousand fans were on hand to witness the Red Sox defeat the rival New York Highlanders, later known as the Yankees, 7–6 in 11 innings. It was an event that may have made front page news in Boston had it not been for the sinking of the *Titanic* five days earlier.

Since that day, the oddly-shaped stadium at 4 Yawkey Way has played host to nearly 8,000 Red Sox games, including fifty-five in the postseason, launching the legends of Tris Speaker, Jimmie Foxx, Ted Williams, Carl Yastrzemski, Jim Rice, Wade Boggs, and Pedro Martinez, and making the ballpark a worldwide destination for legions of baseball fans in the process.

From the Green Monster to Pesky's Pole, The Triangle to the lone red seat marking the longest home run ever hit in the stadium (a 502-foot blast off the bat of Ted Williams in 1946), Fenway Park's unique charms have captivated generations of sports fans. Through vivid full-color photographs and illuminating prose, *100 Years of Fenway Park* tells the story of the most cherished American stadium.

$29.95 Hardcover

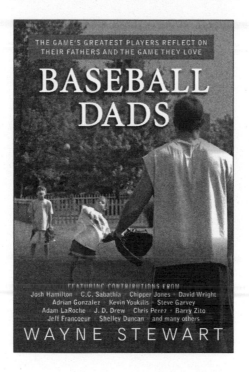

Baseball Dads

The Game's Greatest Players Reflect on Their Fathers and the Game They Love

by Wayne Stewart

Baseball Dads is a heartwarming collection of notable major league players' favorite baseball-related memories about how their relationships with their fathers shaped them, not only as players, but as the men they are today. From superstars like David Wright, Josh Hamilton, CC Sabathia, Adrian Gonzalez, Chipper Jones, and Kevin Youkilis, to journeyman big leaguers like Adam LaRoche, J. D. Drew, Shelley Duncan, Barry Zito, and Jeff Francoeur, this inspiring book reveals, through its fifteen vivid profiles, the profound impact fathers can have on the lives of their children on and off the diamond.

An ideal Father's Day gift, *Baseball Dads* offers a rare, intimate glimpse into the private lives of some of the game's best players.

$19.95 Hardcover